D1496085

THE PENNSYLVANIA NAVY, 1775–1781

Commodore John Hazelwood by Charles Willson Peale. *Independence National Historical Park Collection, Philadelphia.*

THE PENNSYLVANIA NAVY
1775–1781

★ ★ ★ ★ ★ ★ ★ ★ ★ ★ ★ ★ ★

THE DEFENSE
OF THE DELAWARE

John W. Jackson

RUTGERS UNIVERSITY PRESS

New Brunswick, New Jersey

Library of Congress Cataloging in Publication Data

Jackson, John W
  The Pennsylvania Navy, 1775–1781.

  Bibliography: p.
  1. Pennsylvania (Colony). Navy. 2. United States
—History—Revolution—Naval operations. 3. Delaware
Valley—History. 4. Pennsylvania—History—Revolu-
tion. I. Title.
E271.J26   973.3'5   73–18029
ISBN 0–8135–0766–9

To
my wife
Kathryn
whose assistance and encouragement
made this book possible
and
in loving memory
of our
Misty

Preface

The American Revolution produced many heroes and it is the object of this book to rescue one small band of them from oblivion. A definitive study of the Pennsylvania navy, which antedated the United States Navy by nearly six months, is long overdue. Most histories of the period ignore or accord only casual treatment to actions of the State fleet. Historians who have referred to the navy have usually been critical of the command and implied a lack of resourcefulness on the part of the officers and men of the boats. Careful research in the correspondence and documents of the time would have dispelled the cloud under which the little navy has been cast for nearly two centuries.

The active period of the fleet extends for three years (summer of 1775 to summer of 1778), although elements would remain in service for another eighteen months.

October and November 1777 witnessed some of the most dramatic battles of the Revolution—Saratoga, Brandywine, Germantown, and the defense of the Delaware River. Unfortunately, the Delaware engagements have been dismissed as unimportant, except for a few special studies by local historians. Casualties were significant but small compared to Brandywine and Germantown. However, in the eight-week period from September 27 to November 15 probably the heaviest cannonading seen on the North American Continent until the American Civil War thundered across the Delaware. For this period, unless prevented by weather, daily contact was made between the wasp-like Patriot galleys and the heavier British men-of-war. British land batteries maintained a steady bombardment of Fort Mifflin, reaching a crescendo during the siege of November 10 through 15. The brilliant defense by two Rhode Island Continental regiments of Fort Mercer on October 22, and several other minor actions should place this campaign in its proper place in the annals of the American Revolution.

To understand the importance of the defense of the Delaware River passes and the need to prevent British shipping from reaching the port of Philadelphia, it is necessary only to examine the correspondence of Washington and his officers. Washington was hopeful, but not optimistic, that the river could be held against the best the British could throw against it. Many "ifs" conditioned his thinking and, finally, his decisions. He was firmly committed to a policy of maintaining the main Continental army at a strength to contain Howe in Philadelphia. To assign additional reinforcements to the forts would weaken the army at Whitemarsh without gaining an advantage along the river. If reinforcements from the north had reached Washington in time and in sufficient numbers, he could have made a diversionary attack on the British positions on Carpenters' and Province Islands. If the needed reinforcements had been available a larger contingent could have been placed on the State galleys. Increasing the river command to division strength would have permitted Washington to place this independent force in more capable hands. Amid all this speculation on what might have been, moved the little navy. To chronicle the beginnings, vicissitudes, and the final dissolution of the Pennsylvania navy is the main purpose of this book.

Wherever possible I have permitted the participants in the narrative on the State navy and the defense of the Bay and River Delaware, to tell their own story, in their own way. No effort has been made to modernize the orthography or punctuation except where necessary to clarify the meaning of a letter, document, or statement. Eighteenth-century writers wrote detailed, involved, and flowery sentences; however, to cut up or change their sentiments would lose the life and color of their thoughts.

In the preparation of the manuscript, I received help from many whose courtesy I would like to acknowledge. Mr. Howard I. Chapelle and Mr. Thomas Hornsby made many helpful suggestions on the construction of boats during the Revolutionary period.

My thanks are extended to Mr. Donald H. Kent and his staff at the Pennsylvania Bureau of Archives and History, including Mr. William H. Work, Mr. Henry Bown, Mr. Harry Whipkey, Mrs. Barbara Philpott, and especially Miss Martha Simonetti. The excellent resources of the Historical Society of Pennsylvania were made available through the kindness of Mr. Nicholas B. Wainwright. Mr. Peter Parker of the manuscript section and Mr. John Platt of the printed material section and their staff members, Miss

Linda Stanley, Mr. Anthony Roth, and Mr. Gary Christopher, were gracious and helpful, especially on my repeated visits to the Society to recheck various sources.

To single out any one person is difficult, but I am deeply grateful for the counsel and suggestions of Dr. Whitfield J. Bell, Jr., of the American Philosophical Society. Through the courtesy of Dr. Bell, Mrs. Gertrude Hess, Mr. Murphy D. Smith, Mr. Willman Spawn, and Mr. Carl Miller an interlibrary loan of the microfilm reels of the George Washington Papers was made available for my use. For the privilege of reproducing for the first time the Benjamin Franklin-Robert Erskine correspondence and the drawing of Erskine's "Marine Chevaux de Frise," I am indebted to the American Philosophical Society, Mr. Smith, and Mr. Spawn. I am also indebted to the Library of Congress and the West Chester State College for granting this privilege.

At the Department of the Navy, Historical Research Section, Dr. W. J. Morgan made every facility at his command, including the galley proof of a forthcoming volume of the Naval Documents of the Revolution, available for my examination. To Mr. Robert L. Scheina and the balance of the staff, Mr. Robert I. Campbell, Mr. Gordon Bowen-Hassell, Ensign Kristen G. Tryon, Yeoman First Class Dean Crosby, and Miss Jacquelyn L. Long, my thanks for guiding me on a very delightful excursion into the naval archives.

Mr. Edwin Wolf and Mrs. Lillian Tonkin of the Library Company of Philadelphia extended their fullest cooperation in making available several rare and out-of-print volumes on the Revolution.

I wish to thank Mr. Elmer Parker, Mr. Harry Swartz, and Miss Marie Booknight of the National Archives for their efforts to seek out records germane to this study.

Miss Barbara Berthelsen and Mr. Evan Young of the Olen Library, Cornell University, graciously assisted in my examination of the Fleury maps in the Jared Sparks Collection.

My thanks are also extended to several individuals who contributed information in their specialized fields. Mr. Leon de Valinger, Jr., State Archivist of Delaware, help in identifying modern locations of Revolutionary sites in Delaware. Mr. Robert I. Alotta, President of the Shackamaxon Society, the administrator of Fort Mifflin, granted me freedom of the old fort and the use of his compilation of eighteenth-century military terms. My niece Miss Judy Gersteneker helped me with translating certain abstruse eighteenth-century French expressions. My thanks to Mr. A. Modelski of the Library of Congress, Geography and Map Division, for his patience and assistance in reviewing their excellent Revolutionary map collection.

The Mariners Museum, Newport News, Virginia, purchased the Bailey collection of 254 watercolors in London, England, in 1940. This collection is attributed to Charles Turner Warren and or his son Alfred William Warren. It is believed that the watercolors were intended to illustrate a history of the United States Navy. The Warrens began painting these watercolors in the late eighteenth century with the last one completed in the mid-nineteenth century. The watercolors cover the period from 1775 to 1823 with exception of one dated 1745 and one 1850. Through the courtesy of Mr. Barnes, Beulah Tisdale, Katherine Fox, and Carolyn Ritger and the Mariners Museum, I have reproduced in this volume five of the watercolors depicting naval actions on the Delaware River during 1777. While somewhat at variance with the known facts of the engagements, they provide the only near-contemporary portrayal of the Pennsylvania galleys.

To my good friend John Squillace, artist, the Chosen Freeholders of Gloucester County, New Jersey, and the Gloucester County Historical Society, I extend my gratitude for permission to reproduce the "Burning of the *Augusta*." Mr. Squillace has also graciously granted permission to reproduce his painting, "The Battle of Fort Mercer, 1777."

My friend Mrs. Kurt (Edith) Hoelle spent many hours delving into the archives of Gloucester County, read a portion of the manuscript and made several excellent suggestions which served to clarify part of the narrative; my sincerest thanks.

To another friend, Mrs. Robert (Merry Rose) Pollsen, I am deeply grateful for reading the entire manuscript. In no small measure the clarity of the narrative is the result of her diligence and excellent recommendations.

As is customary, I have reserved mention of my wife Kathryn until the end. In addition to typing the manuscript, her encouragement, patience, and dedication made the completion of the book possible. This book is dedicated to her in partial appreciation of the suffering and exultation we experienced in preparing the manuscript.

JOHN W. JACKSON

Flourtown, Pennsylvania
August 1973

Contents

Illustrations

THE PENNSYLVANIA NAVY, 1775–1781

I

War Threatens the Delaware Valley—1775

THE BLOODY confrontations between British troops and embattled New England farmers at Lexington and Concord, and later at Bunker Hill, brought into public focus the common dissatisfactions felt in all thirteen colonies. For the English, the immediate shock of these setbacks had a paralyzing effect on their commander, Sir William Howe, thus providing the Continental Congress and the individual colonies time to organize for defense. Every colonial American who thought about the matter realized that the British government and King would not accept this affront to the royal arms; the humiliation suffered by professional British army units at the hands of country bumpkins was not to be swallowed. The upstarts in Massachusetts and the other colonies who supported them would have to be taught a severe lesson. Punishment would surely be swift and painful —no more wrist-slapping; also it would presumably be severe enough to preclude any colonial Englishman's daring to defy the authority of His Majesty's government at some future time.

The bloodletting in Massachusetts was of course actually a result, not the cause, of the existence and growth of a revolutionary movement in America. Many Americans did believe that war with Great Britain was inevitable, but others fervently hoped that an accommodation could be worked out; still others were committed to the policy of reconciliation and so exhibited their loyalty by accepting all mandates from the British government. And, as in all revolutionary situations, there existed also a neutral group, uncommitted and content to accept any outcome, hoping to weather the rough seas without disturbing their personal status quo. Equally alert along the sidelines were those opportunists who always wait for any signal to jump on the winning bandwagon.

Of these groups, two figured prominently in the eight years of warfare which were heralded by the first shot at Lexington. The Patriot party was composed of both radical and moderate elements. The radicals welcomed any action that would make reconciliation difficult, if not impossible; they had one objective —independence. The major Patriot strength was in New England, but there was a sizable scattering of sympathizers throughout the other colonies. Everywhere they welcomed the shedding of American blood as a means to the end of drawing followers from the more moderate elements of the Patriot citizenry.

These moderates were more numerous and stronger outside the Northeast. They approached the question of independence prudently. Believing that in time complete separation from Great Britain was inevitable, they considered that undue haste could lose friends for the Patriot cause. The need to proceed with caution, and to take no action that would create greater divisiveness was evidenced by the fact that at this time not more than one-third of the population was committed to the Patriot cause in any degree of absoluteness. Indeed, John Adams estimated that the citizens of the thirteen colonies were divided into approximately equal thirds—Patriots, Tories, and neutrals. While this estimate could serve as a yardstick, the percentages varied with the individual colony. Thus, in 1775 the Patriot party in Pennsylvania undoubtedly represented less than one-third of the population of the State.[1]

The Tory party, though numerous, was disorganized; it was almost customarily ignored by the British military authorities. A recent study has indicated the impotence of the Tories, and their lack of the leadership needed to prosecute a war successfully. There was complete absence of unity among the Tories; a failure to understand the problems facing them as a group or the need to organize and to provide arms and men to aid the British cause. Instead, there was a fatal willingness of the great majority to place full reliance on the British army rather than on Tory initiative. True, Loyalist regiments—self styled—were organized, but except as partisan corps they were never very effective. They preferred to display their snobbery toward the Patriots. The extent of their sense of superiority, and the contempt in which the Patriots held them, is exhibited in their desire to be called Loyalists whereas the Patriots disdainfully designated them as Tories.[2]

Joseph Galloway, the most prominent Tory in Pennsylvania, epitomized the lack of preception and the misunderstanding exhibited by Tory leadership. Galloway wrote that he was "convinced that . . . if the British troops were withdrawn and the people left to themselves and their free and unbridled suffrage, that nine persons out of ten in the whole revolted colonies would vote for a constitutional union with and dependence on the British state."[3]

Too often it is claimed that the culture of the colonies and that of the mother country were homogeneous. Certain aspects of colonial culture were similar to that of Great Britain, but for the most part, thirteen new societies had been created. Except for the first-generation settlers, whose memory of the mother country was fresh, most Americans obtained their knowledge of English culture and conditions from books and not from experience, and they had developed their own culture, in many ways different from that of Great Britain. Failure to understand this fact caused most of the British civil authorities to miscalculate the temper and habits of the Americans.

In Great Britain, nothing resembling a representative form of government existed—election to the House of Commons was principally a matter of favor extended by the royal family, whereas in British America, as the colonies increased in population, some form of popular election took shape. The typical town meeting form of government generated a trend toward representative government at higher levels. In spite of all the efforts by royal governors, they could neither delay nor defeat these efforts toward political freedom. They could, if the occasion demanded, prorogue or dissolve the various colonial Assemblies; but the colonists could always circumvent the royal appointees by holding either open or clandestine rump assemblies.

Pennsylvania, being a proprietary colony, enjoyed some privileges not available to royal provinces. Penn had offered religious freedom and political franchise to all settlers in his proprietorship. Unfortunately, his plans for complete equality in the province failed of fruition.

The historian Charles H. Lincoln wrote that Pennsylvania was a microcosm of the British Empire, with comparable racial, religious, and economic differences and such differences lead to the development of the revolutionary party in the State. The leadership of this party was, at least in the beginning, as much interested in freedom from the domination of the proprietary leaders and the Quaker Party as in discarding British affiliation.[4]

However, the feeling for independence was actually stronger in the province than in those colonies where the extension of English government and religion were stronger. Penn had provided a government that was semidemocratic, but the concentration of the government in the hands of the Philadelphia Quakers laid the foundation for the resistance movement in the third quarter of the eighteenth century.[5]

The Quaker Party was dominated by a coalition of Quakers and Anglicans and included practically all the aristocrats of the three easternmost counties. This was a rather uneasy partnership, as little affection existed between the two religious groups. Self-interest was the sole factor that overcame personal animosity. The Quakers were supported by the majority of the German settlers in the eastern counties, principally because these settlers lacked leadership of their own.

The so-called anti-Quaker party was composed of the Scotch-Irish and German settlers of the frontier countries. They were joined by the artisans, mechanics, and the more moderate elements of the merchant and lawyer classes in Philadelphia. The Scotch-Irish, lawyers, and merchants supplied the party leadership, with the lawyers and merchants exerting a moderating influence on the radical frontier leaders. The Scotch-Irish had come to Pennsylvania imbued with a distrust of anything English, and a determination to sever all connections with Great Britain. From this wellspring of political independence would eventually come enthusiastic support for the Patriot cause. On the other hand, the Germans were content, at least in the beginning, to follow. This attitude led to a schism among the Germans. However, after the Declaration of Independence, the Germans became one of the most cohesive groups advocating full independence and almost to a man threw their support to the American cause.[6]

The Eastern party, or Quaker coalition, by careful manipulation and management had retained control of the Assembly. Little was done to provide full representation for the frontier countries; in fact, everything was maneuvered to prevent the back-country settlers from receiving a proportional voice in their government. The result was a three-way struggle for control of the province with the Quaker Party, Proprietary representatives, and anti-Quaker Party contending for political domination. While this is somewhat of an oversimplification of the political make-up of the State at the beginning of the Revolution, it nevertheless indicates why the Quakers moved toward a closer alliance with the mother country, and a number of them became Tories. Many openly avowed loyalty to the British cause; others attempted tactfully to straddle the fence, secretly hoping for a British victory. It should be mentioned that many Quakers subordinated their personal interests to the public good and became staunch Patriots, later styled "Free Quakers." A Philadelphia newspaper in May 1775 observed: "It is impossible to describe the military ardor which now prevails in this city. A considerable number of the Friends have joined in the military association. There is one company composed entirely of gentlemen belonging to that religious denomination."[7] It has been pointed out by one authority that individual Quakers, as distinguished from the Quaker party, favored America rather than England in the struggle.[8]

The Quakers were unfitted for leadership in situations involving outside influences and especially those which might lead to war. They were competent in leading a fight if it involved only a constitutional change, but, according to an authority on prerevolutionary Pennsylvania, they made more Patriots than Tories by their writings and arguments.[9]

As war with Great Britain became inevitable, individual leadership in the various factions assumed greater importance. The

Proprietary representatives and the Penn family were devoid of any dynamic personalities, and survived mainly through sufferance of the British monarch. The Quaker party controlled the Provincial Assembly, not through aggressive leadership, but rather as a result of the disproportionate representation granted the three eastern counties. Benjamin Franklin, Pennsylvania's outstanding statesman, was the recognized leader of the Patriot party. He attempted to direct the aggressive segment of the party, but, as the desire for independence gained momentum, Franklin merely mirrored the thoughts of the Patriots. A moderating influence was exerted by such statesmen as the merchant Robert Morris and the conservative Quaker John Dickinson.

The stage was set in early 1775 for the establishment of a revolutionary organization to plan for the defense of the province. Either the Assembly must be remodeled along lines more sympathetic to the American cause or a new one established. To prevent a complete takeover by radicals, moderate men like Franklin, Dickinson, Wilson, and McKean worked for reform from within the Assembly. The fact that the Assembly entertained a petition in May 1775 to provide £50,000 toward putting the province in a posture of defense was evidence of the changes taking place.[10]

Pennsylvania was now ready to join the other states in the upcoming conflict. On June 30, 1775, the Assembly yielded to the demands of the Patriots and appointed a Committee or Council of Safety. The resolution stated: "That this House approves the Association entered into by the Good People of this Colony for the Defence of their Lives, Liberties and Property."[11] Of course such action did not reflect the attitude of all Pennsylvanians; it was the result of concerted efforts by a minority. In fact, Timothy Pickering at this time called Pennsylvania "enemy country" because of the large number of neutrals and Tories.[12]

Committees or Councils of Safety were the bridge between the crude but necessary revolutionary committees of the colonies prior to 1775 and the organization of permanent state legislatures following the Declaration of Independence in 1776.[13] Committees of Correspondence, Observation, or Intelligence were the more important of the initial political bodies engaged in the common effort of intercolony cooperation and decision.[14]

Pennsylvania was a belated member of this chain of mutual cooperation. The other colonies had formed their committee systems, with varying degrees of effectiveness, by February 1774.[15] The Committee or Council of Safety was the first organized and Assembly-approved revolutionary group to function in the state. However, many prominent Patriots had aided in the deliberations of the Continental Congress and the early efforts to establish intercolony unity.

The resolution creating the Committee of Safety contained sixteen articles assigning specific areas of responsibility for defense against attack or invasion by British armed forces.[16]

With few exceptions, the appointees to the Committee were the most outstanding members of the Patriot party. First and foremost was Benjamin Franklin, who was unanimously chosen president of the Committee. Other members were John Dickinson, George Gray, Henry Wynkoop, Anthony Wayne, Benjamin Bartholomew, George Ross, Michael Swope, John Montgomery, Edward Biddle, William Edmunds, Bernard Daugherty, Samuel Hunter, William Thompson, Thomas Willing, Daniel Roberdeau, John Cadwalader, Andrew Allen, Owen Biddle, Francis Johnston, Richard Riley, Samuel Morris, Jr., Robert Morris, Thomas Wharton, Jr., and Robert White (Whyte).[17] Thus was gathered the most capable leadership in the state, a combination not attainable again during the Revolution. A slow deterioration would set in as some of the most able members would resign to enter the Continental Congress and foreign diplomatic service; others would leave to serve in the Continental army; and a few would renounce their allegiance to the American cause after the Declaration of Independence; and at least one would be attainted with treason.[18]

The zeal for service by the Committee did not match its talents. The first meeting of the Committee was held at the State House in Philadelphia on July 3, 1775, with only nine members present. They planned to meet every day but Sunday at six A.M. This early meeting time was necessary so as not to interfere with the sessions of the Continental Congress, which was also using the chambers of the State House. With twenty-five members on the Committee, it was seldom that half of them were present. The attendance averaged seven to nine, with occasionally only three or four present. A quorum of seven was necessary to conduct business.

The nine members who attended the first meeting of the Committee proceeded with the business of organization. In addition to choosing Franklin president, William Govett was selected as clerk. The following day they resolved that the Committee, as a whole, should survey the river and islands on July 5. Accompanying the Committee was a group of leading merchants, shipbuilders, and Colonel Lewis Nicola, an engineer. They were to seek first-hand information on the status of Mud Island, determine other sites for fortifications, and recommend any other forms of defense necessary. While no record of their deliberations has survived, certain specific resolutions were adopted on July 6 which developed the plans for river defense, and the formation of a State navy.[19]

II

Building the Fleet—1775

T HE AMERICAN colonies' survival depended, in large measure, on their maritime interests. To succeed in any issue with Great Britain, they must keep open the diplomatic and commercial channels with other European powers. All major American cities were seaports or riverports and must be defended against the world's greatest naval power.[1] At the outset of hostilities, while Congress was preoccupied with raising an army, the defense of the seacoast became the responsibility of the individual colonies. Eleven of the thirteen colonies organized state navies; New Jersey and Delaware were the exceptions.

In designing boats for the state navies, first consideration was given to defense; offensive action against the British fleet would have been suicidal. Later the Continental navy would be involved in engagements with individual ships of the British navy, almost exclusively with their small frigates. The main offensive efforts of the state navies and the more ambitious privateersmen, however, would be directed against the commercial fleets of Great Britain.

The lack of an effective central authority naturally led each colony to take separate action.[2] These independent actions by

Pennsylvania and the other colonies reflected the degree of urgency with which each colony viewed the need for defending its shores. The Pennsylvania Council (or Committee) of Safety on June 30, 1775, passed resolutions providing for the defense of the Delaware River from invasion by hostile armed ships and vessels.[3] After an on-the-spot review of the defensive needs of the province, a subcommittee for the "Construction of Boats and Machines" was appointed on July 6. Robert Whyte and Owen Biddle were assigned this responsibility, with the recommendation that they employ John Wharton, Joseph Marsh, Emanuel Eyre, Jacob Miller, Thomas Davis, and Joseph Govett.[4]

This action was taken almost two weeks before the following resolution was passed by the Continental Congress:

That each Colony, at their own expense, make such provision by armed Vessells or otherwise, as their respective Assemblies, Conventions or Committees of Safety shall judge expedient and suitable to their Circumstances and situations, for the protection of their Harbours and Navigation on their Sea Coasts, against all unlawfull invasions, attacks and depredations from Cutters and Ships of War.[5]

The subcommittee of Whyte and Biddle on July 7, 1775, asked John Wharton to purchase materials for building a "Boat or Calevat," and that he bring a model of same before the full Committee on July 8. Wharton presented a model as requested and was immediately authorized to build a "Boat or Calevat" of "47 or 50 feet keel, thirteen feet beam, and four and a half feet deep." [6] The next day Emanuel Eyre presented another model and was authorized to proceed with its construction.[7] The submission of models by different shipbuilders might suggest a difference in the basic construction, but all existing evidence indicates that changes in specifications were minor. The subsequent eleven galleys built by Wharton, Eyre, and other Philadelphia shipbuilders were apparently based on the first two models submitted.

Similar to the Continental Congress, the states were poor and could not compete with mercenary privateersmen. While it was acknowledged that neither monies nor supplies were available in sufficient quantities, the chief obstacle to the success of both the Continental navy or the state navies was lack of mariners.[8] A large segment of American men were conditioned to the sea, but as Gardner Allen points out, regular naval service, with its discipline and restraints, did not offer the allure that the almost total freedom of a privateersman could guarantee.[9] Owners of privateers could afford to be more liberal; prizes often provided more money than many crew members could earn in a lifetime. Also, owners frequently by-passed the tedious processes of admiralty courts by appropriating parts or all of the prize cargoes. Prizes taken by Continental ships of war were closely governed by a code which allowed one-half of the proceeds, or sometimes one-third, to the crews.[10] In the end, this made recruiting for state navies even more difficult. Although they too had codes regulating prizes, little opportunity for taking them would ever present itself to the shallow-draught craft of a riverboat navy.

Research by Allen has revealed that at least two thousand letters of marque or commission were issued by the several states. Of this number, Pennsylvania authorized over five hundred. Allen further estimated that the total privateering venture employed seventy thousand men and carried armament of approximately eighteen thousand guns.[11]

Added to these problems confronting those Patriots organizing Pennsylvania's navy was the low pay scale offered officers and men. As we shall see later, only after several increases did the level of the state payment to the navy become comparable to the Continental establishment. This did not evenuate before several of the best state officers had resigned to enter the Continental service.

The members of the committee were utterly lacking in military or naval background. Most of their martial experience had been gained as junior partners in the wars of the mother country, with Great Britain supplying the professional soldiers and mariners. In common with the other states, Pennsylvania had many capable merchant sea captains and sailors, but they were completely ignorant of the demands of naval warfare; a few had some privateering experience gained in the French and Indian War. The state's most valuable resource was its many capable shipbuilders, and their skill, coupled with the common sense characteristic of such leaders as Benjamin Franklin, assured the birth of a navy.

With the authorization of the first row galleys, quickly followed by instructions to build eleven more, the navy became a reality. These shallow-draught boats would become the nucleus of the fleet. While the galley would be the most effective boat because of its maneuverability above and below the chevaux-de-frise, it would also be the most criticized of all the boats in the fleet. There were obvious limitations to the galley's effectiveness, and these were evident especially during the actions of October and November 1777. Nevertheless, they performed valiantly and served the purpose for which they were designed.

The nomenclature of the period presents a confused picture, and some of the boats defy description. Correspondence, journals, diaries, and minutes of the various civil committees show little consistency in describing the different classes of boats. The popular galley or row galley was variously described as "armed vessel," "armed boat," "gundola," "gunboat," and occasionally "floating battery." Contemporaries and historians have variously described the same sailing vessel as "schooner," "sloop," "brigatine," "brig," or "ship." When the Committee of Safety desired to build two ships to cruise the Delaware Bay between Cape Henlopen and Cape May, they instructed the subcommittee to build two galleys for this purpose.[12] As a result of this order, the armed schooner *Delaware* and the brig *Convention* were constructed.

Robert Whyte and Owen Biddle began their work of supervising the building of the State navy promptly and with enthusiasm. Contracts were assigned for building thirteen galleys, and all were launched by September 29, 1775.[13] Gala ceremonies attended the launching. The Committee of Safety ordered all members to attend the launching of the *Bull Dog* at the Eyre shipyard in Kensington on July 26. Thirteen members of the Committee embarked and went down to Gloucester, but found it inconvenient to hold a board meeting.[14] Christopher Marshall on September 28 observed: "About one [o'clock,] went down to [the] wharf to see the gondolas sail by, the delegates being aboard, with a great number of others. Two of them, about Masters' Wharf, each carried away a mast."[15]

The Committee and subcommittee apparently received many plans and suggestions outlining boat types to be built for defense of the river. On July 6, 1775, Colonel Nicola, an engineer and later commander of the Continental Invalid Regiment and for a time commandant at Mud Island, presented a plan for defending the Delaware River. He suggested that two ships of eighty guns be built and anchored abreast as floating batteries across the channel of the river. All armament was to be removed except from the side facing downriver, with pig iron used as ballast on the other half of the ships. He further recommended that all top masts, yards, and other appurtenances be removed, except for higher crow's-nests from which sharpshooters could cover the decks of enemy ships. The British adopted a somewhat similar plan with the *Vigilant* in October and November 1777.[16]

Other plans for a boat were submitted by a Mr. Hulings.[17] Nathaniel Irish presented a model of a boat or gondola, and a gentleman signing himself "Nauticus" produced a plan for a fire ship.

Irish was concerned that the approved galleys would be defenseless against an enemy ship which might come broadside. The major deviation from the galleys then being constructed was a four-foot-high breastwork, four feet thick and with a porthole for cannon.[18]

The principal feature of "Nauticus's" plan for a fire ship was a method of fixing the ship to the enemy man-of-war so that it could not be turned adrift. Other points included the types of combustibles. Features of this proposal were apparently incorporated in part in the fires ships of the Pennsylvania navy.[19]

As Philadelphia shipbuilders were busily engaged in readying the galleys for service on the Delaware, some modifications in specifications were considered. The boats would need decking, sails, quarters for the men, and a myriad of other armaments and supplies.

The Pennsylvania galleys were smaller than many of those built by other state navies.[20] Apparently all were patterned on the models submitted by John Wharton and Emanuel Eyre and measured forty-seven- to fifty-feet keel, thirteen-feet beam, and four-and-one-half-feet depth amidships.[21] The galleys were double-enders, pointed at bow and stern. Their flat bottoms were ideally adapted for maneuvering over the obstructions placed in the Delaware River. Each galley was decked over and the hold was divided by bulkheads into cubicles designed to serve as cabins. Under the aft deck was a small area for the officers. This cabin was probably little more than a refuge from bad weather, as the area under the aft section must be shared with the ballast. The state galleys were ballasted with junk iron and pig iron to trim the galley by the stern and to counteract the weight of the large cannon placed in the bow.[22] Amidships, divided by the platform for the oarsmen, were bunk-like areas for the crew and possibly the junior officers. Under the bow was another cubbyhole used as a storage area for supplies and extra ammunition. As the greatest depth was four and one-half feet, these quarters must have been extremely uncomfortable.

The galleys rowed twenty oars double banked and were equipped with two short masts with a long yard on each for a lateen sail. Various individuals, Patriots and British sympathizers, wrote accounts describing the galleys. A letter appearing in the *London Evening Post* on November 9, 1775, mentioned "a number of galliots [galleys] and floating batteries . . . carrying two lateen sails and from 16 to 32 oars each." As this letter was dated Philadelphia, September 9, 1775, this observer could only have seen galleys at that date.[23] A letter to a Philip Stephens dated Philadelphia, July 1775, read: "This day saw one of the Floating Batteries [galleys] . . . in length they are 40 feet keel, flatt bottomed & are to row twenty oars double banked."[24] Charles Carroll of Maryland, in writing to his father on March 4, 1776, observed while on board one of the galleys: ". . . has a 24 pounder in the prow, & several swivels. They lie low in the water."[25] The archives do not furnish specifications or the exact number of oars used on the galleys. However, we do know that the oars were twenty-two feet long and could only have been used in a double-bank position.[26]

On the foredeck the galleys carried one large cannon. One galley had a thirty-two-pounder, four were equipped with twenty-four-pounders, and the remaining eight carried eighteen-pounders.[27] The caps along the rails were fitted with tholes for the sweeps and were capped for the swivel pivots.[28] The armament of each galley, in addition to one large cannon and swivels, included two howitzers, pikes, cutlasses, and muskets.[29] On September 29, 1775, an itemized list of Provincial expenditures included £169 for twenty-six howitzers, and £2,500 for swivels and small arms for the armed boats.[30] Along the rail flanking the large cannon were chests for the ammunition. There were sockets in the rail caps for stanchions to support weather cloths or awnings which protected the gun crews from enemy sharp-shooters; sailcloth was used for this purpose.[31] A small quarter-deck platform was provided in the aft section for the helmsman and officers. Each galley was provided with a small iron hearth[32] which was housed in a camboose.[33] The location of the camboose and hearth was probably on the port side and slightly abaft of the mast position.

All ships in the Pennsylvania navy were painted black and yellow, with no other colors allowed.[34] When the thirteen galleys were fully launched and equipped for active service, the estimated cost totaled £7,150, or £550 for each boat. An additional cost of £202 6s 3d per month was allowed for pay and victualing each of the galley crews of fifty-three officers and men—although the boats rarely had more than thirty-five officers and men on their musters.[35]

It has been assumed that Betsy Ross made the first flag for the galleys and floating batteries of the State navy. This assumption was based on an entry in the minutes of the Navy Board for May 29, 1777,[36] which paid Mrs. Ross £14 12s 2d for making ships' colors. Edwin S. Parry, in his life of Betsy Ross, comments that these flags were probably delivered weeks before, and there was the normal delay between delivery of material and approval for payment.[37] Assuming that this is correct, these flags were probably in the hands of the fleet in March 1777. There is in the State archives a receipt from Cornelia Bridges acknowledging payment of "£6 13s for making colors for the Floating Battery [*Putnam*], Warren & Bulldog, £2 3s for former & £2 5s for later [sic] two."[38] This receipt is dated May 25, 1776, and, allowing for Mr. Parry's contention, would mean that these flags were delivered about March 1776, or one year before those made by Betsy Ross. A contemporary study on the flags of the American Revolution states that the floating batteries of the Pennsylvania navy sailed under a flag with a green pine tree in the center of a white field, with the motto, "Appeal to Heaven." This flag, or variations of it, was used by most of the state navies, including the Pennsylvania fleet. It was superseded by the Betsy Ross flag, the first "Stars and Stripes," in 1777.[39]

The galleys were the wasps of the navy and often were effective out of proportion to their size. Their appellation of "row galley" indicates their main dependence on the oar for overall ability to maneuver, especially in the planned defense of the river. Their lateen sails were only useful when riding before the wind. The respect these little men-of-war engendered is evident from the high regard the other colonies had for their effectiveness. Maryland, New Jersey, and Connecticut sent representatives to observe the Pennsylvania galleys,[40] and with the exception of New Jersey, adopted modified versions of them. Because of the rough water in Long Island Sound and Chesapeake Bay, they recommended the same general construction, but larger and with different rigging. Philadelphia shipwrights were regarded so highly that the Continental Congress employed them to supervise the building of galleys for the Continental establishment. Benjamin Eyre was employed in this capacity to build three galleys and start the construction of another in New York before the British occupation of that city.[41] Finally, in July 1776, Captain (later Commodore) John Hazelwood was one of three persons sent to New York by the Committee of Safety to assist in the obstruction of the Hudson River and the construction of fire ships. Hazelwood was singled out for his contribution in designing the fire rafts and advice in general on river obstructions. In appreciation, he was given the sum of three hundred dollars by the State of New York.[42]

Of even greater significance was the request for a Philadelphia shipbuilder to assist in supervising the building of Benedict Arnold's galleys on Lake Champlain. Thomas Casdrop (or Casdorp) of Casdrop & Fulleton had built the *Chatham* and *Effingham* for the State navy. His employment as a shipwright on Lake Champlain in the summer and fall of 1776 suggests that certain features of the Pennsylvania galleys were incorporated in Arnold's Fleet.[43]

With the launching of the last galleys on September 29, 1775, the Committee of Safety realized that other boats would be needed to defend the chevaux-de-frise and support the land forts and batteries. Fire rafts were considered an effective weapon against wooden ships, and a committee was appointed to inquire into the construction of as many as needed to defend the city. In addition to Robert Whyte and Owen Biddle (already members of the subcommittee on boat construction), James Biddle and Samuel Howell were added to the fire-raft committee.[44]

An undated manuscript in the Pennsylvania archives describes the fire rafts:

The Rafts 35 feet long and 13 feet wide—the floor to be close and caulk'd—with a washboard and rails to confine the Materials—to be loaded with hogsheads and other Casks—the Staves of tarbarrels, Oil barrels, turpentine and Rosin Casks with hay [or] Straw, turpentine, Brimstone and other Combustible Substances thrown into the hogsheads and between them—a quantity of pine wood intermixed, and Powdered Rosin Strew'd over the whole to convey the fire with greater rapidity to every part.[45]

In spite of this detailed description, apparently all rafts were not thirty-five feet long and thirteen feet wide. On July 4, 1776, Fullerton & Moran were paid £28 4s 5d for one fire raft thirty feet by eleven feet and £23 5s for one twenty-seven and a half feet by eleven feet.[46] An intelligence report by British Vice-Admiral James Young, compiled from information gathered in conversations with masters and others belonging to captured American vessels, furnished additional details on the fire rafts:

They are to have five Men in each Lighter (with a boat to attend) to set fire to the Train. The Lighters are secured by Chains one to another, each link to Weigh One hundred Weight, and are to be Moored by heavy Anchors on each side the River, with Cables sufficient to hold them, 'til they want to put their Plan in Execution, then to cut their Cables and fall down.[47]

On December 28, 1775, Hazelwood was appointed to the command of the ten fire rafts under construction and to superintend all the rafts to be built.[48]

The exact number of fire rafts in service at any one time cannot now be determined. Gross exaggeration by British spies does not agree with what records are extant today.[49] We have documentation to support the building of eight chains of fire rafts, with substantial surplus of logs earmarked for building additional rafts. As these were of simple construction, other rafts may have been built by independent shipwrights. The chains, which measured 250 to 280 feet in length, were loaded with combustibles and linked together, six rafts to a chain. The bows of each had prongs of barbed iron, which, when the fire rafts were driven against an enemy ship, fastened the burning raft to the ship and would defy efforts to separate the two.[50] Old sailcloth was used to cover the rafts and keep the combustibles dry.

Fire raft chains were cumbersome and difficult to handle; crews seem to have been of a nondescript character and given to panic. The appointment of Hazelwood assured closer supervision of the motley assortment of individuals in this branch of the service. As they became available, he assigned a guard boat or half galley to the direct command of each chain. Their immediate station was near Fort Island and the Schuylkill River. Later, prior to the British invasion, they received specific assigned stations.

The guard boats or half galleys—the latter a British designation —were apparently similar to but much smaller than the galleys. Their area of effectiveness was limited to patrolling the mouths of the creeks flowing into the Delaware, to prevent intercourse between Tory sympathizers and the British army and the carrying of provisions or other supplies to the British army. Later they were assigned to protect the alarm posts established along the bay and river, as well as the command of the fire raft chains. These small boats never ventured on the river if there was the slightest swell, as they were easily swamped. It is believed that their general lines were modified miniatures of the galleys.

We can only conjecture as to their appearance; specifications or lines are no longer extant. It is a matter of record that shipbuilders contracted to build guard boats at a cost of forty shillings per foot; keel, oars, sails, cannon, provisions, and other equipment were not included in the construction cost. Records of payment have been found which provide some idea of the physical appearance of these small boats. Hill & Merritt received payment for a flat-bottomed boat in November 1776. As guard boats are occasionally referred to as flat-bottomed boats, and Hill & Merritt were prime contractors in the building of guard boats in early 1777, it is probable that this boat was the *Fame*. Records for those built during the first half of 1777 furnish some information as to size and cost for constructing the guard boats.

Hill & Merritt built the *Tormentor* and *Lion*, each thirty-five and one-half feet keel; also, a third boat, the size not determinable. Bower Brooks constructed the *Firebrand* and *Dragon;* one was thirty-five feet keel, the other thirty-seven feet. Dunn & Hale built three guard boats, the *Resolution* and *Viper* and one not identified; two were thirty-five feet keel, and the other thirty-seven feet. Samuel Robins built the *Argus*, *Repulse*, and

Wasp; no details of measurement are shown in the record of payment. Williams & Clinton built the *Thunder* and John Coles constructed one not identified. No specifications are available for these two. These records account for the twelve guard boats ordered by the Committee; but fourteen were launched and placed in service with the fleet. In this connection, Hill & Merritt and Dunn & Hale each constructed a barge twenty-nine and one-half feet keel and it is possible these two barges were equipped as guard boats. This conclusion is further strengthened by the occasional reference to specific guard boats as barges. They were only about six feet shorter, and may have conformed in other areas of design to the guard boats. Of the fourteen boats launched, only four (the *Basilisk, Hawk, Hornet,* and *Race Horse*) cannot be identified with a specific shipbuilder. However, as indicated, Hill & Merritt and John Coles built two unidentified guard boats, and the former with Dunn & Hale two large barges; this could account for the four guard boats not identifiable with a specific shipbuilder.

The accounts of the navy paymaster, William Webb, indicate that bare construction costs averaged approximately £80 to £90. As the builders included general repair work on galleys and the making of oars and other expenses in their invoices, a cost can only be arrived at by accepting the contracted per foot cost and auditing the final payments, eliminating, where possible, all extraneous expenses which were not pure construction costs. As the barges were eight-oared, it is reasonable to conclude that the guard boats were never equipped with more than ten or twelve oars, and, due to their small crews, normally fewer. It was the opinion of Commodore Caldwell that a guard boat of less than twelve oars would be unable to turn the fire rafts.[51]

There were no accommodations for quartering the men aboard the guard boats and the only protection was the awnings. Each boat was supplied with a small iron pot for cooking.[52] Their crews never exceeded fifteen officers and men, and usually less than ten, including captain and gunner. They were a true row galley; however, it is probable that they were equipped with a single lateen sail. Otherwise, it is difficult to reconcile the fact that several were included in Hazelwood's escape up the river on the morning of November 20, 1777. Leaving the vicinity of Fort Mercer at three o'clock in the morning, they were carried by a favorable wind and the flood tide past Philadelphia in about an hour and a half [53]—a feat impossible for a boat propelled by oars only.

These small boats were armed with either a two-, three- or four-pounder cannon, two swivels and small arms. It has been generally assumed that all guard boats were armed with four-pounders. Historians have tended to accept Faden's map for the armament and number of boats and ships comprising the American fleet in 1777. On this map neither the armament for the galleys or guard boats is accurate, nor the number of guard boats; instead of twenty-six indicated by Faden, a diligent search of all muster rolls reveals only twenty-one built for the Pennsylvania navy.[54]

The first small guard boat was built some time between December 1, 1775, and March 1, 1776. Apparently well satisfied with the design and usefulness of this boat type, the Committee on March 13, 1776, ordered the construction of five additional guard boats of the same specifications as the one already built.[55] These guard boats were in service and manned by June 1; on this date Hazelwood was ordered to employ persons to build a seventh guard boat. In October, it was decided by the Council to construct an additional twelve boats to guard the fire rafts. Four months later, with little progress in their construction, the newly appointed Navy Board ordered two of its members, Manuel Eyre and Joseph Marsh, to see that those under construction were completed, and to contract for the rest. It was recommended that some alterations be made in the design, but no evidence exists to support any changes.[56] Instead of twelve, fourteen guard boats were launched, ten before April 1, 1777, and the remaining four in the second quarter of 1777.

The exact service performed by some of the small boats is questionable. At least three were probably never in service, several were lost during the actions on the Delaware in 1777, and at least one deserted to the British. Because of their limited effectiveness, Hazelwood may have taken some of their crews for service on the galleys, especially in October and November 1777.[57]

One of the boats about which we know least was the floating battery. An investigation of contemporary sources and discussions with modern authorities have failed to uncover a satisfactory description of this boat. About 1850, Benson Lossing was given a drawing by Peter Force of a floating battery in use during the siege of Boston. This drawing was used as an illustration in Lossing's *Pictorial Field Book of the Revolution*. While the general construction of this floating battery may have been adapted by Philadelphia shipbuilders, certain important changes were incorporated in the Pennsylvania batteries. The Massachusetts floating battery carried two heavy cannon, one in the bow, the other in the aft section. Constructed of strong planks, it was pierced above the water line for oars, five to a side; openings were evident for light and muskets. It also carried four swivels on top.[58]

As we have no specifications for our floating batteries, we must accept some generalizations by British spies and the few vague references found in the Pennsylvania archives or made by Patriot leaders. Two British intelligence reports compiled in 1776 give descriptions, although somewhat exaggerated. One states that the floating battery was "120 feet long, 20 feet wide, the Parapet of which is only Plank"; [59] the other: ". . . 105 feet in keel, which is to mount 18 eighteen-pounders, row fifty oars, and carry 300 men." [60] Charles Carroll, on March 4, 1776, wrote that he had been on board a floating battery of ten eighteen-pounders, which would draw from two and one-half to three feet.[61] A contemporary document on the state of defenses in Pennsylvania lists a floating battery of ten eighteen-pounders with a crew of 116 men.[62] All of these references are to the *Arnold*.

On April 19, 1776, it was decided that further defenses were necessary for the river. Agreeing that another floating battery of a similar or nearly similar construction to the one then in service be built, a committee was appointed to supervise the construction.[63] Arthur Donaldson was given the contract, and the new floating battery was to be named the *Putnam*. The *Putnam* carried twelve eighteen-pounders; both batteries carried at least two swivels.[64] Each was provided with sails [65] and was ballasted with iron junk.[66] It is difficult to determine the use or type of sails employed on the floating battery. While one observer has noted that the crew and marines were protected by a parapet of two-inch plank,[67] the sails may still have been used as protective awnings to screen the crew from enemy sharpshooters. They were unquestionably clumsy craft and difficult to handle, although of shallow draught. Their maneuverability depended on the dexterity of the oarsmen and helmsman.

Romanticists would describe the rowing section (albeit it had auxiliary sail) as the glamorous element of the fleet. All the action participated in by the State navy was with the galleys, floating batteries, and fire rafts. The experiment with the fire rafts and fire ships was annoying to the British, but completely devoid of tangible results. Perhaps Washington, in a report to Congress, best expresses the opinion most prevalent at the time:

The fire-ships, also, will contribute to this end [defense of the Delaware and Chevaux-de-frise]; for though there are many obstacles to render their success precarious, and a happy concurrence of circumstances is necessary towards it,—any of which failing may disappoint the project,—and there is, therefore, no room to be sanguine, yet there is some possibility of its succeeding; and they will be at least an embarrassment and terror to the enemy, and will oblige them to use precautions inconvenient to them and serviceable to us.[68]

As the manifest objective of the navy came into focus, emphasis was placed on those sailing vessels principally needed to supply and victual the fleet. Both the Committee—and later, in 1777, the Navy Board—directed their attention to ships to be purchased for use as victualling schooners, ammunition and accommodation sloops, shallops and the questionable fire ships. Excluding the fire ships, this part of the fleet represented the service arm of the navy. The various small sailing vessels, in addition to supplying the fleet, were employed in transporting men and supplies to the fort, assisting in the laying of the chevaux-de-frise, and a variety of special assignments by the Committee and the Navy Board.

A number of small shallops were owned by the State, but not carried on the muster rolls of the navy.[69] In addition, some shallops, with their owners and crews, were employed by the Committee on a monthly basis.

The first step to add a man-of-war to the fleet was taken by the Committee on November 7, 1775, when a committee was appointed to contract for the building of a ship for river service capable of mounting twenty eighteen-pounders.[70] Acting with characteristic speed, the committee, which included Thomas Wharton and Robert Morris, reported later that day their estimate that such a ship would cost £9,000 exclusive of armament and provisions. On November 10, the Committee decided that, due to the lateness of the season and other difficulties, they should purchase a suitable ship.[71] Apparently the type of ship desired was not available, and in either December 1775 or January 1776, Simon Sherlock was assigned the contract to build an armed ship-of-war. Captain John Barry is said to have been employed to superintend the construction.[72] This vessel was later launched as the fleet's flagship *Montgomery*, and initially carried fourteen eighteen-pounders, sixteen cohorns, and eight swivels.[73] The *Montgomery* had a unique career as a fighting ship, undergoing several changes: In October 1776 her heavy cannon were changed to sixteen twelve-pounders.[74] In early 1777 she was stripped of all armament, her crew temporarily transferred, with Captain William Brown and his company of marines assigned to the floating battery *Putnam*.[75] On May 5, 1777, the Navy Board instructed Commodore Hazelwood to fit out the *Montgomery* as a guard ship: "to mount sixteen nine pounders, which are already proved and lye [sic] in the State House Yard; the Carriages lay on Huddle's wharfe, . . . take in what Ballast[76] necessary, and to equip the ship with every necessary article, as also to procure his [Captain Dougherty's] hands with all possible Expedition."[77]

Two other ships capable of operating below the chevaux-de-frise, and protecting American commerce in Delaware Bay, were authorized on May 14, 1776.[78] John Williams built the armed schooner *Delaware*, and Samuel Robins the brig *Convention*.[79]

The balance of the fleet (fire ships, fire sloops, fire brigs, fire brigatine, victualling schooners, accommodation sloops, ammunition sloop, sloops and shallop), as far as the records reveal, were all purchased vessels. The archives are sprinkled with notations recording the purchase of vessels to be adapted to the use of the State navy.[80] Little of the romantic can be attached to this arm of the naval force, but its contribution to the effectiveness of the fleet cannot be minimized. Constant replenishment of matériel and supplies to the fleet was vital, as they were never abundant, nor could the size of the boats comprising the fleet provide storage for sufficient supplies for a protracted period. These small ships served as a vital factor in the fleet's survival; they also provided an important link to the garrison on Fort Island and the workmen laying the chevaux-de-frise.

III

Organization—1775-1776

W ITH AN abundance of capable shipbuilders in the Philadelphia area, the design and construction of the first elements of the State navy were relatively problem free. However, this was only the beginning of the manifold requirements for implementing a naval force capable of complementing the forts and river obstructions. Men must be recruited to man the boats, and armament obtained—heavy and light cannon, swivels, howitzers, muskets, and ammunition. Rules to govern the conduct of officers and men; housing for the crews, as the boats could only provide emergency shelter and some not that; supplies, food, rum, or beer; clothing and other necessities were only some of the problems to which the Committee must direct its efforts. Indirectly, as vital to the naval effort, attention must be given to building and strengthening the river forts [1] and batteries, superintending the laying of chevaux-de-frise,[2] and providing for an alarm system to alert the defense elements of the approach of British men-of-war. While not germane to this study, the Committee was beset with many needs other than the direct defense of the river and city. Enlisting Continental regiments and local militia companies and the coordination of civil matters with the

State Assembly were only a few of the other demands on their time and talents.

Every few days during July, August, and September 1775 one or two galleys came down the ways to be equipped for service on the river. Captains were usually appointed before the galleys were launched, their first responsibility being the enlistment of crews. The enthusiasm generated during the first weeks and months probably gave some impetus to the recruiting program.[3]

Despite the initial fervor, the ultimate success of the program would be determined by the conditions of the enlistment. Inexperience or the paucity of funds may have prompted the Committee to offer recruits a pay scale far below that available on board a privateer.

Confronted with this competition for available manpower and later by the Continental navy (although the Continental ships also had their problems with the independent privateersmen), the officers of the fleet and civil authorities planned a program of recruitment that carried them into all counties of the State. Recruiting officers were sent to New York[4] and other states, and rendezvous were established throughout Pennsylvania at taverns, residences, and other buildings as rallying centers for recruits. Each officer on this service was assigned a fifer and drummer[5] to stimulate interest and announce a place where the rendezvous would be held. This method of recruiting was continued throughout the life of the State navy.

Difficulty in manning the boats and preventing desertion arose before the last galley was launched. On September 30, 1775, one day after the *Burke, Hancock,* and *Camden* were commissioned, it was noted that the fleet was only partly manned.[6] In an effort to place the fleet on a full war standing, the Committee asked all captains to appear before them to plan ways to encourage good seamen to enter the service, and to caucus and determine what the service should do to attract more volunteers.[7] One month before, on September 1, the Committee had ordered that each galley have a crew of not less than thirty nor more than fifty officers and men. At the same time, a pay scale was established,[8] ranging from thirty dollars per month for the fleet commodore, with the galley captains receiving twenty dollars, down to six dollars for the private or seaman. Each crew member, regardless of rank, received a weekly food allowance.[9] These provisions for wages and rations had obviously not been sufficient to spur enlistments. The captains recommended that each able seaman be given a bounty of fifteen shillings after he had served one month in the fleet.[10]

None of the suggestions for improving the recruitment picture promised immediate success; but other urgent problems were also demanding attention, among them that of the conduct of officers and men of the fleet. On August 29, "Rules and Regulations for Governing the Administration of the Navy" and the guidance of the crews was presented to the captains.[11] They were to insure that these rules were read to the men and that they understood their responsibilities to the State and fleet. In the stilted language of the eighteenth century, the preamble to these instructions reads:

WHEREAS, the Arbitrary and Tyrannical proceedings of the British Ministry, in attempting to reduce the good people of America into a state of abject Slavery and Vassalage, has met with a righteous and Spirited Opposition from the twelve united Colonies by their Delegates in Congress, who, by their resolves of the 18th July, recommended to the Assemblies or Conventions, or in their recess, to the Committees of Safety, to devise & provide such means for defending the Lives, Liberties, and properties of their respective inhabitants, as may to them seem best in compliance with this recommendation; and in consequence of the powers vested in this Committee by Resolve of the Assembly of this Province, they have caused Sundry Boats to be Built and Armed for the defence of the Same, and the protection of its commerce; which Boats being now ready for service, it remains that they be immediately manned and equipped; *Therefore*, to encourage good and brave Men to engage freely in this Glorious Service, the following Rules and Regulations are offered by the said Committee.

This preamble is followed by thirty articles of conduct, which are little more than a penal code. They cover drunkenness, profanity, and other misconduct; mutiny, desertion, or carrying on a treasonable correspondence with the enemy; waste of stores or supplies; careless handling of firearms, or falling asleep on duty—all punishable through conviction by a court-martial. Courts-martial for capital offenses were to be composed of thirteen officers, and require a decision by at least two-thirds. In returning a verdict, officers of the lowest rank, or youngest, voted first. Death sentences for other than mutiny or cowardice must be approved by the Assembly, or, if it were in recess, by the Committee (Council) of Safety. A court-martial could pronounce no other punishment than "degrading, cashiering, drumming out of the fleet, whipping, not exceeding thirty-nine lashes, fine, not exceeding two months' pay, and imprisonment not exceeding one month." All fines were to be turned over to those disabled in the service, or to the support of widows and families of those killed in performance of duty.[12]

It must be recognized that no precedents existed which could serve as guidelines for preparing the resolutions and instructions to govern the navy. With the added responsibility of the militia and Continental regiments to be raised, the results reflect the unusual capabilities of the members of the first Committee of Safety. A commission form for fleet officers was printed and sent to each officer.[13] In October it became apparent that many services of the fleet were woefully deficient and a muster master, paymaster, and ship's husband were appointed.[14] Dr. Benjamin Rush had been commissioned fleet surgeon[15] and Edward Chamberlain master-at-arms and amourer.[16]

In mid-October, a set of general instructions was released to the galley captains. They provided for the well treatment of crews without relaxing discipline. Constant vigilance was to be observed; crews were to maintain a decorous attitude toward all inhabitants, and good manners used in examining all in-bound vessels, but still permitting a search and seizure of those exhibiting hostile intentions. Each captain was to apply himself diligently to ensuring that proper and fresh rations were furnished his men. They were to be constantly alert to repel any of the "King's Ships, Sloops, Cutters, or armed vessels" attempting to proceed up the Delaware in a hostile manner. Finally, they were admonished to have all officers and men "attend the public worship of Almighty God as frequently as in their power."[17]

Concurrent with the problems of administration was the ever-present threat that the enemy could bring a naval force up the river before the State defense units were ready. To ensure a prompt and efficient warning system, Henry Fisher[18] of Lewes, Delaware, was selected to effect a method of alerting the Committee to the approach of British men-of-war.[19] He was empowered to supervise the pilots in the lower Delaware Bay, and to make certain that none was assigned to a mission that might place him in a position to be taken by the British. This was a constant source of irritation to the British navy, as they were always seeking a river pilot to guide them up the bay and river; and later, when the secrets of the chevaux-de-frise were revealed to a handful of pilots,[20] the British were again frustrated. Fisher was instructed to provide a system of riders [21] and alarm posts to quickly inform the city of any news of the British. He assisted in the establishment of thirteen alarm posts between Lewes and Point No Point, at the mouth of Frankford Creek.[22] These were:

1. Cape Henlopen (Lewes)
2. Boat at Mushmellon (Mispillion River)
3. Boat at Motherkill (Murderkill River)
4. Bombay Hook
5. Steep Water Point (Port Penn)
6. Long Point
7. Dalby Point
8. Chester
9. Thompson Point
10. Billingsport
11. Gloucester
12. Market Street Wharf
13. Point No Point (Frankford Creek)

The lower alarm posts all seem to have had small boats, probably pilot boats, in addition to a three- or four-pounder cannon. From Alarm Post 5 north all were equipped with cannon. Later the guard boats of the navy were assigned to complement and protect these posts. Usually these were one-man posts, consisting of a crude cabin on a promontory or point of land. Exceptions to this type of station were the redoubt at Billingsport and the Market Street Wharf. As no agency was assigned to supervise the alarm posts, it became the responsibility of the State navy, and later was under the direct administration of the Navy Board.

During the fourth quarter of 1775, with galleys partly equipped but undermanned, the entire posture of the river defenses was under constant scrutiny by the Committee. The land defenses were undergoing strengthening, additional chevaux-de-frise were added to the channel obstructions, and additional ships were being considered for the navy. A flagship for the Commodore was authorized which became the *Montgomery;* and a floating battery, subsequently named the *Arnold*, was ordered built.

On October 23, the Committee recommended to the Assembly that Captain Thomas Read be named Commodore of the fleet,[23] but the archives do not include any record of his appointment. On January 13, 1776, Andrew Caldwell was appointed Commodore,[24] and Read second in command and captain of the *Montgomery*. On May 25, 1776, Caldwell resigned because of ill health; the next day the Committee issued instructions to Captain John Read (Thomas Read, sometimes Thomas Reed, has now become John Read) that, for the present, command of the fleet would devolve on him. Ten days later Read resigned to enter the Continental navy as commander of one of the new frigates, then building. His ostensible reason was to be of greater assistance in the dispute with Great Britain.[25] Could he have been discouraged with the vacillating policies of political preferment in appointments—or the pressures of the galley captains?

To retrace our steps chronologically, when Read was recommended for Commodore on October 23, 1775, the captains of the galleys protested his appointment. In a memorial to the Committee of Safety, they apologetically denied any attempt to question the motives of the Committee, nor did they wish to cast any aspersions on the gentleman (Read) appointed to command of the armed boats, but rather they were merely seeking to advance their own claims to consideration for promotion. They pointed out that advancement should be based on seniority, especially as several of the captains were as well qualified as the appointee. There had never been any want of harmony among the captains before, but now many were discouraged that a stranger to the service had been selected over them. Acknowledging that the final right to appoint must rest with the Committee, they closed their memorial with the request that their case be given consideration.[26] Their appeal was apparently heard. Read's recommended appointment never was approved, and he served only as acting Commodore. The badgered Committee might have obtained some consolation if they had received a letter from Washington similar to one he wrote the complaining Schuyler:

From my own experience I can easily judge of your difficulties to introduce order and discipline in troops, who have from their infancy imbibed ideas of the most contrary kind. It would be far beyond the compass of a letter for me to describe the situation of things here upon my arrival [Boston]. Perhaps you will only be able to judge of it from my assuring you, that mine must be a portrait at full length of what you have a miniature.[27]

Insubordination, jealousy, and problems of recruitment were distractions to the Committee, but nothing could daunt the resourceful Doctor Franklin and his colleagues; they steadfastly carried on the work of building a navy. As frigates and other elements of the British fleet were momentarily expected to enter the capes, the armed boats must be equipped and ready for action. The scarcity of arms and cannon made uniform supplying of the boats impossible. A list of military stores for each galley was prepared for the State Commissary, and if stores were unavailable in sufficient quantity, they were to furnish an equal proportion of whatever was on hand.[28] The scarcity of ammunition and large cannon was to be a constant source of argument and recrimination between the civil authorities and the navy.

Food and rum were constantly in short supply. Contracts were let to victualling agents, each contract to be advertised in the newspapers and remain in effect for three months, unless the men were discharged before that date. This last provision of the contract reflected the hope and expectation that the Committee had for an accommodation with Great Britain. Clement Biddle had the first contract. When this expired on December 7, 1775, Francis Wade submitted the lowest bid, four shillings eleven pence per man per week. Apparently it was economically impossible to supply the fleet at this figure, as three months later, when the contract again expired, John Mitchell was the low bidder at six shillings per man. Mitchell was awarded the contract for subsequent renewal periods on the same terms. Extra rations were offered the officers, the Commodore receiving six rations per day, second in command and galley captains three rations, other officers two.[29]

The personal comfort of the officers and men was a constant factor in the morale of the crews and, when deficient, a major contributor to desertion. Short supplies in clothing and blankets were ever present to haunt the galley captains.

I have not found any mention of a specific uniform for the navy. It has been posited by editors of the Second Series of the

Pennsylvania Archives that the marine uniform was "a brown coat faced with green, letter I.P.B. on the buttons, and a cocked hat." [30] Support for this statement cannot be found; possibly the record has been lost or misplaced. Orders dated December 30, 1776, were issued to deliver to Captain William Brown jackets, underjackets, check shirts, trousers, stockings, and shoes for his men on the *Putnam*.[31] This issue of clothing to Brown's marines corresponds to uniform requisitions for the seamen; the same description of jackets and trousers is found in all existing records. The return of articles lost by the marines during the Trenton and Princeton campaign are of no value and suggest little that would indicate a regulation uniform.[32] Evidence is not available to designate an official uniform for the navy, nor to document the claim for the marine uniform. Recognizing the difficulties encountered in clothing the Continental forces, it is logical to assume that State authorities would accept any warm clothing that allowed freedom of movement. Jackets, designated as sailors, outside or under, with lincey (linsey-woolsey) trousers, and check shirts were the items issued. Such articles of dress were commonly used in a seaport city, and would be considered adequate for the fleet.[33] On February 28, 1776, the paymaster, in cooperation with the galley captains, was directed to see that the men were properly clothed, and that the cost of the articles furnished each man be deducted from his pay. Generously, not more than half of his pay could be stopped at a time.[34]

An authorized uniform may have been designated for the officers. A portrait of Commodore Hazelwood in Independence Hall, painted by Charles Willson Peale about 1785, shows a somewhat portly gentleman with gray hair and brown eyes. He is wearing a blue coat with buff facings and buff waistcoat. The brass or horn buttons bear an anchor. As Peale is noted for his historical accuracy, this is most likely to be Hazelwood's uniform as an officer of the State navy. It is known that all officers were furnished greatcoats.

If clothing was frequently in short supply, the men were experiencing even greater discomfort from lack of blankets. A return of blankets on hand, made in early 1777, revealed that on the thirteen galleys there were 130 blankets for 458 men. Even if the men could double up and share a blanket, there would be almost two hundred men with no cover.[35]

Of even greater concern, as if the lack of clothing and blankets were not enough, was the need for housing and other comforts for the boat crews. Many recommendations were discussed but the Committee finally decided to convert the old jail on Green Street to a barracks for the militia and galley crews. Speed was essential, as desertion and disciplinary problems were occupying a large percentage of the officers' time. On December 12, the Barrack Master, Joseph Fox, was ordered to secure immediately two hundred blankets or rugs, one hundred bed cases or a sufficient quantity of straw, one hundred cords of wood, and other necessaries for accommodating four hundred men.[36]

The problem of discipline was so serious that each boat was allotted six pairs of handcuffs to restrain the most incorrigible.[37] Assigning the crews to the barracks did little to help the disciplinary situation; officers who were given quarters with their men were often absent from their posts. Some, obtaining more comfortable lodgings in the city, could therefore exercise little control over their commands.

In an effort to relieve the monotony of garrison life, men were assigned guard duty at various storehouses throughout the city, including the State House. To further aid in reducing the boredom, a plan of rotation for the galleys on duty was ordered. Three galleys were to be on duty at Fort Island,[38] relieved every three days.[39] Improvised quarters of a temporary nature were planned for the crews on duty at the fort. An old house on the island was divided to provide a place for the men to "dress their victuals and dry themselves in bad weather." These arrangements proved unsatisfactory and the crews were later transferred to the Pest House on Province Island until more permanent quarters could be built in the fort.[40]

Earlier, on October 14, the Managers of the Pennsylvania Hospital had generously agreed to receive all sick or wounded men of the fleet, offering to minister to them without charge except in the treatment of venereal cases, when the patient was usually asked to pay £3 10s for his cure.[41] As the fleet would be operating in the vicinity of the forts and river obstructions, a facility would be required downriver for emergency purposes. Dr. Duffield, surgeon's mate, was instructed to examine the facilities of the Pest House on Province Island. He reported that the quarters were in good order and had sufficient supplies and equipment to accommodate forty patients.[42] A delay of about four weeks ensued before negotiations were closed with the overseer of the Pest House. He agreed to attend the sick, furnish them with provisions and drink, and wash them at the rate of ten shillings per week per man and an additional two shillings per week for firewood. Dr. Duffield informed the Committee that he and Dr. Rush would attend the sick and wounded men in rotation.[43]

With plans underway or completed for the comfort of the boat crews, the Committee faced the new year of 1776 with a determination to enlarge the navy and keep the river and bay open to commerce. It was imperative that commercial vessels arrive with regularity, as they carried the supplies which represented the life blood of the Continental as well as State cause. As early as June 1775 the British Admiralty had shown interest in placing an embargo on vessels entering the capes carrying provisions and supplies. Admiral Samuel Graves instructed Captain John Collins of the *Nautilus* that the provinces were being assisted in their rebellion by these illegal cruisers. He was to stop and examine all vessels suspected of carrying what might be judged as contraband, and to give every assistance to those subjects loyal to the Crown.[44] It was impossible to prevent spies and certain opportunists from keeping the British informed as to the plans of the State authorities. Much of the information relayed to London, or to the British military in America, was exaggerated, but in some cases it provides us with descriptions not available from other sources.

In early 1776 Captain Andrew Hamond of His Majesty's frigate *Roebuck*, of forty-four guns, was assigned the station in the lower bay. As early as March 3 he requested the aid of troops to operate on both sides of the river; and, as his objective was the taking of Philadelphia, he asked for more ships and a few howitzers or cohorns. Acknowledging the impossibility of navigating through the chevaux-de-frise, he bemoaned the lack of success in decoying a pilot off Cape Henlopen.[45]

The imminence of danger from British men-of-war accelerated recruitment efforts. On January 19 Commodore Caldwell was directed to recruit four hundred seamen and landsmen for the naval establishment. A week later the captains of the galleys advised the Commodore that they were of the opinion that one of the principal objections to entering the service was the fifteenth article of the regulations governing officers and men of the armed boats.[46] This article provided that the proceeds from all prizes were to be distributed as the Assembly should deem proper. In an apparent effort to correct this condition, the Committee, on February 3, resolved "that all [enemy] ships or vessels of war, with their guns, boats, furniture, and good on Board, that shall be taken . . . in the River Delaware by any vessels or armed boats fitted or fitting out for this Province," were to be condemned as lawful prizes. Two-thirds of the proceeds were to be awarded to the officers and crew, the remaining one-third was to be applied to the maintenance and support of such officers, soldiers (marines) and seamen as should be disabled in action and to the widows and children of those killed. Of course, all distributions were to be made at the discretion of the Assembly or Committee (Council) of Safety. They further resolved that if any commercial vessels were taken, they could be condemned in a like manner and distributed according to the resolutions adopted by Congress. Was this wishful thinking? Only three ships of the State navy were ever capable of effective action below the chevaux-de-frise, and the added reference to those ships operating in the Delaware River obviously recognizes the limitations of the armed boats.

An added incentive, raising the captains and lieutenants salaries,[47] was passed at the same time.

In early February, Commodore Caldwell was given £120 for the recruiting service. Officers were to be sent into the country to obtain recruits for the fleet, each officer to be given an allowance of twenty shillings each week for traveling expenses. In lieu of all recruiting expenses they were to receive ten shillings for each man enlisted. An additional ten shillings was allowed for the subsistence of each recruit. These allowances were to continue while recruiting in the country and until the recruits were delivered to their proper commands.[48] To add to the handicaps of recruitment, Tories were visiting the rendezvous and attempting to discourage men from entering the service.[49]

The first marines to be recruited for the fleet were authorized on March 3. Captain Brown was granted the same financial arrangement as that of the galley captains. He was further admonished to select only healthy men, none to be under sixteen years of age. No indentured servants were to be recruited without consent of their masters. A number of complaints were registered by owners of indentured servants and runaway slaves, which were often resolved by remitting the servants' pay to the master. Many of the indentured servants and Negroes served with credit during the conflict. It is impossible to determine the number of servants and black men on the boats, as no attempt is made to single them out on the muster rolls. Occasionally, when sent to the hospital, or claimed by a master, a man's identity was revealed.[50] Several times, when a seaman was considered undesirable or an officer took offense at a particular seaman, he would order him to Philadelphia, with the understanding that he obtain another man in his place. The replacement was usually no better[51] than the man he replaced.

Finally, in a desperate effort to man the boats, the Committee raised the seamen's wages to seven dollars a month, and they were to receive a two-dollar bounty. All recruits were to remain in service until discharged by the Committee. Seamen serving on the boats were to receive the increase allowed the new recruits.[52]

Henry Fisher, ever on the alert at Cape Henlopen, was in constant communication with the authorities at Philadelphia. Almost daily, British sloops and tenders were observed under the capes. On March 25, Captain Andrew Hamond of the *Roebuck* entered the capes and proceeded up the bay. Fisher, probably due to bad weather, thought that it was a sloop-of-war, and relayed this information to the Committee at Philadelphia.[53] Without hesitation, Caldwell was ordered to prepare four of the best equipped galleys, having nearly their full complement of men and arms, to proceed, if necessary, as far as Reedy Island, and to cooperate with Captain John Barry of the Continental brigatine *Lexington*.[54] Fisher soon observed that it was a frigate and too formidable for any American ship in the bay or river. Quickly dispatching express riders for Philadelphia, and pilot boats to alert all alarm stations and residents along the bay, he prepared to defend his post at Lewes.[55] Fortunately for Barry, he received the correct information as to the identity of the

British frigate shortly after passing through the chevaux-de-frise.[56] Realizing that the *Lexington* was no match for the *Roebuck*, he changed his plans to engage the British. Leaving the four galleys at Reedy Island, he proceeded down the bay, hugging the shore, where he would be safe from the *Roebuck*. Arriving at the capes and seeing that he could not prevent the British from occupying their old position in the bay, he decided to go to sea for a cruise against enemy shipping. Keeping the shoals between the brigatine and the frigate, he slipped to sea.[57] This might have been the first action of the State navy, but Hamond was not anxious for contact, as he was waiting for reinforcements. The first engagement must wait until early in May.

IV

The *Roebuck* Affair—1776

UNTIL THE scouting excursion in the upper bay by the
British frigate *Roebuck*, no enemy vessel had ventured so close
to Philadelphia. The possibility of an attempt to force the river
obstructions roused the Committee of Safety to greater attention
to the river defenses. They fragmented their committee assignments by appointing nineteen subcommittees, the duties of several sometimes overlapping.[1] The lookout boats and stations in
the lower bay were placed on constant alert and supplied with
muskets and swivels. No chevaux-de-frise pilot was permitted
to pass below Chester without written permission from the
Committee or the Commodore.[2]

Work on the land defenses at Fort Island and Billingsport was
stepped up, the existing chevaux-de-frise were examined, and
two additional obstructions ordered built and sunk to close a
passage between those already in position. A large channel,
or passage, was spotted and two hulks were ordered purchased
and sunk to close it. Contemporary maps show two hulks sunk
in the river, but these maps were published three years later,
and as subsequently other hulks were sunk, it is not possible to
verify whether those ordered in April 1776 were actually

placed in the river.[3] The channel between the chevaux-de-frise and Fort Island was ordered closed by a boom attached to piers to be built on Fort Island.[4]

Additional craft were considered or actually authorized to be built for the State navy. A fascination for fire rafts and fire ships was demonstrated by increased activity in the outfitting and equipping of these craft, despite their questionable value. Most of these arrangements were of a temporary nature, born of inexperience and haste, and based on trial and error.

As the spring of 1776 approached and the threat of British invasion or raids became more real, it was evident that the fleet must be stationed at Fort Island and the crews quartered there, available for immediate action.

Several incidents on the river at this time were symptomatic of a developing strain in relations between the Committee of Safety and galley captains, which had started with the protest of the suggested appointment of Captain Read as Commodore. Now the captains were accused of a breech of their code of conduct as laid down by the Committee. A number of masters and skippers of vessels bound for the city were stopped by the galleys and, presumably, rather rudely treated. The captains were accused of demanding compliments (a form of obeisance or tribute), a practice common to British officers commanding ships assigned to the Delaware station. The captains were also guilty of firing on vessels coming upriver to bring them to without sufficient cause. The Commodore was commanded to admonish his officers to let all vessels pass without hindrance, unless there was clear evidence of a ship's hostile intentions.[5]

Before the crews could be quartered on Fort Island, the second British threat to the Delaware Valley was received by the Committee. Henry Fisher had been attentive to the activities of the *Roebuck* and other British men-of-war; in fact, his letters are a virtual log on the activities of the *Roebuck*.[6] On May 5 Fisher dispatched an express rider with a message for the Committee and the alarm post at Port Penn:

On yesterday one of the British Pirates with two tenders stood out to sea, and took a schooner and sent in here, this morning with her two tenders, at 10 o'clock this morning the Roebuck and the other ship [*Liverpool*] with the wind at E.S.E., and went out of the Road and are making up the Bay, they have got the Sloop, tender, Dawson's Boat and Prize Schooner all ahead

of them, with intent I believe to sound the Channel, the wind is fresh, therefore the Whale boat from here can be of no use. But I am in hopes as Mr.
Edward's Boat is at Mother Kill she will give the alarm by water, and I
have sent a Letter to Cantwell's bridge to be forwarded to Port Penn to the
Alarm Post there.[7]

The relay express rider arrived Monday, May 6, about nine
A.M. The alternate message, transmitted through Port Penn,
reached the Committee at about the same time.

The Committee immediately ordered the Commodore of the
fleet and the commander of the artillery company at Fort
Island to call all boats with their crews, and all soldiers to their
stations, to be ready for action. Officers and men of the navy on
leave or on duty in the city were ordered to report to their
boats. Captain Hazelwood was directed to send the fire vessels
and two chains of fire rafts down to Fort Island.[8]

An apprehensive group of men met in the State House at dawn
on May 7 to consider the latest news from Port Penn. British
frigates and smaller ships-of-war had been sighted the day before sailing north toward Philadelphia. The Committee was certain that the destination of the British was the river defenses—
to test the chevaux-de-frise and attack the city and shipping if
successful. In reality, Captain Hamond had no intention of
proceeding up the river beyond the present Wilmington area.
He was interested in scouting out the upper bay and filling his
water casks.[9]

Having received information concerning the whereabouts of
Hamond's flotilla, the Committee ordered Captain Read to proceed down the river with the thirteen galleys. (Commodore
Caldwell was ill.) Read was instructed to decide on the best
method of destroying the enemy ships without exposing the
galleys to capture or destruction. Captain Gamble of the fire
sloop *Aetna* was to be taken down with the galleys. Provisions
were ordered sent to Fort Island for the boat crews and artillerymen. The shallop carrying the provisions was also to take
twenty rounds of powder and ball for two guard boats and
thirty rounds of cartridges for each galley; two-thirds of the shot
was to be cross bar, if available. Colonel Samuel Miles of the
Chester County militia, stationed at Marcus Hook, was to receive
a quantity of ammunition for his battalion.[10]

Read, upon receipt of his orders, called a council of the captains on board the *Montgomery*. Upon conveying the Committee's instruction to the council, several of the galley captains complained of undermanned boats, and requested complements of seamen to bring them up to fighting strength. A muster of the fleet on May 1 revealed that one galley, the *Washington*, had a full muster of fifty men; the remaining twelve galleys ranged down to twenty-two on the *Warren*, or a total of 446 on the thirteen galleys. The *Montgomery* had a complement of 117 men, and the floating battery *Arnold* 116 men. Also available, at Fort Island at the time of the muster, was Captain Thomas Proctor's artillery company of 119 men. To supplement the short-handed galley crews, Captain Davidson of the *Arnold* furnished seventy-four seamen, and Read transferred the marine contingent of the *Montgomery*, under command of Captain William Brown. Brown's muster at this time indicates six officers and fifty-eight men fit for duty. The addition of the men from the *Montgomery* and *Arnold* brought the galleys up to 584 men or about forty-five men in each galley.[11]

Captain Dougherty, as senior captain of the galleys, was given the Committee's instructions to drop downriver to resist the advance of the British ships. The galleys were to rendezvous below Hog Island and receive orders before proceeding further. Captain Gamble of the fire sloop *Aetna* was ordered down to report to Dougherty. To assist Gamble in maneuvering the fire sloop, Third Lieutenant Greenway and four men of the *Montgomery* were chosen to man a six-oar boat; men on the flagship were so enthusiastic that the entire crew had volunteered for this service. Great expectations were held for the effectiveness of the fire sloop, due in large measure to the confidence of Captain Gamble.[12]

The naval and military forces gathering at Fort Island were augmented by two chains of fire rafts and fire vessels. Captain Hazelwood had been ordered to send these elements of the fire fleet to Fort Island and station them where they could be of the greatest service. The order to send down the fire vessels would indicate that two or more were in service in May 1776. However, only two were on muster during 1776, the *Aetna* and the *Vesuvius*, and the *Vesuvius* was not in service until July 1. On May 7, Captain Read wrote the Committee that crews were needed for two pilot boats and two fire boats. The fire boats were probably shallops or barges to be used in maneuvering the chains of fire rafts. As no guard boats were available at this time to aid Hazelwood in bringing the fire rafts into position, it was necessary to provide crews and boats for this purpose.[13]

The Committee of Safety had appealed to the Continental Congress for assistance from the Continental ship *Reprisal*, under command of Captain Lambert Wickes. Their request for men to fill out the complements of state galleys was granted by Congress, and instructions were forwarded to Wickes to assist Read in every way possible. Unfortunately, the order was delayed but eventually reached Read about ten o'clock on the evening of May 7. He immediately went on board the *Reprisal* and presented the order to Wickes, "which he complyed with." Lieutenant Robert Harris and ten seamen were placed on board the fire boats while Captain Miles Pennington, two sergeants, and twenty-four marines were dispatched to the pilot boats. As reported by Read, all were "equipped with small arms, all in great Spirits." [14]

Captain Read was encountering numerous petty delays in his frantic deployment of the *Montgomery* and other sailing ships, and he was becoming excited and irritable. Other officers exhibited an equally excitable temperament in their first experience under fire. The frustrations of commanding a fleet so devoid of equipment necessary to face frigates would have discouraged and upset men of greater experience than Read or the galley captains. As indicated, a major shifting of manpower had been necessary to bring the galleys to a combat posture; ammunitions and supplies of all kinds were in short supply; hospital supplies and medicine chests were sent on board ship without keys to unlock the chests. These annoyances were enough to thwart any commander, but the greatest vexation would be meddling by the Committee of Safety.

Between five and six o'clock on May 7, the Committee held a special session and appointed a subcommittee of four with instructions to board the province sloop and proceed to Fort Island, or the flagship *Montgomery*, and establish headquarters "with full and ample power to enforce such orders as have already been Issued, or may Issue from this board to the Commanding officer of the Naval armament of this Province." The committee of Colonel John Cadwalader, Alexander Wilcocks,

James Mease, and Captain Robert Whyte were also empowered to suspend any officer refusing to obey the orders of the commanding officer and to appoint the suspended officer's successor. Also, they were fully authorized, with the commanding officer, to issue whatever orders to the fleet were deemed necessary.[15]

With the arrival of the Committee members on the sloop at 10 P.M. on May 7, Read went on board to receive his orders. Final plans were worked out with Captain Dougherty, who was instructed to proceed downriver with the galleys and the fire sloop, to intercept the British ships. The *Montgomery*, the floating battery *Arnold*, and the Continental ship *Reprisal* were to anchor north of the chevaux-de-frise and serve as a second line of defense.

Read, Wickes, and Captain Davidson of the *Arnold* were badly in need of men, as a sizable part of their crews were now with Dougherty. Orders were received to get the undermanned *Reprisal* through the obstructions to assist the galleys, if needed. To accomplish this, seamen were to be transferred from the *Montgomery* and *Arnold* to the *Reprisal*. Apparently adverse winds or tide prevented this maneuver as the *Reprisal* was still in line above the chevaux-de-frise on May 8. At six o'clock on May 8, Dougherty and his flotilla dropped down the river, to seek out the British ships-of-war.

In the meantime, the British had been beating their way up the bay and river. With the *Liverpool* leading the way, the *Roebuck*, two tenders, and the brig *Betsey* following, the British fleet engaged in land forays and side excursions to capture small American ships. Cattle were butchered and the area foraged in general to replenish depleted larders; it was reported that the cattle were of poor grade but were nevertheless greedily eaten. The most important prize, the Continental armed schooner *Wasp*, commanded by Charles Alexander, formerly captain of the state galley *Bull Dog*, eluded Hamond and escaped up the Christiana River.[16] Hamond and his ships arrived off the mouth of the Christiana during the evening of May 7. Next morning he sent a flag of truce to Philadelphia in an effort to effect an exchange for the bearer [17] of the flag and a Lieutenant George Ball. He also carried an undated letter from Captain Bellew of the *Liverpool*, to obtain a safe-conduct pass for Mrs. Bellew to travel to her relatives in New England.[18] Of interest is the reaction of Bellew after the engagement with the Pennsylvania galleys, when Captain Walter Stewart was sent by the Continental Congress to escort Mrs. Bellew to Philadelphia, preliminary to granting her permission to go to New England. Stewart, finding Bellew in very bad humor, reported that the Englishman said he would not permit his wife to go among the Americans "as their damned gondolas had treated him so ungenteely." [19]

The morning of May 8 was breezy and hazy, turning to calm and fog before noon and lifting somewhat before one o'clock. Hamond observed the State fleet approaching with, as he believed, the intent of attacking the British ships. He reported, "Their fleet consisted of 13 Row Galley's, each carrying a Gun, from 32 Pounders to Eighteen, a Floating Battery of 10 Eighteen Pounders, and a Sloop fitted as a fire ship." Hamond was in error, as the floating battery *Arnold* remained at the chevaux-de-frise. His intelligence undoubtedly had advised him that the State navy included such a boat and he assumed it was in the approaching flotilla.[20]

Hamond recorded that "We met them under Sail (as the Tide ran too rapid to lie with a Spring upon the Cable) and being obliged to engage them at the distance they chose to fix on, which was scarcely within point blank shot."[21] Hamond further noted that the galleys were such low objects in the water that it was difficult to hit them. William Barry, an American seaman, and John Emmes, a Delaware pilot, were prisoners on board the *Roebuck*. Barry noted the disdain with which junior British officers regarded the galleys, believing the small boats could inflict little injury on the larger British ships. Hamond and Bellew had more respect for the galleys and they cleared the decks for action. As the approach of the galleys was unexpected, the decks were littered with water casks. It was necessary to stave in some and place some on the brigatine captured coming up the bay, while others were put in the ship's hold.[22]

The action was started by the row galleys about two o'clock; several shots were fired before the *Roebuck* responded with her stern chasers. According to Emmes, the British brought their ships to a broadside position, with the *Roebuck's* bow to the east and the *Liverpool's* to the west. Firing was rapid and without intermission for over two hours.[23] The galley captains never approached nearer than one mile and maneuvered their boats in shallow water to prevent the frigates from closing the gap. Apparently Dougherty stationed the galleys so that only part of the flotilla was engaged at any one time. A well-directed broadside from the *Roebuck* could have destroyed the entire flotilla of galleys if they had been permitted to fight in close formation. The captains resented a statement published in the *Pennsylvania Evening Post* on May 11, implying a lack of judgment in handling the galleys. Many criticisms were noted on the conduct of the galleys in the first day's action: firing too soon and out of effective range; wasting powder and not following up advantages gained when the *Roebuck* went aground that night. This was their first time under fire and the mistakes must be attributed to lack of experience. All acted bravely, some with greater credit than others.[24]

After two hours of heavy firing and with their ammunition exhausted, the galleys retired upriver, with the intention of renewing the action the next morning. The sole account received from the galleys stated that the *Camden* was the only galley struck by British shot, and the damage was slight. It was officially reported that one man in the fleet was killed during the action.[25] The British damages were light: Emmes commented that most of the shot fired by the galleys at the *Roebuck* failed to reach her. He further remarked that one ball struck the hull of the *Roebuck* and some damage was seen in the rigging and sails. On the other hand, Barry claimed she had some shot in her sides, and considerable damage to the rigging.[26]

The action on the eighth presented a gala occasion for residents on both sides of the river. Charles Biddle recorded in his autobiography that the banks were lined with spectators, of course at a discreet distance from the line of fire. Many of the onlookers brought chairs and refreshments as though they were attending a fair, each rooting for his favorite. A letter written shortly after the engagement related that it afforded a most interesting spectacle to several thousand people who stood on the shores.[27]

As darkness fell on the eighth of May, frustrations beset both American and the British commanders. A minor disturbance to Hamond was the loss of a small brig, although his journal indicates that he was unaware that Alexander, in the *Wasp*, had captured her. More important events occupied Hamond's attention; in an effort to get close to the galleys, the frigate had run aground. She was fast aground "on the [New] Jersey shore, near Kearney's [Carney's] Point, a little above Deep Water Point."[28] Great concern was felt on board the British ships as the *Roebuck* lay helpless in shallow water. Hamond ordered the *Liverpool* in position to cover the *Roebuck*. With approaching twilight, the frigate's boats were deployed to form a protective screen and warn the ships if galleys came downriver during the night.

In this defenseless position, Hamond and Bellew had their crews employed in a frantic effort to refloat the *Roebuck*. The frigate heeled so far that her gunports were closed to prevent flooding, which made her guns useless. The crews were cheered throughout the night by the frequent return of the scouting boats reporting that the galleys were still upriver. If the galleys appeared, plans were to abandon ship; the crew was to transfer to the *Liverpool*. After many attempts with the *Liverpool* anchored close by, they got the frigate's stream cable on board; finally between three and four o'clock in the morning they succeeded in getting her off into deep water.[29]

The question has often been raised as to why the galleys and fire sloop did not come down and attempt to destroy the helpless frigate. Hamond assumed that they were short of ammunition. Much criticism has been directed to the galley captains on the extravagant waste of the fleet's fire power. Such criticism may be rationally sound, but logic does not govern the human factors inherent in war. The galley captains unquestionably wasted ammunition and no excuse can negate the fact that a golden opportunity was lost to destroy the *Roebuck*. In extenuation, certain factors must be considered. The galleys were clumsy and difficult to maneuver; they were designed to operate in smooth water and in cooperation with the forts and obstructions, and not in the open river or bay below these defenses. The crews of many of the galleys were strange to their officers, having been transferred to the boats the previous day. The first time under fire for officers and crews undoubtedly created a condition in which cannon were fired too soon, and too often, without due regard to the location of the target. It is reasonable to assume that a frenetic atmosphere prevailed on board the galleys—but no panic.

Other factors made night attack on the *Roebuck* questionable, if not impossible. The galleys could carry only a limited supply of ammunition; fifty rounds of shot had been placed on board each boat in October 1775.[30] Each galley captain was instructed to maintain this quantity at all times, and to replace powder or shot which might become wet. As the supply in the hands of the commissary of stores was usually inadequate, it was frequently impossible for the captains to maintain sufficient ammunition to engage in combat. According to the galley captains, there was an average of twenty-eight rounds on board the boats at the start of the engagement with the *Roebuck*.[31] Colonel Miles wrote that he estimated three or four hundred shot were exchanged between the two flotillas.[32]

The Committee of Safety ordered Robert Towers, commissary of stores, to obtain a shallop and put on board cartridges and shot for the militia and navy, and to proceed to Fort Island. A minimum of thirty rounds of shot for each galley, two-thirds to be cross bar, if available, were to be included in the shipment. The shallop, upon reaching the flagship, was dispatched downstream by Read to supply the galleys. In addition, Read forwarded all ammunition on board the *Montgomery*, retaining only six rounds for each cannon. All ammunition on the floating battery was also sent down.

Read was ordered to pass through the chevaux-de-frise with the *Montgomery* to be available to assist the galleys, if needed. He reluctantly complied, although undermanned and with only the six rounds of ammunition per cannon. As the powder was received, Read wrote the Committee it was not usable as no cartridges were sent to fill with the powder.[33]

If an excited state existed in the fleet, it was also apparent in the Committee of Safety. They were making strenuous efforts to obtain ammunition; but, as Read reported, what was received could not be used. They attempted to direct the fleet from the State House, finally sending their subcommittee of four to enforce the instructions of the Committee, and, because of the high incidence of desertion and insubordination, to ensure obedience to the captain's orders. As Christopher Marshall wrote in his diary, everyone was in a state of suspense. To further exasperate Read, John Barry and his crew from the *Lexington*, with a large number of volunteers, was sent down to augment the crews.

While Barry's crew could be of assistance, the volunteers were useless. Read wrote the Committee that the "want for Seamen is Terrible," but "As for Volunteer[s], I will not be in the Ship with them, they know nothing and will do nothing they are ordered." [34]

One of these volunteers, Charles Biddle, recorded his impression of an attempt to man a ship for service:

We had about one hundred and fifty men on board, but we were very badly fitted. Our guns were a great deal too long, and our crew chiefly landsmen. There were not more than twenty seamen including officers on board, so that we would have made a bad hand at fighting. Having some apprehension of being taken, I took on board only a few shirts and trowsers, being determined . . . to make my escape by swimming.

Biddle further states that they never sailed, as they were informed that the *Roebuck* was afloat—then he remarked that he was never put to the trial.[35]

In order to observe the conduct of the galleys, the sloop with the Committee of Safety members had passed through the chevaux-de-frise and proceeded downriver. No record has survived to indicate their opinion of the activities of the galleys and their officers and crews; however, the subcommittees' opinions unquestionably influenced the Assembly's findings in the subsequent controversy between the Committee and the galley captains.

As morning dawned on May 9, it was extremely foggy and it was well after eight o'clock before the British commander saw the galleys at anchor, two miles up the river. Hamond ordered the *Roebuck* and *Liverpool* under full sail and to close with the galleys. According to Hamond the galleys "industriously plied their oars and sails to avoid us." The wind failed and as the galleys rowed near the western shore of the river with the frigate in hot pursuit, suddenly Hamond discovered that he had less than six inches of water clearance over the shoal. Fearing a repetition of yesterday's mishap he withdrew downriver where the British ships would have the advantage of the greater width and depth of the river.[36]

The British command did not anticipate further offensive action by the Americans. William Barry noted that the belief on board the *Roebuck* was that considerable damage had been in-

flicted on the American fleet the day before.[37] Later in the
afternoon, the British were astounded to see the galleys advancing to attack. Hamond recorded that the American fleet had increased to twenty-two sail. No American account has survived
to describe the nine additional sail observed by Hamond. The
Province sloop with the Committee of Safety members, the fire
sloop, and probably a number of private sloops, as described by
Charles Biddle, were the other sail accompanying the galleys.
They were, however, well in the rear of the galleys and had
little inclination to become involved in the engagement.

The Americans were eager for action and confident that they
could give a good account of themselves. They had replenished
their ammunition; Read and Davidson had stripped their ships
of powder along with the supply on board the shallop, putting a
quantity approximating forty-five rounds on board each galley.[38]

Captain Thomas Houston, in the *Warren*, led the van of the
State fleet.[39] Approaching to within three-quarters of a mile of
the British ships, the Americans opened fire, and at that distance
were hitting with greater accuracy than the day before. Starting
between four and five o'clock in the afternoon and continuing
for over four hours, the galleys showed considerable spirit in
pressing the attack on ships with the firepower of the *Roebuck*
and *Liverpool*. It was observed by an unknown correspondent
that the galleys were never engaged as a unit, "not more than
one half can be said to have been engaged at any one time." [40]
He continued by commenting that this use of the galleys showed
a lack of ". . . judgment somewhere, in stationing them properly,
and at proper distances, is at the same time an additional argument in favour of the real service of boats." [41]

Christopher Marshall offers a second-hand account of the
conduct of the officers and crews: ". . . that our officers of six
of the gondolas have done their duty with credit, both officers
and men having distinguished themselves nobly and gained
great reputation. The others not showing the same bravery and
resolution, I hope will be enquired strictly into." [42] These comments, along with the scarcity of ammunition, were soon to be
the cause of a public dispute between the galley captains and
the Committee of Safety.

The *Roebuck* and *Liverpool*, as the galleys approached, had
weighed anchor, and getting under sail, attempted to turn to

windward. The wind was fresh to the southwest, and the maneuver thus headed them downriver; giving chase, the galleys prudently maintained a distance of about three-quarters of a mile, and were hitting with greater accuracy and inflicting considerable damage, especially to the *Roebuck*. It was later observed that this action established the proper distance for galleys to engage ships of war.[43]

While Hamond claimed only superficial damage, eyewitness accounts, both on board the *Roebuck* and from observers on shore, recorded substantial damage to the British ships. William Barry reported that

the Roebuck received many shots betwixt the wind and water: some went quite through, some in her quarter, and was much raked fore and aft . . . one man was killed by a shot. . . . Six were much hurt and burned by an eighteen-pound cartridge of powder taking fire, among whom was an acting lieutenant, and several were hurt by splinters. . . . During the engagement, the Captain ordered several of the guns to be loaded with round and grape shot . . . the carpenters . . . having taken . . . forty of the row-galleys' balls out of the Roebuck, and some cannot be come at.

John Emmes noted that one eighteen-pound shot

was lodged in the Roebuck's side, about three streaks above the water's edge, and another like it on the opposite side nearly as low. That one eighteen-pound shot entered an upper port, ruined the carriage, dismounted a nine-pound cannon, killed one man, and wounded two others; that five others were wounded, two of them considerably, by a cartridge taken fire; that another eighteen-pound shot also entered the stern and lodged on board the ship, and that two other shot also struck the ship, seven in all. . . . That the rigging, sails, and spars, of the Roebuck were often struck, damaged, and cut; particularly one mizzen shroud, one of the foretopmast shrouds, and two of the back stays were cut off; the main stay cut as far as a strand and a half, and much running rigging broken; the mizzen yard twice wounded, so that it cannot be depended on, the sails pierced several times, not easy to be numbered. The long boat had been damaged in the first fight.[44]

A visitor to the *Roebuck* noted that "the Roebuck's quarter sails were carried away, and a number of plugs were in her side." Barry mentioned that the carpenters were using a substance called "plaster" to cover the holes to prevent the ship from receiving water. Others commented that the carpenters were busily engaged for at least a week after the action. On the other hand, Hamond, writing to Sir Peter Parker, said that the Americans "fired away Seven Tons of Powder without doing us the least mischief. . . . Report says they received much damage." Several of the galleys were slightly damaged, but all returned to their stations on the following day. One man had been killed in the galleys on the first day, and two or three wounded on the second day.[45]

It was about ten o'clock in the evening when all firing ceased. The British had retired to the vicinity of Reedy Island. The Americans stopped near New Castle. The British were having difficulty in sighting their guns and, in the darkness, were unable to see the galleys. On the other hand, the galleys' ammunition was again in short supply and they were in an area where their effectiveness would be impaired. Dougherty and the galley captains were fully aware of the dangers attendant upon the flotilla being caught in the broad reaches of the upper bay. However, they remained at anchor near the New Castle bight, ready to contest a return upriver by the British.

The British ships lay at anchor for three days, refilling water casks and making temporary repairs to the hulls and rigging. Hamond then dropped down to the Capes, arriving in the road near Lewes about noon on May 15. On the sixteenth they set sail and went to sea; later, on May 22, the *Liverpool* returned, but was scared away on the twenty-seventh as Captains John Barry and Charles Alexander of the Continental navy arrived in the road.[46]

The galley captains had taken stock of their conditions and determined to contest any attempt by the British to come upriver. Captain Dougherty and the galley captains held a council of war on May 11, and decided that it would be suicidal to commit the galleys to an attack on the British ships without assistance from the *Montgomery* and the Continental men-of-war. With the *Roebuck* close in to the New Jersey shore and the *Liverpool* near the Pennsylvania shore, they had spread the galleys across the river to forestall an attempt by the British to return upriver. Their situation was extremely precarious; some of the boats with eighteen- and twenty-four-pounder cannon were without one shot, although all galleys had twenty rounds of powder, most of which was received that day.

The condition of the river at this point presented some problems and three or four of the galleys almost foundered.[47] Captain Read wrote to the Committee on the same day requesting plank to repair the galleys, and chains and anchors for mooring the boats in the rough water of the upper bay and lower part of the river. He further commented on the cartridges being of inferior quality, falling to pieces at the slightest touch, and the need for seamen, not the undependable volunteers. Apparently beer was in good supply and he sent a boat down to the galleys with a quantity of it and some wads for the cannon. The beer was obviously the fourteen barrels of eighteen-shilling beer ordered sent down by the Committee. While good for the morale, it would certainly not make the galleys a formidable fighting force.[48]

As the captains were planning their strategy, they were reviewing the cause of their failure to destroy the *Roebuck*, and possibly the *Liverpool*. They were unaware that a tempest was slowly brewing beneath the surface. Forces which they could not control would bring them in direct confrontation with the Committee of Safety. The seeds of disagreement had been planted as early as October 1775. Recriminations would fly back and forth, the boat would be rocked, but the navy would not sink.

The Philadelphia newspapers, private correspondence, and journals would soon carry accounts of the two-day engagement. Correspondents would be both candid and, in certain instances, constructively critical. But the oversensitive captains were in no mood to accept comments which reflected on their abilities or courage.

As recriminations were exchanged, they ostensibly centered on the subject of ammunition; had the Committee been derelict in their duty to furnish the galleys with enough ammunition to destroy the British? Or had the galley flotilla wasted shot and powder by firing before they were in effective range of the *Roebuck* and her consorts, and continuing the action when it was obvious that the volleys were falling short of their target? These points were the manifest reasons for the public enquiry which followed, aggravated by the subtle inferences of mismanagement of the fleet. Actually, when the smoke cleared, much had been learned about the most effective ways to use the galleys. The majority of the officers and crews, in their first experience under fire, had given an excellent example of courage. Any deficiencies in performance were directly attributable to inexperience—both naval and civilian.

The galley captains had neither the patience nor the resolution to submit to the will of the civilian authorities for the public good; they felt compelled to defend their reputations. On May 16, they prepared a memorial to the citizens of Pennsylvania defending their handling of the galleys in the *Roebuck* action, resting their entire defense on the lack of ammunition. According to their memorial, they had on hand an average of twenty-eight rounds of cartridges as they went into action on May 8. At the time the *Roebuck* went aground, the supply on some galleys was exhausted and only a round or two left on the remaining boats. If more adequately furnished with ammunition, they thought they could have captured the *Roebuck*. But, in their condition, they were obliged to retreat. Early that evening they received a supply equivalent to eight rounds for each galley. This was the quantity forwarded by Read and Davidson from the *Montgomery* and the *Arnold*. On May 9, a second supply was received, bringing the average quantity to forty-five rounds on each galley. Unfortunately, by this time the *Roebuck* was off the reef and under sail down the river. Advancing to the attack, they found themselves operating at a disadvantage and were forced to

cut up blankets, jackets, trowsers, stockings, &c. to supply the defect of cartridges; and for want of wads, some were necessitated to cut up cables and take the oakum out of the netting, this supply likewise also expended about sun-set, and after a very close engagement, when some retreated to look for fresh supplies, and meeting with a barge, three of us got seven rounds there from and returned to the attack, which was continued until the enemy was below Newcastle.[49]

Since the captains had stated their position in the Philadelphia press, the Committee of Safety felt called upon to clear their good names. They must prove that every effort had been made to keep the fleet supplied with cartridges and shot. Correspondents who had commented on the conduct of the galleys wrote retractions or explanations of their statements.[50]

A special meeting was called to consider the proclamation of the officers of the galleys.[51] Requests were made to John Nixon and Robert Whyte to present a report on the ammunition supplied the galleys by the Committee and through Captain Read. All captains of the galleys were ordered to attend this meeting.[52] Following the special meeting, a subcommittee of seven members was appointed to prepare a memorial to the Assembly of Pennsylvania. On May 27, the petition was submitted to the Assembly, stating the opinion of some observers that it was in the power of the galleys to have taken or destroyed the *Roebuck*, and that in extenuation of their failure the captains of the boats had attributed it to misconduct on the part of the Committee of Safety in failing to supply them with sufficient ammunition. The Committee requested an enquiry to fix proper blame, by which verdict they would abide.[53]

In the meantime, many civic organizations had passed resolutions commending the galleys for their spirited behavior in the engagement. One delayed its vote on its resolution to await an unprejudiced study by the Assembly. The galley captains petitioned the Assembly for a hearing but apparently were never called to testify.[54]

On May 28 the Committee of Safety's memorial was laid before the Assembly and a special committee was chosen to enquire into the conduct of the Committee of Safety.[55]

The report of the committee of the Assembly appeared in the *Pennsylvania Packet* on June 24. It exonerated the Committee of Safety and implied that any failure to take the *Roebuck* was the responsibility of the galley captains. To quote from the committee's report:

... before and at time of their engagements with the Roebuck and Liverpool ... that it appears from incontestible evidence, that, before the first engagement, the gallies were supplied with thirty-three pounds of powder each; at the proportion of one third weight of powder to the ball; that during the said first engagement, they received in cartridges and two kegs of loose powder, the quantity of eight rounds more beyond their first stock, and there was then ready to be delivered, and was supposed delivered to them, immediately after the first engagement, while the Roebuck lay aground, the quantity of eleven rounds each, besides three hundred weight sent from Wilmington, and what remained unexpended in the engagement. That on the day of the second engagement, each galley had sixty seven rounds of powder, including the supplies sent them, in addition to what remained on hand, after the first days engagement. Your committee are farther of opinion, that, during both the engagements, the gallies were sufficiently supplied with all other kinds of necessary ammunition; that their not having taken the Roebuck, was not owing to any deficiency in the above articles, and that the conduct of the Committee of Safety, on that occasion, evidenced the greatest zeal and attention to the public service.[56]

The conclusions of the Assembly are somewhat difficult to reconcile with the statement of the captains, especially regarding the number of rounds of ammunition available on the second day.

Except for the ammunition the Assembly stated was on board each galley on May 9, there is little difficulty in reconciling quantities. As the controversy centered upon the first day's action and the failure to destroy the *Roebuck*, the areas of dispute can best be confined to the available amounts on that day. The captains claimed they had an average of twenty-eight rounds "fit for service"; the Assembly noted that they had thirty-three rounds and received an additional eight rounds during the engagement; the latter quantity was received after the action had broken off, according to the captains. Captain Read had reported that the cartridges received were of such poor quality as to fall apart at the touch. The qualitative question had long been a source of irritation to the captains. As early as December 12, 1775, they had written to the Committee of Safety that powder in the magazines of all the galleys was in poor condition because of the dampness of the boats. They further implied that the type of construction employed in building the galleys contributed to this condition. Also, they claimed, the damp powder was not replaced often enough to keep the fleet at top fighting strength.[57]

James Mease, a member of the committee to observe the conduct of the fleet, laid part of the blame at the feet of the Commodore, although Commodore Caldwell was ill and had been temporarily relieved of command. Mease also contended that on the night of the eighth a meeting was held to discuss the feasibility of a night attack on the British, and nothing was said concerning the shortage of ammunition.[58]

These explanations failed to resolve the controversy. The Assembly's verdict absolving the Committee of misconduct may have been a face-saver, but it widened the gap with the captains. Nothing was resolved by an investigation of this sort, as the fundamental problems of administration and supply were ignored. Each faction was ignorant of the problems of the other, jealous of its prerogatives, and watchful of any attempted usurpation of its authority.

The Committee was attempting to operate a revolutionary organization with too many problem areas to cover efficiently. Certain functions were delegated to good Patriots, but dedication was not a substitute either for ability or matériel. Later in 1777, when the British threatened the city, a Navy Board would be created to handle naval affairs. The Committee would have been better served by the creation of such a board in 1776.

Neither side had recognized the urgency of the situation. The land defenses were woefully weak; the navy had not developed an esprit de corps, and insubordination and desertion were daily problems. Whether the captains were attentive to maintaining a "tight ship" or, as with the Continental service, supplies in needed quantities were just not procurable, cannot be stated with accuracy.

It would appear that some responsibility must be assumed by all participants, naval and civilian. The captains probably never considered the possibility that they could destroy the *Roebuck* until after they had retreated upriver and were informed of the frigate's plight. And it is ridiculous to believe that the Committee was sanguine enough to have entertained any such hope before the unhappy controversy began. The prevailing holiday spirit among the citizenry who lined the banks of the river to watch the action and the patriotic groups who commended the spirit and bravery of the galleys' crews show that there was enough credit for all concerned and the dispute need never have occurred.

Many of the lessons that might have been learned from the action were lost, as everyone was too busy justifying his own conduct. The value of the galleys, however, was not lost on some discriminating observers. If used under the proper conditions, and in the narrow confines of the upper river, they could be an effective force in defending the city. Never again would they venture below the lower chevaux-de-frise to engage the heavier armed ships of the British fleet. They would remain in the vicinity of Fort Island and serve creditably, supplemented by the forts and river obstructions.

Wounds did not heal and the Committee's ill-advised appointment of Samuel Davidson as Commodore would soon bring the captains and Committee into another confrontation.

V

Building and Rebuilding
A Navy—1776

NO RELAXATION was possible while awaiting the verdict of the committee appointed by the Assembly of Pennsylvania to investigate the matter of whether adequate ammunition had been furnished the galleys in the *Roebuck* action. Little could be done to reconcile the differences between the galley captains and the Committee of Safety. However, dedication to the American cause kept both groups working together for the common good, although not without some petty moves on both sides.

The Committee of Safety had no way of knowing, at the time, that Hamond did not intend to try to force the chevaux-de-frise or attack the shipping at Philadelphia, and the *Roebuck* action had dramatically focused attention on the weak points in the river and city defenses. A memorial was prepared and presented to the Continental Congress, in which the Committee outlined the steps they had taken: galleys, guard boats, a large ship (*Montgomery*), and a floating battery (*Arnold*) with a great number of fire rafts had been built; fortifications had been erected on Deep Water Island (Fort Island); a large artillery company recruited; and chevaux-de-frise sunk in the channel. Other militia companies had been raised for duty on the banks of the Delaware. They conceded, however, that this was still insufficient and that additional defenses could not be financed by Pennsylvania alone.

The Committee recommended that larger naval vessels, capable of navigating in the Delaware Bay, be built and that another floating battery be added to the fleet. To provide an anchor for the river obstructions, land fortifications must be constructed on the New Jersey side of the Delaware River. These and any other defenses that Congress might consider necessary would require Congressional financing.[1]

Assistance from Congress would ·be forthcoming eventually, but in the meantime the Committee concluded that they must proceed regardless of subsequent action by Congress. The financing of the river defenses was always a source of minor friction between Pennsylvania, on one side, and the Continental Congress and New Jersey on the other. All three governmental bodies were sorely pressed to finance the bare necessities to prosecute the war, and Congress and New Jersey believed that Pennsylvania had the major stake in the defense of the Delaware. Congress was absorbed with the needs of the Continental forces, and New Jersey's close proximity to New York and the British forces there occupied most of that state's attention and resources. The more sparsely populated South Jersey counties cooperated to the best of their ability, recognizing the danger of an invasion of the Delaware Valley by the British. As early as December 1774, a Committee on Observation had been organized in Old Gloucester County; a year later this Committee was reorganized. In the meantime, a group of dedicated Patriots in the county had donated several hundred pine logs to be used in the construction of the chevaux-de-frise.[2]

Workmen were rushed to Fort Island and Billingsport to complete new fortifications and strengthen the existing ones. The Continental Congress entered into negotiations with Margaret M. Paul, widow of John Paul, and her son Benjamin Weatherby to purchase ninety-six acres of a tract of one hundred acres called Billingsport. A deed dated July 5, 1776, is on record in the Gloucester County Clerk's office at Woodbury, New Jersey, conveying this tract of land to George Clymer and Michael Hillegas, Treasurers of the Thirteen United Colonies, for a consideration of £600, Pennsylvania currency. Ten days later

Weatherby transferred title to a house on the tract for £50. This was probably the first land purchased by the United States after the Declaration of Independence.[3]

In early June 1776, Robert Smith was instructed to begin construction of a fort or redoubt on the land purchased from Mrs. Paul. After erecting temporary shelters to house his carpenters and laborers, Smith spent several weeks building barracks. The questionable value of the fortification at Billingsport will be covered in detail later; suffice it to say that in 1776 the authorities believed that a fort at this point, to protect the chevaux-de-frise, was indispensable.[4] On June 14, the Continental Congress resolved that the Committee of Safety be empowered to erect a redoubt at Billingsport, and that a boom or some obstruction be laid across the channel, all to be constructed at Continental expense.[5]

There was even greater activity at Fort Island. As early as 1762, £5,000 had been appropriated to erect a twenty-gun fort on this site. Captain John Montresor of the British engineers arrived in Philadelphia on April 21, 1771, and on the twenty-third laid a plan before the Committee, appointed by Governor Penn, to provide for the defense of the Delaware River. He proposed a five-star redoubt on Mud or Deep Water Island, the foundation to be laid on piles driven into the soft mud of the island, and costing £20,000 in Pennsylvania currency. He further recommended that batteries be raised at Gloucester in New Jersey, Gloucester Point in what is now South Philadelphia near the present Walt Whitman bridge, and on Windmill Island, the three to cost £10,000. He also suggested twenty floating batteries, fire rafts and other military stores to cost an additional £10,000. The Pennsylvania authorities favored economy over defense and would appropriate only £15,000, providing for the building of the fort on Mud Island without piers, and deferring action on the other recommendations. Mud Island was purchased from Joseph Galloway, the colony's most celebrated Loyalist. Montresor laid out the plans for the fort and returned to New York. His plans called for thirty-two cannon, four mortars, four royal howitzers and a garrison of four hundred men.[6]

When hostilities with Great Britain were initiated in 1775, Mud Island became more frequently called Fort Island, and efforts were begun to strengthen the fort. At first militia companies served as garrison; later Captain Thomas Proctor and his artillery company were assigned there. Proctor and his men were to assist the workmen in improving the defenses. The fort became a beehive of activity with carpenters, ditchers, and other workmen busily erecting blockhouses, altering the gun emplacements, building drawbridges and piers, raising a flagstaff, and widening and deepening the ditches.[7]

As activity on the land fortifications proceeded, the naval establishment was not neglected. With Commodore Caldwell still ill and unable to assume command, he tendered his resignation, which was accepted by the Committee on May 25 (although his letter was dated May 27). Captain Thomas Read was again asked to accept temporary command of the fleet.[8]

Read was admonished to keep the fleet in a constant state of preparedness. No officers were to absent themselves from their boats without Read's permission. All boats of the fleet were to be stationed at Fort Island. The barracks at the fort were completed and could accommodate the officers. The Committee ordered Thomas Cuthbert and John Britton to purchase four flat-bottomed boats to be used as hulks to house the boat crews. Orders were issued to outfit them with light timber and ordinary hay and to purchase the necessary anchors and cables to moor them near Fort Island. At the same time, Captain James Montgomery was directed to purchase and equip two shallops to house the officers and crews of the guard boats, each shallop to accommodate forty men. These were needed because six new guard boats had been commissioned.[9]

The resignation of Commodore Caldwell was the occasion for the Committee of Safety again crossing swords with the galley captains. With both sides waiting to hear the Assembly's decision on the misconduct allegations in the *Roebuck* affair, the Committee members were not anxious to have another confrontation with the officers. The verdict released on May 28 was probably known to the Committee when they accepted Caldwell's resignation and appointed Read as temporary commander of the fleet.

It would appear that the interim selection of Read was planned as a convenient means of retaining harmony with the captains. If this was their expectation, they reasoned without Captain Read. Not wishing always to be second in command, or a temporary commander until the Committee could select another Commodore, he had been soliciting a command with the Continental navy. On June 5, he resigned from the State navy, having been recommended for command of a Continental frigate.[10]

Read's resignation precipitated the last important disagreement between the Committee and the captains. On June 15, Captain Samuel Davidson was commissioned Commodore. The reaction to his appointment was immediate and acrimonious. On June 20, Davidson addressed himself to the twelve galleys stationed at Fort Island, presenting the written orders announcing his commission.[11] Eight of the captains refused to accept his orders, three were absent in Philadelphia, and only one (the master of the ammunition sloop) agreed to recognize his authority.[12]

On June 18, the captains presented a remonstrance, outlining their objections to the choice of Samuel Davidson as Commodore. They protested that he was totally unfit to command, that he was without military or naval experience, and his commission was junior to those of the vast majority of galley captains; they further accused him of weakness of character and charged that he had taken no part in the recent action with the *Roebuck*. They expanded on their demand that all promotions be based on seniority. This last appeal was with the foreknowledge that larger ships were to be built.[13]

Samuel Davidson had been appointed captain of the galley *Warren* on September 22, 1775, and was a party to the captains' protest to the selection of Thomas Read as Commodore. Samuel Mifflin had requested a leave of absence for Davidson on November 28, to make a cruise in his ship employed in the Continental service. Davidson returned in March 1776, and was immediately offered command of the floating battery *Arnold*,[14] a position he held when appointed Commodore.

Anger, jealousy, and indignation were evident in the captains' protest. Obviously, the Committee was not going to consider one of the protesting captains for Commodore, although there were in their number several qualified officers. The captains were emphatic in their declaration of loyalty to the American cause, and assured the Committee that they would serve faithfully and abide by the final decision. The only senior officers in the service other than Davidson were Captain John Hazelwood and Captain William Brown of the marines. At this time little was known of the abilities of Hazelwood and Brown, whereas Davidson was not a member of the galley officers' coterie. Regardless of fault, the feuding between Committee and captains resulted in lowered morale and was a direct cause of several of the better captains' resigning to enter the Continental service. In fact, feelings were so intense that no galley captain was ever offered command of the state navy. The dissatisfaction of the captains is indicated in the relatively high turnover of the galley command.

On August 1, before the Davidson affair could be resolved, two galley captains, James Montgomery of the *Chatham* and John Hamilton of the *Congress*, resigned.[15] Hamilton was involved in the charges against Davidson. He was supposed to have alleged that Davidson offered his men an opportunity to run away to serve on a privateer.[16]

Differences arising between the two public bodies had to be aired in the press or other public media before tempers could cool or explanations be offered. With the captains' memorial in the press, the Committee again felt called on to defend its position and prerogatives. In the late afternoon of June 18, the Committee of Safety, sitting as a whole in regular session, considered the objections to Davidson's appointment, summarily dismissed the petition as frivolous, and instructed Robert Morris, as presiding officer, to sign the Commodore's commission. On the following day, Davidson was given broad instructions to govern his conduct. As previously noted, these instructions and the commission as Commodore triggered the first open defiance of Davidson's authority.[17]

Accompanying the instructions to Davidson were orders to deliver fifty rounds of ammunition to the galleys, replacing those quantities on board. Martin Wert, master of the ammunition sloop *Sally*, was instructed to proceed to Fort Island with the replacement powder in cartridges. Arriving at the island, he attempted to make delivery. Somewhat petulantly the captains refused to accept the powder, claiming their stock of powder was in good condition. They then ordered him to anchor his sloop on the inside of the island. Complying with these orders, Wert soon received counterinstructions from Davidson to remove his sloop to the eastern side of the island. In this he was prevented by the captains. Leaving his sloop, with 650 cartridges for eighteen, twenty-four, and thirty-two-pounder cannon, and 1,040 cannon balls and one hundred pounds of matches, he hurried to Philadelphia to report his frustrations.[18]

In the meantime, a Conference of the Revolutionary Committees of the Province of Pennsylvania was sitting at Carpenter's Hall. A nonpartisan subcommittee was selected to investigate this latest dispute between the captains and Committee of Safety. In session from June 18 to June 25, the subcommittee and the Conference of Committees, as a whole, interrogated all interested parties. Accused of boarding Davidson's flagship, the *Montgomery*, to take down his personal pennant, the captains did not deny this charge, but categorically contradicted testimony that they used force of arms—a rather fine line to draw between the accusation and the act, which bordered on mutiny. They were equally adamant that under no conditions would they accept the appointment of Davidson. Considering all the testimony and the other objections put forth in the memorial, and listening to rebuttal statements by the Commodore and the Committee representatives, the Conference passed a resolution which was forwarded to the Committee of Safety on June 25:

Resolved: That it be recommended to the Committee of Safety of this province to confine the Command of Commodore Davidson to the ship-of-war and floating battery belonging to the province, and to issue no orders to the Captains or other officers of the row-gallies, fire-ship or fire-rafts, through the said Commodore, until the convention [a convention to draft a constitution for Pennsylvania would sit from July 15 to September 28, 1776] meets, and that it be recommended to the Captains and the other officers of the gallies etc., to pay all due obedience to the Committee of Safety until that time, and until a new appointment shall take place.[19]

The Conference of Committees recognized that petty family quarrels could seriously endanger the war effort and hoped that their resolution would permit a cooling-off period. But they had not reckoned with the temper of the Committee of Safety, who, rather than being conciliatory, were astonished and angry. A face-saving gesture was necessary. On the Conference's recommendation, orders were reluctantly issued to limit Davidson's command and to appoint Captain Dougherty, as senior galley captain, to temporary charge of the galleys.[20] They now determined to put their arguments before the people of the city and a special committee drafted an "Address to the Public." This wearisome and at times intemperate diatribe began with a lengthy preamble, avowing devotion to their trust, regretting the vilification they had endured, and recognizing that all their decisions would not be popular. Exhibiting a certain pique that their authority should be questioned, and being men of honor, they felt obliged to—as we say today—set the record straight.

The Committee set forth the reasons for their unanimous approval of Davidson's appointment. He was devoted to his duty, maintained a strict discipline, had the affection of his crew and kept a fully manned boat (a questionable statement as the *Warren* usually carried one of the smallest musters of all the galleys). They elaborated on their reasons for refusing to consider seniority as the only criterion for promotion; next, a sharp attack was leveled at the Conference of Committees, claiming interference and an attempt to curry public favor by supporting the captains' position. Then the Committee complained that a rebuttal was impossible as the Conference had dissolved before they could justify the soundness of their decision. Printing the Conference's resolution in full, they attempted to soften their criticism by saying they never doubted the purity of the Conference's intentions.

They closed their remonstrance by admitting that qualified sea captains were not available to fill the vacancies which would occur if the galley captains were dismissed from the naval service. Therefore, though "wounded and dishonored," they would abide by the resolution; but should any misfortune occur as a result, they would disclaim responsibility. In a final gesture of humility, they offered to perform their duties for the few short weeks until the Committee would be dissolved. (On July 22, a reorganization would take place with some changes in personnel; however, many of the Committee would remain on the new Council of Safety).[21]

As many outstanding men were members of the Committee of Safety, and several would become figures of national prominence, it is sometimes difficult to account for their whimsical deliberations. The Committee certainly had the authority to make appointments and promotions without consulting the officers of the fleet. Americans have always resented actions which have overtones of military domination. Several of the galley captains were sources of trouble throughout their careers and did not always perform to the standards demanded by their commissions. A number of the better officers resigned to enter the Continental service and until the pay scale was placed on the same basis as that of the Continental service, this was to be expected. Also, the prestige to be gained from the bridge of a frigate, matched against a small row galley, does not tax the imagination.

The Council of Safety, successor to the original Committee of Safety, apparently pursued their efforts to vindicate their right to make all promotions with the approval of the Pennsylvania Constitutional Convention then sitting in Philadelphia. Matters reached a climax about August 27 and the now Council of Safety released a memorandum dealing with the dismissal of Davidson—again asserting their confidence in Davidson and the opinion that all charges against the Commodore were frivolous and indicative of a dangerous spirit of insubordination. But as the officers had neither respect for nor confidence in Davidson, they conceded that it would be impossible for him to give the necessary spirit and vigor to the command. They concluded with a strange statement in view of all their protestations, "Yet the charge of incompetency to so important a trust is not altogether without foundation." [22] About one month after this announcement Samuel Davidson apparently resigned from the navy.[23]

One internal problem seems to have arisen during Davidson's brief tenure. The printed archives of Pennsylvania designates marines as serving on several of the galleys. Regrettably, later historians have accepted these lists without a critical check of either the manuscript muster rolls or the organization of the State navy. This is undoubtedly a mistake in editing as no marine contingents were assigned to the galleys. The *Montgomery*, the floating battery *Arnold*, and later the State privateering ship, the *General Greene*, were the only elements of the fleet to have marine companies. Captain William Brown and the marines stationed on board the *Montgomery* were transferred to the new floating battery *Putnam* as the naval crew. A few illustrations of this editing error will suffice to prove the point. The manuscript muster rolls designate ordinary seamen as seamen, landsmen, mariners, marines, and privates, with the last in the majority. The printed muster rolls when edited were occasionally changed to list privates as seamen, privates, or marines. Landsmen are always recorded as marines. The inconsistency continues with marines listed as seamen on the *Franklin*; the Congress registers some seamen as marines. No consistent pattern in the editing is discernible. A generalization of the editors' reasoning might be that all designations of seamen or mariner would be listed as seamen; marines, privates, and landsmen as marines—but unfortunately not consistently. Further, there are no officers listed for the marines on the galleys. Marines were always recruited by marine captains and specifically for that service. The wide use of different designations for the crewmen may be the mistake of a captain's clerk or junior officer in preparing the muster roll. Finally, to accept the rosters in the printed archives would make for a ratio of three or four marines to one seaman on each galley listing marines, an impossible condition for the proper handling of the boat.[24]

In May and June 1776, when the *Montgomery* and the *Arnold* were in service and under the command of Davidson, he attempted to exercise direct command over the marines, and members of his staff endeavored to discipline individual marines—apparently even going so far as to strike the men for an act of insubordination or misbehavior. The marine officers objected to disciplinary action taken against their men other than that initiated by themselves. The marine contingents were assigned to specific ships under the command of a marine captain, subject to the overall direction of the ship's captain. No central command was established for the marines as they were part of the State navy. Davidson was in the right in assuming overall command, but he is certainly subject to criticism for permitting the disciplining of men other than by their own officers. While the marines were not part of the protest to Davidson's appointment, these disputes did not endear him to the officers and men of the marine detachment. After the objections raised by the marine officers, the Committee of Safety, in a directive to the commanding officer and dated only 1776, ordered that this practice be discontinued at once and all disciplinary measures administered by marine officers.[25]

Cognizant of the difficulties that had affected relationships between the civil and naval authorities, the Constitutional Convention on August 19 passed a resolution which they hoped would put to rest for the duration of the war any further disputes:

Resolved, That the officers in the naval and land service of this state ought not, in all cases, to rise in command according to seniority, although a proper regard should be had to that circumstance in promotions where there are equal merit, and equal military abilities, of which the Council of Safety is to judge. And that the said council have full authority to use their best discretion herein, so as most effectually to promote the service. And all officers and others concerned, are hereby strictly required and enjoined to yield, and pay full and implicit obedience to all their appointments, regulations, and orders at their peril.[26]

The effectiveness of this resolution can only be judged by the fact that disputes between the Council of Safety and the captains ended at this time—at least on the surface.

The Convention recognized the right of the Council to appoint all officers, including the Commodore, and to assert civilian control over military and naval forces. On the other hand, the captains, in spite of their unorthodox and somewhat mutinous methods, received endorsement of the seniority system and were able to force the withdrawal of Davidson's appointment. It was a somewhat hollow victory, as subsequent appointments as Commodore were made outside the naval establishment, except for that of John Hazelwood.

With the status of Samuel Davidson resolved, many other problems of naval administration demanded the attention of the civil and naval authorities. Desertions were a constant source of concern, a condition common to Continental and State forces throughout the war, especially during periods of unusual enemy activity. This condition, and the addition of new elements to the fleet, placed added emphasis on the recruitment program. It would be necessary to select a new Commodore acceptable to the navy and the Council of Safety. The river fortifications needed strengthening, and additional obstructions must be placed in the channel of the river. The Council of Safety was entertaining plans for new naval units to cruise in the bay to protect incoming ships and take enemy prizes.

The British were determined to break up what they considered to be illegal traffic in vital supplies being carried through the capes to the rebels. Most of the American ships were small sloops or brigs and were able to pass close to the Delaware or New Jersey shore, thus eluding capture. Early in 1776, the British stationed large ships-of-war, usually of the frigate class, in the road between Capes Henlopen and May, and manned their barges and tenders to cruise in the shallow waters close to shore. They were handicapped by their unfamiliarity with the bay and river channels. Every effort was made to capture a pilot but because of the vigilance of the Patriots, they were unsuccessful. The Committee of Safety was constantly warning Henry Fisher not to permit pilots to expose themselves to possible capture. Fisher took all precautions in his power to thwart the small enemy cruisers, but the resources at his disposal were inadequate, and he asked the Committee of Safety for the loan of "one of your small barges that carries a four-pounder, such a craft would be of Service here to attack their barges." [27] The Committee instructed Captain Hazelwood to send Captain Lawrence with the *Salamander* and Captain Hause with the *Eagle* to Lewes and deliver the *Eagle* to Fisher for his use. Lawrence was to return immediately, returning Hause and his crew to the fleet. All supplies and the guard boat *Eagle* were to be placed at Fisher's disposal, for which he was to be accountable to the Committee. His plan was to man the *Eagle* with his pilots, which the Committee objected to on the grounds that "it would be dangerous to suffer any Pilot to cruize in our bay." With the arrival of the guard boats at Lewes, Fisher was handed the letter from the Committee. Deeply disturbed by the order preventing him from using his pilots as the crew of the *Eagle*, he dispatched a note asking the committee to reconsider. He wrote that his pilots were of a different character from those employed in Philadelphia and "as the Boat is to be Stationed at our Creeks mouth I cannot see there will be the least Danger in letting Six Pilots go in her and the Remainder Landsmen as the Pilots are acquainted with the great gun and they can always see their Danger Before they can be Suppressed." [28]

Fisher's woes were not confined to the British frigates and the Committee of Safety; roving bands of Tories had disrupted his express service from Lewes to Philadelphia, and he must use the slower whale or pilot boats. It was customary to send the boats north after midnight to elude the enemy's cruisers.[29]

The period between July 1, 1776, and December saw every effort expended by the civil authorities to improve the morale of the naval establishment. With the galleys undermanned during the recent *Roebuck* and *Liverpool* engagement and only able to face the enemy with supplemental crews borrowed from the *Montgomery* and the *Arnold*, the captains were struggling to maintain their crews at the May 1 muster. Desertions continued and advertisements were placed in the newspapers offering a four-dollar reward for anyone apprehending and delivering a deserter to the galleys or the Philadelphia workhouse.[30]

To provide the basic comforts necessary to maintain a reasonably high spirit among the crews, as previously noted, old hulks, sloops and shallops were purchased and converted into barracks.[31] Sloops were added to the fleet to insure the prompt delivery of rations, and the commissary was importuned to keep on hand a sufficient quantity of good rations for delivery to the boats. The use of the sloops permitted a regular flow of rations on a day-by-day basis. For the period September 10, 1776, through February 10, 1777, the fleet and the artillery company stationed at Fort Island received over 200,000 pounds of beef and the same quantity of other rations.[32]

To further improve morale among the crews, the Council of Safety on September 30, following the example set by the Continental Congress, granted half pay to all seamen incapable of performing their duties because of illness contracted or wounds received while on active duty. Prior to this time, these men had been discharged without compensation or provision for their care. The new arrangement was to remain in effect until both the Continental and the State authorities enacted permanent legislation to provide for men in this condition.[33] Scattered entries in the archives indicate that some assistance was rendered families of the seamen as early as October 1775.

Inflation was another problem, especially in cost of uniforms and clothing, and to alleviate this condition the pay of the men was raised to £3 a month, effective November 1, 1776.[34]

The captains were encouraged to scour the countryside for recruits. Attractive allowances for recruiting expenses and bounties were offered to lure men into the service. Searching for a crew for the new floating battery *Putnam* was accelerated by the use of a recruitment poster:

Volunteers for the Floating Battery

All gentlemen, volunteers and others, who are free, able, and willing to serve their country in this grand struggle for liberty, yet may not choose to be far removed from a parent, family, wife, or sweetheart, have now an opportunity to show that laudable desire, and gratify their tender feelings by entering on board the new Floating Battery fitting out under the commend of Captain William Brown, for the particular defence of the State of Pennsylvania, and will never be stationed more than six or seven miles down the river Delaware. Those who are thus inclined to serve themselves, their country, and posterity, let them repair to the rendezvous opened by said Brown, at John Stoops's, at the sign of the Two Tuns, opposite the New Market, where they shall be well entertained, have a month's pay advance, and a dollar or a dollar's worth of drink, to drown all their sorrows, and drive away care. Their pay and subsistence will be fifty shillings per month, and that paid monthly; ten pounds of beef, mutton, or pork, seven pounds of bread, sixpence worth of vegetables, and seven half pints of rum, per week.

This battery is well constructed for defence, and for the preservation and accommodation of her men. If any industrious tradesmen, whose business is of a sedentary nature, should incline to enter this service, he may here have his house-rent, firing, victuals, and drink free, besides his pay and a great deal of time, in which he may employ himself for the emolument of his family (should he have one) or to fill his pockets for his own amusement. This is encouragement no other service on the Continent can give.

Philadelphia, October 2, 1776.[35]

In what appears to have been a political appointment, the new Council of Safety on September 2 selected Samuel Mifflin as Commodore. Major Mifflin was serving with the Continental forces at Perth Amboy in New Jersey and he declined. The offer to Mifflin was probably made with the full knowledge that he would not accept it, but was proffered in recognition of past services to Pennsylvania's armed forces. Mifflin's refusal was received on September 20, and Thomas Seymour was chosen Commodore on September 26. Neither Mifflin nor Seymour had been officially connected with the navy, but no protest seems to have been raised by the captains. Concurrent with the Council's instructions to Seymour, he was advised to report to the fleet that all officers of the State navy would be allowed the same pay as those in the Continental service, effective October 1.[36] This announcement may have silenced whatever opposition existed.

Many of the galleys, all having been in service for over a year, required repairs and were laid up at Philadelphia shipyards. The method employed in withdrawing the boats from active service is not clear, but it is reasonable to assume that probably two or three were detached for repairs at a time.[37]

In November 1776 Commodore Seymour informed the Council of Safety that the Continental vessels *Wasp* and *Fly* were receiving and detaining a number of men who had deserted from the galleys. The Continental officers also declared that it was their intention to accept as many as sought to enter their service. Seymour was instructed to request the Continental Board of War or Marine Committee to order these men returned. The exact disposition of the runaways is not in the records, but the practice was apparently discontinued, at least openly.[38]

On November 22, the pay for men below the rank of commissioned officer was raised to the Continental base and made retroactive to October 1. The wages were again raised, with the increase of the officers effective January 1, 1777, and the men February 1, 1777.[39]

As November approached, each bit of news from New York was more depressing. The British were in possession of New York City. Daily rumors indicated their determination to invade New Jersey. Little hope was held that Washington could mount a drive to keep the enemy off balance or erect effective defensive works short of the Pennsylvania side of the Delaware River.

The Council of Safety prepared to assist in Washington's strategy to defend the Delaware, to defend the city, furnish the Continental army with reinforcements, and to strip the area on both sides of the river of any commodity or article of war that might serve the enemy.

Owners of cattle or other stock residing near the river were to remove their stock at least five miles inland. Many residents of New Jersey drove their cattle into the pine woods in the hope of escaping the sharp eyes of British or Hessian foragers. Stores of all types were ordered removed from Philadelphia. Matthew Brooke, Leonard Stoneburner, and Jacob Engle were empowered to provide teams for this purpose for which they were authorized to pay two shillings, ten pence, per mile for carrying two thousand pounds. For their personal services they were to be allowed fifteen shillings a day.[40]

No ships were permitted to leave the port while the emergency existed without written approval of the Council of

Safety. The Commodore was given the authority to stop all vessels attempting to pass through the chevaux-de-frise. The Continental navy had advised the Council that no help could be expected from Continental vessels to protect commercial traffic through the capes. Henry Fisher was keeping the Council alerted to the activities of British "pirates" but he was handicapped by increased Tory activity. Captain John Rice, in the brig *Convention*, was ordered to drop down to Lewes and give protection to American merchant ships, endeavor to capture British prizes, and cooperate with Fisher.[41]

The upcoming campaign would raise the American cause out of one of its greatest moments of despair, and the State navy would have an important, if not outstanding, role to play.

VI

Trenton and Princeton—1776

PHILADELPHIA became the apparent objective of Sir William Howe after the fall of Fort Washington on Manhattan Island and Fort Lee atop the New Jersey palisades in November 1776.

Washington retreated across northern New Jersey, plagued by the intrigue and machinations of General Charles Lee. Lee had exploited his past service in the British army to the fullest possible benefit to himself. Many Americans, in comparing the English-born Lee to native-born officers, saw what they believed to be America's only hope for victory. This was a belief Lee was only too willing to foster, and, at every opportunity, he insidiously undermined Washington's authority and extolled his own superior ability as a military commander.

The Congress and the army were not taken in by the scheming of a few ambitious men. Fleeing to Baltimore, the Congress had invested Washington with dictatorial powers to prosecute the war. He was faced with the expiration of the enlistment of a large contingent of the army on December 1, and the remaining regiments on January 1, 1777. Many soldiers were not waiting for their enlistments to expire, but were deserting in large numbers.

As this study is not related to the movements of the Continental army, suffice it to say that the retreat toward the Delaware River was a series of marches and thrusts and counterthrusts by both armies. Washington received some small reinforcements from the New York camps, and fortunately for the American cause, Lee foolishly allowed himself to be captured at a North Jersey tavern. His dilatory tactics had prevented his division from joining Washington; it was now rushed forward to merge with the main Continental army. It is somewhat of an oversimplification to call Washington's men and the added reinforcements an army; contemporaries have described them more as a tatterdemalion mob. Most were without some accouterment of war, and many were without shoes, shirts, tents, or blankets. Practically all intrenching tools had been lost when the Hudson River forts fell to the British.

The Council of Safety was frantically trying to raise militia to reinforce Washington, and on December 5 the Pennsylvania Associators and a regiment of Pennsylvania and Maryland Germans arrived at camp.

On December 2nd, Captain Thomas Houston with the galley *Warren* was ordered to proceed up the Delaware and remove all ships and boats to the Pennsylvania side of the river. He was to clear the river as far as Trenton of any craft that might be serviceable to the British.[1]

In mid-December, as Sir William Howe and his commander in New Jersey, Lord Cornwallis, started garrisoning towns in North Jersey, it became obvious that they had no hostile intentions toward Philadelphia that winter. Washington, fighting rear-guard actions across the state, finally reached the Delaware, and began ferrying his command across the river, aided in this effort by the galleys of the Pennsylvania navy.

The Continentals were without everything necessary to fight a war but their spirit and belief in the man who had shared their every trial and suffering. One of the men in the ranks was Thomas Paine, a distinctly better pamphleteer than soldier. In mid-December he published his tract *The Crisis*, a dynamic and patriotic appeal which animated the Continental soldier's faith and hope in his cause:

These are the times that try men's souls. The summer soldier and the sunshine patriot will, in this crisis, shrink from the service of his country; but he that stands it *now*, deserves the love and thanks of man and woman. Tyranny, like hell, is not easily conquered; yet we have this consolation with us, that the harder the conflict, the more glorious the triumph.

With the realization that their capital city was no longer in danger of British occupation, the Council of Safety turned its attention to assisting Washington in the defense of the Delaware River. The navy was ordered to proceed to Trenton to report to the Commander-in-Chief. Major Proctor, commandant of the artillery company at Fort Island, was ordered to detach fifty privates with officers and two brass field pieces, camp equipage, and other stores, under the command of Captain Thomas Forrest, and send them to Washington without delay.[2]

Commodore Seymour had proceeded upriver and anchored his little flotilla of galleys and the *Montgomery* in the Delaware opposite Trenton. He was immediately employed in ferrying men and matériel across the river to the Pennsylvania shore. The exact number of galleys used in this service cannot be verified, but it is known that the *Congress, Burke, Camden, Franklin, Experiment, Washington, Warren, Chatham,* and *Ranger* were stationed at Trenton. The remaining galleys, the *Bull Dog, Effingham, Dickinson* and *Hancock,* were patrolling the Delaware River from the northern limits of Philadelphia to Bordentown, New Jersey. They were to report any movement of British and Hessian troops, destroy all bridges over the New Jersey creeks which might serve the enemy, and bring off any boats that remained on the eastern bank of the river. Their orders were to destroy all boats they were unable to move, and to prevent British sympathizers or spies from crossing the river to convey information to the enemy.[3]

There was some apprehension in the American camp that the British might push south on the New Jersey side of the Delaware. The Americans did not take into account the custom of eighteenth-century European armies of going into hibernation. To circumvent either an attempt on the part of the enemy to push toward Philadelphia, or to permit their using the small towns along the river bank as winter quarters, militia companies were ordered to harass the enemy and destroy all bridges, not previously demolished by the galleys, over the numerous creeks.

Meanwhile, Seymour's galleys were patrolling the river with orders to bombard any town that welcomed the enemy.

Margaret Morris, a resident of Burlington, New Jersey, has left us a sprightly little journal which describes a brief but bloodless engagement of the galleys with the Hessians. Before daylight on December 11, Colonel Von Donop of the Hessian army left Trenton for Bordentown with a contingent of over four hundred troops. His advance was hampered by the wasp-like attacks of the Burlington county militia. Pursuing the militiamen, he passed Bordentown and continued toward Burlington; the Americans eluded Von Donop and escaped across the river to Bristol, Pennsylvania.[4]

With the approach of the Hessians, a delegation of the townspeople advised Von Donop that if he occupied the town, Seymour would probably cannonade it. Captain Moore of the galley *Hancock* was on shore at the time and agreed to accompany the citizens to confer with Seymour. In the meantime, while awaiting the outcome of the conference with the Commodore, Von Donop with his staff and a small guard were granted the hospitality of the town. The main Hessian detachment was halted near the bridge on the outskirts of Burlington. Mrs. Morris recorded that four galleys approached the head of Main Street and opened fire. It was her belief that only civilians and Captain Moore were in sight, but galley crews claimed they saw Hessian soldiers in the town. An effort was made to persuade the galleys to cease firing, but to no avail, as apparently they too were fired upon. The appearance of Hessian officers at the river's edge obviously did not contribute to an abatement of the firing, but rather added to its briskness. Mrs. Morris records that the Hessians being seen

. . . induced the people on board to believe that the Houses were full of Hessians, & a Canonade was continued till almost dark in different directions, sometimes along the Streets, sometimes across it—Several Houses were Struck & a little damagd, but not one liveing Creature, either Man or beast, killd or Wounded—about dark the Gondolas fell down alittle way below the Town & the night was passt in quiet.[5]

Von Donop was without artillery, and being advised that the Americans were threatening to destroy the town, withdrew his forces. His action was undoubtedly dictated by the presence of a large Tory and neutral element in Burlington. So ended what might be called the first act of the Trenton and Princeton campaign.

In the meantime, Major Thomas Proctor, commander of Fort Island, was warned that a British fleet might attempt to force the river defenses. The Council of Safety was faced with a dilemma: all available manpower had been sent to Washington. The only reinforcements they could offer Proctor were the floating batteries *Arnold* and *Putnam* and Captain Rice's brig *Convention*. Rice had been stationed near Cape Henlopen and he brought back the information that a British fleet of eight men-of-war and three tenders had arrived in the lower bay.

Proctor advised the Council that his command, weakened by the detachment of Captain Forrest's company to the Continental army and by desertions, was incapable of defending the fort. He requested extra ammunition for the floating batteries, as they had only fifty rounds per gun, and he could not supply them. Proctor also expressed concern about Red Bank and Billingsport, as he would not be able to support them.

The British fleet, however, had no intention of forming a junction with Howe at Philadelphia. Their presence in the lower bay was to intercept inbound and outbound merchant ships.[6] The Council apparently became aware that the British objective was the shipping and made plans to protect those merchantmen which had taken refuge in the Christiana River. Captain Rice, as senior officer, was instructed to take the *Convention*, and Captain Eyre the armed schooner *Delaware*, and drop down to the Christiana. Eyre had some difficulty in recruiting enough volunteers to man his schooner. Rice was to destroy, if necessary, the ships of the fleet as well as all merchantmen, to prevent their falling into enemy hands. As the British did not intend to carry out a search-and-destroy mission in the upper bay or river, he was not called upon to take this action.

Washington's plans for surprising Colonel Rall and his Hessians quartered in Trenton are well known. Aware that his small force would virtually disappear on December 31, Washington decided on one bold stroke to surprise the Hessians in Trenton and those stationed around Bordentown under Von Donop.

Dividing his force into three sections, he hoped to develop a pincers movement which would trap the unsuspecting Hessians. The main body 2,400 men, under Washington, would cross the Delaware at McKonkey's Ferry, about nine miles above Trenton, and approach the town from the north. This detachment represented the flower of the little Patriot army.

In the center, opposite Trenton, was General Ewing with a force of over seven hundred Pennsylvania militia, with a few from New Jersey. Ewing was to cross at Trenton Ferry and secure the bridge over Assunpink Creek on the south end of town, to prevent the escape of the Hessians in that direction. They were to be aided in the crossing by units of the State galleys.

The right wing was under the command of General Cadwalader and consisted of nine hundred Rhode Island Continentals, a thousand volunteers called the Philadelphia Associators, a small militia company from Delaware, and two artillery companies. Stationed at Bristol, Pennsylvania, they were to cross over to Burlington and engage Von Donop's Hessians near Mt. Holly, diverting their attention from the attack on Rall's regiments and, if successful, to drive the remnants into the unified force of the left and center. Four of the Pennsylvania galleys were detached to ferry Cadwalader's command over the river and protect the landing of the troops.[7]

During the night of December 23, in a blinding snowstorm, Seymour moved his galleys up to the Bordentown area. There he was in a position to maneuver his flotilla to aid either Ewing or Cadwalader. The men on the boats were suffering from lack of clothing and blankets. Urgent appeals were directed to the Council of Safety for help. Hugh Montgomery of the *Effingham*, on December 17, wrote that he had only three blankets and three rugs for twenty-eight men.[8] While no evidence exists to indicate any relief for the *Effingham*, blankets were forwarded to other galleys at this time and presumably Montgomery received his allotment.[9]

The brilliance of Washington's planning and the courage of the Continental soldiers on Christmas night, 1776, have rarely been excelled in American military annals. The capture of 948 Hessians, with twenty-two killed and ninety-two wounded, compared to casualties of four American wounded, certainly demonstrates the effectiveness of the surprise and the completeness of the victory. Approximately five hundred Hessians escaped over the Assunpink creek and joined Von Donop near Bordentown.

This victory had been achieved without assistance from the divisions of Ewing and Cadwalader. The storm of Christmas Day increased in intensity and made it impossible to land these divisions on the east shore of the Delaware. The river was packed thick with ice that extended three hundred feet from the bank at Burlington, making it impossible for Cadwalader to land his artillery. Captain Thomas Rodney of the Delaware militia company describes the events at Dunks Ferry and Burlington:

It was so severe a night as I ever saw, and after two battalions were landed, the storm increased so much that it was impossible to get the artillery over, for we had to walk one hundred yards on the ice to get on shore. General Cadwalader therefore ordered the whole to retreat again, . . . and by this time the storm of wind, rain, hail and snow with the ice was so bad, that some of the infantry could not get back till next day.[10]

President Wharton of the Council, writing to Cadwalader on December 25, expressed regret that the weather prevented the galleys from keeping their stations. The dating of this letter is an obvious mistake as Wharton is replying to Cadwalader's letter of December 26 describing the failure of his attempt to cross the river. Wharton's letter further stated that men from the boats would be organized in companies to serve in the campaign.[11]

It has been suggested that the failure of these divisions actually contributed to the surprise victory over Rall. If Ewing had succeeded in secretly crossing the Delaware and concealing his command until morning, he would have made prisoners of those escaping over the Assunpink. However, there is little likelihood that he could have found a place of concealment for his command after daylight, as the Hessians had several outposts near the river. If they had been discovered, any chance of surprise by Washington would have been lost.[12] On the other hand, Christopher Ward contends, and with some justification, that Ewing and Cadwalader were too timid, that it took a Washington to cross the Delaware on a night like Christmas, 1776.[13] It is interesting to reflect what the results might have been if the galleys had been stationed close enough to the Assunpink Creek bridge to subject the retreating Hessians to a cross fire as devastating as that at Fort Mercer in October 1777.

As the storm abated and Washington had safely removed his prisoners and captured matériel to the Pennsylvania side, he was considering a return with the Continental army to New Jersey. On December 27 Cadwalader crossed over and landed above Burlington, unaware that he was alone and unsupported. He was unable to locate Von Donop and his Hessians. In the meantime, the Hessian colonel, hearing of the disaster to Rall, had hastily retreated. Two days later Washington recrossed to the New Jersey side and took position on the south bank of Assunpink Creek.

The floating batteries were clumsy and ineffective under the conditions prevailing on the Delaware at this time. Captain William Brown of the *Putnam* was instructed to organize all the marines fit for duty to march and join Washington's army. He had repeatedly written to the Council of Safety of the need for clothing, hospital services, and doctors to attend the men. As late as December 26, he had over forty men unfit for duty.[14]

There are conflicting reports as to the exact units of seamen and marines of the Pennsylvania fleet who served with Washington during this campaign. It has been believed by some historians that Captain William Shippin, killed at Princeton, was commanding a detachment of Pennsylvania marines from the galley *Hancock*. Shippin was not an officer in the State navy or marine service and, as previously stated, marines never served on the galleys. William Shippin was a merchant of German descent who kept a store near the Market Street wharf in Philadelphia. In May 1776 he was appointed captain of marines on board the privateer *Hancock*. Sailing from Philadelphia in June, the *Hancock* returned from its cruise about December 1, 1776. Shippin, with his marines, immediately repaired to the camp of the main army. Apparently his detachment was incorporated into the Second Battalion of Pennsylvania Militia.[15]

Captain William Brown had gathered a force of marines from the *Arnold* and the *Putnam*. It has been assumed that Brown's command included marines from the *Montgomery*. The marine detachment under Captain Brown had served on the *Montgomery* until September 21, 1776, when the contingent was transferred to the *Putnam*, with Brown taking command of the floating battery. Brown's command consisted of a detachment from the *Arnold* under Lieutenant Joseph Rice, and one from the *Putnam* commanded by Lieutenant James Morrison. A study of the muster rolls of the floating batteries, and a record of clothing lost by the men of the *Putnam,* reveals that Brown had a contingent of at least sixty marines.[16]

In addition, some sailors who were familiar with handling cannon were assigned to the artillery companies. Soldiers returning from Trenton gleefully noted that about forty Tories had been impressed as oarsmen on Seymour's galleys. This drastic action may have been necessary because of the absence of many seamen at the main camp.[17]

The smart engagement at Assunpink Creek and the brilliant march around Cornwallis's left again demonstrated Washington's ability as a tactician. The small British garrison at Princeton was the target of the Continental army. Included in Cadwalader's division was the Pennsylvania marine contingent. The gunners and seamen from the galleys were scattered in the various artillery companies.

Nothing is known about the actual part played by the men from the Pennsylvania navy in the Battle of Princeton. As soon as the Pennsylvania division arrived on the field of battle, Cadwalader attempted to form them into line. But at this very moment General Hugh Mercer had fallen and his brigade broke and streamed to the rear—right through the Pennsylvanians. They transmitted their panic to Cadwalader's men who bolted with the remnants of Mercer's brigade.

At this moment Washington rode among the retreating troops and appealed to them to stand firm, meanwhile exposing himself to the enemy. He was aware that these men were untried militia, hungry, tired, and overawed by their first exposure to possible disaster. Heartened by Washington's personal heroism, they rallied and formed a line of Cadwalader's Pennsylvanians, soon to be joined by Mercer's men and Mifflin's brigade, and helped to turn defeat into victory.

The State navy's contribution to the success of this campaign was important if not spectacular. Their presence on the Delaware prevented the British Army from occupying the river towns. Tory sympathizers and spies were unable to cross the river with information concerning the movements of Washington's army.

The galleys proved invaluable in transporting troops and supplies. By their constant patrol of the Delaware between Trenton and the outskirts of Philadelphia they served as the eyes of the army. Rough weather was especially severe on December 25, 1776, preventing the galleys from taking a position to rake the retreating Hessians. Of added importance were the volunteers who served so courageously with Cadwalader's brigade.

Early in January 1777 a severe freeze made the upper river hazardous for the galleys. They were ordered down to Philadelphia and Fort Island. Christopher Marshall reported their arrival at the city waterfront, January 9, 1777: "The gondolas returned to this city and brought some Tory prisoners with them taken in the Jerseys." [18] These prisoners were undoubtedly those impressed to serve as oarsmen on the galleys.

VII

The Navy Board—1776-1777

THE ARMED schooner *Delaware* and the galleys *Congress*, *Dickinson*, *Effingham*, *Experiment*, *Ranger*, and *Warren* arrived at the Philadelphia waterfront on December 28, 1776. They were tied up at wharves belonging to James C. Fisher for periods ranging from six to ten weeks.[1] The balance of the fleet followed in a matter of days and anchored at other city wharves and at Fort Island.

Winter was the time for planning the upcoming summer strategy. For the professional European officers, it was a time of conviviality, an indulgence rarely available to Washington's army or the State organizations. Starving and without proper clothing or shelter, it took a Herculean effort on the part of officers and men merely to sustain a semblance of an army.

The Pennsylvania navy was not suffering the agonies of Washington's Continentals, being safely housed in the Green Street barracks and private homes, and receiving regular rations. While the crews were comparatively comfortable in their quarters, the Council made plans for the coming summer campaign. It seemed obvious to the Continental command that the 1777 campaign would find Sir William Howe marching up the Hudson to join General Burgoyne. However, Washington also kept in mind that Howe's perennial target was the seaport cities. In addition, Howe concurred with certain European strategists who believed that an enemy's cause would be weakened if it's capital were occupied. Washington must, therefore, maintain a mobility that would permit the movement of his army in either direction. Of necessity, he had to place reliance on the states to forestall diversionary raids by the British commander.

As the new year approached, the Council of Safety was engaged in deliberations to streamline the civilian bodies concerned with the war effort. The Council was now a lame-duck body, as the Pennsylvania constitution, drafted and approved at the Constitutional Convention of the previous autumn, had created a new body to supersede the Council on March 1, 1777. The changeover was two months away, however, and much valuable time would be lost unless the Council took immediate steps to improve the defense of the city. Many of the difficulties between the naval and civil establishments had arisen because of the inability of the Council and its predecessor, the Committee of Safety, to devote enough time to the problems of defense. Civil matters were complex and manifold and, hampered by certain personal inadequacies, the Council had allowed a communications gap to develop between the two groups. Coming to this realization, they created a Navy Board on February 13, to be responsible for all matters pertaining to the naval service. It was patterned after the Marine Committee of the Continental Congress.[2]

The Board consisted of six members, with three to constitute a quorum. Andrew Caldwell, former Commodore; Joseph Blewer, member of the Council of Safety and a merchant captain; Joseph Marsh, ship's carpenter; Emanuel Eyre, shipbuilder; Paul Cox, merchant; and Robert Ritchie, a prominent Philadelphian, were appointed. Their duties included responsibility for the fleet, to provide for all defensive armaments and supplies. Other duties assigned to the Board were to put Fort Island in a posture for defending the passage of the river, to examine the river channel, and to cause chevaux-de-frise to be sunk wherever required. The new Supreme Executive Council reappointed this board on March 14 and increased the number of members from six to eleven. Those added at this time were Samuel Massey, former member of the Committee of Inspection and Observation; Samuel Morris, junior, former member of the Committee of Safety; William Pollard, merchant; Thomas Barclay, merchant; and William Bradford, printer. William Bradford and Joseph Blewer were to prove the most active members of the Board, virtually serving as a two-man board during the heated actions of October and November 1777. Blewer and Bradford both served as chairman, commissary, and paymaster, and remained with the fleet during the engagements with the British. Bradford's letters provide some of the best eyewitness accounts of these actions.[3]

The Board would now be able to devote its undivided attention to the many problems of defense. After the hard campaign in the upper river, many galleys and other elements of the fleet required extensive repairs. The boats and ships were undermanned, and the common evil besetting Continental and State forces, desertion, continued without appreciable diminution. There were still some disagreements over rank which would never be completely resolved until after a real need for the navy no longer existed.

In the transition period, several details concerning the fleet were brought to the attention of the Council. Thomas Casdrop presented a model of a swivel skid for the gun carriages. When building galleys at Ticonderoga the previous summer, he had offered it to Generals Arnold and Gates. Casdrop received their approval but does not indicate whether the skids were actually installed on the galleys in Arnold's flotilla. Neither is there a record of acceptance by the Pennsylvania authorities.[4]

At this time William Richards, ship's husband, precipitated a mild crisis by criticizing the signal method employed by Henry Fisher at Lewes, Delaware. He was of the opinion that Fisher used his express riders when the look-out boats should have been utilized, which placed added expense on the State. The value of the express riders was self-evident to the Council, as experience had demonstrated the speed and dependability of the horsemen, whereas the boats were slow and often forced into small creeks or coves in rough weather. Apparently the Council chose to ignore Richards and placated any injured feelings, as Fisher functioned capably throughout the war.[5]

As the reconstituted Navy Board took office on March 14, it was joined by another body, the Board of War. This latter board was to exercise full responsibility for the land defense of the State.

John Hubley, of the Supreme Executive Council, was requested to administer the oath of allegiance required of all officials, judicial, executive, and military, under the authority of the Pennsylvania Constitution of 1776. This oath, found in Section Forty of the Constitution contained the clause: "And that I will not, directly or indirectly, do any act or thing prejudicial or injurious to the Constitution or Government thereof, as established by the Convention." At a meeting of the Board, with William Pollard absent, the ten members in attendance affirmed their loyalty to the Patriot cause. They agreed to take an oath of allegiance to the United States as well as their oath of office, but objected to taking the oath prescribed under the State Constitution. Many officers of the State refused to take this oath of allegiance because they were of the opinion that if they did so it would prevent their advocating a better method of improving or amending the Constitution. A memorandum from the Board, written on March 14, indicated nine of the members present refusing to accept the oath, although Joseph Blewer reluctantly agreed to do so. On March 21, the Supreme Executive Council conceded that the Board was not required to take the oath to the Constitution. However, each board member was requested to take the oath of office.[6]

The concern uppermost in the minds of the new Navy Board was the posture of the State's defense and what would be the summer target of Sir William Howe. As the State fleet was their major responsibility, a review of the status of the naval establishment was conducted. On March 27 Fitzsimmons and Ritchey appeared before the Council and presented specific recommendations for improving the navy and defenses of the State.[7]

They found a majority of boats and ships in need of extensive repairs and "shamefully deficient in their complement of men," the latter deficiency caused by the competition between the State service and the merchantmen. The merchant service was offering seamen fifteen to eighteen pounds per month and landsmen ten to twelve pounds, whereas the State navy could only proffer twelve dollars a month and a bounty of twelve to those agreeing to serve for the duration of the war.[8] They therefore

recommended that an embargo be laid on all outgoing merchantmen until the boats and ships of the fleet could fill their rosters.
While this embargo was to be of only a few days' duration,
there is no record of what action was taken by the Council.

Commodore Seymour was the object of some criticism at this
time. His age and poor health rendered him unable to provide
dynamic leadership for the fleet, and several officers protested
that they did not wish to be subordinate to the Commodore.
Among them was Captain John Hazelwood. As commander of
the fire ships, fire rafts, and guard boats, he requested an independent command, as he did not believe the Commodore offered
any direction to this arm of the fleet. He also was averse to accepting orders from one of the other captains, if an accident
should happen to Seymour. Although it would create a divided
command in the face of an enemy attack, the Navy Board recommended that Hazelwood's protest be given consideration. They
commented that he had great merit and ability.

On April 5 the Council advised Seymour that the fire fleet
would not be under his direction, except in combat. Ten days
later, Hazelwood was recommended and appointed second in
command of the fleet. The Council issued orders to the captains
to direct all requests and other business through "Commodore
Hazelwood." "Commodore" was apparently a slip of the pen,
although it appears several times in the minutes of the board in
April 1777, probably a foreshadowing of things to come. Andrew Caldwell and Thomas Fitzsimmons were instructed to advise Commodore Seymour that the resolution was made because
his infirmities prevented him from assuming his duties. For the
present, at least, he would continue as Commodore.[9]

Many officer vacancies existed in the fleet, and the Board
inquired as to whether the prerogatives of their office included
the recommendation of these appointments. Receiving an affirmative response, numerous recommendations were submitted.[10]

The Board requested an audit of all transactions, to protect
the State against possible loss from the contracts negotiated or
partially consummated.

Only one land fortification was included in their report.
They pointed out the impossibility of completing the ambitious
works planned for Billingsport before the expected appearance
of an enemy fleet. Commenting on the military viewpoint that

this fort was untenable and could provide little defense against enemy men-of-war, they asked whether it should not be abandoned.

This last observation of the Board was contrary to a resolution of the Continental Congress, which had authorized the old Council of Safety, on February 15, to erect a fortification at Billingsport. The command of the work parties and soldiers was to be left to the discretion of the Council, with the recommendation that one person be entrusted with the dual responsibility for supervision. The Council appointed John Bull "Colonel Commandant of the Fortifications at Billingsport and Superintendent of the Works," and Blathwaite Jones Chief Engineer.[11]

As the Navy Board entered on their duties, a distressing condition was reported by Henry Fisher at Lewes. Unaware of the formation of the new Supreme Executive Council, he had appealed to the old Council of Safety for aid. The Executive Council forwarded his letter, outlining the conditions at his station, to the Continental Congress. Apparently the presence of an increasing number of British frigates and other men-of-war was weakening the resolution of some officials of lower Delaware. He cited one instance where, when with a dozen men he attempted to present a proper posture of defiance to the British, two members of his Council of Safety, whom he styled as magistrates, came up and ordered him to lay down his arms and submit to the British. He vowed to do everything in his power to resist the enemy, but implored the Pennsylvania Council for assistance.[12]

Certain insurmountable problems made Fisher's position vulnerable to British incursions and the machinations of disaffected or timid Delawareans. Undoubtedly this led to the Board's decision to effect a change in supervision of the alarm posts and the various small boats responsible for alerting the authorities of the approach of enemy ships. April 15 saw the appointment of Captain Leeson Simmons as supervisor of all intelligence and coordinator of the alarm stations, with headquarters at Reedy Island. Simmons's selection left Fisher free to devote his resources to the outlook post at Lewes, where he remained throughout the war.[13]

The Navy Board, on March 27, was asked to provide protection to the Pennsylvania saltworks located at Toms River, New Jersey. The proposal of Thomas Savadge in the spring of 1776 to make 60,000 bushels of salt annually had been approved by the Committee of Safety. Captain Richard Eyre, with the armed schooner *Delaware*, was sent to Toms River to protect the saltworks against British cruisers. Eyre and the *Delaware* apparently remained on this station until July when they were relieved by a detachment of Pennsylvania militia commanded by Captain John Nice.[14]

The surviving minutes of the Board begin on February 18, 1777, and end on September 24. The entries are replete with the daily chores confronting the naval service. Daily records of the Board, naval officers, and supply officers to the boats reveal unusual activity during this period. Numerous indents of the boat captains for sundries and provisions are recorded in the minutes. The accounts of William Webb, paymaster, and John Mitchell, commissary, incorporate hundreds of items to make the operation of the navy efficient. Every page of the minutes contains reference to the work on the chevaux-de-frise, the Schuylkill Bridge, and supplies for the forts. As previously described, this was the period when the majority of small guard boats were built and the various supply sloops purchased.[15]

Additional land defenses were planned, existing ones strengthened, and added obstructions were placed in the river channel. The positioning of the various elements of the fleet was discussed with Hazelwood. After serious deliberation, Hazelwood was given instructions to dispose the fleet according to his best judgment. The chains of fire rafts were stationed in part in Darby and Mantua Creeks and the Schuylkill River with at least one guard boat assigned to each chain. The galleys and ships were to take position in the vicinity of Fort Island, soon to be called Fort Mifflin.[16]

A subcommittee of the Board directed that a four-gun battery be erected at Darby Creek for the protection of the fire rafts, and that a flanking wing be added at Fort Island. On March 29, Hazelwood was instructed to proceed with building the battery at or near Darby Creek. He selected a location on Tinicum Island, which commanded the back channel. A fascine or earthen redoubt was built and wooden barracks constructed to house the detachment to be stationed there. At approximately the same time, a two-gun battery was erected on Bush (also called Woodbury) Island. This small island was in the Delaware a few hundred yards off Fort Mercer. Pennsylvania Militia Artillery companies were stationed at these two posts. Colonel Jehu Eyre and his artillery companies were assigned to these posts as well as to Billingsport and Fort Mifflin in early September. When the British occupied Philadelphia late in September, the Darby Creek battery was abandoned and the fire rafts were towed upriver above Fort Mifflin.[17]

Fisher's position at Lewes was in an ever-increasing state of danger. Enemy cruisers were unmolested in their attacks on American shipping, and Fisher made frequent appeals for assistance. The Board ordered Captain Rice with the brig *Convention* and Captain Roach with the armed schooner *Delaware* to drop down to Cape May. They were to cruise as far north as Great Egg Harbor Bay and south to Sinepuxent Inlet in Maryland, never to be out of sight of land, nor more than forty-eight hours from their station. If an enemy fleet should enter the bay, they were to observe its activities as long as they were not in jeopardy. The Continental Navy Board sent six cannon to Cape May to aid in the protection of the merchantmen. A request was received from the Marine Committee of the Congress to send additional naval units down to the Capes to assist in keeping British ships out of the lower bay. The State Navy Board advised the committee that only two ships in the State fleet could operate in the waters of the bay, and that they were presently on duty at the Capes.[18]

The perennial problem of undermanned boats and ships and desertions was again rearing its ugly head. Several galleys reported more men sick or absent than those available and fit for duty. The *Montgomery*, floating batteries, and sloops usually suffered a 20- to 50-percent absence. A payroll return for the month of May 1777 shows a disbursement of £4,974 16s 3d. The return further indicated that if all crew complements had been complete, an additional £1,350 would have been needed. As the deficiencies in the crews were principally in the seaman class, this would indicate an overall need for 20 or 25 percent increase in enlistments. A ration return at the same time lists fifty-one boats and ships in service; of this number, two were accommodation sloops rented for a short period. One month later four guard boats, two fire brigs and a fire brigatine would be added, making a fleet of fifty-six vessels of all sizes and descriptions, exclusive of the fire raft chains.[19]

Several expedients were initiated to provide full complements of men on all units of the fleet. An ideal condition, unfortunately it was never realized. Captain Henderson, with the galley *Bull Dog,* was ordered to proceed to Reedy Island and search every outbound or inbound vessel for deserters from the fleet. A directive was sent to Hazelwood instructing every captain not on active duty to pass into the country and establish recruiting stations. They were to be allowed twenty shillings as an expense allowance for each recruit who passed muster. Several records showing the accounts of the various captains with the navy paymaster are in the State archives. Prior to the creation of the Navy Board, £3 15s was paid each recruit; later this amount was increased to £4 10s. In the early months of 1777, amounts varying from fifteen shillings to one pound were paid "for shipping him [the recruit]." These payments were either an advance on the seaman's wages or the bounty authorized effective February 1 of twelve dollars for all who would serve for the duration of the war. According to J. Bennett Nolan, it was at this time that the Reading boatmen, "a rough untutored breed, ready for a fight or quarrel," enlisted on the galleys. These river boatmen were experts in river navigation and, if recruited in substantial numbers, would have been a worthy addition to the galleys.[20] As the fire ships were the least attractive branch of the fleet, a bounty of twenty dollars was offered to those who would enter on board these vessels.[21]

A contributing factor to the high rate of absence among crew members was the request of Council and Continental authorities for those men with special skills. The muster rolls reveal that men were away working as ropemakers, blacksmiths, ironworkers, and as special guards at the State House. Several with unusual talents were employed on the chevaux-de-frise or at the forts.

Most of the men were in their twenties, although a scattering of teenagers was noted; some thirteen and fourteen were enrolled as "boys"—probably as cabin boys, although the size of the galley cabins would hardly accommodate the captain. The oldest members of the crews were in their mid-fifties.

Hazelwood's and the Board's disciplinary problems were not

confined to the enlisted men. A number of the officers were insubordinate and derelict in their duties. Many were inattentive to their recruiting responsibilities, allowing their boats to fall below fighting capability. Officers and men were frequently committing some infraction when quartered in or near the city. Certain captains were more interested in the conviviality of the local taverns than in the performance of their routine duties. They failed to attend morning and evening musters, neglected to exercise their crews daily, and ignored the systematic replenishing of their larders. Hazelwood ordered all boats, except those being repaired, to proceed to Fort Island, attend all musters, and exercise the crews and give strict attention to the needs of their men and boats. Further, each captain was to leave a proper recruiting officer with drummer to establish a rendezvous in the city. Finally, no officer or seaman was to absent himself from his post without special permission from Hazelwood. A typical case in point, which well illustrates the indifference of some captains, was that of Rice of the brig *Convention*. Rice was ordered to the Capes to protect shipping and, arriving at his designated station, discovered that the shot on board did not fit his cannon. He was suspended for his negligence, but later reinstated.[22]

On April 2 the Board was requested to construct a temporary bridge over the Schuylkill River in the vicinity of Philadelphia south of Market Street. For this purpose, the board employed Thomas Casdrop and Thomas Davis. This bridge was to be hinged so as to be detached from either bank of the river upon the approach of enemy troops.[23]

Greater alertness was demanded of the alarm posts as British men-of-war were making more frequent incursions into Delaware Bay. Raiding as far as Reedy Island and Salem, appropriating cattle and farm products, these cruisers were the cause of concern to the Navy Board. Inspection of the alarm posts was imperative. Several attendants were suspected of being drunk and absent from their stations. Two or three were dispossessed of the houses used as their headquarters. Unknown was the condition of the cannon, look-out boats, or Fisher's express riders. Captains Simmons and Allen, on the guard boat *Eagle*, commanded by Captain Murphy, was ordered to conduct a thorough inspection of all thirteen posts. Fisher's post was inspected first and his boat, horses, and men were found in a constant state of readiness. Proceeding up the bay, inspecting each post in turn, varied problems were revealed. Men found derelict were replaced, and log houses were built for those needing quarters. Powder and supplies were furnished and all posts put on an instant alert. Alarm guns were not to be fired unless the British fleet entered the Capes. Other communications were to be relayed by the express riders or look-out boats. It was expected that the enemy would conduct sporadic nuisance raids to keep the countryside in a turmoil, and to steal livestock, but the major concern was an anticipated invasion by the British army and navy. Simmons and Allen reported all alarm posts were in a state of readiness to alert Philadelphia the instant an enemy fleet appeared off the Delaware Capes.[24]

The Navy Board had diligently worked for four months to improve the fleet, perfect the alarm system, construct and sink additional chevaux-de-frise and, in cooperation with the State Board of War, strengthen the river forts. However, clouds were forming on the horizon; the State treasury was exhausted as it became increasingly evident that the city was the next objective of the British. Support, both military and financial, would be needed to avert a catastrophe. This assistance must come from Washington's army and the Continental treasury.

VIII

Summer of Decision—1777

THE GAME of feint and counterfeint was played by Washington and Howe throughout the spring of 1777. To mask his true objective, the British commander-in-chief sent an army of some eighteen thousand men over to Amboy, New Jersey. Marching to New Brunswick, he divided his force into two columns, one under Lord Cornwallis, the other commanded by the Hessian General von Heister. Howe hoped to lure Washington from his strong position at Middlebrook and divide the American army. Washington was not fooled by Howe's maneuver, as his intellligence had reported the British landing at Amboy without baggage or equipment to bridge the Delaware. Several skirmishes resulted but the British were forced to evacuate New Jersey before the end of June.

In the meantime, Sir William Howe, who had the overall command, had been assembling a large fleet in New York Harbor. Washington had received detailed reports of the enemy's activities. Howe's previous excursion had not deceived Washington, but his present movements puzzled the American Commander-in-Chief. A fleet of the strength gathered by the British could have only one use, and that would be to transport the

British and Hessian troops under Howe. Would they go up the Hudson to join Burgoyne, advancing from Canada? Would they endeavor to conquer the southern colonies by sailing to Chesapeake Bay or Charleston? Or possibly their objective was the Capital of the United States, Philadelphia. Washington was at first unwilling to move the American army and, operating on interior lines, believed he could march to Albany to aid Gates, or to the defense of Philadelphia ahead of Howe. Military logic said a union with Burgoyne would be Howe's first consideration and even after Howe embarked his troops and sailed south past Sandy Hook, Washington was not convinced he might not suddenly reverse his direction and sail up the Hudson River.

With the enemy's fleet at sea, Washington set his army in motion toward the Delaware. The civilian authorities of Pennsylvania and the Continental Congress were equally aware of the strategic value of the Delaware Valley and the danger to the young nation's Capital. Engineers and other military specialists on Washington's staff would be needed to survey and make recommendations for strengthening the defenses of the river approaches to the city.

Congress had appointed a committee to evaluate the defenses of the Delaware River, and on June 11, 1777, it moved to implement certain of the committee's suggestions. Governor Livingston of New Jersey was instructed to order out five hundred militia to assist in completing the fortifications at Billingsport. The Supreme Executive Council of Pennsylvania was requested to assist Generals Thomas Mifflin and Philippe Trouson du Coudray to prepare the river defenses. The Continental Navy Board and Marine Committee were directed to order all Continental naval captains to cooperate with the State navy in defending the Delaware Capes against enemy attempts to enter the bay.

At last the Council and state of Pennsylvania were to receive competent engineering advice, albeit some of it would be impractical and rejected. Financial and material aid would be forthcoming, but consistent with the experience of the army and navy throughout the war, neither enough nor of the best quality. But now at least Pennsylvania would not have to assume the burden of defense alone.

Philippe Charles Trouson du Coudray, a general in the French army, had arrived in America in May 1777. Stopping at the Continental encampment at Morristown, New Jersey, he met Washington and then proceeded to Philadelphia to present his credentials to the Continental Congress. His entourage included eighteen commissioned officers and ten sergeants. He had negotiated a contract with Silas Deane in Paris, guaranteeing him command of the Continental Artillery. An explosive situation developed as the contents of du Coudray's contract was revealed to Washington and his generals. Henry Knox, commander of the Artillery, and general Nathanael Greene and John Sullivan wrote to Congress submitting their resignations from the army if du Coudray's agreement with Deane were honored.

Congress complained to Washington that Knox, Greene, and Sullivan demonstrated little confidence in the integrity and justice of that body. Washington was to convey to the officers the displeasure of Congress and request that they acknowledge the error of their ways. No apology was forthcoming. Congressional annoyance was expressed with Silas Deane; he had been authorized to recruit military specialists, but not to enter into agreements superseding American officers.

As always, the man in the middle was Washington. In addition to admonishing the generals, he was instructed to placate du Coudray until Congress could resolve the Frenchman's status. Du Coudray was eventually given a staff assignment with the title of Inspector General of Ordnances and Military Manufactories, a capacity in which he was to figure prominently in the plans for defense of the Delaware River.[1] This assignment was apparently acceptable to du Coudray as he readily entered into a review of the fortifications, the naval force, and chevaux-de-frise. He submitted several detailed recommendations for Congressional consideration and approval.

It was at this time that a British deserter came into the camp of the Continental army. Recently arrived from England, Thomas Bowman had taken the first opportunity to desert. In reporting on the activities of the British in New York, he called attention to the cutting down of a vessel called the *Empress of Russia*. She was to be converted to an ocean-going galley or floating battery, mounting twenty-four thirty-two-pounders, and displacing 1,300 tons.[2] We will meet this ship when she arrives in the Delaware to play a decisive role in the reduction of Fort Mifflin. At that time she will be called the *Vigilant*.

Returning to the activities of du Coudray,[3] the Continental Congress, on June 11, 1777, had passed a resolution authorizing the presentation of the report of "The Committee for Viewing the Works Erected for the Defense of the River" to the Supreme Executive Council of Pennsylvania.[4] On June 21, du Coudray and Mifflin, accompanied by interpreter Nicholas Rogers, laid a copy of their report before the Council.[5]

The plan submitted at this time was du Coudray's "Observations on the Forts intended for the Defense of the Two Passages of the River Delaware." While this report is variously dated in June and July, 1777, a study of the correspondence and plans of du Coudray makes it chronologically impossible to assign this plan to any other time than June 21. Other recommendations of the French engineer reflect a good technician, but one unable to comprehend the American division between civil and military authority or the care exercised by Washington in consulting Congress on all matters.

Du Coudray recommended that the major defense of the river be made at Billingsport, which commanded the river at its narrowest point and therefore was the easiest to defend. This observation he was later to waver on when Washington's opinions became known. Washington noted that the layout and projection of the fort were very poor. It was not properly planned so as to defend the chevaux-de-frise, which should have been its main objective and it would be incapable of withstanding a protracted siege. It was also obvious that it was extremely vulnerable to attack by land.

While considerable effort had been expended on this fort, Washington pointed out its many shortcomings. Planks used to support the sand embankments were not half as thick as they should have been, and, as they were set in a perpendicular fashion, many had already fallen down. The loose sand used would not provide protection for the garrison; guns were placed so as to make them less effective and expose them to a more destructive enemy cannonade. Finally, as situated, the work was totally wasted as a protection for the river obstructions.

For the moment, only the State navy galleys and floating batteries could be relied on to defend the river pass. Du Coudray recommended that the two demi-bastions of the fort be immediately reworked and made into redoubts covered by palisades and with a protecting ditch. These batteries would require a smaller garrison, thereby relieving men for duty in the main army. To execute this project, a labor force of fifteen hundred to two thousand workers would be needed for a minimum of twenty days.

Also, a half-moon battery of fifteen or twenty guns should be placed at the tip of Billings Island to anchor the west end of the chevaux-de-frise. This first line of defense later would be made subordinate to the defense of the second line anchored by Forts Mifflin and Mercer, aided by the galleys and floating batteries.

In commenting on the works on Fort Island, du Coudray's remarks were brief: it was badly situated, its main battery improperly directed, rendering half the guns useless. It could only be effective when directing its fire at shipping approaching the main battery.

Red Bank (Fort Mercer) was considered to be better conceived, directed, and executed than any of the other forts. He complimented Colonel John Bull who, without engineering experience, had laid it out. It was his opinion that this work would be in a posture of defense in two weeks, but he was at a loss to see of what value it would serve in defending the river. In fact, he thought the British would by-pass the fort and not attempt to take it. In common with almost all the general officers of Washington's staff, he was incapable of seeing the real worth of Fort Mercer. As a supply point for men and matériel, it would permit Fort Mifflin to continue resisting the British fleet and army for several weeks.

Finally returning to his original suggestions, du Coudray proposed making a respectable stand at Billingsport, with support from the State navy, and the construction of the recommended half-moon battery on Billings Island. He wanted to transfer to Billingsport most of the cannon from Forts Mifflin and Mercer, leaving only a few of the poorest guns in those forts. He believed they should be retained to present an illusion of resistance as the second line of defense and to sustain civilian and military morale. The latter was important in view of all the expenditures and effort that had gone into these works and the reliance everyone had placed in their effectiveness.[6]

On July 17, 1777, the Continental Board of War returned du Coudray's plans to the Council and recommended that they be put into execution immediately. Approval for this plan resulted from a series of meetings between the State Board of War and a committee from the Continental Congress. These conferences extended over a period of six weeks, beginning in early June. To assist workmen employed by Pennsylvania, militia from New Jersey and Pennsylvania and Continental troops from North Carolina and Virginia under General Nash were ordered to Billingsport. Fortunately, other circumstances brought Washington into the picture about this time, permitting him to take direct command of the situation.[7]

While this study is mainly concerned with the State navy, it cannot be separated from the land defenses. The defense of the river would be only as successful as the coordinated activities of the fleet, forts, and obstructions. A weak link in the chain would result in the destruction of the remaining links.

Approval was given to du Coudray's first plan, and at this point we might briefly review what had happened to improve the defenses during the first two years of war. The State fleet was in service and ready for enemy attack, assuming that the boat crews could be maintained at their full complements. The archival records, both printed and manuscript, report a steady stream of workmen, material, and money being poured into Billingsport and Fort Island. Many manuscripts dealing with this period are lost or missing, or a more complete picture could be drawn of the work done on these fortifications. Some valuable work, especially at Fort Island, was completed but, without qualified military engineers, much of it was misdirected. At Fort Mifflin, in particular, they would create major problems for the defending Continental troops in October and November 1777.[8]

The fort at Red Bank, to be named Mercer, was started in mid-April 1777, under the supervision of Colonel Bull. As we have seen, du Coudray was impressed with the progress at this fort and believe it could be completed before July 1, 1777. It would later be decided that the fort was too large and would need a larger garrison and more cannon than could be made available.[9]

The fort on Tinicum Island, generally referred to as the Derby (Darby) Creek fort was little more than a redoubt. Originally planned by the Navy Board in the spring of 1777 to protect the fire rafts and guard boats stationed in the mouth of Darby Creek, its effectiveness was limited to defense against small ships and cruisers. A major invasion of the British fleet would leave this post isolated.

Some of the shortcomings of these fortifications will be seen as Washington and his generals review the basic strategy to be employed to thwart an invasion by the Howe brothers.

In the meantime, feverish activity extended to the far reaches of the Delaware River. All fords above Trenton were surveyed to determine which were the most easily fordable, which could be readily bridged, and which had the best roads leading to and from the ford. Benedict Arnold was placed in command of the forces defending them.[10]

The citizens of Philadelphia were apprehensive about the British plans, some secretly hopeful that Sir William Howe would occupy the city. Others, the Patriots, were deeply concerned and many were preparing to leave the city. However panic was not present and would not be until mid-September, when a general exodus of Patriot leaders and their families would take place.

Their apprehension did not prevent the Patriots from staging a massive demonstration to celebrate the first anniversary of the Declaration of Independence. A local newspaper reported on July 8, 1777:

Last Friday the 4th of July, being the Anniversary of the Independence of the United States of America, was celebrated in this city with demonstrations of joy and festivity. About noon all the armed ships and gallies in the river were drawn up before the city, dressed in the gayest manner, with colours of the United States and streamers displayed. At one o'clock the yards being properly manned, they began the celebration of the day by discharge of thirteen cannon from each of the ships, and one from each of the thirteen gallies, in honor of the United States.[11]

Turning from the enthusiasm of the Independence Day Celebration to the more somber prospects on the military front, Washington was uncertain whether the apparent indecisiveness of Howe was a subterfuge. Even after all elements of the British fleet were out to sea on July 23, he was careful not to commit the entire American army to either direction until Howe's intentions were known.

Meanwhile, the State navy was busily employed in transporting troops and assisting the Continental navy in patrolling the lower reaches of Delaware Bay. On July 18, the Navy Board instructed Hazelwood to convoy Potter's Pennsylvania Militia from Chester to Billingsport to join the elements of the New Jersey Militia already there, and lend a hand in the construction of the fort. The accommodation sloops *Sally* and *Industry*, Province sloop *Speedwell*, and shallop *Black Duck* were assigned this task. In a few weeks many of these same troops would be transported back to Fort Mifflin.[12]

Fear for the guard boats at Lewes was expressed by the Navy Board, not so much from the British as the disaffected residents of lower Delaware. It was believed an attack by enemy barges would give occasion for an attack by Tory sympathizers on shore. Nevertheless, Fisher was allowed latitude to keep the boats at their stations or return them to Darby Creek. The Continental Navy Board had persistently urged the State Navy Board to send galleys, fire ships and other units of the State fleet to the Capes to assist the Continental fleet under Captain Isaiah Robinson. Careful consideration was always accorded the Continental requests, but the State officials were fully cognizant of the dangers in sending any part of the State fleet to the Capes. It would be suicidal for the galleys to operate in the open waters of the bay. As for the State ships, their armament, even when added to the available Continental fleet, would be totally incapable of opposing Lord Howe's fleet. The danger was expressed by Joseph Blewer, Chairman of the State Navy Board:

. . . run a very great risque of the Fleet down in the Cape May Channel, unless we can procure an equal force with the Enimy for it often happens that a Vessel taking the first of a Southerly breeze, from Sea will push up so fast as to over hawle any Vessels that may be miles higher before they feel the Wind, by which means the Enimies Ships may cut off our retreat.

Finally it was agreed to send the brig *Convention*, Captain Rice, and the armed schooner *Delaware*, Captain Eyre, with the fire ship *Hecla*, Captain Perkins, and fire brig *Volcano*, Captain Brice. The last two were a loan with the understanding that the Continental Navy Board would replace them, as these fire ships were designed for defense of the river at its narrow passes. However, the State Board had little expectation they would either survive or be effective at the Capes. Although these ships were ordered down on July 12, they were not outfitted and manned until August 4, at which time they dropped down to the bay.[13]

Captain John Montresor, the British engineer who had drawn plans for the original fort on Mud Island, is our authority for certain movements of the British fleet. He records that with the *Eagle*, Lord Howe's flagship, in the van, the fleet followed in two divisions. The number of ships vary according to the observer; Montresor claimed 260 sail. Reports from Henry Fisher and Captain Hunn at Lewes and Cape May respectively, vary from 199 to 226. A return included in Montresor's journal indicates 266 transports and ships of war; seventeen thousand troops including one thousand artillerymen; three hundred rounds of ammunition for the cannon, and provisions in each transport for three months.[14]

To provide additional intelligence for the Council, Captain John Hunn was appointed to serve in the same capacity at Cape May as that of Henry Fisher at Cape Henlopen. He was given his instructions on July 24 and left forthwith for his post, journeying through Great Egg Harbor, arriving at Cape May on the twenty-sixth. Instructed that all movements of the enemy fleet were to be transmitted to Washington accurately and promptly, he was further advised to use great care in selecting express riders. Two riders were to be sent to headquarters to ensure delivery in the event of an accident to one.[15]

Arriving at the Cape, Hunn found a house to serve as his headquarters. It was situated in an area where he could establish his observation post without revealing the nature of his assignment, a difficult feat when it was revealed that seven occupants of the lodginghouse were British seamen, prisoners from the frigate *Roebuck*. Hunn was immediately beset with problems, as a heavy fog hung over the Capes for three days. However, constant vigilance paid off on August 29 when thirty sail were seen. The next day forty-five ships were sighted and on the thirty-first he counted 190 sail. On the same day Fisher had reported sighting 228 sail.[16]

In Philadelphia the report of the British fleet entering the Capes created great consternation. The Supreme Executive Council instructed the city magistrate to collect all wagons, in and near the city, and prepare to remove stores, provisions and other supplies that might aid the enemy, except those absolutely needed for the residents. Militia and naval captains were ordered to report to their stations and to place the forts and river in the best defensive position possible.[17]

Our old antagonist Captain Sir Andrew Snape Hamond, with the frigate *Roebuck*, was still on station at the Capes. With the arrival of Sir William Howe, Hamond reported in person to the Commander-in-Chief on the conditions of the Delaware River and Bay. Historians and students have debated what precisely transpired at this meeting of the British command. Some students, buttressed by at least one British officer's statement, have contended that Hamond deliberately overstated the strength and size of the American river defenses. Assuming this to be true, was his report colored by the nightmare of May 1776?

Howe had written to Lord George Germain before leaving New York that "I propose going up the Delaware." Why did he change his mind? Hamond had reported that the defenses of the Delaware were strong; the bay and river possessed swift and strong tides, sand banks, and shallow channels. But the British armada was powerful and could have forced a landing south of the first line of chevaux-de-frise in either Pennsylvania or New Jersey.

The terrain in New Jersey presented many obstacles, including numerous creeks with but few bridges, which could be easily destroyed. The land was crossed with many marshes. Even if these natural obstacles could be overcome, the British would still be on the east bank of the Delaware. Most Americans believed Marcus Hook, Pennsylvania, to be the logical landing site. This landing would place the British army in easy approach of Philadelphia, and capable of support by the British fleet. However, the river would still be barred to the enemy. Except for the State navy, other defenses were in a deplorable condition and garrisoned by a handful of militia and would have presented a much easier target than they did two months later.

Without a doubt, Hamond's persuasiveness must be accepted as the principal, if not the only, reason for Howe's change of mind. The fleet now headed south along the coast to the Chesapeake Bay. Howe in his narrative recorded:

that, finding it hazardous to sail up the Delaware, he agreed with the Admiral to go to Chesapeake Bay, a plan which had been preconcerted in the event of a landing in the Delaware proving upon our arrival [illegible].

He also wrote again to Germain at the end of August that when he arrived off the Capes of the Delaware Bay certain information he received made it more advisable to proceed to the Chesapeake Bay.

A different opinion was offered by Joseph Galloway, Pennsylvania's most talented Tory. In 1779 he was a vitriolic critic of the conduct of war by Sir William Howe. A native Philadelphian, he was convinced that the city would have been easy prey for a more aggressive commander in early August 1777. He wrote:

The fort at Mud Island was garrisoned only by 130 militia, and Billingsport with 90. The floating batteries were not manned, the lower Chevaux-de-frize were not placed in the river. The chain was not finished; the passage from the Capes to Philadelphia was open; Red Bank was not fortified or occupied in short, there was nothing to oppose the taking possession of Mud Island fort, the city of Philadelphia, and all the rebel water guard in the Delaware.

There was much truth in this observation, but foreknowledge and hindsight are two unbeatable adversaries. While Howe should have proceeded up the bay and landed in the neighborhood of Marcus Hook, the information volunteered by Galloway was not available to him—another instance of where communications between Tories and British commanders was imperfect or did not exist.[18]

Meanwhile, Washington had set the Continental army in motion, arriving with his aides in Philadelphia on the morning of July 31. Proceeding south to Chester, he received the perplexing news that Howe had left the Capes for parts unknown. To do other than await developments would have been senseless, as his army at that time was nearing Philadelphia and in need of rest and refreshment. As it was inconceivable that Howe's objective was not the capital city, Washington requested opinions from his generals on the condition of the river defenses and the best method of adapting them to a defense of the river and city. Washington was not entirely satisfied with du Coudray's original proposal, and realizing that the French engineer had been surveying and working on the river defenses for two months, he asked him to update his plans.

Several officers submitted detailed observations on the river defenses. Opinions varied as to the value of the different works, although there was a broad basic agreement on the relative merits of the defense system. To students of Pennsylvania and New Jersey history, they present a vivid picture of the physical characteristics of the Delaware River and its adjacent terrain and forts.[19]

The consensus was that the first line of defense at Billingsport, including one line of chevaux-de-frise, would be unable to withstand a British attack. Another line would soon be placed in the river. The main dependence for defending this line must rest with the State galleys and floating batteries. Still dissenting from the majority, du Coudray again recommended a half-moon battery on Billings Island, and with the naval force stationed behind the obstructions they could hold out for fifteen days, giving the main army a chance to come up. Du Coudray's principal reason remained the narrowness of the channel at Billingsport, which would prevent the British from bringing more than three frigates into line at one time. Again he believed that the galleys presented such a small target that they would, with heavier cannon, be more than a match for the enemy.

The majority opinion was that the second line was more easily defended, despite the badly executed works at Fort Mifflin, where the only effective battery was at the southern tip of the fort. Much could be done if time, men, and materials were available. The existing stone facing on the south and east sides offered excellent protection for batteries placed there. Fear was expressed for the exposed western wall. It could be easily covered by cannon placed on Carpenters' and Province Islands, but it was generally believed that these islands could be flooded and made untenable for enemy batteries. But time was running out and the flooding would prove ineffective.

General but somewhat guarded confidence was placed in the State navy and the chevaux-de-frise. Most opinions were that the navy would be a vital part of the defense force if properly employed, but there was some apprehension regarding the river obstructions. According to du Coudray, Hazelwood is the authority for the statement that certain of the chevaux-de-frise were placed thirty to forty feet apart. Spread at such a distance, small enemy ships could penetrate them. Additional chevaux-de-frise were available and it was planned to sink them to close these gaps.

In early August Washington conducted a personal survey of the river defenses. He inspected the Billingsport line with one row of chevaux-de-frise and the Fort Mifflin-Fort Mercer line with three rows of obstructions. Conferences were held with officers and civilian authorities respecting the weakness and strength of each fort. Washington assiduously reviewed the condition of the chevaux-de-frise, especially those at Billingsport. If that post should fall, could the State flotilla of galleys and floating batteries prevent the British from removing enough stockades to permit passage of their frigates? With the benefit of his on-the-spot examination, and the opinions of members of his official family, he prepared a comprehensive report on the Delaware River defenses. His report reflected a degree of military astuteness often denied by his critics. Writing to Congress from Germantown on August 10, he presented an excellent summation of his personal observations and the suggestions of the officers, interspersed with his conclusions and recommendations. While this letter is lengthy, it so graphically describes the state of conditions on the river, it is worthy of quoting:

. . . It is generally a well founded maxim, that we ought to endeavor to reduce out defence as much as possible to a certainty, by collecting our strength and making all our preparations at one point, rather than to risk its being weak and ineffectual every where, by dividing our attention and force to different objects. In doing this, we may disable ourselves from acting with sufficient vigor any where, and a misfortune in one place may pave the way for a similar one in another. In our circumstances, we have neither men, cannon, nor any thing else to spare, and perhaps cannot with propriety hazard them on objects which being attended with the greatest success we can promise ourselves, can be productive of only partial and indicisive advantages, and which may possibly fail of the end proposed, may have some serious ill-consequences, and must at all events have some disadvantages.

It is then to be considered, where our defence can be most effectually made,—whether at Billingsport, or at Fort Island.

It appears to me, that the last deserves greatly the preference. Billingsport has but one row of Chevaux de frize, Fort Island has three; and in addition to the, a boom and another Chevaux de frize, ready to be sunk in the channel, on the approach of the enemy; of course the obstructions in this respect are four times as great at the one as at the other. The Gallies and floating batteries, that could be brought for the defence of the chevaux de frize at Billingsport, would be unable to maintain their station, when once the enemy were in possession of the commanding ground on the Jersey side, to which they would be entirely exposed, and notwithstanding the works raising there, even supposing them complete, the strongest advocates for making our defence in this place do not pretend, that that event can be protracted more than fifteen or twenty days at most, at the end of which time, we should be obliged with the loss of our cannon at least to abandon the defence, and leave it in the power of the enemy to remove or destroy the chevaux de frize at pleasure. Nor is it by any means certain that a single row of chevaux de frize would be an impenetrable barrier to the enemy's ships. Experiments have been made that lead to a contrary supposition, and if they should hazard one, which it might be well worth their while to do, with some of their less valuable ships, under favor of a leading breeze and tide, and should succeed in it,—the consequence might be the loss of our gallies and floating batteries, which I apprehend might be intercepted, and with the assistance of their gallies and small armed vessels, taken and this would greatly weaken the opposition we might otherwise give at Fort Island, and tend powerfully to render it abortive. But if they should not attempt this, contenting themselves with safer though slower operations, I have already observed, that it is agreed, on all hands, in fifteen or twenty days they would be able to possess themselves of infallible means of frustrating our opposition there, by the capture of our works; and if we add to this, that it might very possibly happen in less time,—if from no other cause,—yet from the garrison being intimidated, by a consciousness of its own inferiority and inability to support itself against a so much superior force of numbers,—which might occasion a conduct destructive to itself—there will remain no sufficient reasons to justify the making this the principal point of defence.

At Fort Island the boom and chevaux de frize are an ample security against any forcible impression of the enemy's ships which it would be imprudent in them to attempt. On the Jersey side the situation of the ground is such, that the gallies, floating batteries and forts employed in the defence of the obstructions would have little to fear from any batteries erected there. Red-bank seems, by its elevation to be the only advantageous spot for annoying them; but as it is computed to be above 1900 yards from Fort Island, the distance is rather too great to allow any battery raised there to act with so much effect as to be able to silence our fire. On this side, the ground by dykes and sluices may be laid under water to so considerable an extent as to leave no danger of our River force being annoyed from thence; for which purpose suitable precautions ought, at once, to be made, against it may be necessary to carry them into effect.

But, though a battery upon Red-bank, would not in my apprehension, be able to prevent the efficacy of our defence or give any material disturbance to Fort Island, in particular, yet it might serve to make the situation of some of our gallies rather uneasy; and this perhaps makes it worth while to pre-occupy it in order to keep it out of the enemy's hands erecting a small, but strong work there capable of containing about two hundred men, with six or eight pieces of light cannon, and a proportionable quantity of stores. As the approaches to it are difficult on account of the adjacent creeks, and a communication can be kept open between it and our army, by which means the garrison might receive succors from time to time, though we could not expect to make it impregnable, yet we should have a prospect of holding it . . . much longer than we could the work at Billingsport.

. . . The comparative extent of the River at Billingsport and at Fort Island has been assigned as a motive of preference to the former, the river being narrower there than at the latter, and supposed to admit of fewer ships oper-ating at a time; but as it is asserted by the gentlemen in the River department, that the sand banks and shallowness of the River in most places near Fort Island, compensate for the width of it and make it impossible for more than three ships to act together at a time, this reason of preferring the position at Billingsport seems to have no foundation. And if we consider, that our whole force of gallies and floating batteries, would be collected at Fort Island, assisted by the fort itself and that it would not be safe to trust them all out for the defence of Billingsport, for fear of the disaster already suggested, it seems evident enough that this is the place where our defence may be most successfully made. . . .

On the whole I am of opinion that the obstructions in the River, with the help of gallies, floating batteries, and with tolerable industry to put the land works in a proper state, will be extremely formidable to the enemy and authorise a reasonable expectation of their being effectual. . . .[20]

Washington had implored the Supreme Executive Council to employ surveyors to map the region and do it promptly. On July 9, writing to Thomas Wharton, he requested: "Draughts or Maps of the Country which is or may be the seat of War so essentially necessary, that I must beg leave to recommend such a measure with all possible Expedition, so far as regards the shores of the Delaware where the Enemy may probably land & march." Later du Coudray, on learning of Washington's opposition to Billingsport as the first line of defense, stated that his favoring that line was based on inaccurate maps.[21] The absence of reliable maps unquestionably led to the general delusion that the flooding of the low west shore islands would prevent any enemy from approaching from that direction—at least close enough to erect batteries. The entire area covering Carpenters' and Province Islands had been diked and embankments of earth erected so that this low swampy ground was converted to rich meadow land—

all at a considerable expense to local residents.[22] A competent survey would have revealed certain elevations which would be above the flooded waters, where small redoubts could be raised. As we shall see, much effort was to be expended in flooding these islands, and, in spite of this, British batteries were erected on both islands.

If Washington had had knowledge of the elevations on Carpenters' and Province Islands, could he have spared men and cannon to fortify those locations? Cannon were in such short supply that suggestions were made literally to strip Forts Mercer and Mifflin of all but the poorest guns to supply Billingsport. Many of the cannon at these posts, and the redoubt at Darby Creek, were in poor condition. More important, the Continental Army had no surplus to supply the forts. Patently undermanned, Washington could not have spared soldiers for these extra posts; facing the main British army, he would need every man in his command.

Receiving only casual notice was the possibility of the British gaining the rear of the river defenses and occupying the city without reducing the river fortifications—a circumstance that came to pass and made Fort Mercer the lifeline for Fort Mifflin.

While these points are omitted from Washington's letter to Congress, it would appear at this time, early August 1777, that he tacitly recognized that the most he could expect of the river defenses was a holding action. He could only hope that the forts and little navy could hold out long enough to permit the Continental Army to choose their own battleground in defense of the city. Knowing the deplorable state of the forts, with the possible exception of Fort Mercer (and that was too extensive a work to defend), and with the undermanned little fleet of galleys and floating batteries, who could have expected them to stand against the might of a British fleet? And yet, two months later, they did just that and for over seven weeks resisted the most bitterly contended siege of the war. However, in August, Sir William Howe must be thanked for any assistance a time delay gave Washington and his army.

Before returning to the activities of the State Navy Board and fleet, we will review the activities of du Coudray and his persistent effort to make Billingsport the main line of defense. After submitting his letter on the status of the river defenses,

Washington received a communication from the French general outlining his reasons for preferring Billingsport, but admitting that he was not possessed of the same information as the Commander-in-Chief. In turn he described a weakness in the defense of Fort Mifflin. A channel between two sandbars on the east side of the fort provided four to four and-one-half fathoms, allowing three frigates to lie between the banks and enfilade the exposed river side of the fort. Two solutions were offered: either sink additional chevaux-de-frise or build a battery on the east flank of the fort. The former was preferable because if properly sunk it would make success more certain. A battery would be difficult to raise because of the marshy character of the island and the shortage of cannon. In addition, a battery might be destroyed by the fire of British men-of-war.

Again, about August 20, du Coudray with Arthur Donaldson conducted a survey of the river, taking soundings in all channels. Donaldson was familiar with the river, having been instrumental in sinking most of the chevaux-de-frise. One week later the Navy Board made similar soundings, which confirmed those taken by du Coudray and Donaldson. The result of these surveys strengthened du Coudray's opinion of the feasibility of defending at Billingsport. At the request of the Continental Board of War, on August 29, he submitted another proposal. Little that was new was contained in this plan. He elaborated at some length on the information given Washington concerning the channel depths before the second line of defense anchored by Forts Mifflin and Mercer. He literally pontificated on the short-comings of Fort Mifflin in an attempt to justify his position. He further considered Fort Mercer too far above the second line of chevaux-de-frise to offer any defense. The battery on Bush Island was nothing but a toy. He had discussed this plan with Washington before sending it to the Board of War and then, on August 30, forwarded a copy of the proposal to the Commander-in-Chief.[23]

Du Coudray addressed a petition to Congress on September 7. Somewhat querulously he called the solons' attention to his proposal of August 29, and the fact that the Board of War and the Supreme Executive Council had not honored him with their decision. He reiterated the willingness of his engineers and himself to serve in the current campaign and called attention to their previous service. Observing that the British had landed at the head of Chesapeake Bay, he still considered Philadelphia their objective. He suggested placing a fortification near Wilmington, Delaware, and offered, with Congressional approval, to superintend its construction. The balance of his communication outlined the possible movements of the British and the lack of heavy artillery in the Continental Army. About one week after writing this letter the unfortunate du Coudray was drowned in the Schuylkill River.

Du Coudray had steadfastly clung to his contention that the Billingsport line was defensible and that the narrowness of the river prevented the British from approaching with more than three frigates at one time. He consistently maintained that Billingsport could hold out for fifteen days, enough time to permit Washington to plan his overall strategy. Washington recognized that the fort was vulnerable on the land side and would be fortunate to withstand an assault from that direction for two or three days, a point to be demonstrated in a few weeks. Du Coudray deferred to Washington's decision but retained his low opinion of Fort Mifflin, and believed that Fort Mercer was located too far from the chevaux-de-frise to be a factor in its defense. In fact, he suggested building another battery or fort on an eminence south of Fort Mercer (probably near the mouth of Mantua Creek where fascine batteries were later erected). This location would provide the eastern anchor to the second line of obstructions and prevent enemy frigates from advancing up between the sand banks to enfilade Fort Mifflin. He suggested a work of twelve or fifteen cannon; because of the distance, they should be eighteen- or twenty-four-pounders. Also, attention should be given to a strong fortification on the western shore—a point seldom made by American officers. Even if desirable, lack of time, material and manpower would have prevented this ambitious undertaking. No records exist to indicate that these recommendations received serious consideration. All programs involving du Coudray came to an abrupt halt with his untimely death.[24]

To return to the situation in early August and the activities of the State navy and its Board, we find feverish efforts being made to ready the fleet for its part in the coming action.

After the British fleet disappeared southward along the Maryland-Virginia coast, frantic attempts were made to strengthen the small Continental flotilla in the bay. The Continental Navy Board, with Congress's approval, was authorized to purchase twelve vessels to be fitted out as fire ships. The State Navy Board was asked to outfit the vessels and an advance of £1,000 was made to the State navy paymaster for this purpose. Continental Stores was ordered to furnish the Navy Board with boards, scantling, planks, and other stores to expedite the conversion of these ships.[25]

These exertions by the Continental authorities were enthusiastically received by State officials. However, they were emphatic in their insistence that the Continental Congress assume all costs for the fire ships. Whether these ships were outfitted remains a mystery, as no record exists to show their participating in the actions on the Delaware. It is more probable that before the Continental Navy Board could procure the necessary vessels, time would preclude converting them to fire ships. On August 6, 1777, the Continental Board appealed to the Council to appoint an impartial committee to appraise vessels in port adaptable for this purpose, commandeer them, and pay the owners accordingly. Council refused, contending this would be an exercise of power that they wished to avoid. They suggested paying what may even be judged as an extravagant price, rather than irritate friend or foe.[26]

Apparently a few vessels were purchased. On August 20, Colonel Lewis Nicola, city marshall, was ordered to furnish a sergeant's guard to protect the combustibles and fire ships. They were lying at Jones's and Thompson's wharves in Southwark below the *Gloria Dei* Old Swedes' Church.[27]

While assisting the Continental Navy Board, the State Navy Board was also deeply involved in affairs of the State navy. Sickness was a major concern to Hazelwood and his officers. The crews on the galleys and guard boats were exposed to the vagaries of the weather on the river. Dr. James Dunlap, fleet surgeon, was forced to quarter men in private homes because the hospital on Province Island could not accommodate all the sick. Facilities were undoubtedly taxed because of the needs of the militia as well as the navy. In fact, on September 4 this hospital would be placed under the care and direction of the Navy Board.

Henry Fisher was beseeching the Council for additional assistance against enemy cruisers and tenders. These small war ships were infesting the creeks and coves of lower Delaware Bay, taking prizes and bringing supplies to the Tories of that region.

A message received from Fisher at this time recounts the only known engagement of a State guard boat with the enemy. Fisher advised the Navy Board that four frigates, with their tenders, were cruising in the road between the Capes and virtually curtailing activity by American ships. A few days previously, the *Eagle* with Captain Murphy had gone up to Cedar Creek, above Lewes, to seize certain small craft that the Tories used to go out to the British frigates to engage in trade. Arriving at the creek he found a sloop with a cargo of sugar, salt, rum, coffee, tea, and other supplies to be delivered to local Tories. The sloop's crew ran away on the approach of the *Eagle*. Seizing the sloop and an assortment of Tories who arrived to trade farm produce with the British, he headed back for Lewes. Darkness and rough weather prevented him from entering the creek near Lewes until daylight. At dawn he observed a schooner and three cutters approaching to retake the prize sloop and to engage the *Eagle*. A hot action ensued; the *Eagle's* gun was skillfully handled and, although the enemies' armament was much heavier, managed to inflict considerable damage on the British. Fisher noted that the British cutters were forced to tow away the disabled schooner. The *Eagle* suffered very little damage; in fact, the only injury was to Captain Murphy who sustained burns of the face when his cannon blew sparks from the touchhole. Fisher observed that the British schooner and sloop types engaged in this action usually carried two six-pounders plus several swivels. He concluded his report with a request for a small galley, as the schooners and sloops ordinarily, if properly handled, carried armament too powerful for the guard boats.[28]

The Council commended Captain Murphy but, as in the past, contended that the galleys could not operate safely in the bay.[29] As the smaller guard boats never operated in open water, but always near shore or more often in the mouths of creeks, there was little danger to them from rough weather. Although objecting to the use of a galley, the Council granted the Navy Board permission to send one or more guard boats to Lewes.

The guard boats *Eagle*, with Captain Murphy, and *Salamander*, with Captain Lawrence, were already on station in the lower bay at Lewes. On August 11, 1777, five additional guard boats were sent to join the *Eagle* and the *Salamander*, subject to orders from Fisher. The *Brimstone, Porcupine, Viper, Fire Brand,* and *Thunder,* commanded by Captains Watkins, Tatnall, Beasley, Rue, and Gilbert respectively, moved south to their rendezvous. Again our attention is called to the fact that not all the guard boats were equipped with four-pounder cannon; the *Brimstone* and *Thunder* had three-pounders and the *Fire Brand* a two-pounder.[30]

Neither the Continental ships nor the small State guard boats operating in the bay could prevent the British from penetrating at will the upper reaches of the bay. Leeson Simmons, at 6 A.M. on August 21, reported a frigate and two schooners off Bombay Hook. At 2 P.M. the Continental and State flotillas got under way to engage the enemy. The State brig *Convention* and armed schooner *Delaware* with the fire ship *Hecla* and fire brig *Volcano* were still members of this little fleet, commanded by Captain Alexander of the Continental navy. No record of contact between the two forces can be found. Simmons reported at 5:30 P.M. that the British were dropping downstream with the Americans in pursuit about one and one-half miles astern.[31]

Continuing to importune the State Navy Board for assistance, the Continental Navy Board reported their request for galleys and fire ships. On August 23, the Navy Board asked permission to send three galleys and two fire ships down to Alexander. Reluctantly the Council agreed, but not without the perennial admonishment about employing galleys in the bay: ". . . the Council think it necessary to observe, that the Galleys are not constructed for rough water, & that they hope the Boats will not be run into unnecessary danger." [32]

The instructions recorded in the minutes of the Navy Board as to the galleys ordered down to Alexander do not agree with facts verified elsewhere. Captain Thomas Moore of the *Hancock* was to command the State boats, and accompanying him would be the *Franklin,* Captain Boys, and the *Hancock,* Captain Roach. The latter assignment was impossible as the *Hancock* was Moore's galley. Roach, at this time, is listed as the captain of armed schooner *Delaware,* another inconsistency, as the *Delaware* was already down in the bay under command of Captain Eyre. Roach commanded the Congress galley on this expedition.[33]

Moore's instructions call for two fire ships but only lists the fire-sloop *Strombello*, Captain Jones. As Jones was under arrest at this time, and facing dismissal from the service, James McKnight was unquestionably in command. McKnight had been assigned to the fire brigatine *Blast* on July 29, but was unable to recruit a crew and was reassigned to the *Strombello*. His official appointment as captain of the *Strombello* was dated September 1, the same date Jones was discharged.[34]

Preparatory to their departure, the accommodation sloop *Sally* was ordered to furnish each boat with one hogshead of rum and as much beef, pork, and bread as needed for a six-weeks' cruise. They were to stop at Reedy Island where Simmons or Benjamin Hall was to furnish whatever fresh vegetables they needed. As a parting remonstrance, Moore was ordered to advise Alexander that: ". . . you are not order'd . . . into ruffer water than your Vessels will be . . . safe in." [35]

These preparations would not contribute to the protection of Philadelphia or its defenses. Their main purpose was to buttress the resolve of the area patriots on both sides of the river and bay to resist British depredations. If by their presence in the bay they could counteract the harassment tactics of the small enemy cutters and an occasional frigate, the forage and produce which would otherwise fall into enemy hands would be available for the undernourished Continental army.

Nominal command of the fleet was still vested in Thomas Seymour, although he had exercised little control for several months. It has generally been accepted that Seymour's incapacity stemmed from advanced age and a persistent illness. It would also appear that he was engaged in a dispute with the Council over salary and quietly resented the independent command exercised by Hazelwood. Council, out of compassion, was apparently reluctant to discharge him, and was willing temporarily to permit Hazelwood to serve as acting Commodore. Little validity can be attached to offering age as a reason for his failure to function as Commodore. When appointed a few months before, his age had not been considered a factor. However, combined with his infirmities suffered during the previous winter's campaign, it had produced a condition which incapacitated him for active duty.

Seymour had constantly petitioned the Council to redress his salary misunderstanding and ration allowance, at least to what Seymour considered fair and proper. In July 1777 he memorialized the Council claiming that a few days after his appointment as Commodore, on September 26, 1776, his commission was read before the captains and other officers, along with a resolution stating that all officers in the State service would receive the same pay and rations as those in the Continental establishment. He mentioned that Commodore Hopkins of the Continental Navy was paid $125 per month. Was it a coincidence that the State Commodore's pay was increased to the same rate concurrent with Seymour's petition? (Adjustments had been made to the pay scale of the fleet, to bring it in line with the Continental navy, in November 1776 and again in January and February 1777. Paydays were often delayed but never omitted.)

He concluded his petition with recalling the contentious condition of the navy when he assumed command, and how much morale had improved under his administration.

As late as September 3, 1777, he was still seeking his current and back pay. It remains a mystery why Seymour was denied his pay, although he laid the blame at the door of the Supreme Executive Council. A search of the archives fails to reveal whether his account was ever settled. A letter of Seymour's from Dunks Ferry dated December 15, 1777, would seem to indicate that the ex-Commodore was still active at this date. This, however, is either a mistake in editing or by Seymour in dating the letter. This letter was undoubtedly written in December 1776, when Seymour was engaged in the Trenton-Princeton campaign.[36]

Shortly after receiving the September 3 communication from Seymour, the Council decided to retire him and on September 6 appointed Hazelwood in his place.[37]

An interesting sidelight to this pay controversy was the payment to Hazelwood of a bonus of £100 for "extra trouble and great attention" to fitting out the fire fleet—a payment made only ten days before Seymour was relieved of his command.[38]

In the meantime, the British army was approaching southeastern Pennsylvania with Philadelphia the apparent objective. Again consternation bordering on panic gripped the city. Prominent Patriots were planning to move to inland towns. Supplies and materials which might benefit the British were re-

moved to Reading and other towns in the back country.
Congress and the State authorities made arrangements to move
to Baltimore and Lancaster, respectively.

The State galleys and ships in the bay were ordered back to
Fort Mifflin, and Fisher was instructed to return the guard boats
to their station in Darby Creek. Washington, in need of every
man he could muster, had recalled all Continental and much of
the militia to the main Continental army. Even with these small
reinforcements, he would confront Howe at the Brandywine
with an inferior force.

Stripping the river forts of their garrisons left them defenseless. A muster taken at the various locations on September 5 indicated at Billingsport thirty Continental artillerymen, fifty Philadelphia militia with eight days to serve, and fifty laborers
and carpenters. Fort Mifflin also had thirty Continental artillerymen, fifteen militiamen, and fifteen laborers. Fort Mercer had no
garrison, only a few laborers. Bush Island and Darby Creek redoubts reported no garrisons.[39] Hazelwood was ordered to survey all the fortifications and, if necessary, throw sufficient men
into them to protect the cannon, ammunition, and other
stores.[40] Colonel John Eyre was instructed to cooperate with
Hazelwood, to accept responsibility for placing the forts in a
defensible posture, and to await the arrival of an officer to be
appointed to their command by Washington.[41]

On September 5 the Navy Board, believing that some part of
the British fleet would attempt to invade the city, offered some
suggestions to strengthen the defense. They recommended flooding Hog Island and the meadows (Province and Carpenters'
Islands), and this they were later instructed to do. They suggested flat boats to bridge the channel between Fort Mifflin and
Province Island; the appointing of someone to take charge at Fort
Mifflin, as this fort was in a bad state of repair (a constant
complaint); putting garrisons of one hundred men into the
Darby Creek redoubt and thirty artillerymen on Bush Island,
(this latter post had two unattended eighteen-pounders); and
placing additional cannon in Billingsport.[42] The Board was later
authorized to build a floodgate on Mud Island as a safe winter
harbor for guard boats.

Washington requested that the Middle Ferry bridge on the
Schuylkill River be removed to the Delaware and all boats be

moved to prevent their falling into enemy hands. At the same time, Washington ordered Colonel Joseph Penrose to cut the banks of Darby Creek to overflow the lands on Province Island.[43]

After the defeat at Brandywine, plans previously formed to flee the city were put into operation and all Patriot officialdom departed. Before leaving on September 13, Congress hastily passed a resolution authorizing Washington to complete the defenses on the Delaware, using whatever agencies he thought proper. John Hancock was in such a hurry that he transmitted the resolution with a terse note stating: "I have only time to transmit your the above resolve." [44]

Responding to Hancock the same day, Washington expressed a wish that the river defenses could be completed, but believed the cause would be injured if Continental troops were diverted for this purpose. He contended that all his resources were needed to oppose Howe in the field and, if he were successful, further work on the forts would be unnecessary; if he were defeated, Howe could easily possess himself of the forts. Washington had taken limited steps to comply with the lawmakers' request by ordering the meadows flooded and instructing General John Armstrong and the Pennsylvania militia to construct redoubts at the fords over the Schuylkill and provide their garrisons.[45]

He also wrote to Thomas Wharton on September 13, reiterating his inability to furnish troops to complete or garrison the river forts. Repeating sentiments expressed in his letter to Hancock, he again stated that little reliance could be placed in the forts if his army should be defeated: ". . . he [Howe] will take possession of the Forts of course and turn our own Guns upon our Ships, Galleys and floating Batteries." He advised throwing the city artillery companies into Fort Mifflin and drawing the fleet up behind the chevaux-de-frise, as the best water defense possible.[46] Washington occasionally experienced periods of hopelessness, and now two days after the defeat at Brandywine, he undoubtedly viewed any division of forces as certain military suicide. It would be impossible to defeat Howe and prevent his entrance into Philadelphia and to defend the river forts simultaneously. Time would tell if either were possible.

IX

Preparations for the Assault—1777[1]

WASHINGTON and the Continental Army were desperately maneuvering on the east bank of the Schuylkill River to prevent the British Army from crossing to take Philadelphia or the principal storehouse for the American Army at Reading. General Potter and the Pennsylvania militia were on the west bank of the river to harass British cavalry on foraging expeditions. Potter was also entrusted with removing boats, building redoubts at fords, and confiscating farm produce that otherwise might fall into British hands. While all this activity was intended to thwart Howe's efforts to capture the young nation's capital, little was being done to strengthen the river forts.

All authorities, Continental and State, military, naval, and civilian, were fully apprised of the status of the city's defense by the water approach. Washington and his generals had put the situation in proper focus, but nothing had been done—at least no important program for making the forts impregnable to attack by the British fleet or army had been planned. Blame cannot be easily assigned. Panic was rife among the citizenry; both the Continental Congress and the State authorities were hastily packing to depart for a safer climate. Money was an unknown commodity and manpower unobtainable. With Patriots fleeing in all directions, and Washington's army undermanned, but not demoralized, there is little wonder the State forces were having difficulty in obtaining recruits for the State fleet or to work on the river defenses.

Washington would later throw Continental troops into Forts Mifflin and Mercer and assume responsibility for their defense. He would also provide Hazelwood with men from the Continental Regiments to man the galleys. But, as events were to prove, he would be handicapped by an insufficiency of men and matériel to act on anything but the defensive. His losses at Brandywine, Paoli, and Germantown, and the detachment of units of the army to assist Gates at Saratoga, depleted his already small force so that those units transferred to river service left him with but the shadow of an army.

Captain Alexander of the Continental frigate *Delaware*, anchoring off Billingsport on September 15, noted that one hundred men could take the fort. Unless a person of knowledge was given command the condition of the fleet would further deteriorate.[2] The latter comment is the first intimation we have of a possible developing feud between Hazelwood and the Continental naval officers. Alexander, a former galley captain, had resigned from the State service in April 1776, at the height of the controversy between the galley captains and the Committee of Safety. Whether his criticism was the result of personal differences with Hazelwood or of a long-standing distrust of the State naval establishment is unknown.

Contributing to the worsening relations between officers of both navies was a decision by the Continental Marine Committee, on September 26, to place the Continental naval captains in the Delaware under Hazelwood.[3] With the need for coordination of all naval elements, it was the Committee's opinion that Hazelwood's familiarity with the river made him the ideal choice to command the combined fleet. Unexpressed, but a certain factor in their selection of the State Commodore, was the knowledge that the most effective elements of the naval establishment would be the galleys, floating batteries, and the fire ships—all elements of the State navy. This view had been shared by Washington's generals and was certainly known by the Marine Committee.

Hazelwood was enjoined to conduct a vigorous defense, and, if necessary, to assist in removing troops from Fort Mifflin to a place of safety. His knowledge of the river made him best fitted to sink hulks or other obstructions to fill vacancies between the chevaux-de-frise.

Although Hazelwood's appointment was intended to unify the naval command in the face of the enemy, it actually created a schism. Hazelwood did not permit this to interfere with his command and would later express astonishment at carping critics. He always expressed satisfaction with the assistance rendered by Captain Robinson and the Continental officers.

The war of personalities was probably fed by certain army officers who were later assigned to the river forts. The situation was further complicated by the natural distrust Continental officers held for any State force, a condition which was to become more obvious during October and November 1777.

In the meantime, the British were slowly but inexorably closing the trap to isolate Philadelphia from the Continental army. All was haste and confusion in the city. Boats of every type were quickly gathered and loaded with military supplies, private property—in fact, anything portable. Three Continental ships, the frigates *Effingham* and *Washington*, commanded by Captains John Barry and Thomas Read, and the packet *Mercury* joined this heterogeneous fleet. The frigates were without rigging, cannon, or crews, and the captains were directed to secure them at a distance safe from the enemy. On September 25, the day before the British entered the city, the flotilla headed upriver. The supplies and other property were landed at Trenton and the frigates were moored off White Hill, New Jersey, with the *Mercury* continuing upriver to Bordentown.[4]

Robert Morton recorded in his diary on September 26, "About 11 o'clock A.M. Lord Cornwallis with his division . . . amounting to about 3,000 marched into this city, accompanied by Enoch Story, Jos. Galloway, Andw. Allen, William Allen and others, inhabitants of this city. . . ."[5] Mrs. Henry Drinker noted that they came down Second Street, "without opposition."[6] Cornwallis's contingent included two battalions of British and Hessian Grenadiers, two squadrons of the Sixteenth Dragoons, and artillery.[7]

Howe, with his headquarters at Germantown, was apprehensive and suspicious of Washington's every move. No one realized better than the British commander-in-chief that he was the prisoner and not the conqueror of Philadelphia. He must contain the Continental army while his army, with the assistance of the British fleet under his brother Lord Howe, endeavored to open the Delaware River to provide provisions and supplies to sustain his army. Failing to accomplish this, he would be forced to evacuate the city under difficult, if not disastrous, conditions.

The Pennsylvania galleys were patrolling the river and they had placed four of them in position to rake four streets in the center city. To complement the galleys the Americans had on September 24 installed two field pieces on the Market Street wharf.[8] Cornwallis anticipated that, with control of the river, the other galleys would return to harass his troops and possibly attempt to destroy the city. Orders were issued to erect batteries to prevent the galleys or other American ships from approaching the city's waterfront.

Redoubts or batteries were built south of the city, one near present Reed and Swanson Streets and one near Swanson and Christian; and the old Association Battery, located at what is now the foot of Washington Avenue, was reactivated. Montresor reported that six medium twelve-pounders and four Royal howitzers were installed in these works. Another battery was placed on a wharf near Cohocksink Creek north of the city. This was in the neighborhood of present Noble Street and Delaware Avenue.[9]

As the result of a conference of State and Continental Naval captains, it was decided to send a small flotilla up to the city to harass any British troops attempting to enter. If the enemy were preparing fortifications along the riverfront, they were to be warned to desist or the American fleet would fire on the city. Captain Alexander of the *Delaware* was entrusted with command of this expedition. His small fleet also included the Continental sloop *Fly*, the State guard ship *Montgomery*,[10] commanded by Captain William Allen (not the Tory William Allen), and four galleys.[11]

Hazelwood's letter of September 27 to Alexander indicated the desires of the Council and further instructed him to appropriate all watercraft along the shores of the river and send them down to Fort Island. Alexander was left with the discretionary authority—"the whole to your prudent and effectual management." From the foregoing instructions to Alexander, and the fact that Cornwallis had started erection of the river batteries on September 26, it would appear that Hazelwood and the Council were in the dark regarding the enemy's activities.

It is difficult to comprehend this absence of intelligence on the British movements in the city. Pennsylvania galleys had been patrolling the river as far as Windmill Island, and as late as the 26th a galley was stationed at Gloucester Point (Pennsylvania). Any activity in areas where the British batteries were erected could not have gone unnoticed.[12]

Lieutenant Francis Downman, in command of one of the batteries, later stated that he had orders not to bring on an engagement. However, Montresor recorded that as soon as "two of the Rebel Frigates and 5 row Gallies [neared city wharves]. . . . Fortunately the two lower Batteries were just completed as they approached us within cannon shot, when we opened upon them. . . ." He commented on the well-directed fire of the British artillerymen. Robert Morton confirmed that the British batteries opened up when the Americans came within range.

In maneuvering, either to avoid the fire of the batteries or to gain position to more effectively use his cannon, Alexander ran the *Delaware* aground.[13] Another contemporary wrote that the *Delaware* went aground through falling of the tide.[14] The *Delaware* was damaged and on fire when Alexander struck his colors and surrendered to the enemy. She had one man killed and six wounded. One report stated that the dead man was the ship's cook, who was decapitated by a cannon ball. The British dispatched men on board to extinguish the fires and secure the vessel. In the engagement, which was reported variously as lasting from one-half to one hour, the *Fly* was hit several times and lost her mast. She went ashore on the New Jersey side of the river but was refloated during the night, and, with the *Montgomery* and galleys, dropped down to Fort Mifflin. Four men were killed and six wounded on the *Fly*. No British casualties were noted, although one house in the lower part of the city was reported struck by a shot.[15]

Whether Alexander mishandled the *Delaware* has never been determined, although in the spring of 1778, after he had been exchanged, his performance in this engagement worked to his disadvantage. He proposed operating against the British merchant shipping in the bay while the ice handicapped the larger British ships of war. Remembering his experience with the *Delaware*, the Continental Navy Board entrusted the project to Captain John Barry.[16]

A minor action, except for the loss of the *Delaware*, it had major implications in the defense of the river. It gave the British a frigate carrying more armament than any single ship in the combined State and Continental fleet. Howe now controlled the ferry to New Jersey and could dispatch troops to the east bank for action against Fort Mercer or to forage without American interference. Wasting no time, on September 28 Lieutenant Colonel Monkton and a detachment of six hundred grenadiers were sent to Chester to escort seamen to man the *Delaware*. Returning the next day, they escorted Lieutenant Watt, two midshipmen, and fifty crewmen from the *Roebuck*, to be followed in a few hours by fourteen additional seamen.[17]

Alexander, now confined in jail in Philadelphia,[18] had obviously been unable to secure the small boats in the creeks and near the wharves on the west bank of the river. The British found about fifty boats of all descriptions including a Durham boat in Frankford Creek. Others were located in the marshes to the south of the city and on Windmill Island.[19] Now that Howe was assured of access to New Jersey above the river defenses, the next move would be to take Billingsport and break through the lower chevaux-de-frise.

Before considering the assault on Billingsport, a review of the defenses will reveal the herculean task confronting Hazelwood and the navy and the defenders of the river forts. Washington had made recommendations on August 9, but little or no attention was paid to his suggestions. General du Coudray had been entrusted with the defense of the river, although Washington would have preferred General Duportail. He, however, carefully assigned Duportail to other areas, knowing full well the jealous nature of du Coudray. (The Commander-in-Chief was constantly smoothing the ruffled feathers of one or more of his officers.)

The drowning of du Coudray had brought the work on much of the fortifications to a virtual standstill. The forts were incapable of withstanding a determined assault by the British. Without dependable engineers, the Americans had given little attention to the military needs of the various works. All the forts were too large—it would have required over three thousand men to garrison the three forts.

Pennsylvania expanded large sums to support the State navy and to erect the river forts and sink the chevaux-de-frise. A cost study of the navy or the defense of the Delaware River is not possible with any hope of accuracy. Many items of payment are not identifiable, others have disappeared. Considering the cost of the navy, Silas Deane estimated that the fleet cost Pennsylvania £100,000 a year. He offered the gratuitous observation that this amount was never recovered in prizes or security against the enemy. His comment on the cost was conservative; but, as his evaluation of the navy's effectiveness was made after the actions of 1777, it was probably based in part on the criticisms originating with General Varnum and Colonel Smith.[20]

To estimate an annual operating cost for the fleet would be difficult. No year of the navy's existence could be described as typical. Starting in July 1775, when the navy was born, until September 1777, it was in the process of reaching a fighting strength sufficient to defend the river passes. The losses in the engagements with the British fleet in October and November 1777 and the subsequent burning of certain ships and floating batteries to prevent their falling into the hands of the enemy caused the virtual disintegration of the navy as an effective fighting force. William Webb, paymaster for the Navy Board, submitted a record for the period March through September 1777, indicating payments of £69,432 16s 6½d.[21] An audit of Webb's accounts reveals that all payments were for the Navy Board, although a few minor items were not related to the navy.

Expenses paid by Webb did not include rations furnished the fleet by Commissaries John Mitchell or William Crispin.[22] As individual boats were occasionally stationed in the lower bay or on patrol at other points on the river, on returning to their base at Fort Mifflin or Darby Creek, they would receive several months' rations at one issue. Many records of ration deliveries are found in the archives, but they provide little aid in establishing reliable figures for rations issued in any calendar period. Other than the individual indents of boat captains, the recapitulations are on scraps of paper, usually unsigned and undated. One return for this period, unsigned, but probably Mitchell's, indicates 198,632 rations delivered between September 11, 1776, and March 10, 1777, of which 178,289 were issued to the fleet. A less reliable return is printed in the archives and lists over 150,000 rations delivered to the navy for one month in 1777. This return must be for several months. A minimum of thirty thousand rations were issued each month to the fleet during the first nine months of 1777, the only period in which any reasonably reliable figure can be documented.[23]

The navy was beset with morale problems. The service had always been plagued with a percentage of recruits who were incapable of developing an esprit de corps. The crews were filled with dregs of the waterfront taverns and those interested in escaping service in the army, men who were always ready to decamp at the first sign of action or disaster. The problem of desertion was not confined to the State navy. Letters of the Revolution from Washington to the lowliest lieutenant constantly bemoan the frequency of desertion. After the burning of the Continental fleet on November 21, 1777, it was reported that their crews went up to Bordentown and a large number deserted.[24] But while desertions handicapped and sometimes crippled many actions by Hazelwood, he still retained a hard core of patriotic seamen who served throughout the life of the navy. These were valorous men who deserve a more conspicuous niche in the hall of American heroes.

Although desertions would continue to plague the fleet, September of 1777 would see the State navy reach the peak of its fighting capability. The fleet was a nondescript collection of fifty-six boats and ships with several fire-raft chains.[25] Hazelwood would also have available the Continental fleet under Captain Isaiah Robinson. Robinson was senior Continental captain since Alexander had been taken prisoner by the British.[26] One Continental xebec was commanded by Captain James Josiah, a former lieutenant in the State navy.

It would be fallacious to assume that Sir William Howe and Lord Howe were unfamiliar with the strength and weakness of the river defenses. Information not revealed by their reconnaissance or reported by spies would be furnished by prominent Tories like Joseph Galloway and the Allens. After the British victory at Brandywine, little doubt existed in the minds of the Howes that Philadelphia would fall, but it would require the joint effort of the army and navy.

Lord Howe and the main elements of the British fleet had been anchored at the Head of the Elk, in the upper Chesapeake Bay. Receiving reports of the victory at Brandywine, he raised anchor and placed the fleet in motion for the Delaware.

With Congress and the State authorities in Baltimore, York, and Lancaster, full responsibility for river defense was shifted to Washington and the Navy Board. Certain members of the Navy Board had been faithful in attendance at the daily meetings and assiduous in their attention to various duties. The official minutes of the Board end on September 24, two days before the British entered the city. Subsequently, the Board would meet wherever and whenever an opportunity presented itself, frequently on board a galley or ship at Fort Mifflin or Fort Mercer or later at Bordentown, Bristol, or Trenton. Such makeshift meetings were unofficial and conducted under conditions which permitted members to serve as observers with the fleet. During this turbulent period, Bradford and Blewer usually served as a two-man Navy Board. During the hectic months from the first meeting on February 18 to September 23, the duties of the Board were performed by six members; four others attended occasional meetings and two members apparently never graced a Board meeting.[27]

The Navy Board and other civilian authorities of Pennsylvania had called to the attention of the distraught Washington the condition of the forts and fleet. He was importuned to furnish Continental troops, especially those with some knowledge of the sea, to serve on the boats and take over defense of the forts from the undependable militia. Washington, anxious to take the offensive against Howe, resorted to his favorite War Council on September 23 to obtain the consensus of his general officers on the feasibility of attacking the British. He outlined their current weakness—lack of ammunition and need for reinforcements. Smallwood and Wayne's brigades were on detached assignments and McDougall was expected in a few days from Peekskill. Also a contingent of one thousand New Jersey militia was momentarily due in camp. It was agreed that the army was not in a condition to advance toward Germantown until the additional troops arrived.[28] Concurring with his officers, Washington decided to detach a contingent of troops to garrison Fort Mifflin. This would be only the first of several decisions to support the river defense.

On the same day he dispatched a letter to Hazelwood requesting that he secure Fort Mifflin and "to take out of the Ships and the Row Gallies, two or three hundred Men and Garrison the Fort with them until I can relieve them with some Continental Troops."[29] Hazelwood was also enjoined to place the galleys around the Fort to prevent the enemy from landing on the island. Further, Washington recommended that all boats on the river be secured and placed out of reach of the British to prevent their foraging in New Jersey.

Also on September 23, Washington appointed Colonel Heinrich ("Baron") d'Arendt to command at Fort Mifflin. D'Arendt was selected for his reputed engineering ability, a quality sadly lacking in most American officers. The selection turned out to be an unfortunate one as the Baron was either incompetent or his ability was warped by mental fatigue brought on by his infirmities. In any event, his illness prevented him from taking immediate command. D'Arendt's appointment would create another personality problem for Lieutenant Colonel Samuel Smith.[30]

Writing to Smith on the same day, Washington appointed him second in command and ordered him to proceed at once with his detachment, by way of Dunk's Ferry (Bristol), to Fort Mifflin. Smith later noted that when he arrived on the parade ground to pick up his detachment, he discovered Majors Robert Ballard of Virginia and Simeon Thayer of Rhode Island,[31] Captain Samuel Treat of the Second Continental Artillery and his (Smith's) lieutenant with two hundred infantrymen and their officers.[32] Crossing at Bristol, Smith and his men marched to Gloucester where they were ferried over to the fort. Smith was carried over by the barge from the *Andrea Doria*, commanded by an old acquaintance, Captain Robinson. He arrived at the fort on September 26 or 27, as Washington indicates in his letter to the President of Congress on September 29: "Lt. Colo Smith must have arrived at Fort Mifflin two days ago"

Lieutenant Colonel Samuel Smith by Charles Willson Peale. *Independence National Historical Park Collection, Philadelphia.*

and on October 1 he wrote to Smith acknowledging his letter of September 27 and commenting, ". . . am sorry to hear that you found matters so much out of order at Fort Mifflin." [33]

Sir William Howe, realizing that he must breach the lines of chevaux-de-frise, made preliminary plans to reduce the fort at Billingsport. The fall of this defensive work would permit the British fleet to work on the lower obstructions and allow the frigates and other men-of-war to approach Fort Mifflin and the upper chevaux-de-frise. Captain Hamond of the *Roebuck* had pointed out the weakness of the fort to a land assault, and insisted that he could cut his way through the chevaux-de-frise if that post were destroyed.

Admiral Lord Howe had dispatched Hamond and the *Roebuck* back to the Delaware to join the frigates *Pearl, Camilla,* and *Liverpool.* Hamond arrived on station below the chevaux-de-frise and assumed temporary command of the advance squadron. He was well acquainted with the Delaware River, having been stationed in the bay and river intermittently for over eighteen months. Possessed of much valuable (and some erroneous) information secured from prominent Tories along the lower reaches of the bay, he was confident of success.

On September 29, Sir William Howe had ordered two regiments, the 10th and 42nd, under command of Colonel Stirling, with a battery of light cannon, to march from Wilmington to Chester. At that point they were to be ferried over by the ships in Hamond's squadron. Landing near Raccoon Creek on October 1, they proceeded to march up to the fort at Billingsport.[34]

Colonel William Bradford of the Pennsylvania militia, who was also chairman of the State Navy Board, arrived at the fort on either September 28 or 29 and assumed command. He wrote: "I found there Colonel Will of the Fourth Battalion with about 100 men, & Captain Massey's Company of Artillery which was reduced by desertion to 12 men, after I got in was reinforced by 100 Jersey Militia and the next day with about 50 more." [35] Bradford was aware of the landing of the British regiments and on the afternoon of October 1 dispatched a contingent of sixty New Jersey militia to scout the movements of the enemy and harass them on the march.

Bradford underestimated the strength of Stirling's detachment, but with his undermanned fortification he could offer little

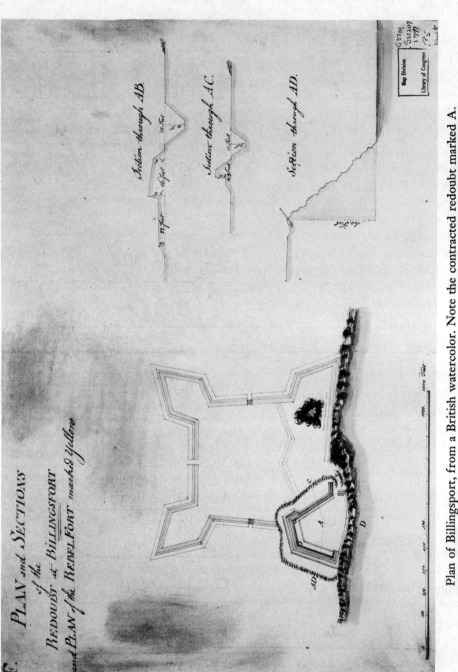

Plan of Billingsport, from a British watercolor. Note the contracted redoubt marked A. This was the section of the fort defended by Colonel William Bradford and the Pennsylvania militia on October 1, 1777. *Peter Force Collection, Geography and Map Division, Library of Congress.*

defense, regardless of the size of the British force. Before the British appeared, General Silas Newcomb of the New Jersey militia arrived at the fort and withdrew the balance of his militia. He said he had one field piece and a small body of men and intended to harass the British. That was the last Bradford was to see of Newcomb. Captain Massey of the Pennsylvania militia and Captain Nathan Boys of the galley *Franklin* were sent out to locate the militia general, but he had evidently seen the size of the British force and decamped.

Newcomb flits across the scene throughout the defense of the Delaware, never where he should be, and indecisive in the extreme. A very pious and well-meaning individual, he should never have been entrusted with a military command. He would later create a command problem for Governor Livingston. His indecision and other poor qualities of leadership had caused Washington to remove him from command of the First New Jersey Brigade of the Continental Line. At that time Washington wrote Livingston: "Notwithstanding I believe that Colonel Newcomb is a Gentleman of great goodness and integrity, and cannot entertain the Slightest doubts of his bravery yet I am to well persuaded he is not equal to such a Command. Many qualities, independent of personal Courage, are requisite to form the good officer." [36]

Billingsport was indefensible from the land side. The plans of the work had been overambitious and sufficient forces were not available for a garrison. To accommodate the militia on hand, the northwest salient of the fort was converted to a redoubt. A contemporary map of the fort indicates that a row of abatis was added to the defenses of the redoubt.

Bradford, with his garrison reduced to about one hundred men, recognized the futility of resistance and ordered an evacuation of the fort. In addition to the militia, a number of guard boats and galleys were stationed above the chevaux-de-frise under the escarpment of the fort. Bradford had requested their assistance in the event the garrison's escape by land was cut off. Captain Isaiah Robinson of the Continental navy was with Bradford as an observer. There is some question as to whether he accompanied Bradford on one of the galleys, or on his brig, the *Andrea Doria*. However, there is no record of the sailing units of the American fleet going below the upper chevaux-de-frise.

Bradford wrote:

I ordered the People into the Boats and sent most of them to Fort Island, spiked up all the Cannon we could not carry off, and set the Barracks & Bake House on Fire, but the Dwelling House some how escaped—We took off all the Ammunition—I stayed myself with Capt. Robeson [Robinson] of the Continental Brig on shore for some more certain advice; about 12 o'clock the Enemy come so close thro' a corn field that they were not more than thirty yards from us, and began to fire on us before our Boat [Franklin] put off the shore, we returned the fire with 6 muskets we had on board, and a Guard Boat we had with us also fired on them, and all got off, one man only being wounded.[37]

Colonel Smith, writing to Washington on October 2, commented on the reason Billingsport had not been abandoned previously:

Our Reason for not Dismantling Billingsport was the great discontent in the State fleet who already are much scar'd & from whom the greatest desertions of Captains, Lieuts., & men has been. So general a discontent and Panic run through that part of the fleet that neither Officers nor men can be confided in, they conceive the River is lost if the enemy gets Possession of Billingsport. ...[38]

Bradford verifies the desertions and confirms that the morale of the fleet reached its nadir at the beginning of October 1777.

Stirling took possession of Billingsport and began to dismantle the works to permit Hamond to commence removing a section of the lower chevaux-de-frise. Completing a reduction of the fort, he abandoned the works and retired to the west bank on October 5.

With the fall of Billingsport, the Delaware defenses were there for the taking by an aggressive British command. Galloway later insisted that Stirling had requested permission to advance on Fort Mercer, but his request was denied. Fort Mercer and Bush Island were ungarrisoned, the cannon and works were without even a caretaker, having only a few laborers at the former location. If the British occupied Fort Mercer, the evacuation of Fort Mifflin would follow within a few days. Smith advised Washington on October 3 that unless he could send a detachment of Continental troops to occupy Fort Mercer "the enemy will have this pass. All we can do is to prolong the time which will I suppose be about One Week." [39] The moment of decision for the British passed and

Captain Hamond of the British frigate *Roebuck* attempting to remove the lower chevaux-de-frise in early October 1777. In the background upriver can be seen the Pennsylvania galleys under Commodore Hazelwood, who successfully resisted Hamond for three weeks. Watercolor attributed to Charles Turner Warren or his son Alfred. *Courtesy Mariners Museum, Newport News, Virginia.*

Forts Mifflin and Mercer were saved for a more heroic place in history.

Howe was nonplussed by the audacity of Washington in attacking the British position at Germantown. When victory seemed in the grasp of the Americans, an elaborate three-pronged attack was thwarted by inexperience, a drunken general, and an early morning fog. However, the fact that the tatter-demalion force of Washington's, lacking everything but courage, could attack and roll back the flower of the British army caused doubts to arise in the mind of the cautious General Howe. Stirling was ordered to abandon Billingsport and join the main army; it has been said that Howe contemplated an evacuation of the area until circumstances forced the American army to withdraw from Germantown.

Admiral Lord Howe arrived in the Delaware on October 6, and elements of the main fleet anchored between Newcastle and Reedy Island. Howe with his flagship, the *Eagle,* took station off Chester.

The partial success of American arms at Germantown, and the pride in their own accomplishments in driving the British frigates from the chevaux-de-frise at Billingsport, produced an immediate improvement in morale. Most letters written by the forts' commanders and Hazelwood at that trying period appealed for reinforcements and sought to find a solution to the ever-present problem of desertion. However, with the improved morale, Colonel Smith, the little navy's most consistent critic, wrote Washington: "We have now no more Desertions, on the contrary some who went from the fleet have returned. . . . One of their ships has just now come in close to the chevaux-de-frise with intent I suppose to weigh it, the Gondolas are down to annoy her." [40]

Smith had suggested that Washington send troops to Fort Mercer to protect the lifeline to Fort Mifflin. Smith's position was far from enviable. His troops were quartered in an extremely unhealthy area on the low mud island and would need frequent relief. His letters to Washington repeatedly called attention to the high percentage of sick in his garrison.

About this time good news reached Washington in the form of a letter from General James Mitchell Varnum. Varnum reported that he had arrived at Coryell's Ferry with his brigade of 1,251

Elements of Lord Howe's fleet at anchor off Chester, Pennsylvania, September 1777. This represents the advance flotilla of light frigates under Captain Hamond of the *Roebuck.* Watercolor attributed to Charles T. or Alfred Warren. *Courtesy Mariners Museum, Newport News, Virginia.*

officers and men and one hundred men under Colonel Bradley of McDougall's brigade.[41] Washington, his dilemma solved, dispatched orders to Varnum to forward Colonel Christopher Greene's and Colonel Israel Angell's regiments to Fort Mercer. He gave explicit directions on the route they were to follow to reach the fort. His concern was so great that he forwarded two additional dispatches to Varnum on October 8 urging speed in placing the Rhode Island regiments in the fort.[42]

On the same day Washington sent a detailed letter of instructions to Greene. He was ordered to cooperate with Smith and Hazelwood, and the General suggested that the galleys or Fort Mifflin could furnish any additional cannon he needed. Captain Blewer of the State Navy Board would see that Greene's garrison was supplied with provisions. Washington also sent Captain du Plessis-Mauduit, a competent artillery officer and engineer, to assist Greene.[43]

Meanwhile, the British were busy planning the reduction of Fort Mifflin. General Archibald Robertson, accompanied by Lord Cornwallis, records the first effort to reconnoiter the area near the mouth of the Schuylkill River on September 29.[44] On October 3, Montresor, with Captain Moncrieff and twenty grenadiers, approached Webb's Ferry, and the officers with nine of the soldiers crossed to Province Island in two skiffs. In the face of this small detachment, the Americans abandoned the island and their hospital.[45] Montresor's party surveyed the high ground in the flooded meadows for sites to erect redoubts and batteries.

Concurrent with activities at the forts, Hamond began his campaign to break through the chevaux-de-frise. The British naval commander recognized the value of Hazelwood's little fleet to the defense of the river. In an effort to eliminate this major obstacle, Hamond, on October 4, offered amnesty to the Commodore and his men. Hazelwood reported that Hamond "sent me a flag to surrender up the fleet and not to destroy any part of it that it was in vain to pretend to hold out against such a force as was against us and that we soon should have no retreat and now we should have the king's pardon and not only that but our liberty also. . . ." Hazelwood returned the flag commenting that he recognized the "valour and bravery" of the British navy and army, but that he would "endeavor to gain their esteem by a glorious defence." He requested that they refrain from sending any more flags; he expected to defend against larger forces than he had thus far encountered.[46]

Hazelwood's summary rejection of Hamond's offer served to increase the latter's effort to remove the chevaux-de-frise, and he returned daily to the lower obstructions, only to be continually harassed by the galleys. From October 4th through the 12th, except on the 9th and 10th when fresh gales and constant rain made it dangerous to bring the galleys into action, daily contact was made between the galleys and British frigates. Hazelwood also brought chains of fire rafts into the engagements but, other than to make Hamond more cautious, they had little effect on the enemies' operations.[47]

Contemporary observers reported the almost constant daily cannonading between the opposing fleets. Philadelphia residents complained of the night-long roar of cannon fire between the galleys and British men-of-war.[48] Montresor records on October 6: "This night almost a continued cannonade between the Enemies Row Galleys and our Ships of war, between Fort Island and Chester." An unknown officer attached to the British General Staff notes in his journal on October 5 that "a considerable firing was heard last night down the river." The next day he states: "The rebel gallies keep up a hot fire upon them, but with little effect." On the 7th Smith wrote to Washington: "The Commodore engaged their Shiping last night and chased them down to Chester." On the same day Bradford wrote: "Commodore Hazelwood went down and attacked the ships very smartly; they got under way and fell down to Chester, where nine of them now lay." [49] Hazelwood was making Hamond's task difficult, and in spite of the previous dire predictions that the crews would desert at the first sign of danger, those remaining were giving a good account of themselves.

Bradford noted on October 7 that the State fire ships were almost destitute of crews, some ships being without one hand. The fire brig *Vesuvius* and fire sloop *Strombello* were without crews and had been stripped of rigging, ready to sink to block openings in the channel at Billingsport. In spite of the persistent cannonading by the galleys, Hamond had made some progress in moving and canting one obstruction.

Bradford's letter of October 8 to Wharton has been offered as proof that these hulks had been sunk and that Hamond removed them as early as October 7. However, a more careful study of this letter would reveal that Bradford was referring to two chevaux-de-frise and not the hulks. He wrote: "Yesterday we sent down to examine the chevaux-de-frise at Billingsport, and find that the two last that were sunk to stop up the Gap are remove higher up and put one side, so that a Ship may warp thro'. A Ship & Brig [*Strombello* and *Vesuvius*] are now preparing to be sunk in Gap, which, if we can Effect, will stop the Channel." There is no record that these fire ships were used to block the channel, and contemporary maps show no hulks near the lower chevaux-de-frise. On October 11 Bradford and Hazelwood, in a joint letter to Wharton from Fort Mifflin, mention that: "The Enemy lays so near the chevaux-de-frize at Billingsport that we have not been able to sink the Ship I mentioned . . . indeed we have hardly had time, for the whole defence of this Fort against the Enemy . . . depends on the Fleet and not much on the troops in it." [50]

The statement by Bradford in his letter of October 8 that the last two obstructions sunk by the Patriots had been moved and placed to one side as early as the 5th is confusing. This letter is reproduced in the published archives, but the original cannot be found. Some doubt as to the accuracy of this survey is manifest, as it would have been impossible for the British to remove two frames in the twenty-four-hour period immediately following the fall of Billingsport. Under constant attack by the galleys, floating batteries, and fire chains, they were repeatedly driven back to their anchorage near Chester. To add to the mystery, Bradford's letter states that the obtsructions were "remove high up," a virtual impossibility in view of the frigates, again, being constantly under the guns of the galleys. In addition, ignorance as to the location of the second row of chevaux-de-frise would have made such an undertaking hazardous in the extreme. The British exercised extreme caution throughout these operations, making no attempt for over two weeks to warp through.

Further, if two frames were removed as indicated, a passage of over 120 feet would have been opened; to infer that one had been removed from each row at this time would be absurd. Logs of various British men-of-war, and especially the *Roebuck*, give no indication on this date of even partial success in removing the frames. Later, on October 13, Bradford wrote to Wharton advising that one chevaux-de-frise had been removed and another "rumored" removed—but he doubted that the latter was true. As the first British frigates were unable to warp through until October 19 or 20, the information in the letter of October 13 would appear to be more accurate.

As indicated, on the 12th the British had succeeded in removing one of the chevaux-de-frise frames. The *Roebuck*, assisted by the *Liverpool* and *Vigilant*, had succeeded in moving or canting a second frame by the morning of the 13th. (The survey of the Port Wardens of Philadelphia in 1784 revealed that a total of three frames had been removed from the river by the British.) Hazelwood immediately attacked with the galleys, guard boats, floating batteries, and chains of fire rafts. At least two chains were taken by the British guard boats or tenders and towed to the river bank and destroyed. A heavy fire was maintained all night until the enemy ships dropped down to the main fleet near Chester. Aiding the State fleet in this action was a small fascine battery with one gun by New Jersey militia under command of Samuel Hugg of Gloucester. The British thought the Americans had placed cannon in the old works at Billingsport. Hugg engaged the British for a full day, losing one man. Unfortunately, he suffered from the same scarcity of ammunition as faced Smith and Hazelwood.[51]

Bradford and Hazelwood could annoy and harass, but eventually Hamond would be able to bring the British frigates above the lower obstructions. The British would have to proceed with caution as they were ignorant of the location of frames above Billingsport; one obstruction could be removed only to run a ship on another immediately above. Their men-of-war were frequently running on the chevaux-de-frise or shoals in the river.[52]

To prevent the British army from establishing batteries on Province and Carpenter's Islands, Hazelwood faced the necessity of splitting his little navy into two squadrons. Leaving a token force of galleys with a few guard boats to work close into shore near the mouth of Mantua Creek, his instructions were to annoy the British frigates in their attempts to remove the Billingsport chevaux-de-frise. He employed his main force of galleys and floating batteries to frustrate the British efforts at erecting redoubts on the western shore. The only specific citation that a unit of the Continental or State sailing fleet was engaged with the British is with the Webb's Ferry Battery at the mouth of the Schuylkill River. Thomas Paine mentions being "on board the Champion Continental galley [xebec], which was stationed at the mouth of the Schuylkill." [53] As all engagements in this area were well above the chevaux-de-frise, it may be assumed that with favorable winds other sailing elements of the fleet were also involved.

October 7 witnessed the first attempt by the British to establish batteries on the higher elevations in the flooded meadows. An engineer with an escort of one hundred grenadiers passed over the Schuylkill at Webb's Ferry and selected sites for the batteries. At sundown on the following day, workmen were employed to erect a battery at Webb's Ferry to protect the passage to Province Island. Men were recruited from the civilian population of Philadelphia to work on the various redoubts and batteries facing Fort Mifflin. They were paid eight shillings per day and provisions. Work on the battery had barely started when three American galleys approached, throwing grapeshot among the workmen, causing a temporary cessation of activities. The 10th Regiment was dispatched to protect the workmen. Montresor reported that two attempts were made to ferry the regiment from Gray's Ferry but both were unsuccessful. In the first try the galleys captured the boats and wounded several British soldiers. The second attempt was foiled by the incoming tide.[54]

Smith informed Washington:

Our Intelligence informs that Six Boats were ready to come down from the lower ferry and in the evening we heard that a large Body with 20 pcs of Artillery and boats on carriages from the City were marching down to Webb's ferry, in consequence of these Accounts the Commodore sent some arm'd Boats & Gondolas in the mouth of the Schuylkill, who discovered the enemy at work along the bank. The Boats kept up a fire on them all night, in the morning they opened a small Battery and fir'd briskly for Some time. The Commodore intends attacking them at high Water and try if possible to silence them.[55]

Smith concluded his letter by noting that it would be impossible to defend the fort if the British established batteries in the meadows opposite the works.

Temporarily frustrated, the British during the night moved heavy equipment to the rear of the Webb's Ferry battery, which consisted of three hundred grenadiers with one light six-pounder, escorting two eight-inch howitzers, two eight-inch mortars and two medium twelve-pounders. They also carried several hundred fascines with planks and tools to erect batteries on Province and Carpenter's Islands.[56]

Smith, at this period, apparently had a satisfactory relationship with Hazelwood. Smith's petulant and jealous nature would eventually bring him into open conflict with many Continental and State officers. He was constantly criticizing the fleet's morale and subsequent desertions, and, more seriously, writing his opinions to Washington. This undoubtedly led to the open break between Hazelwood and Smith. Washington, writing to Smith on October 7, opened his letter with: "I am favoured with both yours of the 3d. and am sorry to find that so dastardly a spirit prevailing in the Navy, but I hope there will still be good men enough left to defend the Fort and obstructions till we can give them a decisive stroke by land."[57] Smith's carping disapproval of the little navy and possibly Washington's ill-advised comments ultimately reached the attention of Bradford and Hazelwood. If these gentlemen confronted Smith with these facts, a schism would quickly develop. Smith was not malicious but the damage was done. Washington's letter was read by Smith to the officers of the navy, apparently to boost morale, as it contained an account of the action at Germantown. It is hoped that Washington's opening remarks on the navy were deleted.

Washington was having a difficult time carrying water on both shoulders, and his letters are filled with admonishments to both men to conduct themselves in the best interests of the country. Writing to Hazelwood, also on October 7, he informed the Commodore that he was sending Continental troops to garrison Fort Mercer—nothing about any dissatisfaction with the morale of the navy.[58]

The American galleys, with their wasp-like thrusts, were constantly harrying the British work parties. On October 9, in spite of heavy rain, nine galleys attacked the Webb's Ferry battery, killing one grenadier and wounding three. On the 10th, the first battery was constructed on the Carpenter's Island dyke about five hundred yards west of Fort Mifflin, with one eight-inch howitzer and one eight-inch mortar.[59]

As soon as Hazelwood discovered the erection of the battery

on the dyke, he ordered three galleys and a floating battery to attack. After a bombardment of nearly two hours the commander, Captain John Vatass (or Vatap) of the 10th regiment, with his detachment of one hundred grenadiers, surrendered. Before all the prisoners could be secured, a contingent of fifty or more Hessians, under Captain James Moncrieff, was seen approaching across the meadows. Smith opened fire from the northwest blockhouse at Fort Mifflin and in the confusion a number of the prisoners escaped. Bradford and Hazelwood were somewhat critical of Smith's conduct, believing that Moncrieff's party was coming to surrender. They later acknowledged their mistake when informed that the Hessians were a rescue party intending to attack the galleymen on the dyke. They were able to bring off Lieutenant William Finch and Ensign Richard Hawkins of the 27th Regiment with fifty-six enlisted men. Vatass was eventually tried at court-martial and forced to sell his commission much below the going rate.[60]

Undaunted, Hazelwood again attacked this redoubt on October 12. After a severe cannonade, a landing party attempted to storm the redoubt. Using the dyke for cover and supported by the galleys, the detachment on shore tried for about one hour to drive the British from their position. Finally, they were forced to withdraw after having two men killed and five wounded. The British acknowledged a loss of four killed and three wounded.[61]

Washington had written to Hazelwood on October 11 requesting that he cut the meadow banks along the Schuylkill as high as Hollanders Creek. This would lay the entire area under water where the British had recently constructed the Webb's Ferry battery and the area to the rear, which they were using to marshal men and matériel for the Province and Carpenter's Island redoubts. To further swell the flood, he suggested a night diversionary raid to cut the dyke that served as a dam for Hollanders Creek. Hazelwood replied the next day that he was so short of men, that the men from four galleys would hardly provide a crew for one galley. He further stated that he lacked confidence in any action which would include a landing operation, as it would result in widespread desertions. Considering his manpower problem, a condition that no one could appreciate more than Washington, he affirmed that he was still capable of upsetting the British attempts to build redoubts and open the chevaux-de-frise at Billingsport. He closed with an urgent plea that the Commander-in-Chief furnish him with 150 men acquainted with the maritime service.[62]

The cannonades between the British and American naval and land forces quickly pointed up a scarcity of ammunition on both sides. The seven weeks of action on the Delaware would witness the greatest and most effective use of artillery in the Revolutionary War. Smith wrote Washington on October 7 that American spies in the city reported Howe's troops to be very low in ammunition. On the 16th, Montresor recorded that the lightness of their artillery fire resulted from a short supply of ammunition and hinted that Howe was forced to change his plans for conquering the Delaware River defenses. The American supply was almost exhausted. Smith observed that the Commodore consistently drove the British frigates from the chevaux-de-frise at Billingsport, but they always returned to renew their work; that it took large quantities of ammunition to make them retreat, and the little fleet did not possess a reserve. On the night of the 12th, Hazelwood, with several galleys and two chains of fire rafts, dropped down to the chevaux-de-frise and engaged the *Roebuck* and two other British men-of-war. In a brisk action they forced the British to retire, but Hazelwood had to cut off the engagement, partly because of almost exhausted ammunition racks.

It was rumored that the British returned the next morning and succeeded in removing the second frame from the channel. Desperate for ammunition, Emmanuel Eyre, the builder of part of the fleet, had been sent off several days before to obtain a supply. As nothing had been heard from him, two visitors to the fleet, James Wharton and Jonathan Penrose, volunteered to find ammunition. Bradford entreated Council President Wharton to use his authority to forward a supply immediately. Hazelwood also implored Eyre to forward ammunition as he had only one hundred rounds left.[63]

Smith's position in Fort Mifflin was becoming more critical each day; his men were almost naked. On October 14, he had 175 officers and men including the militia; over one-third of this small garrison was without breeches. He acknowledged that without clothing furnished by Captain Blewer of the State Navy Board most of his men would have been physically disabled. In

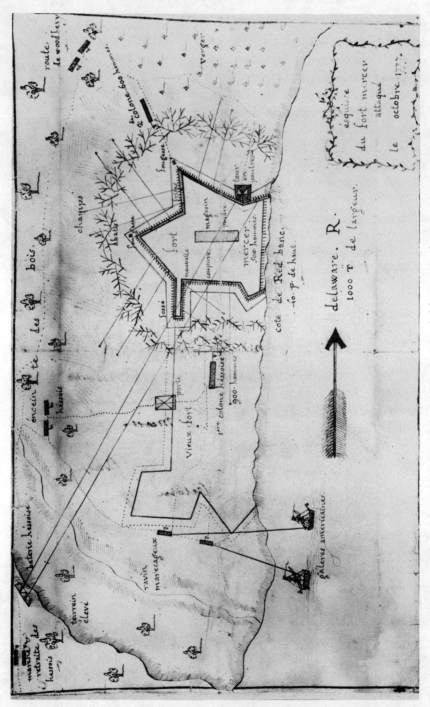

Plan of Fort Mercer by Mauduit du Plessis. Mauduit's map is the most accurate extant depiction of the fort. *Courtesy Historical Society of Pennsylvania.*

spite of this assistance, thirty-four men were sick and the remainder were suffering from fatigue. He requested additional support and suggested that Colonel Israel Angell's Rhode Island regiment be forwarded. The unpredictable Colonel Smith then recommended that Colonels Angell and Greene should first supply the navy and then spare him whatever troops were available.[64]

On this date, October 14, Smith received a valuable reinforcement in the form of Major François Louis de Fleury.[65]

Colonel Smith had been carrying on an almost daily correspondence with Washington. With a penchant for the querulous, he nevertheless punctuated his plaintive comments with resolutions to defend the fort to the last extremity. The Commander-in-Chief's letters were models of patience and direction, carefully guiding each move of Smith without upsetting the peevish colonel. Fleury, an enterprising engineer officer, would furnish a talent much needed at the fort—ability Smith of which readily acknowledged a lack.

Washington had received Hazelwood's request for men with a maritime background to man the galleys, and he ordered a return prepared of all seamen in the Continental Army. A letter was sent to Colonel Greene on October 14, asking him to draft any seamen in his regiment for service with Hazelwood, adding, "the men cannot possibly be more usefully employed than with him." Greene was obviously aware of Hazelwood's need for men, and may have discussed this situation with the Commodore. Greene, needing reinforcements at Fort Mercer, had requested that Angell's regiment be added to his command. He pointed out that Angell had many seamen in his regiment, and he would spare as many of Angell's seamen as needed to man the fleet for an attack, to be returned after the attack was over.[66]

Washington had directed Benjamin Eyre to obtain seamen from the unfinished Continental frigates *Washington* and *Effingham* anchored in Bordentown Creek. Eyre found one hundred seamen on the two frigates and appealed to the Continental Navy Board for twenty. The Board refused, claiming that none of the crews could be spared as they were needed to ensure the safety of the Continental ships.[67]

The attention of the Continental Congress had been drawn to the brave conduct of the officers and men of the State navy

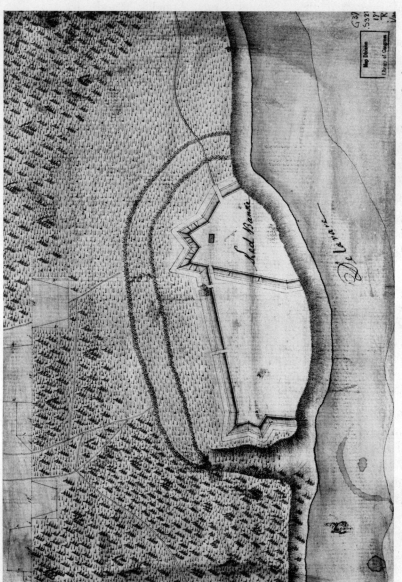

Plan of Fort Mercer, probably the work of the same British cartographer who made the painting of Billingsport. It differs in detail from the Mauduit map and erroneously shows two rows of abatis around the entire fort. In the upper left-hand corner is a purported profile of the fort, which also differs from Mauduit's version. *Peter Force Collection, Geography and Map Division, Library of Congress.*

in defending the pass at Billingsport and their efforts to prevent the British from establishing batteries on the west bank of the Delaware. A resolution was passed in Congress on October 17: "Resolved that Congress highly approve the brave and spirited conduct of Commodore Hazelwood and the other officers and men concerned in the defence of the River Delaware—and of their undaunted perserverance and resolution to maintain that pass to the City of Philadelphia to the utmost extremity." [68]

While the State flotillas were daily engaged with the British frigates and land batteries, the garrisons of Forts Mifflin and Mercer were being strengthened. The British were also vigorously constructing batteries and redoubts on the high points in the flooded meadow lands.

To go back in time and follow Colonel Greene's movements before he reached his command post at Fort Mercer, Washington had reconsidered the size of the Continental garrison for the fort and ordered the return of Colonel Angell's regiment. Greene promptly placed Angell's detachment in motion toward the main camp, and proceeded on to Fort Mercer, arriving on October 11. In the meantime, Alexander Hamilton had directed a note to General Newcomb with Washington's instructions to furnish the garrison with one hundred to 150 men to complete Greene's command. He was also ordered to hold the remainder of his troops in readiness to assist in the defense of Fort Mercer if threatened by the British. [69]

When Colonel Greene and Captain Mauduit viewed the dimensions of Fort Mercer, they were dismayed; their pitiful handful of men would not be able to garrison such works. To defend a fort of that size would require a garrison of fifteen hundred men. The earthen fort extended along the east bank of the Delaware River for 350 yards. Situated on a bluff well above the river, the measurement of the works from the edge of the bluff to the outer ramparts varied with a maximum depth of about seventy-five yards. [70] The greatest depth was in the lower or southern section (except for a salient at the extreme northern limit) of the fort. The lower section would presently be reconstructed to accommodate the available garrison.

The fort could be approached by land on three sides; the water—the Delaware River—extended along the entire western side of the works. Mauduit recorded that the bluff was forty feet

Fort Mercer today is much smaller than the Revolutionary fortification. The ramparts are marked by a line of hedge and the ditch, or trench, is not as deep as in 1777. The area depicted in the photograph is the remains of the lower redoubt defended by the Americans. Excavated and restored in the 1930's, it reasonably follows the line of the original ramparts. To the left of the modern concrete walkway entering the redoubt was the fort's main three-section iron gate. In the background is the battle monument dedicated June 21, 1906. *Courtesy Board of Chosen Freeholders, Gloucester County, New Jersey, and the Gloucester County Historical Society.*

high, a height that undoubtedly varied. On the north, east, and
to a lesser degree the southeast, land had been cleared for a
distance of four hundred yards to permit a field of fire for the
fort artillery. Beyond this clearing were thick woods. The
cleared area was in part the orchards and fields of James Whitall.
To the south was the homestead of Whitall.[71]

After the evacuation and destruction of the fort, little or no
attempt was made to restore the earthworks until the 1930's
when they were reconstructed to their present appearance. About
1900 the visible remains of the fort were few; a contemporary
historian visited the area and described it as "a rounded ridge,
a tangle-hidden ditch and a few hillocks." [72] The present lower
redoubt was undoubtedly scaled to the reduced reconstructed
over-all Fort Mercer of today. The approximate maximum dimensions of the 1777 lower redoubt were about seventy-five
yards from the bluff to the eastern parapet and about 110 yards
north to south. Measurements for the same areas in today's
reconstruction are thirty-five and fifty-seven yards, respectively,
with the over-all fort extending two hundred yards to a cyclone
fence erected at the edge of a gully. The present east-west di-
mension of thirty-five yards is less than one-half of the original
depth.

Early observers recorded in their memoirs or related to later
historians that the action of the water and ice caused a constant
erosion of the bluff. After the battle of Fort Mercer, the Hessian
dead were buried along a path well back from the bluff; that
area has long since been washed into the river. John G. Whitall,
in an interview in 1914, recalled that he had seen at least thirty
or forty feet of the bluff washed away.[73] The process of erosion
continues today but apparently at a slower pace.

The gully forming the northern boundary of the present fort
is a modern intrusion and is all that remains of a road which
lead down to a wharf (no longer in existence). The old fort
extended an additional 150 yards beyond this point to what is
now Monument Avenue, in National Park, New Jersey. Monument Avenue is part of the original ravine or gully at the north
end of the abandoned portion of the fort where the State galleys
wrought such destruction among the retreating Hessians.

Greene, with the assistance of Mauduit, laid plans to scale down
the fort to accommodate the available garrison. Greene's im-

Whitall mansion on the Fort Mercer battlefield. *Courtesy Board of Chosen Freeholders, Gloucester County, New Jersey.*

mediate command consisted of his regiment, the First Rhode Island Continental of about 252 officers and men,[74] and Captain Cook's Continental artillery company accompanied by a few French artillery officers numbering sixty-five to seventy effectives. Mauduit was assigned by Washington to direct the artillery and engineering activities of the garrison, subject to Greene's orders. Upon Greene's arrival at the fort, he was joined by a company of the Second Battalion, Gloucester County militia, commanded by Captain Felix Fisler and several detachments of local militia, approximately one hundred to 150 men. Newcomb, under orders from Washington, had been requested to support the garrison. The addition of the Gloucester County militia raised Greene's garrison to about 425.

At this time the fort had no barracks, hospital, magazine, or storage buildings.

Mauduit found that neither materials or tools were available to carry out his assignment. On October 13, Greene instructed Quartermaster Cook to collect all tools in the garrison and make an exact return the next morning. Cook reported to Greene that evening that there were virtually no tools in the fort. The Colonel ordered Cook and Ensign Greene to take a detachment and call upon all nearby residents to obtain carpenter's tools. They were to be purchased with orders on the Quartermaster General of the Continental Army. If any civilian refused to sell, the tools were to be taken and a certificate given as proof of preemption, with a copy returned to Greene.[75]

At least by October 15, tools in sufficient quantity were available for Mauduit to recruit carpenters from the ranks and probably local citizenry to begin work on the new redoubt. A double board fence was built across the fort from east to west, reducing it to about one-third of its original size and making it somewhat pentagonal in shape. The space between the fences was filled with hay, old lumber, and any other unwanted materials at hand. Sharpened stakes or pickets were placed on the top and an abatis around the land sides of the redoubt. Branches of trees and bushes placed on the ramparts and partly covered with earth concealed the fort's fourteen cannon. The lumber and other materials used in the contraction of the fort and the strengthening of the new redoubt were appropriated from the fort's neighbor, James Whitall.[76]

The fourteen cannon were situated on the different angles of the parapet to provide a complete field of fire of all land approaches to the fort. A curtain or flank of the rampart of the old fort was retained and a hidden battery of two guns installed to enfilade a force attacking through the abandoned area of the fort. A fosse or moat encircled the land sides of the fort from river bank to river bank. Fraises were implanted around the parapet as a second line of resistance in the event the abatis was breached. Mauduit indicates that fougasse or mines were placed at the eastern and southeastern salients of the redoubt. The French engineer constructed a magazine in the center of the work, which was secure against a bomb of thirteen inches.[77]

The south rampart was partly faced with brick and a gate with three sections was hung to provide access to the redoubt. Some contemporaries have described this as a drawbridge. However, Jonas Cattell, who is credited with warning Greene of the Hessian approach, mentions the three iron gates at the south end being closed and locked.[78]

The soldiers lived in tents outside the fort. Greene wrote to Washington on October 16, asking for instructions in regard to building permanent barracks. Washington's opinion was academic, as the course of events dictated the decision as to whether barracks should be constructed.[79] A marquee was placed in the fort for Greene, and tents for his staff officers. The detachment on picket duty and the artillery were also quartered inside the fort.

Almost immediately Greene was beset with recalcitrance on the part of the local militia. Newcomb advised him that the militiamen expected to be relieved every three days. In addition, Newcomb was of the opinion that Washington only desired that the militia be used to harass the enemy's rear in the event of an attack on the fort. Greene was aware that under these conditions the militia would simply dissolve in the face of danger. Newcomb, as usual, placed his own interpretation on the intended use of the militia, whereas Washington had specifically instructed Newcomb and Greene that the militia was to report to Greene and become an integral part of the fort's garrison. Greene's order to reinforce Hazelwood and Smith with detachments from his regiment was based on his ability to obtain militia replacements. Governor Livingston was frustrated with

Newcomb's attitude, and General Forman of the New Jersey militia withdrew in disgust at the reluctance of the inhabitants to defend their own countryside. Greene's quandary at being unable to carry out the Commander-in-Chief's orders, and to finish the work on the redoubt, forced him again to plead for Angell's regiment of Continentals.[80]

An attack on the fort was considered imminent and Greene was concerned that even with the contracted fortification, he was woefully weak in manpower to resist an all-out assault. This did not deter him from ordering sixteen Continental infantrymen from his regiment and sixteen militiamen to report to Captains Mauduit and Cook to be trained as artillerists. It is to be hoped that these militiamen remained beyond their three-day tour of duty. All accouterments and arms were examined and repaired. The drummers and fifers were issued arms and trained in their use, as it was expected they would be vital to a defense of the fort. The undermanned garrison was exhausted. The demands of fatigue duty, work on the fortifications, and the exercise and drills were beginning to take their toll.[81]

Washington had apparently indulged in some wishful thinking in respect to expected help from the militia. Acceding to the importunings of Greene, Smith, and Hazelwood, he decided to order Angell's Second Rhode Island Regiment to Fort Mercer, and Colonel John Green with two hundred men of the Sixth Virginia Continental Regiment to Fort Mifflin. In the meantime, Greene was asked to reinforce Smith and Hazelwood until the arrival of Angell and Green. Washington's dilemma is obvious in his letter of October 17 to President Thomas Wharton, Jr., of the Pennsylvania Supreme Executive Council: "Without the free Navigation of Delaware, I am confident that Gen'l Howe will never remain in Philadelphia, and I am as confident that had I a sufficient force to afford as much assistance to the Forts upon the Delaware as their importance deserves, that he would not be able to possess them. I have spared as many of the Continental Troops as I possibly can, without endangering the safety of this Army. . . ."[82]

Angell had been ordered forward on October 16, and instructed to cross the river at Bristol to avoid attempts by the British to intercept his movement. He probably arrived at the fort on the 18th, or at latest on the 19th. Greene sent Major

Simeon Thayer, three captains, nine subalterns, and 137 sergeants and rank-and-file of Angell's regiment to relieve a detachment of Greene's regiment previously sent to Fort Mifflin. The arrival of Green's Virginia Continentals, expected within forty-eight hours, would permit Thayer's contingent to return to Fort Mercer.[83]

To return to Fort Mifflin, when Colonel Smith and his staff entered the fort on September 27, their reaction was one of shock and dismay. Although none of the officers present were military engineers, the glaring weaknesses of the fort were obvious to all. Without taking time to establish his command, Smith dashed off a letter to Washington bemoaning the deplorable state of his inherited post.[84]

Fort Mifflin had been designed by the British officer who was now planning its reduction, Captain John Montresor. About June 4, 1772, Montresor completed his plans for a fortification on Mud or Deepwater Island. This island had been purchased by the Province from Joseph Galloway, speaker of the Assembly and later to become the State's outstanding Tory. The usual apathy of the Quaker Assembly prevailed and construction on the fort progressed in a desultory manner. Finally, on January 22, 1774, Governor John Penn appealed for action by the Assembly to provide funds to complete the work.[85]

The principal accomplishment was the zig-zag freestone wall facing the river on the east and south sides (the only feature of the modern Fort Mifflin remaining from the Revolutionary period). There had been some ditching and other minor work performed when the Committee of Safety assumed responsibility for the defense of the river in July 1775. For the next two years work on Fort Island progressed, but somewhat sporadically, activity usually stepping up on every rumor of danger.

When Smith took command of the fort on September 27, 1777, the stone wall on the east and south had been joined by a line of palisades made of pine logs fifteen inches thick, extending along the northern and western perimeter. Fleury and other contemporary military cartographers depict the northern third of the east wall as an earthen embankment, without stone facing or palisades. Later, when Fleury added banquettes to the inner facing of the stone wall, they were extended along the entire eastern wall and embankment to the northeast blockhouse. A battery had been constructed in advance of the south wall, but was poorly conceived, being open on the east to enfilade and ricochet fire from enemy men-of-war. Barracks for the men were built inside the palisades, on the west and north sides of the fort and fronting what would have been the parade ground. Quarters for the officers had been constructed near the south wall and also faced the parade. Wooden blockhouses were placed in the northeast, northwest, and southwest corners of the fort, leaving the southeast exposed. A ditch had been dug on all sides except the south, where great hopes had been placed in the battery. To prevent an assault from the Pennsylvania side by landing parties, a floating chain projection extended along the entire west side of the fort. A magazine had been built along the east wall near the officers' quarters and at least three necessary houses or latrines were added near the same wall.[86]

The work, authorized by the Committee, reflected the lack of military engineering, and resulted in a fort more suited for frontier defense. In fact, the placing of blockhouses at the salients and the building of palisades suggests the weakness of planning for defense against artillery. It has been contended that the Patriots did not contemplate an assault from Province or Carpenters' Islands, or shipping in the back channel—a specious argument, as events were to prove.

The island was a mud flat with the fort on the southern tip. Frequently under water at high tide, the entire island including the fort could be flooded for an indefinite period by cutting the dikes.

Smith, who claimed no expertise as an engineer, eagerly welcomed Major Fleury. For nearly five weeks this enterprising French engineer labored day and night to strengthen the fort. At first he concentrated on correcting the obvious flaws in the fortifications. Later, as the British artillery bombardment increased, and especially during the last five days when it reached a crescendo never before seen on the North American Continent, he nightly repaired the damage of the day.

Fleury was a voluminous correspondent, writing several informative letters to Alexander Hamilton and keeping an illuminating journal of the day-to-day activities of the five weeks' siege. Fleury's first impression of the fort was anything but optimistic. His first two days in the garrison were spent surveying the defensive needs of the post. Writing to Hamilton on the 16th of October, he was critical of the time wasted in delaying the improvement of the fort. He angrily emphasized each neglected point with "we might have" when the enemy was quiet and intent on building their own redoubts and batteries: The bank or dike of the western ditch could have been raised to protect the palisades; the main fort [battery] should have been secured against ricochet or horizontal shot; an interior work should have been built as a last resort defense in the event the enemy breached the fort's walls; a fraised work could have been placed in a ditch dug at low tide to protect the battery; fougasses or mines should have been planted and blinds constructed to secure the garrison from bombs or small shells. To somewhat soften his censorious remarks he called attention to his seconding the zeal of Colonel Smith.[87]

Smith, in command for eighteen days before the arrival of Fleury, had done nothing to strengthen the fort except to open a battery of two eighteen-pounders outside the fort near the northwest blockhouse, and a battery of two four-pounders (some authorities report eight-pounders) at the Province Island Ferry Wharf. Smith's extant letters for this period offer a running commentary on the actions at Billingsport, the chevaux-de-frise, the British batteries on Carpenters' and Province Islands, criticism of the State Navy or the need for provisions, clothing and ammunition—but not one word was written about defensive changes or improvements. A caustic critic himself, Smith saw nothing remiss in leaving undone for eighteen days all engineering work on the fort. It may be argued that Smith candidly acknowledged his youth and lack of engineering skills, but it is difficult to accept this as an excuse for his negligence. The situation called for immediate and drastic action which should not have been deferred while waiting the arrival of Fleury. Smith was brave and patriotic but, at this stage of his career, not an officer of the capacity of Colonel Christopher Greene.

As Fleury observed, the British were pushing their construction of batteries and redoubts on the islands opposite the fort. Montresor was continuing to use civilian work parties with covering detachments of up to five hundred British and Hessian troops. All work was performed at night, although activity was limited on clear nights, as Montresor feared an attack from

American boats cruising in the back channel. By October 15, four batteries were completed: the Webb's Ferry battery of two medium twelve-pounders; at the Pest House on Province Island two iron eighteen-pounders, and on Carpenters' Island two batteries each equipped with one eight-inch howitzer and one eight-inch mortar.[88]

The enemy's first bombardment of the fort and the galleys and floating batteries was opened at seven o'clock on October 15. Montresor wrote that the cannonade forced the State boats to change their anchorage, except one floating battery which continued the engagement for about one hour. During this action one of the eighteen-pounders at the Pest House burst, killing one artilleryman and wounding three. The British fired one shell every half hour, a practice they continued to follow throughout the siege.[89]

A fifth redoubt had been built by the British on the elevated land near the Blakely house, slightly over one mile west of the fort on Carpenters' Island. This fortification was intended principally to control the road leading to Philadelphia.

At this time a rumor was current that Lord Cornwallis intended to batter down the palisades with his cannon and lead a landing party to storm Fort Mifflin. This information was relayed by two Patriots from Gloucester, New Jersey, to Bradford, who forwarded it to Washington but advised that it be treated with caution. Some Patriot informer was reported to have overheard the plotting in Cornwallis's headquarters on Second Street in Philadelphia. As the attack, if the rumor were true, was imminent, Bradford consulted with Hazelwood and Smith and the Commodore placed galleys around the fort on the night of October 14 to repel a landing attempt.[90]

With the establishment of these and subsequent batteries, Hazelwood changed his strategy. Up to this time he had daily attacked British attempts to build their batteries, but Smith at Fort Mifflin could provide little firepower to help, as most of his heavy armament was directed downstream. Once the British had completed their works, Hazelwood's anchorage near Fort Mifflin became dangerous. The galleys, guard boats, and floating batteries were "sitting ducks" for the heavy cannon, mortars, and howitzers in fixed positions. Smith and Fleury were unable to understand the reason why the Commodore moved his station

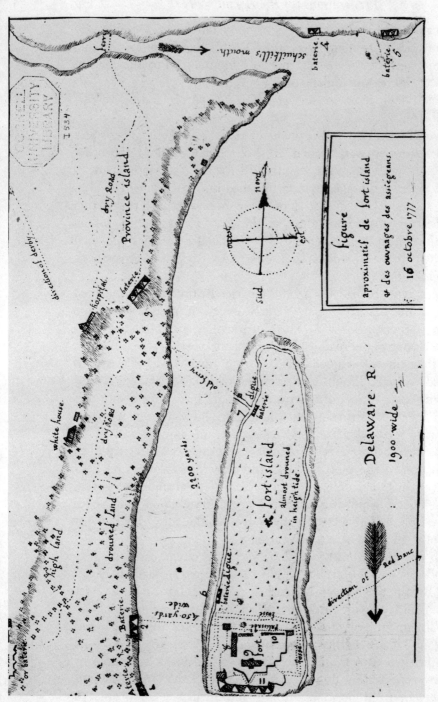

Plan of Fort Island and the British positions on Carpenters' and Province Islands, October 16, 1777, by François Louis de Fleury. A preliminary sketch made by Fleury two days after his arrival at Fort Mifflin. *Jared Sparks Collection, Cornell University.*

for the fleet to the anchorage between Woodbury (Bush) Island and Fort Mercer. Fleury complained that the State fleet engaged the British frigates instead of defending the fort—unaware or unwilling to recognize that the principal function of the fleet was to defend the chevaux-de-frise. If these river obstructions were breached the fall of Fort Mifflin would shortly follow. Once again, Hazelwood directed his main effort to defend the river pass, although he occasionally sent galleys to the back channel to assist the fort.

The British used their scanty supply of ammunition sparingly, concentrating on specific targets rather than attempting to knock down the palisades or breach the walls. At this time, October 16 and 17, Fleury was of the opinion that their prime target was the magazine and barracks. Montresor noted that they were still firing ten shells every twenty-four hours and several rounds of hot shot at the barracks. Their objective was merely to harass and fatigue the garrison. Montresor wrote that Howe was displeased with the slow progress that had been made toward the reduction of Fort Mifflin, and the General had commented "that three weeks were now elapsed and nothing done." Some British officers were critical of Howe's maintaining his headquarters at Germantown and blamed their reverses on the General's absence from Philadelphia. Howe later noted that "On the 19th October I found it advisable to remove to Philadelphia, to expedite the reduction of Mud Island, which proved to be more difficult than was at first supposed." He then decided to alter his strategy; he would direct a land assault at Fort Mercer and a large-scale diversionary naval attack on Fort Mifflin. Several days elapsed before these plans were placed in motion. The major obstacle was the lower chevaux-de-frise. Hamond, while partially successful, had not breached these obstructions to a sufficient width to warp through the big frigates; four more days would see the first of the two-deckers north of the Billingsport line.[91]

For the period of October 17 through 20, the British were beset by problems of high water in the meadowlands on the Pennsylvania side. The tides were so high that the gun platforms of the batteries were under water. Galloway, in his stricture on the conduct of Howe, reported that Montresor had made surveys of the shores of the Delaware and had advised Howe that before

Handwritten title on image: "View of Mud Island before it's Reduction 16.th Nov.r 1777 und[...] taken from the Dyke in the Front of[...]"

Label on image: Red Bank

"View of Mud Island before its reduction 16th Novr 1777 under the Direction of Jo[...] Montresor Esqr Chief Engineer in America taken from the Dyke in the Front of t[...] Six Gun Battery on Carpenter's Island." This watercolor by Montresor is an inset *ion of John Montresor Esq.ʳ Chief Engineer in America*

Battery on Carpenter's Island.

FORT

"Survey of the City of Philadelphia and its Environs." *Geography and Map Division,*
rary of Congress.

any substantial progress on the construction of batteries could be made, the dykes must be repaired. A citizen of the city, familiar with the river meadowlands, agreed with Montresor and offered to make the repairs in a few days. Galloway charged that Howe, for some unexplained reason, ignored the suggestion. Howe, in his narrative, denies that this offer was brought to his attention. The workmen were laboring under great handicaps, a condition which, when brought to the attention of Lord Cornwallis, prompted him to order the dykes repaired. A month had been lost, the holes in the dykes were twice as large, but the work proceeded and the repairs were finally made.[92]

Fleury's letters to Hamilton included his daily journal, which along with Smith's letters provide the only eyewitness accounts of the daily happenings at Fort Mifflin. Supplementing these accounts are the letters of Bradford and Hazelwood. Working under a daily but intermittent shelling, Fleury was engaged in strengthening the fort's defenses and repairing the damages caused by the British shells and howitzers. Frequent hits were made on the barracks, although most shells were fired at what Fleury believed were "fifteen degrees elevation or thereabouts for their Shots fall in the manner of Bombs." Most of these bomb-type shells fell in the soft mud or burst in the air without causing any damage. On the 17th, a shell hit a barracks, killing two men. All accounts mention the presence of galleys in several actions around Fort Island. Many of Hazelwood's letters for this period are dated "off Fort Island," although he found it safer to keep large elements of the fleet stationed off Fort Mercer.[93]

Fleury reported that by October 19 some improvements had been effected. Certain areas of the bank had been raised to protect the palisades; they had raised the wall on the side [west] the galleys should defend; the barracks had been joined by ditches and parapets of reunion which made a second enclosure; a center redoubt or flanked work was constructed in the middle of the fort, made of earth and timber surmounted with barrels filled with sand, surrounded by a ditch, as Fleury said, to defend inch by inch. Some of the embrasures were also raised. He had recommended that the most vulnerable section of the fort, the battery, be framed with palisades. Smith rejected the suggestion because men and materials were not available. Approval had been

Fort Mifflin or "Mud Forte" from the British positions on Carpenters' Island (the drawing is incorrectly labeled Province Island). A wash drawing inset on the map of the Delaware River from Chester to Philadelphia by John Hunter. *Howe Collection, Geography and Map Division, Library of Congress.*

given to erect a small redan on the left of the battery for one
piece of cannon to protect the battery from enfilade fire.[94]

On the 19th Fleury forwarded Hamilton a sketch of Fort Island and the British batteries. This sketch is dated October 16
and is in the Sparks Collection at Cornell University. It is a good
depiction of the British batteries and the two batteries erected
by Smith outside the fort. He humorously apologizes for the
poor drawing, commenting that a bomb burst and disordered
his apparatus and destroyed the wheelbarrow upon which he
was sitting.[95]

Smith appealed to Washington for a diversionary attack on the
British batteries. He asserted that the enemy rarely garrisoned
more than five hundred men in the redoubts and batteries. It
was his opinion that such an attack would cause Howe to raise
the siege. He believed the British were having little success in
breaching the chevaux-de-frise and would continue to have difficulty if the fleet had sufficient ammunition. Smith was more
aware of the value of river obstructions than his subordinate
Fleury. The latter commented in his journal the following day
that the Commodore "is gone to make a fruitless cannonade
against the Fleet [British]." The scarcity of ammunition is mentioned in virtually every letter at this period. Shot, while not
plentiful, was in better supply than powder. Washington and
State authorities were importuned to make up the deficiency.
Hazelwood wrote to Eyre noting that he was daily engaged with
either the British batteries or fleet. Pleading for ammunition, he
vowed to defend the river pass against all odds "we are all that's
left of us in High Spirits and you may Depend Nothing shall
be wanting in my Power to Defend this pass." [96]

At this time there occurred another of those inexplicable happenings in the worsening relations between Hazelwood and
certain Continental officers. On October 19, the Commodore
called a council on board one of the galleys, to be attended by
all captains of the fleet. The captains assembled with Isaiah Robinson heading the Continental officers. The galley became over-
crowded and Hazelwood is reported to have adjourned the meeting and ordered all to reconvene on one of the floating batteries.
It is reported that Robinson resented the tone of the order and
remarked that the Continental officers were not needed and with
his captains stalked off the galley and back to their respective

commands. Obviously something other than this order, no matter how brusquely given, triggered the withdrawal of Robinson and his officers. We have little information on the character of Hazelwood; his contemporaries in the State establishment are high in their praise of his accomplishments. Certain Continental officers are critical of his handling of the fleet but only one, Colonel Smith, would carry his animosity beyond the current campaign.

Whatever the reason for Robinson's actions, he wrote to Washington the next day complaining of the lack of harmony and confidence in the Continental officers. Washington replied with his usual appeal for mutual understanding and cooperation for the common good. He probably came closer to the truth than we are able to today, by suggesting that "fatal miscarriages, that have been produced in many instances by a different disposition. . . . [He enjoined] the officers detach'd to the Forts, to observe a good agreement with those of the Navy; at the same time, I recommended to the Commodore that it should be mutual." [97] Washington's admonishments for understanding and harmony are almost exclusively directed to Continental officers. This may result from the deep-rooted conviction of Washington of the preeminence of civil authority and his belief that only Continental officers were his direct responsibility.

Apparently Robinson and Hazelwood had a forthright relationship, although sometimes in disagreement. Hazelwood obviously had dismissed the incident from his mind, but on visiting Robinson the latter advised him of his letter to Washington. Hazelwood on October 26 wrote to Washington desiring to explain the incident:

On the 19th day of October, I hoisted a signal for all Captains to come on board the galley [his correspondence indicates that he was using the Chatham as his headquarters at this time] in which the flag was hoisted. They came, among whom was Captain Robinson, and some other officers of the Continental fleet. Finding the galley too small, I desired the Captains to remove on board the floating battery, where we should have more room; and acquainted Captain Robinson that my design was to hold a Council. He then replied, he supposed there was no occasion for him or his officers. I told him there was, and I expected him to attend; but he left the galley, and did not come to the Council. This is the state of facts, which he represents as a partial and absurd Council; and says, I knew he would not give his consent, when he, nor myself could possibly tell what the determination would be.

Captain Robinson and myself have always had an exceeding good understanding; but I am astonished at his unkind treatment, in his letter to your Excellency. But, as I look on him as a good officer, this shall not in the least interrupt that harmony I have hitherto kept with him.[98]

William Bell Clark suggests that the difference may have originated in Hazelwood's failure to give credit to the Continental vessels. This may be true, but is difficult to accept, as all naval personnel were aware that the sailing elements of both fleets could not be employed at the chevaux-de-frise. They were used sparingly near the mouth of the Schuylkill until the British batteries were fully operational. Necessity dictated that the shallow-draught galleys, guard boats, and floating batteries were to be the foundation of the American fleet. It is possible that battle fatigue had taken its toll. After almost four weeks of constant action, day and night, Hazelwood may have been somewhat peremptory; on the other hand Robinson, equally exhausted, may have been oversensitive.

Concurrent with Hazelwood's misunderstanding with Robinson, Fleury was making his final plans to make Fort Mifflin impregnable. With the engineer's practiced eye he readily discovered the weakness of the main battery, a detached work at the southern tip of the island open to assault by a landing party, subject to enfilade fire on the east from British frigates and to a relentless cannonade on the west from the enemy land batteries.

On the night of October 20, Fleury put fatigue parties to work digging a ditch in the marsh area in front of the battery. Pushing the men at a feverish pace, the work was barely finished before the first streak of dawn disclosed them to the British on Carpenters' Island. A brisk fire by the enemy forced a discontinuance of work until night could again obscure their efforts.

In spite of inclement weather and high tides, Fleury pushed the men to greater exertions on the night of the 21st. Possibly, as Private Martin later noted, the major liberally applied "his cane in his hand and woe betided him he could get a stroke at." Large pickets or stakes were driven into the river bed about twenty feet from the west side of the battery and spaced at fifteen-foot intervals. Fleury began stretching a double chain (removed from the fire ships), but the work was again interrupted at dawn.

The next night the double chain was completely installed and the intervals closed with floating beams of timber fastened by their ends to the pickets. Small pickets (or fraised work) were then placed on the southeast and southwest embankments of the recently dug ditch, facing horizontally downstream. A double ditch with a double parapet or embankment was excavated on the east side of the battery and fraised to withstand a storm. He traced out and started construction on a demilune near the center of the north palisade to provide a salient work to defend against an approach from that direction.

Finally, during the night of October 23, three traverses were constructed within the battery to protect the gunners against ricochet shot. Fleury surveyed the result of his efforts and, probably with a prayer, hoped for a miracle. From this time until the fall of the fort on November 15, he was forced to direct all labors of the weary garrison to repairing at night the damage wrought by British cannon during the day.[99]

X

Fort Mercer and the *Augusta*—1777

TIME WAS the one factor not favoring Howe and the British army. The dangers to river traffic increased as winter approached; in colonial days the river frequently froze over and was perilous to the wooden ships of the period. If their merchant ships failed to reach the city before freezing set in, starvation faced the army and the citizens of Philadelphia.

With the removal of his headquarters to Philadelphia on October 19, Howe issued orders for a simultaneous attack on the river forts and fleet. Hamond was urged to redouble his efforts to breach the lower chevaux-de-frise. Montresor pushed to completion those batteries already under construction on Province and Carpenters' Islands. Two infantry and grenadier detachments were to make concurrent assaults on the two forts. The largest detachment, a Hessian brigade under the command of Colonel ("Count") Carl Emil Kurt von Donop, was to attack Fort Mercer. Lord Howe apparently informed Sir William that Hamond would be able to warp several frigates through the obstructions by October 21 or 22.

The British fleet and shore batteries were to make a joint effort to annoy the State fleet and Fort Mifflin and prevent their sending assistance to Fort Mercer. The fall of the New Jersey fort would herald the forced evacuation of Fort Mifflin, for without Fort Mercer as a post from which reinforcements and matériel could be forwarded, the western anchor of the river defenses was lost.

According to Admiral Lord Howe:

It was intended that the Vigilant should pass through a shallow and very confined channel between Hog Island and the Pennsylvania shore; to arrive and act upon the rear and less defensible part of the work . . . a diversion was proposed to be made at the same time by the advanced frigates, together with the Isis and Augusta, in the eastern or main channel of the river, as well for engaging the attention of the enemy at Fort Island and the redoubt [Fort Mercer], as to restrain the motions of the gallies and other armed craft which had retired under the works at Red Bank, when they discovered the danger they would be exposed to in their former stations near Fort Island from our batteries on the western shore.[1]

Sir William Howe, commenting on the plan of operation of October 22 wrote: "It has been asserted, that an early possession of Red-Bank must have been immediately followed by the reduction of Mud-Island, to which I in some measure agree." [2]

By October 19, Hamond had breached the lower chevaux-de-frise sufficiently to warp the frigates through. That afternoon, or the next morning, the *Roebuck, Pearl* and *Liverpool* anchored about two cable lengths above and near the eastern side of Billings Island. Unfamiliarity with the channel forced the *Liverpool* aground and the *Roebuck,* in warping back below the obstructions, also went aground. It has usually been presumed that the first British frigates warped through on October 21, but the logs of the various British men-of-war indicate that three frigates were north of the chevaux-de-frise on October 19 or 20.[3]

The lighters of the British fleet were in constant use warping the men-of-war off various spits and sand banks. The *Isis* was aground twice in twenty-four hours.

On October 20 the *Vigilant, Zebra,* and galley *Columbus* sailed up the western channel and took station off Hog Island. Eight Pennsylvania galleys dropped down about four in the afternoon to contest the advance of this small squadron; but as they were also under the guns of the shore batteries, they were forced to retire.[4]

During the afternoon of the 21st and the morning of the 22nd, the British fleet began to warp into position for the attack on Hazelwood's galleys and floating batteries and Fort Mifflin.

In the meantime, at four in the morning on October 20, Captain Clayton conducted twelve flat-bottomed boats up the western channel to be used in ferrying the Hessian battalion across the Delaware. Montresor reported that their progress was hotly contested by the gunners at Fort Mifflin and two galleys.[5]

Colonel von Donop was one of the most distinguished officers among the Hessian mercenaries. He had been an aide-de-camp and favorite of the Landgrave of Hesse. Stationed at Bordentown in December 1776, a detachment of his command had suffered the humiliating defeat at Trenton. Tradition has it that he had subsequently served under a cloud and was seeking an opportunity to expiate what he considered his tactical mistake. Howe noted that Donop had "entreated Lord Cornwallis, in whose corps he served, to express his wishes for an opportunity to signalize himself, and the Hessians under his command." [6]

Howe consented to assign the Hessian colonel and his brigade to the attack on Fort Mercer, but insisted that Donop thoroughly understand the nature of his mission. Before embarking on Captain Clayton's flat-bottomed boat flotilla, Donop asked Cornwallis if he was to attack at all hazards. He was told to use his own discretion but that the attack was to be made unless a good reason existed for not doing so.[7]

Colonel von Donop's brigade comprised three battalions of grenadiers, von Minnigerode, von Lengerke and von Linsing; a regiment of infantry, von Mirbach; four companies of chasseurs or Jägers. A small scouting party of one officer and twenty mounted chasseurs remained in Philadelphia; otherwise Donop's brigade was complete and numbered about 1,200 officers and men. Each Hessian battalion or regiment was assigned two brass three-pounder cannon. In addition, there were two English Royal howitzers commanded by Captain Downman. After inspecting his brigade, Donop was prepared to start his mission on the afternoon of October 21.[8]

Howe decided to have the Hessian brigade cross the river from Philadelphia to Cooper's Ferry (Camden) because the State galleys controlled the river below the city. The difficulties experienced by the British fleet in attempting to contain Hazelwood's galleys convinced Howe that the captured frigate *Delaware* would offer little protection to Donop's force if it were ferried across at Gloucester Point. Landing in New Jersey, the Hessian colonel marched his troops east to Haddonfield and bivouacked beyond the village near Hopkins millpond.[9] Their progress was under fire from snipers and small militia detachments which concentrated on the rear guard under command of Captain Ewald. Donop selected the residence of John Gill for his headquarters, and other citizens willingly entertained Hessian officers as the best insurance against looting by the soldiers.

The Hessians marched out of Haddonfield about four o'clock on the morning of Wednesday, October 22,[10] accompanied by two volunteer guides, a white man named John McIlvaine and a black man, "Dick" Ellis, a slave owned by Colonel Joseph Ellis of the Gloucester County militia. Another black man, "Mitch," was impressed unwillingly into service as a guide. Tradition relates that McIlvaine and Dick frequented the local tavern and were outspoken in their vilification of the Americans.

In Haddonfield the local Tories hastened to the Hessian headquarters to point out all active partisans in the American cause. Young men who had served in the militia, or were known for their unflinching devotion to independence, were taken prisoners. They were forced to remain all night by a campfire in the middle of a street, surrounded by a strong guard of Hessian soldiers. This surveillance was intended to prevent one or more of the Patriots from leaving town during the night to alert the garrison at Fort Mercer. As the Hessians marched out of town at dawn, they were released. Jonas Cattell, one of the young men detained, immediately set out to warn Colonel Greene. Avoiding the line of march of the Hessians, he reached Timber Creek and discovered that all boats along the stream had been scuttled to prevent the Tories or Quakers from taking produce to the British at Philadelphia. He pushed off in a boat partially filled with water and safely crossed, although his boat sank when he reached the other side of the creek. Heading for the fort, he arrived before noon and advised Greene that the Hessians could be expected soon.[11]

Several excellent studies have been made of known eighteenth-century roads and their relation to modern highways in an effort to determine the exact route of Donop's brigade to Fort

Mercer. They proceeded along a road which closely paralleled modern King's Highway toward the bridge over Timber Creek at present Westville. The Gloucester County militia detachment guarding the bridge were warned of the approach of the Hessians in time to dismantle the structure. Learning of the destruction of the bridge, Donop filed to the left, and going about four miles, crossed at Clements Bridge near Westcottville. Turning to the northeast they followed modern Caulfield Avenue and skirting Woodbury, they passed over the road from Gloucester to Woodbury a short distance above the latter town. Following in a general direction over what is now called Hessian Avenue, they arrived in the woods before the fort shortly after noon.

Donop had taken precautions along his route to the fort to forestall a warning of his approach being sent to Greene. The volunteer guides and other Tories singled out all Patriots along the line of march. These individuals were forced to accompany the brigade and were released without injury when the Hessians arrived in the vicinity of the fort.[12]

Captain Felix Fisler's Gloucester County militia destroyed the Timber Creek bridge, but neglected to send a courier to the fort announcing the approach of the Hessians until after Cattell had warned Greene. Greene had been alerted to expect an attack and he was aware that a British force had crossed the Delaware into New Jersey. However, he was uncertain whether it was a foraging expedition or an advance on his fort. Before the arrival of Cattell, he had sent Captain Oliver Clarke of the First Rhode Island Regiment to scout the movements of the Hessians. Cattell's warning caused Greene great concern for the security of Clarke. He had, in fact, been taken prisoner by the advancing Hessians about three miles from the fort.

Greene issued orders for (all Continentals of) the two Rhode Island regiments to promptly repair to the fort. Orders were sent to Fort Mifflin to return immediately the command of Major Simeon Thayer.[13] Militia camped outside the fort could not be accommodated inside and were instructed to file off toward Woodbury to avoid the Hessian advance. They were cautioned to secure their persons, but if possible harass the enemy's flanks. Arms were inspected, cannon were primed, loaded with grape, and sighted, provisions and livestock were brought into the fort in anticipation of a siege.[14]

Job Whitall recorded in his diary for October 22:

Day pleasant and fair. Father and I hung the gate then finished the stocks—then got up horses and wagon and loaded up the goods because the English troops on the Delaware are coming nearer. After dinner my wife and children went with me to Uncle David Cooper's near Woodbury—David Cooper sent his wagon to aid me moving the goods. They drove away 21 heads of cattle. The people of the fort drove away from Father and me 47 sheep into the fort.[15]

In his claim for damages, James Whitall (Job's father) did not include the appropriation of these sheep.

Almost simultaneously with the appearance of the Hessians, it has been asserted that Lieutenant-Colonel Charles Simms and 120 Virginia Continentals arrived at Fort Mercer. Authorities for this statement are then Captain Henry ("Light Horse Harry") Lee and Samuel Smith. Lee in his *Memoirs of the War* mentions Simms's arrival at the fort and his volunteering to serve, but Greene, having been advised by Washington that the Virginians were intended for Fort Mifflin, declined and insisted they immediately pass over the river and report to Smith. Smith, in relating to his son his Revolutionary War experiences a half-century after the war, placed Simms in Fort Mercer during the battle. On the other hand, Thayer was ordered back to Fort Mercer as soon as the Hessians were sighted. Some recent studies have accepted the reminiscences of Smith as placing Simms in the fort during the attack.[16] Too much credence is placed in the recall ability of Smith after a lapse of over fifty years.

No separate order can be found in the writings of Washington ordering Simms to Fort Mifflin. He unquestionably was a member of the detachment of Colonel John Green and the two hundred Virginia Continentals ordered to the fort on October 18. At the same time, Colonel d'Arendt was leaving to assume command at Fort Mifflin. If Green's detachment advanced in two contingents, then it is possible that one was commanded by his second in command, Simms. Lee and Simms were Virginians and friends and Simms is undoubtedly the source of Lee's information. A more cogent argument that the garrison did not include any Virginians is found in the casualty list. If Thayer had remained at Fort Mifflin, Colonel Angell's regiment at Fort Mercer would have been reduced to about seventy men. Yet the casualties suffered by the Second Rhode Island Regiment were twenty-three which would have represented a loss of almost one-third—an impossibility for a force sheltered in a redoubt and under the conditions of the Hessian attack. On the other hand, not one casualty was listed for the Virginia Continentals, a contingent of 150 men. Major Robert Ballard of the Virginia Continentals wrote to Washington on October 23 from Red Bank, outlining their part in the defense of Fort Mifflin on the 22nd: "I am just arrived at this place, on command from Fort Mifflin. . . . Our battery, in concert with the Commodore's fleet, playing on them the whole time; in short we ply'd them with 18 and 32 pound shot so closely, that they, I believe began to give ground. . . ." [17] In addition, the reconstructed redoubt could not possibly have accommodated Greene and Angell's regiments, Cook's artillery company, and Simm's Virginia Continentals.

Donop, on approaching the fort, had divided his command near where the road from Woodbury to modern National Park intersects Hessian Avenue. The larger force comprising the battalions von Minnigerode and von Lengerke with the Jägers and artillery proceeded to the thickly wooded area, within four hundred yards of the northeast salient of the fort. The battalion von Linsing and the regiment von Mirbach filed off near present Hessian Avenue to approach the fort from the east and southeast. Donop ordered earthworks erected to protect his artillery of eight three-pounders and two English howitzers. One Hessian authority stated that each attacking battalion or regiment was preceded by their two three-pounders at a distance of one hundred steps to provide a covering fire for the grenadiers and infantry. However, Mauduit's map of Fort Mercer depicts only one Hessian battery and that above the northeast salient of the abandoned section of the fort—but no cannon with the advancing columns of Hessians. A study of his map reveals the line of fire of the fort cannon, although only twelve of the known fourteen cannon are indicated.

The batallion von Lengerke was selected as a reserve and a shield for the artillery against an incursion by landing parties from the American galleys. The attack was to be carried out simultaneously by von Minnigerode from the north, von Mirbach from the east, and von Linsing was to assail the main gates of the fort on the south. Each was ordered to prepare one hundred fascines to fill the ditches and permit easier access to the fort.[18]

Donop, anxious to remove the blot on his military career, probably viewed the task confronting him with mixed emotions. He had supreme confidence in his Hessian brigade, a formidable and proven fighting force. On the other hand, he had no cannon of a caliber sufficient to breach the walls of Fort Mercer. He saw walls almost nine feet high, well protected by an abatis and fraised; without scaling ladders he must have recognized the fearful loss of life that must attend any assault on the fort's walls. The fascines piled in the ditches might permit a few men to scale the walls, but would not provide the means for a mass assault.

It required about four hours for Donop's troops to make preparations for the attack. In the meantime Colonel Greene was busy readying his garrison; he was especially concerned with their morale. To inspirit the men, he mounted the ramparts and walked up and down inspecting the works, exposing himself to possible enemy sharpshooters. He would stop on the rampart, take out his small pocket spyglass and calmly survey the activities of the Hessians. Dr. Peter Turner, surgeon in Greene's regiment and present in the fort during the attack, always relished this story of the cool and calm demeanor of Greene. He further related that when Greene jumped down from the ramparts he said, "Fire low men, they have a broad belt just above their hips—aim at that." [19]

At four o'clock Donop decided to send a flag ordering the fort to surrender. One source recorded that Donop set two summonses to the fort, one when he arrived about twelve o'clock, the other at four o'clock.[20] For this purpose he selected a British officer, Lieutenant-Colonel Alexander Stewart, who had been assigned to his staff to serve as an interpreter. Stewart, accompanied by a drummer, approached the fort and Lieutenant-Colonel Jeremiah Olney was instructed to meet the flag and determine its meaning. Captain Stephen Olney said that the meeting took place about ten or twelve rods from the ramparts. Stewart demanded the unconditional surrender of the fort and said, "Their force was amply sufficient to take it, and if we persisted in defence, they would give no quarter, therefore our blood would be on our own heads." Colonel Olney is reported to have answered, "We shall not ask for nor expect any quarter, and mean to defend the fort to the last extremity." The Hessians were so infuriated by the effrontery of the American reply that Colonel Olney barely had time to reach the ramparts before the enemy artillery opened with a "tremendous discharge of grape shot and ball." [21] Local tradition has offered other versions of the confrontation between Olney and Stewart, each trying to outdo the other in flamboyant language.

At this point, Donop's decision to attack without a more extensive cannonading or waiting for the British fleet to provide the heavy armament necessary to soften the garrison for an assault, seems a matter of poor military judgment. In fact, the journal of Grenadier Battalion Commander von Minnigerode states that Donop had received orders not to attack until October 23, to allow time for the British frigates to engage the American galleys.

Donop was fatally wounded and, while surviving for three days, he never revealed the reason for his impetuous decision to attack the fort. Greene had left the northern section of the fort vacant except for a few sentries; could this situation, coupled with Donop's contempt for the Americans, make him envision an easy victory? Henry Lee offers another version of what caused Donop to attack. He wrote that Greene's order to Simms to cross to Fort Mifflin was carried out about four o'clock; Donop saw the Virginia Continentals file out of the Fort Mercer gates and board boats to be transported to Fort Mifflin, and the Hessian Colonel thought the Americans were abandoning the fort and ordered an immediate assault.

One British officer was extremely critical of Donop's impetuosity, writing:

The attack also at red bank, appears to have been carried on with more resolution than conduct—for had colonel Donop contented himself for the present, with securing a lodgement in the outer work, and covered his flank from the fire of the rebel gallies, to which he was much exposed—he might very soon in that situation, by throwing a few shells from the howitzers into the work, have obliged them to surrender. . . .

The officer further commented on the statements by Hessian officers that they had not been provided with implements to storm the fort.

Another account, by an anonymous British officer attached to Sir Henry Clinton's staff, mentioned that Donop had surveyed the ramparts and was sensible of the strength of Fort Mercer. But his officers and soldiers were eager to distinguish themselves and wipe out the memory of Trenton. This desire, coupled with the recent report that Clinton had stormed Forts Montgomery and Clinton on the Hudson River, raised the fear that the army would accuse him and his brigade of a want of spirit. All things considered, this reporter said, Donop was induced to act against his own better judgment and sacrifice his life rather than his honor. Whatever Donop's reason, events proved that his action was hasty and doomed to failure.[22]

The Hessian artillery fire continued for about fifteen minutes, after which the attack commenced. In front of each attacking battalion or regiment marched an officer in command of the sappers and one hundred men each carrying a fascine and trailing his arms. Johann Carl Buettner, a deserter from the American army now serving with the Hessians, wrote in his narrative that the galleys were keeping the fort informed of the Hessian movements through speaking tubes (trumpets).[23]

With little daylight remaining, Donop had decided to attack at 4:45 in the afternoon. Did he believe the Americans were abandoning the fort, did he fear the character assassins more than death, or had he heard the first cannon shots from the British frigates thudding into the bluff below the fort? Regardless, his three converging columns began their advance with a precision acquired through years of backbreaking drill and discipline.

The right wing, Grenadier Battalion von Minnigerode, proceeded to the northern wall of the abandoned section of the fort and, meeting no resistance, scaled the walls. Because the rampart was intact, they believed they had driven the Americans into the inner redoubt. Waving their hats and shouting "Victoria!" the Hessian soldiers advanced with self-assurance toward the abatis protecting the ditch of the redoubt.[24]

Donop accompanied the regiment von Mirbach which advanced in a soldierly fashion toward the east wall of the former fort. Either climbing the rampart or filing through the postern gate, they emerged in the center of the abandoned fort and joined forces with von Minnigerode's grenadiers. Equally elated at their apparent easy victory, von Mirbach's infantrymen rushed toward the abatis.

The professional European soldier never learned that the Americans were, in most cases, dead shots and would withhold their fire until certain of their target. No one could out-shoot an American when stationed behind cover. Except for the Colonials living in urban areas, the need for expert marksmanship was the difference between life and death on the frontier of Colonial America. On the other hand, the British and Hessian professional soldier was rarely trained to be a marksman; rather, they relied on the bayonet as their principal weapon. The Hessian Jägers were an exception, but even their skill was limited against an intrenched enemy.

Confidently advancing, the Hessians reached the abatis and began pulling the trees and branches aside to permit passage through to the rampart. The American lines were shrouded in a mantle of deathly silence—a silence reminiscent of Bunker Hill. Colonel Greene had seen service at Bunker Hill and remembered the devastating effect of the New England militiamen under a similar situation. After all, his Rhode Island Continentals were a more effective fighting team than the poorly trained militia.

The ripping aside of the branches made the first break in the lines for the Hessians. As they stumbled forward, encumbered with their enormous trappings, huge knapsacks, and large hats, they began to waver. At virtually the same moment the air was punctuated with a murderous fire of grapeshot and musket balls which swept their lines. They continued to move forward, mostly through instinct, but no one could long withstand the devastating fire from front and flank. The dead and wounded were piled in heaps in the ditch [25] facing the wooden rampart of the redoubt. Eyewitnesses reported that the arrogant English Colonel Stewart and his drummer were among the first of the attackers to fall. A few did reach and climb the rampart, but the smoothness of the facing and the fraised work, coupled with the deadly fire, made a mass assault impossible. Stedman, an officer in the British army, wrote, "The redoubt was found to be more than eight [nine] feet high, with a parapet boarded and frized, and could not be forced without scaling-ladders." Stedman continued with the observation that no foothold is possible in this type of wall. [26]

"The Battle of Fort Mercer, 1777," by John B. Squillace. *Courtesy of John B. Squillace.*

Inside the fort Captain Stephen Olney was stationed in the flank or curtain which created a salient on the northern rampart, permitting the enfilading of any assailants in the abandoned section of the fort. His contact was principally with those Hessians attacking through the old fort. As his manuscript narrative records, he and Lieutenant Colonel Jeremiah Olney were assigned to defend the northern rampart and the flanking curtain which had been added by Mauduit. This would assign the overall defense of this area to the Second Rhode Island Regiment commanded by Colonel Angell. The eastern and southern ramparts with the fort's main gate was defended by Colonel Greene's First Rhode Island Regiment.

Stephen Olney has left a graphic description of the action against Minnigerode's grenadiers and Mirbach's infantrymen, recording in his manuscript:

The enemy had placed their field pieces or artillery (said to be twelve) [actually eight brass three-pounders and two English Royal Howitzers] on the edge of the woods, within point-blank shot, and their first general discharge was tremendous. It made the gravel and dust fly from the top of our fort, and took off all the heads that happened to be in the way. They then instantly advanced in two solid columns [Olney is considering the converging columns of Minnegerode and Mirbach as one column]. Their left [von Linsing] came first within musket shot, when we gave them a serious well-directed fire, which rather disordered their column. Still they continued to advance, and one or two officers were killed or wounded on the brim [berm] of the breastwork, but the column became so broken that they were obliged to retreat. By this time the other column had made its way into that part of the fort which we had evacuated, and supposing they were masters of the fort, huzzaed! and came on, perhaps, to cut up their prisoners. When within 50 or 60 paces, we began a fire upon them. They were put in disorder by getting over the fort. The officers persisted in pushing forward the men, until within about two paces of our breastwork, when our fire proved so destructive that they gave it up and retreated, leaving their dead and wounded. Eighty-seven of the former were buried in the ditch the next day. . . .

I believe Asa Potter, of our company, was killed by our own men. My company was stationed in a salient angle, connected within the curtain of the breastwork, to rake the ditches on each side. When fighting, I thought my company quite secure, as the enemy looked to the bastions on each side; therefore my men were deliberate, except one little Irishman, who was frightened out of his senses, but a few strokes with the but-end of my gun brought him to his duty.

While the enemy were in confusion, not more than 20 paces off a man by the name of Sweetzer insisted that I should see him kill when he fired. I indulged him four or five times, and his object fell. I then directed him to fire at an officer, and he only made him stagger a little. We fired at the column that came first [von Linsing]. Our men partly on my left and rear fired across my station. When that column retreated and the other came up, I fired and fired upon it, and our men on the other side of the works, also fired across my station. Next day, Lieutenant Samuel Whipple told me he counted 12 musket balls lodged within the breastwork, where it was impossible the enemy could have lodged them. The first line of the enemy's artillery intimidated some of the men so much they were afraid to show their heads above the breastworks, raised their guns and fired by guess work, notwithstanding Colonel Jeremiah Olney was busily employed thrashing them with his hanger.[27]

As Olney stated, one Continental soldier was probably killed by a member of the garrison. As the Hessian column attacked from the south, Angell's men, standing on the banquette of the northern rampart, fired over the heads of their comrades defending the south wall. After the attack of von Linsing on the south was beaten back, Greene's men apparently reversed the situation and provided a strong musket fire to aid the defense of the north rampart.

The Hessians meanwhile, seeing the difficulty of a frontal attack on the rampart, attempted a flanking movement near the escarpment, but were driven off by two galleys.[28] The severity of the fort's fire was so great that panic suddenly seized the Hessian soldiers. Trained to follow and obey their officers, the sight of many of their superiors falling was too much for the Hessians, who broke and fled. The compactness of their ranks and the closeness to the American marksmen made the execution frightful. It was said that wads from the fort's muskets were blown entirely through the bodies.

One Hessian soldier with von Minnegerode's battalion relates that as they approached the north wall of the abandoned section "a few faint-hearted ones showed signs of wishing to run away." They finally helped each other over the wall and pressed forward to "a palisade [abatis] made of fruit trees, the branches of which had been sharpened." He recorded two attacks and in the second assault Donop was wounded. This would indicate that the second attack was carried out by the joint commands of von Minnigerode and von Mirbach. After the fall of Donop our narrator recalled, "This accident only increased the help-lessness of his men." [29]

During the entire time the assault was in progress, three galleys lying just below the bluff of the northern section of the fort kept up a fire of grapeshot and ball.

The Grenadier Battalion von Linsing, attacking from the south, was the first column to reach the ramparts of the inner fort. Without the obstacles facing von Minnigerode and von Mirbach, they were soon pulling aside branches to breach the abatis. As an opening was made the Hessians swarmed through and quickly reached and climbed the berm. The pointed pickets (or stakes) in the rampart permitted only a handful of men to reach the top of the wall, where for a brief moment a bitter hand-to-hand struggle ensued. The wall's fraised work caused the majority of Hessians to recoil and fall back on those im-mediately following, throwing all into confusion. Added to the disorganized state was fire as devastating as the slaughter later witnessed in the attack on the north. Bodies were piled high before the main gates. Twenty Hessian soldiers, so terrified that they neither attempted to advance nor retreat, crouched be-neath the berm where they were eventually found by members of the garrison.

Little thought was given to re-forming the regiment or bat-talion. With a large number of the officers dead or wounded and the attacking columns shattered, the remaining officers were in-capable of doing anything but leading the survivors to a place of relative safety. A rallying place was provided by the von Lengerke battalion, the Jägers, and the artillery company. These units had escaped with a minimum of losses and those were sustained by the fire of the galleys. In their retreat to this refuge northeast of the fort, they were again raked with grapeshot by the galleys. As reported by Sir William Howe, the de-moralized Hessians were "much galled by the enemy's galleys and floating batteries in the retreat." [30] No floating batteries were present near the fort; they were busily engaged with the main force of galleys in fighting the British fleet.

The battle had lasted between forty and forty-five minutes and broke off as suddenly as it began.[31] Surprised and suspecting a trick, the garrison, unaware of the panic among the Hessians, hesitated to venture outside the gates. It was now past five-thirty in the afternoon and darkness had set in; Greene feared the Hessians would return to the attack. Ammunition was running low, although probably not as reported by an area resident who said he was in the fort during the attack. He recalled that the Hessians ". . . fired a few shots and hastily retired, just as the Americans had fired their eight rounds of ammunition—and they had but nine rounds to a man." [32] Greene did instruct Lieutenant Colonel Adam Comstock to write Washington and mention their shortage of musket cartridges and request a supply of twenty thousand. [33]

Different versions of the first move outside the gates by Greene's soldiers have come down from contemporaries and eyewitnesses. The Marquis de Chastellux, recording the events as related by his friend Mauduit three years after the battle, writes:

M de Mauduit wanted to replace some of the stakes which had been torn out; he sallied forth with a few men, and was surprised to find about twenty Hessians standing on the berm and glued against the face of the parapet. . . . He beheld, insofar as the darkness of the night allowed, the deplorable spectacle of the dead and dying heaped one upon another. A voice rose from the midst of these corpses, and said in English: "whoever you are, take me out of here." [34] It was the voice of Colonel Donop: M de Mauduit had the soldiers lift him up and carry him into the fort, where he was soon recognized.

Continuing, Chastellux noted that the American soldiers taunted the Hessian Colonel saying, "Well now, it is agreed that no quarter will be given?" He has Mauduit imposing silence on the soldiers after Donop said, "I am in your hands. You may take your revenge." Donop is credited with recognizing a foreign soldier in Mauduit who, on this occasion, said the Hessian spoke in bad English, "Sir you appear to be a foreigner, who are you?" "A French officer," replied Mauduit. Donop replied, in French, "I am content I die in the hands of honor itself." [35]

On the other hand, Stephen Olney recounted that "Count Donop, the German officer, who led these Hessians to the attack, fell on this day; he received thirteen musket ball wounds and retreated out of the works, 20 or 30 rods, where he fell, but was brought into the fort after dark by Major Thayer, at the request of the Count's servant. . . ." [36] Thayer's description of his encounter with the mortally wounded Hessian Colonel was paraphrased by Stone, "Major Thayer commanded according to his rank during the action, and was detached about the dusk of the evening, with a small force to bring in the wounded. As he was employed in this humane service, two Hessian grenadiers approached and told him that their commanding officer, Count Donop, was lying wounded in the edge of the woods, near where their artillery played." Thayer suspected a trick, and placed the grenadiers under arrest, with the threat of being put to instant death if their information was false. Agreeing, they led Thayer to a tree where Donop was lying. "The Count asked the Major if he was an officer, and of what rank, of which being satisfied he surrendered himself a prisoner. Major Thayer caused six men to take him in a blanket and carry him with all possible care to the fort, where he was received by Col. Greene." [37]

The majority of historians have accepted the Mauduit version as told to de Chastellux of the finding of the wounded Donop. There is little basis for accepting Mauduit's account and then in an offhand manner dismissing the statements of Olney and Thayer. In fact, all three narrations may be accurate as both Thayer and Mauduit may have been ordered to reconnoiter the area outside the fort to inspect the state of the defenses and offer succor to the wounded Hessians. Language differences may account for the confusion in the narratives. Thayer's description of finding Donop is a matter-of-fact record of recovering a wounded officer. He may have had some difficulty in communicating with the grenadiers or the Hessian Colonel and summoned Mauduit to assist in a better understanding of Donop's needs. The flamboyant language Mauduit attributes to Donop at this time, and later on his deathbed, are not necessarily consistent with the Hessian's writings. Mauduit's words have become intertwined with the inventions of historians and local tradition.

Donop's final words have been elsewhere reported, "It is finishing a noble career early; but I die the victim of my ambition and of the avarice of my sovereign." [38] The letters of Count Donop were studied by Doctor Hans Huth. Huth commented on Donop's growing disapproval and failing confidence in the strategy and generalship of Sir William Howe—although in no way detracting from his personal loyalty to the English commander. He also exhibited growing respect for the professional ability of Washington and the Continental army. Continuing, Huth notes: "But if, on his deathbed, he cursed the avarice of his own sovereign as he was alleged to have done, or questioned why he had chosen to come so far to fight in a war which did not concern him, he was then giving voice to an idea quite inconsistent with those which he had been habitually committing to paper." [39] It is apparent from this study that the stilted language attributed to Donop was not in character with his writings.

Donop lingered for three days before expiring from his wounds. He was at first placed in a tent in the fort but was soon transferred to the home of Joseph Low across Woodbury Creek. During this period it is probable that Mauduit offered the only means of communication with his American captors. Baron Ludwig von Closen notes that the Frenchman was given Donop's sword in appreciation of the courtesies extended to him.[40] It would appear that Mauduit may have been given to a little self-praise, but our knowledge of events would indicate that there. was enough credit for Thayer and Mauduit to share.

To return to the retreat of the Hessians to Philadelphia, Colonel von Linsing [41] quickly gathered the shattered remnants of the brigade under the protecting wing of the Jägers and the von Lengerke grenadiers. His efforts to restore order were futile, under the constant raking by grape and ball from the galleys.

Panic was speedily transmitted to those troops not engaged in the assault on the fort. The contribution of the galleys to the defense of the fort is confirmed by friend and foe alike. Sir William Howe wrote, "The detachment, in moving up and returning from the attack, was much galled by the enemy's galleys." [42] Joseph Reed observed, "The gallantry of our brave fellows in the fort has been emulated by the Row Gallies every mouth is open in their Praise and I can assure from the best Intelligence that they will come in for a full Share of the honor acquired in the defence of the River." [43]

Before his command entirely disintegrated, von Linsing took action to move off to Haddonfield en route to Philadelphia. He dispatched a detachment of the von Lengerke battalion to secure the Clements Bridge over Timber Creek. Following the advance contingent, von Linsing lead a confused and disorderly column in the direction of the bridge.

Some mystery surrounds the form of transportation used in the retreat. Hessian diarists recorded that Donop did not bring any form of conveyance to transport the dead or wounded; von Linsing evidently used their gun carriages to carry those wounded unable to walk. Later the most serious cases were transferred to wagons appropriated along the line of march. Jonas Cattell observed their arrival in Haddonfield with wagons and gun carriages, but without their cannon.[44] (Tradition has sent many relic hunters searching for these cannon near and in Timber Creek.) The last of the Hessians crossed over Clements Bridge on Timber Creek about midnight, six hours after the battle ended.[45]

Haddonfield residents have left vivid descriptions of how quietly and orderly the Hessians were on their arrival before the attack, contrasted to their disorderly conduct in retreat, fighting each other for food and acting like wild men.[46]

Little time was wasted in Haddonfield, von Linsing pushing on toward Cooper's Ferry, arriving there late in the afternoon of October 23. Before daybreak on that date, Howe had sent the 27th Regiment and the 1st Battalion of light infantry across the river to cover the retreat of the Hessians.[47]

It is somewhat puzzling as to why the Gloucester County militia did not harry the retreating Hessians. Possibly the indecision and lack of resolution on the part of General Newcomb accounts for the failure to follow up. On the day of the battle Washington wrote Newcomb, "If they have or attempt to invest the Fort, I hope you will be able to fall on their Rear with such a respectable number of Militia, as to make them decline the project." [48] Newcomb may not have received this communication before the attack by Donop. However, this cannot excuse the militia commander, stationed near Woodbury and in easy access of the Hessian line of march; he knew from previous correspondence what was expected of him. It is impossible to determine what impact he could have had on an already demoralized enemy by a constant harassment on their flanks and rear. Chaplain Ebenezer David of the Rhode Island Continental Line was absent from the fort and visiting in the small village of Cohansey; but hearing of the approach of the

Hessians, he hastened back to his post before Donop invested the works. Nearing the fort he met Newcomb and later reported:

I said all in my [power] to B.G. [Brigadier General] Nucum urging the importance of a few men if more was not attainable falling on the Enemies rear in time of the attack—But such stupidity such infamous Conduct I never saw—if the Salvation of the Brave Men in the Fort if the Salvation of America had ought depended upon them all had been lost—for they appeared lost to all sensibility....[49]

The pusillanimous conduct of the militia was further illustrated on the morning of the 23rd:

[A] small Party from the Enemy, under pretence of a Flagg, cross'd Coopers' Ferry Arm'd, and approached within 5 miles of this Fort took away a Number of wounded Hessians left on the road in their retreat, took In Militia Officers preforce which were afterwards retaken, But the Militia not having resolution enough to take the Party, they marched back to the Ferry & recross'd with their wounded before we had the inteligence.[50]

Meanwhile, at daybreak on the 23rd, the garrison beheld with horror the area surrounding the fort; the night had been cold, which added to the suffering of the wounded. Our chronicler, Stephen Olney, describes the emotions of the garrison on seeing the suffering and devastation of the battle:

I had charge of the guard on that night after the battle. My sentries were placed round the whole fort. The part we had evacuated on the preceding day, was covered with dead, wounded and dying Hessians. The groans and cries of the wounded and dying, were dreadful music to my ears; and but for the reflection of what would have been our fate had they been victorious, our sympathy would have been truly distressing.[51]

Elated with victory, but faced with the task of caring for the wounded and burying the dead, Greene and his garrison set about their melancholy job. The fort was small and without any structure to serve as a hospital facility. The wounded were cared for in tents, with the majority transferred to the Whitall house. A few less seriously wounded officers were granted parole pending an exchange of prisoners. Job Whitall notes in his diary, although no reference is made to the battle, that the Americans "had filled the kitchen, shop, big room, the long room upstairs

and two other rooms down stairs which forced us to move out—
we took loads of goods to John Murdock's near Woodbury." [52]

Nicholas Collin, a clergyman, visited the fort on the 23rd
and narrowly escaped being arrested as a spy. Apparently due
to the treachery of McIlvaine and Ellis in guiding the Hessians
to the fort, all strangers to the garrison were suspect. Being
conversant in the German language, he entered the house to give
comfort to the wounded Hessians. Hearing of the presence of a
clergyman, they requested he pray with them. Collin describes
the scene in the house as:

a pitiable sight. About two hundred were lying on straw in two large rooms,
some without arms or legs [a footnote indicated two piles of arms and legs
lay outside the house] and others again with their limbs crushed like mush
by langrel, some floated in blood, and told me that some had died for lack of
something to bandage their wounds with. While I was there several men
died in great agony and convulsions. The Majority of those who could do
so lay and read their little prayerbooks and seem to be good Christians.[53]

Johann Buettner, one of the Hessians wounded, recalled:

All wounded soldiers were carried on stretchers inside the earthworks.
Messengers were then dispatched to the Hessian army division for surgeons
to take care of us. A few of these arrived that same day, and were able to
help at least a few of us. Some of us were promptly bandaged, and on others
amputations of legs or of arms were performed.[54]

At least one Hessian surgeon, accompanied by a British surgeon
to act as interpreter with the Americans, was sent to assist the
American surgeons.[55] Under the same flag of truce granted by
Hazelwood, Lieutenant Heister arrived to inquire into the condition of Donop.[56]

The compactness of the Hessian advance, the unerring marksmanship of the Continental soldiers, and their fatal waiting until
their targets were so close that a miss was virtually impossible,
the serious condition of the wounded, and the large proportion
of dead compared to wounded again make this battle comparable to Bunker Hill.

Many estimates and pure guesses have been made as to the
Hessian casualties suffered in the battle. The Hessian estimates
are, of course, the most conservative and possibly more reliable.
Knyphausen's official report and Baurmeister's letter to von

Jungkenn agree on 377 killed and wounded with no reference to those missing.[57] Von Jungkenn wrote that 127 were buried in front of the trench, a figure supported in an unsigned letter to Earl Harcourt.[58] Other authorities and contemporaries have produced statistics numbering from three hundred to one thousand. Several soldiers and area residents, who either assisted in the burial of the dead Hessians or were present as spectators, vary significantly in their estimates. Samuel Smith, a soldier in the Rhode Island line, has left one version of the aftermath of the battle and the burial detail:

The night following the battle we were all on duty, either in scouting parties or on trails. It fell to my lot to go with a party on trail, and in going about half a gun shot from the fort we found Count Donop wounded and concealed behind a pine, attended by his two waiters. We took him and carried him into the fort. He lived but a short time and died of his wounds after having been shot through both knees with small grape shot. The next day the whole regiment was employed, except those on guard and on scouting parties, in digging a trench and burying the dead. Here we buried between four and five hundred; so many Hessians having fallen in the engagement.[59]

Mauduit told de Chastellux that nearly three hundred were buried in front of the fort.[60] On October 25, Comstock advised Washington that the Hessian dead and wounded were greater than first thought. A gentleman on board the province sloop Speedwell wrote, "[T]he enemy buried one Colonel [officer?] and twenty-one privates [local tradition claims at least forty], between this fort and Cooper's ferry, and carried over not less than two hundred wounded." [61]

Greene requested an officer of his command, Samuel Ward, to advise Washington of the action of October 22. Ward wrote that eight officers and seventy privates were killed and four officers and upwards of seventy non-commissioned officers and privates wounded. Writing on October 23, his figures were considered conservative by Comstock on October 25.[62]

The Hessian losses of 377 in the official report by Knyphausen can be accepted as the minimum. The Hessian general, in reporting to his sovereign, would attempt to be as accurate as possible as the Landgrave of Hesse received extra compensation for each man killed or wounded. Baurmeister, in his letter of October 26, reports the same figure; although the total of casualties may have remained fairly constant, the death toll would unquestionably increase. Baurmeister's letter clearly indicates that total losses were many more than reported, as this figure does not include those missing or deserted. Throughout the Revolution Hessian soldiers took advantage of opportunities to desert. He reported that only 190 men were fit for duty in the two grenadier battalions of von Minnigerode and von Linsing and that the regiment of von Mirbach had 112 killed and wounded.[63] Ward noted that at least seventy-four were wounded and prisoners; this probably included the twenty Mauduit found cringing under the berm. Joseph Reed, in his letter of October 24 to Thomas Wharton, added a postscript on the 25th and said a Hessian deserter from the city reported that eight hundred were killed, and probably more accurately, that eighty soldiers deserted.[64] A number of non-combatants' observations have been reviewed, but they frequently are apocryphal, having a tendency to see one thousand where one hundred really existed.

The American losses were small and were reported to Washington by Ward in his letter of October 23. Colonel Greene's regiment ". . . has two serjeants, 1 fifer, and 4 privates killed, 1 serjeant and 3 privates wounded, and one Captain (who was reconnoitering) taken prisoner. Col. Angel has one Captain killed, 3 serjeants, 3 rank and file; and 1 ensign, 1 serjeant, and 15 rank and file wounded; 2 of Capt. Duplessis company were slightly wounded." Ward continues with high praise of Mauduit and the information that the garrison had secured almost three hundred muskets from their vanquished enemy.[65]

One interesting anecdote of the battle concerns Ann Whitall. Some historians have denied her presence and others have insisted that she remained in the farmhouse during the battle. The confusion probably exists because early historians used the diary of Job Whitall, Ann's son, as printed in the *Atlantic Monthly* for July 1903. Logan P. Smith apparently edited out what he considered trivia and paraphrased certain daily entries. The entry for October 22, 1777, includes "after dinner my wife and children went with me to Uncle David Cooper's near Woodbury." This led to the conclusion that Ann Whitall was the wife of Job and had left the farm to find safer quarters. Frank H. Stewart located the original diary and published it in his *Notes on Old Gloucester County.* The entry for the 22nd affords a clearer description of Mrs. Whitall's whereabouts on that date. "We ate some dinner and my wife, children and myself went off in our wagon. Father, mother, and ye boys stayed." Stewart contends that this is proof that Ann Whitall, who was Job's mother and not his wife, remained on the farm during the battle.[66]

About seventy years ago an excellent short biography of Ann Whitall was prepared by Mrs. Wallace McGeorge. Her study was based on family papers and traditions. On the day of the battle Mrs. Whitall, a very pious Quaker, decided to go about her chores and ignore the happenings a couple of hundred yards away. Tradition says she took her spinning wheel to the southeast room. An errant cannonball penetrated the north gable of the house, causing the elderly matron to remember that God favors those who help themselves. Hastily picking up her spinning wheel, she adjourned to the cellar to continue her work.

Abhoring violence and having little sympathy for either American or Hessian, nevertheless her Christian training demanded that she serve the wounded. Her house soon became filled; even the attic was crowded. She worked far into the night and when the wounded complained, she would remind them that they had brought their present condition on themselves. Apocryphal or not, the story of Ann Whitall offers a bit of human interest to the horrors of warfare.

Greene was concerned with what to do with the Hessian prisoners. Apparently he first decided to send the officers to Burlington, New Jersey. Washington, on learning of Greene's plans, took steps to secure the prisoners in a safer place. He ordered Daniel Clymer, Deputy Commissary General of Prisoners, to proceed to Fort Mercer and take the Hessians into custody. The prisoners were to be confined at Morristown, New Jersey, with the wounded taken to hospitals in Princeton, Morristown, and other nearby communities. However, before Washington's letter or Clymer could reach the fort, Greene had paroled the officers.[67]

A fitting climax to the attack on Fort Mercer was the October 31 trial of John McIlvaine and Dick Ellis. They were accused of conducting the enemy through the country, and of being traitors and spies. Found guilty, they were sentenced to be hanged on November 1 at ten o'clock in the morning. A gallows was constructed between the fort and the Whitall farmhouse, upon which the execution was carried out at the appointed time.[68] According to Samuel Smith of Rhode Island, McIlvaine confessed that his pay for guiding the Hessians was a tankard full of British guineas.[69] "Mitch," the other black man who was forced to accompany the Hessians, lived for many years and enjoyed recounting his experiences at the battle of Fort Mercer.

Returning to the river activities, it should be noted that the difficulty of warping and sailing the British ships between the lower and upper chevaux-de-frise had forced Lord Howe to limit the size of the squadron which could be brought into action at one time. There was little room to maneuver the larger sixty-four-gun ships and the danger of going aground on one of the sand bars was always present, which happened several times, and eventually led to the loss of the *Augusta* and *Merlin*.

Lord Howe had assembled a well-balanced squadron to co-ordinate the navy's effort in opening the river passes.[70] The passage in back of Tinicum and Billings Islands was to be patrolled by the frigate *Camilla* and sloop *Zebra*. Their presence would prevent surprise night raids by the American galleys and protect the nightly passage of flat-bottomed boats with provisions and supplies bound for Philadelphia. Their draught would not allow them to go above Hog Island. The *Vigilant* and *Fury* were to be used only in a flanking action against the poorly fortified west wall of Fort Mifflin.

The main flotilla was to operate in the central channel above the lower chevaux-de-frise. Captain Francis Reynolds of the *Augusta*, as senior captain, was in command. By six o'clock on the afternoon of October 22, Reynolds had the *Augusta, Roebuck, Pearl, Liverpool, Merlin* and galley *Cornwallis* in position to open a bombardment on the galleys and forts. There had been sporadic cannon fire beginning at five o'clock, but a severe cannonade began at six and was continued for two hours. At seven o'clock several flat-bottomed boats, manned by volunteers, were sent up the river to augment the crews on the frigates. The frigates, fighting fresh northeast winds, warped into position in the main channel west of the sand bar, while the *Merlin* and *Cornwallis* were positioned in the eastern channel between

the sand bars to prevent the shallow-draught galleys from flanking the frigates.[71]

The logs of the various British men-of-war mention a severe
cannonade between their frigates and the American galleys and
floating batteries, but omit any reference to the Fort Mifflin
battery being engaged on the night of the 22nd. Fleury's diary
makes no reference to the fort being under fire from the enemy's
fleet on October 22. His entry for that day is concerned only
with repairs to the fort's defences. On the 23rd he records that
the British fleet and land batteries opened an "incessant bombardment" at daybreak. Colonel d'Arendt, on the other hand,
wrote to Washington on October 24 that the enemy kept up a
"brisk fire" on the fort, probably from the land batteries.[72]

Shortly after eight o'clock, seemingly by mutual consent, the
action ceased. As the British squadron attempted to move downstream, the *Augusta* and *Merlin* went aground, but this was unknown to Hazelwood until the next morning. Stedman recalled that

as soon as Donop's attack commenced these ships slipped their cables and
moved slowly up the river with the flood tide; but the natural course of
the channel having been altered by the artificial obstructions thrown across
it and sand-banks being collected where there were none before, two of
these ships the Augusta and the Merlin, unfortunately got aground a little
below the second line of Chevaux de frize.[73]

Lord Howe commented, "The diversion was endeavoured to
be continued by the frigates, at which the fire from the enemy's
gallies were chiefly pointed for some time. But as the night
advanced, the Hessian detachment having been repulsed, the
firing ceased." [74]

Lord Howe further observed that "the rebels discovering the
state of the Augusta and Merlin in the morning of the 23rd, re-
newed the fire from their gallies, works and floating batteries." [75]

Every effort was made during the night to refloat the *Augusta*
and *Merlin*, but unsuccessfully. At six o'clock the next morning
the *Roebuck, Liverpool, Pearl* and *Cornwallis* came through the
chevaux-de-frise. Although the prevailing north winds were
continuing to give the frigates trouble, the *Roebuck* threw a
stream cable to the *Augusta* in an effort to get her off the
shoal. The effort, while unsuccessful, alerted Hazelwood to the
plight of the *Augusta*. Opening a relentless fire, the galleys,

Interesting but inaccurate portrayal of the burning of the British men-of-war *Augusta* and *Merlin*, October 23, 1777. The *Augusta* was destroyed at noon whereas the *Merlin* was set on fire and blew up at three o'clock. The *Merlin* was stationed near Mantua Creek and the *Augusta* was aground near the upper chevaux-de-frise. Ignoring the American fleet and Fort Mifflin, the artist places Fort Mercer near Mantua Creek. Watercolor attributed to Charles T. or Alfred Warren. *Courtesy Mariners Museum, Newport News, Virginia.*

floating battery, and the main battery at Fort Mifflin raked the *Augusta* and *Roebuck,* forcing the latter to shift her position. Hope was not abandoned to refloat the sixty-four-gun ship,[76] but Lord Howe and Reynolds recognized that little time could be wasted if she was to be saved. Empty transports were ordered upriver to lighten the *Augusta* preparatory to another attempt to refloat her.[77]

Hazelwood sent three fire ships down in an effort to set fire to the *Augusta.* He sent another fire ship down about ten o'clock (the four fire ships were the fire brigs *Comet, Hellcat,* and *Volcano* and the fire sloop *Aetna*). However, they were ineffectual, as Bradford writes, ". . . but their shot flew so thick around them and indeed cut their rigging so much, that the crews got frightened and set them on Fire so soon, that they were burnt in vain." [78]

The bombardment from the galleys continued to be extremely heavy and again forced the *Roebuck* to drop farther downstream. Considerable damage was noticed as she had been hulled several times. She reported six killed and ten wounded. Hazelwood believed that if she had not changed her position the galleys would have "had her in the same situation [as the *Augusta*]." [79]

Between ten-thirty and eleven o'clock fire was noticed on the *Augusta.* The British immediately placed all emphasis on removing the crew, using the transports and the boats of the *Augusta* and *Roebuck.* The cannonade continued and apparently hampered the rescue efforts. An anonymous British officer reported, "The crew suffered extreamly in their boat by the rebels inhuman fire upon them." [80] This officer was not an eyewitness, being attached to the staff of Sir William Howe. He uses "boat" in the singular and was probably referring to the *Augusta* in her period of greatest distress. The logs of the several British ships and American accounts stress that there was no slacking in the cannonade on either side. Lord Howe contended that the galleys remained at such a distance as only to score with a random shot. The ridiculousness of his statement is self-evident when the damage to the British fleet is considered. Joseph Reed noted that he was "well informed none of them [galleys and floating] batteries lay farther then ½ a mile from the enemy & many much nearer." [81]

"Victory off Redbank, 1777," by John B. Squillace, depicting the burning of the *Augusta*, October 23, 1777. Now in the Whitall mansion on the Fort Mercer battlefield. *Courtesy Board of Chosen Freeholders, Gloucester County, New Jersey, and Gloucester County Historical Society.*

At noon the *Augusta* blew up and Lord Howe ordered Captain Hamond to set fire to the *Merlin* to prevent her falling into American hands. The *Roebuck* accomplished its mission and removed the crew. About this time the *Isis* warped through the lower chevaux-de-frise and entered the engagement. A spasmodic firing continued until nearly three o'clock when the *Merlin* blew up, after which the firing soon ended. Hazelwood was forced to recall his little fleet as he had almost exhausted his ammunition.[82]

There has been much speculation as to what caused the fire on the *Augusta*. Fort Mifflin used mostly hot shot and the galleys and floating batteries hit the *Augusta* enough times to have struck some inflammable materials, the magazine, or some loose powder. From the American viewpoint, the cause of the fire is relatively unimportant as the victory was significant enough for all to share the laurels. Most British accounts claim that the *Augusta* took fire by accident. However, three British versions are of interest. Ambrose Searle, secretary to Lord Howe, observed, ". . . caught Fire upon the Poop by a marine firing into a Hammock, wch, being unperceived, communicated to the Shrouds, & from thence to other Parts past all prevention." Montresor recorded that the powder magazine blew up at 10:30 A.M., the earliest time reported. He noted that many seamen jumped overboard, ". . . but the Chaplain, one Lieutenant [Baldock], and 60 men perished. . . ." He added that the *Merlin* had run on a chevaux-de-frise. Lord Howe contended that the fire was probably caused by wads from her guns.[83]

It is difficult to reconcile the British efforts to rescue the crew with Montresor's report of sixty-two men lost. Some British sources intimate that all men lost could have been rescued. This would assume that no fatalities had occurred on board the frigate. How many of the sixty-two were dead before the *Augusta* blew up and therefore not removed by the rescue teams will never be determined. Also, if casualties were this high, in excess of 12 percent, the damage to the *Augusta* from the constant cannonade by the Fleet and fort must have been extensive. In any event, it is a testimonial to the accuracy of the American gunners.

The reaction to the explosion of the magazines of the *Augusta* and *Merlin* were felt for miles around Philadelphia. Hugh Smyth, postmaster at the main Continental army camp noted, "The shock was felt at camp; several windows were exploded. . . . Headquarters are 16 miles from Philadelphia on the old York Road." [84] Elizabeth Drinker, attending Quaker meeting, recorded that "many were not sensible of any shock—others were . . . appeared to some like an earthquake." [85] Thomas Paine wrote to Benjamin Franklin, "A cannonade, by far the most furious I ever heard, began soon after daylight . . . on the road between Germantown and Whitemarsh we were stunned with a report as loud as a peal of a hundred cannon at once . . . saw a thick smoke rising like a pillar and spreading from the top like a tree." [86] Other residents of the area recorded the roar of the explosions and broken windows. When J. F. Watson was preparing his annals of Philadelphia he interviewed many individuals who resided in the city during the British occupation, among them J. P. Norris, who related,

[T]he blowing up of the Augusta was attended with a Shock Similar to that of an Earthquake—Immediately Started for the Schuylkill Point where the British had a Battery & saw some firing—the officers appeared much chagrined at the events of the Day—On our way down we met several waggons with wounded Soldiers—Many of them in great pain—their moans and cries were very distressing—these men had been wounded before Red Bank fort.[87]

If Norris is correct that these wounded were from the action at Fort Mercer, then some of the Hessian wounded must have been ferried across from Gloucester, New Jersey, to Gloucester Point in what is now South Philadelphia.

While the engagement was progressing, the *Vigilant* was slowly sailing up the western channel. Fresh to strong north winds had prevailed for several days, creating problems for the British fleet and especially for Hazelwood's galleys, which were in constant danger of being swamped. These winds forced the *Vigilant* on a reef and aborted any attempt of the armed ship to come in back of Fort Mifflin, in support of the land batteries.[88]

The British land batteries had kept up a steady bombardment of Fort Mifflin. Colonel d'Arendt reported that their fire destroyed a blockhouse, overset cannon, set fire to the barracks, and set the palisades on fire. Fortunately, he reported only one casualty, a wounded officer.[89]

Two hundred British grenadiers were poised at the ferry on Province Island where boats from the British fleet were ready to receive them. When the *Vigilant* failed to pass the channel at Hog Island, the attempt at landing the grenadiers on Fort Island was abandoned.[90]

Apparently the fire on the *Augusta* continued for several days. When the weather permitted, Hazelwood ordered Bradford with five galleys down to salvage any articles remaining on the wreck of the frigate and the *Merlin.* He was accompanied by many volunteer officers and men from the fleet, and they found many items salvagable.

Bradford wrote on October 26,[91] "I had the pleasure of being on board of Part of a 64 Gun Ship—most of her Guns are in the wreck and we brought off two of her 24 pounders, and are this day preparing to get the rest, if the ships do not come near us—The smaller ships guns are also easily to be got. . . ." Hazelwood advised Washington that "yesterday, I went down to the wrecks, and I find the guns of both ships may be got out, if the enemy's ships can be kept at a proper distance. We brought off two twenty-four pounders. . . ." Joseph Blewer, Navy Board Chairman, noted on October 23 that Hazelwood had removed two twenty-four pounders and sundry supplies from the two ships two days after the engagement. Remarking that the Commodore anticipated going down again "to get the rest of guns, &c., but for four days past, we have had nothing but a constant storm of Rain & Winds, in which we were continual apprehension of losing our Galleys and Guard boats." [92]

Daniel Clymer, Deputy Commissary General of Prisoners for the Continental Army, wrote to Washington on October 26 that twenty-seven twenty-four pounders were taken the day before "from the Wreck of the Augusta Man of War. The Enemy came forward to plunder her but were prevented by the Gallies whose men in driving down the Shipping took that which the British were willing to save." As Bradford and Hazelwood only mention salvaging two twenty-four pounders on October 25, it is evident that Clymer was misinformed. It is worthy of mention only because it was officially acknowledged by Washington. No subsequent correction or confirmation can be found in the correspondence of the principals involved.[93]

These four letters are the only records extant which specify the cannon removed from the wrecks. Weather and the enemy permitting, other cannon were removed between October 25 and November 7, 1777. Rain must have immobilized the galleys from midday on October 26 until late in the day on October 30. All ships logs and many diaries record an almost continuous rain for over four days. A British diarist reported that the storm was so violent that the Schuylkill River was above flood stage and the pontoon bridge at middle ferry was carried away.[94] On January 9, 1779, the Supreme Executive Council authorized George Henry to sell at reasonable value all cannon removed from the *Augusta* that were unfit for further use and could not be repaired.[95]

Dr. Wallace McGeorge, a researcher at the turn of the century, made a detailed study of the *Augusta*. He was advised by the Lord Commissioners of the Admiralty that the *Augusta* carried twenty-six twenty-four pounders on the lower deck; twenty-six eighteen-pounders on the upper deck; ten nine-pounders on the quarter deck; and two nine-pounders on the forecastle.[96] When the *Augusta* was raised and dragged ashore in 1876 at Gloucester, McGeorge reported that only a few twenty-four pounders were found. His deduction was that as they were on the lower deck they would have been more difficult to remove. He further believed the British removed the other more accessible cannon. The accessibility of the cannon would not depend on the deck location, but rather on the position of the frigate. Bradford's letter mentioned being on part of the *Augusta;* the ship may have been split by the explosion and possibly both sections careened to either starboard or port, making all decks accessible. The order by the Council to Henry in 1779 certainly indicates a fair quantity of cannon in the possession of the State fleet. When, or under what conditions, is not ascertainable except that we can establish that Hazelwood made several trips to the wrecks between the dates of October 25 and November 7, 1777.

McGeorge examined the account book of Joseph Blewer, who was also serving as naval storekeeper in October 1777. As this valuable document was lost at the turn of the century we must rely on the notes McGeorge made at the time. He lists all the articles (except the several cannon) salvaged, their disposition, and the amounts received for them:

Invoice of Sundrys from the Burnt ships, we note the following articles saved, 1 Uniform Coat, 49 Red Coats, 6 Blue Coats, 6 Waistcoats, 164 Jackets, 4 Striped Jackets, 1 pair velvet bretches, 1 pair white bretches, 40 pairs Bretches, 3 Frocks, 44 plain shirts, 6 ruffled shirts, 5 white shirts, 2 check shirts, 22 pairs Drawers, 46½ pairs of stockings, (silk, thread and cotton) 18 pairs shoes, 2 stocks, 2 cravatts, 1 hat, 1 handkerchief, and 2 walking cains. Of other things saved there were 154—24 pound shot, 3 gun barrels, 2 Ensigns, 1 Union Jack, Sundry Doctors Instruments, 24 shillings, besides brass, copper, canvass, one rugg, and "The Ship Merlin's main awnin."

Those who saved these articles were Captains John Mitchell, William Watkins, Hugh Montgomery, and Martin Vest. Thomas Townsend, Joseph Best, Richard Eyre, Hugh Stewart, Thomas Moore, Nathan Boys, William Potts and Thomas Huston were /with/ the crews.

In this same Account Book can be seen the names of the purchasers, and the prices paid for much of the clothing saved from the wrecks. John Rice paid £3 for a Blue Coat, £2 for a Red Coat and £1 for another coat, 15 shillings for 1 pair of Bretches and five shillings for another pair. Frederick Burd bought a Marine Coat for £3 and a white shirt for 15 shillings. Joseph Wade paid 15 shillings for a Blue Coat, and £1 for a white shirt. John Thornton paid 10 shillings for a Blue Coat, 12 shillings for a Linsy Jacket, and £1 for a white shirt. Jonathan Copland bought a Red Jacket for 2s. 6d, a Blue Jacket for 7s. 6d, a Linsy Jacket for 2s. 6d. and a pair of Blue Bretches for 3s. 9d. M. Smith secured a Blue Jacket for 7s. 6d, a pair of bretches for 3s. 9d, a white shirt for 5 shillings, and a check shirt for 2 shillings and 6 pence.

Cash bought a good many articles at these prices: Blue Jackets, £1, 15s., 10s, Green Jackets, 10s. White Jackets, 7s. 6d. Linsy Jackets 16s, 15s., 12s, 10s., 7s. 6d., 5s., 3s. 9d., 2s. 6d. Frocks brought 10s. and 7s. 6s. White shirts were sold for £1, 15s, 10s. 5s. and as low as 2s. 6d. The check shirts brought 10s and 7s. 6d. Drawers went at 7s. 6d. and at 2s 6d. The Table Cloth was sold for 10s.

Four wagon loads of Sails, and four wagon loads of "parcells of old iron," were wnt to Burlington, New Jersey, for safe keeping as the following invoice will show:

Red Bank, Nov. 7, 1777.

Sir—You have inclosed an invoice of Sundry Articles that was saved out of the Ships Augusta and Merlin, Men of War, which please to put into Some dry Store Until further Orders, by Order of Commodore Hazlewood.

Yrs,

Nathl Gatt.

To Emanuel Eyres, Esq.[97]
    Burlington.

It is probable that different galleys and at least accommodation sloops accompanied Hazelwood on his salvage operations, the latter to bring off the cannon and heavier articles. Of the captains listed by McGeorge, Hugh Stewart and Joseph Best do not appear on any muster rolls for the fleet. Either McGeorge erred in his transcribing, or these were civilian or Continental ship volunteers. The variety and number of the items salvaged suggest the accuracy of Bradford's observation: "The people on board the Augusta must have got off with great Precipitation, as we have found among the rubbish great number of Cloaths, part of their Books, &c., &c., that they seem to have taken nothing with them but what they had on." [98]

XI

Aftermath of Victory—1777

THE DESTRUCTION of two British men-of-war and the disaster to Donop's Hessians at Fort Mercer produced a feeling of overoptimism in segments of the civilian population. Henry Laurens enthusiastically wrote to Washington, "Is not the Knight of the Bath [Sir William Howe] . . . toward a shameful retreat or a more shameful surrender . . . as now in all probability we shall [be], Masters of the Rivers he will in a few days have nothing to eat. . . ."[1] Even Washington contributed to the general elation, albeit with tongue in cheek, by writing to the President of Congress (Laurens), "The damage the Enemy have sustained in their Ships, I hope will prevent their future attempts to gain the passage of the River, and the repulse of the Troops under Count Donnop and his Captivity, I flatter myself will also be attended with the most happy consequence."[2]

This may have been an effort to placate civilian emotions, but Washington and the officers defending the river did not underestimate the importance of the Delaware as the lifeline of the British army in Philadelphia. In writing to General Forman on October 25 he commented on the fortunate turn of events in the defeat of the British of October 22 and 23. He admonished

Forman that Howe would not be dissuaded, but would probably devise a slower and more effectual means of making "themselves perfect Masters of the River and the defences of the chevaux-de-Frieze it is essential to them to occupy that spot." Pointing out the importance of Fort Mercer and the need to contain any attempt to lay seige to the fort, he requested Forman to raise a respectable force of militia. Colonel Greene, confined with his command in the small fort, had little fear of another assault; however, an investiture would be catastrophic, as artillery could easily reduce the garrison's ability to resist. Forman was requested to throw his militia on the flanks and rear of any besieging force.[3]

Hazelwood had engaged in a sporadic correspondence with Washington concerning the needs of the navy, especially for reinforcements with marine experience. While his critics had accentuated the low morale of his crews, no one was more aware of their shortcomings and the high rate of desertion than Hazelwood. These facts he candidly described to Washington, at the same time reiterating the need for a strong water force to defend the river passes. Washington had ordered a head count of Continental soldiers with maritime service. Preoccupied with the British in Philadelphia and the recent actions on the river, he temporarily deferred further action in recruiting men for the fleet. Now that the emergency was over he resumed his efforts to forward replacements to Hazelwood.

On October 25 he wrote to the Continental Navy Board[4] suggesting that the seamen engaged on board the unfinished frigates *Washington* and *Effingham* would be of greater service with Hazelwood. Assuming that the sailors were kept on board to ensure the security of the frigates, he was of the opinion that in the unfinished and unwieldy condition of the ships the men were unequal to the task. He recommended scuttling the frigates, because if captured they would provide a formidable force in the river above the little State navy.[5]

The more Washington contemplated the possibility of the frigates falling into British hands, the more the thought distressed him. Without waiting for a reply to his letter of the 25th he again communicated with the Navy Board on October 27. He reemphasized the fatal consequence of the loss of the frigates—how the little fleet would be surrounded and at the mercy of the British. Apologetically he closed with a request that they be immediately sunk and asked their forgiveness if he had stepped out of the sphere of his responsibility.[6]

In the meantime, the Navy Board had written to Washington on October 25, stating that Captain Robinson of the Continental Navy had appealed to them for "cartridges and Ball." Robinson had probably discussed the condition with Hazelwood. Hazelwood could not request assistance from the Continental Navy Board, but Robinson could and did. The Navy Board was unable to comply and urged Washington to honor whatever requisitions for ammunition the situation demanded.[7]

The Navy Board answered Washington's letter of the 25th on October 26, enclosing muster rolls for the two frigates, listing twenty-nine officers and men, many of them militiamen, on the *Effingham* and a crew of eighteen on the *Washington*, including thirteen soldiers and landsmen. Of the forty-seven crewmen, the majority were not seamen and, even if available, would have been of little help to Hazelwood. They agreed to comply with the Commander-in-Chief's request, if he insisted, but privately thought little danger was imminent, supposing that the frigates were safe until the British fleet reached Philadelphia. Regardless of their opinions, they would make preparations to scuttle the frigates if necessary. Washington's attention was called to the fact that a number of shallop men and a few sailors on private vessels were tied up at the wharves at Bordentown.[8]

Receiving the letter and muster rolls on the 27th, Washington dispatched his second letter of that date to the Navy Board. Acknowledging receipt of the muster rolls, he thought the need for scuttling the frigates even more pressing, as the few men on board could not hope to defend them if attacked. He recommended that they be sunk as well as all other vessels capable of being converted into men-of-war. The soldiers on board were to be sent, under command of an officer, to their respective regiments, the few seamen down to Hazelwood. He also urged the recruitment of the "watermen" on the private vessels to serve until frost. He suggested a handsome stipend be offered, "but not so much as to occasion jealousy and uneasiness in those already in the service." [9]

The Continental Navy Board, acting with characteristic indecision, turned Washington's request over to the Continental Congress, who acted on the recommendation on November 4. (With over a week lost after the Commander-in-Chief's recommendation, the British could have raided and possibly taken the frigates and other vessels at Bordentown and Burlington.) The Congressional resolution ordered the frigates to be run up some convenient creek and lightened as much as possible. A battery should be constructed on shore with the cannon from the *Washington* to defend them. The frigates were to be charged with combustibles and a vigilant officer placed in command to destroy them on the approach of the British.[10]

Washington presented the resolution from Congress to his Council of War and, agreeable to their opinion, wrote on November 9 to the Continental Navy Board. The Council concurred with Washington's original suggestions and believed that the Congressional resolution gave weight to the Commander in Chief's direction. Replying the next day, the Navy Board advised Washington that they had already scuttled the frigates and were engaged in sinking the other vessels and planned to sink a larger vessel across the mouth of Crosswicks Creek as a barrier to raising the scuttled ships. The crews on board the frigates could not be released as they were needed to effect the program underway. In the meantime, delay had made the need for the frigate crews academic. A detachment of mariner-soldiers had gone on board the galleys and in a few days the fall of Fort Mifflin would reduce the need for additional men.[11]

Hazelwood, desperate for reinforcements, pleaded with anyone having correspondence with the Commander-in-Chief to use his influence to obtain recruits for the fleet. Benjamin Eyre advised Washington that he was forwarding eight wagonloads of powder to the fleet and added that the Commodore was in need of a few men. Hazelwood summarized the manpower problem in his letter to Thomas Wharton. Thanking the Council "for their good opinion of the fleet," he hoped their future conduct would meet with equal approval:

[A]ltho' we have lost 250 or more men thro' cowardice or disaffection, yet with the remaining few we have left, we are determined to spend the last drop of our blood in the defence of this pass & our Country. . . . Dear Sir, if you have any influence on General Washington, I beg you will use it with him to send me 250 men to reinforce our fleet, for we cannot mann half our

Galleys to go to action. I have repeatedly wrote him, but have nothing but promises from time to time . . . how can a man discharge such a trust as I have on me, half mann'd, without being disgraced. . . .[12]

Wharton knew that Washington had forwarded a contingent to reinforce Hazelwood, so did not relay the Commodore's impassioned plea.

Washington had been hopeful that an interchange of men in Greene's and Angell's regiments would relieve the distressing problem of reinforcements for the fleet. As previously indicated, he had instructed Greene on October 14 to draft any men in his command who were "accustomed to water" to serve with Hazelwood. The demand by Greene for the return of all men on loan to the galleys after every action, which in October was daily, could create a crisis either with the fleet or at Fort Mercer. This situation arose in late October and early November when Greene and Varnum were almost daily expecting an attack on the fort. On October 26 Hazelwood advised Washington:

The fleet is now so poorly manned, and the constant cry from Fort Mifflin is to guard that post, that I know not how to act without more assistance. Colonels Greene and Angell can spare no men, as they are afraid of being attack; and as to the vessels at Bordentown, I am informed they have not twenty private men on board, so that I expect no assistance from there.[13]

Hazelwood, in common with Colonels Smith and Greene, was probably so blinded by his own needs that he failed to realize the crises facing the Commander-in-Chief. Washington, while not responding promptly to the Commodore's request, was endeavoring to raise men to augment the faithful crews on board the galleys and floating batteries. On October 28 he wrote to Hazelwood advising him that he had located more than one hundred sailors in the army and would send them forward as soon as the weather moderated. The violent weather was hampering operations on land as well as on the river.[14]

Soldiers with maritime experience were located in the Muhlenberg, Weedon, Woodford, and Scott brigades of Virginians and Pennsylvanians, Smallwood's Second Maryland Brigade, and the North Carolina regiments under McDougall. Alexander McDougall was promoted to major general on October 20 and, though a native of New York, was given temporary command of the North Carolina regiments. Thus the contingent of "more than 100" men ordered as a replacement for Hazelwood included soldiers from Pennsylvania, Virginia, Maryland, and North Carolina.[15] There is some reason to believe that the majority were from the North Carolina line. In March, 1778, Bradford, in answering Washington's request for the return of the men assigned to the fleet, referred to them as from the North Carolina regiment. The soldier-seamen were instructed in the General Orders of October 29 and ordered to have three days' rations cooked and to hold themselves ready to march on short notice. The next day's orders directed the men to accompany Varnum's brigade on their march to Woodbury. The reinforcement reached the fleet on November 2.[16]

With reinforcements on the way, Hazelwood and the State Navy Board turned their attention to supplying the fleet with provisions and matériel. Desertions were to be avoided; the remaining crews must be kept happy and healthy. The sailors on the galleys and floating batteries, with those borrowed from other elements of the State and Continental fleets and the addition of the Continental soldiers, gave Hazelwood enough men to make his shallow-draught boats operational.

William Crispin, commissary, had moved into Fort Mercer, and by the end of October had acquired a sufficiency of cattle and fresh provisions for the navy. His only item in short supply was rum. Constant complaints of profiteering were raised against farmers who regulated their prices for cattle and grain to take advantage of the needs of the navy. The State Navy Board's funds were exhausted after purchasing supplies to provision the State and Continental fleets. Apparently some waste was evident, and, to conserve some of the meat previously thrown away, Crispin was ordered to salt a reserve of beef and pork.[17]

William C. Bradford was appointed paymaster to the fleet to replace the missing William Webb, who was suspected of having accepted protection of the British in Philadelphia.[18]

Colonel d'Arendt arrived at Fort Mifflin on the day before the assault on Fort Mercer, thus creating another problem for the rank-conscious Smith. Smith remarked that he had not been notified of d'Arendt's coming, even though the "Baron" had been assigned to the command of the fort on September 23. In dictating his reminiscences, Smith alluded to d'Arendt as a coward. Smith's jealousy and penchant for dispute with those not agreeing with him could have jeopardized the defence of the fort; fortunately it never did.

Colonel d'Arendt commanded Fort Mifflin during the relentless cannonading of October 22 and 23. In the exchange of artillery fire he received two wounds and, with his already weakened condition, advised Washington that he would have to go to Woodbury for rest and treatment.

Like all who had observed the fort on Fort Island he said, "The Fort is the worst I have ever seen. . . ." Enumerating the works' deficiencies, he concluded that little could be accomplished because there was neither time nor men and materials to make the necessary repairs. Before leaving the island he made two engineering changes. First, he ordered wolf traps dug in the space between the fort's walls and the water's edge. These were holes dug in the ground and shaped like a cone or sugar loaf; into these holes pointed stakes were driven. It is interesting to note that a committee appointed by the Council of Safey had made the same recommendations six months before. These could be very effective in breaking up an orderly assault on the fort. He then ordered the dikes cut to flood Fort Island. This action, of doubtful value, would later cause great discomfort to the garrison.[19]

Colonel d'Arendt held a conference with Hazelwood and requested a constant night patrol around Fort Island to prevent a surprise attack by the British. Hazelwood agreed to provide as much assistance as possible, but the actions of the 22nd and 23rd prohibited him from providing this protection.

Apparently, on October 23, Hazelwood dispatched four galleys and four armed boats to take station at Fort Mifflin. Weather permitting, they would patrol the area near the fort, returning each morning to their anchorage off Fort Mercer. On the 26th he informed d'Arendt and Smith of his manpower problem. His available seamen could provide crews for only five galleys and the same number of guard boats. He reminded the officers that "if there is much wind and sea going . . . [I] cannot keep the river with them, but must make a Harber . . . still weather they can lay to gard you but when it Blows & you cannot defend the Island with the Trupes, you cannot depend on us. . . ."[20]

Smith is the sole authority for the statements that d'Arendt insisted that he, Smith, assume command during the action with the British fleet and also that he had volunteered to lead a force after the retreating Hessians. The latter proposal was ridiculous, as Fort Mifflin was under a severe cannonade and threatened with invasion by British troops gathered at the wharf on Province Island. With the fort needing every man in the garrison, the most charitable explanation is that Colonel Smith's memory after fifty years was defective.[21]

Fleury was actively working on the weaknesses of the fort but was hampered by bad weather and Smith. Although Fleury always protested that he respected Smith's zeal, his writings disclose the antagonism between the two officers.

Colonel d'Arendt and Fleury, worked in harmony but with so little to work with and under constant shelling by the British batteries, were forced to use what materials were available and perform their work at night. They advised Washington that they could not make a "vigorous Resistance with the present garrison." [22] They had requested that Colonel Greene lend them one hundred men each night, to be returned the following morning. Defenseless against a night attack, they asserted that their only security was the fleet. Showing their lack of knowledge of the operational strength of the galleys and other shallow-draught boats, they complained that the Commodore sent only galleys and at other times only guard boats, and contended these would be good as look-out boats but ineffective for defense. By their own admission, Hazelwood was sending galleys and guard boats each night and their own experience of October 22 and 23 should have demonstrated to their satisfaction the fighting capabilities of the galleys. Pressed for reinforcements, they should have realized that Hazelwood was equally in need of men. As this was the period of the heavy storm, it is somewhat unusual that the galleys, and particularly the little guard boats, would venture into open water. In fact, d'Arendt stated that Greene did not send his one-hundred-man reinforcement on the night of October 27 because the water was too rough.[23]

Colonel d'Arendt and Fleury were of the opinion that the British batteries across the back channel could easily batter a breach in Fort Mifflin's palisades. The only defense they could bring to bear would be the southwest and northwest blockhouses. The British had brought up over two hundred wagonloads of fascines and d'Arendt was of the opinion that they were to fill the ditch in an attack on the fort. Fearing a night attack, they agreed that defense of the fort "consists on this single point, *to prevent the Enemy from Landing,* this is the business of our Fleet especially at night—at which time the Cannon of the Fort would do but little good."[24]

The storm interrupted repairs to the fort and caused more damage than enemy action. On October 29 the rain cut the bank in several places, inundating the fort and putting the entire island under water. While this would be a deterrent to an attempt by the British to storm the fort, it also flooded every area near the walls where the garrison sought shelter from the cannonading of the land batteries and made communications between the various sections of the fort next to impossible.

The British batteries were experiencing similar difficulties. Their works were flooded, making it impossible to use some of their artillery. Believing that these batteries were assailable, it was determined to storm the works on the Province Island dikes. Fleury observed that three galleys came to help the landing party but after the exchange of a few cannon shot, "The firing ceased by mutual consent." He said that the lack of boats to carry the soldiers forced them to call off the planned attack.[25]

When d'Arendt left the island, he recommended to Washington that Colonel Green of the Virginia Continentals be given the command, a deliberate affront to Smith.

Extant correspondence indicates that Fleury and d'Arendt worked well together, while, on the other hand, Smith interfered with Fleury's effort to function as an engineer. In an attempt to clarify his status, Fleury unburdened himself in his Journal of November 3, knowing that the contents would be brought to Washington's attention. He commented on the enthusiasm with which Washington accepted him as an engineer but, inasmuch as a specific order appointing him in that capacity had not been issued, all he could do was act as an advisor ". . . without being heard. While Baron Arendt was present he understands the Military Art, and my Opinions in point of fortifications were his—but he is absent, and you know there are persons who know a great deal without having ever learnt —and whose obstinacy is equal to their Insufficiency." His journal reached headquarters the next day and a concerned

Washington instructed his aide John Laurens to send an unsealed letter to Smith with a postscript to Fleury clarifying
the latter's status. He admonished Smith to recognize and properly use Fleury's abilities as an engineer. His postscript to Fleury,
"You were sent to Fort Mifflin in the capacity of Engineer . . .
left unsealed for the perusal of Col. Smith who will in consequence vest you with the proper Power for carrying into execution such plans. . . ." [26]

With d'Arendt's departure imminent, Smith was concerned
about his rank as commander. He addressed Washington posing
a hypothetical situation involving the command at Fort Mifflin:

> Whether Coll. Green or I are to Command I know not. I presume I am to
> have the Command untill an express order from your Excellency to the
> Contrary, even should he be an Elder Officer, for if an Elder Officer (for
> instance Coll Green of Red Bank) was to throw in his Regt. to our Assist-
> ance would not d'Arendt Command. I believe so if he would, then I cer-
> tainly after him have the Command by your Excellency's Order. . . . I am
> clearly of the Opinion if we had a Commodore who would do his Duty, it
> would be impossible for the Enemy ever to get Possession of this fort.[27]

The problem of command is presented in some detail to illustrate Washington's quandary, which poses the question not as
to the success of American arms but the remarkable fact that
such successes were achieved. Washington's admonishments to
the officers involved illustrate the complexity of his dilemma.
Writing to Smith on October 28, he acknowledges that he has
requested Lieutenant Colonel Green of Virginia to waive his
seniority in the interest of the service. Continuing, he cautions
Smith, "You seem to have mistaken the Commodore's meaning.
From his letter I understand he will always assist you. . . . He
tells you, that in rough Weather his Gallies and Armed Boats
cannot live and therefore guards you against expecting much
assistance at that time." Exasperated and obviously depressed, he
dispatched a note to Varnum on November 4, "I thank you for
your endeavours to restore confidence between the Com^r. &
Smith. I find something of the same kind existing between Smith
and Monsr. Fleury, who I consider as a very valuable officer.
How strange it is that Men engaged in the same Important
Service, should be eternally bickering, instead of giving mutual
aid!" [28]

It was unnecessary to remind Washington that reinforcements were needed for the river defenses. A combination of elements made his position anything but enviable. Pennsylvania militia had failed to turn out in any significant numbers and there had been consistent command problems in the New Jersey militia. To make it impossible for the British to send out foraging parties, and to keep local farmers from clandestinely entering the city to sell their produce for British gold instead of Continental promises to pay, it would be necessary to station a cordon of troops on the perimeter of the city. To contain Howe's army and to cope with any reconnaissances in force, the main Continental army must remain intact; troops assigned to patrols or scouting expeditions and to augment the garrisons in the river forts would have to come from the Pennsylvania and New Jersey militia.

All was not sweetness and light in the Continental establishment in the fall of 1777. While machinations were evident in both the army and Congress, there is some question whether there was an organized conspiracy or "cabal" to replace Washington. The details of the so-called Conway Cabal are not germane to this study. However, there was much foot-dragging and a conspicuous lack of cooperation given Washington, which made a more effective defense of the river impossible. Many sincere Patriots, and others whose importance to the American cause existed only in their own fancy, resented what they styled the "Fabian" tactics of Washington. There was little understanding of the needs and sufferings of the Commander-in-Chief and his men among little coterie living in relative comfort at York, Pennsylvania.

The crux of the problem is not whether there was a conspiracy, but rather why Gates failed to release certain contingents so vital to the defense of the Delaware. An egocentric whose value to the American Army existed mainly in his own mind, he may have visioned himself a savior of the Patriot cause. It was finally necessary for Washington to dispatch Alexander Hamilton to Gates and order him to forward certain Continental brigades to the main camp—another classic example of too little and too late.

Meanwhile, Washington could not wait for reinforcements from the north, and he ordered General Varnum's brigade to

New Jersey. Varnum was directed to establish headquarters at Woodbury and supply relief units for the forts. It was especially urgent that Fort Mifflin receive replacements every twenty-four to forty-eight hours. Until Varnum arrived at Woodbury, Greene was sending a contingent to Fort Mifflin every forty-eight hours.[29] Ordered forward on October 28, Varnum was delayed by the weather, arriving in Woodbury on November 2. On the 26th Lieutenant Colonel Ralston was directed to take his detachment of three hundred Pennsylvania militia and report to Greene.[30] No further mention is made of this contingent, and Greene's returns of October 27 and November 17 do not mention Pennsylvania militia being stationed at Fort Mercer.[31] In case of attack on Fort Mercer, Varnum was to act against the flanks and rear of the attacking force and not make the mistake of throwing his brigade into the fort.[32]

Varnum, on arriving at Woodbury, made a tour of inspection and, surprisingly, reported the forts in a good state of defense, but quickly sensed the lack of harmony between Hazelwood and Smith. He sent a detachment of 236 officers and men into Fort Mifflin. He was apprised that the British had repossessed Billingsport to protect their shipping and obstruct Hazelwood's efforts to salvage cannon from the *Augusta* and *Merlin*. Newcomb was also reported camped near Woodbury with between one hundred and two hundred militia.[33]

Varnum surveyed the area south of Fort Mercer as far as Mantua Creek. He decided to erect a small battery on an eminence on the east (north) side of the creek near its confluence with the Delaware River. Erecting the battery on November 4, he planned to drive the British shipping below the chevaux-de-frise at Billingsport. He dispatched a small contingent of artillery under Captain James Lee of the Second Continental Artillery, with one eighteen-pounder and one twelve-pounder to occupy the battery. The eighteen-pounder upset on the way and did not arrive until the next afternoon. At 9 A.M. on the 5th, Lee opened up with his twelve-pounder on the *Isis*, *Pearl* and galley *Cornwallis*.[34] On the other hand, Varnum mistakenly thought his battery was engaged with the *Somerset, Roebuck*, and a galley.

The British ships were driven downstream about one-and-a-quarter miles with the *Isis* going aground. Several galleys came down about noon and engaged the frigates, albeit, Varnum thought, at too great a range to be effective. At five the next morning the galleys re-entered the fight and, although accused of wasting ammunition, did score at least one hit on the large man-of-war. Varnum believed that if the galleys had been more aggressive the sixty-four-gun ship would have suffered the fate of the *Augusta*.

Varnum was probably attempting to be constructive in his evaluation of the fleet's effectiveness. Whether Smith's complaints affected the judgment of Varnum is difficult to determine; the latter admitted that "Smith is continually complaining of the Remissness of the Fleet." If Varnum's comments are accurate and the galleys wasted ammunition and failed to press their attack, then the galley captains were guilty of cowardice. Of course many of the crews were under fire for the first time, having arrived only two days before with Varnum's brigade. Varnum could not understand why the Commodore would not commit the galleys to the western channel under the guns of the British batteries on Province and Carpenters' Islands. To somewhat soften his criticism, he offered the observation that Hazelwood was a kind man, whose good nature permitted his subordinates to take advantage of him.[35]

Varnum's survey convinced him that the British would not storm Fort Mifflin even if the palisades were battered down—rather, the defense of the fort would rest with the galleys. He wanted to attack Billingsport; for some unexplained reason he considered that fort the vital link in the river's defense. Apparently he disregarded the bitter lesson learned at that post the month before—that it was indefensible from the land side and impossible to supply when under siege. Varnum closed his report with "I must beg Liberty to repeat that Billingsport is of far more Importance than all the Forts and Gallies put together."[36]

On November 5, Henry Laurens, President of the Continental Congress, wrote to Hazelwood: "I feel a very singular satisfaction in obeying the order of Congress by transmitting the inclosed Extract of Minutes testifying to the high sense entertained by the Representatives of the Thirteen free & Independent United States of your Merit and bravery."[37] A similar communication was sent to Greene and Smith in compliance with resolutions passed the day before. The resolution to Hazel-wood stated:

Resolved, That Congress have a high sense of the merit of Commodore Hazelwood, the commander of the naval force in the Delaware River; in the service of the commonwealth of Pennsylvania, and of the officers and men of his command, in their late gallant defence of their country against the British fleet, whereby two of their men of war were destroyed, and four others compelled to retire, and that an elegant sword be provided by the Marine Committee, and presented to Commodore Hazelwood.[38]

These commendations and awards involved Smith in two trivial controversies. General John Armstrong may have been the source of one of these. In a letter to Thomas Wharton, Armstrong noted that ". . . Smith will not accept his sword . . . because one hath been ordered for Hazelwood, as to the Fleet he imputes the loss of Fort Island." [39] Smith did not refuse his sword, so this may have been another of his bombastic outbursts or merely some grist thrown in the rumor mill.

A more acrimonious dispute was engendered by the Rhode Island friends of Major Simeon Thayer. Contending that Thayer was the real hero of Fort Mifflin, they castigated Smith for accepting his sword. They overlooked the main point that the sword was awarded to Smith on November 4, almost a week before Thayer took command at the fort, and was intended as an award for his conduct on October 22 and 23. The guilty party in the failure to honor a gallant officer for his courageous defense of Fort Mifflin was the Continental Congress. For some strange reason Thayer's defense went unrecognized, but bravery in lost causes is rarely rewarded.

Sensitive to the discord between the Commodore and Smith, Washington was anxious that Hazelwood not permit their differences to affect his deployment of the fleet. He cautioned that the enemy would probably attack the upper chevaux-de-frise to divert attention from their main attack on the western palisades of the fort. The obstructions would temporarily withstand an effort to break through and thus permit the majority of the galleys to operate against troops attempting to land on the island. Washington had temporarily forgotten his own advice of August—if the enemy frigates were permitted to approach close to the chevaux-de-frise they could enfilade the fort's main battery from the east.

Continuing, he warned that while a daytime storm of the fort would be difficult to repel, it would be impossible to thwart a nighttime attack. To ensure security against night forays by the British, the galleys must control the channel. He suggested a regular nightly patrol. Also, Washington believed that the former American frigate, the *Delaware*, taken by the British in September, was a menace to the galleys. He acknowledged, however, that Hazelwood was the best judge on the use of the galleys, but strongly recommended that if possible his requests be effected.[40]

Hazelwood had always insisted that his galleys and guard boats were defenseless against artillery in fixed positions and had hesitated when asked to station them in the western channel in daylight hours. Not averse to a night patrol, he had agreed with d'Arendt to provide galleys each night to anchor off the north end of Mud Island. His only fear at night was turbulent weather, the galleys' worst enemy.

Rumors had been circulating that Howe was planning an all-out assault on Fort Mifflin and an investment of Fort Mercer. On November 7 Washington advised Varnum that the attack was expected at any time, but he was convinced the enemy would concentrate on Fort Mifflin. Varnum was of a different opinion, as his informants had declared that the British would land one force below Timber Creek, while the garrison at Billingsport, reinforced by two Hessian regiments, would move up from the south.[41]

Varnum evidently held a meeting with Hazelwood to determine the best method of deploying the fleet. The Commodore agreed to lay a chain between Hog and Province Islands; it was to be buoyed with logs and anchored. For some unexplained reason, unless it was that weather prevented the galleys and guard boats from operating, the chain was not laid in the channel. Fourteen guard boats were to lie in the passage in back of the chain. This would have been a gamble Hazelwood would not normally have agreed to with boats which were easily capsized. The Commodore, using one of the galleys (probably the *Chatham*) as his flagship, with the balance of the galleys, would anchor close to the north end of Mud Island. The floating batteries and xebecs were to guard the upper chevaux-de-frise. The Continental ships and the sailing units of the State navy under Captain Robinson, were to be stationed in two sections, one near the mouth of the Schuylkill River and the other at the mouth of Timber Creek.[42]

Robinson probably did not approach the mouth of the Schuylkill, as the sailing units of the fleet would not have been able to withstand the fire of Webb's Ferry battery. A few days previous, one of his xebecs had been badly mauled by this battery and forced to retreat to the anchorage near Fort Mercer.[43] Both American and British commands had difficulty in recognizing the effectiveness of land batteries; only a few days before, the little one-gun battery had driven the men-of-war *Isis* and *Pearl* from their anchorages near Mantua Creek.

Unable to spare additional reinforcements for the defense of the river, the distraught Washington relied on the New Jersey militia to augment Varnum's Continental brigade. As in past crises, the obstinate Newcomb refused to cooperate with either General Forman, of the New Jersey militia, or the Continental command. Governor Livingston was forced to intervene in the dispute and demand that Newcomb relinquish his command to Forman. This controversy resulted in only a trickle of militia joining the Continental service for the campaign.[44]

Fort Mifflin possessed so many inherent weaknesses that all the engineering skills of Fleury were taxed to provide mere shelter for the men against British shells and bombs. Neither time, materials nor manpower was available in sufficient quantities to strengthen the fort's most vulnerable areas. Forced to work on the ramparts and barracks each night to repair the damage done by enemy fire during the day, Fleury and Smith realized that this was only the dress rehearsal for the main performance. Fleury's frustrations prompted occasional outbursts about the dereliction of the fleet—sometimes justified, and on other occasions without understanding that Hazelwood also had problems.

Fleury and Smith were convinced that the British were raising a battery of heavy cannon on the hulk of the *Augusta*. They protested that the galleys were making no effort to interrupt the enemy's activities. The erection of a battery on the hulk would create a serious menace to the fort, as it could enfilade the main battery from the east where there was no shelter for the garrison. Discovering that he and Fleury had made a mistake, Smith hastily penned a note to Washington acknowledging their error. He explained that they were deceived by the river being lower than usual.[45] Unquestionably, the British had been on the hulk endeavoring to remove cannon, and may have salvaged a few pieces. After removing the two twenty-four-pounders on October 25, Hazelwood had returned to the hulk and removed additional cannon, some of which were taken into Fort Mifflin.[46]

Boats were passing in both directions every night, hugging the shore line of Province and Carpenters' Islands. Fleury lamented that the fort could not fire on them as ". . . the shade of Trees prevents our being informed of their passage, otherwise than by the noise of oars. . . ." Lord Howe reported that officers and seamen were assigned to the flotilla of flat-bottomed boats and sloops to transport ". . . previsions, artillery and stores to the Schuylkill, between Fort-Island and the Pennsylvania shore. . . ." He further indicated that the sloops were used to carry six twenty-four-pounders from the *Eagle* and four thirty-two-pounders from the *Somerset* to the new batteries opposite Fort Mifflin. The thirty-two-pounders were intended for use on two floating batteries the British were building.[47]

The water route up the west channel to the area of Webb's Ferry was probably used on dark and overcast nights to transport cannon. On clear nights the boats carrying provisions entered Bow Creek and unloaded their cargoes at the lower end of Carpenters' Island. They would then be transported over the Bow Creek road, improved by Montresor, to the Schuylkill and then ferried over to the Philadelphia shore. This multiple handling was not preferred, but the fear of the fort's and galleys' cannon and weather forced this alternate route.[48]

General Potter and the Pennsylvania militia were constantly harassing the British along the roads leading to Province and Carpenters' Islands. On November 1 he cut a dam flooding areas of Carpenters' Island and destroyed sections of the road to Bow Creek. Potter and Henry Lee reported on the 8th that the British were forced to find a new route to bring up their supplies. The change was necessary as the planned all-out attack on Fort Mifflin would make it extremely hazardous to use the channel between the batteries and the fort. Also, Potter's foray had made the Bow Creek road impassable for wagons. The boats were to enter Bow Creek and unload their supplies ". . . and careys it up the Creek to Giers Wharff [Geyer or Guier, sometimes referred to as Blakely] thence to Mingas [Mingo] Creek and into the Schulkill at Everleys. . . ." The log of Howe's flagship, the *Eagle*, records almost daily flotillas of boats going up the back channel.[49]

Fleury's journal consistently confirms that the majority of the boats used the western channel, passing without interruption unless challenged by the galleys, as the fort's garrison could not see distinctly. They could only hear the oars and would waste precious ammunition if their fire was directed at the sound of the oars. Fleury mistakenly assumed that the erection of new batteries on Province Island indicated that the British intended to winter there if they were unsuccessful in their attempt to take Fort Mifflin. Believing the British position on the island insecure, he suggested that Washington attack them from the rear while a diversionary raid was made by the fort's garrison. With his knowledge of the island, he volunteered to act as guide to the expedition.[50]

The batteries Fleury judged to be defensive in nature were actually part of Howe's plan to reduce Fort Mifflin. Montresor was working day and night to complete the construction of these works. He later commented, "During 23 campaigns . . . this service was by far the most severe, not having been in bed for nine nights together, and remaining in general in the midst of a swamp. . . ."[51] On November 3, he started a heavy battery to contain six twenty-four-pounders (from the *Eagle*) near the dike on Carpenters' Island. Montresor recorded that on November 4 the galley with Hazelwood on board was struck by a shell from a medium twelve-pounder.

The work parties of British troops were suffering similar discomforts to those of their American counterparts in the fort, except that they had uniforms to cover their nakedness. Standing all day in water, plagued with fatigue and sickness, the British command was forced to send relief detachments each morning. Flood water and rain turned the high ground and dikes into quagmires; Montresor was compelled to suspend work on November 5 and 6. On November 7, the weather turned clear but extremely cold and work was rushed to completion on the heavy battery on the dike and a second one near the Blakely (Geyer) house.[52]

Washington was certain that Howe could not defer the appointed time for reducing the river forts and fleet. With winter approaching, the British command was becoming desperate. Washington's informants had observed unusual activity in the city, and the garrison at Fort Mifflin had noted the feverish haste with which the handicapped Montresor was building redoubts and batteries. Wagons, except for military use, were disappearing from the streets of Philadelphia; thirty-five were observed loading ammunition on the State House lawn. Hessian and British reserves were moving up to the east bank of the Schuylkill, preparatory to crossing to Province Island. Two floating batteries were nearing completion. Because of inclement weather and the activities of the galleys, the British could not bring up their pontoon bridges. Major John Clark advised Washington that the enemy was building three bridges of boats with timbers laid on them. A British source more accurately describes a new bridge at Middle Ferry to be made of spare masts and logs forty-four feet long and lashed together with timber laid across the frames.

The elements of the British fleet anchored near New Castle and Reedy Island were ordered up and anchored between Chester and Marcus Hook; one officer reported over 209 men-of-war and transports were seen, mostly the latter. Intense activity was noted on board in repairing small boats and shallops, apparently anything that could be used for landing parties. In an effort to prevent American patrols from observing their activities, the British had posted vedettes (mounted sentinels) on all roads, and constant skirmishing was reported.[53]

One of Potter's spies reported a fleet of thirty-seven sail in the upper Delaware Bay, anchored off New Castle. On board was Major General Sir Thomas Wilson and Brigadiers Leslie and Pattison with five regiments, including one of light dragoons. These reinforcements numbered slightly more than three thousand men.[54]

At dawn on November 10, the British were to begin their last desperate offensive to open the river to their shipping. All reports from Philadelphia indicated that the population was on the verge of starvation and the army never had more than two days' provisions on hand at any time. After the river froze, even this trickle of provisions would cease.[55] The upper chevaux-de-frise must be breached to permit passage of the supply ships.

The Americans were expectant and apprehensive. However, everyone knew what Howe must do. Informants had alerted Washington and Varnum that the enemy had assembled large numbers of men and ships, and vast quantities of materials of war. The only question remaining was where, when, and how would the first blow be struck?

XII

Fort Mifflin and Fort Mercer—1777

U NCERTAIN both as to the British plans and his own future, Smith wrote to Washington on November 9, with his observations on the garrison. If Fort Mifflin were not attacked before November 20, the works would be in a "good posture of defence," at which time he would request that his detachment and the Virginia Continentals be relieved. He had arrived at the fort on September 27 with over two hundred officers and men; of this number only four officers and sixty-five privates remained in the garrison. The Sixth Virginia Regiment had arrived with 120 rank and file,[1] of whom on November 9 only forty-six were fit for duty. Varnum's replacement had already sent twenty officers and men to the hospital at Woodbury. The men were exhausted from overwork on guard duty; one-half the garrison was on constant duty. Smith, so fearful of night attacks, remained up all night and slept when he could in the daytime, a procedure certain to aggravate fatigue.[2]

At the same time, Fleury was taking advantage of a dark and cloudy night to raise the bank covering the palisades on the west side of the fort. Knowing that the British attack, when launched, would be against this most exposed part of the fortifications, he wanted to afford better protection to the palisades.[3]

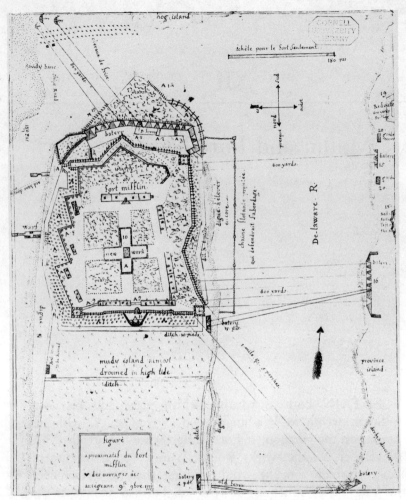

Map of Fort Mifflin, November 9, 1777, by François Louis de Fleury. This map presents in detail the state of the defenses of Fort Mifflin just prior to the all-out bombardment by the British land and naval forces. Fleury endorsed the map: "the engineer author of this imperfect draugh, begg indulgence for it; Considering, that he has not paper, pen, Rule neither Circel, and being disturbed by good many Shells, or Cannon's balls, flying in the fort." He detailed all the improvements he made to the fortification, indicating each with an *A. A. 1, 2, 3.* Traverses to defend the Battery from Ricochet Shot. *A. 4, 5.* Ditches to close the Left of the Battery which was open. *A. 6.* A double Iron Chain which incloses the right of the battery. *A. 7.* Pits with sharp upright Stakes, to defend the approaches to our Inclosure. *A. 8.* Banquet raised round the Wall. *A. 9.* Ditches and Parapet of Reunion between our Barracks, which will make a second Inclosure, and be furnished with loop-holes. *A. 10.* Last Retreat in the middle of the Fort made when we had only 120 Men in the Garrison. *A. 11.* Demilune to flank the front, substituted to the Blockhouse which was blown up. *A. 12, 13, 14.* Fraise-work.

Fleury's description of British positions: *15.* Enemy's battery of 2 Mortars. *16.* Enemy's battery of 5 pieces of large Cannon 1 Mortar. *17.* Enemy's battery of 2 pieces Cannon—1 Mortar. *18.* Unfinished Redoubt at a mile and a third from the Fort, near the Road. *19.* A pretty extensive work at about the same distance. *20.* Epaulements for the Guards. *Jared Sparks Collection, Cornell University.*

The fort was in as good a state of defense as Fleury could make it. His every improvisation was made out of desperation. He had completed traverses in the main battery and excavated ditches fronted with a fraised earthen rampart on the southeast salient to protect the gunners from enfilade and ricochet shot. A double chain had been installed at the water's edge to afford some security to the right of the battery.

Fraised work had been placed on the earthen ramparts of the north and west sides and in front of the main battery which, together with the wolf pits, would offer a degree of protection from storm by British troops. Fleury's demilune would permit the riflemen to rake the flanks of the northern rampart. Smith had added two batteries outside the fort before Fleury joined the garrison. A battery of two eighteen-pounders had been placed near the northwest blockhouse and another battery of two four-pounders at the old ferry wharf.

In the fort, the banquette raised along the stone wall allowed the riflemen a field of fire for assault from the east. However, the ramparts on the north and west were ill-conceived and the loopholes were constructed in such a position that it was impossible to rake or provide enfilade fire to the approaches from those directions.

If the outer walls were breached, the garrison could fall back on the parapets of reunion built between and including the northern and western barracks. The last resort would be a redoubt, shaped like a Greek cross, constructed in the center of the parade ground.[4]

In his reminiscences, Smith claimed credit for several of the improvements to the fort. However, all major changes originated with Fleury, except the wolf pits which were ordered by d'Arendt. Nevertheless, little can be made of Smith's statement, as he was recalling events a half-century later.

Smith recalled that the main battery contained eighteen-pounders pointing downriver and one thirty-two-pounder aimed at Province Island. In the blockhouses he remembered there were eight-pounder French guns. General Samuel Cleaveland, commander of the British artillery, reported after the fall of Fort Mifflin that they found considerable ordnance. On traveling carriages, they found one thirty-two-pounder; one twenty-four-pounder; seven eighteen-pounders, two unserviceable; one

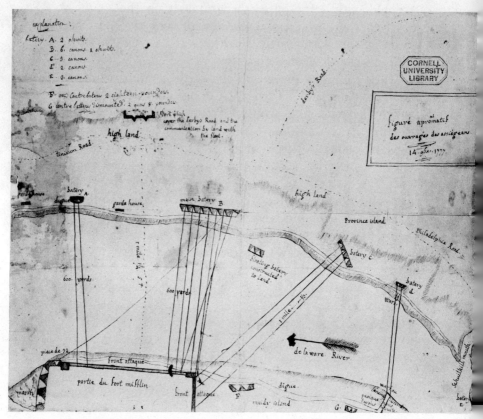

Fleury's other plan of Fort Mifflin, November 14, 1777, showing the British gun positions and their field of fire. *Jared Sparks Collection, Cornell University.*

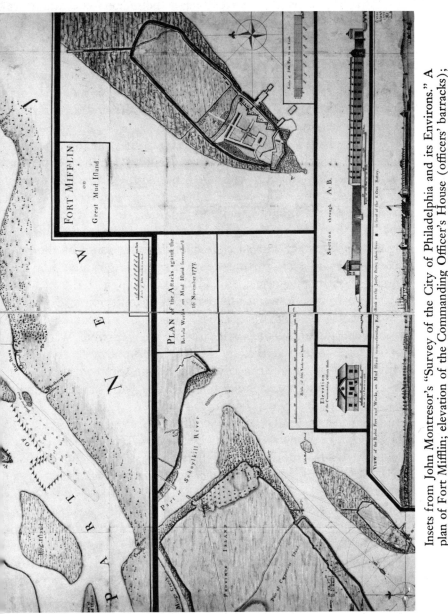

Insets from John Montresor's "Survey of the City of Philadelphia and its Environs." A plan of Fort Mifflin; elevation of the Commanding Officer's House (officers' barracks); soldiers' barracks and a profile of the fort offer interesting detail not available elsewhere. *Geography and Division, Library of Congress.*

twelve-pounder; and two four-pounders. They also salvaged, on garrison carriages, fourteen eight-pounders, one unserviceable. Cleaveland also reported that a scow carrying ten cannon from the fort was sunk. No records exist to determine the exact armament in the fort on the eve of the attack. Cleaveland's return was made on November 16, and with extracts from Fleury's Journal must be accepted as representative of the fort's ordnance.[5] Such was the condition of the fort and its armament as the garrison awaited Howe's attack.

Montresor had the British batteries ready for the bombardment. He had built three batteries fronting on the Carpenters' Island dike and directly opposite Fort Mifflin, at a distance of six hundred yards. The heaviest battery was constructed a short distance below Mingo Creek. In addition to six twenty-four-pounders brought up from the *Eagle*, the battery contained an eight-inch howitzer and an eight-inch mortar. South of the main battery was a small fortification with one eight-inch howitzer and an eight-inch mortar. Still farther south was a thirteen-inch mortar battery. Between the batteries, Montresor had erected epaulements (earthen barricades) for the protection of the grenadiers guarding the artillerists. Two redoubts were built on a bench near the Blakely House, over one mile from Fort Mifflin. They were primarily designed to protect the patrols on the roads and creeks supplying the city with the few supplies the flat-bottomed boats could bring up to Carpenters' Island. André maintained that at the confluence of Mingo Creek and the western channel of the Delaware River a thirty-two-pounder, taken from a floating battery, was placed on a wharf. If a cannon was placed at this position, it was probably on November 14.

On Province Island, Montresor had originally erected a battery of two eighteen-pounders near the Old Pest House. Apparently, in testing the cannon on October 15, one burst, killing one man and wounding three. He later replaced the eighteen-pounders with thirty-two-pounders, probably brought up from the *Somerset*. The serviceable eighteen-pounder was installed on the old ferry wharf on Province Island.

At Webb's Ferry, sometimes referred to as Schuylkill Point, there was a battery of two medium-twelve-pounders and a battery with one eighteen-pounder.[6]

As dawn broke on November 10, it was overcast and damp. The British ordnance in the five batteries on Province and Carpenters' Islands opened fire at 7:30 A.M. Each piece of artillery was to fire eighty rounds of round shot, shell, and carcases.[7] With fourteen cannon, howitzers and mortars in action, the fort would be hit by 1,120 projectiles, although Varnum said that some of the British fire was directed at the fleet. Fleury and Smith observed that the greatest damage to the fort and the flanking batteries was caused by the enemy's main battery of six twenty-four-pounders and the hospital battery of two thirty-two-pounders. Montresor asserted that the two flanking batteries were silenced by noon, except for one cannon. Smith and Fleury mention that one eighteen-pounder was struck on the muzzle and rendered useless.[8]

The British twenty-four-pounders raked the western ramparts, knocking down four or five palisades with each shot. By early afternoon a large section of the wall had been destroyed, and the barracks paralleling the wall were virtually leveled. Looking at the destruction of the palisades with a degree of optimism, Fleury commented that the damage would save him the trouble of cutting them down to the height of a man, to make the loopholes more effective. Varnum occasionally offered interesting observations contrary to the opinions of others. After noting the incessant cannonade of five hours, which tapered off about two o'clock in the afternoon, he maintained there was little damage to the fort. Amazingly, he suggested that Smith quarter the men in the barracks, commenting that if a few men were killed it was better than exposing the entire garrison to the inclement weather, a rather unusual suggestion, inasmuch as the barracks were a death trap.

A steady and destructive fire had been maintained by the two thirty-two-pounders in the hospital battery. Great havoc had been wrought to the northeast and northwest blockhouses, and three eight-pounders had been knocked off their carriages. The northern palisades and barracks were badly damaged.[9] The cannonade was so heavy that a citizen of Germantown recorded that it was "still shaking the earth." [10]

In the early afternoon a heavy downpour began, accompanied by strong gusts of wind out of the southwest, forcing the galleys and guard boats to seek shelter.

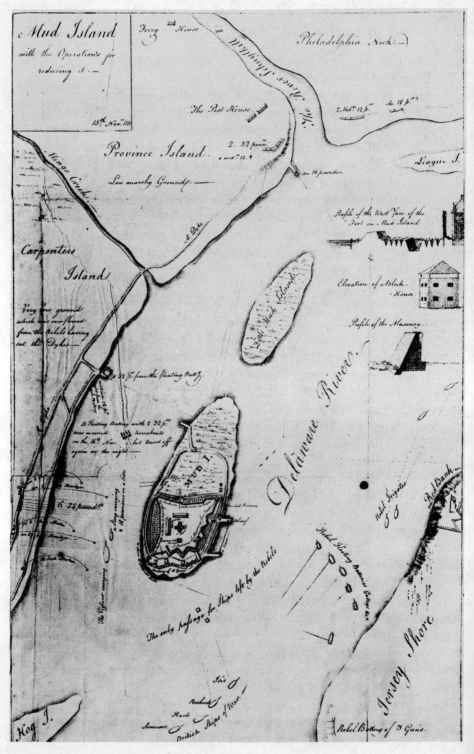

"Mud Island with the Operations for reducing it—15th Nov: 1777," by John André
This map offers interesting profiles of the walls and blockhouses of Fort Mifflin
Courtesy Historical Society of Pennsylvania.

"A Plan of the Attacks Against Fort Mifflin on Mud Island." This map is attributed to Ensign Wheeler, although Captain John Montresor's name is stamped on the verso of the original map. Wheeler's map presents a "List of the Rebel Fleet," which incorporates many errors. Unfortunately, the use of this inaccurate inset by other contemporary British cartographers has misled many historians. A copy of this plan, with some variations, may be seen in the collections of the Historical Society of Pennsylvania. *Geography and Map Division, Library of Congress.*

Varnum employed his troops in preparing fascines and making palisades to be transported to the fort each night. Fleury utilized the garrison to replace the destroyed or damaged palisades under cover of darkness. The engineer was disturbed that the promised palisades and fascines had not arrived at midnight; it was absolutely necessary that they be received before dawn. His workmen were completely exhausted from spending their nights on the alert or at work on the fortifications.

Varnum decided to discard his plan to have Hazelwood stretch a chain to block the channel between Fort and Province Islands. Fleury criticized Hazelwood, stating that it would be of "little consequence," not knowing that it was the decision of a council of war presided over by Varnum. Fleury requested and received the chain, saying it would be used to strengthen the western approaches to the fort.

As Smith surveyed the damage of the first day's bombardment, he was conscious that it would take a miracle to hold out for five or six days. Convinced that an attack must be made on the rear of the British batteries, he was joined by Varnum in beseeching Washington to assault the enemy's position. He admitted that the galleys could not operate in the western channel and therefore the fort must look to its own resources. It was futile to expose the shallow-draught boats of the fleet to the fire of the batteries. Smith's acknowledgment of the danger to the galleys is evidence that a complete break with Hazelwood had not occurred on November 10. This would come later, after Smith relinquished command of Fort Mifflin.

If a diversionary attack could not be made on the British force in the meadows, Smith recommended the abandonment of the fort. He suggested moving all transportable cannon and supplies to the New Jersey shore, and establishing batteries to sweep the shipping lanes in the river. The battery on Bush Island, which had been stripped of its cannon and probably taken to Fort Mifflin, could be reoccupied. The fleet was using the small natural harbor between Bush Island and Fort Mercer as its anchorage, a perfect sanctuary from which the galleys could sally forth and attack British shipping. It was Smith's opinion that an effective defense of the river could be made without dependence on Fort Mifflin.[11]

Fleury recorded that the British maintained a regular cannonade every half hour during the night—a program calculated to prevent the garrison from gaining either a well-earned rest or time to repair the damages to the fortifications.

Strangely, in spite of the continuous bombardment, not one member of the garrison had been wounded. Except for the gunners, who gallantly served their cannon until they were destroyed or rendered useless, the garrison was ordered to take refuge under the stone wall. Only one partial description of this shelter has been found, and this pen picture places it on the wrong side of the wall. Private Joseph Plumb Martin recorded in his memoirs:

Between the stone wall and the palisadoes was a kind of yard or pen, at the southern end of which was a narrow entrance not more than eight or ten feet wide, with a ditch about four feet wide in the middle, extending the whole length of the pen. Here, on the eastern side of the wall, was the only place in the fort anyone could be in any degree of safety.

Three months after the evacuation of Fort Mifflin Colonel Angell wrote, "It may be proper to observe here that there was no place of safety in any part of the fort . . . the only covering the troops had was *without the fort under the wall,* and this afforded a shelter from nothing but the enormous balls. . . ." Such an area of refuge is mentioned in several contemporary accounts, but only Angell and Martin place this shelter outside the fort along the eastern wall. The ditch referred to by Martin was probably the one Fleury dug as a protection to the main battery, at the southeast salient of the fort. The confusing point is the reference by Martin to palisades being placed outside, and the length of, the stone wall. No map or other account refers to palisades in this section of the fort. Wolf pits were dug outside the masonry wall, but palisades would have added nothing to the defense of the wall. The most reliable map, one which offers the best description of the fort, was prepared by Fleury on November 9, 1777. The only area on the map fitting Martin's description is the space between the front or south wall and the palisades which extended the entire length of this wall, from the ditch at the southeast salient to the south-

Fort Mifflin today. The east wall, facing the river with the exception of the bastion in the upper left-hand corner, represents the Revolutionary wall. During the siege of November 10-15, 1777, this wall was breeched in several places; however, it is believed that the wall was restored with the original stones. The south wall, to the right, was leveled by British cannonfire and was completely rebuilt after the war, again presumably with the original stones. The balance of the present outline of the fort was constructed between 1790 and 1802. *Courtesy The Shackamaxon Society, Inc.*

Portion of wall at Fort Mifflin, rebuilt during the early 19th century, using stone from the 1772 wall. *Courtesy The Shackamaxon Society, Inc.*

west blockhouse. This line of palisades was provided to protect the rear of the main battery from the devastating fire of the hospital battery, and to afford a second line of defense if the battery should be overrun by the enemy.[12]

During the night of November 10 the rain increased in intensity and a strong west-northwest wind developed. Toward morning the rain stopped and it turned extremely cold, with a heavy frost and ice one-half inch thick in some areas adding to the discomfort of the garrison.

British batteries picked up the tempo of their cannonading of the previous day with the exception of the two eight-inch howitzers, which had been partially disabled by American cannon fire. Sufficient damage was done to the land batteries in the meadows to require considerable repair work during the night.

In mid-morning a small tender, the *Elk,* and the galley *Cornwallis* moved above the lower chevaux-de-frise and began firing on a small battery being erected above Mantua Creek. As no cannon were as yet installed in this battery, and those in the former battery at the mouth of the creek had been withdrawn, the British engaged in a one-sided cannonade in an effort to discourage the construction of the new battery. Slightly above the old battery, but still on the property of Tench Francis, it was intended to afford an eastern anchor for the upper chevaux-de-frise.[13] No damage was reported to the fortification, but one sergeant was killed and one man wounded.

Overnight Montresor had changed the direction of the embrasures in their main battery of twenty-four-pounders and the hospital battery of thirty-two-pounders. Fleury said that instead of a frontal cannonade to batter down the palisades protecting the northern embankment, they were taking them obliquely and causing "great injury." The oblique fire also produced extensive damage to the northeast blockhouse, near the John Reed house. The blockhouse became untenable and with the cannon dismounted, the gunners were forced to flee.[14]

Captain Samuel Treat, a competent and valiant officer and commander of the artillery contingent in the fort, was the first fatality of the siege. According to Smith, he and "Captain Treat of the Artillery were conversing, near the thirty-two-pounder [main battery], when a ball, from the enemy, came. It lodged in the traverse. Captain Treat tottered and was upheld by the Colonel. A slight squeeze of the hand and he expired. No wound was apparent." [15] One private was also killed during the morning hours.

As the day progressed the damage became more extensive and confirmed, at least in the minds of Varnum and Smith, the hopelessness of defending the fort. The two blockhouses nearest the enemy would be completely destroyed before another twenty-four hours elapsed. Only one cannon in these structures was still capable of answering the British cannon. The Batteries outside the main fort were out of action and the palisades were leveled. However, the optimistic Fleury still contended that he could make repairs each night if supplied with new fascines and palisades. Varnum wrote Washington that the "enemy have battered down a part of the Stone Wall." Smith noted that the wall was "broke through in different places." [16]

Varnum was positive that Fort Mifflin could not withstand another day of the punishment inflicted by the British ordnance. He called a council of Colonels Greene and d'Arendt, the latter still the titular commandant of Fort Mifflin, to decide on the future course of the defense. It is strange that the Commodore of the navy was not included in a conference affecting the overall defense of the river.[17]

Smith had received a minor wound along with Fleury, Lieutenant George of the artillery, and several privates. Smith was forced to leave the fort and go to Woodbury for treatment. He described his injury as occurring when he entered a blockhouse to answer a note from Varnum (strange behavior, to which Smith agreed, when the barracks were considered so dangerous as to be declared off limits). Smith said, "I imprudently went into my Barracks." Writing with his left hand behind him and with his back to a chimney "a ball came through the stockade, the barracks, and two stacks of chimneys: and, nearly spent, it struck him on the left hip and dislocated his wrist. He fell covered with bricks, by which he was severely bruised." [18] George accompanied Smith to the mainland, but Fleury refused to leave the garrison.

Death and destruction were not confined to the Americans. The British batteries had been pretty roughly handled by the

Fragment of 18-pounder cannon from the British frigate *Augusta*. This cannon was placed in Fort Mercer and exploded on November 11, 1777, while firing on the British batteries on the west bank of the Delaware River. *Courtesy Gloucester County Historical Society*.

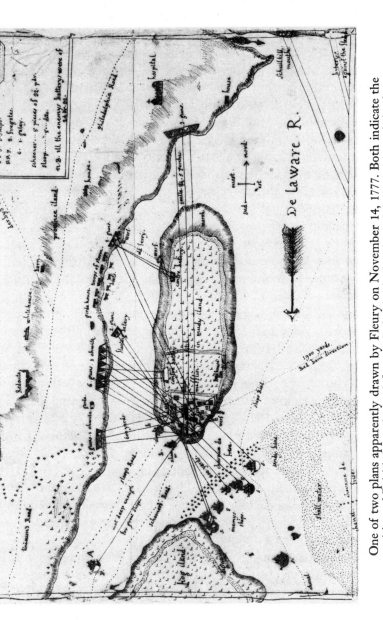

One of two plans apparently drawn by Fleury on November 14, 1777. Both indicate the position of British batteries and fleet and clearly depict the helpless position of the fort, which was surrounded except for the northeast and directly east, where the Pennsylvania galleys and floating batteries were in position. While not on Fleury's maps, the correspondence of Thayer, Hazelwood, Bradford, and Fleury indicate the presence of the American boats in this quarter. *Jared Sparks Collection, Cornell University.*

American gunners. One artillery sergeant was killed in the main battery, one corporal was killed, and two sergeants wounded near Blakely's house.

On November 11 an accident occurred at Fort Mercer when an eighteen-pounder, said to have been removed from the *Augusta*, burst in the act of firing, killing one man and wounding several others.[19]

At ten o'clock that night, two brigs and two sloops loaded with provisions and ammunition passed up the channel and entered the mouth of the Schuylkill River. One sloop had her rigging shot away and went aground, but her cargo was saved. Montresor estimated that the ships brought up provisions enough to last the army three weeks.[20]

As darkness fell on November 11, Fort Mifflin had a new commanding officer, Lieutenant Colonel Giles Russell of Durkee's Connecticut Regiment. One contemporary account states that Lieutenant Colonel Simms of the Virginia Continentals assumed temporary command pending the arrival of Russell.[21]

Logs of British frigates and diarists record that on November 12 strong gales prevailed throughout the day. The water was very rough and restricted the activities of the fleet, as Smith wrote, "Such weather as this the gallies can give no assistance." [22] In spite of the danger to the galleys, Hazelwood took them down the shallow eastern channel between the sand bars, in an attempt to drive the British ships below the lower chevaux-de-frise. The *Isis, Cornwallis*, and two tenders had returned to shell the undefended battery above Mantua Creek. The weather, however, limited the effectiveness of both sides, and after a desultory exchange of shot, both flotillas returned to their former anchorage. One of the guard boats deserted to the British, and Montresor noted that the boat carried a four-pounder and four swivels.[23]

The British attack was not proceeding according to plan; the accuracy of the fort's gunners had caused more damage to the batteries than expected. The howitzers were still not repaired and to replace this lost fire power, Montresor built a battery on the Province Island wharf to house a medium twelve-pounder. No thought of storming the island fort was contemplated until the *Vigilant* could be brought up to soften the fort's garrison and prepare for an assault that would be certain of success without excessive losses. The bad weather and adverse winds prevented the *Vigilant* from making her way up the western channel; in fact she touched ground but was refloated.[24]

Unfamiliar with the British plans, but conscious of the havoc wreaked on the fort, Smith and Varnum continued their recommendations that the post be abandoned. At the same time, Fleury labored unceasingly to repair the damages. By early morning, Fleury had activated one gun in each of the outside batteries. The barracks and blockhouses were ruined and could not be rebuilt, but the energetic engineer was certain he could repair the ramparts and palisades each night.

When Varnum and Smith's recommendation to abandon the fort reached Washington, he called a council of war and it was the decision of the general officers that the fort be held to the last extremity. Varnum was ordered to relieve all injured and fatigued members of the garrison, and to induce the militia to go to the fort each night and work on the fortifications. These instructions had just been dispatched when Varnum's communication, written at midnight, arrived at headquarters. A hastily reconvened council reversed its decision and Washington quickly forwarded a second dispatch to Varnum ordering him to remove all cannon and stores and place everything in order to destroy the works on a minute's notice. A word of caution from the Commander-in-Chief counseled Varnum that every day the fort was held would further the strategic plans of the army.[25]

Anxious to comply with Washington's order, even though it was contrary to his own position, Varnum dispatched one hundred fresh troops to the fort on the night of November 12. He planned to follow, with the balance of Durkee's and Chandler's regiments physically able to endure the rigors of the siege, the next day. At the same time, he would pull out the last of Smith's original detachment and the Virginians.

The lot of the private soldier in Fort Mifflin was not an enviable one. It was bitter cold, residents of the area avowing that the wintry blasts and light snow which fell during the day was the earliest arrival of winter in their memory. To warm themselves, the men gathered up splinters broken off the palisades by British shells and built small fires in the area under the wall. Sleep was impossible, as there was no place to lie down, and those few hardy souls who attempted to steal a nap in the partially demolished barracks seldom emerged unscathed. No soldiers were fully clothed and few had shoes. Those brave Continental soldiers who served in Fort Mifflin deserve greater recognition than the one-line notices recorded in most accounts of the Revolutionary War.[26]

Russell found that he was physically unable to continue in command, and requested Varnum to send relief. The latter had intended offering the command to Colonel Durkee, but he decided that the time was not propitious to adhere to the service policy of assignment by rank and seniority; instead, an officer capable of animating the garrison and directing a spirited defense was needed. That Varnum intended to seek a volunteer who possessed the desired talents was soon known, and Major Simeon Thayer is reported to have volunteered. Thayer, who had served at Fort Mifflin, was an ideal choice and the offer was immediately accepted. Early on the morning of November 13, Thayer, accompanied by the remaining fresh troops in Durkee's and Chandler's regiments and Captain James Lee and his artillerymen entered Fort Mifflin. According to the same contemporary account, Thayer's command consisted of 286 rank and file and Lee's artillery company of twenty men.[27]

Characteristic of the prevailing weather, November 13 dawned with a wind of gale force that continued all day. Coming from the north-northwest, it drove the *Vigilant* back to the shelter of Tinicum Island. Although the British were continuing their unremitting shelling of the three previous days, the Americans continued to operate one eighteen-pounder in the mud battery near the northwest blockhouse. Occasional shots were also fired by the little four-pounder battery on Mud Island's ferry wharf. The American fire was apparently still annoying, as one British twenty-four-pounder had been disabled in the truck.[28]

Elements of the British fleet again came up to bombard the little battery under construction on the New Jersey shore. The *Isis*, *Cornwallis* and two tenders, later joined by the *Liverpool*, kept up a steady cannonade, occasionally harassed by the American galleys. As in previous days, the weather seriously hampered the activities of both fleets.[29]

Much of the Commander-in-Chief's time was devoted to the

defense of the Delaware, as is manifest in his voluminous correspondence with those participating in its defense. As he advised the President of Congress on November 17, "Nothing in the Course of this Campaign, has taken up so much attention and consideration of myself and all the General Officers, as the possibility of giving a further relief to Fort Mifflin, than what we had already afforded." Desperate measures were necessary if the American position was to be maintained. Any over-all strategy which employed both the Continental army and the forces defending the river would jeopardize the containment of Howe in Philadelphia. One suggestion was to move the main army toward Philadelphia and feint an attack on the British lines north of the city. Howe's engineers had laid out a series of ten redoubts extending from the Delaware to the Schuylkill, with abatis linking each redoubt with the next one and supported by British artillery. This plan presupposed that Howe would be forced to withdraw a large part of the garrison in the redoubts facing Fort Mifflin. Then the garrison of the fort, with the fleet, could make a sortie and destroy the British works on Province and Carpenters' Islands. Washington rejected this proposal, as he was apprehensive that instead of a diversionary action it would bring on a general engagement—one he was not prepared for until reinforcements arrived from Gates. He was hopeful that the fort could hold out a few more days until the "arrival of Reinforcement from the Northward."

A minority of the generals on Washington's staff believed an assault on the British positions on Province and Carpenters' Islands would take the pressure off Fort Mifflin and make Howe's position in Philadelphia untenable. Anthony Wayne, the most articulate member, had volunteered to command the attacking force. He was outspoken in his criticism of the reluctance of the council of war to take the offensive, believing such councils vacillated and were productive of nothing. He stated, ". . . an over stretched caution, which is often times attended with as fatal Consequences; as to much rashness. . . ." Wayne continued, commenting on what to him were the most cogent reasons why such an undertaking was necessary. As frequently happened, the cautious council of war vetoed the overaggressive suggestions of the Wayne coterie.

Before accepting the council's decision, Washington decided

to send his most trusted general, Nathanael Greene, to reconnoiter the British position on the islands. Greene with Generals Wayne and Cadwalader, and Thomas Paine as volunteer aide, escorted by a troop of light horse, were to determine whether an attack would be successful. Greene wrote that all agreed that an effort must be made, but a difference of opinion existed as to the proper method of attack. Some of the party thought the project would be dangerous unless supported by the main army. Others believed a series of hit-and-run raids would force the enemy from their batteries. Washington decided that a force of at least fifteen hundred would be necessary to attack the British batteries on the near shore islands. With control of the bridges over the Schuylkill, the enemy could dispatch a sufficient force to get to the rear of a raiding party and cut off its retreat. The enemy could make this movement without seriously weakening their lines above the city. To cover the attacking party with the main Continental army would leave the entire countryside to the north and east of Philadelphia, including the main American storehouses at Easton, Bethlehem, and Reading, and the several Continental hospitals, an easy prey to the enemy.

In the meantime, writing to Varnum for the third time in less than twenty-four hours, Washington reaffirmed his desire that Fort Mifflin be held as long as possible; and that while Varnum had certain discretionary powers, he hoped his orders would be respected. Offering a counter proposal to an attack on the British from the main army, and emphasizing that his thoughts were only for consideration, he recommended a descent on Province Island. This would offer an opportunity to spike the British cannon and destroy their batteries. Volunteers and picked men should make up the force, which with assistance from the fleet, could seriously embarrass the enemy and gain valuable time for Washington. This suggestion reflects the desperate straits to which Washington was reduced; with the boisterous winds, high rough water, and firepower of the British guns, an assault from the river side was doomed to fail with heavy losses. Conversely, even with most of Fort Mifflin's guns on the channel side silenced and the defenses a shambles, the British were not willing to accept the losses involved in a frontal attack. All plans were made with one objective in mind, to hold Fort Mifflin and the river pass until winter set in. In the eighteenth century the river usually froze over in November, so a project which would gain a few days' grace might immobilize the British shipping until spring. This would force Howe to evacuate Philadelphia or face starvation for his army and the residents of the city.[30]

Fleury and Martin combine to present a vivid account of the constant efforts made to repair the various areas in the fortification. On the night of November 13—maybe he was using a wheelbarrow as a desk, it is known that he did use one on occasion—Fleury sat down to record in his diary the accomplishments of that night's work. The workmen labored under a bright moon which revealed their position to the British gunners, who kept up a steady fire most of the night. Disregarding the danger from shot and shell, the workmen applied themselves to the job at hand. They covered the western blockhouses with joists both on the inside and outside with the interstices filled with rammed earth (mud). Fleury had closed the breaches made by British shells in the palisades with planks, sentry boxes, and rafters, and then strengthened the ramparts with earth. Lamenting that again Varnum had not forwarded the promised axes, fascines, palisades, and gabions, he stated that it would be impossible to make ramparts of mud capable of resisting the shells of enemy thirty-two-pounders. The workmen, probably members of the garrison as well as any militia present, constantly tried to escape the watchful eyes of Fleury. Whenever they thought he might not be vigilant, they would sneak into the space under the wall to escape the cold and the shells. When the engineer noticed a considerable number of men missing, he would go to the entrance of the wall pen and call them out, belaboring each in turn with his cane.[31]

Meanwhile, the British were having their problems; Montresor was forced to employ a work party of one hundred to labor all night repairing the damages to the batteries. Suffering was widespread among the British troops. Provisions, clothing, and firewood were in short supply, in spite of the optimistic reports of the day before, when the four brigs and sloops arrived in the Schuylkill. Many horses had succumbed to the hard work in the heavy mud, the extremely cold weather, and no pasture or grain.[32]

Apparently Varnum visited the fort during the evening to

survey the damage and, upon return to Woodbury, dashed off a note to Washington at 4:30 A.M., November 14. Varnum wrote that the garrison had three killed and seven wounded on November 13, and that the river was so high and rough that it had been impossible to get supplies and workmen to the island during the night.

The battery under construction above Mantua Creek was near the mouth of Little Mantua Creek and Varnum expected it to be in operation, with three guns, on November 14. The British General Archibald Robertson, with a contingent of fifty men, left Billingsport on November 12 and "reconnoitered Manto Creek and a Battery the Rebels were Erecting about 800 yards from the mouth of it." Unforeseen delays would prevent the battery from engaging the enemy before November 15.[33]

A cold and cloudy day greeted Thayer on November 14, and as he looked out upon the channel he saw a British floating battery with two thirty-two-pounders about to join in the bombardment. Montresor laconically noted, "Our batteries continued as usual against Fort Island." Thayer ordered Fleury to raise a battery of two eighteen-pounders on the western side of the fort to counteract the fire power of the floating battery. These cannon were taken from the fort's main battery, which reduced the ordnance in that work to seven guns. The enemy's floating battery fired a few shots but received such a hot fire in return that the crew jumped overboard and waded ashore.[34]

Fleury, wounded and a victim of complete exhaustion, retained confidence that the fort could be defended. Beset with problems he believed were unnecessary, he unburdened himself to his journal on November 14. Smith, always contentious, was attempting to exercise command from Woodbury. He continued to throw roadblocks in the way of Fleury's efforts to improve or strengthen the defenses. Fleury candidly reports Smith transmitting orders to the garrison ". . . we want a Commanding Officer, ours is absent and forms projects at a distance. . . ." and later that night, "I repeat it, our Commanding Officer issues orders from Woodbury." It was well known that Smith was jealous of his rank and authority. However, all official orders and correspondence of the period name Thayer as in command at Fort Mifflin.

Certain questions are raised by Smith's conduct in attempting to command in absentia. Did Thayer, a major in Varnum's brigade, volunteer or was it suggested that he present himself for the command? Varnum originally planned to offer the command to Colonel Durkee, but this would have created a problem as he would outrank Smith; on the other hand, Thayer would be subordinate to the caustic Smith. Also, the real commander of the fort was still in Woodbury, and if the command was to be exercised from Varnum's headquarters, why not d'Arendt? Unquestionably a behind-the-scenes clash of personalities was present and certainly not to the best interest of the American cause.

Was Varnum capable of assuming the responsibilities of an independent command? Varnum may have questioned his own ability, as he asked for the assistance of a general officer whose superior standing would be advantageous. He also requested a commanding officer of artillery, as he expressed it not ". . . because I am not fond of commanding,—But more from a Consciousness that the Service demands it." [35]

Meanwhile, Fleury enumerated all the tools and materials needed to continue his improvement of the fort. He bemoaned the unnecessary weaknesses of Fort Mifflin and stressed its importance as the key to the river defense. He pointed out the need for reinforcements to defend a work so extensive, and the fact that additional ordnance was essential. The main battery had nineteen embrasures, but only seven cannons, and two of those were dismounted. Fleury had also come to appreciate the place of the State navy in the defense of the river.

His observation was that the fort's defense had been effective and that the main British battery was in no better condition than the fort's blockhouses. Commenting that the latter presented a pitiful sight, he planned to cover the lower story of each with fascines to make flanking works out of the blockhouses.

Concerned about the suffering of the men, Fleury described how the garrison had been neglected; as an example, no firewood had been received in the fort in seven days. He noted that the supply of cartridges was woefully deficient. Only those for eighteen-pounders were available.[36] Thayer joined his voice to that of Fleury and Varnum and requested a reinforcement of at least one hundred men.

Another longboat or barge deserted from the fleet and raised some concern that the deserters would reveal the condition of the fort. During the siege Lieutenant Samuel Lyon of the galley *Dickinson* and seven men went over to the British. Lieutenant Samuel Ford of the galley *Effingham* also deserted during this period. Both officers were subsequently retaken and tried for desertion, found guilty, and shot on board a guard boat on the Delaware in September 1778.

British shipping was patiently marking time waiting for the *Vigilant* and the *Fury* to make their way up the west channel. Lord Howe's strategy was basically the same as that of October 23. The *Vigilant*, in concert with the land batteries, was to deliver a massive bombardment on the western and least defensible side of the fort. The frigates were to warp through the lower chevaux-de-frise to constitute a diversionary factor in softening the fort for an assault by British troops. The weather had at last changed, and it appeared that a favorable wind would permit the *Vigilant* to move up to the southwest salient of the fort on November 15.

General Greene's party, on Carpenters' Island in the late afternoon of November 14, observed that the *Vigilant* was working her way up in back of Hog Island. Erroneously they reported that the armed ship came up without her guns. Greene wrote, ". . . by the best observation we could make her guns were taken out and follow'd her in a sloop." The American officers could see only the port side, which was ballasted, so made the natural mistake that she was without ordnance, whereas the cannon were all placed on the starboard side. The sloop following the *Vigilant* was the three-gun armed hulk *Fury*.[37]

Great concern continued in the councils of American officers in Varnum's command over the state of affairs on the river. Washington had received many gratuitous opinions on the feasibility of supporting or evacuating Fort Mifflin. On November 15, d'Arendt joined the parade of officers submitting recommendations to preserve the garrison and provide facilities to make nightly repairs of damages brought about by the daily cannonading. He suggested that the garrison use the area outside the lower stone wall for shelter, although it was badly damaged and sections had fallen. Only a handful of sentries and gunners should be exposed to the British artillerists. As a morale booster, d'Arendt said that men should not be required to serve in excess of forty-eight hours without relief. Armed militia detachments of one hundred men should be sent over each night for fatigue and work duty. D'Arendt vetoed a previous proposal to erect a battery on the wall, believing this would draw enemy fire on the men's shelter area. Instead, a battery should be placed on the river side to operate more effectively against the British ships. Only a few days' supply of ammunition and provisions should be kept on the island. Reserves should be stored on accommodation vessels to be available at a moment's notice. Finally, he said, the interruption of the nocturnal movements of the British boats in the channel must be the responsibility of the galleys.

Evidently, the many facets of this plan were worked out with Hazelwood, as d'Arendt refers to the Commodore several times in his communication. In one instance he states ". . . this is the opinion of the Commodore." He also added a postscript stating that several of his ideas had been communicated to Varnum and Smith.[38]

This proposal is another indication of the independent attitude adopted by the commanders of Fort Mifflin. Appointed by Washington, they consistently by-passed Varnum. They might consult with the brigade commander, but reported directly to the Commander-in-Chief. No such concern confronted Varnum with Greene and Thayer, who were members of his brigade. Greene did communicate with Washington before the arrival of Varnum on November 2. Varnum was forced to exercise forebearance under difficult conditions. He was not in an enviable position, especially with prima donnas of the ilk of Smith and d'Arendt. Washington always hoped that his officers would place the American cause above personal aggrandizement. The inner struggle between patriotism and ambition disturbed Smith, as he wrote to Varnum on November 11. "Tis true I fight for glory, but at the same time must study the general good." Perhaps a more aggressive Varnum might have demanded more respect for his authority.[39]

Hazelwood called a council of the navy captains on the galley *Chatham* on November 14, in response to a letter received from Washington, of the day previous, asking whether the river pass could be held if Fort Mifflin should fall to the British. He also wished to know whether the fleet could prevent the enemy from erecting works on the ruins of the fort.

The council was of the opinion that the navy could hold the

river and frustrate an attempt to breach the upper chevaux-de-frise, if the army could hold Fort Mercer and the batteries at Mantua Creek and opposite the chevaux-de-frise. They would not be able to control small boat traffic on the back channel near the Pennsylvania shore, but would check any movement in force by the British fleet. They reiterated their dependence on the army holding the New Jersey shore, otherwise the fleet would be cut off and destroyed. Anchorage and shelter for the boats and ships could be found in Timber Creek, from which the galleys could sally forth to intercept small sloops or boats that might come through the obstructions. The conclusions of the council of naval captains would, after the fall of Fort Mifflin, influence Washington to send several general officers to determine the feasibility of defending the east bank of the river.[40]

Dawn of November 15 was clear, but very cold and with strong westerly winds, a condition which would severely hamper the movement of the galleys. Thayer and Fleury had worked all night removing debris and making a few temporary repairs to a fortification almost beyond repair. Rest for the garrison was virtually impossible since the only place for sleep was on the slime which formed the floor of the fort. With heavy eyes the men watched the gradual encirclement of the fort by British land and sea forces. Every man in the garrison was fully conscious that no reinforcements would be forthcoming, that the fate of the garrison was in his hands. The troops with Varnum at Woodbury were physically incapable of relieving the Connecticut Continentals in Fort Mifflin— consisting only of detachments of Smith's command and the Virginia regiments. To have stripped the Rhode Island regiments in Fort Mercer would have been to court disaster. The British were again at Billingsport, and, with reconnaissance detachments constantly prowling the Mantua Creek area, Varnum could not afford to weaken the fort at Red Bank.

As the first streaks of dawn came up over the tops of the trees along the New Jersey shore, the enemy batteries began a vigorous shelling of the ruins that had once been Fort Mifflin. The garrison, except for a few sentries and the artillerists, sought shelter under the fragment of the stone wall. The main British squadron sailed upriver and took station according to their plan to place the fort in a cross fire, and attempt to divert the galleys

Attack on Fort Mifflin, November 10, 1777. The artist shows an exchange of broadsides between the British fleet and the Pennsylvania galleys, with Fort Mifflin dimly seen at the right. This is a fanciful portrayal of the action, as the galleys were incapable of delivering a broadside; their only heavy armament was one cannon in the bow. Watercolor attributed to Charles T. or Alfred Warren. *Courtesy Mariners Museum, Newport News, Virginia.*

and floating batteries from coming to the defense of the fort. The *Isis* took station abreast of the fort about six hundred yards off the southeast salient of the main battery; the *Somerset* took position near the upper end of the sand bar, with the *Pearl* and *Liverpool* off the battery near Mantua Creek. This battery of three guns (some accounts say two) opposite the upper chevaux-de-frise on the property of Tench Francis went into operation on this day, although for some inexplicable reason Varnum advised Washington on November 16 that it would go into operation that day. All accounts, British and American, including another letter of Varnum's have the battery engaging the British fleet on November 15. Later the *Roebuck* joined the *Isis*, and the galley *Cornwallis* moved into position near the *Pearl* and *Liverpool*.[41]

At eleven o'clock the *Vigilant* and *Fury* warped up back of Hog Island and took position off the southwest salient of the fort. Eyewitnesses said they were anchored so close to the works that marines in the crow's-nest threw hand grenades into the works. They were stationed off the fort's most vulnerable side which had only two embrasures for cannon. A thirty-two pounder was in position and an eighteen-pounder would soon be wheeled into place at the other embrasure. Both cannon opened fire before the British could bring their guns to bear on the fort, striking the *Vigilant* several times; some say at least fourteen shells hit the armed ship. After the British were in position, they delivered several broadsides, each successive round of cannonading causing great destruction to the parapet, battery, and cannon. The topmasts of the armed ship were occupied by about forty riflemen, marines from the frigates, who poured an incessant musketry fire on the garrison, killing and wounding many of the gunners and driving the rest from the platforms. When the artillerists returned to their stations, they were caught in a devastating cross fire from the land batteries. In addition, they soon discovered that their supply of powder and cartridges was almost exhausted.

This section of the fort, the main or water battery, was in command of Captain Lee, who also took personal command of the two guns on the right of the battery. His lieutenant commanded the center and Captain Dickinson the two guns on the left. Fleury was assigned the best marksmen in the garrison to attempt to dislodge the enemy sharpshooters from the tops of the *Vigilant*. Major Talbot (later Commodore Silas Talbot of the United States Navy) was assigned the inner work, to command the last-ditch defense in the event of a storm by British troops.[42]

Varnum, probably on the authority of Thayer, reported that during one twenty-minute period more than 1,030 twelve- to thirty-two-pounder cannon shots were discharged. Nothing like this bombardment had ever been seen in America. Philadelphia residents, said it sounded like one constant roll of thunder.[43]

About eleven o'clock the ammunition was almost exhausted, and the gunners could only sporadically answer the British fleet or land batteries. Mercilessly the shot and shell rained down on the defenseless garrison. So desperate was the situation that Fleury, assisted by the commissary and other volunteers, began a frantic search of the magazine for cartridges. Their efforts uncovered one thirty-two-pounder and several eighteen-pounder cartridges. If used sparingly, they would postpone the inevitable for an hour or two.[44]

The brave and resolute Thayer believed that the fort must fall and, wishing to retire with the fewest casualties possible, ordered the flag lowered preparatory to hoisting the distress signal. Fleury and Lee hastened to entreat Thayer to reconsider, and informed him they had found a few cartridges. Observing that momentarily the Americans had lowered their flag, the British slackened their fire, believing the fort was about to surrender. Their elation was quickly dispelled as the flag was again raised. Due in part to frustration and disappointment, they opened fire with increased intensity, determined to subdue the garrison of Fort Mifflin. In an effort to deceive the enemy, Fleury and Lee suggested sending boats to Fort Mercer on the pretense that it was a routine mission for supplies.[45]

The small windfall of cartridges was soon gone and by one o'clock the ammunition was exhausted, although an occasional cartridge was found throughout the afternoon. Even if adequate supplies of powder and cartridges had been available, only two cannon remained capable of being fired. The fort was a shambles, a sloop (probably what the British later described as a scow sunk with ten eight-pounders removed from the demolished blockhouses) was badly damaged and sinking, and the banks and palisades were leveled. Enemy troops were seen assembling, ready to embark on the Pennsylvania shore, and a storm was momentarily expected.[46]

Thayer, the realist, called a council of war at two o'clock. Attending the council were Talbot, Fleury, Lee, Dickinson, and an anonymous Connecticut captain of infantry. The council resolved that they must either have *supplies of ammunition or boats*. The garrison's officers were brave and resolute, and, at this juncture of the siege, somewhat foolhardy. With only two cannon serviceable, ammunition obviously could not save the fort. Evacuation was inevitable and could not be delayed beyond nightfall. One hour after this council, the galleys would make their eventful appearance on the western side of Fort Island, only to face the same devastating fire that had leveled the fort.[47]

Enemy fire continued and by mid-afternoon the stone wall was half demolished. The air was filled with splinters from the block-houses. As Fleury and Lee were standing in the fort, a flying timber struck them, knocking the former unconscious and killing the latter. Talbot, running to their assistance, was wounded in the thigh and arm with grapeshot.[48]

Between two and three o'clock on the afternoon of November 15, Thayer asked Hazelwood for assistance in driving the *Vigilant* downstream. The Commodore, with twelve galleys and two floating batteries, had been engaged with the British frigates since eleven o'clock. Before going into action, he augmented his galley crews with men borrowed from Captain Robinson and the Continental ships. Assisted by the battery on the New Jersey shore, a severe cannonading had been carried on for over three hours. He ordered six galleys to warp around the north end of Fort Island to engage the *Vigilant* and *Fury*. He continued the attack on the frigates with the remaining six galleys and two floating batteries, although he later dispatched one of the latter to assist the galleys fighting the *Vigilant*.[49]

As the galleys warped around the island and entered the back channel, they were subjected to a severe cannonading from the batteries on Province Island and a floating battery near the hospital wharf. Damage was extensive and several men were killed. A hasty council was held and, as there was no prospect of support from the fort, the captains decided to retire. As Hazelwood described the action to Wharton: "Six Battery's playing on us from the shore to Westward besides two nine inch mortars, & two floating Batterys, & Seven Ships, & two of these [their] Galleys that with their shot from their batterys & ships, the River was cover'd with shot on all sides of us and cross Fire in such a manner I was surprised the Fleet never gave way." Without support, six small galleys with one cannon each could not be expected to face an armed ship, from which one well-directed broadside could have blown them out of the water. Also, while confronting the *Vigilant*, they were at the mercy of the land batteries. Hazelwood had dispatched a floating battery to aid the galleys, and as the battery warped around the island, her warps and lines were shot away and she was forced to retire. Seeing the floating battery coming to their assistance, the galleys made one final attempt to board the *Vigilant*, but, receiving additional damage and casualties, retired. In the meantime, Hazelwood received a note from Thayer requesting that he concentrate on the frigates and attempt to drive them below the chevaux-de-frise. Although buffeted severely by strong winds, the galleys were able to warp to the east side of the island and join the rest of the fleet engaged with the frigates. Thayer, in his memoirs, noted that the galleys made two unsuccessful attempts to attack the *Vigilant*.[50]

Admiral Howe came up the back channel that morning and landed on Province Island. From his vantage point near the main battery, he directed the attack on the fort. One British report called the cannonade the "severest . . . perhaps ever heard." Nothing could have long withstood the rain of shot and shell which fell on the fort. Varying times have been mentioned when the British fire slackened. Some British officers thought it lasted almost twenty-four hours; Morton observed that the fire was heavy until six o'clock; Fleury notes that "Fire continued until night"; and the gentleman on board the *Speedwell* wrote, ". . . cannonade . . . continued till evening." After all other artillery-fire had ceased, the *Vigilant* kept up a steady cannonading all evening. This was done to mask the preparations under way on Province Island for a storm of the island fort the next morning. With the fort cannon silenced, the action had become somewhat one-sided, except for the engagement between the State navy and the battery on the New Jersey shore with the British fleet.[51]

The British fleet called off the action about five o'clock and dropped downstream below Billingsport. Several of the frigates had suffered considerable damage and their official returns reported twenty-five seamen killed or wounded. Almost simultaneously with the withdrawal of the fleet, the land batteries had become silent. It was obvious that the fort was indefensible and further cannonading, except from the *Vigilant,* would only result in useless slaughter. The fort was theirs. The only question was when. It was "all tore to pieces, having scarce a stockade standing, the blockhouses almost beat down, and every gun dismounted or broken." In addition, the south section of the stone wall was virtually leveled. As observed by Benjamin Rush, this was where the garrison was forced to take refuge, "the cover of the stone wall (built by Mr. Galloway) on wet ground without fires or any covering other than a blanket." Sections of the wall on the river side were breached or shattered.[52]

Early in the evening Varnum dispatched "Ferry boats . . . instead of Reinforcement." Thayer was given the discretionary authority to determine when the fort should be evacuated. Surveying his exhausted troops (all artillery men were either dead or wounded), the fort's ordnance silenced and without ammunition, he realized that to postpone the inevitable would merely be an unnecessary sacrifice of life. Varnum had not sent supplies or ammunition, so that the discretionary power granted Thayer was a mockery—even the feeblest of resistance was impossible. He therefore decided to abandon the works, and loaded the boats with what remained of the arms (probably small arms), ammunition and provisions, and the entire garrison, except for forty picked men, and sent them over to Fort Mercer. They reached the New Jersey fort about seven o'clock and for the first time in several days were able to find rest and refreshment on dry land.[53]

Thayer and his small detachment wasted no time in spiking the cannon, destroying the carriages and setting fire to what remained of the barracks. Many gallant defenses in the annals of American arms have received more attention from historians; but none was more valiant than that of the men of the army and navy who resisted the might of the British army and navy for eight weeks in the fall of 1777. Observers in the British fleet mention seeing the fort in flames between midnight and one o'clock, although Montresor records the time as eleven-thirty. It was probably shortly after eleven-thirty, as Fleury recorded that they abandoned the fort at that time. Angell, writing two years later, said Thayer arrived at Fort Mercer about midnight.[54]

As the last troops were evacuating, Fleury thought he heard the oars of an approaching landing party. However, he was probably mistaken, because with normal British caution, no storm of the fort was contemplated before daylight. Why make a sortie that would involve unnecessary casualties when the fort was theirs for the taking the next morning? At seven-thirty on the morning of the 16th, sailors, probably from the *Vigilant*, landed on Fort Island, lowered the American flag, and hoisted British colors. Sir George Osborne had been charged with carrying the fort by storm on the morning of the 16th if any resistance were evident. At nine o'clock Osborne, with his aides, accompanied by Montresor and the detachment assigned to take the island, embarked in eight flat-bottomed boats. A force of 280 rank and file with engineers, and a company of carpenters carrying fascines, scaling ladders, a flying bridge, and other materials needed to build a battery for four thirty-two-pounders, landed on the island. The battery was to prevent the American galleys from interfering with the removal of the upper chevaux-de-frise.[55]

The attempt by six galleys to attack the *Vigilant* elicited the most caustic denunciation of the State navy and it's Commodore. Varnum, Smith, and Chaplain David, of the Rhode Island regiments, claimed that the senior captain of the galleys retired without making any effort to relieve the fort, but they admitted several men were killed on the galleys. They attributed the loss of the fort to this one incident in the siege. Varnum and Smith's allegations were the most damaging to the fleet's reputation. Varnum's letter to Washington, on November 16, became the official report and accused the galleys and their Commodore of want of resolution. He wrote, "The Commodore gave positive Orders to six Gallies to attack and take the ship. They warp'd over to the Island, & there held a Council, lost a few of their men & then returned without attempting any Thing." Adding a postscript he said "Col⁰ Greene offered to Officer and Man three

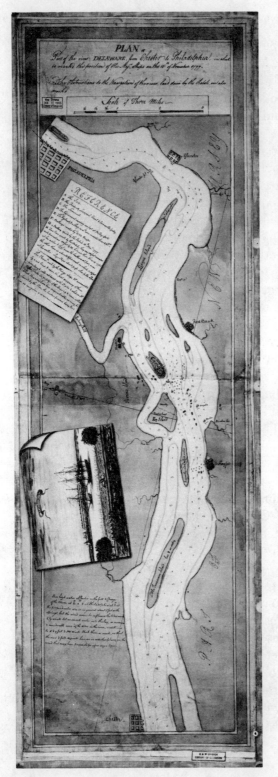

"A Plan of Part of the river Delaware from Chester to Philadelphia in which is marked the position of His Majesty's Ships on the 15th of November 1777." Prepared by John Hunter in 1781. *Howe Collection, Geography and Map Division, Library of Congress.*

Gallies, that would destroy the Empress of Russia, or perish to a Man. Capt. Robinson, of the Continental Fleet, offered to go himself & the Commodore proposes a fine Disposition, but cannot command his Fleet." His words were echoed by David, who said that Greene volunteered to man the galleys, as his men were trained to obey. Curiously, Greene made no mention of this episode in his letter to General Potter on the night of November 15, nor in his letter to Washington of November 17. His only reference to the fleet was "Our Shipping have kept up a warm Fire, and a two Gun Battery about 2½ miles from this has annoyed the Enemy very much. . . ." Smith added his usual vitriolic comments that the fort would not have fallen if the galleys had not lacked courage and resolution. When Varnum's communique reached headquarters, John Laurens wrote to his father (President of Congress), "I hate to blame without sure grounds; but as far as I can judge at this distance, the naval department has been deficient in its duty. The Commodore is brave, but he has no command." Such sentiments expressed by Continental officers caused opprobrium to be heaped on the navy, and subsequently these sentiments were picked up and repeated by historians.[56]

Hazelwood would naturally reject any suggestion that his captains relinquish their commands to army volunteers. It was not a question of resolution on the part of his captains, but the ability of the galleys to withstand the full force of the British artillery and naval cannon fire without support from the fort or army. In addition, the strong westerly winds made it difficult to maneuver in the back channel. The State navy had nothing to do with the fact that the fort had not been furnished with an adequate supply of powder and cartridges. No competent observer could have expected the fort, a complete shambles by one o'clock, to be capable of a successful defense. When the six galleys entered the back channel they were on their own, against the entire enemy force. Their total ordnance was one cannon in each bow and a few swivels. If they had proceeded down the channel, they would have been subject to an enfilade fire from the batteries, with no way of replying. Facing an armed ship and a hulk with three times their fire power, the wonder isn't that they made two efforts to attack the *Vigilant*, but that they entered the channel at all!

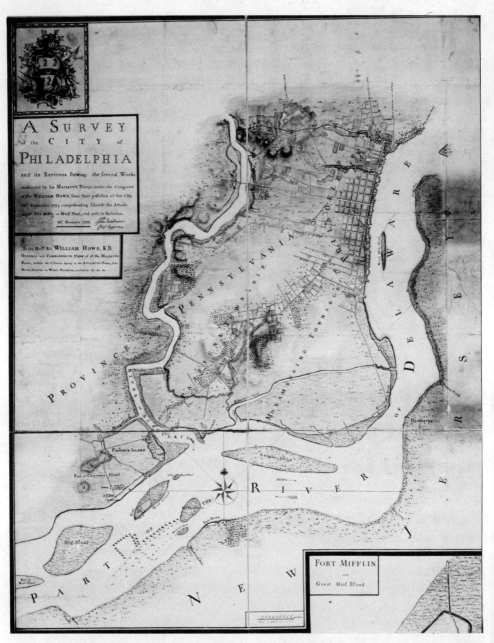

"A Survey of the City of Philadelphia and its Environs shewing the several Works constructed by His Majesty's Troops, under the Command of Sir William Howe, since their possession of that City 26th September, 1777, comprehending likewise the Attacks against Fort Mifflin on Mud Island, and until it's Reduction, 16th November 1777." Signed by John Montresor, Chief Engineer. Insets of this map are shown separately and are especially interesting for a profile view of Fort Mifflin and certain of the barracks and blockhouses. *Geography and Map Division, Library of Congress.*

When General Samuel Cleaveland entered the fort on November 16 to catalogue the ordnance and shot left by the garrison, he found a surprisingly large quantity of shot but no cartridges. Fleury had bemoaned the paucity of heavy ordnance, with nineteen embrasures in the main battery but only nine cannon available. Of these guns, two eighteen-pounders were moved on November 14 for installation in a counter battery to be raised on the western embankment, to oppose two British floating batteries each carrying two thirty-two-pounders. Remaining were two eighteen-pounders on the left of the main battery, a thirty-two-pounder in the center facing downriver. Of the four in the main battery, two were dismounted, leaving the works virtually defenseless to the fire of the frigates. Inability to oppose the cannonading from the British fleet was what prompted Thayer to request a concentration of the galleys on the east side of the fort near the chevaux-de-frise.

The ten cannon found in the scow sunk near the wharf on the east side of the island were eight-pounders used in the blockhouses. Cleaveland's return confirms that they were on garrison carriages and therefore must have been of this caliber. If they had been heavier ordnance, Thayer would have mounted them in the embrasures of the main battery. With the fourteen eight-pounders found in the fort, a total of twenty-four were accounted for, which suggests that each blockhouse was equipped with eight of these cannon. An unusually heavy concentration of the fort's ordnance seems to have been mounted in the easily destructible blockhouses.

Sufficient shot was available but no powder or cartridges, and there was a deplorable lack of heavy ordnance. Further, inattention to details of supply is observed in the statistic of 1,475 twenty-four-pounder round shot, when only one cannon of that caliber was in the fort. If Fort Mifflin was the keystone for the river defense, who was derelict in failing to provide adequate ordnance, cartridges, and other matériel? Correspondence of Varnum and Smith to Washington offer many suggestions to abandon the fort, or at least remove the heavy ordnance and merely engage in a delaying action before evacuating the works. Vacillation and indecision characterized the defense. Varnum, responsible for the on-the-spot tactics for river defense, seems always to have waited for direction from headquarters.

Camp stove, cannonballs, bar and grapeshot found at Fort Mercer during excavations for the battle monument in 1905. The bog-iron stove, made at Batsto, is believed to be the only one of its kind in existence. It has elaborate scrollwork, with the letters "Batsto," it is twenty-four inches high, and thirteen and one-half inches wide. These stoves were not made after the first third of the 19th century, but were common during the Revolution. Owned and exhibited by Gloucester County Historical Society, Woodbury, N.J. *Photo by E. B. Fisler.*

The over-all strategy of the campaign for containing the British was of course the responsibility of Washington. However, decisions to make certain specific areas more tactically capable of defense rested with the individual field commanders. If manpower and supplies were in short supply, or not available from the main army, then a plan should have been formulated for the withdrawal or abandonment of a position no longer defensible. Under the most favorable conditions, Fort Mifflin would probably have succumbed to British power in a few days, but to place the blame for failure of November 15 on the shoulders of the navy is absurd.[57]

Those castigators were shifting the blame to cover their own deficiencies and ignoring the reality of the situation. Varnum and Smith, instead of placing the responsibility for the fall of the fort on one act of the galleys on the afternoon of November 15, might have referred to their own prophecies of doom. On November 11 Varnum wrote Washington, "I expect we shall cause an evacuation this Night." Later the same day he reported, "I am this moment returned from Fort Mifflin.—Every Defense is almost destroyed . . . cannot hold out more than two days." Also on the 11th, Smith wrote to Varnum, "By tomorrow night everything will be levelled. . . . If you should be of my opinion [to evacuate] send boats . . . to get over the cannon and before day take off the men." Smith suggested that a temporary force of fifty men could keep up the appearance of defense. The next day Smith wrote to Washington, "All guns in Block Houses are render'd unfit . . . the Houses almost destroyed. . . . We shall perhaps be able to keep the fort three days in which time it will be levell'd to the Ground." In a reversal of mood on November 14, Varnum dashed a note to Washington saying the fort was defensible until the Commander-in-Chief sent a second relief of five hundred troops—something Varnum knew Washington did not contemplate. At dusk on the 15th he noted, "We shall be obliged to evacuate the Fort this Night." Also on this date, Smith advised Washington that "It [Fort Mifflin] is now one Heap of Ruins & must be defended with musketry in Case of Storm. With six hundred Men *I think we could defend it as an Island.* (Italics are the author's.) Our great dependence must be Their being afraid to storm." Both officers were obviously aware of the hopelessness of defending Fort Mifflin. Individually, most of the defenders had conducted themselves bravely, but the odds were insurmountable and the inevitable came to pass after eight heroic weeks.[58]

Varnum, a courageous and dedicated officer, served with distinction during the war. However, his correspondence indicates a certain lack of decision and poor judgment. Unsure of his own ability as a commander, he succumbed to the charm of Smith and accepted his evaluation of the navy. The appointment of Major Thayer made possible a magnificent defense of the fort. Varnum's selection as commander of this post is only another indication of the difficulties besetting Washington. He had many brave and patriotic general officers, but few capable of exercising independent judgment. With half of Varnum's brigade already garrisoning Fort Mercer, he was the logical brigadier to command the river defenses.

In addition to Greene, there were two participants who did not criticize Hazelwood or the navy. Fleury, who had occasionally in times of stress questioned the navy giving so much attention to the British frigates, did not mention the fleet in his journal for November 15. In fact, he was to be associated with the Commodore in a scheme to destroy British shipping. Thayer's memoirs recorded that the galleys made two unsuccessful attempts to attack the *Vigilant*. It would appear that those most involved in the fort's defense considered the failure of the galleys to destroy or drive the *Vigilant* from her position to be just another disappointment in the uneven struggle.[59]

Washington was slow to condemn, while awaiting an inquiry into the conduct of the galley captains. Hazelwood was unaware of the official complaint until advised on November 17 by President Wharton of the Supreme Executive Council. Hazelwood called the accused galley captain and started an investigation to determine the degree of fault. He was satisfied that the captain (unfortunately it is impossible to determine the name of the man) had exercised good judgment and was blameless, a fact confirmed when he reviewed the extensive damage to the galleys.[60]

Hazelwood was incensed at the unjust accusations, citing that all galleys, except one, had been badly shattered by shot; in fact, on December 1 two were still on shore at Bristol being repaired of damages received in the actions of November 15. The fleet had lost thirty-eight men killed and wounded on that date, with a ratio of over two killed to one wounded. Thus, almost 10 percent of those engaged on the galleys and floating batteries were casualties.[61]

A little-known incident occurred, probably on November 15 or shortly thereafter, at Fort Mercer, which throws some light on the deep-rooted and unremitting hatred Smith held toward Hazelwood. Our only authority for the confrontation is found in Hazelwood's letter of February 8, 1778, to Wharton:

I have been informed by Capt. Blewer & some others That a Col° Smith, who was in Fort Mifflin for some time, has made free with my character, which surprizes me much. He received some hurt in his arm in the Fort, came over to Red Bank, & another officer sent to take the command at the Fort in his place. One day Gen¹ Varnom sent for me on shore to meet him at Col. Green's, at Red Bank Fort. I went, & after doing my business with him, Col. Smith mention'd something to me about the Galleys that I knew to be false. I told him he was a lying scoundrel, with that he made a stroke at me, & nothing prevented me for treating him as he deserved but Gen¹ Vernom constantly begging me to make the matter up, & even brought him on board the Province Sloop one night after dark, where part of our board was present, & insisted that we should be friends. After a great deal of persuasions of both sides, the matter was settled; we drank together & parted friends. I heard no more of it until lately, but I cannot find any person who heard him say it, or I should call him to a proper account for it.[62]

What was specifically said, or the degree of guilt, is impossible to determine. Smith was noted for his differences with numerous officers, but this is the first evidence of such disagreements almost turning to violence. His quick temper, according to Wallace, involved him in at least two duels. Smith's son offers some insight into the fact that his father had not accepted the mediation of Varnum:

Colonel Smith always held the Commodore in great contempt thinking that he did not discharge his duty with becoming zeal. They had several animated altercations, during the siege; and after the evacuation of the Fort, the Colonel refused to return his salutation in the streets of Philadelphia. Colonel Smith was walking with Colonel N. Rogers of Maryland when this insult was offered. And so gross was the insult, that Colonel Rogers expected, confidently, that Colonel Smith would be challenged the next day, and so told his son, my friend, L. N. Rogers, who communicated it to me.

No matter who was at fault, the American cause would suffer from such conduct on the part of its officers.[63]

No criticism was leveled at Hazelwood by his superiors. The Navy Board, headed by Bradford and Blewer, ardently defended the Commodore and the fleet, conscious as they were of the limitations of the galleys, and the weaknesses inherent in the officers and crews. All captains were not of equal ability; while the majority were resolute and brave and brought honor to the fleet, a few were weak and required constant direction. The greatest recalcitrance was noted among the guard-boat and fire-ship captains. Some were, according to Bradford "good for Little." These were never stationed in a position of trust or responsibility. The board was satisfied that for eight weeks the Commodore and his little fleet had performed in a courageous manner and made a substantial contribution to the defense of the river. In fact, the Continental Congress had twice cited the fleet and its Commodore for conspicuous bravery under fire.

The Supreme Executive Council considered Hazelwood's inquiry and subsequent explanation of events to be satisfactory, and Wharton advised him on December 20:

I greatly lament the Situation the Fleet had been reduced to, I know every exertion in your power has been made to render it serviceable to your Country, and I am now well convinced, from many Circumstances, that both Officers and Men, in Many of the Boats, merit praise, rather than deserve Censure—the reproaches of some has proceeded, I dare say, from Ignorance of the Orders given, or want of knowledge of their circumstances; and of Others from a desire to throw the blame from off their own shoulders on to those of others. When I wrote you from Head Quarters it was in consequence of a Letter shown to me by his Excell^y. from Gen. Varnum, wherein some reflections were cast on some of the Boats as not obeying your signals, it was proper you should be made acquainted with that Gentlemans opinion of them, in order that if he was mistaken, you might have an opport^y to say so; if otherwise that the proper punishment might be inflicted on the delinquents. Your letter to me, which was read in Council, has satisfied them that the Officers and Men of your Fleet, generally, have behaved with a Spirit and Vigor that does them great Honor, and that the thanks of the Country is due to their services. And the Council desire you will in our name thank them accordingly in the most respectful terms. There are others, it is too true, who have disgraced the American Arms, but it would be hard that the brave & Virtuous should bear the Infamy of the base Conduct of Cowards and Traitors.[64]

Criticism of the State navy ranged from charges of dereliction of duty and wholesale desertion to hints of cowardice on the part of some officers. The critics forgot that the failures of the navy were not peculiar to the fleet. Many of the comments resulted from a difference of opinion between army officers and Commodore Hazelwood on the proper use of the shallow-draught boats and their sphere of effectiveness. The galley was the most effective of the boats, and was designed primarily for patrol duty. In case of combat, its most profitable use was at night. An earlier historian remarked that they were effective against larger vessels, temporarily aground, at which time they could attack the bow and stern, causing considerable damage. The galleys gained such an advantage against the *Roebuck* in May 1776 and again in October 1777, when the *Augusta* was aground. State authorities, not the galley captains, had repeatedly warned Continental officers that the galleys were in danger of capsizing in rough water. With these limitations, the navy would be involved in the actions of November 15 and be cast in the role of scapegoat by Varnum.[65]

Varnum and Hazelwood were confronted with enemies that neither guns nor ammunition could fight—fatigue and virtual nakedness. The troops commanded by Smith had been exposed to the ooze and cold of Fort Mifflin for over six weeks and were anxious to return to the main camp of the Continental army to recuperate. Half of Varnum's brigade had been badly mauled, the two Connecticut regiments had suffered many casualties the last four days of the siege and especially on the fifteenth. Greene's garrison in Fort Mercer were the only troops in physical condition to assume an offensive posture, and Varnum never considered withdrawing any detachments from that post. The garrison of 565 included 211 of Greene's regiment, 215 of Angell's regiment, sixty-five New Jersey militia from General Forman's brigade and a train of artillery of seventy-four officers and men. The fleet, composed of seamen from the State and Continental vessels and Continental troops on loan, was equally exhausted and in need of clothing, provisions, and rest. In addition, a number of the galleys and the two floating batteries were in need of immediate repairs.[66]

Confused but conscious of the importance of defending the river and retaining control of Fort Mercer, Washington on the 17th ordered three of his major generals to the fort. Arthur St. Clair, Baron Johann de Kalb, and Henry Knox were instructed

The destruction of the Continental and Pennsylvania ships and floating batteries attempting to pass Philadelphia during the night of November 20, 1777. In the foreground is the frigate *Delaware*, captured from the Americans on September 27. Watercolor attributed to Charles T. or Alfred Warren. *Courtesy Mariners Museum, Newport News, Virginia.*

to consult with Varnum, Hazelwood, and other officers of the garrison who could contribute to a defense of the river. He was disappointed, perplexed, and in a measure irritated with the immaturity manifest in certain areas of the river command. With reinforcements arriving from the north and his patience exhausted, Washington would soon come to the conclusion that he must send additional troops to New Jersey and appoint a new commander.

The three generals were instructed to determine whether the chevaux-de-frise could be protected without the Americans having possession of Fort Mifflin, and ascertain what, if anything, the main army could do to assist. Could Hazelwood remain at his anchorage if the British established batteries on Mud Island, or if Varnum's brigade was forced to evacuate the batteries and Fort Mercer? Latitude was granted the generals to explore the western channel, and could a hulk or other obstruction be sunk to block the channel between Mud and Province Islands? If it was decided to abandon the area, an effective withdrawal plan should be designed to ensure the safety of the garrison at Fort Mercer. Latitude was granted the generals to explore any phase of the Delaware River's defense they considered pertinent to containing the British army in their present lines, or the British fleet below the chevaux-de-frise.[67]

Arriving at the fort, the generals called a council and after several sessions with the officers, issued a report on their deliberations at 9:30 P.M. on November 18: It was the unanimous opinion of Hazelwood, Robinson, and their captains that the fleet could be of little service if the British were permitted to fortify Fort Island. The generals recommended that the Commodore attempt to pass up the river with the first favorable wind, and try to destroy the frigate *Delaware* with the fire ships as they passed Philadelphia.[68]

Hazelwood offered a different version, maintaining that if the New Jersey posts could be held and reinforced, the navy could hold the pass. But the generals were quoted as saying this was impossible as reinforcements could not reach the area before the British moved up from Billingsport. Intelligence had alerted the officers that Cornwallis had crossed the Schuylkill with about two thousand troops marching for Chester on the evening of the 17th. Then crossing to Billingsport he was joined by Sir Thomas Wilson with an additional three or four thousand, making a force of approximately 5,500 troops.

A study of contemporary accounts and of Clinton's attack on Forts Clinton and Montgomery on the Hudson River on October 6 (most of the regiments with Wilson were in these attacks), permit a reasonable reconstruction of the components of the British army Wilson brought to Billingsport. He was accompanied by the 26th, 27th, and 63rd Regiments, the 17th Light Dragoons, 7th Royal Fusiliers and two battalions of Anspach Grenadiers. Robertson wrote that Wilson's force also included three hundred Jägers, five hundred convalescents and recruits, and seventy guards, but omits any reference to the 27th Regiment. Cornwallis with a slightly smaller force included the 5th, 15th, 33rd, 45th and 56th British Regiments, 1st Light Infantry, a draft of guards and some Hessian Jägers, with twelve cannon and several howitzers. The inclusion of artillery caused an alarm at Varnum's headquarters, as it became obvious that Cornwallis did not contemplate a storm of Fort Mercer, but rather was planning a siege.[69]

Receiving the generals' decision, Hazelwood and Robinson met with Greene and his staff to define the strategy of the fleet and fort. They returned to the fleet and were alarmed early on the morning of November 19, when an officer of the fleet came on board the flagship and reported that the garrison was planning to withdraw, thus exposing the fleet to a land attack from the east. It was decided to move the fleet up to Ladd's Cove, the mouth of Big Timber Creek a short distance above the fort, and await a favorable wind before attempting to proceed upriver.[70]

Shortly after the fleet came to anchor in the cove, Hazelwood and Robinson called a council of the naval captains on board the *Speedwell*. It was unanimously agreed that an attempt should be made the next morning, the 20th, before dawn to pass the fleet up the river. Separated into two squadrons, the Continental ships and the larger units of the State navy would be compelled to take the main channel and sail close to the British batteries and the frigate *Delaware*. Each ship and boat in this flotilla was to be prepared with combustible materials, so that if the wind was unfavorable or a ship was damaged by enemy action, any one or all were to be set on fire and abandoned. The galleys and smaller vessels were to take the eastern channel, hugging the Jersey shore until past Cooper's Ferry, and the galleys were similarly prepared for destruction.[71]

The winds were not favorable to a passage of the larger ships. Seeking some protection for the ships which were becalmed in Ladd's Cove, Hazelwood and Robinson went ashore to confer with Varnum but found the latter had withdrawn to Haddonfield. At three o'clock on the morning of the 20th, Hazelwood ordered the thirteen galleys and nine guard boats upriver. Taking advantage of what little southerly wind prevailed, and riding the incoming tide, they diligently plied their oars, closely hugging the eastern shore, and arrived at Bristol at ten in the morning without molestation by the British.

After seeing the galleys off, Hazelwood made plans for the balance of the fleet to follow. His attention was called to the accumulation of ordnance and stores at Ladd's Cove and on the Continental ships. Unless immediate provision was made to move these supplies to a place of safety, they would fall into the enemy's hands. Borrowing a horse, he hastened to Bristol, intending to obtain wagons and, if necessary, return some of the galleys to Ladd's Cove to move the stores to Bristol. Arriving late at night, he decided to wait until daybreak before forwarding the wagons or galleys. Unfortunately, the turn of events would prevent the rescue of the stores.

In the meantime, Robinson had seen Varnum, who would offer no protection until the fleet was well above the city near Rancocas Creek. Even at this time, Varnum apparently had made up his mind to retreat to Mount Holly. The fleet would have to pass the city or fall into the hands of the enemy; in accordance with his agreement with Hazelwood, Robinson issued orders for the balance of the fleet to proceed up the river that night (November 20). Unlike the previous night, the boats were spotted by the British as they passed the northern section of the city. Opening a heavy fire, the enemy artillerists drove two small sloops on shore, where one was captured and the other set on fire by its crew. One schooner, four sloops, and the brig *Convention* safely passed the city. Two shallops and a few guard boats remained in the cove to transfer stores to wagons. At least three of the guard boats later succeeded in reaching Bristol. The remainder of the fleet, consisting of the Continental

ships, the State armed ship *Montgomery*, and two floating batteries, were destroyed according to plan.[72]

Before the arrival of Hazelwood at Bristol, the galleys had
been employed in ferrying the Continental troops from Bristol
to Burlington. General Greene made a mild complaint about the
management of the boats and scows at Burlington. He was not
referring to the galleys, but to the undisciplined crews of the
Durham boats brought down from Coryell's Ferry by the Continental Navy Board.[73]

The reports that reached Fort Mercer had caused great concern to Varnum and Greene. Varnum was apprehensive of being
trapped between Mantua and Big Timber Creeks. He advised
Washington that Greene would write and describe the attitudes
and viewpoints of the garrison officers on the situation at Fort
Mercer. In passing, Varnum could not refrain from making a
sarcastic reference to the navy: "Was our Fleet to continue under
the Cover of this place, the Enemy's Shipping would be in a
worse Situation; but as they seem to be on the Wing, the
enemy will soon be able to open Bomb Batteries from Fort
Mifflin." Again he seems to have chosen to ignore the requirements of the fleet. At this time the fleet was anchored in Ladd's
Cove, and Hazelwood was making temporary repairs to the
galleys. The enemy's battery had been safely ensconced behind
the stone wall on the 16th, before repairs to the galleys were
completed. The Commodore and Robinson were also anxious
to know what Varnum's plans were but had had singularly bad
luck in their attempts to locate the general.[74]

Greene submitted the consensus of the garrison's officers on
the ability to defend the fort—that it was safe from storm, but
could not hold out against a heavy artillery attack. The cramped
quarters of the fort made it impossible to house more than
one-third of the garrison in tents. The bomb-proof magazine
and a new partly constructed breastwork on the river side had
drastically reduced the available space on the floor of the fort.
A previous proposal to build a bomb-proof shelter for the garrison in the bank was no longer feasible since the fall of Fort
Mifflin. Greene, by inference, advised Washington that Fort
Mercer was indefensible unless a strong force of Continentals
could contain any British army should it land in New Jersey.[75]

By November 19, Cornwallis was probing the area around

Mantua Creek. Later in the day considerable skirmishing was reported between the creek and Woodbury. The previous night Washington had issued simultaneous instructions to Hazelwood and Varnum. Hazelwood had promptly complied by patrolling the waters near the fort. Varnum was ordered to place his command on the upper side of Big Timber Creek to avoid the possibility of the British trapping him in Woodbury. He was to station his troops so as to offer succor to Fort Mercer, which was to be held until its fall was imminent. The garrison was then to be withdrawn and the works destroyed.[76]

Varnum had been beseeching Washington for advice and specific instructions. Late on the night of the 18th the Commander-in-Chief ordered Varnum to discuss the problems of defense with St. Clair, de Kalb, and Knox. Washington would be governed by the recommendations of the generals on the proper role of the main army.

Returning to the camp on the 19th, the generals reported directly to Washington. Their advice was to retain possession of Fort Mercer as long as possible without jeopardizing the garrison. This concurred with Washington's viewpoint, as he had already dispatched General Huntington's brigade to reinforce Varnum. After meeting with the generals, he decided that additional troops would be needed to contain Cornwallis. General Greene's division of Muhlenberg's and Weedon's brigades, to be augmented by Glover's brigade on its way from the north, were ordered to join Varnum and Huntington, with Greene in command. A detachment of 170 sharpshooters from Morgan's riflemen was also sent to join Greene. Washington dashed off quick messages to Hazelwood and Varnum, admonishing them that the fort must be defended to the last possible moment.[77] His instructions reached the Commodore and General after the fort's fate had been sealed.

Varnum visited Fort Mercer during the evening of November 19, and found Greene greatly concerned by a rumor that the British had forded Mantua Creek and penetrated to the area around Little Mantua Creek. With this information, Greene ordered the fort abandoned, and Mauduit was charged with scattering powder over the entire works. Reconsidering their decision and anticipating that Washington would make a major diversion to relieve the fort, the garrison agreed to delay the evacuation. They intended to gather the scattered powder the next day, forgetting that the very presence of this powder made their position untenable; the discharge of a musket or the bursting of a shell would ignite the powder and destroy the fort and a large segment of the garrison with it. The sound of oars alarmed Varnum and Greene and they quickly decided to withdraw. Since no British boats were known to be in the channel between Bush Island and the fort, it was probably the American galleys or guard boats on patrol. A degree of panic seems to have seized the command, and making a somewhat precipitous withdrawal, they left behind a strong guard to fire on the boats, a dangerous undertaking in view of the strewn powder. Fortunately, the boats pulled away and, according to Varnum, the rest of the garrison agreed to return to the fort. They took a second look at the situation, but with their fear of an investure of the fort by Cornwallis, and the knowledge that they had made the situation untenable by strewing powder over the fort, they marched off toward the Big Timber Creek bridge.

Varnum reported that a few men were left to ignite the powder upon the approach of the British. He was apparently mistaken or confused, as the fort appears to have been unoccupied for several hours. An entry in Greene's orderly book for November 20 asks for a volunteer detachment of fifty-five officers and men, drawn equally from his regiment and Angell's to be commanded by a captain from the latter regiment. They were to proceed to Gloucester Point (New Jersey) and embark on boats for Fort Mercer, where they were to act as a guard, and destroy the works rather than permit the British to occupy them. The boats were to be retained as a means of escape if necessary. Varnum's patrols were ordered to alert the detachment when the British arrived in the vicinity. The detachment destroyed the, fort on the afternoon of November 20.[78]

Varnum returned to his headquarters at Haddonfield and quickly proceeded to move to Mount Holly with Colonels Christopher Greene and Israel Angell's regiments, arriving there either late on the 20th or early on the 21st. Feeling that his precipitate move required an explanation, he dashed a note off to Washington justifying his change of headquarters so as not to be trapped between the creeks. He had been joined by

Huntington's brigade and had received information that General Greene was at Burlington. He concluded his observations with uncomplimentary comments on the attitude of the militia, and asserted that most of the stores were brought away when the fort was evacuated—a misleading statement when the return of ordnance and military stores recovered by the British is scrutinized. (Over the last two centuries a number of cannon have been found in the ruins of the earthworks.) [79]

Cornwallis had made his headquarters at the home of John Cooper in Woodbury, with outpost detachments extending from Mantua Creek to Little Timber Creek. Units were also at Billingsport and Fort Mercer. The latter were marines assigned to complete the destruction begun by the Americans.[80]

Distressed and somewhat aggravated, Washington acknowledged Varnum's communications of the previous two days and instructed the General to look to General Greene for his orders in the future. His displeasure was evident:

> I am at a loss to determine upon what Principle the Powder was strewed over the fort at Red bank as I expected that if an Evacuation was found necessary it might be brought off, & if that was impracticable I considered the best mode of destroying it was to throw it into the River unless it was determined to blow up the Works with it, which could never be effected by the mode which was adopted.[81]

Others criticized the apparent haste of Varnum. Bradford wrote, "It is astonishing to think of the Precipitate retreat from Fort Mercer, they seemed determined not to see the Enemy. How General Varnum will account for his conduct, others must judge." [82]

General Greene had temporarily established headquarters at Burlington, awaiting the arrival of his division. His troops were ferried over on November 21, and the baggage and artillery followed during the night. He planned to march to Mount Holly the next morning to join forces with Varnum and Huntington. While at Burlington he had a conference with Hazelwood and informed Washington, "The fleet are greatly disgusted at the reflections thrown out against the officers; the Commodore thinks the Officers are greatly injured, he asserts they did their duty faithfully." [83]

At Mount Holly, Greene made plans to intercept the advance

of the British beyond Haddonfield. He was perplexed by the apparently sluggish movements of Cornwallis. The British General had taken two days to advance from Billingsport to Woodbury, where he set up his headquarters. The American command was unaware that Cornwallis's mission was to destroy the batteries and Fort Mercer and force the withdrawal or capitulation of the American fleet. He planned to remain in the vicinity until his objective was accomplished, and then withdraw to Philadelphia by way of Gloucester Point (New Jersey).

Without this knowledge Greene placed his defensive line along Rancocas Creek, and sent patrols of New Jersey militia ranging as far as Haddonfield and Little Timber Creek. His efforts to enlist large numbers of local militia were meeting with little success. The Continental commissary was ill equipped to subsist Greene's Continentals and the local farmers refused to sell provisions for Continental promises to pay. The militia was unwilling to turn out without more definite assurances of subsistence.

Washington urged Greene to attack the British if an opportunity presented itself for a reasonable prospect of success. Greene was anxious to take the offensive, but believed he should await Glover's brigade and Captain "Light Horse Harry" Lee's troop of light horse. He considered his division of three thousand inadequate to attack a British force of what he estimated to be five thousand. Lee's light horse were particularly needed to offer a screen for any movement he might make. Until Lee's arrival, he employed Morgan's riflemen as a cover to frustrate a possible attempt by Cornwallis to penetrate beyond Haddonfield.[84]

Uncertain and desirous of undertaking an attack only if success seemed assured, Greene wrote a somewhat plaintive letter to Washington on November 24. Although his independent command permitted Greene full latitude to take whatever action he deemed proper, he hesitated to move unless assured of Washington's approval, especially in the event of defeat. He wrote,

Your Excellency observes in your last, you must leave the Propriety of attacking the enemy to me. Would you advise me to fight them with very unequal numbers. . . . For your Sake, for my own Sake, & for my Country's Sake I wish to attempt every thing which will meet with your Excellency's Approbation—I will run any Risque or engage under any Disadvantages if

I can only have your Countenance if unfortunate. With the Publick I know Success sanctifies every thing and that only. I cannot help thinking from the most Dispassionate Survey of the Operations of the Campaign that you stand approved by Reason & justified by every military Principle.—With Respect to my own Conduct, I have ever given my Opinion with Candour & to my utmost executed with Fidelity whatever was committed to my charge.

Greene was then unaware that the course of events would relieve him of the responsibility of making a decision to attack Cornwallis. However, his letter reflects the apprehension that possessed the generals who were close to Washington. Sensitive to the criticism that had been leveled at the main Continental army and especially the Commander-in-Chief, Greene realized that an abortive attack would only add fuel to the fire.[85]

Colonel Ellis of the New Jersey militia reported to Greene on November 24 that the British were still on a line from Mantua to Little Timber Creek with their main encampment at Woodbury. Artillery pieces were set up on all roads leading to their headquarters. A detachment of British marines were completing the destruction of Fort Mercer. Ellis's report was undoubtedly delayed as Weedon's brigade arrived in Haddonfield on the same day and discovered the British army above Big Timber Creek. Job Whitall recorded in his diary on November 22 that the British soldiers had left Woodbury. Having completed their razing of the American fortifications, Cornwallis filed off toward Gloucester preparatory to crossing the Delaware. Jonas Cattell said that Cornwallis carried a portable bridge by which means he crossed Big Timber Creek. Cattell observed that "It was made of copper plates united together by hinges and when not in use folded up in leaves upon a wagon. It was stretched across the creek by means of ropes and tackle. It was wide enough for a wagon to pass with three feet to spare."[86]

Detachments of British troops were constantly roaming the countryside garnering forage and provisions. They would take their plunder to Gloucester and load it on boats to be ferried to Philadelphia. Poor Job Whitall, who experienced heavy losses and sufferings from the depredations of the garrison at Fort Mercer, was again to feel the heavy hands of soldiery. The British took bread, pies, milk, cheese, dishes, cups, spoons, shirts, sheets, blankets, and other apparel. They appropriated livestock, taking two mares, both with foal, and all their cattle, though through some fortuitous circumstance, all but one of the cattle wandered back.[87]

As early as November 24 Cornwallis, safely ensconced in Colonel Ellis's house in Gloucester, was embarking his troops to cross back to the city. The 17th Light Dragoons and the Royal Artillery were among the first contingents to cross over early on the 25th. To prevent the Americans from disturbing his operation, Cornwallis established strong outposts of three to four hundred troops on the perimeter of his camp.[88]

Lafayette had joined Greene's official family as a volunteer, and at his insistence was given the command of a reconnaissance detachment. His command included ten light horse, 150 of Morgan's riflemen, commanded by Colonel Butler, and two companies of local militia under Colonels Hite and Ellis—a total not exceeding three hundred. He was also accompanied by four French officers, including Mauduit, one of the heroes at Fort Mercer. About two-and-a-half miles from Gloucester, they came upon a picket of 350 Hessians supported by artillery. Without hesitation Lafayette attacked, driving the Hessians back a half-mile where they were reinforced by a contingent of British support troops. Flushed with success, the Americans pressed their advantage and the enemy once more withdrew, only to be again reinforced. Not daunted, the attacking riflemen and militia pushed the larger force back until darkness compelled Lafayette to recall his troops. Varying estimates of casualties were reported. Lafayette said his losses were one militia lieutenant killed and five men wounded. He claimed between twenty-five and thirty enemy killed and about the same number wounded, with fourteen prisoners; other accounts credit more prisoners. Montresor reported thirty-one Jägers killed, wounded, and missing. Possibly some of the prisoners could be accounted for by the tendency of the Hessians to take advantage of every opportunity to desert. Lafayette was aware of the reputation of Morgan's riflemen, but they exceeded even his fondest hopes; as to the militia, he said they were "above all expectations." [89]

The skirmish at Gloucester concluded Cornwallis's venture into New Jersey. As soon as Greene was assured that the British had returned to Philadelphia, he made an orderly withdrawal from New Jersey. He expressed some concern that the hospitals and the many loyal residents would be at the mercy of British raiding parties.

Washington was exploring the possibility of taking the offensive against the British and wanted Greene to return to camp as soon as practicable. The enemy had abandoned Province and Carpenters' Islands, leveling the works and removing the cannon. Howe had concentrated his army in the environs of the city in preparation for a winter of pleasure and comfort.

As the curtain fell on the campaign to open the Delaware, a postscript to all the internal disputes was added by d'Arendt. Smith had been honored for his part in the heroic defense of Fort Mifflin on October 22 and 23 and d'Arendt had been ignored. He claimed it had been intimated that he was absent from his post during the engagement. He informed Washington that he did not object to Smith's receiving a sword, but his honor had been sullied, especially when a subordinate officer had been cited and his superior overlooked. He added, "Your Excellency must be the best Judge of my Conduct . . . if my Conduct has deserved censure I am unworthy of serving under your orders . . . that you will undeceive the Congress." [90]

XIII

Navy in Eclipse—1778

ON DECEMBER 1 Commodore Hazelwood surveyed the remnants of the little fleet resting at anchor off the small Pennsylvania town of Bristol. A number of galleys needed repairs and two required extensive renovating. Bradford was beset with a multitude of problems in provisioning and refurbishing the boats. With Blewer absent, the task of keeping the navy afloat was in the hands of the faithful Bradford and Hazelwood.

Hazelwood reported that the fleet had suffered seventy killed and wounded in the various engagements with enemy ships and land batteries. Dr. Valentine Standley, in a memorial to obtain his salary as chief surgeon of the fleet, asserted that he first attended the wounded seamen on Mud Island, then in the neighborhood around Fort Mercer. After the fall of the latter post, the wounded were removed to Burlington and then to a temporary hospital in Bristol. Because of the exposed position of this hospital, facilities were provided in Trenton for the winter. Later, the more seriously wounded were removed to Lancaster, and, after the evacuation of Philadelphia by the British, they were transferred to the capital city.[1]

The morale of the men was noticeably depressed and Bradford was having trouble raising funds to purchase provisions and pay them. Local tradesmen and farmers avoided the naval commissary, who had nothing more tangible than promises to pay. Dissatisfaction with the lack of provisions and pay was blamed for the increasing desertions. The Supreme Executive Council, heeding the entreaties of the Navy Board chairman, forwarded money to Crispin, the commissary, for provisions, and to Bradford to pay the men.[2]

The problem of quartering the fleet for the winter was causing concern at the temporary state capital at Lancaster, as well with Bradford and Hazelwood. Hazelwood had requested an early decision by Council, as the river at Bristol would soon freeze over. Wharton suggested the wharves at Trenton but left the final determination to Hazelwood and Bradford. On December 19 the Navy Board decided to send the fleet up to Bordentown Creek.

Upon arrival at Bordentown the stores and ordnance were dispersed at various locations some distance from the river, on orders of the Council. The fleet was vulnerable to a large raiding party of British, and the decision to winter the Continental army at Valley Forge would not permit adequate coverage for the fleet by the military. All sails, rigging, stores, and guns were removed, and the boats scuttled in some convenient creek, where they could be raised and placed in commission at short notice.[3]

Council was surprised that Hazelwood had five hundred galleymen available, and they proposed that the men be usefully employed in erecting a breastwork to protect the sunken craft. Some of the naval cannon could be used on carriages to serve as field pieces and, with a sufficient supply of small arms and ammunition, thwart attacks by enemy raiders.

Other branches of the navy were not so well situated. Bradford reported that all the fire ship captains were without command, many guard boats were without crews, and a few guard boat captains were without boats. Many of those without command were of little value, and the Navy Board would have discharged them, but considered it would be a hardship after faithful, if not spectacular, service.

Crispin had been complaining that his credit was exhausted, and with the receipt of the first funds on December 17, he purchased provisions and rum. This money was soon disbursed

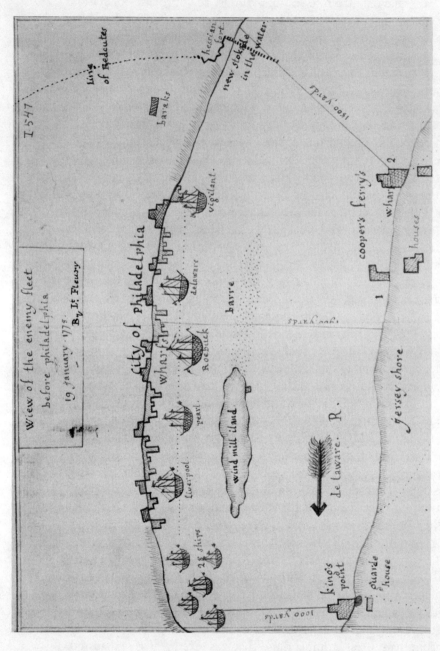

Plan of the Philadelphia waterfront by Fleury, January 19, 1778, submitted with his plan for destroying British shipping. *Jared Sparks Collection, Cornell University.*

and the needs of the navy were as great as ever. Rum was clearly the most important ingredient in the daily diet of the fleet, Crispin noting that it consumed between two and three hundred gallons each week. As Crispin expressed it, ". . . how we are Distressed for the Necessary article. . . ." [4]

In mid-January another effort was made to keep some of the galleymen from a winter of indolence and discontent. Hazelwood was ordered to send thirty men to Toms River, New Jersey, to act as a guard for the State saltworks. [5]

As the month progressed, inactivity and the dilatory tactics of furnishing the Navy Board with funds to feed and pay the men was exacerbating the morale problem. The Council was not always in a position to raise the money to relieve the navy's wants, payments being made sporadically but never in sufficient amounts. To occupy the time of some of the officers and men, several of the former requested the loan of a guard boat to take down to the bay as a privateersman. They proposed lying in the mouth of a small creek to pounce upon unsuspecting British merchantmen.

A loan of two guard boats was requested by Captain Boys. The Navy Board consented and manned each boat with an officer and ten men. They were to proceed to Cooper's Creek, whence they were to be taken overland to the vicinity of Salem and refloated. Unfortunately, after they arrived at Coopers Creek, while the officers took a nap, the men deserted. One other boat was sent overland from Burlington under command of Captain Robert Collings. Collings had been first lieutenant on the armed ship *Montgomery*. According to Clark, three additional boats were dispatched on this service, one commanded by Captain Joseph Wade. [6]

John Barry, with the same idea, had borrowed two Continental barges and was granted permission to recruit volunteers from the Continental seamen at Bordentown. Taking his favorite subordinates, Lieutenant Luke Matthewman, Midshipman Matthew Clarkson, and Lieutenant James Cokelys, he issued a call for volunteers. As he had anticipated, they were reluctant to come forward and he could only raise twenty-five men. He needed a twenty-man crew for each barge and appealed to Hazelwood for the fifteen additional men, and his request was granted. [7]

In a short biographical sketch of Colonel John Eyre, Peter G. Keyser states that Hazelwood was a partner in a group of Patriots interested in purchasing two guard boats to cruise for prizes in the bay; that on January 22, Colonel Eyre, Thomas Bradford, Manuel Eyre, Paul Cox, James Longhead, Commodore Hazelwood, and Joseph Blewer purchased two boats at Trenton, and by February 2 they were outfitted and on their way downriver. Another boat was reputedly purchased but Hazelwood was not a party to this transaction. A search of the records does not produce substantiation for Keyser's claim. If these Pennsylvanians purchased boats for privateering (a common practice during the Revolution) they could not have been State guard boats as all can be accounted for in the subsequent disposal of the fleet.[8]

With the British in possession of Philadelphia, the galleys and ships were locked in the river above the city. Guard boats had been the only elements of the navy capable of reaching Delaware Bay and they had to be taken overland from either Burlington or Cooper's Creek to Salem and from there launched in the bay.

Fleury was in Trenton in mid-January and he developed a plan for destroying the British shipping at Philadelphia. Initially he considered enlisting five or six determined militiamen to cross the river on the ice from Cooper's Ferry and set fire to one or two of the enemy's ships by using two sulphur-filled shirts he had prepared for that purpose. Because of the mild weather the river had not frozen over. Disappointed, Fleury discarded the idea.

He appealed to Colonel John Laurens to present a second plan to Washington for approval. The river, while not frozen over, was dangerous for shipping near the shores, especially on the New Jersey side and near Windmill Island, where accumulated ice was a hazard. There were only two places where boats could safely land on the east bank, the wharf at King's (Kaighn's) Point and Cooper's Ferry. Fleury proposed to install an eighteen-pounder on the King's Point wharf and two others on a slight elevation, twenty yards in the rear of the wharf. Hazelwood said that the cannon from the galleys were on the shore at Bordentown and two carriages for eighteen-pounders were at Trenton. To frustrate a British raiding party, he contemplated moving in fascines, gabions, and the cannon during the night. Colonel Ellis of the militia offered to garrison the battery. In an emergency the cannon could be safely withdrawn across Cooper Creek and the bridge destroyed.

Fleury suggested two types of fire boats. The first kind was to be loaded with tons of powder and directed to burst in the middle of the British shipping. He was certain it could be directed "by one Strong Racket [rachis] filled with particular composition, & fasten'd in the very middle of the head of the boat, to give him [the boat] direction and velocity . . . one mast in the Stern of the boat, horisontaly under the water & to which one sail would be circularly bound would hinder the current to drive it out the way." He further suggested that the head of the boat have a sharp point of iron to fix itself in a ship's side until the powder would explode.

His second type of fire boat would be effective only if employed immediately when favorable winds prevailed. Adverse northwest winds could be expected in February and March. He proposed to load several flat-bottomed boats with tar and other combustibles at a sand bar (probably an extension of Windmill Island) during the night, and taking advantage of the wind and tide, let them drift into the city's wharves where the British shipping was anchored.

His plan was discussed in detail with Hazelwood and the latter agreed to assist him if approval was received from Washington. Hazelwood's knowledge of the construction of fire ships for the State and Continental navies would be invaluable in the construction of the fire boats. The galleys had quantities of saltpeter and powder and their crewmen would make the inflammable composition. He concluded his presentation by requesting permission to make a model, and authorization to test it secretly be granted to the Commodore and himself. "We will work friendly and loyally, together." [9]

On January 23, Fleury again wrote to Laurens that he was ready to construct a model at the Commodore's headquarters and was awaiting approval. Explaining his plan in more detail, he proposed that bombs, carcases, and a mine be placed in each of twelve boats. A slight amplification of the guiding mechanism and the hoped-for attachment of the fire boat to the enemy's ships were described. The main purpose of his letter appears to have been to express his impatience in securing approval.

Laurens replied on the 25th and gave approval to conduct a test. Washington was of the opinion that if "some desperate fellows" could be employed the sulphured-shirt idea held the most promise of success. Washington sadly remembered the failures of fire ships and candidly stated that he believed little could be expected of them. But he was not adverse to experimenting with anything that might embarrass the enemy, and he wished Fleury and Hazelwood success.[10]

Fleury's plan either failed in the subsequent test or, if an attempt was made to fire the British ships, it was abortive, as no contemporary chronicled the attempt. Hazelwood's private opinion is not known.

Infernal machines were favorite brain children of certain scientifically minded Americans. David Bushnell, the principal advocate of submarine warfare in the Revolution, had worked on an underwater mine to destroy the British shipping at Philadelphia. Under the aegis of Colonel Joseph Borden of Bordentown, he had perfected a system of mines, connected by lines of ropes with buoys or kegs. The instruments of destruction were supposed to float just beneath the surface of the river and attach themselves to the sides of a ship so that the movement of the ship in the water would jar the mine sufficiently to explode it. The mines and hardware were made by a local gunsmith and blacksmith under the watchful eye of Bushnell. It is a local tradition that the kegs were made at the home of Mrs. Hunter near the west end of the Academy in Bordentown.

A few days after Christmas, Bushnell, with a companion, started down the river towing their mines and kegs. Bushnell's biographer says that more than twenty kegs were used.[11] Apparently the men were unfamiliar with the river and released the kegs too soon; this caused them to scatter rather than float into the British shipping en masse. Two young boys out in a small boat saw the floating objects and decided to investigate. Either they tried to pull one into their boat or touched it with their oars; in any case, it instantly exploded, causing consternation along the waterfront and blinding the boys, although both eventually recovered. Other accounts of the extent of the injuries to the boys are more nebulous. Captain Coates, living in Philadelphia, reported in 1826 that the boys were James Wilson, a ship's carpenter who died in 1825, and a mulatto.[12]

A few days later, January 5, more of the kegs floated into view. A contemporary anecdote, possibly apocryphal, describes the activity of the British in the city: "The day the 'Battle of the Kegs' occurred the alarm and consternation of the British was extremely great—The *Military* of every kind & order was seen in an instant, running in every degree of confusion & in every direction,—perhaps to assigned posts, but to the eye of an *observor*, as without predetermined object." [13]

Other descriptions confirm that a certain degree of confusion reigned in the city. One account facetiously describes the gallant defense by British officers and men against the kegs. A letter written from Philadelphia described the *Roebuck* and other men-of-war pouring entire broadsides into the *Delaware*. "In short, not a wandering ship, stick, or drift log, but felt the vigor of British arms." It was claimed an old market woman accidently dropped a keg of butter in the river and as it floated into view the cannon fire increased in intensity. Others with British sympathies castigated the maker of these instruments of destruction saying, ". . . the fellow who invented the mischief may quit his conscience of the murder or injury done the lads, as well as he can." One account dismisses the activity as a few shots fired from some transports and accuses the Patriot accounts as being the inventions of fertile imaginations.[14]

This abortive incident has long been celebrated in the poem written by Francis Hopkinson, entitled "The Battle of the Kegs." Hopkinson, member of the Continental Navy Board, lived near Colonel Borden and was an interested observer of the activities of Bushnell.

A puzzling fact in this somewhat ludicrous incident is the failure to ask assistance from the State navy. The gentlemen sponsoring Bushnell knew that Hazelwood was thoroughly familiar with the river. Bushnell's unfamiliarity with the river obviously made the attempt abortive and, as it merited serious consideration, Hazelwood's assistance should have been solicited, as Fleury would do in a few days.

Discontent was increasing among the seamen. A few had been satisfied with the special guard boat assignments downriver or as guards at the saltworks. These detached details accommodated less than 25 percent of the men available for duty. A number of the original galleymen were gravely disturbed by reports from

their families. Many reported that their wives and children were
in great distress for want of food and other necessities. Hazelwood and Bradford realized that inactivity, frequent moneyless
pay days, and anxiety for the welfare of their families would
soon result in large-scale desertions. To provide activity for the
men, the Navy Board and Hazelwood decided to raise the
scuttled galleys and refit them for combat. By February 8
Hazelwood was able to advise Wharton that a number of the
galleys were equipped with stores and ordnance and would be
ready to proceed downriver in a few days. He was enthusiastic
and believed the time was propitious for a successful stroke
against British shipping, as the river was free of ice.[15]

Hazelwood's dream of attacking the British ships with the
galleys was never to be fulfilled. On March 2 Washington wrote
the State Navy Board recommending the virtual disbandment
of the fleet. He specifically suggested:

As the Gallies can now be of no service in the River, and the enemy have
it in their power to get them into their possession, with all their cannon and
stores, I beg leave strongly to recommend it to the Board, without delay, to
evacuate them of their cannon and stores; and removing these to a place of
security, in some interior part of the country, to carry the Gallies up into
some of the creeks and have them sunk. If there should be any other vessels,
belonging to the state in the river, I would mean to comprehend them; and
if there should be any stores at Bordentown, or other places on the river,
these also ought to be removed to a place of safety. We can reap no advantage from keeping the Gallies, cannon and stores in such an exposed
situation; and if they should fall into the hands of the enemy, which they
would in all probability do, the gallies would be useful to them, and the
cannon and stores would be no inconsiderable loss to us.[16]

The courier bearing Washington's letter was instructed to
request the return of the North Carolina soldiers serving with
the galleys. This was a follow-up to a request by the Adjutant
General to Hazelwood in early February. The Commodore had
promised to send the men back to Washington as soon as they
returned from downriver.

This communication would open an animated correspondence
on the merits of the galleys. Bradford wrote to the Council,
enclosing a copy of Washington's letter. The indefatigable Bradford protested scuttling the navy, calling the Council's attention
to the safety of the fleet headquartered at Trenton. A number

of galleys were fully manned and equipped and were stationed at Bordentown as a first line of defense and to guard against surprise. He warned that the river towns and inhabitants in the vicinity of the river relied on the galleys for protection, and if the fleet were scuttled the entire countryside would be open to British depredations. A few more galleys could be manned, and he recommended this to be done for security of the river. Bradford and Hazelwood appealed for support to Governor Livingston of New Jersey. Livingston agreed that the galleys should not be sunk, but refused to intercede with the Commander in Chief.[17]

Council wrote to Washington and enclosed a copy of Bradford's letter. Captain Thomas Houston, one of Hazelwood's most capable officers, was ordered to carry these dispatches to Washington and offer to particularize on any facet of the fleet's operations. Council's covering note informed Washington that the State was unwilling to lose its little navy, but they would defer to Washington's wisdom and were ready to obey his orders.[18]

A joint committee of members selected from Council and the Assembly was formed to discuss Washington's recommendation to scuttle the fleet, and decide what action the State should take. Nothing concrete resulted from their meetings, but it was intimated that the State would offer the galleys and xebecs to the Continental Congress. There were never any xebecs in the State navy; two belonging to the Continental navy were destroyed in attempting to pass the city on November 21, 1777. The politicians were unaware of the composition of their own fleet and apparently were ready to use this device to transfer responsibility for destroying the galleys to Congress. Sufficient objections were raised when Council and the Assembly met to table the recommendation of their special committee.[19]

In the meantime, Houston had arrived at Washington's headquarters. Houston must have been persuasive as Washington wrote a conciliatory letter to Bradford on March 15:

I yesterday received a letter from Governor Wharton inclosing Copy of one from you to the Council on the subject of keeping five or six Gallies manned for the protection of the upper part of the River. The Govr. has very politely left the matter to my determination, but I would not wish to interfere in a Business which is out of my line any further than by giving my advice. I cannot help thinking now, as I did before, that should the Enemy come up the River, they will do it with a superior force and certainly carry them. But Captn. Huston thinks, with the assistance of a small work upon land, under cover of which they can run in case of necessity, that they may be protected. I would wish you to consult Govr. Livingston and the Gentlemen in the Naval line upon this matter and do what to you seems best. But you will not fail to secure the Guns and Stores of those Gallies that you strip, in the safest manner until means can be fallen upon to carry them away.[20]

Before Washington's letter reached Bradford, he had written to the Commander-in-Chief reiterating the need for the galleys to protect the inhabitants and property contiguous to the river. He particularly emphasized the great number of private vessels anchored near Bordentown. The North Carolina troops were on duty downriver and he pleaded for their service for a while longer. Washington, however, insisted that the troops be returned as soon as they were back in to Trenton.[21]

Oddly, Washington must have been cognizant of the fact that in withdrawing the soldiers on loan to the galleys, several of those boats would have to be deactivated. In spite of the apparent harmonious understanding on the future of the fleet, concern was evident among the naval officers. Writing on April 20, Washington expressed his understanding about the galleys: "I have already given my opinion on the subject of dismantling the Gallies, in concurrence with the Sentiments of Gov'. Livingston and Commodore Hazelwood. It is understood that those Gallies only are to be dismantled that are destitute of crews." [22] Regardless of plan, the fleet would gradually be dismantled through attrition.

In compliance with Washington's original recommendation of March 2, six galleys had been dismantled. When the galleys returned to Trenton from patrolling the river at Burlington, soldiers on board were discharged and marched off to Valley Forge. Two galleys returned before April 16 and were quickly stripped. The eight galleys were plugged and made ready to sink in half an hour. Shot and other nonperishable stores were buried in a safe location, but convenient enough to be available in an emergency. Most of the surplus powder and perishable stores were taken to Pittstown, New Jersey, and later removed to Allentown, another New Jersey hamlet. On April 16 the effective fleet was reduced to four galleys and four guard boats stationed at Burlington.[23]

With the passing of another week the State fleet was completely dismantled and the idle crews quartered in Trenton. Idle hands were a cause of great concern to Hazelwood and he solicited the assistance of the Navy Board and Council to provide employment for the men. Council suggested they be employed as guards in the interior of the State or used as ferrymen on the continent's major rivers to transport troops and supplies. They ordered the Navy Board to send all privates (seamen) to Lancaster by way of Reading. Wagons and carriages were to be furnished the sick and handicapped and for the baggage. Crispin was instructed to ensure that subsistence be provided for the men on their march.

All except fifteen or twenty officers were to be dismissed. Those discharged were to receive a bonus of two months' pay and all arrearages. The parsimonious Council considered this ample compensation and noted that the season most propitious for obtaining employment was approaching.

The discharged officers were angry and considered that their peremptory dismissal was unfair and worked hardships on them. Even the men had become disturbed and Bradford noted that again a number had deserted. The officers determined to present a remonstrance to the Council and deputized Hazelwood, Houston, and Captain Brown to represent them. Their memorial recounted their devotion to duty; the heroic conduct of officers and men during the engagements of October and November 1777; and the enterprise demanded in passing the British batteries and the frigate *Delaware* on the early mornings of November 20 and 21. The men of the navy had performed individual acts of bravery and devoted their lives to the public good and their country. They did not consider themselves discharged, rather suspended from their commands, and believed they were entitled to the same emoluments as those still employed in the fleet. Eleven officers signed the memorial and asked that all officers be covered in their petition for a commutation of their service to half-pay.[24]

The memorial was presented to the Assembly on May 23, 1778, and tabled. A second reading was made on the 25th, at which time it was unanimously resolved that the officers be continued in the pay of the State until the next session of the Assembly.[25]

The officers remaining on duty at Trenton were to conduct the impending courts-martial of officers and men accused of treason or insubordination. They were also to supervise and provide care for the more seriously wounded in the area hospitals.

Concern was expressed for the stores and arms which were the property of the State and were lying in exposed locations. Council ordered them removed to a safer site and placed under the jurisdiction of State officials. Easton was recommended as an ideal location.[26]

The distress of Governor Livingston and residents along the river was exacerbated by the loss of the protective screen provided by the galleys. The owners of the private vessels moored off Bordentown had not heeded the suggestions to scuttle their craft to prevent them falling into British hands, and they were "sitting ducks" for any British raiding party.

Several factors probably influenced Washington to make his recommendation that the State fleet be scuttled. It was well known that the British would soon evacuate Philadelphia and that a treaty of alliance with France was being negotiated. He was anxious that all soldiers on detached service be returned to camp, so that he could have the army at full strength to take the offensive against the British.

Quiet naturally the State and naval authorities would be in disagreement with any decision which would have the effect of wiping out the State fleet. It is possible that Washingon privately had little confidence in the fleet to defend itself or the river communities, a viewpoint that was vehemently opposed by Hazelwood, Bradford, and the Council. Whatever opinion Washington had, it is to be hoped he did not give credence to the acrimonious complaints of Varnum and Smith. Rather, it is likely his decision had to encompass the whole spectrum of the area defense, although dismantling the fleet would give the British an uncontested minor victory. If the galleys had been patrolling the area between Bristol and Trenton, they would probably have deterred the British from their raid on Bordentown in early May. (The brothers Howe, with long memories, would have recalled October and November 1777.)

The fate of the State navy was soon known in the Continental

Congress and little time was lost in soliciting the use of the galleymen. Richard Peters, of the Continental Board of War, asked if any able-bodied seamen were available for transfer to the Continental service. Galleys belonging to the states of Maryland and Virginia were operating in Chesapeake Bay and, while possessing sufficient officers, were weakly manned. These galleys, temporarily assigned to the Continental navy, were not intended for combat but to transport provisions from Virginia to the head of the bay.

On May 2 Council President Wharton wrote to Henry Laurens, President of the Continental Congress, stating the State's position relative to the use of the galleymen. He pointed out that the State galleymen were originally landsmen, but diligent application of the oars had made them "tolerable watermen." They were expected in Lancaster in eight or ten days at which time their usefulness to further State service would be determined. Before making a decision, Council must decide whether it was advisable to permit their absence from the State in the event of an emergency. Possibly, until such an eventuality arose, they could be gainfully employed on the Susquehanna or Schuylkill Rivers. Ten days later the Board of War pressed for a decision; however, no response from the Council is known. It is known that the galleymen never left the jurisdiction of the State.[27]

Intelligence reached Philadelphia that the State fleet had been scuttled, and no naval opposition would be encountered by a British raiding party to the upper Delaware River. Sir William Howe promptly organized a joint army and naval expedition to destroy the American frigates and shipping at Bordentown and in the surrounding creeks. Admiral Lord Howe contended that the prime objective was four American galleys patrolling between Bordentown and Burlington, but he was either misinformed or confused, as it was known at British headquarters in Philadelphia that the galleys were all sunk. Lord Howe was on the *Eagle*, anchored near Billingsport, and may not have possessed this information. The British had had many opportunities to attack the galleys, but had refrained from sending expeditions up the river; so this premise is specious and misleading.

Major John Maitland, with the 2nd Battalion of light infantry and two field pieces, embarked on eighteen flatboats on the night of May 7. Captain John Henry, who had commanded the *Vigilant* on that fateful day, November 15, 1777, was in command of the escort squadron with the galleys *Hussar*, *Cornwallis*, *Ferret*, and *Philadelphia*, the armed schooners *Pembroke* and *Viper*, and four gunboats—a force which would not have dismayed the State galleys, particularly if the long-discussed shore battery had been erected. Henry's official communique declared that the flotilla left Philadelphia on May 6, but all other contemporary reports, both British and American, report the departure as May 7.

Between eight and ten o'clock on the night of May 7, Henry and Maitland proceeded up the river to the vicinity of Rancocas Creek and dropped anchor. The passage had been difficult, with a strong head wind accompanied by frequent gusts and heavy rain. At five o'clock next morning, a shift in the wind permitted the British to get under way, and they rowed or sailed up the river arriving at Whitehill, about two miles below Bordentown, shortly before noon. Henry placed his galleys, armed schooners, and gunboats in a position to cover the landing of the light infantry and field pieces. Whitehill was the anchorage of the Continental frigates *Washington* and *Effingham;* they, together with a brig and sloop, were set on fire and destroyed. The frigates had been sunk on the recommendation of Washington and later raised to house nearly four hundred officers and men of the Continental navy. It was believed that most of the Continental sailors had deserted after the destruction of their ships on November 21. However, the majority managed to evade British patrols and drifted singly and in groups into Bordentown. Washington had grudgingly permitted the frigates to be raised to serve as barracks. Hopkinson's biographer contends that Washington acquiesced, even though he realized that the British would make an attempt to destroy the American shipping. This was curious reasoning in view of the sinking of the galleys.

Maitland then set his battalion in motion for Bordentown. New Jersey militia had gathered to oppose the British and had set up a defense line supported by a five-gun battery. A brisk but erratic musket fire was exchanged with the British. The battery fired one shot and the gunners decamped along with the militia, leaving fourteen dead on the field. British officers reported that they had suffered no casualties. Advancing into

Bordentown, Maitland's troops set fire to four warehouses containing provisions, tobacco, military stores, and camp equipage. The flames engulfed the palatial home of Colonel Borden, the show place of the town. Maitland and Henry deplored the destruction of private residences. However, their protestations suggested the probability that certain malicious elements of the soldiery may have deliberately set fire to the Borden house. Borden's prominent position as a Patriot was well known, and he was a prime target for vandalism. According to some American sources, it was the spiteful work of a young woman with Tory sympathies.

Completing their destruction at Bordentown, Maitland's troops boarded the flatboats and the entire flotilla moved upstream. Proceeding to Crosswicks Creek, they destroyed all shipping anchored along the shore or in the mouths of the various creeks, then crossed to the Pennsylvania shore, where they made camp for the night.

Early the next morning, May 9, the galleys *Hussar* and *Ferret* with the gunboats rowed up to Biles Island Creek and completed their work of destruction by burning every boat or ship encountered along the way. They crossed over to the New Jersey side and scouted the area near Watson's Creek, but found the galleys and other State craft too deeply submerged to destroy. Their movement was sharply contested by General Philemon Dickinson of the New Jersey militia, assisted by a two-gun battery. Apparently the increased activity of the militia made the British overly cautious, as they abandoned their plan to destroy the shipping and stores at Trenton.

At noon on May 9 Maitland set the light infantry in motion for Bristol, where they embarked on the flatboats and, joined by Henry's squadron, dropped downstream. They arrived in Philadelphia at six o'clock on the morning of the 10th. On the march to Bristol, Maitland's troops wantonly burned private residences, notably among them the home of Colonel Kirkbride of the Bucks County militia.

"Too little and too late" were General Maxwell and a detachment of Continental infantry, who arrived at the Delaware after the British had left the area for Philadelphia. Hamilton mildly chided Maxwell about his delay in leaving camp and mentioned that Washington was chagrined that he failed to take his artillery, but still hoped he could forestall further depredations by the British. Washington bemoaned the loss of the frigates, but the dubious wisdom of several decisions affecting the defense of the river had made the result inevitable.

The total number of vessels destroyed was forty-four, according to Henry. Maitland listed two frigates, nine large ships, three sloops of sixteen guns, three sloops of ten guns, twenty-three brigs and a number of other sloops and schooners destroyed.[28]

The first court-martial held at Trenton, on May 19, was presided over by Captain Thomas Moore of the galley *Hancock* and a court of fifteen captains and lieutenants. The accused was John Gilfroy, boatswain of the *Montgomery*. Gilfroy was accused of inciting mutiny and deserting to the enemy in Philadelphia. Adjudged guilty, the majority of the court recommended the death sentence, which was approved by Hazelwood and transmitted for final disposition to George Bryan, Vice-President of the State and acting as President of the Council. As Gilfroy was the first defendant accused of a capital crime against the navy, Council on July 25 pardoned him. In line with this decision, Hazelwood was authorized to offer amnesty to all deserters from the fleet who would return to their commands by September 1.[29]

In the meantime, following the British incursion up the river on May 9, it appeared that in certain quarters many State officials approved of the galleys being raised, manned, and refitted. About May 25 the crews of the galleys had arrived at the temporary state capital, Lancaster. Council declared that although the men had been requested by the Continental Congress for service in Chesapeake Bay, the Council preferred that they be employed in State services.[30]

The Patriot cause suffered a severe loss on May 23 when Thomas Wharton, Jr., President of the Supreme Executive Council, died. The officers of the navy journeyed to Lancaster and joined in the funeral procession to Evangelical Trinity Church. Bryan had been acting as President of Council since May 15 and would continue in that capacity until December 4.[31]

By mid-June Hazelwood was actively engaged in an effort to raise the galleys, obtain cannon and stores, and locate former crewmen and officers. The few officers and men remaining at

Trenton were bitterly complaining that their pay was in arrears and were fearful there was little prospect of receiving it soon. The paymaster of the navy was William C. Bradford, nephew of Board Chairman Bradford. He was adamant in his refusal to pay the men until ordered to do so by the Board. Hazelwood, anxious to relieve the anxiety of the men and hopeful of removing any threat of desertion, urged prompt payment. Addressing Bryan, he declared that two galleys were raised, properly officered, and ready for service. He requested that twenty or thirty men and two lieutenants be forwarded to Trenton to assist in raising two additional galleys and a sloop, and he observed that with a sufficient number of men he could raise all the galleys. It was common knowledge that the British were in the process of evacuating Philadelphia. Hazelwood stated that he wished it was in his ". . . Power to give them a scowering before they get out of the river." [32] The final detachment of British soldiers crossed the Delaware to Gloucester Point (New Jersey) on June 18. About June 20 the remaining crewmen and officers left Lancaster and headed for Philadelphia to join the fleet.

For the first time in more than nine months commercial vessels were arriving at the wharves of the city, bringing much needed merchandise and supplies to the Patriots. Apprehension was expressed for the safety of these merchantmen. Council on July 24 ordered two or three galleys to the Delaware Bay to intercept British cruisers attempting to enter the bay. They were also to collect intelligence and, if fortunate, take British merchantmen. Following up Hazelwood's requests made in June, they ordered as many galleys as could be manned and equipped to fall down and join those previously ordered to the bay to form a protective screen against enemy cruisers. The brig *Convention* was ordered fitted out and directed to cruise in the lower bay. On July 31 the Council, by a six to one majority, selected Captain Richard Eyre to command the *Convention* over Captain Thomas Houston, who was recommended by the Navy Board.[33]

After the fall of the river forts the navy had become a veritable political football. Threatened danger from British men-of-war would bring the navy into a posture of defense, only to be decommissioned or scuttled when the danger passed.

Obviously these political maneuvers depressed the morale of officers and men. In early August the Assembly again reappraised the danger to the Delaware and were convinced that little peril existed from incursions by British cruisers. Finally, on August 15, a number of resolutions were passed in the Chambers of the Assembly. All supernumerary officers with their crews were to be discharged on August 20. No attention was to be paid to rank or seniority. At least one officer, Captain Hugh Montgomery of the galley *Effingham*, lost little time in seeking civilian employment. Montgomery petitioned the Council for the privilege of keeping a tavern and caring for the ferry horses on Province Island. Three galleys, three guard boats, one sloop, and the brig *Convention* were to be retained; the balance of the fleet was to be drydocked or sold.

The Assembly was at odds with the Navy Board because the *Convention* was not ready to sail after seven weeks had been spent refitting the brig for a cruise. It was resolved to dismiss the Board, a rather puzzling development in view of the faithful service of its chairman, William Bradford. Captain Joseph Blewer and Colonel Robert Knox were commissioned to complete the equipping of the brig. Either Captain Eyre declined the command of the brig or the Assembly reversed its decision, as they offered the command to Captain Thomas Houston.[34] These resolutions were similar to the actions taken by the Council at the end of April. While August 20 was the effective date, temporary exceptions were permitted for the good of the service.

At this time the attention of Council was directed to the use of guard boats in the Delaware Bay by private individuals. Permission for this activity had been first granted in January 1778, with preference awarded to officers and men of the State naval service. Outfitted as privateers, they apparently had some success. As late as August a ship was sent up to Philadelphia to be libeled as a prize.

With British shipping out of the bay and river, except for an occasional ship, Council was of the opinion that the need for the guard boats to cruise for prizes was past. Their principal solicitude was that certain men of the fleet were unfairly profiting at the expense of those not privileged to serve on the guard boats in the bay. Concern was expressed that these men were drawing their navy pay and ration allowance while benefiting from their privateering ventures.[35]

On August 13 Philadelphia was the scene of the most celebrated court-martial of the State navy. Lieutenant Samuel Ford, of the galley *Effingham*, was tried for deserting to the British during the siege of Fort Mifflin. Along with Ford, separate trials were held for Lieutenants Lyons and Wilson and gunner Lawrence. All were convicted of desertion and sentenced to death. Protestations were made by leading citizens of the city to the Council, expressing hope that the lives of some of the condemned men might be spared. Their pleadings were partially successful, as Wilson and Lawrence received reprieves and later, in November, pardons. Lyons's and Ford's convictions were upheld and both were shot on board a guard boat in September 1778.[36]

All energies of the State naval authorities were now centered on outfitting the *Convention*. Houston and his crew had visions of rich prizes and were anxious to put to sea. Hazelwood furnished twenty-five galleymen to round out the crew and Council completed the complement of officers. Houston sailed from Philadelphia in late August. Meager records survive of the results of the cruise of the *Convention*. At least two prizes were taken, a brig and sloop. The libeling of the sloop was to become one of the most celebrated cases in admiralty law in the United States.

Four residents of Connecticut, led by Gideon Olmstead, were taken prisoner by the British and carried to Jamaica. There they were transferred to the sloop *Active* to assist the crew on its voyage to New York. Somewhere off the New Jersey coast the four Americans overpowered the captain and crew, even though outnumbered more than three to one. Olmstead assumed command and headed for Egg Harbor, but was soon overtaken by the *Convention* and her consort the *Gerard*, privateer. Houston took the *Active* into Philadelphia and libeled against her as a prize, while the privateer also claimed a share. On the other hand, Olmstead and his friends demanded the entire prize money. A State court awarded the Connecticut seamen one-fourth of the prize moneys and divided the remainder between the *Convention* and the privateer.

Olmstead and his shipmates appealed to the Federal Commissioners who, on December 15, reversed the decision of the State court and awarded the monies to the claimants. Judge Ross of the Pennsylvania Admiralty Court recognized the authority of the commissioners, but refused to change the verdict of the State court. Judge Ross ordered the *Active* and its cargo sold, with the proceeds turned over to the court, pending disposition of the case. Olmstead attempted to prevent the sale of the *Active* by the State-designated marshal. As the marshal was out of the jurisdiction of the Court of Appeals, he ignored the commissioners and proceeded with the sale.

A further hearing was scheduled on January 5, 1779. Prior to the hearing the commissioners were alerted by Benedict Arnold, acting as attorney for Olmstead, that the Judge of the State Admiralty Court was adamant and would insist that the proceeds of the sale be turned over to him. The commissioners then ordered the marshal to hold the funds subject to further instructions from them, but he ignored their order and placed the funds in Judge Ross's hands.

Thus began a case that would not be settled for thirty years —a confrontation between Federal and State authority. The marshal had ignored the Federal government and the Federal court was unwilling to force the issue while the nation was engaged in a war of survival with Great Britain. It was decided to lay the matter before the Continental Congress, but it was obvious that the issue was too hot to handle.

The case dragged through the courts and the funds were eventually deposited with the Treasurer of Pennsylvania, David Rittenhouse. Rittenhouse was to stand security for the money until the Judge of Admiralty made a disposition of the final proceeds. Prize monies were expected to exceed £11,000. The State's portion was to be shared equally with the *Convention*'s crew. Here the matter rested for a few years until Rittenhouse's death in 1802. Olmstead and his companions sued the executrixes of the Rittenhouse estate in the United States District Court for Pennsylvania.

Judge Peters of the district court reviewed the case and declared for the Olmstead party. The State passed legislation ordering the State Attorney General to sue the executrixes, Mrs. Elizabeth Sergeant and Mrs. Esther Waters, daughters of Rittenhouse, demanding they turn the prize money over to the State. In addition, the Governor was instructed by the legislature to protect the executrixes from Federal process servers.

The case was finally carried to the United States Supreme Court in 1809, and in February of that year Chief Justice John Marshall read the opinion, which favored Olmstead and his friends, and ordered the executrixes to deliver the prize money to the claimants.

A small war seemed to be developing as Pennsylvania troops were stationed around the Rittenhouse home at the northwest corner of Seventh and Arch Streets. The house was facetiously dubbed "Fort Rittenhouse." After five weeks of virtual siege during March and April 1809, a Federal marshal eluded the vigilance of the troops and served the writ. Litigation continued for some time, but the award of the prize monies was finally made to the Connecticut seamen.[37]

With the reduction of the fleet to a small patrol flotilla, Council appointed Captain Nathan Boys as squadron commander. Boys assumed personal command of the galley *Franklin* with George Garland on the *Hancock* and Isaac Roach on the *Chatham*. Three guard boats were also included in the squadron: *Fame*, Captain Thomas Hazelwood; *Viper*, Stephen Beasley; *Lyon*, Henry Martin. The sloop *Liberty* was to remain in service as a supply ship to Boys's small squadron. Boys was assigned the security of the chevaux-de-frise and the river passes. Commodore Hazelwood remained available as a consultant and retained administrative supervision of the fleet for several months. The *Fame* was temporarily deactivated in December 1778, when Captain Hazelwood received permission to make an independent cruise to the West Indies.

Typical of wartime, profiteering and self-interest were causing concern to the civil authorities of Pennsylvania. The military and civilian population were hungry and grains, meat, and other provisions were in short supply. The British had confiscated large quantities of foodstuffs, and equally significant amounts were being shipped out by merchants. A thirty-day embargo was declared in August 1778, and repeated several times during the ensuing few years. The Commodore was entrusted with the enforcement of the embargo and was to forbid any vessel carrying foodstuffs to clear the port. In this connection, Hazelwood, on September 18, was requested to station a galley at the Cape May channel to enforce the embargo. His orders contained the usual admonition not to ". . . continue one of the low-built Gallies in so exposed a situation. . . ." for an extended period. Also, a guard boat was to be sent down to Reedy Island with similar instructions. Captain Boys later assumed responsibility for enforcing the embargo.[38]

At the end of August Arthur Donaldson was authorized to raise the wrecks in the Delaware. A number were obstructing navigation, and Council had been petitioned to ensure safe passage for American merchantmen. A number of British ships had been lost on the chevaux-de-frise—a Hessian hospital ship, British merchant ship and brig, and unquestionably others were sunk during the previous year. Before the British invasion several local merchants had lost ships through carelessly attempting to bring their ships through the obstructions without a pilot. Donaldson was empowered to call on Boys for assistance from the galleys and guard boats.

On Monday, December 7, 1778, Council advertised the sale of ten galleys, nine guard boats, brig *Convention*, sloops *Speedwell*, *Sally*, and *Industry*, shallop *Black Duck*, and the schooner *Lydia*, to be held on Friday, December 11, at two o'clock in the afternoon at the Coffee House by public vendue for cash only. Council advised Hazelwood of the proposed sale, adding that all vessels and boats were laid up except one galley still sunk in the waters of Crosswicks Creek. George Henry was selected to supervise the sale of the fleet with all apparel and furniture except the guns. He was to receive the same commission awarded the marshal of admiralty in similar sales. A few days later Council ordered Henry to sell the best galley for £500 and the others at a proportionate value, but none for less than £300. Apparently changing their minds, Council authorized Henry on December 14 to sell all guns under six-pounders in pairs. Henry was ordered to bid in any boats, ships or guns not agreeable to the terms of the auction as set by the State. No record survives of the details of the sale or the amount realized. However, on January 4, 1779, Henry reported to Council that a number of vessels had been sold and part of the proceeds turned into the State Treasurer. A complete accounting was expected by Henry within a few days.[39]

Evidently the Council was satisfied with Henry's performance, as they appointed him Commissary of Naval Stores, with full responsibility for all the vessels not in commission, guns, arms, and naval stores, with a salary of eight dollars per day and expenses.[40]

The question of prize money for the crews was again revived by Commodore Hazelwood. Many of the seamen had been discharged in August, and, finding employment difficult to obtain, were in need of funds to take care of their families. Council recognized their moral responsibility to the men and the legitimacy of their claim to prize monies.

It would appear that Council was desirous of making an equitable distribution of the prize monies to all officers and men of the navy. A sliding scale according to rank was established.

The scale of prize awards prepared by Council was:

Commodore	— one twelfth of the entire proceeds
Chief surgeon of the fleet and director of the hospital (ship excepted— this meant the *Montgomery*, destroyed November, 1777)	— four and one-sixth shares
Captains	— four shares
First lieutenants	— two and one-half shares
Second lieutenants, masters, boatswains, surgeons mate	— one and two-thirds shares
Mates, gunners, clerk and steward of the fleet, boatswains, carpenters	— one and one-third shares
Clerks and stewards of the ship and battery, other petty officers (if any)	— one and one-sixth shares
Armourer	— one and one-twelfth shares
Privates, cook	— one share
Drummers and fifers	— five-sixths share
Boys	— one-half share [41]

XIV

The *General Greene*—1779

WITH THE American capital free of the invader, it was hoped that it could be restored to its preoccupation status. Unfortunately, ugly specters soon arose in the proliferation of greed, black marketing, profiteering, and hoarding. Provisions in all categories were scarce and a number of merchants were shipping out what small reserves of grain, meat, and other foodstuffs were available. Council and the Assembly were forced to place periodic embargoes during 1778 and 1779 to alleviate hunger in the city. Some of the hoarders and black-market operators were detected and sentenced to the city's gaol.

Added to the misery of the inhabitants of the Delaware Valley was the toll being taken by British cruisers. Enemy frigates stationed at the entrance of the bay blockaded the port. Few merchant ships slipped through the capes, and legitimate and profiteering merchants alike were clamoring for protection. Merchants were suffering huge losses, but were willing to gamble. Inflation had sky-rocketed prices and the profits from one successful cruise more than offset the loss of several merchant ships. However, fewer ships were reaching the city's wharves and all merchants were aware that measures must be taken to protect shipping.

The merchants importuned Council for protection, as the residue of the State fleet was capable of little except defensive action above the chevaux-de-frise. The few elements of the fleet that had been capable of operating in the lower bay, or venturing to sea, had been either sold or destroyed, and Council took steps to lease or buy a vessel that could cruise near the capes.

To finance the acquisition of a ship, the merchants agreed to lend money to the State. Blair McClenachan and Matthew Irwin were selected as agents to locate a suitable vessel and equip and man her. They were authorized to receive funds offered to the State on loan and were to stipulate that all monies advanced would be repaid in six months or sooner, if convenient to the State. McClenachan and Irwin were to acknowledge the loans, give receipts, and prepare an accounting of such funds for the Council and State Treasurer, turning the monies over to the latter official.[1]

Inquiries were made as to the availability of vessels adequate for service as ocean-going cruisers. President Joseph Reed [2] of the Council advised the Continental Marine Committee of the State's plight, but it was obvious that no relief was possible from that source. Reed was considering a cutter, the *Revenge*, owned jointly by Nesbitt & Company and the Continental government.[3] McClenachan and Irwin were ordered to examine the *Revenge* and determine whether she were suitable for the State's needs. The Revenge was found to be in a satisfactory condition for a cruise. The Marine Committee had confidentially apprised Reed that the many ramifications of ownership of the cutter would force a sale at public auction.[4]

Undaunted, the Council, on April 1, 1779, instructed McClenachan and Irwin to approach the owners and negotiate for a three-months' cruise in consort with the new ship the Council was interested in purchasing. The agents reported back to Council the next day detailing the owners' terms. They insisted that the *Revenge*'s captain, Gustavus Conyngham, remain in command; that the State fully insure for the owners' cost; that the cutter be returned in as good condition as received or a sum agreed on by three impartial judges be forfeited. Finally, the State must agree to pay £10,000 each month while the ship was in service.[5]

The Eyre Shipyard in Kensington was building a privateer for the firm of Irwin, Barclay, Coxe, and Mitchell. As the ship was nearly finished, and equipped with eight cannon, three pair of howitzers, and some ballast, Council evinced interest. Irwin and his associates agreed to waive their claim to the ship to permit Council to negotiate with Benjamin Eyre for her purchase. An agreement was apparently made about March 23 when the Irwin group asked Council for a final determination on their intent to purchase the ship. Consummation of the sale would await an appraisal of the value of the ship, now called the *General Greene*, by impartial judges. McClenachan and Irwin were assigned to arm and equip the ship. Irwin suggested renaming the *General Greene* in honor of the President of Council, the *General Reed*. Joseph Reed declined the honor out of respect for his friend, General Nathanael Greene.

Joseph Rush and James Craig, Jr., representing the State, and Thomas Penrose and Samuel C. Morris, the owners, were selected to appraise the *General Greene* and submit a certificate of evaluation to be the basis for a settlement. On April 16, the judges submitted an evaluation of £53,057 11s, which was paid Benjamin Eyre and Company on April 26.[6] No evidence exists to show any equity in the ship by Irwin and Associates. If Irwin had made advance payments to Eyre, any liability of Eyre's was probably resolved at the time of the payment for the *General Greene*. Title must have been vested in Eyre, as there would have been a clear conflict of interest on Irwin's part, as agent negotiating to buy his own ship for the State.

The acquisition of the *General Greene* added a privateer to the roster of the State navy. The only reason for its inclusion as a ship of the navy was because it came under the direction of Council. Otherwise, the ship had no connection with the little navy that defended the river passes. In the summer of 1778, Captain Thomas Houston and the brig *Convention* had been dispatched to sea on a similar cruise, which had been planned in part to give employment to the discharged galley and ship crews.

McClenachan and Irwin had proceeded with their recommendations of officers for the General Greene. They submitted three names for consideration: Captains James Montgomery and Thomas Houston, both former galley captains, and John

Green of the Continental navy. On March 30, Council selected James Montgomery. Houston, one of the better galley captains, may have been passed over because of his involvement in what was becoming the celebrated case of the prize sloop. *Active.* Other officers appointed were First Lieutenant Samuel Cassan (from the galley *Franklin*), Second Lieutenant Jacob de Hart, and Samuel Hollingshead, master. A marine contingent independent of the ship's command was established with Robert Caldwell as captain and John Hambright, Jr., lieutenant.[7]

Many problems confronted Council and the agents; men must be recruited, pay scales and prize money distribution established, and guns, ammunition, and ship furniture procured. McClenachan and Irwin appealed to the Continental Marine Committee, to Joseph Stiles, commissary of military stores, and George Henry, naval storekeeper, for cannon, guns, and ammunition. The *General Greene* was finally outfitted to carry fourteen cannon, with howitzers in the tops. The caliber of her cannon were three- and six-pounders with the former predominating. The issue of shot shows one thousand round-shot and six-hundred double-headed shot for three-pounders with only fifty round shot and one hundred fifty double-headed shot for six-pounders.[8]

In the meantime, Council was groping with pay scales and a method of distributing prizes. Competition with privateersmen for the available seamen in port was a losing battle. A pay scale was established for officers and marines without specific reference to able-bodied seamen. Marines on board the *General Greene* were to receive six and two-third dollars per month. At this time seamen on board the galleys and guard boats were paid twelve dollars a month, but with practically no opportunity to share in prize monies. There is little reason to doubt that with the anticipated prize ships to be captured, the seamen of the *General Greene* were paid the equivalent of the marines, but not the galleymen. Brewington contended that the seamen were paid five to eight dollars a month; the amount paid the marines falls within this range. Prize monies were to be distributed according to the method previously declared by Council for the State navy.

To specifically cover the crew of the *General Greene,* Council decreed that all "Officers, Sailors & Marines of the Vessels now fitted, or which may hereafter be fitted out by this State, be subject to the like Articles of War, Regulations and Tryal, as the Officers, Sailors & Marines of the Gallies. . . ." McClenachan and Irwin had recommended that the funds realized from the sale of a prize be distributed in the same proportion as that of the Continental service. Full proceeds on all "Kings ships" and enemy privateers, and one half of all letters of marque and non-commissioned vessels should be awarded the crews. Council accepted this recommendation with one emendation, that if cruising in consort (Council still had hopes an arrangement could be made with owners of the *Revenge*) only three-quarters of the proceeds of the sale of a commissioned vessel would be allowed the crews, the other one-quarter would revert to the State.[9]

The question of taking the *Revenge* on a voyage with the *General Greene* was the subject of long deliberations in Council chambers. It was agreed that the terms were unrealistic and unacceptable to the State. A decision was made on April 15 to return the cutter to her owners.[10]

With pay scales and the method of awarding prize monies established, a rendezvous was opened in the city with the usual fanfare. Fifes and drums furnished music, and the local tavern searched fruitlessly for recruits. None came forward, so Council was forced to top the offer of the privateers. Council advised the agents that an advance could be offered the men as soon as their enlistment papers were signed. Each able-bodied seaman would be paid one hundred dollars and each landsman fifty dollars, to be deducted from the anticipated prize monies. All this added up to one final spree for some, and disappearance for others. Some signed their enlistment papers, received their advance, and promptly enlisted on a privateer and put to sea. The number of deserters compelled Council to place an embargo on ships leaving port until the *General Greene* was fully manned. This decree brought a few more men to the recruiting-officers; however, many of them took their bounty money and ran away to other states. Deserters were taken in Baltimore and forced to return. Two Baltimore sea captains were forced to post bond to prevent them from impressing seamen from the *General Greene* on the pretense that they were merely recruiting.[11]

On April 26 recruiting instructions for the marine contingent were released to Captain Caldwell. He was advised that his company was to consist of himself, one lieutenant, three sergeants, four corporals, one drummer, one fifer, and thirty-five privates—a total of forty-six officers and men. He was to enlist only able-bodied men, with age limits of eighteen to fifty years.

Marines were to take the following oath, which was probably identical for the seamen:

I [AB] do swear that I will be true and faithful to the State of Pennsylvania and that I will be obedient to such officers as may be appointed by the State over me, that I will make known any mutinies and conspiracies which may come to my knowledge in the said Service, and in all things do my duty as a faithful Subject and Soldier of the State of Pennsylvania, so help me God.

No men were to be recruited from the Continental army and navy or the State galleys. They were to serve on the *General Greene* as long as the ship was in the State's service. Each marine was eligible for a proportionate share of prize money. They were to receive a bounty of fifty dollars when mustered into the service, wages would be at the rate of six and two-thirds dollars, with rations on board or shore equal to that of marines in the Continental service.

Deviation from the instructions by an officer would make him liable for all monies expended.[12]

Frustration beset the Council, Montgomery and Caldwell compelling them to take drastic action to find seamen and marines for the *General Greene*. Montgomery resorted to the old British custom of impressment. This expedient yielded only a handful of men, and finally Council ordered Montgomery to take men from the city gaol. There Montgomery picked up deserters from the State galleys, British prisoners and deserters, and thieves and hoodlums. Sprogell, commissary of musters, made a return on May 24 showing eighty-three seamen and officers, and for the marines twenty-nine men and officers on board ship. The next day Council informed Montgomery that he should put to sea without further delay.[13]

On May 25 the *General Greene* dropped down the bay and passed through the capes. Montgomery had decided to cruise northward along the New Jersey coast. The sea lanes leading to New York were popular with British merchantmen and privateers, and Montgomery viewed this as a fertile area for the taking of prizes.

Reed had unsuccessfully endeavored to reach Montgomery before he sailed through the capes. He sent a messenger directing the *General Greene* to join a squadron of Continental frigates on a mission to destroy British shipping. The Continental Marine Committee had ordered the frigates *Boston*, Captain Samuel Tucker, and the *Confederacy*, Captain Seth Harding, to cruise between latitudes 40 and 35 degrees and ". . . to take, burn, sink or destroy as many of the enemy's Ships or Vessels of every kind as may be in their power." The squadron would be commanded by Captain Tucker.[14]

Missing Reed's messenger at Lewes, Montgomery cruised for several days, until on June 7 he sighted a sail on the horizon coming from the direction of New York. Giving chase, the *General Greene* soon overhauled the privateer brigatine *Impertinent*, "of ten dubel [double] fortified four pounders Captain Jacob Getshues [Getchus]." The *Impertinent*'s crew of fifty-three were transferred to the *General Greene* and Lieutenant Cassan with a prize crew placed on the captured ship. The *Impertinent* had been sailing in consort with two British frigates and a privateersman, but had become separated in the fog and sailed into the path of the *General Greene*. Montgomery sighted the other British ships but with a strong northeast wind and an ebb tide, he was confident he could outsail them. He ordered Cassan to take the *Impertinent* to New Castle to be libeled as a prize.[15]

Montgomery made all possible speed for the Delaware; en route he found his mizzenmast to be "intiearley Rotton." Since several of his most dependable seamen were on the *Impertinent* with Cassan, he advised Reed that he did not have six able-bodied seamen. Many members of the original crew were British prisoners or deserters, and with the hoodlums from the streets of Philadelphia, were ready to mutiny if an opportunity presented itself. Montgomery had placed the ringleaders in irons and sent them with Cassan, who was ordered to turn them over to authorities in Philadelphia, and inform Reed as to the conditions aboard the *General Greene*.[16]

Fortune again smiled on the *General Greene* as she captured a small schooner from Virginia, the *Humming Bird*.[17]

Entering Delaware Bay, the *General Greene* dropped anchor in the roadstead and while Montgomery anxiously scanned the horizon, two strange sails came into view. As they came closer, they were identified as frigates. Montgomery took stock: the *General Greene* needed repairs, and in her hold were the prisoners from the *Impertinent, Humming Bird* and, most dangerous of all, the mutinious members of the *General Greene*'s own crew. With prisoners outnumbering the loyal crewmen, Montgomery believed his most sagacious course would be to proceed to New Castle for repairs.

The General Greene arrived at New Castle on June 9, and the repairs were speedily completed. Montgomery sent the balance of the recalcitrant crew members to Philadelphia, where they were imprisoned. The success of the first cruise was well known in the city and lured numbers of able-bodied seamen to New Castle to enlist. Only one muster roll of the *General Greene* has survived, covering the period of June 1 through August 31, 1779. Recorded are the names of one hundred seamen and forty marines, including officers. This muster includes, in part at least, seamen who served on the first two cruises of the *General Greene*. At least six seamen listed are known to have deserted while the ship was under repairs at New Castle. The names of the mutineers are probably included, as the muster roll was first taken on June 1, eight days before Montgomery came to anchor off the little Delaware port. The exact number on board when Montgomery sailed on June 15 cannot be determined, but it was certainly a more capable and loyal crew than on the first cruise.[18]

On the 15th Reed again instructed Montgomery to join the Continental squadron under Captain Tucker for a cruise of three weeks. At the expiration of that period, Montgomery was free to return to the roadstead inside the capes or continue at sea. His judgment should be based on the condition of the *General Greene* and the state of her stores, but under no circumstances, except in a dire emergency, should he return to port. Extra stores and ammunition for the *General Greene* would be sent down to Lewes.[19]

Reed entrusted his orders to Captain Tucker, who delivered them to Montgomery off Lewes on June 29. For two weeks the *General Greene* had been fruitlessly cruising between Cape May and Sandy Hook. Montgomery had chased one enemy privateer only to run into a heavily armed British cruiser, which forced the *General Greene* to retreat. Seeking shelter in the roadstead near Lewes, Montgomery was startled by the appearance of two large ships on the horizon. With relief he discovered the approaching ships to be the Continental frigates *Boston* and *Confederacy*. Montgomery was soon exchanging salutations with Tucker and Harding and receiving his instructions from Reed. A short time later the frigate *Deane* was sighted and joined the squadron. As Captain Samuel Nicholson of the *Deane* was the senior captain, he assumed command of the flotilla.[20]

Word had been received that three British frigates were cruising off the capes, and the American captains were anxious to test arms with the enemy. Sighting two sail, they started in pursuit, and gradually the American squadron overhauled the strange ships. The enemy ships quickly ran up the British flag but, to the dismay of the Americans, they discovered not two but three ships; a two-decker (probably in the fifty- to sixty-four-gun class), a small frigate, and a large sloop of twelve or fourteen guns. Decidedly out-gunned, the Americans turned and, with all hands at their battle stations, headed for the capes —Montgomery wrote—"determined to sell their ships dearly if overtaken." [21] Some have questioned the courage of Nicholson on this occasion. Certainly acting in consort with the Continental frigates was not to Montgomery's liking.

The Continental frigates soon received orders and departed on their separate missions, leaving the *General Greene* at the capes. Shortly after the frigates' departure Montgomery set sail for his favorite cruising waters along the New Jersey coast in the vicinity of Sandy Hook. In early July the *General Greene* took a ship, the *William and Ann*, which appears to have been her richest prize. Of three hundred tons, she carried slaves and a cargo of molasses, sugar, and coffee. The ship's cargo was sold at public auction and brought £83,062 12s 11d.[22]

Montgomery's activities for the next two months are shrouded in darkness. However, during this period complaints were regis-

tered with Council of inhuman treatment of the crew and
impressment of private citizens. John Jay, President of Congress,
acting on an official French protest, wrote Reed requesting an
investigation of the case of one Francis Fleury (not the hero
of Fort Mifflin), a French citizen, and his immediate release
if he had been illegally held. Timothy Pickering, on August
20, vigorously protested that two New England seamen
serving on board the *General Greene* had been barbarously
treated, especially by a "Lieutenant Castwind." (Cassan was
Montgomery's most trusted subordinate, all major prizes were
confidently entrusted to him, and he never failed to reach port
safely with his prize ship.) The complainants said they had
served on several ships but had never suffered such inhuman
treatment. They were not interested in compensation, just a
discontinuance of the conditions on board the *General Greene.*
The disposition of these complaints is unknown, but they serve
to show that all was not beer and skittles on board the State
privateer.[23]

In mid-September, while cruising off the Delaware capes, the
General Greene was buffeted by heavy winds from the north.
After four days the storm abated and a relieved crew noted
that the ship had suffered little damage, but the winds had
forced the *General Greene* far down the Virginia coast, and
what was more serious, all food spoiled. Spying a sail on September 18, Montgomery gave chase. The *General Greene,* with
her bottom fouled with barnacles and the crew starving, was
determined to overtake the strange sail. As they came broadside
to the stranger, now identified as a brigantine, all hands were
piped to their stations. Through his trumpet, Montgomery demanded the brigantine's surrender; without hesitation the British
flag was lowered. No resistance had been offered, since the prize,
the *Bayard,* in an effort to ride out the same storm that had
buffeted the *General Greene,* had cast its guns overboard to
lighten ship.

The prisoners were placed in the hold of the *General Greene*
and a prize crew was transferred to the *Bayard.* The most significant find was a well-stocked galley, and for a famished crew
this was more precious than gold.[24]

Entering the Delaware about the 20th, Montgomery again

headed for New Castle to turn his prisoners over to the authorities. After making hasty repairs and loading fresh supplies on board, the *General Greene* again headed for sea.

Returning to Cape May on October 6, Montgomery reported taking three prizes. One was a New York privateer, the *Langolee*. The other two were American vessels captured by the British and now retaken by the *General Greene*, the *Bedford* and the *Generous Friend*. The latter prize was taken in company with a Philadelphia privateer, the *Holker*, Captain Geddes. These would be the last prizes taken by the *General Greene* as a State ship.

Montgomery observed that the rigging of his ship was in need of repairs. After making them he planned to put to sea, but expected that he soon would be forced to return to port. His provisions were low and the increased boisterous weather would prevent "... our poor Egg Shell to Cruze...."[25]

Before Montgomery could put to sea, instructions were received to return to port. Council had decided that the *General Greene* could not withstand the turbulent weather that prevailed off the New Jersey coast in the winter season. About November 1 they determined to sell the *General Greene* at public auction and Irwin was ordered to supervise the sale.[26]

The sum of £67,450 was realized from the sale of the State ship. According to a modern authority, the total cost to the State for the ship, its armament, provisions, and supplies was £80,734 10s 11d.[27]

Council was disturbed by rumors and expressions of dissatisfaction with the methods employed at the sale of the *General Greene*. The critics charged that the ship was sold below its real value because Irwin neglected his responsibilities as the State's agent. On November 3 Council appointed a committee to investigate the actions of Irwin, and particularly the accusation that the *General Greene* was stripped after the sale.

McClenachan, Irwin, George Henry, and Montgomery were ordered to appear before the committee and give testimony bearing on the sale. The special committee made "... all possible inquiry into the circumstances of the sale of the ship *General Greene*...." Unable or unwilling to point the finger of guilt, the committee reported that the purchasers had made honest bids, but nothing was found that would have prevented the suspected loss to the State. Council accepted the committee's findings and, on November 19, resolved, "That the Agents receive the purchase money and deliver the ship, without further loss of time." Suspicion was not put to rest. Many believed the success of the *General Greene* stirred the cupidity of certain people in authority.[28]

The *General Greene* cost the State £53,057 11s in April and in November was sold for £67,450. Expenditures of £27,676 19s 11d were made for cannon, ammunition, supplies, and provisions, making a total outlay on the ship of £80,734 10s 11d. It is always difficult to sift fact from rumors. If there were malfeasance or collusion in recording the bids, it was apparently not discovered by the committee. On the other hand, the specific charge of stripping the ship after the sale, if upheld, would have been a case of defrauding the purchasers, unless the agreement of sale detailed particular equipment.

The returns of four of the prize ships show proceeds of £210,077 13s 5d. The amount and disposition of the proceeds from the two remaining prizes is not indicated. On the other hand, a modern authority has estimated prize monies of £462,080 0s 4d was realized from the ships captured by the *General Greene*. The State's share of these sums is unknown but it would certainly have exceeded any disbursements made to operate the ship.[29]

A list of prizes taken by the *General Greene* was included in a letter from Francis Hopkinson in March 1788. The prizes were libeled and reviewed by Judge George Ross of the Court of Admiralty. He ruled in favor of the State and crew of the State ship and directed the funds be paid to Michael Hillegas, Treasurer of Pennsylvania. The list omits reference to the *Generous Friend* taken in consort with the *Holker*. The list does not include all details of these transactions: however, it does give evidence that the crews received generous shares of the prizes. The report submitted by Hopkinson is of interest:

List of Prizes taken by the Ship General Green whilst she was commanded by James Montgomery & belonged to the State of Pennsylvania.

The Humming Bird — Libel dated June 17, 1779—½ decreed to the State, & to the officers & Crew of the Ship—½ to remain

	till claimed, no return made by the Marshall, or Acct render'd to the Admiralty office
Brig Impertinent	— Augt. 3rd 1779—Nett Proceeds £ 48,491 15s paid as per return to Blair McClenachan & Matthew Irwin, agents for the ship Gen'l Green
Ship Will^{am} & Mary [or Anne]	— Sept. 18, 1779—Nett Proceeds £ 83,062 12s 11d paid as per Return to B. McClenachan & M. Irwin Agents
Brig Bayard	— Nov. 5th, 1779—Nett Proceeds £ 69,816 1s 6d paid as per return, ¼ thereof to Blair McClenachan & M. Irwin Agents for the State & ¾ to William Graham Agent for the Officers & Crew of Ship Genl. Green
Sloop Bedford	— Nov. 15th 1779—Nett Proceeds £ 8,707 4s paid as per return ¼ thereof to Blair McClenachan & M. Irwin Agts for the State & W. Graham Agt. for Officers & Crew of G. Green
The Langolee	— Nov. 13th 1779—Prize to the State & Officers & Crew of the Genl Green—No Return or Acc't render'd.[30]

The officers and crew of the *General Greene* were dissatisfied with the decisions of Council, particularly the abrupt termination of their service. Brusque action where the navy was concerned was characteristic of Council and did not surprise those who had previously served on the galleys. They remembered that in 1778 many dedicated officers and men (some included in the present crew of the *General Greene*) with up to three years of faithful service had been unceremoniously dismissed. To forestall a repetition of such treatment, immediately upon arriving in port they appointed an agent, W. Graham, to represent them in all negotiations. They also petitioned Council to determine their status as officers of the State navy and whether they were covered by the Resolution of March 13, 1779. At that time the Assembly had declared that officers, seamen, and mariners in the naval service of the State would be entitled to the same benefits granted the officers and soldiers of the State in the Continental army. Council denied their petition, declaring that the *General Greene* was not in commission when the resolution was promulgated. At least Montgomery and his men would have their well-earned prize money.[31]

Despite the many obstacles in obtaining and outfitting the *General Greene* and the subsequent threats of mutiny, the State ship fulfilled its mission. Along with the Continental frigates she was instrumental in opening the Delaware to commercial traffic. Merchant ships again docked at the Philadelphia wharves. The needs of the city were satisfied and the specter of hunger disappeared.

Other ships owned by the State or merchants of Philadelphia were usually referred to as State ships. However, Council never made the mistake of considering them elements of the State navy. In reality, they operated as privateers subject to the administration of the Commissioners for Defence of River Delaware (John Patton, Francis Gurney and William Allibone). The most famous of the privateers was the *Hyder Ally*, commanded by Joshua Barney. Her encounter with the British privateer *General Monk* was one of the most spectacular engagements between privateers in the war. The *General Monk* had originally been the American privateer *General Washington*, taken by the British and now retaken by the *Hyder Ally*. Renamed the *General Washington*, she was sold to the Continental navy in September 1782.[32]

XV

Disbandment of the Navy—1779-1783

THE ORDER of August 1778 that the majority of the officers and men be discharged finally took effect in February 1779. Council advised the General Assembly on February 5 that with the sale of the major portion of the fleet in December 1778, and the release of the crews, their cost reduction program had been fulfilled.

The question of prize money due discharged seamen continued to plague the Council. In December 1778, four ex-lieutenants of the State fleet, Thomas Fell of the *Burke*, Thomas Philips of the *Convention*, Alexander Campbell of the *Putnam* and William Rozen (probably William Rogers of the *Volcano*), had petitioned for their share of the prize money for items salvaged from the *Augusta* and *Merlin*. Council ordered the lieutenants to make a formal declaration of their claims, outlining in detail all transactions involving the wrecks. Council contended that they were unacquainted with the items in question and that no proceeds were turned over to the State. This was a strange statement because Joseph Blewer's account book for the State navy, covering the period of October and November 1777, gives an itemized accounting of the material salvaged from the *Augusta* and *Merlin*.[1] It would be interesting to know whether the lieutenants received their prize money.

Captain Boys was ordered to station the remaining galleys and guard boats at Fort Mifflin. Rarely would the three galleys and three guard boats see action as a unit. They would operate principally on detached service, patrolling the river passes, defending the chevaux-de-frise, serving as lookout boats at the capes, on occasion garrisoning Fort Mifflin and Billingsport, and being employed in special services as ordered by Council. Boys's muster roll of March 31, 1779, listed 125 officers and men, a surgeon, paymaster, muster master, and clerk.[2]

Captain Martin, with the guard boat *Lyon*, was assigned to duty at the lookout post at Lewes. The *Lyon* was to patrol inside Cape Henlopen and close to shore on watch for British frigates or privateers. All out-bound merchant ships were to be alerted to potential danger from enemy ships before passing out through the capes. Martin was ordered to remain at his station as long as the service was necessary or until weather forced his return to Fort Mifflin.[3]

A lack of compassion for the wounded and disabled seamen is manifest in the scattered references to their sufferings recorded in the minutes of Council. Some individual seamen requested release when unable to perform assigned duties. This was usually granted without giving the men their back pay. Subsequently undergoing traumatic experiences, unable to obtain employment and in some cases physically incapable of working, they were forced to petition Council for their back wages. Council, with an exhausted treasury, was forced to be parsimonious, but eventually honored the entreaties of the disabled seamen. Although slow to recognize the urgent needs of the veterans of the navy, Council paradoxically expressed deep concern for the invalid seamen who remained on the muster rolls.

John Turner, of the galley *Washington*, lost an eye in the actions of 1777 and was discharged on September 1, 1778. He was forced to petition for his back pay which he received on February 17, 1779. Francis Bryan lost an arm and was compelled to ask for his back pay. Widows of seamen killed in action requested assistance and were granted temporary relief usually in the form of subsistence rations. Captain Tatnall had suffered great hardships as a prisoner of the British. His health was affected by his imprisonment and subsequently caused his death. In April 1779 his widow petitioned for his pay and rations to the time of his death. As late as September 1786 she was still fruitlessly seeking relief. These are a few of the veterans and veterans' widows who were forgotten and ultimately forced to beg for redress of what was rightfully due them.[4]

Legislation had provided certain benefits to the State militia, but the navy had been ignored. Persistent petitions spurred Council to action. On March 25, 1779, Council decreed that naval personnel would receive the same benefits and allowances as the military. Boys was asked to submit a complete return of officers and men, so that a list could be established of those eligible for benefits.[5] No provision was made for those men released because of the fleet cost reduction program of 1778, or those wounded in action and discharged.

The British had removed some of the river obstructions to permit their shipping to reach the Philadelphia wharves. Colonel Bull was ordered to construct six chevaux-de-frise of varying sizes for different depths, and Captain Boys was to furnish him with boats and any assistance necessary. Bull conferred with Boys and galley captains Roach and Garland to determine if six frames were sufficient and to agree on the proper locations to sink them. Improvements were authorized for Fort Mifflin and Bull was to build barracks for the men and apartments for the officers. A new battery was being constructed on the ruins of the old fort and cannon and howitzers were ordered sent to the battery and also to Billingsport.[6]

In the meantime, Washington and the State authorities agreed that the city was vulnerable to British naval attacks, either in force or of the hit-and-run variety. Reed addressed the governors of nearby states asking their cooperation in establishing a defense against British raids on the New Jersey coast and the Delaware River and Bay. The governors were informed that no ships would be permitted to leave Philadelphia until the State galleys and guard boats had full crews. Boys's small squadron was considered the key to the defense of the port.[7]

Washington offered to furnish engineers to make a survey of the river and adjacent terrain, and prepare plans for the location of fortifications and river obstructions. Washington reposed great confidence in the engineering skills of General Louis Le Beque Duportail and instructed him to contact Reed. Accompanied by Baron von Steuben, Colonel Nicola, Colonel Proctor, David Rittenhouse of the Council, and Captain Thomas Hazelwood, Duportail planned to make a preliminary survey of the area. Several aides of Duportail also joined the party. Captain Boys was ordered to place his available boats at the disposal of the survey group. Taking their horses, they crossed at Gloucester Point (Philadelphia) and rode to Fort Mercer, Billingsport, and then recrossed to the Pennsylvania side.[8]

Duportail returned to the main camp and reported to Washington and the Board of War. He outlined to the Continental officers his conditions for carrying out the proposed survey. On March 8, the Board of War informed Reed of the limitations under which Duportail would operate. He refused to accept any map or sounding of the river made by other engineers. He further contended that it would not be possible to plan proper fortifications or river defenses unless he conducted a personal survey. In no other way could he acquaint himself with the river and terrain. Duportail added that the entire transaction must be kept secret until the project was finished. He asked for the assistance of four engineers, but only his aide, Colonel Lewis de la Radière, and himself were to know the details of the survey. With Radière he would conduct the survey by boat; the other engineers would work on shore. To impress Council, he claimed he could complete the survey in a few days while nonengineering personnel (probably an allusion to Colonels Bull and Proctor and other Pennsylvanians working at Fort Mifflin and Billingsport) would take several weeks.[9]

Council refused to accede to Duportail's demand for secrecy. They did not wish to lose the services of the Frenchman but insisted that Duportail, or any person engaged on State business, must keep Council informed. Finally, on March 29, Duportail addressed the Council asking if they desired him to execute Washington's order or, if not, give him their refusal in writing. Two days later Council, spurred by a desire not to offend Washington, passed a resolution apparently granting Duportail many of his demands. (Unfortunately the resolution was omitted from the published archives and is now missing.) Duportail received and accepted Council's offer the next day.[10]

Duportail, assisted by Radière and cartographer Chevalier de Villefranche, conducted the survey sometime between April 1 and May 14. Captain Isaac Roach with the galley *Chatham* was assigned to the survey party, and, with his vast knowledge of the river, was invaluable to Duportail.

The end product of the survey was Villefranche's magnificent map of the river and the proposed fortifications.[11] This map was discovered in 1959 in the Bureau of Land Records, Harrisburg. Its overall dimensions are forty-four by sixty-seven inches with an extension at the upper right hand corner measuring fourteen by eighteen inches. The map depicts in detail the topography of the terrain on both sides of the river and various features of the river and chevaux-de-frise. Proposed sites for fortifications are carefully delineated. Unfortunately, the recommended two small batteries to be erected between Mantua Creek and Fort Mercer have been accepted as the site of the fascine batteries constructed in November, 1777. For the location of the 1777 batteries see Chapter 12, note 33. The outline of the ruins of Fort Mifflin were shown in detail with a small overlay to show the proposed new works.

In recent years two additional small maps by Villefranche have been found and are in the Pennsylvania Bureau of Archives and History, Harrisburg. These maps show two redoubts proposed for Carpenters' and Province Islands and a powder magazine for Fort Mifflin.

With the submission of Villefranche's map to Council on or before May 14, Duportail asked permission for Radière and Villefranche to return to the Continental camp. In appreciation of their services, Council awarded Duportail two thousand dollars, Radière one thousand, and Villefranche six hundred dollars. Reed, in presenting the French officers their honorarium expressed the Council's profuse thanks for their contribution to the defense of the Delaware, and regrets that the depleted State treasury did not permit a larger gift.[12]

Colonel Bull was ordered to proceed with construction of the proposed forts and batteries. He was to observe strict adherence to Duportail's proposals, no deviation to be made without approval of Council. Reconsidering his request to return Radière to camp, Duportail offered his aide's services for two weeks to assist Bull. Work was begun on Fort Mifflin and Billingsport, but no evidence exists that the small batteries above Mantua Creek were ever constructed.[13]

Work on the Delaware River defenses had always been motivated by crisis. Whenever danger threatened, feverish activity would be observed in the chambers of Council, at the various military installations along the river, and in the naval establishment. With the withdrawal of Clinton's army from Philadelphia in June 1778, no danger was anticipated from a land force, and all defensive measures were oriented toward repelling naval sorties. However, no urgency was evident, although Duportail's recommendations gave a momentary spur to the efforts of Council. Following the French engineer's proposal, work progressed steadily on Billingsport and Fort Mifflin as the anchors of the defensive line. Some activity was noted on the Province Island redoubt, but no evidence exists of work on Carpenters' Island. Fort Mercer was ignored in plans for the defense in 1779. Chevaux-de-frise were built although there is some doubt that they were sunk.

Colonel Bull and Major William Armstrong were active in supervising the work on the forts until early 1780, after which there was a gradual diminution of activity. After the surrender of Cornwallis in October 1781, work virtually ceased.

The monotony of life on the small boats and the need to overcome idleness among both the officers and men were ever present problems. Housing accommodations on board were hopelessly inadequate, and the need to occasionally quarter men on shore created disciplinary problems. Captain Boys was authorized to grant incentives to spur the crews to greater efforts. The men were offered extra allowances of rum and refreshments to assist in sinking the chevaux-de-frise. Council thought that "after liberal treatment they have had from the State, we presume they will cheerfuly labour in a Service of so much Importance to the City." [14]

On May 21 James Hopkins was granted permission to search the various wrecks in the river with the right to remove any materials salvagable. As an added inducement to the galleymen, one condition of Hopkins' agreement was that he employ the galleys; one-third of the proceeds going to the galleys, with the balance shared one-third to Hopkins and the remaining third to the State.[15]

For the first time in the war, the State was in a position to negotiate for State naval officers and men held by the British. The success of the *General Greene* and the guard boats had provided State authorities with a significant number of British prisoners for exchange. Council, on June 16, appointed Thomas Bradford to superintend the exchange of galleymen for those Englishmen being held in Philadelphia gaols or other detention centers.[16]

Efforts to enlist men for the Pennsylvania Continental Line from officers and men discharged from the State navy evidently met with a degree of success. By enlisting in the military, these veterans of the fleet would become eligible for the half-pay granted the military and now extended to those still in service with the galleys by Congress.

Continental Congress, in the spring of 1779, had passed a resolution extending to the officers, seamen, and marines employed in the naval service of Pennsylvania the same benefits and allowances granted the soldiers employed in the defense of the United States. Specifically this gave each member of the State navy who served until the end of the war half pay for seven years.[17]

The summer and fall of 1779 brought a period of relative quiet to the navy. The galleys and guard boats were stationed at Fort Mifflin with individual boats on detached service at the chevaux-de-frise, Lewes, or Billingsport.

In 1779 economy was the watchword of Council. Inflation was rampant and demanded the constant attention of the authorities. The value of a ration was estimated at £46 16s 7d per week. (It may be recalled that in December, 1775 contractors agreed to furnish the rations to the fleet at a cost of six shillings per weekly ration.) Compared to the cost of providing such comforts and refreshment was the mere pittance paid as wages, or £4 10s each month. It is interesting to note the type of rations and refreshments furnished the men and their inflated value compared with the Continental dollar. In the following table a few outstanding examples are beef, nearly five dollars a pound, wood over one hundred fifty dollars a cord, a gallon of rum cost almost the same as a cord of wood. An estimate of the cost of one ration, the amount each private or able-bodied seaman received, is well in excess of one hundred dollars a week. Each captain received three of these rations per week.

Value of Rations, 1779

Estimate of the present value of a single Ration per wk.

10 lbs. Beef, Pork or Mutton @ 37s 6d per lb.		£ 18 15 0
6 " flour	@ 90 £ per cwt.	4 5 8¼
⅓ " Candles	75s per lb.	1 5 0
Vegetables		1 10 0
Original allowance of Rum 7½ pts. per wk.		0 7 0
" " " Salt ½ pt		0 4 8¼
1/12 of a cord of wood at £ 60 per Cord		5 0 0
Allowance of Paper, Quills, and Ink Powder		0 7 6
		£ 31 14 10½

An Estimate of the value of such refreshments as by Act of Assembly those persons in the Naval Service of this State are entitled to receive with each ration of Provisions for one week.

Rum, one pint each Ration per wk @ £ 55 per Gal.		£ 6 17 6
Sugar, ½ lb. " " " " 67s 6d per lb.		1 13 9
Chocolate ½ lb. " " " " 105s " "		2 12 6
Coffee, 4 ounces " " " " 90s " "		1 2 6
Tea, 1 " " " " " £ 30 " "		1 17 6
Tobacco, 4 ounces " " " " 60s " "		0 15 0
Soap, 2 ounces " " " " 75s " "		0 9 4½
		£ 15 8 1½

For which is paid by the Officers & Seamen

One pint of Rum at 5s per gallon	£ 0 0 7½		
½ lb. of sugar " 3s 9d per lb.	0 1 10½		
½ lb. " chocolate " 3s 9d " "	0 1 10½		
4 ounces coffee " 3s 9d " "	0 0 11¼		
1 " tea " 12s " "	0 0 9		
4 " tobacco " 9d " "	0 0 2¼		
2 " soap " 1s 3d " "	0 0 2	0 6 5	
Balance value of the refreshments received for each		£ 15 1 8½	
ration per wk.			
To which add value of a Provision Ration etc.		31 14 10½	18
		£ 46 16 7	

It was impossible to maintain permanent garrisons in the river posts. Colonel Proctor's contingent was withdrawn at the request of Washington, and Council endeavored to replace them with militia companies. However, desertions and short enlistments left the forts destitute of manpower. The situation became so critical that on October 18 Captain Boys was ordered to place an officer and twelve men in both Fort Mifflin and Billingsport. By 1781 and 1782 the forts would be without garrisons and under a caretaker arrangement.[19]

With significant French naval forces in American and West Indian waters, and frigates of the Continental navy frequently patrolling near the capes, the threat to Philadelphia was considerably lessened. As 1779 drew to a close, men on board the galleys and guard boats were becoming restless from inactivity. It was evident that in the interests of economy another reduction in the fleet would soon be effected. On December 3, ninety-nine noncommissioned officers and men requested their discharges, which were granted.[20] The release of these men reduced the active roster to Captains Boys, Roach, Beasley and Martin, four lieutenants, one armourer, the fleet surgeon, and eleven privates; of the privates, three were invalids, incapable of active service.

The reduction of the fleet resulted in the resignation, on December 7, of William C. Bradford, paymaster, and Ludwig Sprogell, muster master. George Henry, commissary of naval stores, announced that there was no need for the continuance of his function. On December 11 he was authorized to sell the supplies on hand except for what was needed by the galleys, after which his resignation would become effective.[21]

The smaller number of men on board the galleys made it impractical to furnish rations to the crews and to continue the heavy expenses of the commissary department. As the men would rather receive money than rations, it was agreed to make a weekly cash distribution based on the following schedule:

	£	s	d
To a Captain three rations of refreshments common rations	82	11	1½
Lieutenant two rations ditto	55	–	9
Dr. Hutchinson (State Surgeon) five rations	137	11	10½
A private a single ration	27	10	4½

William Crispin was to issue rations until January 14, 1780, after which he was to turn excess stores over to Colonel Lewis Farmer and prepare an accounting of his office for Council.[22]

In 1780 the activities of the small naval contingent of twenty-one officers and men was restricted to housekeeping and guard duties. On June 3 the cash allowance, in lieu of rations and refreshments, was increased to £480 for the captains and surgeon, £320 to the lieutenants, £160 for the active privates and £110 for the invalids for each calendar period of four weeks or a total of £5,450.[23]

On February 13, 1781, Captain Boys and Doctor Hutchinson, representing the officers of the State navy, expressed to Council their willingness to be discharged. They reserved their prerogative to be covered under the provisions of half-pay for seven years allowed all State naval and army officers. Council wanted Boys to continue on active duty and ordered: "That the officers and men of the State Navy be discharged, except only Captain Boys, and such of the men who, having been disabled in the State service, are by the laws of the State intitled to support; and that the thanks of the Council be given to the said officers for their faithful service." Council also ordered "that Captain Boys be directed to take charge of the Gallies and Forts at Mud Island and Billingsport untill the further order of Council." [24]

The latter provision made Boys a caretaker. With the discharge of the seventeen officers and men, he was left with three invalided seamen. Possibly they were capable of duty as watchmen.

By December 20 Captain Boys was the only remaining member of the State navy in active service. Council discharged him because "the service in which he was engaged is at an end, and for no other cause." They assured him that his merit as an officer was recognized and that his conduct over six years' service met with the approbation of all Pennsylvanians.[25]

Several issues remained in abeyance affecting the State navy and required the attention of Council. Officers and men of the navy were still held in the prison ships in New York harbor. The inhuman treatment of Americans in these hellholes was a blot on British honor. The barbarous handling of American prisoners was a source of great distress to Washington and the subject of a long and almost fruitless correspondence with the various British commanders-in-chief. Pennsylvania authorities were constantly attempting to relieve the suffering of the naval personnel on the prison ships with shipments of flour and other foodstuffs. It is questionable how many of these relief shipments reached the prisoners. Probably all or the majority found their way into the rapacious hands of the infamous Captain Cunningham and his hirelings. Cunningham would appropriate most of the ordinary rations destined for the prisoners and then if they protested beat them so severely that many died. This brutish hulk was also keeper of the prison at Sixth and Walnut Streets during the British occupation of Philadelphia. The last recorded effort to send food to the naval prisoners in New York was on January 23, 1783.[26]

Continental Congress had agreed to place all soldiers and sailors of the various States on half-pay for life, providing they served until the end of the war. Reconsidering, they revised this plan and substituted five years full pay for the half-pay feature. The officers had repeatedly petitioned the State authorities for consideration under the Continental plan. Their dismissal resulted from the disbandment of the navy and not because they were unwilling to serve throughout the war. The President of the State, John Dickinson, asked the Assembly to honor the officers' petition. Eventually relief was granted men of the navy and State pensions were awarded wounded and disabled veterans unable to obtain gainful employment. Awards to pensioners are found in the dockets of the Orphans' Court of the City and County of Philadelphia for the years 1785 through 1788. Seamen, unable to work because of wounds or sickness received in service, were granted three to five dollars a month. One widow of a navy lieutenant was awarded fifteen dollars, half of his pay as long as she remained a widow. Other settlements reflect similar awards and one or two indicate no action taken.[27]

One of the final acts of the Council representing the State navy was to settle accounts with Henry Fisher. Fisher filed a report on November 28, 1786, showing total expenditures on his behalf for conducting his post at Lewes, between September, 1775, and April, 1782, of £1,645 18s 9d, of which £868 18s 9d was still due him.[28]

Much of the criticism directed at the little navy originated from a single source. A number of historians have accepted the Varnum and Smith version of the handling of the six galleys in the western channel on the afternoon of November 15, 1777. They have accused Hazelwood of not having command over the fleet and the navy of shirking its responsibilities during the siege of Fort Mifflin. Both accusations fall of their own weight when exposed to exhaustive research. Forgotten has been the bravery exhibited by the loyal officers and crews in the preceding eight weeks, and the two Congressional citations for meritorious conduct.

To apply a whitewash to the navy is ridiculous. All degrees of courage were evident on the boats—heroes rubbed elbows with cowards. Many worthy officers served in command positions, others were of mediocre ability—as Bradford stated, "Good for Little"—a condition found in all branches of the Continental armed forces.

Along with the brave Continental soldiers and many of the New Jersey and Pennsylvania militiamen garrisoning the various fortifications, the courageous naval personnel who served throughout October and November, 1777, deserve a special place in the hearts of all Americans.

Appendix A

The Fleet

The printed archives and manuscripts at the State Archives in Harrisburg provide a complete roster of the boats and ships comprising the State navy. A total of fifty-seven craft of all descriptions is listed. However, the few shallops and accommodation craft rented by the Council of Safety or Navy Board are not included, as they were not part of the naval establishment; they were occasionally used to transport militia and workmen to the forts or chevaux-de-frise or to supplement the efforts of the navy's provisioning sloops.

At this date it is impossible to ascertain the exact dates of service for all boats and ships of the fleet. However, an analysis of all sources has made possible an almost complete determination of the pertinent data on each vessel. Information on those elements of the fleet built for the navy are available in most cases, whereas, for the purchased ships—those converted to fire ships, accommodation, provisioning, and ammunition sloops—little physical information is available except as to the classification of the vessel. Many statistics, however, such as armament or builder, are revealed for the first time.

In the interest of conserving space, only the general officers and captains will be listed for the staff function of each vessel. For those interested in other officer and men of the navy and marines, consult the printed Archives of Pennsylvania, especially *P.A.*, Second Series,

Volume I; *P.A.*, Fifth Series, Volume I, and the manuscript muster rolls in the State Archives.

The detail concerning the service period of each officer is as complete as existing records reveal. Many announcements affecting changes in the status of certain offices and officers have vanished, deliberately or inadvertently. The printed and manuscript archives furnished some of the missing information, but, regrettably, some records are either missing or destroyed. To bridge the hiatus dates for each officer, we begin with his first commission, with each subsequent promotion indicated. During 1775 and 1776, a number of officers were apparently discharged for various reasons; others left the service for personal reasons. These captains will show a starting date but no termination date. Termination dates for many captains in service in 1777 are not always determinable; in those instances where an approximate severance date from service cannot be established, it may be reasonably assumed as occurring in 1778, when the fleet was reduced to a token force. Of course a few, particularly guard-boat and fire-vessel captains, may have deserted during the fall of 1777, although no record exists to support this supposition other than those indicated in the narrative.

The galley muster rolls in the printed Archives indicate that marines served on some galleys—a mistake. The only marine contingents in the service were on the floating battery *Arnold*, the *Montgomery*, and later the *General Greene*. The marines, under Captain William Brown, were transferred from the *Montgomery* to become the naval complement on board the floating battery *Putnam*. The inclusion of marines seems to be an error in editing the printed Archives, especially *P.A.*, Second Series, Volume I. A comparison of manuscript and printed muster rolls reveals that ordinary seamen were listed on the manuscript rolls variously as seamen, landsmen, mariners, marines, and privates, with the latter in the majority. In editing, these designations would be changed to list seamen as privates or privates as marines. The entire pattern of editing was inconsistent. No marine officers are listed except on the aforementioned ships and the marines were responsible to their own officers and not to any direction by a naval officer. See Chapter V for additional details.

Caution should be exercised in the use of the muster rolls, both printed and manuscript, as eighteen-century spelling is inconsistent and the orthography difficult to trace. The printed sources occasionally record one or more variants in the spelling of the same name. As the muster rolls are incomplete, it is not possible to determine when many of the officers and men retired from the service. Some unquestionably deserted, others resigned to enter the merchant service or to serve on a privateer. Approximately a score of officers resigned to enter the Continental service, which was more attractive and paid better.

The names of captains commanding each vessel at the time of the 1777 engagements are italicized. Commodore Hazelwood and several captains were discharged in 1778 as supernumerary, when the navy was reduced to a skeleton force.

GENERAL OFFICERS

Commodores

Caldwell, Andrew, January 13, 1776; resigned May 25, 1776, because of ill-health.

Davidson, Samuel, appointed captain of the galley *Warren*, September 22, 1775; obtained leave of absence to make an ocean cruise, November 29, 1775; command of the floating battery *Arnold*, March 9, 1776; appointed Commodore, June 15, 1776; relieved of command as Commodore because of opposition from galley captains, August 27, 1776, and given command of ship *Montgomery* and floating battery *Arnold*. He resigned about October 1, 1776.

Mifflin, Samuel, offered command September 2, 1776; declined September 20, 1776.

Seymour, Thomas, September 26, 1776; discharged as supernumerary due to age and health, September 6, 1777.

Hazelwood, John, appointed Superintendent of fire rafts, December 28, 1775; additional duties added as commander of guard boats and second in command of fleet, October 1, 1776; recommended again for same post with orders for direction of the fleet to by-pass Commodore Seymour, April 1, 1777; to Commodore, September 6, 1777; discharged August 17, 1778.

Before the Committee of Safety recommended the appointment of Captain Thomas Read as Commodore of the Navy on October 23, 1775, the senior captain of the galleys acted as commander of the boats. Read was never officially appointed Commodore, probably due in part to opposition from the galley captains. He served as acting Commodore (second in command) until the appointment of Caldwell. He also served in the same capacity for seventeen days following Caldwell's resignation.

Later, in 1778, after the resignation of Hazelwood and the disposal of most of the fleet except for three galleys and three guard boats, Captain Nathan Boys served as senior officer, without the title of Commodore.

Surgeons

Rush, Benjamin, September 27, 1775; resigned July 1, 1776.

Dunlap, James, July 5, 1776; resigned September, 1777.

Standley, Valentine, appointed surgeon of the *Montgomery*, July 31, 1777; to surgeon of the fleet, October 1, 1777; discharged February 1, 1779.

Hutchinson, James, appointed surgeon's mate July 31, 1778; to surgeon February 1, 1779.

Surgeon's Mate

Duffield, John, October 10, 1775; resigned July 1, 1776.

Hutchinson, James, see Surgeons.

Paymasters

Nesbit, John Maxwell, September 14, 1775.

Webb, William, March 1, 1777.

Bradford, William C., November 6, 1777; discharged December 6, 1779.

Muster Masters

Ross, John, October 6, 1775; resigned February 23, 1776.

Mitchell, John, March 5, 1776; resigned October 21, 1776. (See galley *Ranger* for additional details on Mitchell.)

Sprogel, Ludwig, October 21, 1776; discharged December 7, 1779.

Commissaries

Some confusion exists in attempting to identify those who served in the capacity of commissary. Certain commissaries supplied the navy and military. At other times there were commissaries of provisions and commissaries of stores serving simultaneously. Names appear in the minutes of the various Committees and Navy Board without indication of date of appointment. John Mitchell served as acting commissary, then as commissary and muster master, from March 5, 1776, to October 21, 1776, resigning to take command of the galley *Ranger*. (See galley *Ranger* for details.) During this period and extending through the effective life of the navy, Robert Towers served as commissary of stores for the armed forces of the State. The State Archives list William Crispin as appointed commissary on August 3, 1778; actually Crispin was functioning as commissary as early as 1776. Others were employed to furnish the prescribed rations to the fleet at a contract price, acting as independent suppliers. The last commissary appointed was George Henry, December 22, 1778. Characteristic of all civilian officers attached to the fleet, because of an ap-

336 The Pennsylvania Navy, 1775-1781

parent dearth of capable men available, they often served in more than one capacity. Some reported to the military or Board of War, but served the navy. An example would be Edward Ryves, Deputy Quartermaster General for the fleet and army. (See *P.A.*, Second Series, Vol. I, p. 55). It is known that Ship's Husband Captain William Richards also served as commissary of naval stores.

Ships' Husbands

Long, Peter, October 8, 1775.
Richards, William, May 21, 1776.

Master-at-Arms and Armourer

Chamberlain, Edward, September 23, 1775; resigned March 12, 1776.
Myers, Jacob, February 20, 1776.

Roster of Fleet
Galleys (13)

The thirteen galleys were all commissioned between July 19 and September 29, 1775. For a list of the builders of the galleys see footnote 14, Chapter 2. For a general description of the armament carried on board the galleys and other craft of the fleet see Chapter 2. All galleys survived the actions on the Delaware River in October and November, 1777, although some sustained extensive damage. On December 7, 1778, the Supreme Executive Council ordered ten galleys, *Bull Dog, Burke, Camden, Congress, Dickinson, Effingham, Experiment, Ranger, Warren,* and *Washington,* with the other surviving boats and ships of the navy, to be offered at public sale, for cash only, on December 11. George Henry, commissioned to sell the fleet, was to sell the best of the ten galleys for not less than £500 and the others at a proportionate rate but not less than £300. The best were to be offered first. No record survives to show the exact amount received. (*C.R.*, Vol. XI, p. 643). The remaining three galleys, *Chatham, Franklin,* and *Hancock,* with three guard boats, *Fame, Lion,* and *Viper,* were retained as a patrol unit and to provide naval support for the redoubts at Billingsport and Fort Mifflin. Captain Nathan Boys was commander of this small flotilla. These boats were considered expendable in December 1779, and were probably sold at public auction in the first half of 1780. The crews were discharged with only Captains Boys, Roach, Beasley, and Martin and a handful of men, mostly invalids, retained on the muster roll until February 1781. Boys and three invalids were not discharged until December 1781.

Bull Dog (one eighteen-pounder)

Alexander, Charles, July 24, 1775; to galley *Chatham*, October 2, 1775; resigned April 12, 1776, to enter the Continental navy.

Henderson, Alexander, October 2, 1775; to galley *Dickinson*, October 1, 1776; resigned April 1, 1777; refused to accept orders from Hazelwood.

Potts, William, October 1, 1776; discharged August 17, 1778.

Burke (one eighteen-pounder)

Blair, James, September 19, 1775.

Hardie, Robert, appointed captain of guard boat *Terror*, March 29, 1776; to the *Burke*, August 7, 1777. Hardie was discharged by order of a court-martial for disobedience of orders on December 9, 1777. See *C.R.*, Vol. XI, p. 718.

Camden (one eighteen-pounder)

Eyre, Richard, September 20, 1775; to the armed schooner *Delaware*, October 1, 1776; offered command of the brig *Convention*, July 31, 1778, declined. (See armed schooner *Delaware* for additional data on Eyre.)

Yorke, Edward, appointed second lieutenant of the ship *Montgomery*, March 20, 1776; to captain *Camden*, October 1, 1776.

Chatham (one twenty-four-pounder)

Alexander, Charles, see *Bull Dog*.

Montgomery, James, appointed captain of the galley *Ranger*, August 31, 1775; to the galley *Chatham*, May 29, 1776; resigned to enter the Continental navy, August 1, 1776; returned to command the State privateer ship, *General Greene*, March 30, 1779; discharged October, 1779.

Garland, George, appointed first lieutenant of the galley *Camden*, September 21, 1775; to captain of the *Chatham*, September 26, 1776; to galley *Hancock*, May 1, 1778; resigned April 13, 1780.

Roach, Isaac, appointed a second lieutenant of the galley *Hancock*, October 27, 1775; first lieutenant of the galley *Franklin*, February 16, 1776; to captain of the galley *Congress*, September 28, 1776; captain of the armed schooner *Delaware*, April 14, 1777 (apparently a temporary assignment for one cruise—see armed schooner *Delaware* for details); to the *Chatham*, May 1, 1778; discharged on February 13, 1781.

Congress (one twenty-four-pounder)

Hamilton, John, August 2, 1775; resigned to enter the Continental navy, August 1, 1776.

Roach, Isaac, see galley *Chatham.*

Dickinson (one twenty-four-pounder)

Rice, John, September 14, 1775; to brig *Convention*, October 1, 1776; discharged August 17, 1778.

Henderson, Alexander, see galley *Bull Dog.*

McLean, Lachlan, appointed second lieutenant of the galley *Warren*, May 1, 1776; to first lieutenant, November 1, 1776; to captain of the *Dickinson*, May 5, 1777.

Harrison, John, appointed captain of guard boat *Repulse*, April 7, 1777; to captain of the galley *Experiment*, April 30, 1777; to the *Dickinson*, December 31, 1777; discharged August 17, 1778.

Effingham (one eighteen-pounder)

Moore, Allen, appointed first lieutenant of the galley *Experiment*, July 17, 1775; to captain, August 1, 1775; to galley *Effingham*, August 30, 1775; resigned January 1, 1776.

Montgomery, Hugh, appointed first lieutenant of the galley *Congress*, September 1, 1775; to captain of the *Effingham*, February 16, 1776; discharged August 17, 1778.

Experiment (one eighteen-pounder)

Dougherty, Henry, July 17, 1775; to the galley *Washington*, August 1, 1775; on August 27, 1776, appointed captain armed schooner *Delaware*, never assumed command pending transfer to ship *Montgomery*; to ship *Montgomery*, October 1, 1776; resigned May 14, 1777.

Moore, Allen, see galley *Effingham.*

Webb, John, appointed first lieutenant of the galley *Bull Dog*, October 3, 1775; to captain of *Experiment*, May 7, 1776; resigned April 7, 1777.

Harrison, John, see galley *Dickinson.*

Ross, John, appointed mate on floating battery *Arnold*, March 15, 1776; to master of *Arnold*, April 1, 1777; to captain *Experiment*, September 1, 1778.

Franklin (one twenty-four-pounder)

Biddle, Nicholas, August 1, 1775; resigned December 9, 1775, to enter the Continental navy.

Boys, Nathan (or Nathaniel), appointed first lieutenant of the galley

Washington, August 29, 1775; to captain of the *Franklin*, December 6, 1775; served as commander of the remnant of the fleet from mid-August 1778 until early 1780. This segment of the fleet included three galleys and three guard boats. Boys was discharged on December 20, 1781, the last official act of the Navy.

Hancock (one eighteen-pounder)

Moulder, John, September 22, 1775; resigned October 10, 1775.
Moore, Thomas, October 16, 1775; discharged August 17, 1778.
Garland, George, see galley *Chatham*.

Ranger (one eighteen-pounder)

Montgomery, James, see galley *Chatham*.
Mitchell, John, appointed second lieutenant galley *Chatham*, November 16, 1775; to first lieutenant *Ranger*, February 16, 1776; to captain, October 21, 1776. There is confusion between the identities of Captain Mitchell and John Mitchell, commissary. It would have been virtually impossible for him to have served in both capacities at the same time. Commissary Mitchell made a deposition involving the loss of his records during September and October 1777, in which he claimed to be on duty at the Battle of Brandywine and later on special duty at Valley Forge. The editor of the Archives contends that he resigned as muster master to take command of the *Ranger*, a boat on which a John Mitchell was already first lieutenant. Hazelwood consistently refers to twelve galleys in action during October, 1777; this may account for the *Ranger*. If the *Ranger* was without a crew at this time, Mitchell may have served with the militia at the Battle of Brandywine. In any event, the *Ranger* was later in service and escaped to the upper river with the other galleys on November 21.

Warren (one eighteen-pounder)

Davidson, Samuel, see section under commodores.
Houston, Thomas, appointed first lieutenant, galley *Franklin*, September 2, 1775; to captain of *Warren*, March 11, 1776; to captain brig *Convention*, August 17, 1778 (for purpose of cruising at sea as State privateer); probably discharged in December, 1778.

Washington (one thirty-two-pounder)

Dougherty, Henry, see galley *Experiment*.
McFetrich, John, appointed second lieutenant of floating battery *Arnold*, March 22, 1776; to captain of *Washington*, October 1, 1776.

Guard Boats (21)

All twenty-one guard boats were commissioned by July 1, 1777. Certain guard boats apparently saw no service; in a few instances such as the *Basilisk, Race Horse* and *Repulse*, captains were appointed, but were unsuccessful in their efforts to recruit crews. A crew was assigned to the *Basilisk* for two months, then transferred to the *Hawk*. The *Thunder* with Captain Francis Gilbert and crew deserted to the British in September 1777. The muster rolls of the *Argus* and *Vulture* show all seamen had deserted, been taken prisoner in Philadelphia, or were sick in September 1777. These six guard boats, with the *Firebrand, Resolution* and *Tormentor*, were all lost sometime prior to November 21, 1777, either by enemy action, desertion, or deliberate destruction to prevent their falling into British hands. A few may have been sunk in the action involving the *Augusta* on October 22–23. (See *P.A.*, First Series, Vol. V, pp. 722–23, State Navy Board to Wharton, October 30, 1777.) The remaining twelve guard boats escaped up the river with Hazelwood. A contrary opinion was expressed by William Wallace in his biography of William Bradford (p. 258), where he suggests that the *Tormentor* and *Vulture* also escaped up the river with Hazelwood. To reconcile this difference, a study was made of all muster rolls subsequent to November 1777, and checked with Hazelwood's letter to the Council on December 1, 1777. Hazelwood stated that only twelve guard boats escaped and, as his report is official, this should be the confirmation needed. Muster rolls of some of the lost boats were prepared into early 1778, but these were only paper commands, as they list only a few men as wounded or deserted. The *Brimstone, Dragon, Eagle, Hawk, Hornet, Porcupine, Salamander, Terror,* and *Wasp* were included in the order to sell the fleet on December 7, 1778. (See *C.R.*, Vol. XI, pp. 638, 641.) The *Fame, Lion,* and *Viper* were retained to serve with the galleys *Chatham, Franklin,* and *Hancock* under Captain Boys. This little remnant of the State navy remained in service at Fort Mifflin until the Council resolved to discharge the bulk of the crews in December 1779.

An element of mystery surrounds an armed boat taken by a Philadelphia mariner, Robert Mackey, during the early summer of 1778. Named the *Viper*, it has been confused with the State guard boat of the same name. The misunderstanding results from the minutes of the Supreme Executive Council of January 18, 1779 calling it a retaken boat, although, the minutes of the same Council on July 9, 1778, merely noted it was "brought off from the Vigilant." It was probably a British armed barge left behind when the British fleet sailed in June

1778. The State guard boat *Viper* was in service patrolling the upper reaches of the Delaware River during the winter and spring of 1778. In fact, seamen who had previously served on the lost guard boat *Firebrand* were transferred to the *Viper* in April 1778, before Mackey's prize was turned over to the State Navy Board for salvage. (See *C.R.* Vol. XI, pp. 529, 670; *P.A.* Second Series, Vol. I, p. 293.)

The armament of the guard boats were two-, three- or four-pounder cannon, two swivels, although Montresor recorded that one deserted to the British carrying four swivels (some carried two howitzers), pikes and muskets. (All galleys, boats and ships were issued hand grenades.)

Faden, copied by other eighteenth-century British cartographers and repeated by historians since then, asserted that the guard boats carried four-pounders. No records survive to indicate the exact armament for each specific guard boat, but we do know that *Thunder* and *Brimstone* had three-pounders; the *Firebrand* a two-pounder and the *Eagle* a four-pounder. (See *P.A.*, Second Series, Vol. I., pp. 203, 204, 205; *C.R.*, Vol. X, p. 620.) It would appear that the Navy Board placed whatever size cannon were available on board the boats—strictly a matter of expediency. On March 17, 1777, Captain Blewer was ordered to pick up fourteen three- and four-pounder cannon, the exact number of guard boats under construction. Obviously he substituted, as the *Firebrand* received a two-pounder.

On March 18, 1778 the Tory press in Philadelphia announced the capture of a rebel boat with one three-pounder, the *Fame* (*Royal Pennsylvania Gazette*, March 24, 1778). According to this account, the boats of the British men-of-war *Pearl* and *Camilla* took the *Fame* out of a creek a little above Reedy Point. Assuming this *Fame* was the Pennsylvania guard boat of the same name, it must have been retaken after the British evacuation of Philadelphia. As previously noted, the *Fame* was one of three guard boats retained in service until December 1779.

While guard boat muster rolls have shown a maximum of fifteen officers and men, the official size of the crew, as designated by the Council of Safety, was a captain, gunner and eleven men—a number rarely realized. (See *C.R.*, Vol. X, p. 586.)

Other details on the guard boats, such as builders, will be found in Chapter 2.

Argus

Galt, Nathaniel, April 7, 1777; taken prisoner January 1778; discharged May 8, 1780.

Basilisk

Cowpland, Jonathan, appointed captain of the guard boat *Fame*, October 17, 1776; to the *Basilisk*, February 1, 1777, to the *Hawk*, April 1, 1777.

Brimstone

Watkins, William, May 27, 1776; discharged August 17, 1778.

Dragon

Thompson, Benjamin, April 7, 1777; died September 7, 1777.
Ross, William, September 14, 1777; discharged August 17, 1778.

Eagle

Hanse, Jacob, April 16, 1776; to the guard boat *Vulture*, October 1, 1776; resigned March 6, 1778.
Murphy, Daniel, February 1, 1777; absent on leave November 29, 1777; returned to duty 1778.

Fame

Greenway, William, appointed captain of the guard boat *Vulture*, March 28, 1776; to *Fame*, October 1, 1776; requested discharge to command privateer *Congress*, October 17, 1776; reinstated July 4, 1777, as captain of the guard boat *Hornet;* discharged August 17, 1778.
Cowpland Jonathan, see guard boat *Basilisk*.
Hazelwood, Thomas, February 1, 1777; On August 17, 1778, he was given permission to command a privateer.

Firebrand

Rue, Benjamin, February 8, 1777; resigned February 1, 1778.

Hawk

Cowpland, Jonathan, see guard boat *Basilisk*.

Hornet

Greenway, William, see guard boat *Fame*.

Lion

Martin, Henry, appointed second lieutenant of the galley *Dickinson*, March 6, 1776; to first lieutenant of the galley *Washington*, October 1, 1776; to captain of the *Lion*, March 6, 1777; discharged February 13, 1781.

Porcupine

Tatnall, Robert, May 27, 1776; taken prisoner at Bristol, Pennsylvania, April 7, 1778.

Race Horse

Dunn, Benjamin, no data available.

Repulse

Harrison, John, see galley *Dickinson.*

Resolution

Lyell, William, appointed second lieutenant of the galley *Bull Dog,* November 6, 1775; to first lieutenant of the galley *Dickinson,* October 1, 1776; to captain *Resolution,* April 7, 1777.

Salamander

Lawrence, Charles, April 6, 1776; apparently resigned on February 28, 1778.

Terror

Hardie, Robert, see galley *Burke.*

Erwin, James, appointed second lieutenant galley *Franklin,* June 13, 1776; to first lieutenant, October 3, 1776; to captain of the *Terror,* August 8, 1777; discharged December 15, 1778.

Thunder

Gilbert, Francis, appointed second lieutenant of the galley *Washington,* November 21, 1775; to first lieutenant, February 16, 1776; to ship *Montgomery* as first lieutenant, October 1, 1776; to captain *Thunder,* April 7, 1777. In September 1777, Gilbert deserted to the British with his guard boat and crew.

Tormentor

Brown, James, appointed second lieutenant of the galley *Camden,* March 6, 1776; to first lieutenant of the galley *Bull Dog,* May 7, 1776; to fire brig *Vesuvius* as first lieutenant, October 4, 1776; to captain *Tormentor,* February 1, 1777; resigned March 6, 1778.

Viper

Beasley, Stephen, April 7, 1777; discharged February 13, 1781.

Vulture

Greenway, William, see guard boat *Fame.*

Hanse, Jacob, see guard boat *Eagle.*

Wasp

Bradford, Joseph, July 4. 1777.

Fire Rafts

There are no muster rolls extant for the fire rafts, probably because they were never carried on the rolls of the navy. Certain inferrential comments indicate the probability that waterfront roustabouts were picked up in emergencies; also, occasional volunteers were solicited from local militia groups called Associators. In fact, several men had offered to form companies of volunteers to be available whenever needed for defense of the river. They agreed to serve on any armed boat provided by the Committee of Safety, under their own officers. This is a typical illustration of the problems confronting Revolutionary leaders when men were willing to fight in companies of their own choosing under officers selected by themselves. These volunteer seamen wanted their own boats and would probably have been more dangerous to their fellow countrymen than to the enemy. (See *C.R.*, Vol. X, p. 569.) Ration lists indicate that these volunteers received rations, but no payrolls have been found. However, the greatest reliance was placed on the guard boats for maneuvering the rafts. The responsibility for a chain of fire rafts was assigned to the captain and crew of a guard boat. The method for properly maneuvering these chains of fire rafts was somewhat similar to that employed by today's ocean and river tugs. No precise number of the raft chains is available; a figure between nine and twelve can be documented. The fire rafts were built by Philadelphia shipbuilders. See description in Chapter 2. The fire rafts were all destroyed in action or, as reported by Bradford, most were lost in "tempestuous weather." (See *P.A.*, First Series, Vol. VI, p. 11.)

Floating Batteries (2)

The muster rolls for the *Arnold* and *Putnam* are no longer extant for the period of September through December 1777. Hazelwood, in his letters, comments on the participation of the floating batteries in the engagements during the attacks on Forts Mifflin and Mercer. As in the case of certain other elements of the fleet, which were destroyed, a muster roll showing a paper command for the floating batteries was made for the period May 1, 1778, to June 1778. This was a fleet (not individual boat) muster roll and listed six privates and one boy for the *Arnold* and a quartermaster, boy, and nineteen privates for the *Putnam*. (See Penna. MSS, Various, RG-4, Box 2, "A Muster & Payroll of the Officers and Privates Belonging to the Pennsylvania State Fleet.")

Arnold (10 eighteen-pounders, at least two swivels)

Davidson, Samuel, see section under commodores.
Simmons, Jeremiah, October 1, 1776.

Marines

Forrest, Thomas, captain, March 13, 1776; resigned to command artillery company in Major Proctor's Pennsylvania Militia, October 5, 1776.

Putnam (12 eighteen-pounders, at least two swivels)

Brown, William, appointed captain of Marines on ship *Montgomery*, February 16, 1776; to captain of *Putnam* (with his marine contingent as the crew) September 21, 1776; discharged August 17, 1778.

Ships (2)

The *General Greene* was officially a member of the State navy, but was intended for privateering and made several cruises before being sold on November 1, 1779. The *Montgomery* was the flagship of the fleet, but encountered many vicissitudes in its short existence before being destroyed on November 21, 1777. It originally carried fourteen eighteen-pounders, sixteen cohorns and eight swivels. The eighteen-pounders were apparently too long and incapable of being properly sighted, rendering them ineffective. (See *P.A.*, First Series, Vol. V, pp. 45–46, Major Proctor to Council, October 15, 1776.) In October 1776, her heavy cannon were changed to sixteen twelve-pounders. Later she was stripped of all armaments and in May, 1777, was rerigged and equipped as a guard ship carrying sixteen nine-pounders.

General Greene

Montgomery, James, see galley *Chatham*.

Marines

Caldwell, Robert, April 12, 1779 (probably discharged in October, 1779).

Montgomery, flagship

Read, Thomas, see note under commodore section.
Davidson, Samuel, see section under commodores.
Dougherty, Henry, see galley *Experiment*.
Allen, William, May 15, 1777; discharged August 17, 1778.

Marines

Brown, William, fee floating battery *Putnam*.

Commodore's Barge

Middleton, John (Coxswain), enlisted as ordinary seaman on guard
    boat *Viper*, May 21, 1777, transferred same day to Commodore's
    barge as coxswain; deserted with many of crew in September
    1777; the balance decamped in December, 1777. Apparently the
    barge was destroyed on November 21, 1777.

Armed Schooners (2)

The armed schooner *Delaware* and brig *Convention* were built during the late spring and summer of 1776. Designated as galleys by the
Council, they were actually constructed to cruise in the lower bay
and along the Atlantic coast from Great Egg Harbor Bay in New
Jersey to Sinepuxent Inlet in Maryland. Information on the armament
of these ships is sketchy. Faden, in preparing his map of the Delaware River engagements, lists one galley schooner and one brig
galley, each with two eighteen-pounders in the bow and two nine-
pounders in the stern. Faden's sources are unknown and, at the risk of
belaboring a point, many statistical errors on the Pennsylvania navy
are apparent on his otherwise excellent map. These errors were picked
up by Ensign Thomas Wheeler on his map, "A Plan of the Attacks
Against Fort Mifflin on Mud Island." The *Delaware* and *Convention*
were armed at the same time twelve-pounders were placed on the
Montgomery. We know that the *Convention* was carrying twelve-
pounders in the spring of 1777, when ordered to the lower Delaware
Bay with the *Delaware* to cooperate with Captain Alexander of the
Continental navy. On arriving at Lewes, Captain Rice discovered the
shot he had taken on board at Fort Island did not fit his twelve-
pounders. Both ships were provided with swivels, the *Convention*
receiving five in April and May, 1777. In addition, we have a record
of two four-pounders delivered to the *Delaware*. (See *P.A.*, Second
Series, Vol. I, pp. 89, 135, 149, 155.) It would appear that their heavy
armament was twelve-pounders (number unknown), at least two
four-pounders and swivels.

Delaware

Dougherty, Henry, see galley *Experiment*.
Eyre, *Richard*, see galley *Camden*. (Some confusion exists as to the
    command of the *Delaware* during the actions of October and
    November, 1777, and the subsequent burning of the schooner.

The editors of the Archives indicate that Captain Roach was in command at this time. The misunderstanding was created by the assignment of Eyre to special duties in April 1777, and Roach was given temporary command of the *Delaware*. It is doubtful that Roach assumed this command, as he was ordered down to the Capes with his galley *Congress* in August 1777. Eyre was already down the bay on the armed schooner *Delaware* at that time. Additional proof is furnished by William Bradford in a letter to President Thomas Wharton of the Council, dated November 22, 1777 (*P.A.*, First Series, Vol. VI, p. 27). In this letter he refers to the burning of Captain Eyre's *Delaware*. As Chairman of the Navy Board, and being present during all of the engagements in September, October and November, he certainly was in a position to know the commanding officer of the *Delaware*.

Convention

Brig (1)

Rice, John, appointed captain of the galley *Dickinson*, September 14, 1775; to the *Convention*, October 1, 1776; served until mid-1778.
Eyre, Richard, see galley *Camden*.
Houston, Thomas, see galley *Warren*.

See the descriptive details listed under the armed schooner *Delaware*. The *Convention* was the largest ship in the fleet to escape destruction in November 1777. When the Supreme Executive Council ordered the bulk of the fleet sold on December 7, 1778, the *Convention* was purchased by Blair McClenachan. (See *P.A.* Second Series, Vol. I, p. 237.)

Fire Ships (8)

No elements of the fire fleet survived the actions of 1777; they were either destroyed in action or deliberately burnt to prevent their falling into enemy hands. The crews were of a poor quality and either panicked under fire or deserted when enemy action threatened. In attempting to unravel the mystery of what happened to the fire ships, certain known factors will assist in determining their fate by a process of elimination. The fire fleet on September 1, 1777, included four fire brigs, two fire sloops, a fire brigatine, and a fire ship. In a letter to the President of Council on October 7, 1777, William Bradford stated that the fire brig *Vesuvius* and fire sloop *Strombello* were stripped of all rigging and ready to sink to block any opening in the channel or chevaux-de-frise. Nothing further is known about the disposition of these hulks. Hazelwood does show one hulk sunk in the first row of chevaux-de-frise between Forts Mifflin and Mercer. (See his map *P.A.*, First Series, Vol. V facing p. 721.) Their crews had deserted en masse in early September. The fire brigatine *Blast* was crewless; every effort to recruit men having been unsuccessful. Bradford, writing again to Wharton on October 27, described the events leading up to the burning of the *Augusta*, mentioning three fire brigs and ône fire ship being sent down to assist in the attack on the British ships. He deplored the panic on board the fire ships and wrote that as the "shot flew so thick," they cut their rigging too soon and they burnt prematurely. (See *P.A.*, First Series, Vol. VI, pp. 648, 707–9.) With the *Vesuvius* a hulk, only three fire brigs remained: the *Comet*, *Hellcat*, and *Volcano*. Only one muster roll can be found for the *Comet* and the *Hellcat*. This only lists the captains, and in the case of the *Hellcat* a lieutenant. As Hazelwood did shift crews as men were needed for specific assignments, he may have assigned men from the guard boats or Continental fire ships—where were these elusive fire ships? Probably they were activated in time to participate in the actions on the Delaware and were destroyed to prevent their falling into British hands. This leaves either the fire ship *Hecla* or the fire sloop *Aetna* as the fourth ship Bradford mentions. As the *Hecla's* crew had run away in September, the *Aetna* was the only remaining fire vessel with a crew and must have been the fire ship, (actually a fire sloop) mentioned by Bradford. Thus by self-destruction, being sunk as channel obstructions, or burnt to prevent them being taken by the enemy, the fire fleet was destroyed.

The fire vessels carried little armament. It is known that in April 1777 the *Strombello* was issued two swivels, hand grenades, four blunderbusses and six muskets. (*P.A.*, Second Series, Vol. I, p. 134).

Fire brigs (4)

Comet (no muster for crew located)

Pomeroy, Robert, July 31, 1777.

Hellcat (no muster for crew located)

French, Robert, July 31, 1777.

Vesuvius (crew deserted September, 1777)

Bingley, Edward, June 20, 1776; resigned or discharged September, 1776.

Christie, John, appointed second lieutenant galley *Dickinson*, November 7, 1775; to first lieutenant galley *Chatham*, February 16, 1776; to captain *Vesuvius*, October 1, 1776.

Volcano

Brice, *John*, appointed first lieutenant galley *Warren*, March 2, 1776; to captain fire sloop *Aetna*, October 19, 1776; to captain *Volcano*, March 11, 1777; discharged August 17, 1778. (Many of the crew of the *Volcano* transferred to the galleys *Warren* and *Franklin* in September, 1777.)

Fire brigatine (1)

Blast

McKnight, *James*, appointed lieutenant fire sloop *Strombello*, March 11, 1777; assigned as captain *Blast*, July 29, 1777, to recruit crew. Along with Pomeroy of the *Comet* and French of the *Hellcat*, was unsuccessful in obtaining crews; returned to *Strombello* as captain before September 1, 1777.

Fire ship (1)

Hecla

Perkins, *Thomas*, enlisted as gunner on galley *Hancock*, January 3, 1776; to second lieutenant galley *Washington*, June 20, 1776; transferred back to *Hancock* as first lieutenant, October 1, 1776; to captain *Hecla*, April 26, 1777. The crew ran away in September, 1777, leaving Perkins, the lieutenant, and two men; adding a new boatswain, they remained on muster until November, when the rest of the crew deserted leaving only Perkins and Lieutenant Stetson. Musters were maintained by the officers until February, 1778. (Perkins' name is sometimes shown as Parker.)

Fire sloops (2)

Aetna

Gamble, William, March 26, 1776; discharged October 19, 1776.
Brice, John, see fire brig *Volcano*.
Clark, *William*, April 7, 1777; cashiered January 13, 1778.

Strombello [*Strumbelo* or *Strombeli*] (crew deserted September, 1777)

Jones, Griffity, March 4, 1777; under arrest August 1, 1777; discharged September 1, 1777.
McKnight, *James*, see fire brigatine *Blast*.

Schooners and Sloops (7)

The sloops and schooners were vital in keeping the fleet supplied with provisions, ammunition, and other materials of war—an indispensable role in the defense of the river. As with the fire ships, they were all purchased, either from owners or at public auction. The *Speedwell* served as the Navy Board's flagship during October and November 1777. Of the seven schooners and sloops, five escaped upriver in November 1777. Hazelwood, in a letter to Wharton on December 1, 1777, reported that the *Liberty, Lydia, Sally,* and *Speedwell* and one accommodation sloop passed the city successfully. (See *P.A.,* First Series, Vol. VI, pp. 47–50.) Wallace (p. 258) offers a contrary opinion that the *Defiance, Hetty, Industry, Sally,* and *Speedwell* were the sloops which succeeded in reaching the fleet near Bristol. However, we must accept Hazelwood's statement, as he was in a better position to know; also, the minutes of the Supreme Executive Council, on December 7, 1778, ordered the *Speedwell, Industry, Sally,* and *Lydia* sold at public auction. (See *C.R.,* Vol. XI, p. 638.) The identity of the accommodation sloop mentioned by Hazelwood is thus revealed as the *Industry.* This also accounts for the *Hetty* and *Defiance;* it becomes obvious that they were destroyed to prevent their falling into the hands of the British. A study of all muster rolls confirms this conclusion. The schooners and sloops did not carry cannon. To prevent boarding, swivels, hand grenades, and muskets were issued; as pikes were available, they may also have been used.

Accommodation or Provision Sloops (4)

Defiance

Gardner, Alexander (Master), June 28, 1776; to second lieutenant galley *Congress,* November 3, 1776.

Graff, Christopher, November 21, 1776; not permitted to be master by muster master, December 1, 1776; reappointed by Commodore Seymour, June 2, 1777.

Roden, William, shipped in place of Graff, December 2, 1776, replaced by Graff on June 2, 1777; apparently Roden did not serve until June 2, as two interim masters were appointed, although some confusion is evident in the chronology of the appointments. (See F. Bird and J. Bird.)

Bird, Frederick, February 17, 1777; to fire brig *Volcano* as pilot, May 17, 1777; to captain sloop *Sally,* January 1, 1778.

Bird, Jacob, enlisted as private April 1, 1777; to master May 17, 1777; ran away November 1, 1777.

Hoover, Henry, appointed master sloop *Hetty,* June 11, 1776; discharged March 27, 1777; enlisted as private on *Defiance,* June 1, 1777; to master November 1, 1777; discharged January 1, 1778.

Hetty

Hoover, Henry (Master). See sloop *Defiance.*
Craig, James, March 27, 1777; discharged June 1, 1777.
Hoover, John, appointed steward September 12, 1776; master June 1, 1777.
(The *Hetty* was without a crew in October and November 1777, except for the master and two men.)

Industry

Townsend, Thomas (Master), November 1, 1777.
(The only muster roll extant covers the period from November 1, 1777 to April 1, 1778, although this sloop appears to have been in service until sold in December 1778.)

Liberty

Wert, George (Master), March 7, 1777.
Crawford, David, July 1, 1778; discharged December 15, 1778.

Ammunition Sloop (1)

Sally

Wert, Martin (Master), May 24, 1776; discharged January 1, 1778.
Bird, Frederick. See accommodation sloop *Defiance.*

Province Sloop (1)

Speedwell

Wade, Joseph (Master), September 1, 1777; resigned December 12, 1778.

Victualling or Provision Schooner (1)

Lydia

Simpson, James (Master), May 25, 1776; to second lieutenant brig *Convention,* February 2, 1777; to master, April 20, 1777; reappointed second lieutenant August 19, 1778.
Wert, Philip, February 2, 1777.
(State archives incorrectly lists commanders of the *Lydia* as captains. This classification was not used on the miscellaneous collection of sloops and schooners.)

Shallop (1)

Black Duck

Wade, Robert (Master), September 1, 1777; resigned April 15, 1778.

For some unknown reason Hazelwood omitted the *Black Duck* from his letter of December 1, 1777.

The *Black Duck* was included in the public sale of the fleet ordered by the Council in December, 1778.

For additional data on the schooners and sloops see Chapter 2 and note 81 of that chapter.

Appendix B

Chevaux-de-frise

Chevaux-de-frise, translated literally, means Friseland horses. They were machines used by the people of Friseland, a section of eastern Holland and western Germany, to offset their deficiency of cavalry. Normally used as land obstructions, they were sometimes placed in shallow streams.[1]

In the American Revolution, chevaux-de-frise were sunk in the Delaware and Hudson Rivers to prevent passage of British men-of-war. The inspiration for these river "stackadoes," as the British termed them, originated in Philadelphia, and the first model was built by a Philadelphia architect, Robert Smith. Specialists in the construction and sinking of these obstructions were sent to assist the Continental and New York authorities in 1777 and 1778.

The basic construction of all chevaux-de-frise were similar, but varied in size and detail. Because of the greater depth of the Hudson River near West Point and the New York Bay between the Battery and Governor's Island, larger chevaux-de-frise were built and sunk to obstruct those water passages. This has occasionally led to a misrepresentation of the size of those constructed for the Delaware River.

Notorious for its changing channels, shoals, sand bars, and appearing and disappearing islands, the Delaware offered navigational problems not present in the Hudson. Two distinctly different situations were evident in the building of the chevaux-de-frise. The pass between Billingsport and Billings Island was narrow but somewhat deeper than the second line of defense between Fort Mifflin and the New Jersey shore. At the latter defense line, the river was wider but contained two prominent sand bars which created a main channel between Hog and Fort Islands on the west and the large shoal on the east. East of this shoal was a secondary channel with another sand bar near the New Jersey shore. The main channel was sufficient to permit passage of any eighteenth-century ship, but slightly shallower than the pass at Billingsport. In the beginning, it was believed that no British man-of-war could come up the east channel, a point graphically disproved by Washington and du Coudray, explaining that up to three frigates could approach close enough in this channel to enfilade the works at Fort Mifflin. On their recommendations, a belated effort was made to block the eastern channel.

No contemporary drawing of the Delaware River chevaux-de-frise has survived. However, sufficient information can be gathered from those engaged in their construction and removal in 1784 to establish reasonably accurate dimensions. Old prints of plans and profiles reproduced in early histories and a few sketches found in contemporary letters vary in some detail.[2]

The design for the chevaux-de-frise has been popularly credited to the venerable Benjamin Franklin. The search for some means of obstructing the river navigation unquestionably originated with the Committee of Safety, and, with his creative genius, Franklin may have conceived the idea of the chevaux-de-frise. Search of all published editions of Franklin's writings reveals a paucity of his papers for the period during which he served on the Committee. Only two references to his activity as a Committee member were located. On July 7, 1775, he wrote Joseph Priestly: "My time was never more fully employed. In the morning at six, I am at the Committee of Safety, appointed by the Assembly to put the province in a state of defence; which committee holds till near nine, when I am at the Congress, and that sits till after four in the afternoon. . . ."[3] There is no evidence that Franklin ever claimed credit for designing the chevaux-de-frise.

Franklin did present a model for a pike which was used on the galleys. Often accused of old-granny ideas, he suggested the use of bows and arrows to Charles Lee. The scarcity of muskets and ammunition prompted him to observe that an arrow was as accurate as a musket shot; that four arrows could be discharged in the same time as one bullet; that a flight of arrows was more terrifying and could as easily put a man *hors du combat*.[4] More likely, the idea that the river obstructions were his invention originated with his colleagues

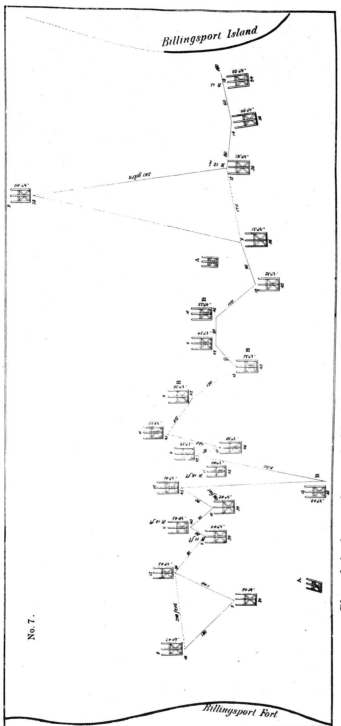

No. 7.

Plan of the lower chevaux-de-frise between Billingsport and Billings Island, removed and destroyed by Levi Hollingsworth and Arthur Donaldson in 1784. The dotted lines represent the distance between frames. The numerals above the spears indicate their depth in feet below the surface of the river, and the figures at the base of the frames indicate the water they lay in at low tide. The frame numbers assigned by Hollingsworth and Donaldson are shown alongside the frames. Those frames marked A were unknown to the Port Wardens; those marked B were either partially removed or destroyed by the British or through natural causes. Pennsylvania Archives, *Second Series, Vol. I.*

in the Continental Congress. Knowing of their effectiveness, he probably urged their consideration for the river and harbor defense of other states. Letters of various contemporaries of Franklin occasionally refer to "Dr. Franklin's boats" and "Dr. Franklin's Chevaux-de-frise." [5]

The adaptation of the European chevaux-de-frise to naval warfare was, in any case, an American idea, and it is likely that the man who built the first model, Robert Smith, was also its originator. Smith, born in Scotland about 1722 came to Philadelphia about 1750. He designed St. Peters Church and the "Old Pine Street" Presbyterian Church, in Philadelphia, and Nassau Hall at Princeton. He also designed the Zion Lutheran Church and the Old Walnut Street Prison, both since razed in the interest of progress. The original design for Carpenters' Hall was submitted by Smith, who also served on the building committee. Franklin, as President, presided over the Committee which on July 24, 1775, approved Smith's model and design for river obstructions. Smith's apparatus was the only one accepted by the Committee, while at least five others were rejected. [6]

Smith also volunteered to supervise the construction of the chevaux-de-frise. Several contractors were employed and at least seventeen frames were completed by August 24, 1775. Smith expressed concern that the completed frames were not as sturdy as had been planned. A report prepared by Captain Robert Whyte and Samuel Morris, Jr., and signed by Franklin, was submitted to the State Assembly, estimating the initial costs of building the fleet and chevaux-de-frise to September 29, 1775. These costs included an estimate of £1,700 for building seventeen chevaux-de-frise. Smith's audit of the contractor's accounts were included in this report and indicated the construction cost was approximately £700. Other costs included stones for ballast; ferrying stones and frames; sinking of frames; logs, planks, scantling, chain and iron spears. [7]

The designation of these machines of obstruction as chevaux-de-frise is first recorded in the minutes of the Committee of Safety on August 5, 1775. [8] The repeated references to chevaux-de-frise in the minutes disprove the accepted belief that this term was first used by French engineers in 1777. It is a more typical bit of Frankliniana, as the eminent Doctor Franklin was, at this time, President of the Committee of Safety. Prior to August 5, 1775, they were referred to as "Machines for defense of the River," or "Machines for Obstructing the Navigation of the River."

Robert Smith with Arthur Donaldson figured prominently in the early construction and sinking of the obstructions. Smith died on February 11, 1777, before the effectiveness of his river obstructions

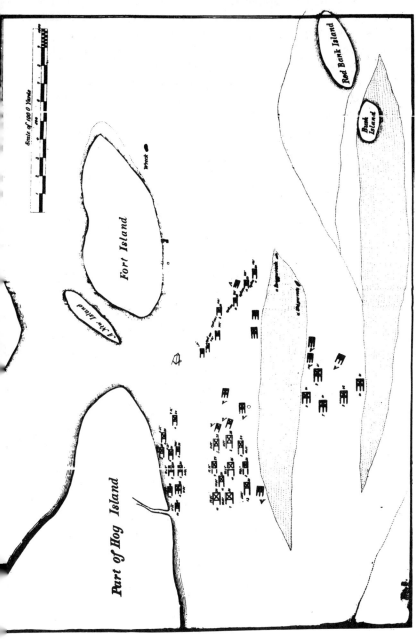

Plan of the upper chevaux-de-frise between Hog Island and Fort Mifflin on the west and the sandbar and the New Jersey shore on the east. These frames were also removed by Hollingsworth and Donaldson. See plan of the lower chevaux-de-frise for details. *Pennsylvania Archives, Second Series, Vol. I.*

could be tested. Later Captain du Plessis Mauduit, the engineer who played a major role in the defense of Fort Mercer, is credited by several historians with supervising the construction of several of the chevaux-de-frise. With the death of Smith, Mauduits' assistance may have been enlisted to supervise the sinking of the last two rows of obstructions at Billingsport and Fort Mifflin. No contemporary citations can be found to support this statement, but he may have been one of the engineers assisting du Coudray in the summer of 1777.

Only three records have survived which offer dimensions to indicate the size of the frames. In reporting on the removal of the chevaux-de-frise in 1784, they were found to be thirty feet wide.[9] As these obstructions were built and sunk over a twenty-seven-month period, variations may have resulted. A few frames were prepared and may have been sunk in 1779.

In June 1776, Robert Smith was ordered by the Council to see "That a Number of Chevaux-de-frise be sunk as soon as possible across the Channel of the River at Billingsport, to be placed sixty feet distance from Center to Center of each of them, and of such height that there will not be more than six feet of Water over them at low tide." [10]

Also in June 1776, the Continental and New York authorities requested assistance in the construction and sinking of chevaux-de-frise in New York Bay between the Battery and Governor's Island. A Pennsylvanian, Colonel Stephen Moylan, stationed with the Continental army in New York, was solicited for assistance. He wrote to the Committee of Safety and they immediately dispatched Arthur Donaldson with several carpenters to Manhattan. Donaldson, an authority on construction, was exceptionally well qualified in the sinking of the frames. To aid Moylan in having an adequate supply of logs and timber available when Donaldson arrived, the Committee wrote: "It takes about 25 or 30 logs from 40 to 65 feet in length, from 12 to 26 inches thick in the Butts for each of the Chevaux de Freize sunk in our River." [11]

These citations furnish some idea on the construction of the frames. Additional data is found in Robert Smith's audit of the carpenters' accounts and in two plats prepared at the time of removal in 1784.[12]

Smith, on August 24, 1775, had advised the Committee that Guion had built four frames fourteen to twenty feet high; Govett seven, thirteen to twenty-three feet nine inches; Robinson four, fourteen to nineteen feet; Tew one of twenty feet. These frames were built at Gloucester and were to be floated and sunk in the main channel near Hog Island and Fort Mifflin (at that time called Fort Island). The varying heights were to ensure the minimum exposure of the spears at low tide.

Remnants of chevaux-de-frise dredged from the Delaware River off Fort Mifflin in the 1930's by the Army Engineer Corps. Note the size of the timbers used to build the frames; the anchors employed to hold the frames in place until filled with stone; chains which were attached to adjoining frames to make canting more difficult; and the iron spike attachment which was affixed to each projecting timber. These relics are on display near the Whitall mansion on the Fort Mercer battlefield. *Courtesy Board of Chosen Freeholders, Gloucester County, New Jersey.*

The plats were prepared to assist in the removal of sixty-three chevaux-de-frise in 1784. Twenty-four frames, in two slightly irregular lines, were located between Billingsport and Billings Island. The spears are shown to be from eight to fifteen feet below water. The frame bottoms are depicted as resting on the bottom in mid-channel from thirty to forty-six feet, at low tide. Those near the shore were at a depth of ten to twenty-four feet.

This plat supports the two lines of chevaux-de-frise, although some were canted and moved aside or destroyed by the British to provide passage for their ships. Others were moved out of position by the action of the water. One frame was 510 yards downstream in 1784 and would have opened a passage of about 140 feet. It was either towed downstream or forced there by the action of ice and tides.

Further upriver, ten chevaux-de-frise were found off Hog Island, fifteen directly opposite near the sand bar, and ten more were located at the upper end of the sand bar and opposite Fort Mifflin. These latter frames served as the river anchor for the piers which were sunk to permit a chain to be stretched across the channel near Fort Mifflin.[13] Between the two sand bars, eight additional frames were found, making a total of forty-three. The frames found in the upper defenses were seated on the river bed at depths varying from thirteen to thirty feet. Those in the channel were mostly in the range of twenty-two to thirty feet with one at thirty-three feet. Near the shoal and Hog Island they averaged thirteen to twenty feet. With one exception, the spears were all four to ten feet below water.

Accounting for sixty-seven frames, all but four were removed by Hollingsworth and Donaldson. The British or the river probably destroyed the other four and possibly a few more. In the 1930's, the Army Engineers removed parts of two or three frames from the river off Fort Mifflin. These may be seen today at Fort Mercer.

In removing them, many were found to have disintegrated in the water with only the bottoms and the spear posts remaining. The upper chevaux-de-frise have been described as being sunk in four rows and are so placed on the map prepared by Commodore Hazelwood in 1779.[14] In surveying the river preparatory to their removal, the frames were found grouped in four areas, not in rows. Staggered and sunk so as to effectively obstruct the river, they gave no evidence of having been placed in four regular rows across the channel.

What did these large frames of destruction look like? Although no contemporary plans have been found, it is possible to offer a reasonable description of a chevaux-de-frise. Large hoppers, boxes, frames or bin-like containers were built approximately thirty feet square. The bottoms of the frames were constructed of huge timbers and floored with two-inch pine plank. On the side, logs were used to build a sturdy frame and lined with pine plank to provide a perfect box for the stone ballast. Stone was ferried in flat boats from quarries on the upper Schuylkill River. Long posts were placed obliquely, mounted with large iron spears facing downstream to rip out the bottom of an enemy ship unwary enough to run upon them. The hypotenuse of these spear posts varied with the depth of the river. Some chevaux-de-frise were known to possess four spear posts. However, the Delaware River frames had only two or three posts; no four-post frames were found. Placed sixty feet center to center, they were chained together to prevent their being easily canted to discharge their ballast or towed away by the British.

The frames were floated to the spot where they were to be sunk, with the use of heavy anchors. Anchors were used to lower the empty frames to the river bed and secure them in place while the stone ballast was lowered into the hopper of the frame. Anchors were not used to permanently moor the chevaux-de-frise to the river bottom. It was reported that fifteen to twenty tons of stone were used to ballast the smaller frames, with greater quantities in the larger frames. Captain Hamond of the British frigate *Roebuck* wrote that forty to fifty tons were placed in the frames. The exact quantity required to safely anchor the chevaux-de-frise was probably determined by trial and error. In January 1776 it was reported that twenty-two chevaux-de-frise were moved from their moorings by the action of the ice.[15]

In November 1776, two crews of workmen—the majority were sailors from the galleys—were engaged in sinking the chevaux-de-frise. A record of the equipment used in this endeavor shows each crew was furnished:

2 Anchors from 11 to 13 or 1400 weight each; 2 cables about 11 inches each; 4 Buoy Ropes about 6 inches & 20 fathoms long; 2 Hedges Anchors 150 to 300 wt. & 2 Towlines of 6 Inches, & 1 towline of 7½ Inches to Heave off by, each 100 to 120 fathoms long; 2 large long Boats with Windlass's & David's [davits], & a Sheave forward in each; 1 Six or Eight Oar'd Barge; Sundry Coils of Rigging 2½ to 3 Inches & 30 or 40 Good Water Cask & Two Shallop.

Anchors weighing 1700 pounds were used in the sinking of the piers at Fort Mifflin.[16]

Other theories as to the size and design of the chevaux-de-frise have been advanced. However, no citations have been offered, nor does search of the Pennsylvania archives support these claims. They are usually based on those built for the Hudson River, and conform to their general design, but are much larger than those sunk in the Delaware River.

Correspondence of Continental statesmen, city residents, and British intelligence officers, emanating from Philadelphia, refer to the sinking of the chevaux-de-frise and their destructive capabilities. With one or two exceptions, they offer little to increase our knowledge of the machines.[17] It is possible that these vague reports, coupled with Captain Hamond's healthy respect for the obstructions, influenced Sir William Howe's decision to land at the head of Chesapeake Bay rather than in the Delaware River.

One British officer has left an interesting and reasonably accurate description of the chevaux-de-frise. Although there are some mistakes in detail, it is the best British version. Roger Lamb recorded in his journal:

Two ranges of Chevaux de frise were also sunk into the channel; these consisted of large pieces of timber, strongly framed together in the manner usual for making the foundation of wharfs, in deep water. Several large points of bearded iron, projecting down the river, were annexed to the upper parts of these chevaux de frise, and the whole sunk with stones, so as to be about four feet under the water at low tide. Their prodigious weight and strength, could not fail to effect the destruction of any vessel which came upon them. Thirty of these machines were sunk about three hundred yards below Mud Island, so as to stretch in a diagonal line across the channel. The only open passage left was between two piers lying close to the fort, and that was secured by a strong boom [chain], and could not be approached but in a direct line to the battery [Fort Mifflin].[18]

To provide a sketch of the activities surrounding the building of chevaux-de-frise, a series of selected passages from the Archives may be of interest: [19]

July 4, 1775:
The Committee of Safety resolved to "go to Red Bank tomorrow to take a view of the River and Islands."

July 6:
Committee "went to Red Bank, Mud or Fort Island, & viewed them and several parts of the River, and find the Channel from the Fort to the Barr to be 150 fathom or there about. . . . [A]t present impracticable to lay a Boom across that part of the River."
Resolved "that Robert White [Whyte] & Owen Biddle be a Committee for the Construction of Boats and Machines."

July 11:
Committee for Construction of Boats and Machines "have been viewing a number of Pine Loggs."

July 13:
Ebenezar Robinson thanked for his plan to stop the river channel.

July 15:
Committee to immediately employ all necessary carpenters and workmen to construct as many machines as necessary to interrupt navigation.

July 19:
Fourteen prominent Gloucester County, New Jersey, citizens contributed 296 logs toward the building of the machines.

July 24:
Robert Smith, architect, appeared before Committee of Safety "with a model of a machine for observing the Navigation of the River Delaware and explained the Construction of it, which was approved of. . . ."

August 5:
Model of machine for lowering and raising ballast into and out of chevaux-de-frise submitted by Robert Smith.

August 24:
Robert Smith reported on condition of seventeen chevaux-de-frise finished and ready for sinking.

September 14:
Chevaux-de-frise [17] to be sunk in river opposite the Fort [Mifflin]; Robert Whyte and Samuel Morris, Jr. appointed Committee to supervise this work.

September 29:
Whyte and Morris ordered to estimate cost of frames sunk; estimate of £1700 for 17 chevaux-de-frise.

October 11:
Ten chevaux-de-frise pilots appointed, all others dismissed.

November 3:
Whyte and Morris ordered to provide logs and plank to build a third tier of chevaux-de-frise.

November 8:
Whyte, Owen Biddle and George Clymer to consider the most effective method of connecting the chevaux-de-frise with chains.

November 16:
Whyte and Morris to purchase logs to build three tiers of chevaux-de-frise, one additional line at Fort Island, two at Marcus Hook.

March 13, 1776:
Arthur Donaldson to launch the frames built at Gloucester, John Cobourn employed to sink them when launched. Captain Rice of the State navy instructed to assist in the sinking of the frames.

March 26:
Donaldson to build two piers to sink in the passage at Fort Island. It was planned to attach a boom to the piers; later this was deemed inadvisable and a chain was stretched between the piers.

March 30:
Whyte, Howell and Nixon to procure two vessels to sink in the passage between the chevaux-de-frise.

June 15:
A number of frames are to be sunk across channel at Billingsport, to be placed sixty feet distance center to center and with not more than six feet of water over the spear points at low tide.

July 16:
Captain Whyte given £150 for outstanding services in connection with building and sinking the chevaux-de-frise. On July 19, Morris was awarded a similar amount. (Whyte attended his last meeting of the Council of Safety on July 1, 1776.)

October 15:
Major Proctor reporting from Fort Island said, ". . . floating Chevaux-de-frise were moored at proper place ready for sinking. Further the boom is worthless, large ships can pass between east pier and observations with ease. East Channel should be blocked with additional Chevaux-de-frise building at Gloucester as enemy ships can go through unchallenged."

December 31:
Some examples of construction costs of the chevaux-de-frise are: for iron work and construction at Billingsport from June to December, 1776, to Robert Smith £2558 15s 2d; to Samuel Morris, Jr., for miscellaneous services and disbursements at same location from April,

1776, to July, 1777, £3,465 8s 11½ d. These are relatively minor when compared with the numerous expenditures represented in the next entry.

January 1777; to September 1, 1777:
Many entries during this period reflect the feverish activtiy of ensuring that the channels were effectively closed to shipping. Numerous entries show the purchase of several hundred logs; thousands of feet of two-inch pine plank (two entries for 30,000 and 23,702 feet with several others for 2,000 and 3,000 feet were noted); many receipts for stone, such as nine and six flat loads another for 180 perch of stone; several miscellaneous payments for cables, six-inch spikes, bolts, spears and iron work were recorded. Also, several surveys of the river were conducted during this period.

February 24, 1777:
James Rhoads was requested to report the current status of planned and finished chevaux-de-frise at Billingsport. One additional tier of frames would be sunk at Billingsport and the same at the Fort Mifflin line of defense. It was recognized that any delay gained at the former location would facilitate the strengthening of the Forts Mifflin and Mercer line. His report stated:

That there are Eight Frames finish'd & plank'd; Eight more to finish, part not rais'd.
He thinks there is as much Plank as will finish two of the Latter, & consequently Plank for 6 Wanted.
There are 42 Loggs at the Water side; and a Certain Woulfe who lives at the place, informs that there are several Loggs along shore.
There are 36 Small Loggs on the ground, which will make floor Timbers, as also Some Scantlings and Boards.
He thinks there are Bolts, Straps, & pins Enough to finish the above frames.
There is One Barrel of Spikes; not sufficient to finish the Frames begun
The Spear Irons are all on.

April 21:
A Committee to repair to Billingsport to decide on width of passage through chevaux-de-frise.

June 6:
Captain Blewer and Joseph Marsh of Navy Board were instructed to survey the obstructions and sound the middle channel. They reported that there was sufficient water for a ship drawing twelve to eighteen feet.

August 29:
Chevaux-de-frise pilots discharged as of this date. Channels closed to all shipping.

October 1:
Fall of Billingsport.

October 4:
Captain Hamond of the British frigate *Roebuck*, with several other men-of-war, began work on the removal of the chevaux-de-frise. For fifteen days they labored at this task and finally effected a passage on October 21.

October 21:
First British ships warped through the chevaux-de-frise. Disagreement as to the size of the opening has persisted for nearly two hundred years, some authorities estimate seven feet, others seventeen. Both measurements of the opening seem too small for a ship like the *Roebuck*. If one frame was removed, and it is known that the Billingsport chevaux-de-frise were thirty feet wide and placed sixty feet center to center, a space of approximately ninety feet would have been made. The plat of the chevaux-de-frise shows three frames from the main channel destroyed or removed, although not necessarily this early in the campaign. On October 13, William Bradford reported that one frame had been removed and another "rumored" removed, but he doubted that the latter was true.

October 22-November 21:
This period saw the assault on Fort Mercer, the burning of the *Augusta* and the *Merlin* and the final glorious six-day defense of Fort Mifflin, events in which the State navy and the chevaux-de-frise played prominent roles.

November 28:
Two channels were discovered near Fort Mifflin permitting passage of small transports carrying provisions, stores, and other supplies up to Philadelphia. Later, with the removal of some chevaux-de-frise frames, the larger ships-of-war reached the city.

August 18, 1778:
John Dickinson, President of the Supreme Executive Council, advised the Assembly that they had requested proposals for removing the chevaux-de-frise, but would not proceed further without Assembly approbation. This resolution was never acted upon.

March 23, 1779:
Colonel John Bull was ordered to have six chevaux-de-frise built for sinking at different depths near Mud Island.

April 19:
A master workman named Francis McClester was authorized to build one frame.

July 9:
Colonel Bull was employed to raise fortifications and prepare chevaux-de-frise for sinking at Billingsport.

July 20:
Bull advises frames are ready and requests advice and assistance; Captain Boys of the State Navy ordered to assist Bull. Little is known of the numbers, or if these frames were eventually sunk in the river.

These are the last recorded chevaux-de-frise authorized to be built or sunk in the river. The great majority of them would be removed or destroyed in 1784.

June 3, 1783:
Thirteen chevaux-de-frise, lying on the New Jersey shore, were ordered removed. Could these have been those Colonel Bull was ordered to build in 1779, but possibly never sunk?

June 10:
Council ordered the Wardens of the Port to adopt some plan for the removal of the obstructions in the river.

August 5:
Wardens were ordered to make exact survey of the river bed to determine the number of chevaux-de-frise to be removed so that a channel could be opened for commerce to the city.

August 10:
Council advertised for proposals to remove the chevaux-de-frise. By the 26th only one man had submitted a plan and that as superintendent at a per diem rate of one guinea.

August 22:
Assembly appointed members to form a joint committee with Council for reviewing subject of removing river obstructions.

November 4 and 11:
de Brussine [sic] and N. Garrison proposed two plans for removing all chevaux-de-frise. One plan was to cut each obstruction down to

the ballast, without removing the stones. Under this plan they would pay all expenses, assume all risks for a consideration of £4,000. The second proposal called for an experiment to completely remove one frame. They were to be advanced £1,200 and if successful £2,000 for the entire removal. While Council approved the first plan, no work was ever done.

November 7:
Francis Gurney claimed £400 was due him for the purchase of a vessel to remove the chevaux-de-frise. He also claimed amounts for buoys, anchors, and chains, and for making a survey of the river near Fort Mifflin.

November 14:
Council instructed de Brussine and Garrison to proceed with the first plan. Payment to be made when Council was satisfied that all frames had been removed. This proposal seems to have ended on this note. Possibly the contractors were dissatisfied with the method of payment.

February 21, 1784:
Merchants exert pressure on Council to have chevaux-de-frise removed. A memorial was presented outlining effect of the obstructions on the economy of the city.

February 24:
Dickinson advised Merchant Committee that plans were going forward to open river.

March 6:
Merchants expressed gratitude and offered assistance.

March 13:
Merchants' advice solicited.

March 19:
Recommended that Wardens of the Port be assigned responsibility for removal.

April 16:
Wardens of the Port again instructed to obtain proposals for removal of the obstructions.

April 20:
Proposals were received from Arthur Donaldson and Levi Hollingsworth and read to Council. Donaldson, having been engaged during the war in placing the chevaux-de-frise in the river, was eminently qualified to be engaged in their removal.

May 1:
Formal agreement was made with Hollingsworth and Donaldson. The Supreme Executive Council agreed to provide the contractors with the vessel purchased by the Wardens (see entry of November 7, 1783) and with any spare timber on Mud Island to a value of twenty pounds, and also the frames of chevaux-de-frise lying on the Billingsport shore. They were to receive £6,000 for removing and destroying forty-nine chevaux-de-frise. Advance of £1,500 was to be made to enable them to purchase needed materials (£400 advanced on April 30 and £1,100 on May 3), £1,500 when the Wardens were satisfied that ample progress had been made (paid June 30);—£1,500 when thirty-six frames had been removed and destroyed (paid September 30); and a final £1,500 when the forty-nine frames were removed and destroyed (authorized payment October 26).

July 23:
Wardens advised that fifteen frames have been removed and are located at: Billingsport, 3; Fort Island, 1; Red Bank, 1; Eagle Point, 2; Gloucester, 3; below Thompson's Wharf, 1; Windmill Island, 1; League Island, 1; buoyed off Timber Creek, 1; 1 cut up by Mr. Conarroe.

September 4:
Wardens advised Dickinson that nearly all chevaux-de-frise were removed; however, they ordered the State sloop, with a skillful pilot and diver, to sweep and carefully examine the river to determine if some frames remained undetected. They added that five previously undiscovered frames remained in the eastern channel preventing navigation.

September 23:
Fourteen chevaux-de-frise not previously discovered were found. Hollingsworth and Donaldson apparently removed most of them before agreeing upon compensation. Those in shallow east channel could not be canted to discharge ballast; they had to be floated into the main channel where the ballast could be removed by canting the frames.

Thomas Conarroe and several associates criticized the efforts of Hollingsworth and Donaldson. They described the ease with which the frames could be removed, saving a considerable sum of money for the State. Donaldson and his partner asked these "Pretenders" to demonstrate but only Conarroe agreed. He spent a considerable amount of money and after several weeks had not raised one chevaux-de-frise. After this failure, criticism stopped and the partners agreed to remove the last fourteen for £1,400.

October 12:
The last of the sixty-three frames was removed on this date.

October 26:

From early September through October 14, pilots and divers had been busy sweeping the river and were satisfied that all obstructions had been removed. The Wardens advised the Council that both channels were now open to navigation and that the contract with Hollingsworth and Donaldson had been fulfilled.

The contractors had removed and destroyed sixty-three chevaux-de-frise; others were destroyed on the shore—apparently never sunk in the river. A few fragments were removed by the Army Engineers in the 1930's. The exact number built and sunk cannot be determined but those removed by Hollingsworth and Donaldson were the major obstacles to commerce.

To retrace our steps, on October 11, 1775, the Committee of Safety appointed ten chevaux-de-frise pilots to conduct ships through the serpentine channel created by the obstructions. All other pilots were forbidden to attempt to bring vessels above Chester. Appointed were Michael Dawson, Joseph Gamble, Daniel Gordon, William Marshall, Nehemiah Maul, William Molletson, James Roberts, William Ross, John Schneider, and Matthew Strong.

The pilots made a proposal to the Committee to work for a monthly wage of £10. They apparently were advised that this amount was excessive, as their demands were lowered to £7 6s, and then a day later to £6. On October 12, they took an oath of office pledging not to reveal any information concerning the chevaux-de-frise, and to avoid any indiscretion which might place them in a position to be taken prisoner. They also agreed to serve until discharged by the Committee.

Rules governing their conduct were released on November 3 and read into the Committee minutes on the 7th.

One incident where an unauthorized pilot successfully brought a ship through the chevaux-de-frise is recorded on November 11, 1775. A John Saunders was ordered taken into custody and confined in the city gaol; after being incarcerated for seventeen days, he was released. He took a solemn oath before a justice of the peace not to reveal how he discovered the passage through the obstructions.

By mid-December 1775, the pilots petitioned the Committee for a salary increase, as they were unable to meet expenses. On December 18 their rate was raised to £7 a month, and on March 19, 1776, to £10. On May 20, 1777, their wages were again increased to £18 a month with three rations a day.

On September 19, 1776, James Maul was appointed a pilot to replace Daniel Gordon, deceased. Matthew Strong's name appears on the early oath but is subsequently omitted from the roster of chevaux-de-frise pilots in the printed archives. These same archives list a Nathan Storey appointed February 20, 1776—possibly a replacement for Strong.

The Supreme Executive Council declared the chevaux-de-frise pilots supernumerary on August 29, 1777, and they were called before the Council the next day and officially discharged.

The rules governing the conduct of the chevaux-de-frise pilots released by the Committee of Safety on November 3, 1775 were:

The Committee of Safety having order'd & directed that ten Pilots only be employed in Conducting all Vessels between Philadelphia & Chester whether Inward or Outward bound, The following are the Rules & Regulations concerning them viz

1st That five of the said Number of Pilots be in readiness at Philadelphia to carry Vessels down to Chester & having performed that Service are immediately to return by land or in their Skiffs to Philadelphia.

2nd That the other five be at Chester to bring Vessels up from thence to Philadelphia & are to return in like manner to Chester.

3rd That no Pilot be allow'd to return to his Station otherwise than as above, unless where it happens that any Vessel shall be in want of a Pilot and there is none other on the Spot, in which case he may take charge of her—

4th That each set of Pilots change their Stations, every ten days unless it be otherwise agreed among themselves—

5th That such of the five pilots at Philadelphia as are not absent upon duty shall attend from 10 to 1 o'clock every day at the House of Clement Humphreys on Pine Street Wharf, and those at Chester at the House of Mrs. Whitby, to receive their Applications from Owners or Masters of Vessels—

6th That the Several Pilots be oblig'd to perform the Services required in Rotation, according to the Number of the Ticket or Certificate of their appointment that each one received from the Committee of Safety unless otherwise agreed among themselves—and that applications made by Owners or Masters of Vessels at the aforesaid houses, be deem'd due & Sufficient Notice—

7th That none of the Pilots so employ'd demand or receive any Pilotage from Owners or Masters of Vessels for such Service, they being in the pay of the Committee of Safety for this Special purpose.[20]

Philad: November 2nd 1775 Thos. Wharton, Jr.
John Nixon
Geo. Clymer
Robert Whyte

A footnote to the story of the chevaux-de-frise is the statement of Francis B. Lee that poles thirty to forty feet long were driven into the mud near Billingsport. At the top of each pole was fastened a long sharp piece of iron. Because these poles would have been easily

Dear Sir   Newark August 16th 1776.—

I beg leave to enclose you a drawing of a new Contrivance for stopping Channels and Rivers, which I call Marine Chevaux de Frise, a model of which was exhibited at Head quarters in New York, the 20th of last month.

After the ships passed the Batteries with such facility, I considered with regret, that the Channel was not obstructed; and since the exigence required something both speedily executed and effectual, the enclosed Construction oc-curred, which I have reason to believe is now putting in practice.

In addition to what is set forth on the drawing, I beg leave to observe, that it may be described as a Tetrahedron with four horned Corners; having three Horns to each Corner; that the Consequence of a Ships running against it, must either be that she will stake upon it, or overset it, in which case the other horns will rise and take her in the bottom, and either overset her, go through her; or else she must break it with her weight; but here it is to be considered, what force it will require to break a Beam 12 or 15 Inches square, standing only 1/3 from the perpendicular; which seems too great for any ship to apply, without injuring her so effectually, as to render her unfit for further service — Such Chevaux dropt here & there in anchoring grounds and Harbours, would render them very unsafe — Supposing the Channels to be obstructed Seven fathoms deep, if it is made of Beams 32 feet long, its perpendicular height would be near 28 feet; the Horns would be within 14 feet of the surface; consequently obstruct any Vessel which drew more than that depth of water — Two Chevaux of these dimensions would stop 10 Fathoms, as the Horns of the one would be within 20 feet of those of the other — 20 would stop an hundred Fathoms, and require only 120 pieces of Timber — As the Current has full liberty to flow under, they cannot injure Channels or sensibly obstruct the tide: indeed they need not be put in till an alarm, for if they are ready prepared, a number of them may be rigged up and thrown into a Channel in a few hours — but I need not enlarge or add a number of Circumstances which will naturally occur to any one Conversant in Mechanics.

I shall think my self happy if any endeavours of mine tend to serve the Cause of Freedom, Humanity & the States of America & am
                        Dear Sir, with the Greatest respect
Hon.ble Dr Benjamin Franklin }   Your most Obed: humble Serv.t Rob. Erskine

The
Marine Chevaux de Frise,

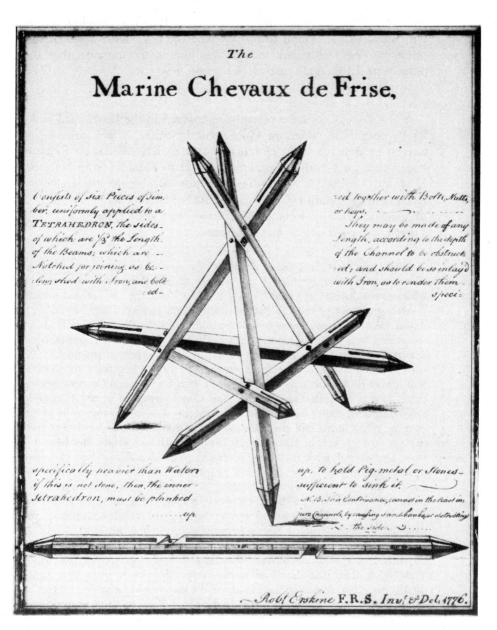

Consists of six Pieces of Tim-ber, uniformly applied to a TETRAHEDRON, the sides of which are 1/3 the Length of the Beams; which are Notched for joining, as be-low; shod with Iron, and bolt-ed

...ed together with Bolts, Nutts, or keys.

They may be made of any Length, according to the depth of the Channel to be obstruct-ed; and should be so inlaid with Iron, as to render them speci-

specifically heavier than Water: if this is not done, then the inner Tetrahedron, must be planked ....up

up, to hold Pig-metal or Stones sufficient to sink it.

N.B. This Contrivance, cannot in the least in-jure Channels, by causing sand-banks, or obstructing the sides.

Robt. Erskine F.R.S. Invt. & Del. 1776.

Courtesy American Philosophical Society.

removed, he claimed that they were strengthened by sinking frames with stone ballast behind them to which the poles were chained. Lee offers no documentations and he was apparently unaware that the poles were an integral part of the frame, being set obliquely to face downriver.[21]

A few documents were recently discovered in the Benjamin Franklin Papers at the American Philosophical Society, which provide an interesting epilogue to the chevaux-de-frise narrative.[22] Robert Erskine, map maker for George Washington, wrote to Franklin from Newark, N. J., on August 16, 1776, offering a plan to obstruct the Delaware River with a "Marine Chevaux-de-frise." Erskine's letter included a drawing of what he sometimes referred to as his "Tetrahedron" and a detail of the efficacy of its performance:

I beg leave to enclose you a drawing of a new Contrivance for stopping Channels and Rivers, which I call Marine Chevaux de Frise; a model of which was exhibited at Headquarters in New York, the 20th of last month.

After the ships passed the Batteries with such facility, I considered with regret, that the Channel was not obstructed; and since the exigence required something both speedily executed and effectual, the Enclosed Construction occurred, which I have reason to believe is now putting in practice.

In addition to what is set forth on the Drawing, I beg leave to observe, that it may be described as a Tetrahedron with four horned Corners; having three Horns to each Corner; that the Consequence of a Ships running against it, must either be that she will stake upon it, or overset it, in which case the other horns will rise and take her in the bottom, and either overset her, go through her; or else she must break it with her weight; but here it is to be Considered, what force it will require to break a Beam 12 or 15 Inches square, standing only ⅓ᵈ from the perpendicular; which seems too great for any ship to apply, without injuring her so effectually, as to render her unfit for further service—Such Chevaux dropt here & there in anchoring grounds and Harbours, would render them very unsafe—Supposing the Channel to be obstructed Seven fathoms deep, if it is made of Beams 32 feet long, its perpendicular height would be near 28 feet; the Horns would be within 14 feet of the surface, Consequently obstruct any vessel which drew more than that depth of water—Two Chevaux & there dimensions would stop 10 Fathoms, as the Horns of the one would be within 20 feet of those of the other—20 would stop an hundred Fathoms, and require only 120 pieces of Timber—as the Current has full liberty to flow under, they Cannot injure Channels or sensibly obstruct the tide: indeed they need not be put in till an alarm, for if they are ready prepared, a number of them may be rigged up and thrown into a Channel in a few hours—but I need not enlarge or add a number of Circumstances which will naturally occur to any one Conversant in Mechanics.

I shall think my self happy if any endeavours of mine tend to serve the Cause of Freedom, Humanity & the States of America.

Sir   Philad. Oct. 16. '6

I should sooner have acknowledged your
Favour of Aug. 16. containing the Drawing of
your Chevaux de Frise: but that I have been so
extreamly occupyed as to be oblig'd to postpone Corresting
to many of my Correspondents

Be so good as Please to accept my
thanks for the Communication of your Contrivance,
which I am persuaded will answer the Purpose where
ever the Bottom is so hard as to prevent the Points
being pressed into the Ground by the passing Ship before the Resistance shall become great enough to force
the upper Points thro' her Bottom. The Ground being
soft in our Channel, we were oblig'd to fix our pointed
Beams to a Floor, in the Chevaux we plac'd there
during the Summer of the preceding Year. That Floor
gives them so firm a Stand, that all the Vessels
which thro' inadvertance have run upon them, have
had such Breaches made in their Bottoms as
immediately sunk them. One was a large
Ship.

I am, Sir, with great Esteem,
Your most obed.t
humble Servant
B Franklin

In compliance with the request of the New York legislature, the Pennsylvania Council of Safety in June 1776 forwarded specifications and technicians to aid in the water defense of the city of New York. As previously stated, Arthur Donaldson and a contingent of carpenters were dispatched to construct and install chevaux-de-frise in New York Bay between the Battery and Governor's Island. Hazelwood accompanied Donaldson to supervise the building of fire-rafts for which each received a generous gratuity from the New York authorities.

Albert H. Heusser, in his biography of Erskine, does not mention the activities of the Pennsylvanians, nor did he see the Erskine-Franklin correspondence. He does give a splendid account of Erskine's contributions in the summer of 1776 to design and install obstructions for the Hudson River between Forts Washington and Lee.[23]

However it would appear that Erskine's contribution was in design and not the installation of the chevaux-de-frise. In his letter he was aware that land fortifications could at best merely delay the British fleet, and that river obstructions were necessary. His design was apparently submitted at Continental headquarters and accepted. As late as August 16 he wrote that "I have reason to believe is now putting in practice," an indication that others were engaged in the actual installation.

It is difficult to determine if Franklin and the Pennsylvania Council of Safety seriously considered Erskine's "Marine Chevaux-de-frise." Pennsylvania had placed the first frames in the river in 1775 and were cognizant of the effectiveness of those designed by Robert Smith. Franklin wrote to Erskine on October 16, 1776, explaining why Erskine's version of the chevaux-de-frise would not be effective in the Delaware River:

I should sooner have acknowledged your Favour of Aug. 16, containing the Drawing of your Chevaux de Frise; but that I have been so extreamly occupy'd as to be oblig'd to postpone Writing to many of my Correspondents

Please to accept my Thanks for the Communication of your Contrivance, which I am persuaded will answer the Purpose where ever the Bottom is so hard as to prevent the Points being press'd into the Ground by the passing Ship before the Resistance shall become great enough to force the upper Points thro' her Bottom. The Ground being soft in our Channel, we were oblig'd to fix our pointed Beams to a Floor, in the Chevaux we plac'd there during the Summer of the preceding year. That Floor gives them so firm a Stand, that all the Vessels which thro' Inadvertance have run upon them, have had such Breaches made in their Bottoms as immediately sunk them. One was a large Ship.

Appendix C

Pay Scale of the State Navy

The pay scale of the State navy was always one of the major problems of recruiting and keeping good officers and men in the service. Owners and captains of the privateers could always offer greater inducements than could the State. The Continental pay scale, especially for officers, was also much more attractive to good officers. The Continental pay scale was based on the armament of the ship: ships with 20 guns and up; ten to twenty guns; and those with less than ten guns. A fine point of distinction was evident to the galley captains as their boats carried only one cannon, thus placing them in the lowest Continental category. Continental ships in this class also usually were commanded by lieutenants.

Several changes in rates paid the various grades of officers, petty officers, and seamen were noted until February 1777. In the early months of 1776, distinctions were made between certain officer classifications on the ship *Montgomery*, the floating batteries *Arnold* and *Putnam*, and the galleys and guard boats. While there is no citation available to document any morale problem caused by this situation, it undoubtedly was another of the irritants in the relations between the Committee of Safety and the galley captains. A complete revamping of the pay scale, effective October 1, 1776, placed all classifications, except a few petty officers included in the roster of the *Montgomery*, on an equal basis.

The fire fleet and accommodation sloops and schooners were treated independently as each ship was acquired. They were never included in the pay scale revisions as approved by the Council or Committee of Safety.

The marines were treated separately; they ceased to exist as a separate unit within the State navy in September or October 1776. The *Montgomery*'s marines, under Captain William Brown, became the crew of the floating battery *Putnam* in October 1776. Captain Thomas Forrest of the marines on the *Arnold* resigned to take command of a Pennsylvania artillery company and his contingent was incorporated into the crew of the *Arnold*. The only other marine company in the fleet was on board the ship *General Greene*, a State privateer. They served for about six months and were then discharged.

Little is known about the surgeon of the fleet. Dr. Benjamin Rush had accepted the appointment, but, finding the duties more than he could handle, recommended Dr. John Duffield as surgeon's mate, to be jointly responsible and to receive equal pay. Later the chief surgeon was in charge of the fleet, artillery companies at Fort Island, and the hospital on Province Island, but not the ship *Montgomery*. The *Montgomery* was assigned its own surgeon until it was partially deactivated in early 1777. At this time the Navy Board was asked to assume responsibility for the hospital. The chief surgeon's salary was charged to the services on a pro-rata basis.

Shown below is the first pay scale of the fleet, effective September 1, 1775, and the last one, approved on February 22, 1777. This latter rate was intended to keep the salaries of the fleet in line with the Continental fleet. A resolution had been passed by the Council to this effect when Seymour was appointed Commodore on September 26, 1776. Allowing Seymour to make this announcement was thought to make his appointment more palatable to the galley captains. Footnote references are provided which permit those interested to study interim changes and, in at least two instances, preliminary drafts of proposed changes and then the final accepted versions.

The masters of the ammunition and provision sloops and schooners received £5 per month and two rations per day (this was equivalent to 13⅓ dollars). The mate, who also acted as clerk, received ten dollars and one ration, and the crew seven dollars and one ration. The master of the shallop was given the same as the schooners and sloops, his steward receiving ten dollars.[7]

Captains of the fire vessels were given 26⅔ dollars per month and three rations per day. Lieutenants received eighteen dollars and two

PAY SCALE
PER MONTH

Galleys, Guard Boats, Ship and Floating Batteries

	September 1, 1775 (in dollars) [1]	February 1, 1777 (in dollars) [2]
Commodore	30	75 (125) [5]
Second in Command	–	– (100) [5]
Captain	20	48
First Lieutenant	12	30
Second Lieutenant	–	20
Third Lieutenant [3]	–	–
Master [3]	–	–
Master's Mate [3]	–	–
Surgeon [3]	–	48
Fleet Surgeon	20 [4]	12s 6d per day [6]
Surgeon's Mate [3]	12 [4]	20
Gunner	10	16
Gunner's Mate [3]	–	13
Carpenter	10	16
Carpenter's Yeoman (mate) [3]	–	13
Boatswain	8	16
Boatswain's Mate [3]	–	13
Quartermaster's Mate [3]	–	13
Armourer [3]	–	13
Clerk	8	16
Steward	10	16
Midshipman [3]	–	–
Drummer	6	10
Fifer	–	10
Privates (Seamen)	6	12
Boys	4	6
Cook	6	12

rations and the crew seven dollars and one ration.[8] It was the hope of Council that the crews of the fire vessels could be augmented by volunteers in times of emergencies.

In an effort to make a distinction between seamen and landsmen, a temporary measure was passed by Council in June 1776 giving seamen eight dollars per month and landsmen 6⅔ dollars. Apparently the experiment was unsatisfactory as all privates or seamen were soon on the same basis again.[9]

Marine pay rates were in force for only a few months; the captains were probably placed on the same basis as the first lieutenants of the galleys and the men were given 6⅔ dollars per month.[10]

Rations were furnished each crew member. The enlisted men received one ration per day. The commodore received six rations, second in command and captains, three; lieutenants, gunners, carpenters, and other petty officers, two rations. The weekly ration allowance of provisions and rum or malt beer was:

Seven pounds of bread per week, or six pounds of flour.
Ten pounds of Beef, Mutton or Pork.
The value of six pence per week in roots or vegetables.
Salt and vinegar.
Three pints and a half of rum, or beer in proportion.[11]

The fleet paymaster was to receive the salary of a galley captain.[12]

The ordinary seamen were charged for their clothing, such charges being deducted from their wages. There was apparently some abuse of permission to withhold amounts from the men's wages as the Council passed a resolution on September 17, 1776: "That the Wages due to the Men in the service of this State, be not stoped by their Officers on any pretense, unless with the consent of the men, or by special orders from this Board." [13]

On April 24, 1779, a pay scale was adopted for the *General Greene*, a State privateer ship.

	(in dollars)		(in dollars)
Captain	50	Midshipman	12
First Lieutenant	30	Armourer	9
Second Lieutenant	24	Cook	9
Surgeon	24	Steward	10
Muster Master	24		
Master's Mate	15	*Marines*	
Boatswain	13	Captain	30
Boatswain's Mate	9	Lieutenants	20
Gunner	13	Sergeant	10
Gunner's Mate	9	Corporal	7⅓
Carpenter	15	Privates	6⅔
Carpenter's Mate	9	with rations equal to those in the
Cooper	9	Continental service.

There is no mention of the pay scale for ordinary seamen in the minutes of the Supreme Executive Council. It was probably the same as privates in the marine detachment. The seamen were given an advance of one hundred dollars on future prize monies. The marines were given fifty dollars bounty and would be entitled to prize according to the ship's articles.

That the Captain of the ship was to be allowed forty dollars each week for subsistance in domestic ports, in lieu of all rations; and when at sea twenty dollars a week for cabin expenses; That the Lieutenants of the ship, Surgeons, Captain and Lieutenants of the Marines, when in actual service and domestic ports, to be allowed twenty dollars each week for subsistance, during such time as the Ship is not in condition to receive them on board.[14]

In 1780, when the naval establishment was reduced to a total of twenty-one officers and men, the pay scale was expressed in pounds. Paid monthly, the fleet surgeon, James Hutchinson, received £33 15s; two galley and two guard boat captains each received £18; three first lieutenants £11 5s; one second lieutenant £7 10s; armourer £4 17s 6d and eleven privates each £4 10s.[15]

Some changes were made in the ration allowances in the years 1779 and 1780. As the office of the commissary was no longer needed, the few remaining men were granted a cash allowance in lieu of rations.[16]

Appendix D

Rules and Regulations
for Administration of
the Pennsylvania Navy

The Articles governing the conduct of officers and men and the general instructions to commanders of the boats are little more than a penal code designed to regulate the State navy. Individual instructions to the Commodore and other specific fleet officers were standardized and submitted to each appointee and for each officer replacement. In the confusion of the impending crisis, no record of official instructions to Hazelwood in September 1777 seems to have been preserved. Subsequent appointments of fleet officers, such as commissary of stores, received little other than an official notice of their selection. It is probable that their duties were verbally outlined in greater detail.

Articles for the Government of the Officers and Men
employed on the Provincial Armed Boats [1]

Whereas, the arbitrary and tyrannical proceedings of the British ministry, in attempting to reduce the good people of America into a state of abject slavery and vassalage, has met with a righteous and spirited opposition from the twelve united colonies by their Delegates in Congress, who, by their resolves of the 18th July, recommended to the assemblies or conventions, or in their recess, to the Committees of Safety, to devise and provide such means for defending the lives, liberties, and properties of their respective inhabitants, as may to them seem best in compliance with this recommendation; and in consequence of the powers vested in this Committee by resolve of the Assembly of this Province, they have caused sundry boats to be built and armed for the defense of the same, and the protection of its commerce; which boats being now ready for service, it remains that they be immediately manned and equipped; *Therefore,* to encourage good and brave men to engage freely in this glorious service, the following Rules and Regulations are offered by the said Committee:

1st. All officers and privates in or belonging to the Provincial armed boats, being guilty of profane oaths, cursing drunkenness or other scandalous actions, shall incur such punishment as the nature and degree of the offense shall deserve, at the discretion of a court martial.

2nd. Any officer or private who shall strike the commander-in-chief or other his superior officer, or draw, or offer to draw, or lift up any weapon, or use any violence against him, or shall behave himself with contempt or disrespect to him, them, or either of them, being in the execution of their office, shall be punished according to the nature of his offence, at the discretion of a court martial.

3rd. If any person, in or belonging to the Provincial armed boats shall raise, or endeavour to raise a mutiny, on any pretence whatever, or shall disobey any lawful commands of his superior officer, he shall, on conviction thereof, suffer such punishment as shall be ordered by a court martial.

4th. Any officer or private who shall, without leave of his commanding officer, absent himself from the boat or other vessell to which he belongs, or from any detachment of the same, or shall advise or persuade any other officer or private so to do, shall be punished, at the discretion of a court martial.

5th. Every person in the fleet who shall mutiny in time of action, or who through cowardice, disaffection, or negligence, shall at such time withdraw or keep back, or not come into the fight or engagement, or shall not do his utmost to take or destroy any ship, boat or other vessell which it shall be his duty to engage, or shall endeavour to persuade or deter others from doing their duty at such a time, shall suffer death.

6th. Every person who shall desert to the enemy, or shall entice others so to do, shall suffer death, or such other punishment as the circumstances of the offence shall deserve, and a court martial think fit.

7th. Any officer or private who shall be convicted of holding any correspondence with, or giving intelligence to the enemy, either directly or indirectly, shall suffer death, or such punishment as shall be ordered by a court martial.

8th. Every officer or private who shall be convicted of having designedly or carelessly wasted or embezzled the ammunition, arms, stores, or provisions belonging to any of the boats, shall suffer such punishment as a court martial shall think proper for the offence.

9th. Whatever officer shall be found drunk on guard or under arms, shall be cashiered; and any private so offending, shall be punished at the discretion of a court martial.

10th. No person in or belonging to the Provincial armed boats shall sleep upon his watch, or forsake his post, on pain of such punishment as a court martial shall think fit to impose.

11th. Any officer or private who shall, by discharging fire arms, beating of drums, or by any other means, occasion false alarms, shall suffer such punishment as shall be inflicted by a court martial.

12th. All officers, of what condition soever, shall have power to part and quell all quarrels, affrays and disorders, though the persons concerned should belong to another boat, and order officers to be arrested, and non-commissioned officers or privates to be confined until their proper superior officers shall be acquainted therewith, and whoever shall refuse to obey such officer, though of an inferior rank, or shall draw his sword, or lift up any weapon against him, shall be punished, at the discretion of a court martial.

13th. If any inferior officer or private shall think himself wronged by the commander of the boat to which he belongs, he may apply to the commander-in-chief, who is to redress his grievance.

14th. All officers shall take rank from the date of their commissions.

15th. All ships and other vessels, and their cargoes, ammunition, artillery, clothing, or other articles taken from the enemy, shall be disposed of or distributed as the Provincial Assembly shall hereafter think proper.

16th. If any officer or private shall commit any crime deserving punishment, he shall by his commanding officer be put under arrest if an officer, or if a non-commissioned officer or private, be put in confinement, till he shall be tried by a court martial or discharged by proper authority.

17th. If any officer under arrest shall leave his confinement before he is set at liberty by the officer who confined him, or by proper authority, he shall be cashiered.

18th. Any officer who shall presume to discharge any prisoner committed to his charge without proper authority for so doing, or shall suffer any prisoner to escape, shall be punished, at the discretion of a court martial.

19th. If any commissioned officer shall be convicted before a court martial of behaving in a scandalous, infamous, cruel, oppressive or fraudulent manner, unbecoming the character of an officer, he shall be dismissed from the service.

20th. All crimes not capital, and all disorders and neglect which officers and privates may be guilty of, to the prejudice of good order and military discipline, though not mentioned in these articles, shall be taken notice of by a court martial, and punished, according to the nature of the offence.

21st. No person to be sentenced by a court martial to suffer death, except in the cases expressly mentioned in the foregoing articles, nor shall any other punishment be inflicted, at the discretion of a court martial, other than degrading, cashiering, drumming out of the fleet, whipping, not exceeding thirty-nine lashes, fine, not exceeding two months pay, and imprisonment, not exceeding one month.

22nd. The commanding officer of each boat shall appoint some suitable person to receive all such fines as may arise within the same, for breach of any of these articles, which fines shall be accounted for to the Assembly or Committee of Safety, and by them be appropriated for the relief of the maimed and disabled in the service, and the support of the widows and families of such as may be killed.

23rd. No court martial for the trial of offences under the degree of capital, shall consist of less than five officers, except in cases where that number cannot be conveniently assembled, when three may be sufficient, who are to determine on the sentence by a majority of voices, and in all trials for capital offences, the court martial shall be composed of thirteen officers, and the sentence be determined by at least two-thirds.

24th. All persons belonging to the boats, called as witnesses in any case before a court martial, who shall refuse to attend and give evidence, shall be punished, at the discretion of a court martial.

25th. All members of a court martial are to behave with calmness, decency and impartiality, and in giving their votes, are to begin with the youngest or lowest in commission, and all officers of different boats are to rank in court martial according to their commissions.

26th. All members sitting in a court martial, shall be sworn or affirmed by the President of said court, which president shall himself be sworn or affirmed by the officer next in rank in said court, the oath or affirmation to be administered previous to their proceeding to the trial of any offender, in form following, viz.: 'You, A. B., swear or affirm that you will well and truly try, and impartially determine the cause of the prisoner now to be tried, according to the Rules framed for the Regulation of the Pennsylvania Fleet, (if an oath add) so help you God.'

27th. The President of the court martial shall administer the following oath or affirmation to all persons called to give evidence: 'You swear or affirm that the evidence you shall give in the cause now trying, shall be the truth, the whole truth, and nothing but the truth (if an oath add), so help you God.'

28th. No person shall suffer death, agreeable to the sentence of a court martial, (except in the cases mentioned in the 5th Article), till the sentence is confirmed by the Assembly, or in their recess by the Committee of Safety.

29th. The commander of each boat shall, in the beginning of every month, make a faithful return to the Committee of Safety, of the men employed in his boat, to be signed by himself, and upon being convicted of having made a false return, shall be discharged from the service, and if he neglect to make a return within the month, shall be fined, at the discretion of said Committee.

30th. No officer or private shall be tried a second time for the same offence.

We, the underwritten, having seen and distinctly heard the foregoing Articles read, and fully understanding the contents thereof, do freely and voluntarily subject ourselves to all and every of the Rules, Regulations, and Restrictions therein contained. In witness whereof, we hereunto subscribe our names.

General Instructions for the Commanders of the Provincial Armed Boats [2]

1. Every Captain or other officer shall give strict attention, that the boat he commands be kept clean and in good order at all times.

2. The officers of the boats are to use the crew well, and to keep strict discipline among them.

3. Each Captain shall appoint all officers under the rank of a commissioned officer, and oblige them to perform diligently the duties of their station.

4. Every Captain and other officer shall be punctual in observing the orders he shall from time to time receive from the Commodore, Committee of Safety, or Assembly.

5. No powder to be expended for exercising either great guns or small arms, without orders from the Commodore, Committee of Safety, or Assembly, and only swivel guns or muskets to be fired for signals, except in cases of immediate danger.

6. The Commodore shall order the crews, or each Captain his respective crew, to be exercised in the use of their oars, great guns,

small arms, and pikes, as often as possible, without impeding the public service, or harassing the men too much.

7. The crew not to be suffered to go on shore, or absent themselves from on board the boats without leave from their officers, nor to disturb any inhabitants, or settlements, on any pretence whatever.

8. The Commodore or Commanding officer shall appoint proper signals, copies of which shall be given to the Captain or Commanding officer of every boat, to all which signals the officers are to pay due obedience and respect.

9. The eldest officer present, where more boats are together than one, to act as Commodore, and have the command of the whole.

10. When a boat is below the city, the Commanding officer on board is to examine all vessels bound up, whether the people on board are our friends or foes, and if they refuse satisfaction in these points they are to be considered as enemies.

11. The officers of the boats are to treat the masters and crews of all vessels, both foreign and others, who have no hostile intentions against us, and who do not violate the laws of the Continental Congress, or the rules and regulations of the Committee of Safety or Assembly, with decency and good manners, nor are they to put them to unnecessary delay or trouble, but if any should be in distress they are to lend them all reasonable assistance.

12. A copy of the Articles, subscribed by the officers and men, shall be hung up in some public part of the boat, for the perusal of the crew, to whom they are to be read once every week, in an orderly manner, all the officers, who can conveniently attend, to be present.

13. The boats are not to leave any particular station assigned them out of port, or when appointed to any duty, without orders from the Commodore, Committee of Safety, or Assembly.

14. The Captain of each boat shall cause his clerk to make out a muster roll of the crew of the boat which he commands, with their names, stations on board, time of entering the service, whether they are sickly or maimed, and what is their ailment, and if any of the crew should die or be discharged, specify the time thereof, all which is to be returned to the Muster Master of the boats, once every month, at least, or oftener if required by him.

15. No Captain or other officer shall discharge any of the boats' crew without leave from the Commodore, Committee of Safety, or Assembly, unless he ships an equal number to those discharged, immediately.

16. The Commander of each boat is by ticket to certify to the contractor, from time to time, the number of rations that are required for his boat's crew; the stewart of the boat is to receive the same from

the commissary upon producing the said ticket, and is to give his receipt, and be accountable.

17. The Commander of each boat is to examine into the quality of the provisions, from time to time, and see that they be good and wholesome, and that the proper quantity be delivered out by the steward, and in convenient messes.

18. If the quality of the provisions should be objected to, the Captain of the boat is to report the same to the contractor, with a desire that they may be exchanged for such as are good and wholesome, but if the contractor is dissatisfied with the report of the Captain, they are to have a survey made by two judicious and impartial freeholders, mutually chosen, who may determine the same if they agree, but if otherwise, they are to call in an umpire, who shall decide upon the quality of said provisions; if they are condemned the contractor shall supply others to equal amount in kind, but if the judgment of the referrers should be otherwise, the men must receive them for their allowance.

19. No warrant officer or private, discharged from the service of the boat he first ships in, shall be admitted in the service of any other boat unless by mutual consent of the Commanders.

20. The Commanding officer of each boat constantly to enforce a due observance of all the articles signed and agreed to by the officers and men, for their regulation in this service.

21. In case of making prisoners, it is recommended by the Committee of Safety to all the officers and men employed in the Pennsylvania fleet, to treat them with humanity, and such kindness as the public good will admit of.

22. It is recommended by the Committee of Safety, to all the officers and men employed in the Pennsylvania fleet, to attend the public worship of Almighty God as frequently as in their power.

23. If any of the King's ships, sloops, cutters, or other armed vessels, shall proceed up the River Delaware in a hostile manner, or with hostile intentions; if they attempt to pass the machines now sunk, or hereafter to be sunk in the River Delaware, or if they attempt to weigh those that are sunk, or obstruct the sinking of others that are, or may be ordered by the Committee of Safety or Assembly, or if they seize or attempt to seize any property of the inhabitants of the United Colonies of America, or to molest, or destroy their property or persons, in any shape or manner whatever, the officers and men employed in this fleet, are hereby ordered to oppose all such proceedings and attempts, by whomsoever made, and to repel force by force, even to the taking, sinking, or destroying all such ships, sloops, cutters, armed vessels, or other force, employed in such designs and attempts against the peace and security of the United Colonies.

Officer's Commission, Pennsylvania Navy [3]

"To ———

We, reposing especial trust and confidence in your patriotism, valor, conduct and fidelity, do by these present constitute and appoint you to be   of the Provincial armed boat called the   fitted out for the protection of the Province of Pennsylvania and the commerce of the River Delaware, against all hostile enterprises, and for the defense of American liberty; you are, therefore, to take the said boat into your charge and carefully and diligently to discharge the duty of   by doing and performing all manner of things thereunto belonging. And we do strictly charge and require all officers, soldiers and mariners under your command, to be obedient to your orders as   and you are to observe and follow such orders and directions from time to time, as you shall receive from the Assembly or Provincial Convention during their sessions, or from this or a future Committee of Safety for this Province, or from your superior officer, according to the Rules and Discipline of War, pursuant to the trust reposed in you; this Commission to continue in force until revoked by the Assembly or Provincial Convention, or by this or any succeeding Committee of Safety.

By Order of the Committee."

Warrant of Muster Master [4]

"To ———, Gentleman:

You are hereby appointed Muster Master of the forces belonging to the Pennsylvania fleet, and authorized to exercise all such powers as may be necessary for the effectual discharge of the said office. You are to repair on board and visit each boat in the fleet, once at least in every month, and oftener if occasion should require, or if directed by this Committee. You are there to require the articles signed by the boat's company, and carefully to call over their names, view each of them separately, examine whether they be actually fit for their respective duty, and see that their numbers, conditions, and abilities, agree with the returns made by the captains, and faithfully certify the same on the said returns. You are also to compare all draughts and orders made on the paymaster by the captains in favor of the officers and privates belonging to the boats, examine whether the time which they have been in the service be truly stated, with their ranks, and certify the same accordingly. And all officers and others belonging to the Pennsylvania fleet, are hereby strictly enjoined and required at all times to admit and receive you on board the boats, and suffer you to proceed in the duties above specified, without hindrance or molestation; and for your so doing this shall be your warrant."

Warrant of Paymaster [5]

"To ———, Gentleman:

You are hereby appointed Paymaster of the Pennsylvania fleet, and impowered to do all such matters and things as may be necessary in the execution of the said office. You are regularly to pay all draughts and orders made on you by the Captains of the armed boats in favor of the officers and privates employed in the service of the said boats, which are properly certified by the Muster Master, having strict regard to the rates fixed and published by this Committee for the pay of the said officers and privates respectively, and keeping exact accounts and receipts of all sums of money by you paid away, and the names of the persons to whom, and the purposes for which they were disbursed; and for your so doing this shall be your warrant."

Warrant of Ship Husband [6]

"To ———, Gentleman:

You are hereby appointed Ship's Husband to the Pennsylvania fleet, and empowered to do all such matters and things as may be necessary for the due execution of the said office.

You are to make known to all Commanders and other officers employed in the said fleet, that they are to apply through you for all stores and necessary's required for the service. You are to receive their indents or lists of what is wanted, report the same as often as necessary to this Committee, and when the approbation of the Board is obtained, you are to procure the sundry articles, of the best quality, each in its kind; and it is your particular duty to buy them on the best terms in your power; you are to take each officers' receipts for the articles delivered to him, and you are to return the bills or accounts of those you purchase for this Board, certified by you that the quantity's are what you received, and the prices what you agreed for, not being dearer than the current rates of each respective articles at the time of purchase.

You are empowered to inspect and inquire on board the fleet at least once in every month, and as much oftener as you may think necessary, whether all stores and necessary's are taken proper care of, and not neglected, wasted or embezzled, and make report according, as you find to this Board.

This Board, being ever desirous to serve the public faithfully, do recommend the most prudent economy in the outfits and supplies of the fleet; they must have every thing necessary, but avoid all expensive superfluities, and in the purchase of what is wanted, give a preference to such persons as are known to be zealous supporters of the American cause, dividing the business amongst as many of such as can be done with conveniency, and consistantly with the public good."

Instructions from the Committee of Safety at Philadelphia,
To Mr. Henry Fisher at Lewis Town [7]

"You are immediately to repair down to Lewis Town, and remain there constantly, (until discharged from this service,) for the purpose of giving advice to this Board of every British man-of-war or armed vessel that may arrive at the Capes of Delaware. We deliver you herewith, an order from the Board of Wardens to the keeper of the light house, directing him to make such signals by day and night, on discovering any ship or vessel standing in for the land as you and he may agree on, and you must immediately repair to the properest place for discovering what they are, and when you are convinced of the arrival of one or more men-of-war intending up this river, you are to send us advice thereof, either by land or water, as you conceive best, mentioning the number of the enemy ships, and their force and manner of proceeding, as nearly as you can ascertain these circumstances; when you send intelligence by water, you should avoid sending pilots, or persons that can serve as pilots to the enemy, lest they fall within their power.

Resolved, that it is the opinion of this Committee, that the buoys in the Bay of Delaware ought to be taken up immediately, and that the Wardens of the Port be desired to give orders for its being done, and to give orders to the keeper of the light to make such signals by day or night, as Mr. Henry Fisher and he may agree on, upon seeing vessels standing inwards.

Resolved, that it is the opinion of this Committee, that six six-pound cannon be lent to the inhabitants of Lewis Town and Pilot Town, near Cape Henlopen, with ammunition for the same, to defend themselves from any hostile attacks; they giving security to return the cannon on demand, and in expectation that the Committee of Safety for the three Lower Counties will repay the quantity of ammunition, or its value in money, in a reasonable time.

Resolved, that it is the opinion of this Committee, that if any pilot, or pilot boat, should be wanted for especial or particular purposes, during the time these resolves remain in force, application should be made to this Board, who will grant a certificate to the pilot or person employed, on finding the public good is connected with his service."

Instructions to Commodore Commanding
The State Marine Forces [8]

"The Committee having thought proper to appoint you Commodore-in-chief of all the Provincial Naval Armaments in the River Delaware, which you are to notify to the officers of the fleet by publishing to them your commission, it becomes necessary to give you some instructions to regulate your conduct in some points of this important trust.

And first, you are by all possible means, to establish such a proper sense of subordination in the fleet, that all the orders you think necessary to issue, be punctually and implicitly obeyed, a loose and relaxed discipline utterly enfeebling every military establishment, however respectable it may otherwise be in the circumstances of number or force.

Secondly, as it is the duty and inclination of this Committee to maintain the fleet in a constant state of preparation to receive the enemy, you must immediately take an exact survey of its present condition, and whatever may be wanting in its equipment to make report of to Capt. William Richards, who is appointed and directed by this Board to supply all its deficiencies.

Thirdly, an attack from the enemy being highly probable, tho' the time uncertain, it is necessary, that every part of the fleet should have its proper station assigned, in such way as to afford mutual support, and that the whole may act to the best effect.

Fourthly, you must particularly attend not only to the situation of the fleet, but take great care that the officers and men are not absent from their respective vessels any length of time and at any great distance, but as it is probable that some of the officers of the boats may be desirous of coming up to this city, you may give leave of absence to them, but only to six officers at one time, and that no more than three of that number shall be captains, who shall not be absent more than forty-eight hours at one time from their respective vessels.

Lastly, should any accident or circumstance happen in the fleet that has the least tendency to effect the service, you are to give the earliest information of it to the Committee of Safety, that, they, if they have the means of remedy, may apply such as the nature of the case may require.

These being the principal matters that have occurred to the Committee, they confide in your prudence and discretion, which have directed their choice, to supply their omission in those numberless circumstances and situations in which you may be placed, earnestly recommending to you, however, that you endeavour to promote the utmost harmony between you and the officers of the fleet, and between one another, on which depends so much the success of every undertaking, where men are to act in concert, and mutual assistance is required."

Appendix E

Captain Robert Whyte (White)

Was Robert Whyte a traitor? Some historians have created a monster only a shade better than Benedict Arnold. Did Whyte sell out the chevaux-de-frise for his thirty pieces of silver? To impartially judge the conduct of Whyte, we must review his career in the service of Pennsylvania and subsequent shift of allegiance to Great Britain.

William Wallace, one of Whyte's most vitriolic critics, made a study of his life. Whyte was a British sea captain trading between Philadelphia and the West Indies. In 1753 he commanded the brig *Susanna* and in 1755 the ship *Hope*. In 1757, during the war with France, he was first officer of a British man-of-war, which, after a smart engagement with three French ships, captured two of them. One of the ships was new and taken into British service, and the command was given to Whyte. For three years he sailed this ship between Philadelphia and the West Indies. In 1760 he was aboard the *Hamilton* making several voyages to the West Indies. Later he sailed to Lisbon, subsequently transferring to the *Snow Britannia*, until September 1768. At that date, he either retired from the sea or sailed from some port other than Philadelphia.

The records of Christ Church show that he married Jane Richardson on March 18, 1758. They were blessed with six children. He was a contributor, in 1758, to the building fund of St. Peter's Church. In 1773 he was manager of The Society for the Relief of Poor Distressed

Masters of Ships, their Widows and Children, a charitable organization established in 1765 for shipmasters trading out of Philadelphia.[1]

It cannot be determined when Whyte made Philadelphia his home, although Wallace suggests at the latest 1774. His basis for this date was Whyte's election to the church parish office in that year. He was again chosen for this office in 1775, 1776, and 1778 during the British occupation. It was undoubtedly before 1774 as Whyte's biographical sketch testifies.

After his service with the Committee of Safety in 1775-76, he left Philadelphia with the British army in 1778. He was attainted of treason and proscribed on October 30, 1778.[2] He entered the British naval service and in April 1782 was in command of a royal cutter. This cutter was captured by New Jersey militia, Captain Hyler, and taken into New Brunswick. Upon hearing that the cutter had been taken, Governor Moore of Pennsylvania wrote to Governor Livingston of New Jersey petitioning for the return of Whyte to Philadelphia, to be placed in the custody of the sheriff.

Without detailing the treasonable acts of which Whyte was accused, Moore wrote Livingston: "Captain White has been an atrocious offender, and as he is a man of address, it will be prudent and necessary to guard against his escape." [3] Fortunately for Whyte, he was already exchanged and out of the grasp of Pennsylvania authorities.

Apparently Whyte went to England after the war, settling in what was then a suburb of London. Two items appearing in the *Gentlemen's Magazine* are the last glimpses we have of Whyte. On September 3, 1795, his youngest daughter Margaret died and in June 1812 an obituary notice appeared announcing his death at an advanced age.

Whyte's services to Pennsylvania and the dedication with which he performed those duties have never been given an objective study. The archives of Pennsylvania disclose a devotion to the patriot cause as sincere as that of any member of the Committee of Safety in 1775-76—a record that has been ignored. To better understand the emotional tug-of-war which led to his decision to leave the city with Clinton's army and choose a life of exile in Great Britain, a somewhat cold but factual analysis of his day-by-day movements in 1775-76 is necessary.

He was named to the first Committee of Safety, which included such outstanding Patriots as Benjamin Franklin, Robert Morris, John Cadwalader, Anthony Wayne, George Ross, Thomas Wharton, Jr., Samuel Morris, and Owen Biddle.

As one of the very few members of the Committee with maritime experience, and the only one with the background of ship's command, he was always chosen for committees on naval affairs.

On July 3, 1775, Whyte was chosen with Robert Morris and Thomas Wharton, Jr., to obtain powder and saltpeter. Following the decision to build a river naval force, Owen Biddle and Whyte were selected as a committee to supervise the "Construction of Boats and Machines" to defend the river. Biddle was a landsman and the responsibility for coordinating the plans, designs, and construction of boats rested with Whyte. For the next two months he served on a number of sub-committees all concerned with arming and equipping the State navy.

With Colonel George Ross he was assigned to draft rules and regulations for the conduct of the navy, specific regulations to govern each officer, and a pay scale for officers and men. Along with Morris, he prepared a projected cost of the navy and river obstructions.

In September, along with Samuel Morris, Jr., Whyte was assigned the responsibility for striking the chevaux-de-frise and closing the channel of the river.

For the next six months he was active on committees: obtaining matériel for the navy, surveying the river, sinking chevaux-de-frise, and supervising certain construction projects on Fort Island. These duties naturally demanded that he spend a considerable amount of time downriver in the vicinity of Fort Island.

On April 16, 1776, the Committee of Safety divided its functions into numerous subcommittees and Whyte was assigned to five, all oriented to the navy and chevaux-de-frise.

From this date until July 1, 1776, he faithfully served on these subcommittees and attended the regular Committee of Safety meetings. A scrutiny of the Committee's minutes and other records reveals a faithful attendance for the year ending July 1, 1776, a record matched but not excelled by any other member. His attendance to duty at the various shipyards, Fort Island, and in constructing and sinking the chevaux-de-frise is not available, but the results of his work are self-evident. Any absence from regular Committee meetings can usually be correlated with a specific assignment. He was absent for about three weeks in late September and early October 1775, at which time he was helping draft the regulations for governing the navy and the rules of conduct for the officers.[4] He was the only maritime-oriented member of the committee engaged in this work. George Ross, Owen Biddle, and Samuel Morris, Jr. were all landsmen.[5]

Faithful in attendance, devoted to detail, constant in the supervision of his assignments, he served until July 1, 1776. The Committee of Safety minutes make only one reference to Captain Whyte after this date. On July 16, a resolution was passed: "The Committee taking into Consideration the extraordinary trouble of Captain Whyte in attending and directing the Building & sinking Chevaux de Frize, and other public services out of doors, are of opinion he is entitled to Receive One hundred & fifty pounds for such services." [6] Three days later, either as an afterthought or oversight, the same resolution was passed granting Samuel Morris, Jr., an identical amount.[7]

Whyte disappears from history for almost two years, his name appearing on October 30, 1778, on a list of those attainted of treason. Why was a patriot of 1775–76 suddenly being proscribed as a traitor? Some historians, like Mr. Wallace, assert that he sold out his country— that he was instrumental in the British finding that the back channel, between Fort Island and the Pennsylvania bank of the Delaware River, was deep enough to bring up the *Vigilant* and *Fury* to bombard Fort Mifflin. Strittmatter says that he was the only one paid for superintending the construction and sinking of the chevaux-de-frise. As has been indicated, Whyte was not the only one paid for these services; Samuel Morris received an identical amount. The charges of blackguard hurled at Whyte are unsupported by documentation.[8]

Independence created an emotional tug-of-war in the hearts of many Americans. A similar decision confronted other Americans in 1861. In the Revolution, a substantial number of Americans served in the Continental Congress, state Assemblies and legislatures and even in the Continental Army, but stopped short at independence from Great Britain. To these Americans the decision was distressingly poignant. They believed that the colonists had a perfect right to protest the arbitrary imposition of taxes and imposts, even resorting to arms. But, independence—no! To them the innate fairness of British justice would permit an accommodation acceptable to all citizens.

With the Continental Congress meeting in Philadelphia, the demands of the militant Patriots for complete separation from Great Britain caused great concern to those opposed to independence. Many signs pointed to the rising demand for autonomy among the artisans, laborers, and frontier citizens as well as a growing number of merchants, lawyers, and large landowners. Fort Island was temporarily renamed Liberty Island by the officers and men of the State navy and artillary companies. Working diligently to correct the usurpation of colonial authority by Great Britain and seeking a just settlement within the framework of the British Empire, were the Whytes, Galloways and Allens.

As that fateful day, July 2, 1776, approached, when a resolution would be passed in Congress declaring these states free, the majority of the State's delegates opposed independence at that time. Robert Morris and John Dickinson, staunch Patriots, believed independence inevitable, but the present action premature. To permit unanimity among the states, they abstained from voting. Pennsylvania, with Franklin, Morton, and Wilson voting for independence and Humphreys and Willing against, made a three for two vote in the affirmative.

Many of those opposed to independence immediately left to join the British in New York. Sacrificing everything and going into exile, they trusted to the success of British arms to restore their property. Others, like Captain Whyte, remained in Philadelphia during the British occupation, leaving with Clinton's army in June 1778. Some prominent Quakers who remained were exiled to Virginia.

This is the extent of treasonable acts which we can attribute to those Pennsylvanians who chose the British side. There is no evidence supporting a sellout by any one of this number. It is alleged that Whyte sold the secrets of the chevaux-de-frise. Was this possible?

Great emphasis has been laid by Whyte's detractors on the charge that he deliberately left open the channel at the rear of Fort Mifflin. Did he also leave open the channel between the sandbars near the New Jersey shore, a channel potentially more dangerous to Fort Mifflin? Whyte was not identified with the construction or sinking of the river obstructions after June 1776. The majority of the chevaux-de-frise were placed in the river after this date. Howe's army and fleet did not arrive in the Delaware until fifteen months later. It is difficult to see collusion in these facts and the time discrepancy.

Washington and du Coudray both conducted surveys of the river and its defenses. It is inconceivable that they could have discovered the threatened danger from the eastern channel and missed that of the western channel. Chevaux-de-frise were sunk in the eastern channel to prevent the passage of British frigates. With the erection of the fort on Tinicum Island and the stationing of fire rafts in the mouth of Darby Creek, guard boats, galleys, and floating batteries were constantly using the back channel. It is unbelievable that with all the activity of the State navy and duCoudray's engineers, the danger of this channel went undiscovered. Either the Americans were negligent or were sincerely convinced that none of the British men-of-war could navigate this channel. However, if the American galleys and small ships could navigate the west channel, so could similar classes of British boats and ships. American intelligence was aware that the British had cut down an East India merchantman (*Vigilant*) for service in shallow draught waters. The *Vigilants'* first attempt to ascend the channel on October 22 was unsuccessful.

To say that Whyte—out of conviction—did not give what information he possessed to Howe is ridiculous, but his information was not up to date. The gossip that circulated in the city was usually a conglomerate of misinformation, as is attested by reading some of the British intelligence reports. Regardless, any Tory could have furnished Howe with the same information, and probably did.

Joseph Galloway, Pennsylvania's most talented Tory, was advisor to Howe on local affairs and was better informed than Whyte. The advice and information offered by these Tories was gratuitous and considered a patriotic gesture. As for payment, if the British were defeated (of course at this date no Englishman believed this possible) their losses would be greater than any small gratuity.

A study of those attainted of treason was made by Wilbur Siebert.[9] In the period from March 6, 1778, to April 27, 1781, nine proclamations were issued declaring 453 Tories traitors to Pennsylvania. While this step was taken to apply the penalties of attainder and forfeiture of property, the Council of Safety could have taken a more militant stand, as those announced as traitors represented only about 10 percent of the inhabitants of the area who joined the British. The 453 were all accused of the same treasonable act, the Proclamation stating: ". . . have severally adhered to & knowingly & willingly aided and assisted the Enemies of this State of the United States of America, *by having joined their armies at Philadelphia, within this State.*" [author's italics] [10]

In each case they were ordered to appear for trial, but it is doubtful that any of the accused were foolish enough to do so. It should be emphasized that the only crime these men were guilty of was joining the British armed forces. Nothing was said about selling secrets or betraying the country. Under conditions of war, such conduct must be considered treasonous, but not with the implications assigned to Captain Whyte.

When Whyte was a prisoner of the New Jersey militia in 1782, Governor Moore's request for the arrest of Whyte described him as an "atrocious offender." This phrase has been repeated and interpreted to imply that he was guilty of selling the secrets of the river defenses. Research in depth would have proved that his treasonous acts were no more nor less than those of any American who joined the British army or navy in Philadelphia. History would then have placed him in the same category as Joseph Galloway or Andrew Allen, and not Benedict Arnold. When a choice became inescapable, he made the decision to throw in his lot with Great Britain. Leaving his home and family in Philadelphia, he accepted the inevitable exile unless British arms prevailed. Apparently his family joined him in England after the war.

The activities of Whyte's wife Jane are not clear. Maintaining her residence in Philadelphia, she apparently visited Whyte in New York

—probably clandestinely as it is difficult to conceive of the Supreme Executive Council granting permission for her to cross the enemy's lines. On December 14, 1779, she was accused of visiting within British lines and bringing to Philadelphia counterfeit money and British manufactured goods, prohibited by the laws of the State. The sheriff was ordered to search her residence and seize any articles of this nature and report to the Council. The disposition of this case and the future activities of Jane Whyte are not recorded in the Council's minutes.[11]

An addendum to the Whyte story is the footnote reference made by George Grieve in his edition of *Travels in North America in the Years 1780, 1781 and 1782* by the Marquis de Chastellux. Grieve is a mystery figure described by his biographer as an "hereditary agitator" and "ardent politician." A prepossessing individual and ardent Whig, he had the opportunity of meeting the leaders of democratic thought on both sides of the Atlantic; he claimed the friendship of such men as Franklin, Washington, and Jefferson. He was apparently forced to live in exile in France. His historical accuracy is suspect but this is probably more a matter of style than intent to deceive. A footnote in his edition of Chastellux's *Travels* states: "The person principally employed in sinking the chevaux-de-frise, and in securing the passage of the river, was one White, who is supposed to have left this channel open designedly, as he afterwards turned out a decided traitor, went over to the enemy, and distinguished himself by every act of hostile virulence against his country." Unfortunately, the usually reliable Wallace cited this along with Governor Moore's "atrocious offender" to label Whyte a Judas, and others have consistently repeated his conclusions.[12]

Appendix F

Howe's Strategy in the Delaware

A different version of Howe's strategy is presented by Ira D. Gruber in his excellent study, *The Howe Brothers and the American Revolution*, pp. 235–36; and W. H. Moomaw, "The Denouement of General Howe's Campaign of 1777," *English Historical Review*, Vol. LXXIX (1964), pp. 502–10.

The role of Hamond of the *Roebuck* in the decision of Howe not to proceed up the Delaware and the conclusion, that Howe's original preference was to approach Philadelphia by way of the Chesapeake Bay, appear to be the principal areas of disagreement. It is agreed that Hamond suggested a landing of the British army near Reedy Island, approximately the same distance from the city as the eventual landing place at the head of Chesapeake Bay (without the month's voyage which was enervating to man and horse). It has been conjectured that Howe considered the Delaware too dangerous because of the American naval force and the natural hazards of the river. This assumes that Howe was ignorant of the real condition of the river defenses. It is inconceivable that Howe was not aware of the true status of the river defenses, both natural and man-made. The only effective arm of the little fleet was the thirteen Pennsylvania galleys and two floating batteries, whose combined armament was only thirty-five cannon, slightly more than half of one of Lord Howe's "64-gun ships." Equally important, they could not maneuver in the open water below the chevaux-de-frise because of the danger of swamping from the slightest swell. These conditions were known to Hamond, the only officer with this knowledge at Howe's council of war, and to all the leading Loyalists in Delaware and southeastern Pennsylvania. Following Hamond's near disaster in May 1776, (see Chapter 4) when the *Roebuck* ran aground near the New Jersey shore with the resultant waspish attack of the galleys, he seemed reluctant to sail above Reedy Island even though he remained on the Delaware station intermittently for another fifteen months. This reveals either an ultracautious nature or great respect for the little American fleet and the natural hazards of the river. Hamond was unquestionably chagrined at Howe's decision to sail to the Chesapeake, but his preference for a landing at Reedy Island must have been accompanied with his reason for not recommending an anchorage thirty miles farther up the river. American naval authorities were amazed that the Marcus Hook-Chester roadstead was not selected, since it was only fifteen miles from Philadelphia and in easy access of the river forts. This could have shortened the campaign by several months. The fortifications were without garrisons except for a skeleton militia force at Fort Mifflin and Billingsport; in fact, as late as September 5 Billingsport had a garrison of eighty artillerymen and militia and Fort Mifflin, forty-five. Fort Mercer and the redoubts at Darby Creek and on Bush Island were abandoned except for three or four laborers. The fall of the forts would have forced Commodore Hazelwood to withdraw to the Bristol area leaving the chevaux-de-frise undefended. To prevent the British from bringing their shipping to the city, all elements of river defense had to remain in American hands. If one fell or was destroyed, the whole fabric of defense would collapse. All of this was known to Howe, regardless of where he preferred to land. The obvious need to open the Delaware River, even if a successful landing was made at the head of the Chesapeake Bay (coupled with the logistical and tactical disadvantages of such a landing), should have been apparent to Howe. Granted that the Elk River landing was about the same distance from Philadelphia as a landing at Reedy Island, the real question was why either was considered. We return to Hamond as the only officer present at the council of war on board the flagship *Eagle* who had the knowledge to influence a negative consideration of the Marcus Hook-Chester roadstead.

Another reason for selecting the Chesapeake Bay, as suggested by Christopher Ward, *The War of the Revolution*, Vol. I, p. 333, was that Howe had some abstruse plan for physically severing communications between the colonies on the line of the Chesapeake and later returning to conquer the Delaware.

Appendix G

ORDNANCE FOUND IN FORTS MERCER AND MIFFLIN

Returns of ordnance and stores found in Mud Island Fort, taken from the rebels by the King's troops the 16th of November, 1777.[1]

IRON ORDNANCE

On traveling carriages: 1 Thirty-two-pounder; 1 twenty-four-pounder; 7 eighteen-pounders, 2 unserviceable; 1 twelve-pounder; 2 four-pounders.

On garrison carriages. 14 Eight-pounders; 1 unserviceable; sunk with a scow, of sorts, 10.

SHOT

Round loose: 1475 Twenty-four-pounders; 843 eighteen-pounders; 165 twelve-pounders; 1100 eight-pounders; 16 four-pounders.

Barr: 6 Thirty-two-pounders; 4 twenty-four-pounders; 169 eighteen-pounders.

Grape quilted: 12 Thirty-two-pounders; 84 eighteen-pounders; 20 twelve-pounders; 110 eight-pounders; 8 four-pounders.

Fixed with powder for twelve-pounders: 11 Case; 9 grape.

Small iron for case: 4 cwt.

Cartridges paper filled: 65 Eight-pounders.
Sponges of sorts: 36.
Ladles ditto: 9.
Wad-hooks: 15.
Aprons of lead: 9.
Linstocks: 6.
Budge barrels: 2.

Samuel Cleaveland,
Brigadier-general commanding
the Royal Artillery.

Philadelphia,
Nov. 18, 1777.

Return of the artillery and military stores found in the Fort of Red Bank, the 22d of November, 1777.

6 Eighteen-pounders, 1 unserviceable; 3 eighteen-pounders, mounted on truck carriages, 2 unserviceable; 2 six-pounders, mounted on ditto, spiked and unserviceable; 1 four-pounder, mounted on ditto, unserviceable; 1 four-pounder, mounted on ditto, with elevating screw, spiked; 3 four-pounders, mounted on ditto, spiked; 1 three-pounder on ditto, spiked and unserviceable; 8 howitzer swivels; 4 howitzer ditto, carried off by a naval Captain; 3 swivels; 1 travelling carriage for eighteen-pounder; 5 trucks carriages for ditto; 1 travelling carriage for nine-pounders; 4 ditto for six-pounders; three limbers for ditto.

SHOT

Round. 536 Twenty-four-pounders; 818 eighteen-pounders; 156 twelve-pounders; 51 nine-pounders; 23 six-pounders; 1301 four-pounders; 173 three-pounders; 20 one-pounders; 32 half-pounders.

Barr. 7 Twenty-four-pounders; 25 twelve-pounders; 50 nine-pounders; 65 three-pounders.

Grape Quilted. 14 Twelve-pounders; 54 six-pounders; 28 four-pounders.

Grape in bags, 24.

Box of different natures, 1.

Round shot fixed to wood bottoms.
5 Twelve-pounders; 6 six-pounders; 6 four-pounders; 16 three-pounders.

Hand grenades, 18.

Wad-hooks. 1 Thirty-two-pounder; 1 six-pounder.

Spunges. 1 Six-pounder; 2 four-pounders.

Aprons of lead, 4.

Drag ropes, 3.
Traversing handspike, 1.
Pikes, 93.
Intrenching tools, 30.
Boxes with ball cartridges, 9.
Cask with musquet balls, 1.

James Pattison, Brigadier-general,
Commander of the Royal Artillery
in North-America.

Camp at Woodbury,
Nov. 23, 1777.

Notes

CHAPTER I

1. Modern Pennsylvania is a legal commonwealth; however, during the Revolution official records refer to it as a state or province. For the purposes of this book, commencing with July 1, 1775, we will use the designation "state." The *Pennsylvania Archives* and *Colonial Records* usually refer to the naval defenses of the Delaware as the "State navy."

2. North Callahan, *Royal Raiders: The Tories of the American Revolution*, pp. 35–36.

3. *The Examination of Joseph Galloway, Speaker of the House of Assembly, Before the House of Commons*, pp. 71–72; Joseph Galloway, *Historical and Political Reflections on the Rise and Progress of the American Revolution*, pp. 13, 18; Callahan, *Royal Raiders*, p. 158.

4. Charles H. Lincoln, *The Revolutionary Movement in Pennsylvania*, pp. 3–4.

5. *Ibid.*, p. 12.

6. *Ibid.*, pp. 28–32.

7. *Pennsylvania Journal*, May 10, 1775.

8. Lincoln, *Revolution*, pp. 184–185.

9. *Ibid.*, p. 38.

10. *Ibid.*, pp. 195, 198–199.

11. *Colonial Records,* Vol. X, p. 279 (hereafter cited as *C.R.*); *Pennsylvania Archives,* Eighth Series, Vol. VIII, p. 7246 (hereafter cited as *P.A.*).

12. Callahan, *Royal Raiders,* p. 37.

13. John C. Fitzpatrick, *The Spirit of the Revolution,* pp. 100–116; *C.R.,* Vol. X, pp. 279–282; *P.A.,* Eighth Series, Vol. VIII, pp. 7245–7249.

14. Fitzpatrick, *Revolution,* p. 100.

15. *Ibid.,* p. 105.

16. *C.R.,* Vol. X, pp. 279–282; *P.A.,* Eighth Series, Vol. VIII, pp. 7245–7249.

17. *C.R.,* Vol. X, pp. 280, 282.

18. The questionable activities of Robert White (Whyte) are covered in Appendix E.

19. *C.R.,* Vol. X, pp. 282–283.

CHAPTER II

1. Charles O. Paullin, *The Navy of the American Revolution,* p. 34.

2. Gardner W. Allen, *A Naval History of the American Revolution,* Vol. I, p. 38.

3. *C.R.,* Vol. X, p. 279.

4. *Ibid.,* p. 283.

5. *P.A.,* Fourth Series, Vol. III, p. 558 (Copy of minutes of Continental Congress, signed by Charles Thomson; *C.R.,* Vol. X, p. 317.

6. *C.R.,* Vol. X, p. 284.

7. *Ibid.,* p. 285.

8. Paullin, *Navy,* p. 145.

9. Allen, *Naval History,* Vol. I, p. 50.

10. *Ibid.,* pp. 50–51; Paullin, *Navy,* p. 147.

11. Allen, *Naval History,* Vol. I., pp. 45–47.

12. *C.R.,* Vol. X, p. 570.

13. Emanuel Eyre built the *Bull Dog, Franklin,* and *Congress;* John Wharton the *Washington* and *Experiment;* Casdrop & Fullerton the *Chatham* and *Effingham;* Warnock Coates the *Burke;* Simon Sherlock the *Camden;* John Rice the *Dickinson;* William Williams the *Hancock;* Samuel Robins the *Ranger;* Joseph Marsh the *Warren.* The *Experiment,* built by John Wharton, was the first galley launched, July 19, 1775, and its name probably indicates the uncertainty which beset the Committee of Safety. A "List of Galley Officers" in the Pennsylvania

Division of Archives and Manuscripts (hereafter cited as Penna. MSS) states that the *Effingham* was built by Caswell (this should be Casdrop & Fullerton). *C.R.*, Vol. X, pp. 284–351; William Bell Clark, ed., *Naval Documents of the American Revolution* (hereafter cited as *Naval Documents*), Vol. II, p. 428; Penna. MSS, RG-4, Military Accounts, Navy, Box 1.

14. *C.R.*, Vol. X, pp. 290–291.

15. William Duane, ed., *Extracts from the Diary of Christopher Marshall*, p. 44.

16. *P.A.*, First Series, Vol. IV, pp. 635–636, Nicola to Committee of Safety, July 6, 1775.

17. *C.R.*, Vol. X, p. 296.

18. *Ibid.*, p. 291; *P.A.*, First Series, Vol. IV, p. 638, Irish to Committee, July 26, 1775.

19. *Ibid.*, pp. 666–667; *C.R.*, Vol. X, p. 366.

20. I am indebted to Howard Chapelle for his suggestions and explanations which aided me in preparing the description of the State galleys. Also helpful were the many descriptions of boat plans in Mr. Chapelle's excellent volumes on the sailing era, *The American Sailing Navy, History of American Sailing Ships*, and *The Search for Speed Under Sail*. I am also grateful for the many suggestions of Thomas Hornsby. However, the author must accept complete responsibility for the specifications and plans of the galleys, and the final descriptions of the State fleet.

21. *C.R.*, Vol. X, pp. 284–285.

22. *P.A.*, Second Series, Vol. I, pp. 99, 117, 163, 189; For a different version of the area below deck, see William Bell Clark, *Captain Dauntless*, p. 79.

23. *Naval Documents*, Vol. II, p. 60 (taken from the *London Evening Post*, November 9, 1775).

24. *Ibid.*, Vol. I, p. 929 (taken from the PRO Colonial Office Class 5/122, 22c, LC Transcripts).

25. *Ibid.*, Vol. IV, pp. 163–164 (taken from the Carroll Papers, Maryland Historical Society).

26. *P.A.*, Second Series, Vol. I, p. 160.

27. *C.R.*, Vol. X, p. 327; undated manuscript in Penna. MSS, "Military Stores and Ammunition Put on Board the Gondolas."

28. Howard I. Chapelle, *History of the American Sailing Navy*, p. 111.

29. Historical Society of Pennsylvania (hereafter cited as HSP), Miscellaneous Statistical Lists, Box 15B, "Accounts of Defenses in Pennsylvania."

30. *C.R.*, Vol. X, p. 350.

31. Chapelle, *American Sailing Navy*, p. 111; Penna. MSS, RG-4, Various, Box 1, Committee of Safety Receipt Book B, May 23 to July 3, 1776.

32. *C.R.*, Vol. X, p. 593.

33. A camboose was a diminutive substitute for the cookroom (galley), a portable shelter lashed to the deck with ropes, with a ring bolt in each corner and four ring bolts on the deck. The Pennsylvania fleet had both wooden and iron camboose, the former costing £2 and the latter £9. While some were lashed to the decks, others were permanently installed with a masonry foundation; *P.A.*, Second Series, Vol. I, pp. 110, 155, 163, 175; Penna. MSS, RG-4, Military Accounts, Navy, Box 2, "Accounts of William Webb, paymaster, Navy Board," "John Nicholson's Remarks on the Revisal of William Webb's Accounts."

34. *P.A.*, Second Series, Vol. I, p. 86.

35. Penna. MSS, RG-4, Military Accounts, Navy Box 1; *P.A.*, Fourth Series, Vol. III, pp. 572–576; *C.R.*, Vol. X, pp. 350–351.

36. *P.A.*, Second Series, Vol. I, p. 164.

37. Edwin S. Parry, *Betsy Ross, Quaker Rebel*, pp. 103–104.

38. Penna. MSS, RG-4, Various, Box 1, Committee of Safety Receipt Book B, May 23 to July 3, 1776.

39. F. E. Schermerhorn, *American and French Flags of the Revolution, 1775–1783*, pp. 6, 21, 31. Mr. Schermerhorn's notes as outlined in the preface to his book failed to reveal the source of his conclusions. However, I agree with him that the Pennsylvania fleet used the so-called "Floating Batteries Flag," or one similar. In the case of the Pennsylvania navy, this flag was made by Mrs. Bridges from a copy submitted to her. A somewhat conflicting picture as to what colors were used is revealed in a letter of William Richards, ship husband, to the Committee of Safety, August 19, 1776: "I hope you have agreed what sort of Colours I am to have made for the Galleys, &c., as they are much wanted." *P.A.*, First Series, Vol. V, p. 13, Richards to Committee, August 19, 1776. Later, on October 15, with no decision having been made, he again writes to the Committee, "The Commodore was with me this morning, and says the Fleet has not any Colours to hoist if they should be called on Duty." *Ibid.*, p. 46, Richards to Council, October 15, 1776. Richards further requests that the Council establish a design acceptable to the State navy. It would appear that the State navy wanted their own flag as distinguished from one copied from another state. This probably prompted the decision to ask Betsy Ross to design a flag for the fleet—a request which was granted five months later. Others than Mrs. Ross and Mrs. Bridges were employed to make colors for the fleet. In May 1777 Ann King made colors for the fire

ship. See Penna. MSS, RG-4; Military Accounts, Box 2, "Accounts of William Webb, paymaster Navy Board," and "John Nicholson's Remarks on the Revisal of William Webb's Accounts."

40. *Naval Documents*, Vol. V, pp. 340–341, 349–350 (from Council of Safety Letter Book, No 1, and Revolutionary Papers, Box 9, Maryland Archives); *Ibid.*, Vol III, p. 1034 (from Minutes of the Connecticut Council of Safety); *Ibid.*, Vol. VI (New Jersey State Papers, 1775–1778, in preparation).

41. These galleys have been confused with those built for the Pennsylvania navy, probably because the Eyres were prominent Philadelphia shipbuilders. Examination of Benjamin Eyre's memorial to the Continental Congress reveals that he was employed to supervise the building of these galleys in New York for the Continental service. They were to be used on the Hudson River and adjacent waterways; also, they were not built until one year after the last Pennsylvania galley had been launched.

42. *Obstructions to the Navigation of Hudson's River*, Munsel's Historical Series, No. 5, pp. 19, 23, 24, 36.

43. *P.A.*, First Series, Vol. V, p. 200, Casdorp to Council, January 24, 1777. Other references are found in the correspondence and diaries of American statesmen. Josiah Quincy wrote to John Adams on September 22, 1775, and said that galleys built by our worthy friend, Dr. Franklin, should be the first line of defense for the colonies. See J. Quincy to J. Adams, Adams Papers, Massachusetts Historical Society. John Adams noted in his diary on September 28, 1775, an excursion on a galley and wrote to James Warren, October 7, that our harbors and rivers should be defended by galleys, floating batteries, and chevaux-de-frise. See Butterfield, ed., *Diary of John Adams*, Vol. II, p. 187, and *Warren-Adams Letters*, Vol. I, pp. 126–129, 366. These citations are to be found in *Naval Documents*, Vol. II, pp. 234, 342, 366. Washington suggested to Ramsay (Dec. 8, 1775) that a couple of row galleys on the Philadelphia plan might be of considerable help on the Potomac. George Washington, *The Writings of George Washington*, John C. Fitzpatrick, ed., Vol. IV, pp. 200–202 (hereafter cited as Washington, *Writings*).

44. *C.R.*, Vol. X, p. 396.

45. Penna. MSS, RG-4, Military Accounts, Navy, Box 2; *P.A.*, Second Series, Vol. I, p. 230, fn.

46. Penna. MSS, RG-4, Various, Box 1, Committee of Safety Receipt Book B, May 23 to July 3, 1776.

47. *Naval Documents*, Vol. III, pp. 790–791 (from PRO, Admiralty 1/309, Vice-Admiral James Young's Intelligence of Naval Preparations in Philadelphia, Antigua, January 14, 1776).

48. *C.R.*, Vol. X, p. 437.

49. *Pennsylvania Magazine of History and Biography* (hereafter cited as *PMHB*), Vol. 85. Gilbert Barkley, a British spy in Philadelphia, reported that there were 150 fire floats at Fort Island.

50. HSP, Miscellaneous Statistical List, Box 15-B, "Account of Defenses in Pennsylvania," and "Account of what has been prepared at the Fire Raft House"; John William Wallace, *Colonel William Bradford, The Patriot Printer of 1776*, p. 132.

51. *P.A.*, Second Series, Vol. I, pp. 119, 171; *C.R.*, Vol. X, p. 779; *P.A.*, First Series, Vol. IV, p. 720; Penna. MSS, RG-4, Military Accounts, Navy, Box 2, "Accounts of William Webb, Paymaster Navy Board," and "John Nicholson's Remarks on the Revisal of William Webb's Accounts." See also Appendix A.

52. *P.A.*, Second Series, Vol. I, p. 121.

53. Wallace, *Bradford*, pp. 251–252.

54. *P.A.*, Second Series, Vol. I, pp. 118, 204, 205, 239–359; *P.A.*, Fifth Series, Vol V, pp. 417–606; Penna. MSS, manuscript muster rolls of the State fleet; William Faden map, 1779, A Plan of the City and Environs of Philadelphia. For armament and of galleys, see sources cited in note 27.

55. *C.R.*, Vol. X, p. 514; for roster of boats of the fleet, see Appendix A.

56. *P.A.*, Second Series, Vol. I, pp. 82, 83.

57. See Appendix A.

58. Benjamin Lossing, *Pictorial Field Book of the American Revolution* (1859 edition), Vol. I, p. 575.

59. *Naval Documents*, Vol. IV, p. 616 (from PRO, Admiralty 1/484, Intelligence on Continental Navy [January 4, 1776]).

60. J. Almon, *The Remembrancer or Impartial Repository of Public Events*, Vol. II, Part I, p. 364, "Intelligence Regarding the Naval Force at Philadelphia, February 16, 1776."

61. *Naval Documents*, Vol. IV, pp. 163–164 (from Carroll Papers, Maryland Historical Society).

62. HSP, Statistical Lists, Miscellaneous, Box 15-B, "Accounts of Defenses in Pennsylvania."

63. *C.R.*, Vol. X, p. 547.

64. *P.A.*, Second Series, Vol. I, p. 131.

65. *Ibid.*, p. 103.

66. *Ibid.*, p. 88.

67. See note 60.

68. Worthington C. Ford, ed., "Defenses of Philadelphia in 1777," *PMHB*, Vol. 18, Part II, July 1894, p. 180, Washington to the President of the Continental Congress, August [9] 1777.

69. *P.A.*, Second Series, Vol. I, p. 87. "That the masters of shallops belonging to this State and under direction of the Navy Board be allowed Seven pounds Ten shillings per month." See Appendix A.

70. *C.R.*, Vol. X, p. 395. Committee included Wharton, Whyte, Nixon, Howell, Robert Morris, and Clymer.

71. *Ibid.*, pp. 397, 401.

72. William B. Clark, *Gallant John Barry*, p. 71.

73. *C.R.*, Vol. X, pp. 486, 488, 495, 505, 521, 525. On February 15, 1776, Sherlock was urged to hasten the completion of the provincial ship. Eleven days later Nixon and Whyte were ordered to procure all the ship carpenters needed to forward the building of this ship in the most expeditious manner. During February and March officers were appointed and marines were ordered recruited to serve on board. On March 26 the ship was officially named *Wallace;* p. 204.

74. *C.R.*, Vol. X, p. 741.

75. *P.A.*, Second Series, Vol. I, pp. 108, 117, 121, 126, 127, 142. Numerous references in the minutes of the Navy Board indicate that she was stripped of all armament and matériel, i.e., the ship's six-oar barge, miscellaneous supplies, swivels, and howitzers. It appears that the terms howitzer, swivel, and cohorn were used interchangeably in the Board's minutes.

76. *Ibid.*, p. 176. She was ballasted with stone. As previously noted, the galleys were ballasted with pig and junk iron, the fire ships with wood. See *P.A.*, Second Series, Vol. I., p. 112.

77. *Ibid.*, p. 147.

78. *C.R.*, Vol. X, pp. 570, 594, 599. As further indication of the confused nomenclature of the times, these ships were called galleys and gondolas by the civil authorities and shipwrights.

79. Penna. MSS, RG-4, Military Accounts, Navy, Box 2.

80. The smaller sailing ships were purchased from owners at public auction or, as in the case of the sloop *Liberty*, directly from the owner, who was then appointed to command her. *P.A.*, Second Series, Vol I, pp. 90–91. On April 6, 1776, Hazelwood was asked to approve Mr. Vernon's brigantine and to take the said vessel into the State service at the appraisers' valuation and equip her as a fire ship. *C.R.*, Vol. X, pp. 535–536. On May 13, 1776, Fitzsimmons and Moulder were requested to purchase two vessels to use, one as a magazine, the other as a provision ship. On May 16, they reported that Arthur Donaldson had a ship ideally suitable as an ammunition vessel for £325, and Thomas Hollingsworth a schooner valued at £200, suited for a victualing ship. No record exists of either purchase, but on May 28 they were ordered to equip the two ships. *Ibid.*, p. 567; *Naval Documents*, Vol. V, pp. 126–127; on February 27, 1777, Hazelwood was ordered to

look for any vessels suitable for fire ships and report to the Navy Board, with a view to purchasing them. *P.A.*, Second Series, Vol. I, p. 85; on February 28 and March 1, 1777, at a public sale at the London Coffee House, Navy Board member Paul Cox purchased the prize ship *King George* for £1,105, to be converted to a fire ship. *Ibid.*, p. 86; on March 5, Samuel Massey was appointed to purchase the brig *Rebecca*, which he bid in at £1,750, and the ship *Sam* at the London Coffee House. *Ibid.*, p. 89; Penna. MSS, RG-4, Military Accounts, Navy, Box 2, "John Nicholson Remarks on the Revisal of William Webb's Accounts"; on April 17, Cox and Massey were ordered to purchase a ship belonging to George Meade & Co. *P.A.*, Second Series, Vol. I, p. 133.

CHAPTER III

1. The river forts at Mud or Fort Island, Red Bank or Fort Mercer, and Billingsport were little more than earthen redoubts, with the exception of the outer or river face of the fort at Mud Island, which was of stone.

2. See Appendix B.

3. Probably certain members of the Committee of Safety were assigned the responsibility of working with the galley captains in recruiting men for the boats. Thomas Boyd states that General Wayne raised crews for the galleys. See Thomas Boyd, *Mad Anthony Wayne*, pp. 12–13.

4. *C.R.*, Vol. X, p. 520.

5. Penna. MSS, RG-4, Various. Box 1. Committee of Safety, Receipts Book B, May 23 to July 7, 1776.

6. *C.R.*, Vol. X, p. 351.

7. *Ibid.*, p. 361.

8. *Ibid.*, p. 329; *P.A.*, Fourth Series, Vol. III, pp. 570–571. See Appendix C for the progressive changes in the pay scale of the State navy.

9. *C.R.*, Vol. X, p. 329; *P.A.*, Fourth Series, Vol. III, pp. 570–571. The weekly ration allowance was seven pounds of bread or six of flour; ten pounds of beef, mutton, or pork; value of sixpence in roots or vegetables; salt and vinegar; three and one-half pints of rum or its equivalent in beer.

10. *C.R.*, Vol. X, p. 385.

11. *Ibid.*, pp. 323–327; *P.A.*, Fourth Series, Vol. III, pp. 565–570.

12. See Appendix D for the complete list of Rules and Regulations for Governing Officers and Men.

13. *C.R.*, Vol. X, pp. 321–322; *P.A.*, Second Series, Vol. I, p. 378.

14. *Ibid.*, pp. 377–378; *P.A.*, Fourth Series, Vol. III, pp. 576–578; *C.R.*, Vol. X, pp. 355–356, 364. John Ross was the first muster master, John M. Nesbit paymaster, and Peter Long ship's husband. See Appendix D for their warrants.

15. *Ibid.*, p. 347.

16. *Ibid.*, p. 343.

17. *Ibid.*, pp. 368–371; *P.A.*, Fourth Series, Vol. III, pp. 578–582.

18. Henry Fisher was one of the unsung heroes of the American Revolution. Born in Lewes, Delaware, in 1735, he early became enamored of the sea. He was asked to select the site for the first lighthouse at Cape Henlopen in 1764. He purchased his own pilot boat and became the recognized leader of the pilots at Pilot Town, Lewes. The Committee of Safety appointed him to take command of all pilots to ensure that none fell into British hands. His active participation in the Patriot cause and supervision of the alarm system placed him in constant jeopardy. Fisher died in Pilot Town in 1792. See *Delaware Register*, Vol. II, pp. 27–32; Christopher Ward, *The Delaware Continentals*, pp. 497–499.

19. *C.R.*, Vol. X, pp. 337–338; See Appendix D.

20. See Appendix B; *P.A.*, Second Series, Vol. I, p. 359.

21. Fisher established stations between Lewes and Philadelphia for change of riders and horses. Each station was to endorse the message, indicating time received and time dispatched. Stations were located at Cedar Creek (Thomas Evans), Dover (Thomas Battell or Battle), Cantwell's Bridge (Matthew Delaney), Wilmington (Thomas Kean, later replaced by James Chandler), and Chester (Richard Kerlin). This eighteenth-century express required about twenty-one hours to reach Philadelphia. The few records available show varying time between individual stations and reflect delays occasioned by ferries, weather, and need for refreshment. *P.A.*, First Series, Vol. IV, pp. 725, 736–737, 740–741, 744–745, 755–756, 769–770, a series of letters, Fisher to Committee of Safety, March 26–June 7, 1776; *Ibid.*, Vol. V, pp. 99–100, Fisher to Council, December 11, 1776; *Delaware Archives*, Vol. III, pp. 1362–63. The express riders employed on this run were Joseph Alison, Edward Cole, Joseph Cowan, Nicholas Cox, John Crampton, John Dawson, Adam Dayet, I. Engan, James Finley, and Ryner Stevenson. See *Delaware Archives*, Vol. II, pp. 987. One rider not mentioned in the *Dela-*

ware Archives was Richard Kane, recorded at Chester and Wilmington, in March 1776. See *C.R.*, Vol. X, p. 725. The orthography of our early chroniclers is frequently inaccurate as they had the phonetic spelling habits of the time.

22. The locations of the alarm posts were discovered in the papers of Frank H. Stewart, well-known Gloucester County, New Jersey, historian, and verified in *P.A.*, Second Series, Vol. I, pp. 81–226. In an effort to identify the present locations of the posts, I am indebted to Leon de Valinger, Jr., Delaware State Archivist, for his assistance. We have been unable to determine the exact location of Long Point or Dalby Point. I believe Long Point was between Wilmington and Reedy Island, and Mr. de Valinger agrees that Dalby Point was probably in the southeastern corner of Pennsylvania near Marcus Hook or Claymont, Delaware. Originally it was believed that Steep Water Point was the same as modern Deep Water Point. However, my research indicates that this post was up the bay from Bombay Hook, whereas Deep Water Point was on the New Jersey side of the river, near the present Delaware Memorial Bridge, but this point was not an alarm station. See *Naval Documents*, pp. 13–14, and the *Constitutional Gazette*, May 11, 1776. I now believe that Steep Water Point was in the vicinity of Port Penn, as correspondence and other archival records of the period indicate that an alarm post was located at that site. Henry Fisher, in a letter dated May 5, 1776, mentions an alarm post at Port Penn and later, during the campaign of 1777, frequent references are noted. *P.A.*, First Series, Vol. IV, pp. 743–744; Fisher to Committee, May 5, 1776; *P.A.*, Second Series, Vol. I, pp. 81–226. The *Pennsylvania Archives* have identified many of the Patriots who were responsible for manning the alarm posts. Besides Henry Fisher at Lewes, George Jackson was at Mispillon River, Samuel Edwards and John Marshall at the Murderkill River, Benjamin Brooks (sometimes written Rook or Books) at Bombay Hook, Lawrence Morris at Steep Water Point or Port Penn (this post in 1777 became the headquarters for the alarm post command under Captain Leeson Simmons), Uriah Paul (later discharged, replacement not known) at Long Point, Baltzer or Poltis Risner (Resner of Riner) at Dalby Point, a Mr. Coburn at Chester, Charles Thompson at Thompson Point, the militia officer in command at Billingsport, Charles Richards and Christopher Ronedollar at Gloucester (Fort Island was not an official alarm station but was expected to assist in forwarding alarm messages), William Hammond at Market Street Wharf. At Point-No-Point the custodian is unknown. *P.A.*, Second Series, Vol. I, pp. 81–226; Penna. MSS, RG–4, Military Accounts, Navy, Box 2, "Accounts of William Webb, paymaster, Navy

Board," and "John Nicholson's Remarks on the Revisal of William Webb's Accounts."

23. *C.R.*, Vol. X, p. 379.

24. *Ibid.*, p. 456.

25. *Ibid.*, p. 506; *P.A.*, Second Series, Vol. I, pp. 230, 239, 318; *P.A.*, First Series, Vol. IV, p. 769; HSP, Gratz Collection, Box 27, Case 5.

26. *Ibid.*

27. Washington, *Writings*, Vol. III, pp. 373–376.

28. The list of military stores considered adequate for each galley was:

4 Chests Powder	300 Musket Cartridges
30 Round Shot	20 Pistol Cartridges
10 Double Headed Shot	500 Musket Balls, loose
20 Chain Shot	2 Cohorns
30 Grape Shot	4 Powder Hours
100 Swivel Round Shot	1 Cartridge Case
15 Stand Small Arms	1 Pouch Barrel
20 Cutlasses	4 Cheeses of Wadd
10 Pikes	Some Tanned Hides for the
10 Pair of Pistols	Magazine

HSP, Miscellaneous, Invoices of Stores, Box 15–B; *C.R.*, Vol. X, p. 363. A manuscript, undated, in the Penna. MSS enumerates the amounts and types of armament and ammunition supplied each boat. This paper reveals the dilemma confronting the commissary agent; each boat received an equal or near-equal assortment and proportion of matériel available. This distribution was made about ten days after the established guidelines were submitted. See *Naval Documents*, Vol. II, pp. 559–564, for the allotment to each galley.

29. *C.R.*, Vol. X, pp. 415, 418, 423–424, 500, 510, 518, 594; Penna. MSS. RG–4, Auditors of Accounts for State, Various, Box 1; MG 92, Mitchell Papers. Box 6.

30. *P.A.*, Second Series, Vol. I, p. 234.

31. Penna. MSS, RG–4, Military Accounts, Navy, Box 6.

32. *Ibid.*

33. *Ibid.*, Box 3, Box 2, and Box 1.

34. *C.R.*, Vol. X, pp. 498–499.

35. Penna. MSS, RG–4, Military Accounts, Navy, Box 2.

36. *C.R.*, Vol. X, p. 427.

37. *Ibid.*, p. 361.

38. Fort Island, called Mud, Liberty, and before the Revolution occasionally Deepwater Island. William Bell Clark in *Gallant John Barry*, p. 60, and *Captain Dauntless*, p. 76, says that the island was renamed

Liberty Island in 1775. It would appear that the rechristening as Liberty Island was the result of a spontaneous reaction of many of the galley and militia officers and a few politicians, from late summer 1775 through August 1776. It was apparently the result of the enthusiasm generated for independence, as after the Declaration of Independence its use gradually disappeared and Fort Island again became the accepted name until it became known as Fort Mifflin. During this period the majority of Pennsylvanians continued to call it Fort Island. For a general sprinkling of the use of Liberty Island see Penna. MSS; *C.R.*, Vol. X; and *P.A.*, First Series, Vol. IV, J. Thomas Scharf and Thompson Wescott, *History of Philadelphia*, Vol. I, p. 306, states that Liberty Island was another island. This is an incorrect assumption as examination of the above sources will confirm.

39. *C.R.*, Vol. X, pp. 427, 434.

40. *Ibid.*, pp. 367, 507.

41. *Ibid.*, p. 366.

42. *Ibid.*, p. 388.

43. *Ibid.*, p. 409.

44. *Naval Documents*, Vol. I, p. 657 (taken from Grave's Conduct, Appendix 440, Massachusetts H.S. Transcript).

45. *Ibid.*, Vol. IV, pp. 151–152 (Hamond Letter Book, 1775–1778, University of Virginia Library).

46. *P.A.*, First Series, Vol. IV, pp. 706–707, Captains of Armed Vessels to Caldwell, January 31, 1776.

47. *C.R.*, Vol. X, p. 476; *P.A.*, Fourth Series, Vol. III, pp. 591–592.

48. *C.R.*, Vol. X, pp. 480–481.

49. *Ibid.*, p. 503.

50. Benjamin Quarles, *The Negro in the American Revolution*, p. 86. Mr. Quarles lists only one Negro serving in the Pennsylvania State navy. My study of the muster rolls has uncovered at least eight or ten more. I believe that others were listed in the muster rolls without identification of race.

51. *P.A.*, Second Series, Vol. I, p. 249; Penna. MSS, RG–4, Military Accounts, Navy, Box 3.

52. *C.R.*, Vol. X, pp. 513–514.

53. *P.A.*, First Series, Vol. IV, p. 726, Instructions to Caldwell, March 26, 1776.

54. *Ibid.*, p. 726; *C.R.*, Vol. X, p. 526; Clark, *Barry*, p. 77.

55. *P.A.*, First Series, Vol. IV, pp. 724–725, Fisher to Committee, March 25, 1776.

56. Clark, *Barry*, p. 77.

57. *Ibid.*, p. 78; *Delaware Archives*, Vol. III, pp. 1362–1363; *Naval Documents*, Vol. IV, pp. 618–619.

CHAPTER IV

1. *C.R.*, Vol. X, pp. 543–544. The subcommittees were: For importing powder, arms, etc.; Accounts; Cannon; Fire Raft; Floating Battery; Ship; for Providing Pikes & Intrenching Tools; Chevaux-de-Frise; for Fitting Out 4 Guard Boats to Cruise at Cape May; for Building Floating Battery; Fort Island; Powder House; Powder House, Out of Doors; Out of Doors for Providing Firelocks; to Superintend Workmen in Gun Lock Factory; Barracks—Fort Island; Armed Boat; for Further Defenses; for Fitting Out Two of the Armed Boats; for Building Two Galleys for the Bay Service.

2. *Ibid.*, pp. 526, 535, 540, 556.

3. *Ibid.*, p. 530.

4. *Ibid.*, pp. 525, 530.

5. *P.A.*, First Series, Vol. IV, p. 724, Committee to Caldwell, March 23, 1776.

6. The best detailed accounts of the action between the British ships *Roebuck* and *Liverpool* and the Pennsylvania navy are in William B. Clark, *Lambert Wickes*, pp. 20–35, and Clark, "The Battle in the Delaware," New Jersey Society of Pennsylvania, *Year Book*, 1930, pp. 51–73. The latter account is an expanded version of *Lambert Wickes*, although the bibliographical references are not always reliable. Hereafter cited as Clark, "Delaware," and Clark, *Wickes*.

7. *P.A.*, First Series, Vol. IV, pp. 743–744, Fisher to Committee, May 5, 1776.

8. *C.R.*, Vol. X, p. 557.

9. *Ibid.*, pp. 557–558; Clark, "Delaware," p. 58.

10. *C.R.*, Vol. X, 557–558.

11. *P.A.*, First Series, Vol. IV, pp. 739, 745–746, Muster Roll of Naval Service, May 1, 1776, Reed to Committee, May 7, 1776; *P.A.*, Second Series, Vol. I, pp. 324–326; Clark, "Delaware," p. 51; Clark, *Wickes*, pp. 20–21.

12. *P.A.*, First Series, Vol. IV, pp. 745–746, Reed to Committee, May 7, 1776; Clark, "Delaware," p. 54; Clark, *Wickes*, p. 21.

13. *C.R.*, Vol. X, pp. 514, 557, 560; *P.A.*, First Series, Vol. IV, pp. 739, 746, 781, Muster Rolls of May 1, 1776, and July 1, 1776. Clark believes that the boats Read reported as fire boats were in reality fire sloops. The musters of the State navy indicate that only two fire vessels may have been in service in 1776: the *Aetna*, a fire sloop, and the *Vesuvius*, a fire brig. There is no record that either of these boats was in service before June 1, 1776. Apparently Clark interpreted fire boats as fire sloops. See

The Pennsylvania Navy, 1775–1781

Clark, "Delaware," p. 55. On May 8 Captain Robert Hardis of the guard boat *Terror* was assigned command of one chain of fire rafts. A muster roll for the fleet prepared on May 1, 1776, does not show any guard boats in service. Six guard boats were manned and available for duty by July 1, 1776: *Terror, Vulture, Eagle, Brimstone, Porcupine,* and *Salamander.* However, one of the boats was in commission early in 1776; the other five were ordered built on March 13, and appear to have been completed, equipped, and manned during April, May, and June. The *Terror* was apparently completely equipped but without a crew until after the *Roebuck* affair. See Appendix A.

14. *C.R.,* Vol. X, p. 558; *P.A.,* First Series, Vol. IV, pp. 745–746, Read to Committee, May 7, 1776; Clark, "Delaware," p. 55.

15. *C.R.,* Vol. X, p. 559: *P.A.,* First Series, Vol. IV, pp. 739, 745-746, 781, Muster Rolls of May 1, 1776, and July 1, 1776, Read to Committee, May 7, 1776. Captain Read mentions the arrival of the Province sloop; however, no sloop or schooner is carried on the fleet muster in May 1776. The *Hetty,* with a muster roll for June 1, 1776, may have been in service with a volunteer crew on May 7. The schooner *Lydia* and the sloop *Sally* were in service on July 1, 1776. See Appendix A.

16. Clark, "Delaware," pp. 58–61; Clark, *Wickes,* pp. 24–25.

17. William Budden.

18. *Naval Documents,* Vol. IV, p. 1470.

19. *Purdie's Virginia Gazette,* May 24, 1776.

20. *Naval Documents,* Vol. IV, p. 1470, Journal of H.M.S. *Roebuck,* Captain Andrew Snape Hamond (taken from PRO Admiralty 51/796); *Ibid.,* p. 1471, Journal of H.M.S. *Liverpool,* Captain Henry Bellew (taken from PRO Admiralty 51/548).

21. *Ibid.,* p. 1470, Journal of H.M.S. *Roebuck.*

22. Peter Force, ed., *American Archives,* Fourth Series, Vol. VI, pp. 809–811; *Naval Documents,* Vol. V, pp. 481–485, 665–669; *Pennsylvania Evening Post,* June 29, 1776. Depositions of William Barry and John Emmes (hereafter cited as Barry and Emmes).

23. *Pennsylvania Evening Post,* June 29, 1776.

24. *Ibid.,* May 11, June 29, 1776. Although many eyewitnesses and some official letters said that the firing lasted four hours, Hamond reported that it lasted two hours (Journal of the *Roebuck*) and Colonel Samuel Miles, in a letter to the Committee of Safety dated May 8, 4 o'clock, said that the engagement was over, and it had lasted two hours. *P.A.,* First Series, Vol. IV, p. 748, Miles to Committee, May 8, 1776. The fact that Hamond and others comment on sighting the galleys at 1 o'clock and firing beginning after 1:30, the action could not have lasted beyond 4 o'clock.

25. *Constitutional Gazette,* May 11, 1776.

26. Emmes and Barry.

27. Samuel Hazard, *Register of Pennsylvania*, Vol. I, p. 239; Charles Biddle, *Autobiography*, pp. 84–86; *Naval Documents*, Vol. IV, pp. 1463–1464.

28. *Constitutional Gazette*, May 11, 1776. The *Roebuck* was aground a short distance north of the modern-day Delaware Memorial Bridge.

29. Emmes; Barry; *Naval Documents*, Vol. V, pp. 15–16 (Narrative of Captain Andrew Snape Hamond, Hamond Papers, University of Virginia); *Ibid.*, Vol. IV, p. 1470–1471, Journal of H.M.S. *Roebuck* (PRO Admiralty 51/796) and Journal of H.M.S. *Liverpool* (PRO Admiralty 51/548); Clark, "Delaware," pp. 63–64.

30. Penna. MSS, Military Stores & Ammunition Put on Board the Gondolas; *Naval Documents*, Vol. II, pp. 559–564.

31. *Pennsylvania Evening Post*, May 16, 1776; *Pennsylvania Journal*, May 22, 1776; *Naval Documents*, Vol. V, pp. 127–128.

32. *P.A.*, First Series, Vol. IV, p. 748, Miles to Committee, May 8, 1776.

33. *C.R.*, Vol. X, p. 558; *P.A.*, First Series, Vol. IV, pp. 745–747, 750, 751, Read to Committee, May 7, 8, and 9, 1776 (2 letters).

34. *Ibid.*, pp. 750, 753, Barry to R. Morris, May 9, 1776, Read to Committee, May 9 and 11, 1776.

35. Biddle, *Autobiography*, p. 83.

36. *Naval Documents*, Vol. V, p. 18, Journal of H.M.S. *Roebuck*, (PRO Admiralty 51/796).

37. Barry.

38. *Pennsylvania Evening Post*, May 16, 1776; *Pennsylvania Journal*, May 22, 1776; *Naval Documents*, Vol. V, pp. 127–128.

39. George H. Ryder, ed., *Letters to and from Caesar Rodney, 1756–1784*, p. 76 (letter from George Read, May 10, 1776).

40. Samuel Hazard, ed., *Register of Pennsylvania*, Vol. I, p. 239; *Pennsylvania Evening Post*, May 11 and 16, 1776.

41. *Ibid.*

42. Christopher Marshall, *Extracts from the Diary of Christopher Marshall*, William Duane, ed., p. 70.

43. Hazard, *Register of Pennsylvania*, Vol. I, p. 239; *Pennsylvania Evening Post*, May 11 and 16, 1776; Emmes.

44. Barry; Emmes; Hazard, *Register of Pennsylvania*, Vol. I, p. 239; *Pennsylvania Evening Post*, May 11, 1776. The correspondent in the *Evening Post* commented on the nearest distance the galley could approach a ship without coming in reach of the grapeshot, and beyond which was a waste of powder. He further noted that if it was necessary to approach within grapeshot range, then the nearer the boat, but out of musket range, the better for both service and safety. Grapeshot, like

small shot, does the most execution at the greatest killing distance and the least at the least distance.

45. *Purdie's Virginia Gazette*, May 24, 1776 (in *Naval Documents*, Vol. V, pp. 240–242); *Pennsylvania Journal*, May 17 and 22, 1776; *Naval Documents*, Vol. V, pp. 460–461 (Captain Andrew S. Hamond, R.N., to Commodore Sir Peter Parker in Hamond Letters and Orders, 1775–1778, University of Virginia Library); Almon, *Remembrancer*, Vol. III, p. 173.

46. Emmes; *Naval Documents*, Vol. V, pp. 108–109 (taken from Narrative of Captain Andrew S. Hamond, Hamond Papers, No. 5, University of Virginia Library); *P.A.*, First Series, Vol. IV, pp. 755–756, 762–763, Fisher to Committee, May 15 and 27, 1776.

47. *P.A.*, First Series, Vol. IV, p. 754, Dougherty to Committee, May 11, 1776.

48. *Ibid.*, p. 753, Read to Committee, May 11, 1776; *C.R.*, Vol. X, p. 562.

49. *Pennsylvania Evening Post*, May 16, 1776; *Pennsylvania Journal*, May 22, 1776; *Naval Documents*, Vol. V, pp. 127–128.

50. *Pennsylvania Evening Post*, May 16, 1776.

51. *P.A.*, First Series, Vol. IV, p. 757, Committee to Cadwalader, May 16, 1776.

52. *C.R.*, Vol. X, pp. 571–572.

53. *P.A.*, Fourth Series, Vol. III, p. 600; *C.R.*, Vol. X, p. 582.

54. *Pennsylvania Packet*, June 10, 1776; *P.A.*, Eighth Series, Vol. VIII, p. 7536; *Naval Documents*, Vol. V, p. 533.

55. *P.A.*, Eighth Series, Vol. VIII, pp. 7521, 7523.

56. *Pennsylvania Packet*, June 24, 1776; *Pennsylvania Gazette*, June 26, 1776.

57. HSP, David McNeely Stauffer Collection (interleaved in copies of Westcott's *History of Philadelphia*, Vol. 6, p. 488).

58. *Pennsylvania Evening Post*, May 16, 1776; *Pennsylvania Journal*, May 22, 1776; *Pennsylvania Packet*, June 24, 1776; *Naval Documents*, Vol. V, pp. 137–138 (taken from Committee of Safety, Navy Papers, Penna. MSS).

CHAPTER V

1. *P.A.*, Fourth Series, Vol. III, pp. 596–598; *C.R.*, Vol. X, pp. 575–576.

2. *Ibid.*, Vol. X, pp. 288–289; Frank H. Stewart, *The Battle of Red Bank*, p. 6. The Gloucester County Patriots were Benjamin Whitall,

John Wood, Nathan Kinsey, Richard Johns, David Paul, Joseph Low, James Brown, Joseph Ward, Joshua Hopper, Isaac Hopper, Levi Hopper, James Wood, Joseph Tatem, and Charles West. They gave a total of 296 logs.

3. *Ibid.*, pp. 6–7; *Gloucester County Revolutionary War Documents*, p. 9; *C.R.*, Vol. X, p. 645.

4. *P.A.*, First Series, Vol. IV, pp. 776, 784, Smith to Committee, June 18, 1776, and July 13, 1776; Vol. XII, Appendix, p. 341.

5. Worthington C. Ford, ed., *Journals of the Continental Congress*, Vol. V, p. 443.

6. *Ibid.*, p. 407; G. D. Scull, ed., *The Evelyns in America*, pp. 253–256 (extracts from the Journals and notebooks of Captain John Montresor); George Smith, *History of Delaware County, Pennsylvania*, pp. 269, 277. Windmill Island, long since disappeared, was in the Delaware River between Philadelphia and Camden.

7. HSP, Miscellaneous, Committee of Safety, Box 15; Penna. MSS, RG–4, Delaware Fortification Accounts, 1775–1778, Box 1 and Box 2.

8. *C.R.*, Vol. X, pp. 581, 587.

9. *Ibid.*, pp. 562, 579, 586, 587, 593. These guard boats were the *Brimstone, Fame, Porcupine, Salamander, Terror,* and *Vulture*.

10. *Ibid.*, p. 595.

11. The communication to the captains is dated May 20, 1776. This has to be an error in dating or editing the archives. In his deposition, dated June 22, the master (Martin Wert) of the ammunition sloop said he would obey orders and deliver the powder in cartridges to the galleys. He further stated that he attempted to deliver his cargo between June 17 and 19, but was unsuccessful. Davidson mentions this master's willingness to accept orders as a footnote to his memorandum of May (June) 20. This is the only explanation for this date, as Caldwell was still Commodore on the 20th of May and Read was made acting commander on May 29. *P.A.*, First Series, Vol. IV, p. 759, Davidson to Commanders of Gallies, May 20, 1776 (should be June 20); *C.R.*, Vol. X, p. 581, 587; *Naval Documents*, Vol. V, p. 684 (deposition of Martin Wert, Penna. MSS, Navy Papers, Committee of Safety).

12. The eight galley commanders who refused to accept Davidson's orders were: Eyre of the *Camden*, J. Montgomery of the *Chatham*, Hamilton of the *Congress*, H. Montgomery of the *Effingham*, Moore of the *Hancock*, Lieutenant Hume of the *Ranger*, Dougherty of the *Washington*, and Henderson of the *Bull Dog*. Blair of the *Burke*, Rice of the *Dickinson*, and Houston of the *Warren* were absent in Philadelphia. Lieutenant Thompson of the *Experiment* agreed to obey orders. Captain Boys and the *Franklin* cannot be accounted for at Fort Island at this time. Later all captains protested the appointment of Davidson. *P.A.*, First Series, Vol. IV, p. 759, Davidson to Commanders of Gallies,

May (June) 20, 1776; *P.A.*, Second Series, Vol. I, pp. 239–359; Penna. MSS, Board of War General Correspondence, August 1777, Box 27; see Appendix A.

13. Penna. MSS, RG–4, Military Accounts, Navy, Box 2. This is a rough draft of the final petition and is headed "Reasons assigned why we pray the Removal of Capt. Davis [sic] from Chief Command." The body of the draft identifies Davidson as "Davison." *Pennsylvania Packet*, June 24, 1776; Force, *American Archives*, Fourth Series, Vol. VI, pp. 966–967; *Naval Documents*, Vol. V, pp. 604–605.

14. *C.R.*, Vol. X, pp. 342, 415, 510; HSP, Simon Gratz Collection, Case 5, Box 27, "Memorial of the Captains of the Galleys." (Also in *Naval Documents*, Vol. II, pp. 654–655.

15. See Appendix A.

16. Penna. MSS, RG–4, Military Accounts, Navy, Box 2.

17. *C.R.*, Vol. X, pp. 606–607, 608–609; see footnote 11.

18. *Naval Documents*, Vol. V, p. 684 (deposition of Martin Wert); *C.R.*, Vol. X, p. 610.

19. *Ibid.*, pp. 615–616; HSP, Bradford Papers, Vol. II, p. 204, "Report of the Commanders of the Provincial Gallies to the Sub-Committee of Conference"; *P.A.*, Fourth Series, Vol. III, pp. 662–663; *Naval Documents*, Vol. V, p. 649; *P.A.*, First Series, Vol. IV, p. 759, Davidson to Commanders of Gallies, May [June] 20, 1776; Vol. V, p. 378, Davidson to R. Morris, June 19, 1776.

20. Dougherty was instructed to anchor the galleys on the east side of Fort Island, to see that they were in good condition, put through frequent training maneuvers, make a prompt survey of supplies and obtain the assistance of the ship's husband to remedy any deficiencies. He was admonished to make certain that all galleys carry fifty rounds of powder and occasionally replace with fresh powder, the replaced powder to be forwarded to the commissary by the ammunition sloop. He was given detailed instructions on the granting of leaves to officers or men, and to ensure that they were of limited duration. Finally, the usual appeal was made for harmony to promote the common cause in which they were all engaged. *C.R.*, Vol. X, pp. 617–618; *P.A.*, Fourth Series, Vol. III, pp. 603–605; Force, *American Archives*, Fourth Series, Vol. VI, pp. 1291–1292.

21. *Pennsylvania Packet*, July 8, 1776 (address was dated July 2); Force, *American Archives*, Fourth Series, Vol. VI, pp. 1295–1296; *P.A.*, Fourth Series, Vol. III, pp. 605–608; *C.R.*, Vol. X, pp. 623–625; *P.A.*, Second Series, Vol. I, p. 234fn.

22. *P.A.*, Fourth Series, Vol. III, p. 611; Force, *American Archives*, Fifth Series, Vol. I, p. 1327; *C.R.*, Vol. X, p. 701–702; *P.A.*, Second Series, Vol. I, pp. 233–234.

23. See Appendix A.

24. *P.A.*, Second Series, Vol. I, pp. 239–259; Penna. MSS, RG–4, Military Accounts, Navy, 1775–1794, Boxes 2, 3, 4, 5, and 6; Various RG-4, Box 2, General Greene, Provincial Store, RD-4, Box 5; see Appendix A.

25. *Ibid.; P.A.*, First Series, Vol. IV, p. 770, Committee to Commanding Officer [Davidson], 1776.

26. Almon, *Remembrancer*, Vol. IV, p. 127.

27. *P.A.*, First Series, Vol. IV, pp. 762–763, Fisher to Committee, May 27, 1776.

28. *Ibid.*, p. 765, Committee to Fisher, 1776; *C.R.*, Vol. X, p. 593; *Delaware Archives*, Vol. II, p. 945, Vol. III, pp. 1364–1365.

29. *Ibid.*, p. 1365.

30. *Pennsylvania Evening Post*, May 2, May 7, and June 6, 1776; *Pennsylvania Gazette*, April 17, 1776.

31. *C.R.*, Vol. X, pp. 562, 567, 586.

32. Penna. MSS, Mitchell Papers MG–92, Box 6; Military Accounts, Navy, Box 2, Records of the Comptroller General, 1775–1794, RG–4.

33. *C.R.*, Vol. X, p. 735.

34. *Ibid.*, p. 759.

35. Force, *American Archives*, Fifth Series, Vol. II, p. 841.

36. *C.R.*, Vol. X, pp. 708, 712, 718, 724, 731–732.

37. Philadelphia Maritime Museum, J. Welles Henderson Collection, Galley Book, Ship Yard No. 3.

38. *C.R.*, Vol. X, pp. 777–778.

39. *Ibid.*, p. 732; Penna. MSS, Records of the Comptroller General, Navy Board, Various (Minutes, 1777) RG-4, Military Accounts, Navy, Box 2. The manuscript records show an early draft giving effect to the raise in officers' pay as of November 15, 1776, later revised to January 1, 1777.

40. *C.R.*, Vol. XI, pp. 4, 21.

41. *Ibid.*, pp. 8, 9, 23; *P.A.*, Fourth Series, Vol. III, pp. 619, 620; Force, *American Archives*, Fifth Series, Vol. III, p. 192.

CHAPTER VI

1. *P.A.*, First Series, Vol. V, p. 84, Resolution of the Council of Safety, December 2, 1776.

2. *C.R.*, Vol. XI, p. 25; Captain Thomas Forrest, former captain of the marines on the floating battery *Arnold*, transferred to Major

Proctor's artillery detachment as captain of the Second Company on October 5, 1776. PMBH, Vol. 47, p. 37. "The Second Troop Philadelphia City Cavalry," by W. A. Newman Dorland; PMBH, Vol. IV, p. 455; "A Sketch of Major Thomas Proctor," by Benjamin M. Nead. Mr. Nead gives the date of Forrest's artillery appointment as August 6, 1776, which would appear to be incorrect.

3. *C.R.*, Vol. XI, pp. 39, 52; Penna. MSS, Mitchell Papers, "An account of provisions Delivered the Gallies lying Near Trenton." RG-92, Box 6; *P.A.*, First Series, Vol. V, pp. 129–130, Instructions of Council, December 22, 1776. The Council was aware of the concern of seamen aboard the galleys for the welfare of their families. Captain Blewer was authorized to make whatever allowances he found necessary for their subsistence.

4. John W. Jackson, *Margaret Morris*, pp. 41–46; William S. Stryker, *The Battles of Trenton and Princeton*, pp. 42–44.

5. *Ibid.*, pp. 44–46; Jackson, *Morris*, pp. 45, 89.

6. *P.A.*, First Series, Vol. V, p. 118, Proctor to Council, December 17, 1776.

7. Christopher Ward, *The War of the Revolution*, Vol. I, pp. 292–293; Alfred Hoyt Bill, *The Campaign of Princeton*, pp. 27–28; Thomas Jefferson Wertenbaker, "The Battle of Princeton," in *The Princeton Battle Monument*, pp. 53–57.

8. *P.A.*, First Series, Vol. V, pp. 120–121, Hugh Montgomery to Joseph Blewer, December 19, 1776.

9. *C.R.*, Vol. XI, pp. 50, 52.

10. William B. Reed, *Life and Correspondence of Joseph Reed*, Vol. I, pp. 276–277fn.; *PMHB*, Vol. VIII, No. 4, p. 394, "General Joseph Reed's Narrative, 1776–77." Reed comments: ". . . began to reimbark. . . . Ice began to drive with such force & in such Quantities as threatened many Boats with absolute Destruction. To add to the Difficulty about Day Break there came on a most violent Storm of Rain Hail and Snow." See also *PMHB*, Vol. VIII, No. 3. pp. 258–259, "Journal of Sergeant William Young."

11. HSP, Cadwalader Papers, Thomas Wharton Letters.

12. *P.A.*, First Series, Vol. V, p. 136, Cadwalader to Council, December 26, 1776; Bill, *Campaign of Princeton*, p. 61.

13. Ward, *The War of the Revolution*, Vol. I, pp. 303–304.

14. *P.A.*, First Series, Vol. V, p. 135–136, Brown to Council, December 26, 1776.

15. William S. Stryker, *The Battles of Trenton and Princeton*, p. 433. Stryker apparently accepted Shippin's service on the privateer *Hancock* as that of the galley *Hancock*. This assumption has been repeated in subsequent studies of this campaign. See *PMHB*, Vol. 42, pp.

263, 265–266, 270–271, 271–273. "Pennsylvania Pensioners of the Revolution," *Ibid.*, Vol. 48, p. 357, "The Provincial and Revolutionary History of St. Peter's Church, Philadelphia, 1753–1783," by C.P.B. Jeffreys in Church War Records extracts from the *Pennsylvania Evening Post*, August 6, 10, 17, 20, and October 31, and *Pennsylvania Gazette*, September 4, October 23, 1776; for Shippin's service in the Second Battalion of Pennsylvania Militia, see *PMHB*, Vol. 38, p. 280, "Charles Willson Peale, his Journal"; *Ibid.*, Vol. I, p. 178fn.; HSP, Cadwalader Papers, Miscellaneous Revolutionary Items, Box C-38, "Provision return of Captain William Shippin's Company of the Second Battalion Pennsylvania Militia Commanded by Colonel John Bayard."

16. *P.A.*, Second Series, Vol. I, pp. 386–387; Penna. MSS, Military Accounts, Navy, RG-4, Box 6, "All of the Sundry Articles lost at Trenton by the Officers and privates belonging to the Putnam Battery While Volunteers in the Country Service"; *Ibid.*, Box 2, "State of the Accounts of William Brown, Esq. Capt. of Putnam Battery." This account for January and February 1777 lists a charge of £346 13s 11d for clothing for the crew. It is possible that these were replacement for the articles reported lost in the previous citation, as they were delivered to the battery on January 22; *Ibid.*, Box 3, "Muster Roll Arnold Battery."

17. Bill, *Campaign of Princton*, p. 132; Stryker, *Trenton and Princeton*, p. 433.

18. Duane, *Christopher Marshall*, p. 111.

CHAPTER VII

1. HSP, Bradford Papers, Vol. II, p. 205.
2. *C.R.*, Vol. XI, pp. 122–123.
3. *Ibid.*, pp. 122–123, 182.
4. *P.A.*, First Series, Vol. V, p. 200, Casdorp to Council, January 24, 1777.
5. *Ibid.*, p. 166, Richards to Council, 1777.
6. *P.A.*, First Series, Vol. V, pp. 252–253, Memorandum, excerpt from *C.R.*, March 4, 1777; *P.A.*, Second Series, Vol. I, pp. 96–97, 97fn., 98, 102; *C.R.*, Vol. XI, pp. 181–184; HSP, Gratz Collection, Box 18, Case 1.
7. *P.A.*, Second Series, Vol. I, pp. 108–110; *C.R.*, Vol. XI, pp. 191–193.
8. Penna. MSS, Military Accounts, Navy, RG-4, Box 2; Records of the Comptroller General, Navy Board, Various (Minutes, 1777).

9. *P.A.*, Second Series, Vol. I, pp. 116, 125, 129, 132.

10. *Ibid.*, pp. 119, 120; *P.A.*, First Series, Vol. V, pp. 293, 303, Navy Board to Council, April 5, 1777, Officers for Appointment, April 9, 1777; *C.R.*, Vol. XI, pp. 193–194, 199–202.

11. *Ibid.*, p. 125.

12. *P.A.*, First Series, Vol. V, p. 263, Fisher to Council, March 17, 1777.

13. *P.A.*, Second Series, Vol. I, pp. 128–129.

14. *Ibid.*, pp. 101, 108; Harry B. and Grace M. Weiss, *The Revolutionary Saltworks of the New Jersey Coast*, pp. 21–26.

15. *P.A.*, Second Series, Vol. I, pp. 81–226; Penna. MSS, Military Accounts, Navy, RD-4, Box 2, Accounts of William Webb, and John Nicholson's Remarks on the Revisal of William Webb's Accounts.

16. *P.A.*, Second Series, Vol. I, p. 99. This volume is devoted almost exclusively to the Pennsylvania navy. There are several editing errors, but for the period of February through September 1777 is the most complete record extant. For other periods of time, various volumes in the *Pennsylvania Archives* (all series) and the *Colonial Records* are helpful, supplemented by the manuscript archives in the Pennsylvania Division of Archives and Manuscripts.

17. *P.A.*, Second Series, Vol. I, pp. 96, 99, 111, 124, 171, 185; Penna. MSS, Accounts of William Webb, John Nicholson's Remarks on the Revisal of William Webb's Accounts, Military Accounts, Navy, RG-4, Box 2; George Smith, *History of Delaware County, Pennsylvania*, p. 299. See map accompanying John Hazelwood's letter of December 9, 1779, reproduced in *P.A.*, First Series, Vol. V, facing p. 721.

18. *P.A.*, Second Series, Vol. I, pp. 127–128, 133; *P.A.*, First Series, Vol. V, p. 346, Navy Board to Board of War, May 20, 1777. Sinepuxent Inlet in Maryland is approximately thirty miles south of Cape Henlopen.

19. *Ibid.*, pp. 392–394; Penna. MSS, Military Accounts, Navy, RG-4, Boxes 2, 3, 4, 5, 6; General Greene, Provincial Store, RG-4, Various, RG-4, Box 2.

20. Penna. MSS, Military Accounts, Navy, RG-4, Boxes 2, 5; Various Minutes, 1777, RG-4, *P.A.*, Second Series, Vol. I, pp. 118–210, 705 *passim;* J. Bennett Nolan, *The Schuylkill*, p. 270.

21. *P.A.*, Second Series, Vol. I, p. 141.

22. *Ibid.*, pp. 84, 88, 115, 132, 134, 142, 149, 156, 157.

23. *Ibid.*, pp. 114, 115, 140, 142, 166, 206; HSP, Gratz Collection, Box 18, Case 1; Penna. MSS, Military Accounts, Navy, Box 2.

24. *P.A.*, Second Series, Vol. I, pp. 88–226 *passim*. The men in charge of the posts received £5 a month for their services.

CHAPTER VIII

1. North Callahan, *Henry Knox, General Washington's General,* pp. 106–109.

2. Library of Congress, George Washington Papers, June 7, 1777, Reel 42. These copies of the microfilm reels of the papers of Washington were made available by the West Chester State College, West Chester, Pennsylvania, and the facilities and loan service of the American Philosophical Society, Philadelphia. This memorandum was included in a letter from Washington to Benedict Arnold (hereafter cited as "G.W. Papers").

3. General Phillipe Trouson du Coudray had a somewhat pathetic and short-lived career in the American army. He gave some evidence of being a competent engineer, but suffered from a lack of rapport with his fellow officers because of the unfortunate circumstances connected with his agreement with Silas Deane. He was also handicapped by a lack of adequate charts or maps of the Delaware River and its environs—a standard complaint of Washington. No competent military engineers to assist him were in the American service; his chief reliance seems to have been on Commodore Hazelwood and General Thomas Mifflin. Another not insignificant obstacle was his inability to communicate with his American counterparts except through interpreters. His drowning in the Schuylkill River was due to his insisting on sitting in the saddle on his horse during the crossing. Although a regrettable accident, it unquestionably eased certain tensions among American generals.

4. *P.A.*, First Series, Vol. V, p. 359, Resolution of Congress, June 11, 1777.

5. *C.R.*, Vol. XI, p. 231.

6. *P.A.*, First Series, Vol. V, pp. 360–363, du Coudray's Observation on the Forts for the Defence of the two passages of the River Delaware; PMHB, Vol. XXIV. Du Coudray's views at this time are outlined in some detail, and several of the submissions offered by American generals in early August are undoubtedly based in part on du Coudray.

Du Coudray undoubtedly deserves the credit for giving the name Mifflin to the fort on Fort Island. Many historians have assumed that the works on Fort Island were not designated as Fort Mifflin until the summer following the British evacuation of Philadelphia. Assisted by General Thomas Mifflin, du Coudray made his first study of the river defenses in early June 1777, the results of which were placed before the Supreme Executive Council on June 21. In this report the fortification on Fort Island was merely called "The Fort." Du Coudray's next detailed study was submitted to the Continental Congress on August 6. In this report he designates the Fort Island works as Fort Mifflin. Therefore, at some time between June 21 and August 6, du Coudray named the fort in honor of his associate, General Mifflin, in appreciation for his assistance. Before mid-September Washington and his general staff were referring to the fortification as Fort Mifflin. (See citations above and *PMHB*, Vol. XVIII, pp. 1–19, 163–184, 329–337, "Defenses Philadelphia").

7. *Journals of the Continental Congress*, Vol. VIII, pp. 414, 451, 538, 541, 553, 557; *P.A.*, First Series, Vol. V, p. 430, Board of War (Continental) to Wharton, July 17, 1777.

8. One instance of the problems stemming from natural causes was cited in a letter of John Read, Commissary of Stores at the fort. In early 1777 he complained of muskrats making large holes in the fort's banks. Penna. MSS, General Correspondence, Board of War, RG-4, Various.

9. Apparently Red Bank was completed and ready for a garrison before June 1, 1777. Captain Nice records in his orderly book on that date that men with their accoutrements were ordered to march to Gloucester. Fifty-seven officers and men were to remain as the garrison, commanded by Captain Carnahan with Lieutenant Gregg, Ensign Becker, three sergeants, drum major and a small fife and drummer, with five privates from each company, or a total fifty men.

An interesting entry in Nice's journal for May 2 mentions a British foraging expedition coming up the bay as far as New Castle and removing, among other things, the alarm gun. As New Castle was not designated an alarm post, could this have been the elusive Long Point cited in Chapter III, note 22? HSP, Orderly Book, American, Captain John Nice, headquarters at Red Bank, Fort Mercer, 1777.

10. *P.A.*, First Series, Vol. V, pp. 375, 441–442, Eyre to Mifflin, June 17, Fords on Delaware.

11. *Pennsylvania Packet*, July 8, 1777.

12. *P.A.*, First Series, Vol. V, pp. 376–377, Arnold to Wharton, June 18, 1777; *P.A.*, Second Series, Vol. I, p. 188; *C.R.*, Vol. XI, p. 248. No muster rolls have been found in either the printed archives or the manuscript musters for the *Speedwell* or *Black Duck* before September 1, 1777. Records for Joseph Wade and Robert Wade also begin at this date. It is certain that the Wades were employed in the ferrying of Potter's troops at this date; therefore the missing muster rolls would

probably confirm that these vessels were in service in July 1777. The editing of the printed archives is unfortunately inaccurate in several instances and must be checked and confirmed. A case in point is a return found in *P.A.*, Second Series, Vol. I, p. 392–393, covering stores issued to the fleet for February 1777. It lists several boats, including the *Speedwell* and *Black Duck*, which were not in service at that date.

13. *P.A.*, Second Series, Vol. I, pp. 190, 198–199; *C.R.*, Vol. XI, p. 247; *P.A.*, First Series, Vol. V, pp. 425–426, 429, Navy Board to Wharton, July 12, 1777, and July 17, 1777; HSP, Gratz Collection, Case 1, Box 18.

14. John Montresor, "The Journal of Captain John Montresor, July 1, 1777, to July 1, 1778," ed. by G. D. Scull, in *PMHB*, Vol. V, p. 396 (hereafter cited as "Montresor"); *P.A.*, First Series, Vol. V, pp. 465, 474–475, Fisher to Navy Board, · July 30, 1777, Hunn to Wharton, July 31 and August 1, 1777.

15. *Ibid.*, pp. 450, 453, Instructions to John Hunn, July 24, 1777, Hunn to Wharton, July 26, 1777.

16. *Ibid.*, pp. 453, 462–463, 465, 467, 468, 474–475, Hunn to Wharton, July 26, July 29, July 30 (2 letters), July 31, 1777, Fisher to Navy Board, July 30, 1777.

17. *Ibid.*, p. 472–473; *P.A.*, Second Series, Vol. I, p. 196.

18. Joseph Galloway, *Letters to a Nobleman on the Conduct of the War in the Middle Colonies* (second edition), p. 70. See also Appendix F.

19. In addition to du Coudray, others submitting opinions were Joseph Reed and Anthony Wayne, both Pennsylvanians, with Wayne a member of the original Council of Safety and deeply involved in the organization of the State navy and river forts. Two of Washington's most trusted generals also submitted reports: Nathanael Greene and Henry Knox, chief of artillery. For those interested in studying these reports in detail, refer to "Defences of Philadelphia in 1777," Worthington C. Ford, contr., in PMHB, Vol. XVIII, pp. 5–19, 163–184 (hereafter cited as "Defences Philadelphia"); HSP, Wayne Papers, Vol. IV.

20. *PMHB*, Vol. XVIII, pp. 174–181, "Defences Philadelphia," Washington to President of Congress, August 9, 1777; Washington, *Writings*. Vol. IX, pp. 45–53 (August 10).

21. *PMHB*, Vol. XVIII, pp. 12–19, "Defences Philadelphia," A Definitive Project upon the Defense of Philadelphia in the Present State of Affairs by du Coudray; *P.A.*, First Series, Vol. V, pp. 419–420, Washington to Wharton, July 9, 1777.

22. Henry G. Ashmead, *History of Delaware County, Pennsylvania*, p. 69.

23. *PMHB,* Vol. XVIII, pp. 330–333, "Defences Philadelphia," Memoir upon the Defense of the two passages of the River by du Coudray, August 29, 1777.

24. *Ibid.,* pp. 330–337, Defense of River, etc., du Coudray, August 29, 1777; du Coudray to Washington, August 30, 1777; du Coudray to Congress, September 7, 1777.

25. *P.A.,* Second Series, Vol. I, pp. 194, 197, 225; *P.A.,* First Series, Vol. V, p. 464, Blewer to Wharton, July 30, 1777; *C.R.,* Vol. XI, pp. 255–256. The official records of the various state authorities indiscriminately use English pounds and American dollars in pricing invoices, memorandums, or in making payments. Apparently, at this time, an English pound was valued at about two and two-thirds dollars. To illustrate, the State Navy Board was paid $8,000 or £3,000 on September 20, 1777.

26. *P.A.,* First Series, Vol. V, p. 459, Council to Hopkinson, Nixon and Wharton (John), August 6, 1777.

27. *P.A.,* Second Series, Vol. I, p. 208; a record of expenditures by the Continental Navy Board of amounts for fire ships, including small disbursements for State guard boats, can be found in Penna. MSS, Military Accounts, Navy, RG-4, Box 2, "The Continental Navy Board for Fire-Ships, to Wm. Rush, July 31-August 31, 1777."

28. *P.A.,* First Series, Vol. V, pp. 504–505, Fisher to Navy Board, August 8, 1777.

29. *Ibid.,* p. 510, Council to Navy Board, August 11, 1777; HSP, Dreer Collection, Governors of the State, Vol. IV.

30. *P.A.,* Second Series, Vol. I, pp. 203, 204, 205.

31. *P.A.,* First Series, Vol. V, pp. 538–539, Simmons to Navy Board, August 21, 1777.

32. *Ibid.,* p. 542, Navy Board to Council, August 23, 1777; *P.A.,* Second Series, Vol. I, pp. 211–212; *C.R.,* Vol. XI, pp. 275–276.

33. See Appendix A. Roach was appointed Captain of the *Delaware,* April 16, 1777, succeeding Captain Eyre. However, as Eyre was still in command of the *Delaware* in November 1777, I do not believe that Roach ever assumed this command. Also, Roach is the only captain listed for the *Congress* subsequent to September 28, 1776.

34. *Ibid.; P.A.,* Second Series, Vol. I, pp. 211–212.

35. *Ibid.*

36. *Ibid.,* pp. 116, 129, 180–181; *P.A.,* First Series, Vol. V, pp. 401, 434–435, 577–578, Seymour to Bradford, June 23, 1777, Memorial of Commodore Seymour, July, 1777, Seymour to Wharton, September 3, 1777; Vol. VI, p. 97, Seymour to Council, December 15, 1777 (1776); HSP. Stauffer Collection, "Extra Illustrated Edition, Westcott's History of Philadelphia," Vol. VII, p. 538.

37. *P.A.*, First Series, Vol. V, p. 594, Council to Navy Board, September 6, 1777; *P.A.*, Second Series, Vol. I, p. 220; *C.R.*, Vol. XI, p. 293; HSP, Dreer Collection, Soldiers of the Revolution, Vol. V.

38. *C.R.*, Vol. XI, p. 277.

39. *P.A.*, First Series, Vol. V, pp. 572–573, Armstrong to Wharton, September 1, 1777.

40. *Ibid.*, pp. 620–621, Council to Hazelwood, September 13, 1777.

41. *Ibid.*, p. 591, Council to Jehu Eyre, September 6, 1777; *PMHB*, Vol. III, p. 490, "Colonel John Eyre, contributed by Peter D. Keyser."

42. *P.A.*, First Series, Vol. V, p. 590, Navy Board to Council, September 5, 1777; *P.A.*, Second Series, Vol. I, p. 219; *C.R.*, Vol. XI, pp. 285–286.

43. *Ibid.*, pp. 305–306; "G.W. Papers," Reel 44, Matlack to Major Casdrop, September 14, 1777; Ashmead, *Delaware County, Pennsylvania*, p. 65.

44. "G.W. Papers," Reel 44, Resolve of Congress, signed by Charles Thomson, transmitted by John Hancock, September 13, 1777.

45. Washington, *Writings*, Vol. IX, pp. 215–216.

46. *Ibid.*, pp. 216–217, *P.A.*, First Series, Vol. V, pp. 617–618, Washington to Wharton, September 13, 1777.

CHAPTER IX

1. While this chapter is based largely on eyewitness and contemporary accounts, the excellent studies of other historians, contemporary and modern, have not been overlooked. Eyewitness and contemporary accounts are invaluable, but if accepted without critical scrutiny by modern historical standards, they will at times produce conclusions that are distorted by prejudice, self-interest, or misconstruction. Contemporary historians benefited through the opportunity of interviewing participants in the events narrated or lived coeval with them. Historians of the last century have been favored with data not available to contemporary writers and have added to our knowledge of the Revolutionary War in Delaware Valley. In preparing Chapters IX, X, XI, and XII, free use has been made of secondary as well as prime sources. In the interest of brevity, unless a direct quotation is made or another historian's conclusions noted, no citations will be made in the notes. Refer to the bibliography for a complete list of these valuable secondary sources.

2. *P.A.*, First Series, Vol. V, p. 626, Alexander to Robert Morris, September 15, 1777.

3. Charles O. Paullin, *Out-Letters of the Continental Marine Committee and Board of Admiralty, 1776–1780*, 2 vols., Vol. I, pp. 157–160.

4. Clark, *Barry*, pp. 123–124.

5. *PMHB*, Vol. I, p. 7, "The Diary of Robert Morton" (hereafter cited as "Morton").

6. *Ibid.*, Vol. XIII, p. 298, "Extracts from the Journal of Mrs. Henry Drinker" (hereafter cited as "Drinker").

7. *Ibid.*, Vol. VI, p. 41, "Montresor."

8. *Ibid.*, Vol. I, p. 7, "Morton."

9. *Ibid.*, p. 42; Vol. I, pp. 8, 9fn., "Morton"; Scharf and Westcott, *History of Philadelphia*, Vol. I, p. 352. Another source mentioned that two medium twelve-pounders, two 5-½-inch howitzers, and four six-pounders of the Grenadiers were in the batteries. William L. Clements Library, Clinton Papers.

10. During the spring of 1777, the *Montgomery* had been stripped of cannon and supplies which were transferred to other elements of the fleet. On May 5, 1777, the old State flagship was ordered refitted and equipped as a guard ship with sixteen nine-pounders. The *Montgomery* was listed on the Faden map as carrying ten eighteen-pounders. Wallace in his life of William Bradford indicates that the *Montgomery* had fourteen eighteen-pounders, sixteen cohorns, and eight Swivels. Unfortunately, the dismantling and later the rearming of the *Montgomery* has been overlooked. See *P.A.*, Second Series, Vol. I, pp. 99–145, "Minutes of the Navy Board," for entries covering the disposition of items removed from the ship. Also, see *Ibid.*, p. 147, for the refitting as a guard ship with nine-pounders.

11. *P.A.*, First Series, Vol. V, p. 637, Instructions, Hazelwood to Alexander, September 27, 1777; Penna. MSS, RG-4, Military Accounts, Navy, Box 4; *PMHB*, Vol. VI, p. 42, "Montresor." Montresor mentions five galleys but he mistakenly types the sloop *Fly* as a galley. *Ibid.*, Vol. I, p. 8, "Morton."

12. *Ibid.*, Vol. VI, p. 42, "Montresor." Montresor noted that on September 26, while reconnoitering near Gloucester Point, he was nearly taken by the galley stationed there. Gloucester Point was in what is now South Philadelphia, near the Walt Whitman Bridge.

13. *Ibid.*, p. 42; Vol. I, p. 8, "Morton."

14. John Marshall, *The Life of George Washington*, 5 vols. (Citizens Guild edition), Vol. II, p. 320.

15. *PMHB*, Vol. VI, p. 42, "Montresor"; *Ibid.*, Vol. XIII, p. 298, "Drinker."

16. Clark, *Barry*, p. 141.

17. *PMHB*, Vol. VI, p. 44, "Montresor."

18. Captain Alexander was probably confined in the old Walnut Street Gaol, now occupied by the Penn Mutual Insurance Company at Sixth and Walnut Streets. Later, when the British were more securely ensconced in Philadelphia, most American officers were imprisoned on the second floor of Independence Hall.

19. *PMHB*, Vol. VI, pp. 42–44, "Montresor." Durham boats were used by Washington in his celebrated Christmas night, 1776, crossing of the Delaware. These boats were forty to sixty feet long, eight feet wide, and two feet deep amidships. They were furnished with two lateen sails for use when the wind was favorable and they were usually poled by a crew of four. Running boards along each side were walked by the polemen, who placed their poles on the river bottom at the bow of the boat and by walking aft pushed the boat at its full length, then walked back to the bow to repeat the process. Some authorities believe that the Durham boat provided some inspiration for the designers of the row galley. Seymour Dunbar, *History of Travel in America*, Vol. I, p. 282. Windmill Island was near the Philadelphia shore and extended from Fitzwater Street on the South to Arch Street on the north. Originally a bar or shoal, it was formed by an accumulation of sand, silt, and refuse brought downriver by ice and spring floods. Later the island was separated by a canal, the upper part being called Smith's Island and the lower portion retaining the name Windmill Island. One John Harding leased the island, building a windmill on its shore, hence the name. However, at the time of the Revolution it was one island, about one mile long. Scharf and Westcott, *History of Philadelphia*, Vol. I, pp. 8–9.

20. *Ibid.*, Vol. I, p. 300.

21. Penna. MSS, Military Accounts, Navy, RG-4, Box 2, "Accounts of William Webb, Paymaster Navy Board," "John Nicholson's Remarks on the Revisal of Wm. Webb's Accounts."

22. William Crispin was listed by the editors of *P.A.*, Second Series, Vol. I, p. 240, as appointed commissary on August 3, 1778. Crispin was serving in this capacity in 1777. The entry in the minutes of August 3, 1778 does not mention his appointment; only that he furnished rations to the muster master. *C.R.*, Vol. XI, p. 546.

23. *P.A.*, Second Series, Vol. I, pp. 392–393; Penna. MSS, Military Accounts, Navy, RG-4, Box 2, "Accounts William Webb Paymaster Navy Board." The same box contains many ration summaries unsigned and undated. "Mitchell Papers," MG-92, Box 6. In a deposition made by Mitchell on November 9, 1779, he certified that a considerable part of his papers were left in Philadelphia, while he was on duty at the Battle of Brandywine. He was later sent to Valley Forge and Pawlings

Ford on orders. The British apparently destroyed or confiscated these papers; it is therefore difficult to compile an accurate summary of expenses.

24. Clark, *Barry*, p. 134.

25. See Appendix A.

26. Confusion exists as to the number and size of the cannon on various ships in the Continental fleet in the Delaware River in October 1777. Authorities differ as indicated:

Andrea Doria, brig: Wallace lists fourteen six-pounders, Chapelle fourteen four-pounders, and Allen sixteen six-pounders and twelve swivels.

Hornet, sloop: ten guns, caliber unknown.

Racehorse, sloop: Chapelle lists ten nine-pounders, Allen twelve guns, no caliber, Wallace, ten guns, no caliber. The *Racehorse* was a British sloop-of war captured off Porto Rico.

Fly, sloop: Chapelle lists six nine-pounders, Wallace six guns, Allen eight guns, no caliber.

Wasp, sloop: Chapelle and Allen list eight guns, no caliber; Wallace ten nine-pounders.

Repulse, xebec: two twenty-four pounders in bow, two eighteen-pounders in stern, and four nine-pounders in waist.

Champion, xebec: same armaments as *Repulse*.

Mosquito, sloop: four nine-pounders.

Sachem, sloop: ten nine-pounders.

Independence, sloop: ten nine-pounders listed by Emmons. This sloop was not in the Delaware in October 1777; it was lost off the North Carolina coast in 1778.

Some authorities question the presence of the *Mosquito* and *Sachem*, but as their regular station was off the coast of New Jersey, Maryland, and Delaware, with Philadelphia as their home port, they may have been with Robinson at this time. In any event, they disappear from marine records after this campaign. Chapelle states that the *Mosquito* was destroyed in the Delaware in 1778. This would probably indicate that it was at Bordentown, New Jersey, when the British raided that river town and destroyed all river boats in May 1778.

Three other Continental ships were in the Delaware, but were neither rigged, manned, nor armed: the unfinished frigates *Washington* and *Effingham* and the packet *Mercury*. All were destroyed in the British raid of May 1778.

Nothing is recorded by the authorities quoted, or others consulted, concerning any Continental fire ships. As indicated in the preceding chapter, twelve were authorized to be purchased and outfitted, but there is no record that this was done. It is known that one fire ship, the *Pluto*, was on the Delaware in August 1777. Its fate is unknown. Also, Lieutenant Douglas Spence of the brig *Convention* resigned to accept command of a Continental fire ship. George F. Emmons, *The Navy of the U.S. from the Commencement*, 1775–1853, p. 2; Wallace, *Bradford*, pp. 204–205; Howard I. Chapelle, *The American Sailing Navy*, pp. 53–55; Gardner W. Allen, *A Naval History of the American Revolution*, Vol. I, pp. 25, 29, 90, 140–141, 160, 241–242; Penna. MSS, Military Accounts, Navy, RG-4, Box 2, "Accounts of William Webb, Paymaster Navy Board"; *P.A.*, Second Series, Vol. I, p. 200.

27. William Bradford, Joseph Blewer, Emanuel Eyre, Samuel Massey, Joseph Marsh, and Paul Cox rarely missed a Board meeting; absence was usually the result of duty with the fleet or militia, supervising the building or repair of boats, or procuring provisions, ammunition, or arms. The remaining Board members attended regularly for the first month, but made rare appearances after April 1, 1777. Andrew Caldwell, Robert Richie, Thomas Fitzsimmons, and Thomas Barclay were possibly serving in other capacities in the civil government or the militia. William Pollard was appointed to the Board by the Council of Safety, but when the Supreme Executive Council was reconstituted as the Board on March 13, his name was omitted. Pollard, along with Samuel Morris, Jr., never attended a meeting, although Morris is known to have been active in the militia and may have been on active duty.

28. *PMHB*, Vol. XVIII, pp. 337–339, "Defences Philadelphia," Council of War, September 23, 1777.

29. Washington, *Writings*, Vol. IX, pp. 255–256.

30. *Ibid.*, pp. 256–257.

31. Neither Major Ballard nor Major Thayer could have been in Smith's original detachment as the former entered Fort Mifflin on October 22 with the Virginia Continentals under Colonel John Green. On the other hand, Major Thayer was with his regiment, the Second Rhode Island, a part of General Varnum's brigade marching from New York to join Washington's army.

Citations from the papers of Colonel Smith must be used with caution. Smith dictated his reminiscences to his son General J. Speare Smith (although some have believed the amanuensis was Jared S. Sparks, a natural mistake since Sparks was an outstanding historian of the time) about fifty years after the war. The original papers are in the Maryland Historical Society and copies, in the handwriting of Henry B. Dawson, are at Columbia University. Dawson, in editing the papers, noted that Colonel Smith's son permitted him to make a copy.

32. Washington, *Writings,* pp. 260–261; Henry B. Dawson, ed., *The Historical Magazine and Notes and Queries Concerning Antiquities, History and Biography of America,* Second Series, Vol. III, p. 86, "Papers of General Samuel Smith (hereafter cited as "Smith Papers").

33. Washington, *Writings,* Vol. IX, pp. 284–285, 292–293.

34. American Philosophical Society, Sol Feinstone Collection, "Diary Revolutionary War: Campaign, 1777"; Galloway, *Letters to a Nobleman,* pp. 79–80; *Continental Journal and Weekly Advertiser* (Boston), March 26, 1778; Almon, *Remembrancer,* Vol. V, pp. 428–429.

35. *P.A.,* First Series, Vol. V, pp. 644–645, Bradford to Wharton, October 3, 1777.

36. Washington, *Writings,* Vol. VII, p. 134.

37. *P.A.,* First Series, Vol. V, pp. 644–645, Bradford to Wharton, October 3, 1777.

38. "G. W. Papers," Reel 44, S. Smith to Washington, October 2, 1777.

39. *Ibid.,* October 3, 1777.

40. *Ibid.,* October 6, 1777.

41. *Ibid.,* Varnum to Washington, October 5, 1777.

42. Washington, *Writings,* Vol. IX, pp. 326–327, 333, Washington to Varnum, October 7, 1777, and two letters on October 8.

43. Ibid., pp. 333–335; Jared Sparks, ed., *Correspondence of the American Revolution,* Vol. V, pp. 86–88, for a slightly different construction of this letter. Captain du Plessis-Mauduit's name has been written either as du Plessis or Mauduit in various accounts of the Revolution. The Marquis de Chastellux recorded his friend's full name but usually, apparently in the interest of brevity, used M. du Mauduit. In this study, we will use Mauduit.

44. Archibald Robertson, . . . *His Diaries and Sketches in America, 1762–1780,* p. 151.

45. *PMHB,* Vol. VI, p. 45, "Montresor."

46. *P.A.,* First Series, Vol. V, pp. 648–649, Bradford to Wharton, October 7, 1777; "G.W. Papers," Reel 44, Hazelwood to Washington, October 10, 1777.

47. The logs of several British men-of-war were studied, and except for minor details, they agree on principal events. The originals of all naval logs are in the Admiralty Records, Public Records Office, London. I had the privilege of studying copies in the Historical Research Section, Department of the Navy, through the courtesy of Dr. William J. Morgan. Of those reviewed, the *Camilla, Roebuck, Pearl,* and *Eagle* offered a greater amount of detailed information. The *Eagle's* log was published in *PMHB,* Vol. XXXVIII, pp. 211–226. Care should be exer-

cised in using the logs of these ships. Entries begin at 12 noon on the day preceding the entry date and extend for twenty-four hours.

48. *Proceedings of the American Antiquarian Society*, Vol. 40, pp. 86–87, "British Account"; *PMHB*, Vol. VI, pp. 46–47, "Montresor"; "Drinker," p. 57; *PMHB*, Vol. XIII, pp. 299–300, "Drinker"; *PMHB*, Vol. I, pp. 15–17, "Morton."

49. *PMHB*, Vol. VI, p. 46, "Montresor"; *Proceedings of the American Antiquarian Society*, Vol. 40, p. 87, "A Contemporary British Account of General Sir William Howe's Military Operations in 1777." Original in Harvard College Library; *P.A.*, First Series, Vol. V, pp. 648–649, Bradford to Wharton, October 7, 1777.

50. *P.A.*, First Series, Vol. V, pp. 649–650, Bradford to Wharton, October 8, 1777, Bradford and Hazelwood to Wharton, October 11, 1777; "G.W. Papers," Reel 44, Bradford and Hazelwood to Washington, October 11, 1777.

51. Logs, *Roebuck* and *Camilla;* Isaac Mickle, *Reminiscences of Old Gloucester*, p. 127; *P.A.*, First Series, Vol. V, p. 668, Bradford to Wharton, October 13, 1777. The British logs mention the American guard boats in action at the Billingsport line of chevaux de frise. Normally it would entail great risks to use these small boats in the open water of the river. The logs of the frigates indicate clear and fine weather for October 11, 12, and 13, a condition which may have prompted Hazelwood to risk their use.

52. Logs, *Roebuck* and *Camilla*, October 20, 1777.

53. *PMBH*, Vol. II, p. 290, Thomas Paine to Franklin, May 16, 1778.

54. *Ibid.*, Vol. VI, pp. 46–47, "Montresor."

55. "G.W. Papers," Reel 44, Smith to Washington, October 9, 1777.

56. *PMBH*, Vol. VI, p. 47, "Montresor."

57. Washington, *Writings*, Vol. IX, pp. 327–328.

58. *Ibid.*, pp. 328–329.

59. *PMBH*, Vol. VI, pp. 46–47, "Montresor."

60. *Ibid.*, p. 48; *P.A.*, First Series, Vol. V, pp. 663–664, Bradford to Wharton, October 11, 1777; "G.W. Papers," Reel 44, Bradford and Hazelwood to Washington, October 11, 1777; *Proceedings of the American Antiquarian Society*, Vol. 40, p. 88, "British Account . . . Howe"; Robertson, *Diaries*, p. 152.

61. "G.W. Papers," Reel 44, Hazelwood to Washington, October 12, 1777; *PMHB*, Vol. VI, p. 48, "Montresor."

62. *P.A.*, First Series, Vol. V, p. 668, Bradford to Wharton, October 13, 1777; Washington, *Writings*, Vol. IX, pp. 358–359; "G.W. Papers," Reel 44, Hazelwood to Washington, October 12, 1777.

63. *Ibid.*, Smith to Washington, October 7, 1777, and October 14, 1777, Hazelwood to Washington, October 15, 1777, Hazelwood to

Emanuel Eyre, October 15, 1777; *PMHB*, Vol. VI, p. 50, "Montresor"; *P.A.*, First Series, Vol. V, p. 668.

64. "G.W. Papers," Reel 44, Smith to Washington, October 14, 1777.

65. *Ibid.* Fleury frequently signed his name "Lewis Fleury." Some scholars have mistakenly read his signature as "Lewis Henry."

66. Washington, *Writings*, Vol. IX, pp. 369, 370; "G.W. Papers," reel 44, State Navy Board (Joseph Blewer) to Washington, October 14, 1777.

67. *Ibid.*, Benjamin Eyre to Washington, October 16, 1777.

68. *Ibid.*, "Resolution signed by Charles Thomson, October 17"; Worthington C. Ford, ed., *Journals of the Continental Congress*, Vol. IX, p. 813.

69. "G.W. Papers," Reel 44, Greene to Washington, October 10, 1777, Hamilton to Newcomb, October 10, 1777.

70. HSP, "Maps and Plans of the Revolution, Willard Estate," map of Fort Mercer by Captain Mauduit; Alfred M. Heston, *Red Bank: Defense of Fort Mercer*, p. 10, "Plan of Fort Mercer drawn by T. S. Saunders, 1842"; Gloucester County Historical Society, "Plan of Fort Mercer by E. W. Bowden, circa 1895"; HSP, "Plan of the Attacks against Fort Mifflin. . . ." (This map is obviously a variant of the Ensign Thomas Wheeler drawing in the Library of Congress.) As the engineer responsible for the construction of the new redoubt, Mauduit's delineation of the fort is the most reliable. However, his main intent was to depict the redoubt's shape and detail its features, without any effort to relate the measurements of the redoubt to the original fortification. Other contemporary and nineteenth-century maps were consulted; unfortunately, in the majority of them no effort had been made to draw the fort to scale. This was characteristic of early cartographers and military engineers like Mauduit. Many map makers omitted details of the lines of the fort. A survey of the area was made by the author in an effort to identify the lines of the original fort and redoubt with the present terrain.

71. James Whitall filed a certificate for damages and theft (Greene would have called this an appropriation for the defense of the garrison) with the State Adjutant General on April 17, 1779, claiming that American troops caused losses to his property of £5,760 1s.

		£	s	d
April 16, 1777	"First Breaking the ground which is Rendered'd unfit for tilling	300	0	0
	Cutting and Destroying the Timber	1200	0	0
	Pasturing Cattle and horses for the use of the Army	26	13	0

	To Pasturing Continental Cattel & Horses			
	while Colonel Green Ocupy'd Fort Mercer	100	0	0
	To 15 Ton of Hay at 30 £ per Ton	550	0	0
	To 63 Bushel of wheat at 6 £ per Bushel	378	0	0
	To 1000 feet of Cedar Boards			
	at 40 £ per Thousand	40	0	0
October	8550 Rails at 12 £ per Hundred	1026	0	0
12, 1777	2048 Stakes also at 4 £ per Hundred	81	18	0
	50 Whiteoak Posts at 3s per piece	7	10	0
	To one Barn & Hayhouse totally Destroy'd &			
	Damages done to Sundry other Buildings	350	0	0
	To two pailed Gardens Cut down			
	and carried to fort Island	200	0	0
	To an orchard near 300 trees			
	all Grafted trees	1500	0	0
		£5760	1	0"

Frank H. Stewart was unable to find any record that restitution for these losses was made to Whitall. Stewart, *Notes on Old Gloucester County*, Vol. II, p. 167.

72. Heston, *Red Bank*, p. 3.

73. Interview with John G. Whitall on December 2, 1914, conducted and recorded by Frank H. Stewart.

74. There are conflicting reports as to the exact number of men in Greene's regiment when he arrived at the fort on October 11. Greene, writing to Washington on October 14, mentioned enclosing a return of the garrison, but this return does not appear in the Washington Papers or in Sparks' *Correspondence of the American Revolution*. The earliest extant return lists 244 officers and men present and fit for duty in Greene's regiment, the First Rhode Island. Colonel Angell's Second Rhode Island had 227 and Captain Cook's Continental Artillery Company sixty-three. Mauduit and the French Artillery and engineer personnel are not listed, although eyewitnesses remembered seeing a number of Frenchmen in the garrison on the day following the battle. Washington's instructions to Greene also mention the dispatch of Mauduit with officers and men to direct the artillery (Washingon, *Writings*, Vol. IX, p. 334).

To add to the confusion, a letter from Washington to General Israel Putnam dated October 8 mentions sending Greene and his regiment of *about 212 effective privates* to Fort Mercer (*ibid.*, p. 350). This is a figure difficult to reconcile unless Washington included sergeants, drummers, and fifers. Greene listed 213 in these classifications, and with the seven killed in the battle, it would indicate that his effective strength on October 11 was about 200, exclusive of the thirty-two officers (thirty-one on the roster and one a prisoner of the British). Cook's artillery company of sixty-three effectives on October 27 excludes the French officers and can be accepted only provisionally as the number on October 11.

The question has been raised as to whether the Rhode Island regiments at Red Bank included Negroes. The answer is found in a tract prepared by Sidney S. Rider, *An Historical Inquiry concerning the attempt to Raise a Regiment of Slaves by Rhode Island during the War of the Revolution,* Rhode Island Historical Tract 10: "The praises awarded the 'black regiment' by Governor Eustis for their defence of Redbank is entirely fictitious. The defense of Redbank took place October 22, 1777. The 'black regiment' was enlisted and purchased in the following year. The act under which their enlistments were made was passed in February, 1778." The "black regiment," while not in service at the battle of Fort Mercer, gave an excellent account of itself in the engagement at Newport, Rhode Island, in 1778.

75. Orderly Book of Colonel Christopher Greene, October 11, 1777, to December 18, 1777, *Year Book, 1928, of the New Jersey Society of Pennsylvania,* pp. 46–47. The original is in the Rhode Island Historical Society (hereafter cited as Orderly Book, Greene).

76. Orderly Book, Greene, p. 47; Heston, *Red Bank,* p. 11. See fn. 71 for detail of Whitall's losses.

77. See du Plessi-Mauduit's map of Fort Mercer; "G.W. Papers," Reel 45, Mauduit to Washington, November 17, 1777. I am grateful to Judy Gersteneker and Robert I. Alotta for a glossary of French fortification terms. Fougasse is an old French term for a camouflaged underground mine. Fraises differed from abatis in that they were pointed stakes driven into a rampart in a horizontal or inclined position.

78. Narrative of Jonas Cattell, Gloucester County Historical Society.

79. "G.W. Papers," Reel 44, Greene to Washington, October 16, 1777.

80. Washington, *Writings,* Vol. IX, p. 370; "G.W. Papers," Reel 44, Hamilton to Newcomb, October 10, 1777, Greene to Washington, October 14, 1777, Hamilton to Greene, October 15, 1777.

81. Orderly Book, Greene, pp. 46–49.

82. Washington, *Writings,* Vol. IX, pp. 392–394, 395–396; *P.A.,* First Series, Vol. V., pp. 678–680, Washington to Wharton, October 17, 1777.

83. Washington, *Writings,* Vol. IX, pp. 380–381, 395–396; Orderly Book, Greene, pp. 47–49.

84. Washington, *Writings,* Vol. IX, pp. 292–293.

85. G. D. Scull, ed., *The Evelyns in America*, Appendix, pp. 253–257, "Extracts from the Journals and note-books of Captain John Montresor."

86. "G.W. Papers," Reels 44 and 45, "Journal and Letters of Major Fleury"; Smith Papers, p. 86; Joseph Plumb Martin, *Private Yankee Doodle, Being a Narrative of some of the Adventures, Dangers and Sufferings of a Revolutionary Soldier*, George F. Scheer, ed., p. 86. Martin's reminiscences were written fifty years later and without recourse to notes. His often quoted description of the fort cannot be accepted as an accurate portrayal of the works as first seen by Smith. Martin arrived in early November, after the major changes in the fortifications had been made by Fleury. His narrative is an extremely interesting one, but not always reliable, unless confirmed by other sources.

Of all the maps of the Revolutionary period and later that were consulted (see Bibliography), the best and most reliable is Major Fleury's in the Jared Sparks Collection at Cornell University.

87. "G.W. Papers," Reel 44, Fleury to Hamilton, October 17 (16), 1777.

88. *Ibid.*, Reel 44, Fleury to Hamilton, October 17 (16), 1777; Smith to Washington, October 16, 1777; *PMHB*, Vol. VI, p. 49, "Montresor."

89. *Ibid.*

90. "G.W. Papers," Reel 44, J. Ellis and R. Harris to Bradford, October 14, 1777, Bradford to Washington, October 15, 1777.

91. *PMHB*, Vol. VI, p. 50, "Montresor"; "G.W. Papers," Reel 44, Fleury to Hamilton, October 17 (16), 1777, Fleury Journal, October 15, 16; Sir William Howe, *Narrative*, second edition, p. 28.

92. Galloway, *Letters to a Nobleman*, p. 78; *PMHB*, Vol. VI, pp. 50–51, "Montresor"; "G.W. Papers," Reel 44, Potter to Washington, October 16, 1777.

93. *Ibid.*, Fleury's Journal, October 15–19, 1777, Smith to Washington, October 16, 1777, Hazelwood to Washington, October 16, 1777, Hazelwood to Washington, October 15, 1777.

94. *Ibid.*, Fleury's Journal, October 19, 1777.

95. *Ibid.*

96. *Ibid.*, Hazelwood to Washington, October 15, 1777, Smith to Washington, October 16, 19, 1777, B. Eyre to Washington, October 16, 1777, Hazelwood to B. Eyre, October 15, 1777, Fleury's Journal, October 20.

97. *PMHB*, Vol. LXXIX, p. 459, "James Josiah," by William B. Clark; Washington, Writings, Vol. IX, pp. 427–428.

98. Sparks, ed., *Correspondence*, Vol. II, pp. 18–21, Hazelwood to Washington, October 26, 1777.

99. "G.W. Papers, "Reel 44, Fleury's Journal, October 19–23, 1777; Martin, *Private Yankee Doodle*, p. 89.

CHAPTER X

1. Almon, *Remembrancer*, Vol. V, pp. 428–431, Vice Admiral Lord Howe to Stephens (of the Admiralty Office), October 25, 1777; also in the *Continental Journal and Weekly Advertiser*, Boston, March 26, 1778.

2. Sir William Howe, *Narrative*, p. 29.

3. Logs, *Camilla, Pearl,* and *Roebuck,* for October 19, 20, and 21, 1777; *PMHB*, Vol. XXXVIII, p. 220, "Log, *Eagle.*"

4. *Ibid.*, October 21, 1777.

5. *PMHB*, Vol. VI, p. 51, "Montresor"; Almon, *Remembrancer*, pp. 428–431, Lord Howe to Stephens, October 23, 1777.

6. Edward J. Lowell, *The Hessians and the other German Auxiliaries of Great Britain in the Revolutionary War*, p. 204. Lowell drew on the manuscript journals of the Jäger Corps, Grenadier Battalion von Minnigerode, Knyphausen's report, and the journal of Captain Johann Ewald for his narrative. Howe, *Narrative*, p. 28.

7. *Ibid.*, pp. 28–29; Almon, *Remembrancer*, pp. 428–431, Lord Howe to Stephens, October 25, 1777.

8. Lowell, *Hessians*, p. 204; *Proceedings of the American Antiquarian Society*, "British Account," p. 89; William L. Clements Library, Von Jungkenn Manuscripts, Vol. 7:5; *PMHB*, Vol. VI, p. 52, "Montresor"; *Ibid.*, Vol. LX, p. 35, "Letters of Major Baurmeister During the Philadelphia Campaign, 1777–1778."

9. Wallace McGeorge wrote that this road was little more than a bridle path in 1777, not being designated a road or turnpike until 1792.

10. Von Jungkenn MSS, Vol. 7:5; Hazard, *Register of Pennsylvania*, Vol. III, p. 181, Samuel Ward to Washington, October 23, 1777. Ward reported that the Hessians left Haddonfield at three in the morning.

11. Frank H. Stewart, comp. and ed., *Notes on Old Gloucester County*, Vol. III, p. 78, "Jonas Cattell's Reminiscences of the Revolution."

12. *Ibid.*, pp. 75–76.

13. Edward Martin Stone, "The Invasion of Canada in 1775," *Collections of the Rhode Island Historical Society*, Vol. VI, p. 75. Stone included a biographical sketch of Major Simeon Thayer based exclusively on the papers of Thayer, and including the major's Journal of 1775.

14. As previously stated, the fort's armament was fourteen cannon (Chastellux, *Travels*, Vol. I, p. 157). The fort is known to have had at various times eighteen-pounders, six-pounders, four-pounders, three-pounders, swivels, and howitzers, but in what precise numbers cannot be determined. The British return of cannon found after the evacuation

of the fort included at least one of each of those enumerated. (See Almon, *Remembrancer*, Vol. V, p. 503.) However, those found by the British on November 23, 1777, cannot be identified as those in the fort on October 22; a few were taken off by the retreating Americans. At least five have been found during the last century, two when the foundations for the New Jersey monument were dug in 1905–06, and a score of years later three were found by using a radio detector. Stewart, *Red Bank*, p. 24, and *Notes on Old Gloucester County*, Vol. II, p. 104.

15. Logan Pearsall Smith, "Two Generations of Quakers" (includes an old diary of Job Whitall, *Atlantic Monthly*, July 1903. For a slightly different version, see Stewart, *Gloucester County*, Vol. II, pp. 258–259. See also note 66.

16. Stone, "Invasion of Canada," p. 75; Henry Lee, *Memoirs of the War in the Southern Department of the United States*, 97–99; Dawson, *Smith Papers*, p. 88.

17. Hazard, *Register of Pennsylvania*, Vol. III, p. 181, Robert Ballard to Washington, October 23, 1777.

18. Von Jungkenn MSS, Vol. 7:5; Lowell, *Hessians*, p. 204.

19. George W. Greene, *Life of Nathanael Greene*, Vol. I, p. 489 (quoting from an interview with Dr. Peter Turner).

20. Lowell, *Hessians*, p. 205fn., quoting the Journal of the Grenadier Battalion von Minnigerode.

21. Mrs. Williams, *Biography of Revolutionary Heroes*, pp. 222–223. One half of the volume is devoted to the life of Captain Stephen Olney. A large portion of the narrative contains direct quotations from Olney's manuscript memoirs of his war experiences.

22. Lee, *Memoirs of the War*, p. 98; Lowell, *Hessians*, p. 206fn.; American Philosophical Society, Sol Feinstone Collection, "Revolutionary War Dairy, Campaign 1777; Proceedings of the American Antiquarian Society, p. 90, "British Account."

23. Johann Carl Buettner, *Narrative of Johann Carl Buettner in the American Revolution*, p. 2; Lowell, *Hessians*, p. 205; Von Jungkenn MSS, Vol. 7:5.

24. Castellux, *Travels*, Vol. I, p. 158.

25. A deep ditch had been dug in front of the new rampart in the abandoned section of the fort. Gloucester County (New Jersey) Archives, Narrative of Thomas Stokes.

26. C. Stedman, *The History of the Origin, Progress, and Termination of the American War*, Vol. I, p. 302.

27. Williams, *Revolutionary Heroes*, pp. 223, 225.

28. Isaac Mickle, *Reminiscences of Old Gloucester*, p. 69.

29. Buettner, *Narrative*, p. 2.

30. Henry B. Dawson, *The Battles of the United States by Sea and Land*, Vol. I, pp. 356–357, Dispatch of Sir William Howe to Lord George Germain, October 25, 1777.

31. Brief summaries of contemporary accounts are found in Hazard, *Register of Pennsylvania*, Vol. III, p. 181, Samuel Ward to Washington, October 23, 1777, Robert Ballard to Washington, October 23, 1777; Dawson, *Battles*, Vol. I, pp. 356–357, Dispatch of Sir William Howe to Lord George Germain, October 25, 1777; Penna. MSS, William Bradford to Thomas Wharton, October 26, 1777 (listed in *P.A.*, First Series, Vol. V, pp. 707–709 as October 27); *Ibid.*, Joseph Reed Papers (originals in New-York Historical Society), Reel 2, Joseph Reed to Thomas Wharton, October 27, 1777" (also in *Life and Correspondence of Joseph Reed*, by William B. Reed); Williams, *Revolutionary Heroes*, extensive quotations from manuscript of Captain Olney; Greene, *Nathanael Greene*, quotes experiences of Dr. Peter Turner and other Rhode Island soldiers; Edward J. Lowell, *The Hessians and the other German Auxiliaries*, and Max von Eelking, *The German Allied Troops in North America* are based on the journals of the various grenadier battalions, the Jäger Corps, and the Knyphausen report and the journals of individual Hessian soldiers; Buettner, *Narrative*, and Chastellux, *Travels* (Mauduit's version); also, many interesting accounts of local residents may be found in the Gloucester County Historical Society and the writings of Frank H. Stewart. See Bibliography for comprehensive list of accounts.

32. Stewart, *Notes on Old Gloucester County*, Vol. II, p. 104.

33. "G.W. Papers," Reel 44, J. Adam Comstock to Washington, October 25, 1777.

34. If Donop was able to converse in English, it raises some speculation as to why Lieutenant Colonel Stewart was assigned to his staff as interpreter, unless it was believed that the presence of an English officer would aid the Hessians in being accepted by the Americans residing along the line of march.

35. Chastellux, *Travels*, Vol. I, p. 159–160.

36. Williams, *Revolutionary Heroes*, p. 225.

37. Stone, *Invasion of Canada*, p. 75.

38. Stewart, *Red Bank*, p. 12. This quotation, sometimes with slightly different wording is found in most accounts of the battle.

39. *PMHB*, Vol. LXII, pp. 500–501, "Letters from a Hessian Mercenary," by Hans Huth, tr. C. V. Easum.

40. Ludwig von Clausen, *The Revolutionary Journal of Baron Ludwig von Clausen*, Evelyn M. Acomb, ed., p. 122.

41. Dawson, *Battles*, Vol. I, p. 356–357, Dispatch of General Howe to Lord George Germain, October 25, 1777; Lowell, *Hessians*, p. 206

(quoting the Grenadier and Jäger Journals). Some Hessian sources spell the name of the new Hessian commander "Linsingen."

42. Dawson, *Battles*, Vol. I, p. 356–357, Dispatch of General Howe to Lord George Germain, October 25, 1777.

43. Penna. MSS, Joseph Reed Papers, Reel 2, Joseph Reed to Thomas Wharton, October 27, 1777.

44. Stewart, *Notes on Old Gloucester County*, Vol. III, p. 79, "Jonas Cattell's Reminiscences of the Revolution."

45. Von Jungkenn MSS, Vol. 7:5.

46. Stewart, *Notes on Old Gloucester County*, Vol. III, pp. 67, 76.

47. *PMHB*, Vol. VI, p. 52, "Montresor"; *Proceedings of the American Antiquarian Society*, p. 89, "British Account."

48. Washington, *Writings*, Vol. IX, pp. 417–418.

49. Ebenezer David, *A Rhode Island Chaplain in the Revolution: Letters of Ebenezer David to Nicholas Brown, 1775–1778*, Jeanette D. Black and William G. Roelker, eds., pp. 53–54.

50. "G.W. Papers," Reel 44, J. Adam Comstock to Washington, October 25, 1777.

51. Williams, *Revolutionary Heroes*, p. 225.

52. Smith, "Quakers," Whitall Diary, October 23, 1777; Stewart, *Notes on Old Gloucester County*, Vol. II, p. 259, "Diary of Job Whitall."

53. Amandus Johnson, tr., *Journal and Biography of Nicholas Collin, 1746–1831*, pp. 240–241. Other eyewitness accounts can be found in the several special studies of the battle and in Stewart, *Notes on Old Gloucester County*, Vols. II and III.

54. Buettner, *Narrative*, p. 4.

55. Von Jungkenn MSS, Vol. 7:5.

56. *PMHB*, Vol. LX, p. 36, "Letters of Major Baurmeister During the Philadelphia Campaign," Bernard H. Uhlendorf and Edna Vosper, eds.

57. *Ibid.*, p. 35; Lowell, *Hessians*, p. 208fn., "Knyphausen Report."

58. Von Jungkenn MSS, Vol. 7:5; Scull, *Evelyns*, p. 247, anonymous letter from Philadelphia to Earl Harcourt, October 26, 1777.

59. Charles I. Bushnell, ed., *Crumbs for Antiquarians*, Vol. I, pp. 9–10, "Memoir of Samuel Smith, 1776–1778."

60. Chastellux, *Travels*, Vol. I, p. 157.

61. *Archives of the State of New Jersey*, Vol. I, pp. 491–493; Stewart, *Notes on Old Gloucester County*, Vol. III, p. 79, "Jonas Cattell's Reminiscences of the Revolution."

62. Hazard, *Register of Pennsylvania*, Vol. III, p. 181, Sam Ward to Washington, October 23, 1777; "G.W. Papers," Reel 44, J. Adam Comstock to Washington, October 25, 1777.

63. See note 57.

64. William B. Reed, *Life and Correspondence of Joseph Reed*, Vol. II, pp. 328–330. The postscript to this letter is also reproduced in *P.A.*, First Series, Vol. V, pp. 702–703, J. Reed to [?], October 25, 1777.

65. Hazard, *Register of Pennsylvania*, Vol. III, p. 181, Sam Ward to Washington, October 23, 1777.

66. Smith, "Quakers"; Stewart, *Notes on Old Gloucester County*, Vol. II, pp. 258–259.

67. Washington, *Writings*, Vol. IX, pp. 422–423, 424–425; "G.W. Papers," Reel 44, J. Adam Comstock to Washington, October 25, 1777.

68. Orderly Book, Greene, p. 51.

69. Bushnell, ed., *Crumbs for Antiquarians*, Vol. I, p. 7, "Memoir of Samuel Smith."

70. Most elements of the British fleet were anchored in the Delaware River from Chester to Reedy Island and had no part in the engagement on the river. Lord Howe's flagship, the *Eagle*, was anchored near Chester. The squadron, which participated in the actions on the Delaware from October 1 through November 15, 1777, was made up of the following men-of-war:

Augusta, Captain Francis Reynolds	500 men, 64 guns
Somerset, Captain George Ourry	500 men, 64 guns
Isis, Captain William Cornwallis	350 men, 50 guns
Roebuck, Captain Andrew Hamond	280 men, 44 guns
Pearl, Captain John Linzee	220 men, 32 guns
Liverpool, Captain Henry Bellew	200 men, 28 guns
Camilla, Captain Charles Phipps	160 men, 28 guns
Merlin, Captain Samuel Reeve	125 men, 18 guns
Zebra, Captain John Tollemache	125 men, 14 guns
Cornwallis (galley), Lieutenant Johnston	40 men, 1 gun
Vigilant (armed ship), Captain John Henry	150 men, 16 guns
Fury (armed hulk), Lieutenant John Botham	— 3 guns

A few historians have listed the *Somerset* as having seventy guns. It was of the same class as the *Augusta*, and all sources checked list sixty-four guns. A roster of the men-of-war in Lord Howe's fleet is found at the American Philosophical Society, Sol Feinstone Collection. All frigates on this roster were not in the Delaware; several were with Admiral John Byron or on detached service.

The *Cornwallis* was a galley constructed along the same general lines as those in the Pennsylvania navy. She carried one thirty-two-pounder in her bow and had several swivels.

The *Vigilant*, a converted merchantman, was armed with sixteen twenty-four-pounders on the starboard side. Her port side carried ballast to offset the weight of the cannon. Both the *Vigilant* and the *Fury* carried skeleton crews. To fill out their complements seamen were transferred from the *Eagle* and other ships on October 22 and November 15. The *Fury* carried three cannons. On November 23, Lord Howe wrote that she carried three eighteen-pounders; On November 28, Sir William Howe wrote that she had three twenty-four-pounders. Such differences are occasionally noted in official records. Lord Howe and Sir William Howe are the best sources for certain details. For information on the armament of the *Vigilant* and *Fury* see Almon, *Remembrancer*, Vol. V, pp. 499–502, Lord Howe to Mr. Stephens, Admiralty Office, November 23, 1777, Sir William Howe to Lord George Germain, November 28, 1777. These letters were also reproduced in Dawson, *Battles*, Vol. I, pp. 364–367.

71. Logs for October 23, 1777, *Camilla, Pearl,* and *Roebuck; PMHB,* Vol. XXXVIII, pp. 221–222, 226, Captain's Log of the *Eagle* and Log of *Eagle,* October 23, 1777.

72. "G.W. Papers," Reel 44, Fleury Diary, October 22 and 23, 1777, d'Arendt to Washington, October 24, 1777.

73. Stedman, *American War,* Vol. I, p. 303.

74. Almon, *Remembrancer,* Vol. V, pp. 428–431, Lord Howe to Stephens, October 25, 1777.

75. *Ibid.*

76. The *Augusta* has variously been described as a frigate, ship-of-the-line, and ship. America's foremost authority on the sailing era, Howard I. Chapelle, in his definitive study *The History of American Sailing Ships,* pp. 51–52, describes eighteenth-century sailing navies, "The largest type was the battleship, known as the 'ship-of-the-line' or, for the sake of brevity, 'liner.' This class included ships carrying from 70 to 140 guns on two or more completely armed decks. . . . At the time of the American Revolution, some navies classed ships carrying as few as 60 guns as of the 'line,' but these ships were dropped from this rating in nearly all navies during the last part of the eighteenth century. . . . In some navies there were vessels carrying from 44 to 64 guns which were classed merely as 'ships' with the number of guns prefixed. The '64-gun ship' of the British navy was an example. . . ." This point was confirmed in discussions with Mr. Chapelle and Mr. Thomas Hornsby, another authority on this period; therefore I have classified the Augusta as a "64-gun ship."

77. Logs for October 23, 1777, *Camilla, Pearl,* and *Roebuck; PMHB,* Vol. XXXVIII, pp. 221–222, 226, Captain's Log of the *Eagle,* October 23, 1777, and Log of *Eagle,* October 23, 1777.

78. *P.A.,* First Series, Vol. V, pp. 707–709, Bradford to Wharton, October 27 (26), 1777.

79. Sparks, ed., *Correspondence*, Vol. II, pp. 12–13, Hazelwood to Washington, October 23, 1777.

80. *Proceedings of the American Antiquarian Society*, New Series, Vol. XL, p. 89, "British Account."

81. Logs for October 23, 1777, *Roebuck, Pearl; PMHB*, Vol. XXXVIII, pp. 221–222, 226, Captain's Log of the *Eagle* and Log of *Eagle*, October 23, 1777; Almon, *Remembrancer*, Vol. V, pp. 428–431, Lord Howe to Stephens, October 25, 1777; Penna. MSS, Joseph Reed Papers, Reel 2, Reed to Wharton, October 27, 1777.

82. Logs, *Camilla, Pearl, Roebuck*, October 23, 1777; *PMHB*, Vol. XXXVIII, pp. 221–222, Log *Eagle*, October 23, 24, 1777; *P.A.*, First Series, Vol. V, pp. 707–709, Bradford to Wharton, October 27 (26), 1777; Sparks, *Correspondence*, Vol. II, pp. 18–21, Hazelwood to Washington, October 26, 1777.

83. Ambrose Searle, *The American Journal of Ambrose Searle*, Edward H. Tatum, Jr., ed., p. 261; *PMHB*, Vol. VI, p. 53, "Montresor"; Almon, *Remembrancer*, Vol. V, pp. 428–431, Lord Howe to Stephens, October 25, 1777.

84. *P.A.*, First Series, Vol. V, pp. 703–704, Extract of a letter from Hugh Smyth, Esq., Postmaster, 1777.

85. "Drinker," p. 61.

86. *PMHB*, Vol. II, pp. 291–292, "Military Operations near Philadelphia in the Campaign of 1777–8, a letter of Thomas Paine to Benjamin Franklin, May 16, 1778."

87. HSP, John Fanning Watson Manuscripts.

88. Searle, *Journal*, p. 261; Almon, *Remembrancer*, Vol. V, pp. 428–431, Lord Howe to Stephens, October 25, 1777; *PMHB*, Vol. VI, p. 53, "Montresor."

89. "G.W. Papers," Reel 44, d'Arendt to Washington, October 24, 1777.

90. *PMHB*, Vol. VI, p. 53, "Montresor"; *Proceedings of the American Antiquarian Society*, New Series, Vol. XL, pp. 89–90, "British Account."

91. Penna. MSS, Bradford to Wharton, October 26, 1777, reproduced in *P.A.*, First Series, Vol. V, pp. 707–709, but dated October 27. This has led to the error of placing Hazelwood and the crews on the wrecks on October 26.

92. Sparks, ed., *Correspondence*, Vol. II, pp. 18–21, Hazelwood to Washington, October 26, 1777; *P.A.*, First Series, Vol. V, pp. 722–723, State Navy Board to Wharton, October 30, 1777.

93. "G.W. Papers," Reel 45, Daniel Clymer to Washington, October 26, 1777; Washington, *Writings*, Vol. IX, pp. 448–449.

94. *Proceedings of the American Antiquarian Society*, New Series,

Vol. XL, pp. 90–91, "British Account"; Logs, *Roebuck* and *Camilla*, October 26–30, 1777.

95. *C.R.*, Vol. XI, p. 662.

96. Wallace McGeorge, *The Frigate Augusta*, Lord Commissioners of the Admiralty to Dr. Wallace McGeorge, May 6, 1905.

97. McGeorge, *Augusta*.

98. Penna. MSS, Bradford to Wharton, October 26, 1777.

CHAPTER XI

1. HSP, Laurens, *Correspondence*, Vol. I, Laurens to Washington, October 25, 1777.

2. Washington, *Writings*, Vol. IX, pp. 422–423.

3. *Ibid.*, p. 431.

4. The Continental Navy Board was headquartered at Bordentown, N.J., and was composed of Francis Hopkinson and John Wharton.

5. Washington, *Writings*, Vol. IX, pp. 436–437.

6. *Ibid.*, pp. 445–447.

7. "G.W. Papers," Reel 44, Continental Navy Board to Washington, October 25, 1777.

8. *Ibid.*, Reel 45, Muster Rolls of the *Washington* and *Effingham* on October 26, 1777; *PMHB*, Vol. XVIII, pp. 346–347, "Defences Philadelphia," Continental Navy Board to Washington, October 26, 1777.

9. Washington, *Writings*, Vol. IX, pp. 447–448.

10. "G.W. Papers," Reel 45, Continental Congress to Washington, November 4, 1777.

11. *PMHB*, Vol. XIX, pp. 75–76, 82–84, "Defences Philadelphia," Continental Navy Board to Washington, November 10, 1777, Washington to Francis Hopkinson and John Wharton, November 9, 1777.

12. "G.W. Papers," Reel 44, Benjamin Eyre to Washington, October 25, 1777; *P.A.*, First Series, Vol. V, pp. 721–722, 747, Hazelwood to Wharton, October 29, 1777, Supreme Executive Council to Hazelwood, November 6, 1777.

13. "G.W. Papers," Reel 44, State Navy Board to Washington, October 14, 1777; Washington, *Writings*, Vol. IX, pp. 369, 370; See note 66, Chapter IX; Sparks, *Correspondence*, Vol. II, pp. 18–21, Hazelwood to Washington, October 26, 1777.

14. Washington, *Writings*, Vol. IX, p. 460.

15. *Ibid.*, pp. 461, 469, "General Orders"; Hugh F. Rankin, *The North Carolina Continentals*, pp. 122, 140.

16. HSP, Gratz Collection, Officers of the Revolution, Box 17, Case 4, State Navy Board (Bradford) to Washington, March 4, 1778. Bradford's reply to Washington's request for return of troops on loan to the State Navy indicated that the North Carolina troops were on duty downriver. The number of men sent by Washington is confirmed by the returns of the North Carolina Line which, for the period of November 3–December 31, 1777, shows an average of 120 men "on command." A few may have been on scouting or foraging expeditions, but the majority were with Hazelwood; see Walter Clark, ed., *State Records of North Carolina*, Vol. XI, pp. 667, 676, 690, 700, 703; *P.A.*, First Series, Vol. V, p. 747, Supreme Executive Council to Hazelwood, November 6, 1777.

17. *P.A.*, First Series, Vol. V, pp. 706–707, 722–723, 748–749, William Crispin to Wharton, October 26, 1777, State Navy Board (Blewer) to Wharton, October 30, 1777, Supreme Executive Council to Crispin, November 6, 1777.

18. William Cornelius Bradford was a nephew of Colonel Bradford of the State Navy Board. Bradford served faithfully until the fleet was disbanded. See Wallace, *Bradford*, p. 260.

19. "G.W. Papers," Reel 44, d'Arendt to Washington, October 24, 1777; Dawson, "Smith Papers," p. 88; HSP, Committee of Safety Papers, 15 C, "Report: Committee for Viewing Fort Island and the Shore Contiguous." This report is in the handwriting of Joseph Reed.

20. "G.W. Papers," Reel 45, Hazelwood to d'Arendt and Smith, October 26, 1777.

21. Dawson, "Smith Papers," p. 89.

22. "G.W. Papers," Reel 44, Fleury Journal, October 23 and 24, 1777.

23. *Ibid.*, Reel 45, Fleury to Washington, October 26, 1777, d'Arendt to Washington, October 26 with added material dated October 27, 1777.

24. *Ibid.*, Reel 45, Fleury to Washington, October 28, 1777, d'Arendt to Washington, October 29, 1777, includes Fleury's Journal for October 27, 28, and 29. At that time d'Arendt was in a house near Red Bank. Italics are d'Arendt's.

25. *Ibid.*, Reel 45, Fleury's Journal, October 29, 1777.

26. *Ibid.*, Reel 44, d'Arendt to Washington, October 24, 1777; Reel 45, footnote of letter Washington to Smith, November 4, 1777, signed by John Laurens. This letter is in *PMHB*, Vol. XVIII, pp. 480–481, "Defences Philadelphia," pp. 472–473, Fleury's Journal, November 3, 1777. Letters from Fleury and d'Arendt were sometimes written jointly, and on other occasions individual letters were dispatched to headquarters under the same cover.

27. *PMHB*, Vol. XVIII, pp. 344–345, "Defences Philadelphia," Smith to Washington, October 26, 1777.

28. Washington, *Writings*, Vol. IX, pp. 458–459; *PMHB*, Vol. XVIII, pp. 479–480, Washington to Varnum, November 4, 1777.

29. *New Jersey Society*, Orderly Book, Greene, p. 51.

30. Washington, *Writings*, Vol. IX, p. 444. Fitzpatrick believes that the officer may be Robert Ralston, adjutant to the First Pennsylvania Brigade. The author has checked the muster rolls of the Pennsylvania militia and was unable to find any officer by this name.

31. "G.W. Papers," Reel 45, Returns of the Muster of Men present and fit for duty in the garrison at Red Bank commanded by Colonel Greene, October 27, and November 17, 1777.

32. Washington, *Writings*, Vol. IX, pp. 455–457.

33. *PMHB*, Vol. XVIII, pp. 475–476, "Defences Philadelphia," Varnum to Washington, November 3, 1777.

34. Logs, *Roebuck* and *Camilla*, November 5, 1775; *PMHB*, Vol. XVIII, pp. 483–487, "Defences Philadelphia," Varnum to Washington, November 6, 1777.

35. *Ibid.*

36. *Ibid.*

37. HSP, Henry Laurens Correspondence, Vol. I.

38. Ford, ed., *Continental Congress*, Vol. IX, p. 862.

39. *P.A.*, First Series, Vol. VI, pp. 30–32, Armstrong to Wharton, November 23, 1777.

40. Washington, *Writings*, Vol. IX, p. 445, Vol. X, pp. 9–10; *PMHB*, Vol. XVIII, pp. 471–472, "Defences Philadelphia," Washington to Hazelwood, November 2, 1777.

41. *Ibid.*, pp. 487–488, 492–494, Washington to Varnum, November 7, 1777, Varnum to Washington, November 8, 1777.

42. *Ibid.*

43. *PMHB*, Vol. II, p. 290, "Military Operations near Philadelphia in the Campaign of 1777–8, described in a letter of Thomas Paine to Benjamin Franklin, May 16, 1778."

44. Washington, *Writings*, Vol. IX, pp. 457, 468–469, 473–474, 485–487; "G.W. Papers," Reel 45, Livingston to Newcomb, November 5, 1777.

45. *PMHB*, Vol. XVIII, pp. 472–473, 476–477, 482, "Defences Philadelphia," Fleury's Journal, November 3, 1777, Smith to Washington, November 3 and 4, 1777.

46. Washington, *Writings*, Vol. IX, pp. 472–473.

47. Almon, *Remembrancer*, Vol. V, pp. 499–501. Lord Howe to Stephens, November 23, 1777; *PMHB*, Vol. XVIII, pp. 478, 494, "De-

fences Philadelphia," Fleury's Journal, November 3 (night), 1777, Henry Lee to Washington, November 8, 1777; *Ibid.*, Vol. XIX, pp. 73–74, Potter to Washington (November 1, 1777); *Ibid.*, Vol. VI, pp. 50–57, "Montresor."

48. *Ibid.*

49. *PMHB*, Vol. XVIII, pp. 494–495, "Defences Philadelphia," Lee to Washington, November 8, 1777, Vol. XIX, pp. 73–74, Potter to Washington (November 8, 1777), Vol. XXXVIII, pp. 222–223, Log, *Eagle.*

50. *PMHB*, Vol. XIX, pp. 72–73, "Defences Philadelphia," Fleury's Journal, November 8, 1777.

51. Scull, ed., *Evelyns*, p. 257, "Extracts from the Journals and Note-Books of Capt. John Montresor."

52. *PMHB*, Vol. VI, pp. 55–57, "Montresor"; *Collections of the New-York Historical Society for the Years 1883–1884*, "Kemble Papers," Vol. I, pp. 526–534.

53. *HSP Bulletin #1*, "Letters from Major Clark, Jr. to General Washington during the Occupation of Philadelphia by the British Army," pp. 5–8, Letters of November 3, 4, and 8, 1777; *Proceedings of the American Antiquarian Society*, p. 91, "British Accounts."

54. *Ibid.*; "G.W. Papers," Reel 45, J. Rumfort to Potter, November 11, 1777; *PMHB*, Vol. VI, p. 57, "Montresor." Apparently, according to these accounts, Wilson arrived off New Castle between November 3 and 5.

55. *HSP Bull.*, "Clark," p. 8, letter of November 8, 1777.

CHAPTER XII

1. Smith consistently refers to the Virginia regiment as having only 120 rank and file, whereas Washington's instruction to Lieutenant Colonel John Green ordered two hundred Virginia Continentals to march to Fort Mifflin. Writing to both Smith and Colonel Christopher Greene on October 18, he stated that "Lieutenant Colonel John Green marched this morning to reinforce the Garrison at Fort Mifflin, with a detachment of two hundred men." Washington, *Writings*, Vol. IX, pp. 392–393, 396.

2. *PMHB*, Vol. XIX, p. 79, "Defences Philadelphia," Smith to Washington, November 9, 1777; Dawson, "Smith Papers," p. 87.

3. *PMHB*, Vol. XIX, pp. 80–81, "Defences Philadelphia," Fleury's Journal, November 9, night, 1777.

4. Cornell University, Jared Sparks Collection, map by Fleury of Fort Mifflin on November 9, 1777.

5. Dawson, "Smith Papers," p. 86; Almon, *Remembrancer*, Vol. V, p. 503, Return of Ordnance and stores found in Mud Island Fort . . . the 16th of November, 1777.

6. *HSP*, Major John André's Map of Mud Island and the Operations for reducing it, November 15, 1777; Cornell University, Jared Sparks Collection, map by Fleury of Fort Mifflin on November 9, 1777; *PMHB*, Vol. VI, pp. 49–57, "Montresor"; Almon, *Remembrancer*, Vol. V, p. 499, Lord Howe to Mr. Stephens, November 23, 1777.

7. Carcase or Carcass, according to Smith, was two feet square, filled with combustibles and having sharp hooks which permitted it to attach itself to the wooden shingles of the barracks and other buildings. Dawson, "Smith Papers," p. 89. Military authorities have defined a carcase as a hollow shell, wrapped with an incendiary material, and use to set fire to wooden buildings and ships.

8. *PMHB*, Vol. VI, p. 57, "Montresor"; *Ibid.*, Vol. XIX, pp. 80–81, 84–86, "Defences Philadelphia," Fleury's Journal, November 10, 1777, Smith to Washington, November 10, 1777, Varnum to Washington, November 10, 1777.

9. *Ibid.*

10. *HSP*, John Fanning Watson Manuscripts, "Diary of Mr. Miller, a magistrate of Germantown, November 10, 1777."

11. *PMHB*, Vol. XIX, pp. 80–81, 84–86, "Defences Philadelphia," Fleury's Journal, November 10, 1777, Varnum to Washington, November 10, 1777.

12. Martin, *Private Yankee Doodle*, pp. 88–89. Martin's recall of his activities is chronologically confusing for this period. He was a member of Colonel Chandler's Eighth Connecticut Continental Regiment. His reminiscences state that he was in Fort Mifflin at the time of the burning of the *Augusta* on October 23, an impossibility as Chandler's regiment was a part of Varnum's brigade, which did not arrive at Woodbury until November 2. Martin claimed that he was in the fort for a fortnight. To have served two weeks in the fort, Martin would have had to enter the fort on November 2, the day of his regiment's arrival in the vicinity, and remain there without relief. Varnum apparently relieved part of the garrison every forty-eight hours, and Martin may have been in one of these relief detachments. However, the only verifiable dates for Chandler's regiment being in the garrison are November 13, 14, and 15. Chandler accompanied Major Thayer when he assumed command, and the earliest assignable date for Thayer arriving at Fort Mifflin is November 12. See Greene, *Nathanael Greene*, Vol. I, p. 502; Benjamin Cowell, *Spirit of '76 in Rhode Island*, pp. 296–297 (extract of

letter of Colonel Israel Angell, February 17, 1778). The greatest value of Martin's narrative is in his graphic description of the vicissitudes in the life of a private soldier at Fort Mifflin; Cornell University, Jared Sparks Collection, map of Fort Mifflin by Fleury, November 9, 1777.

13. Log, *Roebuck*, November 12, 1777.

14. "G.W. Papers," Reel 45, Fleury's Journal, November 11, 1777; *PMHB*, Vol. XIX, p. 238, "Defences Delaware," Smith to Varnum, November 11, 1777.

15. Dawson, "Smith Papers," p. 89–90.

16. *PMHB*, Vol. XIX, pp. 236–238, "Defences Philadelphia," Smith to Varnum, November 11, 1777, Varnum to Washington, November 11, 1777 (2 letters). It would be interesting to know the extent of the damages to the masonry wall and by whom and when the repairs were made.

17. *Ibid.*, John Laurens, *The Army Correspondence of Colonel John Laurens in the Years 1777–8*, William Gilmore Simms, ed., p. 75. In the four letters written to his father, Henry Laurens, Laurens is a reliable chronicler, although he occasionally echoes Smith's evaluation of the navy. His information is a compilation of the letters of Smith and Varnum and the Journal of Fleury.

18. Dawson, "Smith Papers," p. 90; *PMHB*, Vol. XIX, p. 242, "Defences Philadelphia," Smith to Washington, November 12, 1777.

19. *Ibid.*, p. 237, Varnum to Washington, November 11, 1777, 12 P.M. *Ibid.*, Vol. VI, p. 57, "Montresor."

20. *Ibid.*; André, *Journal*, p. 63; *PMHB*, Vol. I, p. 27, "Morton."

21. Lee, *Memoirs*, p. 103.

22. *PMHB*, Vol. XIX, p. 242–243, "Defences Philadelphia," Smith to Washington, November 12, 1777.

23. *Ibid.*, Vol. VI, p. 189, "Montresor." The guard boats *Tormentor*, *Resolution*, and *Firebrand* were lost during the actions of October and November 1777. As the *Firebrand* carried a two-pounder cannon, the boat deserting was probably the *Tormentor* or the *Resolution*. Logs, *Camilla*, *Roebuck*, November 12 and 13, 1777; *PMHB*, Vol. XXXVIII, p. 224, Log *Eagle*, November 12, 1777.

24. *Ibid.*, Vol. VI, p. 189, "Montresor."

25. *Ibid.*, Vol. XIX, pp. 237, 241–43, "Defences Philadelphia," Varnum to Washington, November 11 (12 o'clock), 1777, Varnum to Washington, November 12, 1777, Smith to Washington, November 12, 1777; Washington, *Writings*, Vol. X, pp. 48–50.

26. Martin, *Private Yankee Doodle*, pp. 88–89; *PMHB*, Vol. VI, p. 189, "Montresor."

27. Cowell, *Spirit of '76*, pp. 296, 299; Varnum, writing almost nine

years later, states that Thayer assumed command on November 12. Angell in his letter of February 17, 1778, notes that Thayer went over to the island on November 13. Both officers are undoubtedly correct, as Thayer accepted his command on the night of November 12, but did not pass over to the island fort until the next morning.

28. *PMHB*, Vol. VI, pp. 190–191, "Montresor."

29. *Ibid.;* Logs, *Camilla* and *Roebuck*, November 13 and 14, 1777.

30. *PMHB*, Vol. XIX, pp. 239–240, 243–244, 249–250, "Defences Philadelphia," Washington to Varnum, November 13, 1777. Nathanael Greene to Washington, November 14, 1777 (8 p.m.), Potter to Washington, November 12, 1777; HSP, Wayne MSS, Vol. IV, p. 38, Wayne to Richard Peters, November 18, 1777; Washington, *Writings*, Vol. X, pp. 68–70, 73–77; Charles J. Stille, *Major General Anthony Wayne*, pp. 105–106.

31. *PMHB*, Vol. XIX, p. 244, "Defences Philadelphia," Fleury Journal, November 13, 1777 (at night); Martin, *Private Yankee Doodle*, p. 89.

32. *PMHB*, Vol. VI, p. 190, "Montresor."

33. The location of the second battery has been the subject of much speculation. Villefranche's excellent map of the proposed fortifications for the Delaware in 1779, prepared under the direction of General Duportail, has led many to believe that it was located farther up the river near Leonard's Lane. This map was the result of a 1779 survey and did not purport to identify the location of the forts and batteries of 1777. Some of the 1777 fortifications are shown because their sites agree with those selected by Duportail for 1779 defenses, such as Fort Mifflin. Most contemporary maps are unreliable for pinpointing the locations of these small batteries.

Little Mantua Creek emptied into the Delaware slightly more than one-half mile above Mantua Creek. Today the mouth of this little stream is blocked by fill from the dredging operations of the U.S. Army Engineer Corps and drains into a marsh area. Varnum is the authority for the location of the small fascine battery erected on a slight eminence at the mouth of Mantua Creek. *PMHB*, Vol. XVIII, pp. 483–487, "Defences Philadelphia," Varnum to Washington, November 6, 1777. Robertson, commander of the Royal Engineers, stated that the second battery was 800 yards above Mantua Creek. Robertson, p. 154. Bradford stated that it was near the Tench Francis House. *P.A.*, First Series, Vol. VI, p. 11, Bradford to Wharton, November 16, 1777. The opinion of an eminent military engineer, Robertson, and Bradford's statement that it was near the home of Tench Francis place this battery below the south bank of Little Mantua Creek. There were two houses on the Tench

Francis property, one called Paradise Farm, but both were below the little creek. See also *PMHB*, Vol. XIX, pp. 246–247, "Defences Philadelphia," Varnum to Washington, November 14, 1777 (at 4:30 a.m.).

34. *PMHB*, Vol. VI, p. 190, "Montresor"; *Ibid.*, Vol. XIX, p. 245, "Defences Philadelphia," Fleury's Journal, November 14, 1777; André, *Journal*, p. 63.

35. *PMHB*, Vol. XIX, pp. 241–242, 244–246, 363, "Defences Philadelphia," Fleury's Journal, November 14, 1777, Varnum to Washington, November 12, 1777 (at sunset) and November 15, 1777 (11:00 a.m.)

36. *Ibid.*, pp. 244–246, 247, 248, Fleury's Journal, November 14, 1777, Varnum to Washington, November 14, 1777, Thayer to Varnum, November 14, 1777; Laurens, *Correspondence*, pp. 76–77.

37. *PMHB*, Vol. XIX, pp. 249–250, "Defences Philadelphia," Nathanael Greene to Washington, November 14, 1777 (at 8:00 p.m.); *Ibid.*, Vol. II, p. 292, "Military Operations near Philadelphia, Paine to Franklin, May 16, 1778."

38. *Ibid.*, Vol. XIX, pp. 366–368, Baron d'Arendt on Fort Mifflin.

39. *Ibid.*, p. 238, Smith to Varnum, November 11, 1777.

40. "G.W. Papers," Reel 45, In Council of War held on board the Chatham Galley, Nov. 14th, 1777; *PMHB*, Vol. XIX, pp. 359–361, "Defences Philadelphia," Hazelwood to Washington, November 15, 1777; *P.A.*, First Series, Vol. VI, Council of War on Board the Fleet, 1777.

41. Logs, *Camilla* and *Roebuck*, November 15 and 16, 1777. (The logs of the other British frigates are virtually the same.); "G.W. Papers," Reel 44, Fleury's Journal, October 15, 1777 (should be November 15). Fleury and other American accounts mention six frigates and one galley in the main channel, but this is contrary to British accounts. The *Camilla* and *Zebra* were used as support vessels and were stationed in the lower back channel below Hog Island. Robertson, *Diaries*, p. 155; *PMHB*, Vol. XIX, pp. 363, 370–371, "Defences Philadelphia," Varnum to Washington, November 15 (11:00 a.m.) and November 16 (11:15 a.m.), 1777.

42. Cowell, *Spirit of '76*, p. 297; *New Jersey Archives*. Second Series, Vol. I, p. 495, Newspaper Extracts, Letter from a Gentleman on board the Sloop the Speedwell, dated November 22, 1777. The correspondent to the *New Jersey Gazette* mentioned as being aboard the *Speedwell*, headquarters ship of the Pennsylvania Navy Board, may have been Colonel William Bradford, Chairman of the Board. He was the only civilian known to have been on board the sloop throughout the siege; "G.W. Papers," Reel 44, Fleury's Journal, October (November) 15, 1777; *PMHB*, Vol. XI, p. 87, "The Siege of Fort Mifflin."

43. Drinker, "Journal," p. 63; Cowell, *Spirit of '76*, p. 301, letter of

General Varnum, August, 2, 1786; Stone, "Invasion of Canada," Coll. R.I. Hist. Soc., Vol. VI, p. 77, from memoirs of Major Simeon Thayer.

44. "G.W. Papers," Reel 44, Fleury's Journal, October (November) 15, 1777.

45. *Ibid.*

46. *Ibid.;* André, *Journal,* p. 64; Almon, *Remembrancer,* Vol. V, p. 503, Return of ordnance and stores found at Fort Mifflin, Brigadier General Samuel Cleaveland.

47. "G.W. Papers," Reel 44, Fleury's Journal, November 15, 1777.

48. *Ibid.*

49. *PMHB,* Vol. XIX, p. 359, "Defences Philadelphia," Hazelwood to Washington, November 15, 1777; Cowell, *Spirit of '76,* p. 297; Stone, "Invasion of Canada," Coll. R.I. Hist. Soc., Vol. VI, p. 77; *P.A.,* First Series, Vol. VI, pp. 47–50, Hazelwood to Wharton, December 1, 1777. Hazelwood also had a few guard boats but their range was limited, and the strong westerly winds prevailing on November 15 would have capsized them.

50. *Ibid.*

51. *Rivington's New York Gazette,* December 8, 1777; *PMHB,* Vol. I, p. 28, "Morton"; "G.W. Papers," Reel 44, Fleury's Journal, October (November), 15, 1777; *New Jersey Archives,* Second Series, Vol. I, p. 495, Letter from a Gentleman on Board the Speedwell November 22, 1777; Logs, *Camilla* and *Roebuck,* November 15 and 16, 1777; Almon, *Remembrancer,* Vol. V, pp. 499–501, Lord Howe to Stephens, November 23, 1777.

52. *Ibid.; New Jersey Archives,* Second Series, Vol. I, p. 495, Letter from a Gentleman, November 22, 1777; "G.W. Papers," Reel 44, Fleury's Journal, October (November) 15, 1777; *HSP,* Conarroe Collection, Benjamin Rush to James Searle, November 19, 1777.

53. *Ibid.*

54. *Ibid.;* Cowell, *Spirit of '76,* pp. 296–298; Logs, *Camilla* and *Roebuck,* November 16, 1777; *PMHB,* Vol. XXXVIII, p. 224, Log, *Eagle,* November 16, 1777; *Ibid.,* Vol. VI, p. 190, "Montresor"; *Proceedings of the American Antiquarian Society,* pp. 91–92, "British Account."

55. "G.W. Papers," Reel 44, Fleury's Journal, October (November) 15, 1777; *PMHB,* Vol. VI, pp. 190–191, "Montresor"; *P.A.,* First Series, Vol. VI, p. 23, John Clark, Jr., to Paul Zantzinger, November 20, 1777, quoted Lord Cornwallis as saying, ". . . lost a great number of Brave fellows, & said 'twas a cursed little mud island."

56. *PMHB,* Vol. XIX, pp. 369, 370–371, "Defences Philadelphia," Greene to Potter, November 15, 1777, Varnum to Washington, November 16 (11:15 a.m.), 1777; Black and Roelker, eds., *A Rhode Island*

Chaplain, p. 68; Laurens, *Army Correspondence,* p. 79; Sparks, ed., *Correspondence,* Vol. II, pp. 43–44, Greene to Washington, November 17, 1777.

57. "G.W. Papers," Reel 44, Fleury's Journal, October (November) 15, 1777; Reel 46, "Thoughts of a Freeman," January 7, 1778, an anonymous query listing a number of points concerning the failure to hold the Delaware River forts, all prefaced with "That." The first statement was, "That had proper supplies been given to the forts on the River their Shipping could not have come up, without which they could not have stay'd in the city."; Almon, *Remembrancer,* Vol. V, p. 503; see Appendix F.

58. *PMHB,* Vol. XIX, pp. 236–243 *passim.,* 361–362, 365–366, Varnum to Washington, November 11, 1777 (2 letters), Smith to Varnum, November 11, 1777, Smith to Washington, November 12, 1777, Varnum to Washington, November 15 (6 p.m.), 1777, Smith to Washington, November 15, 1777.

59. Stone, "Invasion of Canada," Coll. R.I. Hist. Soc., Vol. VI, p. 77; "G.W. Papers," Reel 44, Fleury's Journal, October (November) 15, 1777.

60. Washington, *Writings,* Vol. X, pp. 73–77; *P.A.,* First Series, Vol. VI, pp. 47–50, Hazelwood to Wharton, December 1, 1777.

61. *Ibid.,* pp. 11, 47–50, Bradford to Wharton, November 16, 1777, Hazelwood to Wharton, December 1, 1777.

62. *Ibid.,* pp. 246–247, Hazelwood to Wharton, February 8, 1778.

63. Dawson, "Smith Papers," p. 88 fn.; Wallace, *William Bradford,* p. 429.

64. *P.A.,* First Series, Vol. VI, pp. 11, 24, 80–81, 110, 121–122, 246–247, Bradford to Wharton, November 16, 1777, Council to Bradford, November 20, 1777, State Navy Board to Wharton, December 19, 1777, Hazelwood to Wharton, February 8, 1778, Wharton to Bradford, December 9, 1777, Council to Hazelwood, December 20, 1777.

65. Wallace, *William Bradford,* p. 207 fn.

66. "G.W. Papers," Reel 45, Return of the N° of Men present fit for duty belonging to the garrison at Red Bank Commanded by Col. Greene, November 17, 1777; *PMHB,* Vol. XIX, p. 370–371, "Defences Philadelphia," Varnum to Washington, November 16 (11:15 a.m.), 1777.

67. Washington, *Writings,* Vol. X, pp. 77–78.

68. *P.A.,* First Series, Vol. VI, p. 21, to Commodore Hazelwood from St. Clair, de Kalb, and Knox, November 18 (9:30 p.m.), 1777; Friedrich Kapp, *The Life of John Kalb,* p. 133. In spite of the misunderstanding that had occurred on October 19, Hazelwood and Robinson cooperated in the best interests of the American cause. Apparently

Notes
459

an amiable relationship existed, as Hazelwood noted, "Captain Robinson in particular has been always ready to give every assistance with his people. . . ." See *P.A.*, First Series, Vol. VI, pp. 47–50, Hazelwood to Wharton, December 1, 1777.

69. American Philosophical Society, Sol Feinstone Collection, "A Diary of the American Revolution, Campaign of 1777"; *HSP Bull.*, "Clark," pp. 14–15, letter of November 19, 1777; Robertson, *Diaries*, pp. 154–155; Ward, *Revolution*, pp. 516–520; Max von Elking, in *The German Allied Troops in the North American War of Independence*, p. 120, says that the Hessians accompanying Wilson were in the Regiment Bayreuth.

70. *P.A.*, First Series, Vol. VI, pp. 47–50, Hazelwood to Wharton, December 1, 1777.

71. *Ibid.*, p. 21, Council of War held on board the Sloop Speedwell off Red Bank, November 19, 1777.

72. *Ibid.*, p. 27–28, 47–50, Bradford to Wharton, November 22, 1777, Hazelwood to Wharton, December 1, 1777.

73. *PMHB*, Vol. XIX, pp. 498–499, "Defences Philadelphia," Greene to Washington, November 22, 1777.

74. *Ibid.*, Vol. XIX, pp. 481–482, "Defences Philadelphia," Varnum to Washington, November 17 (1 p.m.), 1777.

75. Sparks, *Correspondence*, Vol. II, pp. 43–44, Greene to Washington, November 17 (4 o'clock), 1777. "G.W. Papers," Reel 45, Mauduit to Washington, November 17, 1777. Mauduit wrote to Washington re-emphasizing Greene's position, but implying that if Washington should take Province Island, it would be difficult to capture Mud Island, providing the enemy was permitted to capture Fort Mercer. Mauduit apparently viewed this as something of a reversal of the American position of the previous eight weeks.

76. *P.A.*, First Series, Vol. VI, p. 21, Instructions to Commodore Hazelwood, November 18 (9:30 p.m.), 1777; *Year Book, 1928, New Jersey Society of Pennsylvania*, p. 57, Instructions to Varnum, November 18 (9:30 p.m.), 1777.

77. *PMHB*, Vol. XIX, pp. 486, 488–489, "Defences Philadelphia," Washington to Glover, November 19 (11:00 p.m.), 1777, Washington to Hazelwood, November 19, 1777, Washington to Varnum, November 19, 1777.

78. *Ibid.*, pp. 493–495, Varnum to Washington, November 20 (11 a.m.), 1777; *New Jersey Society*, Orderly Book, Greene, p. 52, November 20, 1777.

79. *PMHB*, Vol. XIX, p. 495, "Defences Philadelphia," Varnum to Washington, November 21, 1777; see Appendix G.

80. *PMHB*, Vol. XX, p. 87, "Defences Philadelphia," Colonel Ellis to

General Greene, November 24, 1777; this landmark has recently been demolished.

81. *Ibid.*, Vol. XIX, p. 501, Washington to Varnum, November 22, 1777.

82. *P.A.*, First Series, Vol. VI, pp. 27–28, Bradford to Wharton, November 22, 1777.

83. *PMHB*, Vol. XIX, p. 496, "Defences Philadelphia," Greene to Washington, November 25 (5:00 p.m.), 1777.

84. *Ibid.*, pp. 498–501, Greene to Washington, November 22, 1777, Washington to Greene, November 22, 1777 (2 letters).

85. *Ibid.*, pp. 503–506, Greene to Washington, November 24, 1777.

86. *Ibid.*, Vol. XX, pp. 87–88, Colonel Ellis to Greene, November 24, 1777, Weedon to Greene, November 24 (7 o'clock), 1777; Gloucester County Historical Society, "Reminiscences of Jonas Cattell"; Smith, "Quakers."

87. *Ibid.*, entries of November 21 and 22, 1777.

88. *PMHB*, Vol. VI, p. 194, "Montresor"; HSP, Gratz Collection, American Officers in the American Revolution, Case 4, Box 18, Comstock to Greene, November 25, 1777.

89. *PMHB*, Vol. VI, p. 194, "Montresor"; Isaac Mickle, *Reminiscences of Old Gloucester*, pp. 63–64; Wallace McGeorge, "The Battle of Gloucester," a paper read before the Gloucester County Historical Society, January 9, 1906; Sparks, Washington, *Writings*, Vol. V, p. 171; *New Jersey Archives*, Second Series, Vol. I, p. 497, Letter of a Gentleman of distinction at Mount Holly, November 25, 1777.

90. "G.W. Papers," Reel 45, d'Arendt to Washington, November 21, 1777.

CHAPTER XIII

1. *P.A.*, First Series, Vol. VIII, pp. 165–166, Petition of Dr. Valentine Standley, January 26, 1779.

2. *C.R.*, Vol. XI. Many entries show advances of monies to Crispin and Bradford. The receipts for these funds are found in a manuscript account at the HSP, Disbursements by William Bradford on account of the Pennsylvania State Navy Board. This account covers the period from October 1777 to January 1780. A total of £39,839 7s 10d was expended during this period.

3. *P.A.*, First Series, Vol. VI, pp. 110, 132, State Navy Board to

Wharton, December 19, 1777, Council to Hazelwood, December 24, 1777.

4. *Ibid.*, p. 203, Crispin to Wharton, January 24, 1778; *C.R.*, XI, p. 387.

5. *P.A.*, First Series, Vol. VI, p. 181, T. Matlack to Hazelwood, January 16, 1778.

6. *Ibid.*, p. 204, Bradford to Wharton, January 24, 1778; Clark, *Barry*, p. 143.

7. *Ibid.*, pp. 142–144.

8. *PMHB*, Vol. III, pp. 422–423, "Colonel John Eyre by Peter D. Keyser."

9. "G.W. Papers," Reel 46, Fleury to J. Laurens, January 20, 1778; HSP, disbursements of Wm. Bradford on Account of the Pennsylvania State Navy Board, October 1777 to January 1780. Hazelwood was paid £350 in December 1777 for outfitting seven Continental fire ships. The elusive Continental fire ships were probably destroyed in October or November 1777, although no mention of them occurs in known sources.

10. "G.W. Papers," Reel 46, Fleury to Laurens, January 23, 1778, Reel 47, Laurens to Fleury, January 25, 1778.

11. Frederich Wagner, *Submarine Fighter of the American Revolution: The Story of David Bushnell*, pp. 84–89.

12. HSP, John Fanning Watson Manuscripts, Captain Coats' account of the British in Philadelphia on 1777/78 (taken in January, 1826).

13. *Ibid.*, Incidents and Anecdotes of the Revolution.

14. Wagner, *Bushnell*, pp. 86–89; Frank Moore, *Diary of the American Revolution*, Vol. II, pp. 5–7. Mr. Moore quotes extracts from letters in the *New Jersey Gazette*, January 21, 1778, and the *Pennsylvania Ledger*, February 11, 1778.

15. *P.A.*, First Series, Vol. VI, pp. 167–168, 246–247, Wharton to Hazelwood, January 8, 1778, Hazelwood to Wharton, February 8, 1778.

16. Washington, *Writings*, Vol. XI, pp. 12–13; "G.W. Papers," Reel 47, Hazelwood to Washington, February 4, 1778.

17. *Ibid.; P.A.*, First Series, Vol. VI, p. 332, Navy Board to Wharton, March 5, 1778.

18. *Ibid.*, pp. 354, 355, Council to Washington, March 11, 1778, Council to Navy Board, March 11, 1778.

19. *Ibid.*, p. 359, D. Roberdeau and J. B. Smith to Wharton, March 12, 1778.

20. Washington, *Writings*, Vol. XI, pp. 88–89.

21. *Ibid.*, p. 105; HSP, Gratz Collection, Officers of the Revolution, Box 17, Case 4, Bradford to Washington, March 14, 1778.

22. Washington, *Writings*, Vol. XI, pp. 283–284.

23. *C.R.*, Vol. XI, pp. 470–471; *P.A.*, First Series, Vol. VI, pp. 421–422, State Navy Board to Wharton, April 16, 1778.

24. *Ibid.*, p. 517, Navy Board to Wharton, May 18, 1778; HSP, Bradford Papers, Vol. II, p. 208, "Memorial of the Officers of the State Navy of Pennsylvania." The memorial was signed by Hazelwood, Thomas Moore, William Allen, William Greenway, John Harrison, John Rice, Hugh Montgomery, William Brown, William Watkin, William Ross, John Brice, and William Potts.

25. *Journals of the House of Representatives of the Commonwealth of Pennsylvania,* beginning the 28th day of November, 1776, and ending the 2nd day of October, 1781, pp. 209–211.

26. *P.A.*, First Series, Vol. VI, pp. 434–435, 440, Council to Navy Board, April 23, 1778, Council to Crispin, April 24, 1778.

27. *Ibid.*, pp. 454, 460–461, 492, 550. Richard Peters to Wharton, April 29, 1778, Council to President of Continental Congress, May 2, 1778, Richard Peters to Wharton, May 12, 1778, Council to Colonel Galbraith, May 25, 1778.

28. *Universal Magazine,* June 1778, Report of Major John Maitland, May 11, 1778, Report of John Henry, May 11, 1778, Letter of Sir William Howe to Lord George Germain, May 11, 1778, Lord Howe to Stephens, May 10, 1778; Washington, *Writings*, Vol. XI, p. 383; "G.W. Papers," Reel 49, Dickinson to Washington, May 9, 1778, Stephen Moylan to Washington, May 8, 1778, Hamilton to Maxwell, May 10, 1778; Everett Hastings, *Life and Works of Francis Hopkinson*, pp. 226–228; *New Jersey Gazette*, May 13, 1778.

29. *P.A.*, First Series, Vol. VI, pp. 527–528, at a Court-Martial held at Trenton, May 19, 1778; *C.R.*, Vol. XI, p. 541.

30. *P.A.*, First Series, Vol. VI, p. 550, Council to Colonel Galbraith, May 25, 1778.

31. *C.R.*, Vol. XI, pp. 488, 498, 499, 635.

32. *P.A.*, First Series, Vol. VI, pp. 598–599, Hazelwood to Bryan, June 13, 1778.

33. *C.R.*, Vol. XI, pp. 529, 539, 543.

34. *Ibid.*, pp. 549–550, 552, 554–555; HSP, Stauffer Collection, interleaved in a copy of Westcott's *History of Philadelphia*, Vol. VI, p. 508.

35. *P.A.*, First Series, Vol. VI, p. 696, Council to Navy Board, August 12, 1778.

36. *Ibid.*, pp. 697–699, at a Court Martial Held at Philadelphia, the 13th of August, 1778; *C.R.*, Vol. XI, pp. 564–566.

37. J. Franklin Jameson, ed., *Essays in the Constitutional History of the United States in the Foundation Period, 1775–1789,* "The Predecessor of the Supreme Court," J. Franklin Jameson, pp. 17–21; John F.

Watson, *Annals of Philadelphia and Pennsylvania in the Olden Times,* Vol. III, p. 93; *C.R.,* Vol. XI, p. 754.

38. *P.A.,* Fourth Series, Vol. III, pp. 692–695, 724–725; *P.A.,* First Series, Vol. VI, pp. 749–750, Council to Hazelwood, September 18, 1778.

39. *Ibid.,* Vol. VII, pp. 100, 112, 139–140, Council to General Assembly, November 27, 1778, Council to Hazelwood, December 10, 1778, Henry to Council, January 4, 1779; *C.R.,* Vol. XI, pp. 638, 641, 643.

40. *Ibid.,* p. 649.

41. *Ibid.,* p. 659.

CHAPTER XIV

1. *Pennsylvania Packet,* February 4, 18, and March 16, 1779; *C.R.,* Vol. XI, p. 741; *P.A.,* First Series, Vol. VII, p. 265.

2. Joseph Reed had become President of the Supreme Executive Council on December 4, 1778.

3. *P.A.,* First Series, Vol. VII, p. 235, Reed to Marine Committee, March 9, 1779.

4. *Ibid.,* p. 241, Marine Committee to Reed, March 12, 1779.

5. *Ibid.,* pp. 281, 285, Reed to McClenachan and Irwin, April 1, 1779, McClenachan and Irwin to Reed, April 2, 1779.

6. *PMHB,* Vol. LX, pp. 230–231, "The State Ship General Greene by M. V. Brewington"; *P.A.,* First Series, Vol. VII, pp. 263, 303–304, 320, Reed to Irwin, March 24, 1779, Reed to James Craig, April 7, 1779, Valuation of Ship General Greene, 1779; *C.R.,* Vol. XI, pp. 724, 751, 756.

7. *Ibid.,* pp. 730, 747; *P.A.,* First Series, Vol. VII, pp. 266–267, M. Irwin and B. McClenachan to Reed, March 27, 1779.

8. *C.R.,* Vol. XI, pp. 730, 735, 775; Charles Henry Lincoln, *Naval Records of the American Revolution,* p. 309. Lincoln said that the *General Greene* carried fourteen guns on December 11, 1779. This would be after the ship had been sold by the State.

9. See Appendix C; *PMHB,* Vol. LX, p. 232, Brewington, "Greene"; *C.R.,* Vol. XI, pp. 659, 740; *P.A.,* First Series, Vol. VIII, pp. 266–267, 285, 289, McClenachan and Irwin to Reed, March 27 and April 2, 1779, Reed to McClenachan and Irwin, April 3, 1779.

10. *Ibid.,* pp. 318–320, *passim,* Reed to McClanahan and Irwin, April 15, 1779, Reed to Andrew Hodge (one of the owners of the *Revenge*), April 15, 1779, Conyngham to Nesbitt, April 15, 1779.

11. *Ibid.*, p. 390, Council of Magistrates to Baltimore, May 11, 1779; *C.R.*, Vol. XI, pp. 761, 770; *P.A.*, Second Series, Vol. I, p. 237.

12. Philadelphia Maritime Museum, J. Welles Henderson Collection, Recruiting Instructions to Captain Caldwell, April 26, 1779.

13. *C.R.*, Vol. XII, pp. 4, 5; *P.A.*, First Series, Vol. VII, pp. 703–704, Thomas McKean to Reed, September 20, 1779. This letter gives a good insight into the typical occupants of the Philadelphia gaol; *PMHB*, Vol. LX, p. 233; Brewington, "Greene."

14. Paullin, ed., *Out-Letters*, Vol. II, pp. 81–82; *P.A.*, First Series, Vol. VII, pp. 454, 487, Reed to Montgomery, June 2 and June 15, 1779.

15. *Ibid.*, p. 476, Montgomery to Reed, June 9, 1779; *Delaware Archives*, Vol. III, p. 1376; *Pennsylvania Packet*, June 12, 1779.

16. *C.R.*, Vol. XII, p. 19; *Delaware Archives*, Vol. III, p. 1376; *P.A.*, First Series, Vol. VII, p. 476, Montgomery to Reed, June 9, 1779.

17. *Ibid.*

18. *P.A.*, Second Series, Vol. I, pp. 300–304; *Delaware Archives*, Vol. III, p. 1376; *P.A.*, First Series, Vol. VII, p. 476, Montgomery to Reed, June 9, 1779.

19. *Ibid.*, p. 487, Reed to Montgomery, June 15, 1779; *Delaware Archives*, Vol. III, p. 1376.

20. *Ibid.*, p. 1377; *P.A.*, First Series, Vol. VII, p. 521, Montgomery to Reed, June 29, 1779.

21. *Ibid.*, p. 533, Montgomery to Reed, July 4, 1779.

22. *Pennsylvania Packet*, July 13, 24, and August 26, 1779; Paullin, *Out-Letters*, Vol. II, pp. 89–93, 101; Penna. MSS, Military Accounts, Navy, RG–4, Box 2, List of Prizes taken by the Ship General Greene, submitted by Francis Hopkinson, March 1788.

23. *P.A.*, First Series, Vol. VII, pp. 552, 656, John Jay to Reed, June 29, 1779, Timothy Pickering to Reed, August 20, 1779.

24. *Ibid.*, p. 706, Montgomery to Reed, September 21, 1779; *C.R.*, Vol. XII, p. 111; *PMHB*, Vol. LX, pp. 239–240, Brewington, "Greene."

25. *P.A.*, First Series, Vol. VII, p. 755, Montgomery to Reed, October 6, 1779; *Delaware Archives*, Vol. III, p. 1378.

26. *C.R.*, Vol. XII, p. 150.

27. *PMHB*, Vol. LX, p. 241, Brewington, "Greene."

28. *C.R.*, Vol. XII, pp. 155, 173, 175; *P.A.*, Second Series, Vol. I, p. 237; *P.A.*, First Series, Vol. VIII, p. 3, McClenachan, Irwin, Henry, and Montgomery, November 3, 1779.

29. *PMHB*, Vol. LX, p. 241, Brewington, "Greene"; *C.R.*, Vol. XI, pp. 751, 756; Penna. MSS, RG–4, Military Accounts, Navy, Box 2, List of Prizes taken by the Ship General Greene, whilst she was commanded by James Montgomery & belonged to the State of Pennsylvania, submitted by Francis Hopkinson, March 1788.

30. *Ibid.*

31. *Ibid.; C.R.*, Vol. XI, p. 727, XII, p. 158.

32. Allen, *Naval History*, Vol. II, pp. 588, 591; Penna. MSS, RG–4, Military Accounts, Navy, Box 2, State of Accounts of John Patton, Francis Gurney, William Allibone, Esq., Commissioners for the Defence of the Bay & River Delaware, Condition of Sale General Washington, William Allibone, August 28, 1782.

CHAPTER XV

1. *C.R.*, Vol. XI, p. 650.

2. HSP, Miscellaneous Society Collection, Box 15–D, "A Return of the Officers and Men belonging to the Pennsylvania State Fleet, March 31, 1779," signed by Nathan Boye.

3. *C.R.*, Vol. XI, pp. 692, 694.

4. *Ibid.*, pp. 464, 530, 555, 583, 678, 701, 750.

5. *Ibid.*, pp. 727, 742.

6. *Ibid.*, pp. 725, 777; *P.A.*, First Series, Vol. VII, pp. 80, 270–271, Council to the Assembly, November 9, 1778, Reed to Proctor, March 29, 1779.

7. *Ibid.*, p. 197, Reed to Governors of Nearby States, February 21, 1779.

8. *Ibid.*, pp. 199–200, 201, Reed to Steuben, February 21, 1779. Board of War to Reed, February 22, 1779. Captain Thomas Hazelwood was the son of Commodore Hazelwood.

9. *Ibid.*, pp. 227–228, Board of War to Reed, March 8, 1779.

10. *Ibid.*, pp. 229, 232–233, 272, 279–281, Reed to Board of War, March 8, 1779, Timothy Pickering to Reed, March 9, 1779, Duportail to Reed, March 29, 1779, Reed to Duportail, March 31, 1779, Duportail to Reed, April 1, 1779.

11. *PMHB*, Vol. LXXXIV, pp. 424–434; "The Villefranche Map for the Defense of the Delaware by Hubertis M. Cummings." Mr. Cummings presents an excellent detailed description of the map.

12. *C.R.*, Vol. XI, pp. 776–777; *P.A.*, First Series, Vol. VII, pp. 400, 403, Duportail to Reed, May 14, 1779, Council to Duportail, May 14, 1779.

13. *Ibid.*, p. 409, Duportail to Reed, May 15, 1779.

14. *Ibid.*, p. 566, Reed to Boys, July 20, 1779.

15. *C.R.*, Vol. XII, p. 1.

16. *Ibid.*, p. 23.

17. *P.A.*, First Series, Vol. VII, pp. 263–264, 291, Resolution of Congress, March 24, 1779, St. Clair to Reed, April 4, 1779.

18. *Ibid.*, pp. 302–303, Value of Rations, 1779.

19. *C.R.*, Vol. XII, p. 134; *P.A.*, First Series, Vol. IX, pp. 330, 554, Wm. Hammel to Reed, August 3, 1781, Matlack to Justices of Gloucester, New Jersey, May 13, 1782.

20. *C.R.*, Vol. XII, pp. 187–188, 190 (34 from the *Franklin*, 23 *Hancock*, 21 *Chatham*, 12 *Lion*, and 9 *Viper*. Others including the crew of the *Fame* had been released at various times during the year).

21. *Ibid.*, pp. 192, 194–195, 227.

22. *Ibid.*, pp. 226–227, 251.

23. Penna. MSS, Military Accounts, Navy, 1775–94, RG–4, "A Return of the Officers and Men belonging to the State Fleet . . . from May 6 to June 3 [1780]."

24. *C.R.*, Vol. XII, p. 627.

25. *Ibid.*, Vol. XIII, p. 151.

26. *P.A.*, Fourth Series, Vol. III, p. 880, Dickinson to Assembly, January 23, 1783.

27. *Ibid.*, pp. 922–923, Dickinson to Assembly, September 9, 1783; *PMHB*, Vol. XLI, p. 468, 472; Vol. XLII, pp. 34, 36, 158, 168, 262, 267, 274, "Pensioners of the State Forces."

28. Penna. MSS, Military Accounts, Navy, RG–4, Box 2, State of the Accounts of Henry Fisher, Esq., November 28, 1786.

APPENDIX B

1. Wallace McGeorge, *The Chevaux-de-Frise in the Delaware*, p. 1.

2. Lossing, *Pictorial Field Book*, Vol. II, p. 86; I. P. Strittmatter, *The Importance of the Campaign on the Delaware During the Revolutionary War, 1777*, P. 13; *Naval Documents*, Vol. IV, p. 1314, illustration, "from a Gentleman of Credit at Philadelphia"; *ibid.*, pp. 163–164, Charles Carroll to Charles Carroll, Sr., March 4, 1776.

3. Benjamin Franklin, *The Writings of Benjamin Franklin*, Albert Harry Smyth, ed., Vol. VI, p. 409.

4. *Ibid.*, pp. 438–439.

5. *Naval Documents*, Vol. II, p. 177, Josiah Quincy to George Washington, October 3, 1775; *P.A.*, Second Series, Vol. I, pp. 750–754.

6. *C.R.*, Vol. X, p. 290; Malone, ed., *Dictionary of American Biography*, Vol. XVII, pp. 335–336.

7. *C.R.*, Vol. X, p. 290; *P.A.*, Second Series, Vol. I, pp. 754–755; *P.A.*, Fourth Series, Vol. III, pp. 572–576; Penna. MSS, Military Accounts, Navy, RD-4, Box 1.

8. *C.R.*, Vol. X, p. 299, "Mr. Owen Biddle presented to this Board, from Mr. Robert Smith, a Model of a Machine for lowering and raising balace [ballast] into and out of the Chivaux de Freis. . . ."

9. HSP, Thompson Westcott, Extra Illustrated set of *History of Philadelphia*, Vol. VI, p. 507, Stauffer Collection, Levi Hollingsworth and Arthur Donaldson to John Dickinson, President, Supreme Executive Council, September 23, 1784; *P.A.*, First Series, Vol. X, p. 607, Wardens of the Port to Council, September 23, 1784.

10. *C.R.*, Vol. X, p. 603.

11. *P.A.*, First Series, Vol. IV, p. 774.

12. *P.A.*, Second Series, Vol. I, pp. 754, 755, and plates between pp. 769 and 771.

13. *C.R.*, Vol. X, p. 750.

14. *P.A.*, First Series, Vol. V, facing p. 721.

15. *Naval Documents*, Vol. IV, p. 1314, illustration, "from a Gentleman of Credit at Philadelphia"; pp. 151–152, Captain Andrew Snape Hamond to Vice Admiral Molyneux Shuldham, March 3, 1776.

16. *P.A.*, First Series, Vol. V, p. 66; HSP, Westcott, *History of Philadelphia*, Vol. VIII, p. 542, Stauffer Collection, "A List of Such articles as are absolutely necessary to Expedite the Sinking Cheveaux de Frize at Billingsport, November 13, 1776"; Woodhouse Collection, Committee of Safety to the Commissioner of Naval Stores, December 14, 1776.

17. *Naval Documents*, Vol. I, p. 929; Vol. II, pp. 342, 661, 757–758, 760–761, 1163–1164; Vol. III, pp. 653–654, 834, 941–942, 1258–1259, 1322–1323; Vol. IV, pp. 151–152, 163–164; *PMHB*, Vol. 85, "A British Spy in Philadelphia [Gilbert Barkly] 1775–1777 by Geoffrey Sand."

18. R. Lamb, *An Original and Authentic Journal of Occurences during the Late American War, from Its Commencement to Year, 1783*, p. 232; David Ramsay in his *History of the American Revolution* copied this description verbatim, p. 29.

19. The chevaux-de-frise diary citations are taken from *P.A.*, Second Series, Vol. I; *C.R.*, Vols. X, XI, XIII, and XIV; *P.A.*, First Series, Vols. IV, V, VII, and X; *P.A.*, Fourth Series, Vol. III; Penna. MSS, Delaware Fortification Accounts, Box 1; HSP, Dreer Collection, Soldiers of the Revolution, Vol. II, Soldiers of the American Wars, Vol. V; Westcott, *History of Philadelphia*, Stauffer Collection, Vol. VI, p. 607, L. Hollingsworth and A. Donaldson to Supreme Executive Council, September 23, 1784; Vol. VII, p. 542, "Situation of the Chevaux de Frize that have been Weighed"; McGeorge, *Chevaux-de-Frise*.

20. *C.R.*, Vol. X, pp. 363, 372, 375, 376–377, 396–397, 402, 416, 430, 520, 723; *P.A.*, Second Series, Vol. I, pp. 163, 214, 215, 359, 501.

21. Francis B. Lee, *New Jersey as a Colony and as a State*, Vol. II, p. 190.

22. I am indebted to Murphy Smith and Willman Spawn of the American Philosophical Society for advising me on the existence of this correspondence.

23. Heusser, *George Washington's Map Maker*, pp. 150–156.

APPENDIX C

1. *P.A.*, Fourth Series, Vol. III, pp. 570–571; *C.R.*, Vol. X, p. 329.

2. *C.R.*, Vol. XI, p. 132; Penna. MSS, Various (Minutes, 1777), RG-4, Records of the Comptroller General, Records of the Navy Board. Preliminary drafts of this pay scale with some changes may be found in *P.A.*, Second Series, Vol. I, p. 394; *C.R.*, Vol. XI, p. 8 (galleys only); Penna. MSS, Various (Minutes, 1777) RG-4, "A List of the Pay of the Fleet in the Services of the State of Pennsylvania"; Military Accounts, Navy, RG-4, Box 2.

3. These junior and petty officer classifications apply to the ship *Montgomery*.

4. In accordance with the agreement between Drs. Rush and Duffield, they each received sixteen dollars per month.

5. On July 2, 1777, the Commodore's salary was raised to $125 per month and Hazelwood, as second in command, to $100, both inclusive of rations. *P.A.*, Second Series, Vol. I, pp. 180–181; *C.R.*, Vol. XI, p. 323.

6. See text for description of chief surgeon's activity.

7. *C.R.*, Vol. X, p. 584, 597.

8. *Ibid.*, pp. 585, 586.

9. *Ibid.*, p. 594.

10. *Ibid.*, p. 650.

11. *P.A.*, Fourth Series, Vol. III, pp. 570–571; *C.R.*, Vol. X, p. 329.

12. *C.R.*, Vol. XI, p. 202.

13. *Ibid.*, p. 720.

14. *Ibid.*, pp. 757–758; Philadelphia Maritime Museum, J. Welles Henderson Collection, Recruiting Instructions to Captain Caldwell, April 26, 1779; *P.A.*, First Series, Vol. VII, pp. 266–267.

15. HSP, Stauffer Collection, interleaved in Westcott's *History of Philadelphia*, Vol. VI, p. 488.

16. See Chapter 15. Other interim changes of new rates for individual classifications may be found scattered through *C.R.*, Vols. X and XI, and *P.A.*, Second Series, Vol. I.

APPENDIX D

1. *C.R.*, Vol. X, pp. 323–327; *P.A.*, Fourth Series, Vol. III, pp. 565–570.
2. *Ibid.*, pp. 578–582; *C.R.*, Vol. X, pp. 368–371.
3. *Ibid.*, pp. 321–322; *P.A.*, Second Series, Vol. I, p. 378.
4. *Ibid.*, pp. 377–378; *C.R.*, Vol. X, pp. 355–356; *P.A.*, Fourth Series, Vol. III, pp. 576–577.
5. *Ibid.*, p. 577; *C.R.*, Vol. X, p. 356.
6. *Ibid.*, p. 364; *P.A.*, Fourth Series, Vol. III, pp. 577–578, 598–599.
7. *C.R.*, Vol. X, pp. 337–338.
8. *Ibid.*, pp. 608–609, 731–732; *P.A.*, Fourth Series, Vol. III, pp. 602–603; *P.A.*, Fifth Series, Vol. II, pp. 74–75; Force, *American Archives*, Fourth Series, Vol. VI, p. 1287. (These instructions were issued to all commodores, although Hazelwood's may have been verbal.)

APPENDIX E

1. Wallace, *Bradford*, pp. 232–233. C. R. Hildeburn had compiled the data in this sketch for Wallace; Lorenzo Sabine, *Biographical Sketches of Loyalists of the American Revolution*, Vol. II, p. 422. He always signed his name Robert Whyte. Later the minutes of the Committee of Safety use both Whyte and White, usually the latter.
2. *C.R.*, Vol. XI, pp. 610–612; *P.A.*, Fourth Series, Vol. III, pp. 695–699.
3. *P.A.*, First Series, Vol. IX, pp. 530–531, Moore to Livingston, April 23, 1782, and Livingston to Moore, April 26, 1782; Vol. X, p. 730, Livingston to Moore, April 27, 1782.
4. See Appendices C and D.
5. *C.R.*, Vol. X, p. 327.
6. *Ibid.*, p. 648.
7. *Ibid.*, p. 650.

8. Wallace, *Bradford,* pp. 228–242; Strittmatter, *Campaign on the Delaware,* pp. 6–7.

9. Wilbur H. Siebert, *The Loyalists of Pennsylvania,* pp. 58–59.

10. C.R., Vol. XI, pp. 483–485, 503, 504–505, 514–518, 587, 610–612; Vol. XII, pp. 27–29, 496, 665, 710; *P.A.,* Fourth Series, Vol. III, pp. 695–699.

11. *C.R.,* Vol. XII, p. 199.

12. Chastellux, *Travels,* Vol. I, pp. 29–35, 316 fn.; Wallace, *Bradford,* pp. 231–232.

APPENDIX G

1. Almon, *Remembrancer,* Vol. V, p. 503; André, *Journal,* p. 64; Stewart, *Notes on Old Gloucester County,* Vol. III, pp. 280–281.

Bibliography

Manuscripts

Historical Society of Pennsylvania

Armstrong, Major William:
Receipt Book, Fort Island, 1779–1780.

Balch Collection:
Shippen Papers, Volume 3.

Bradford, Colonel William (especially Volume 2).

Cadwalader Collection:
General John Cadwalader Papers (especially Box C-38 [2]).
Thomas Wharton Letters.

Conarroe Collection

Clymer, Daniel C., family papers.

Dreer Collection:
Famous Merchants of the American Revolution.
Soldiers of the American Revolution (5 volumes).
American Navy (3 volumes).
Governors of the States.

Esling, Charles, H. A.:
  The Escape of General Wharton at the British Occupation of Philadelphia.

Forts of Pennsylvania:
  Samuel Hazard's letters, notes and maps.

Gratz Collection:
  Pennsylvania Series, Board of War and Navy Board Box 18, Case 1.
  The American Navy in the Revolution. A-L Box 27, Case 5.
  The American Navy in the Revolution. M-Z Box 28, Case 5.
  French Officers in the Revolution.
  American Officers in the Revolution.
  Generals in the Revolution. Boxes 11 to 16, Case 4.

Hildeburn, Charles R.:
  Loyalist Ladies in Revolutionary Times.

Hildeburn, Charles R., Papers.

Historical Society of Pennsylvania, Miscellaneous Collection:
  Revolutionary Correspondence, Statistical Lists 1775–1791, Invoices of Stores, 1775–1779, Box 15 B.
  Committee of Safety, 1775–1778, Box 15 C.
  Council of Safety, 1775–1778, Box 15 C.
  Affidavits and Courts Martial, 1777–1805, Box 15 C.
  Revolution-Return of Troops, 1776–1794, Box 15 D.
  Old Congress Papers, Box 2-B.

Humphreys, Joshua, Papers.

Laurens, Henry, correspondence, 2 vols.

Orderly Books, American:
  Captain John Nice, headquarters at Red Bank, Fort Mercer, 1777.

Pemberton Papers:
  Papers for 1775–1783, Volume 27 through 33.

Provincial Delegates, Volume 5.

Stauffer, David McNeely, Collection:
  Interleaved in copies of Thompson Westcott's, *History of Philadelphia*, Volumes 6, 7 and 8.

Watson, John Fanning, manuscripts.

Wayne, General Anthony, papers.

Wharton Papers.

Woodhouse, Samuel W., Collection.

Pennsylvania Bureau of Archives and History
  Military Accounts, Navy, RG-4, 1775–1794, Boxes 1 through 6.
  Delaware Fortification Accounts, RG-4, 1775–1798, Box 1.
  Various, RG-4, Boxes 1 and 2.
  Minutes and General Correspondence of the Navy Board and
    Board of War, 1777, RG-27.
  Sequestered John Mitchell Papers, MG-92, Boxes 3, 4 and 6.
  Morris, Robert, Papers, microfilm, Reel 12.
  Reed, Joseph, Papers, microfilm, Reels 1 and 2.
  Clinton, Major-General Henry Papers, microfilm.

New York Public Library
  Bancroft Collection:
      Brunswick Papers (includes Journal of Capt. Fr. von Mun-
        chhausen).
  German Papers, von Dincklage Diary.

William M. Clements Library
  Clinton, Major-General Sir Henry, Papers.
  Von Jungkenn manuscripts.

Library of Congress
  Washington, George, papers, especially Reels 43 through 47
    (through courtesy of the American Philosophical Society and
    the West Chester State College).

American Philosophical Society
  Feinstone, Sol, Collection of American Revolutionary Manuscripts.
  Benjamin Franklin Papers.

Philadelphia Maritime Museum
  Henderson, J. Welles, Collection:
      Recruiting Instructions to Captain Caldwell
      Galley Book, Ship Yard No. 3.

Gloucester County Historical Society and Gloucester County Archives
  (typescripts)
  Deposition of Samuel C. Pancoast.
  Narrative of Thomas Stokes.

Narrative of Jonas Cattell.
Family reminiscences of John G. Whitall.

Department of the Navy, Historical Research Section
    Log Books of the *Camilla, Experiment, Eagle, Roebuck, Solebay,*
        and *Pearl* (originals in the Public Records Office, London).

National Archives
    Naval Records Collection, RG-45.
        Operations of the fleet under Lord Howe.
        Operations in the Delaware River in the American Revolution.
    War Department Collection of Revolutionary War Records
    RG-93.

Maps

A number of excellent contemporary Revolutionary War maps of
the Delaware Valley and its fortifications are available for study. A
few of the maps are prepared to scale, but they are not intended to
provide accurate dimensions for the various river fortifications. Certain minor details, such as the location of the land batteries in the
vicinity of Mantua Creek are incorrectly positioned. Faden's map of
the area and its naval activities offer historical information on the
Pennsylvania and Continental navy, much of which is inaccurate.
Other eighteen-century cartographers have perpetuated Faden's mistakes by copying his historical data.

The need for a definitive study of Revolutionary maps has been
partially filled by two recent studies. *American Maps and Map Makers
of the Revolution,* by Peter J. Guthorn, Monmouth Beach, N. J.
1966, and "A Preliminary Study: Maps of the American Revolution,"
by Walter W. Ristow, Chief of the Geography and Map Division of
the Library of Congress appeared in *The Quarterly Journal of the
Library of Congress,* July, 1971, pp. 196–215. Mr. Ristow's article is
especially valuable and it is hoped that additional research may extend
his study. Germane to this book, Mr. Ristow in his article states that
the fort on Fort Island was not called Fort Mifflin until after the
British evacuated Philadelphia in the early summer of 1778. The naming
of Fort Mifflin actually took place between June 21 and August 6,
1777 (see note 6, Chapter 8).

An examination of a number of map collections, including modern
maps, and a personal survey of existing terrain has made possible a

reasonable reconstruction of Revolutionary sites and distances in relation to modern topography. Some collections of importance are:

Cornell University, Olen Library, Jared Sparks Collection
  Fleury Maps

Library of Congress, Geography and Map Division:
  Peter Force Collection
  Howe Collection
  Montresor Map, *Survey of the City of Philadelphia and Environs*

Historical Society of Pennsylvania:
  Willard Estate, Maps and Plans of the Revolution, 1771–1778, Mauduit's Maps
  Mud Island, with Operations for reducing it, 15th Nov., 1777 (John André)
  Plan of the Siege of Fort Mifflin, 1777 (a reissue of the Wheeler map in the Howe Collection, Library of Congress)

Philadelphia Maritime Museum:
  J. Welles Henderson Collection
    William Faden, 1779—*A Plan of the City and Environs of Philadelphia*
    William Faden, 1785—*Province and Carpenters' Islands.*

Pennsylvania Bureau of Archives and History and the Pennsylvania Bureau of Land Records:
  Villefranche Map (1779) and two small auxiliary maps of plans of redoubts on Carpenters' and Province Islands, and for a powder magazine for Fort Mifflin

Gloucester County (New Jersey) Historical Society:
  Plan of Fort Mercer, by E. W. Bowden (circa 1895)

Commodore John Hazelwood's Map (1779) in *P.A.,* First Series, Vol. VII, facing p. 721

Maps of the chevaux-de-frise, see *P.A.,* Second Series, Vol. I, pp. 749–73

Map of Fort Mercer (1854) Barber and Howe, *Historical Collections of the State of New Jersey,* p. 210

J. F. W. Des Barres, *Chart of Delaware River from Bombay Hook to Philadelphia,* (1779)

Several modern surveys and aerial photographs have been invaluable in locating the sites of the Mantua Creek land batteries.

Many other contemporary maps were consulted but offered little information not included in those listed. Maps of this period must be used with care, especially as to detail.

Newspapers

Constitutional Gazette
Continental Journal and Weekly Advertiser (Boston)
New Jersey Gazette
New York Gazette & Weekly Mercury
Pennsylvania Evening Post
Pennsylvania Gazette
Pennsylvania Journal and the Weekly Advertiser
Pennsylvania Ledger
Pennsylvania Packet
Rivington's Royal Gazette (New York)
Virginia Gazette

Printed Primary Sources: Collections

Archives of the State of New Jersey, Second Series. 5 vols., Trenton, 1901–1917.

Burnett, Edmund C., ed. *Letters of Members of the Continental Congress* (7 vols.). Washington, 1921–1934.

Clark, Walter, ed., *State Records of North Carolina*, vols. 11, 12 & 13. Winston, N. C., 1895–1896.

Clark, William Bell, ed. *Naval Documents of the American Revolution* (6 vols.), 1964–197–.

Colonial Records of Pennsylvania (16 vols.). Harrisburg, 1838–1853.

Delaware Archives (3 vols.). Wilmington, 1911–1919.

Force, Peter, comp. *American Archives,* Fourth Series (6 vols.), Fifth Series (3 vols.), Washington, 1837–1853.

Ford, Worthington C., ed. *Journals of the Continental Congress* 34 vols., Washington, 1904–1937.

Gloucester County Revolutionary War Documents, WPA Survey Project, Newark, 1940.

Hazard, Samuel, ed. *Register of Pennsylvania* (16 vols.). Philadelphia, 1828–1838.

Huffington, William, ed., *Delaware Register* (2 vols.). Dover, Delaware, 1838–1839.

Journal of the House of Representatives of Pennsylvania, November 1776 to October 1781. Philadelphia, 1782.

Paullin, Charles O., ed. *Out Letters of the Continental Marine Committee and Board of Admiralty, 1777–1780* (2 vols.). New York, 1913–1914.

Pennsylvania Archives, First Series, 12 vols. Second Series, Vols. I and II; Third Series, Vol. XXIII, Fourth Series, Vol. III, Fifth Series, Vol. I, Eighth Series, Vol. VIII. Harrisburg, 1852–1914.

Publications of Learned Societies, Periodicals

Bellas, Henry H. "The Defenses of the Delaware in the Revolution," *Wyoming Historical and Geological Society Proceedings and Collections,* Vol. 5 (1900).

Brewington, Marion V. "Maritime Philadelphia, 1609–1837," *Pennsylvania Magazine History and Biography,* Vol. LXIII (1939).

———. "The State Ship *General Greene,*" *Pennsylvania Magazine History and Biography,* Vol. LX, (1936).

Clark, William Bell. "The Battle in the Delaware." *Year Book, 1930, of The New Jersey Society of Pennsylvania.*

———. "James Josiah, Master Mariner," *Pennsylvania Magazine History and Biography,* Vol. LXXIX, (1955).

Collum, Captain R. S. "The Capture of Philadelphia and the attack of the British Fleet on the Defenses of the Delaware, 1777," *The United Service, New Series,* Vol. IV (1890).

Cooper, Major Robert. "Attack on Fort Mifflin," *Hazard's Register of Pennsylvania,* Vol. I (1828).

Cummings, Hubertis M. "The Villefranche Map for the Defense of the Delaware," *Pennsylvania Magazine of History and Biography,* Vol. LXXXIV, (1960).

Darlington, William M. "Major-General John Armstrong," *Pennsylvania Magazine History and Biography,* Vol. I, (1877).

Dorland, W. A. Newman. "The Second Troop, Philadelphia City Cavalry," *Pennsylvania Magazine History and Biography,* Vol. XLVII, (1923).

Harris, Joseph S. "Robert Smith," *Pennsylvania Magazine of History and Biography,* Vol. IV, (1880).

Heston, Alfred M. *Red Bank-Defence of Fort Mercer.* (Paper read before Monmouth County Historical Association, July 26, 1900.)

Jeffreys, C. P. B. "The Provincial and Revolutionary History of St. Peters Church, Philadelphia, 1753–1783," *Pennsylvania Magazine of History and Biography,* Vol. XLVIII, (1924).

Keyser, Peter D., ed. "Colonel John Eyre," *Pennsylvania Magazine of History and Biography,* Vol. III, (1879).

Leach, Josiah G. "Commodore John Hazelwood, Commander of the

Pennsylvania Navy in the Revolution," *Pennsylvania Magazine of History and Biography*, Vol. XXVI, (1902).

McGeorge, Isabella C. "The Heroine of Red Bank." (Paper read before the Gloucester County Historical Society, January 11, 1904.)

McGeorge, Wallace. "The Battle of Gloucester." (Paper read before the Gloucester County Historical Society, January 9, 1906.)

————. *The Chevaux-de-Frise in the Delaware.* (Paper read before the Gloucester County Historical Society, July 18, 1911.)

————. *The Frigate Augusta.* Camden, N. J., 1905.

————. *The Siege of Fort Mifflin and a Few of Its Brave Defenders.* (Paper read before the Gloucester County Historical Society, July 9, 1907.)

Moomaw, W. H., "The Denouement of General Howe's Campaign of 1777," *English Historical Review*, Vol. LXXIX (1964).

Nead, Benjamin M. "A Sketch of General Thomas Proctor," *Pennsylvania Magazine History and Biography*, Vol. IV, (1890).

Paine, Ralph D. *The Battle of Red Bank* (Reprinted from excerpts of an article by the Gloucester County Board of Chosen Freeholders, 1967).

"Pensioners of the State Forces," *Pennsylvania of Magazine History and Biography*, Vols. LXI & LXII (1917, 1918).

"Report of Actions on the Delaware, October and November, 1777," *The Annual Register, or a View of the History, Politics, and Literature for the Year 1777.* London, 1778.

Seed, Geoffrey. "A British Spy in Philadelphia, 1775–1777 (Gilbert Barkly)," *Pennsylvania Magazine History and Biography*, Vol. LXXXV, (1961).

Shelton, Frederick H. "Old Fort Mifflin," *Philadelphia Numismatic and Antiquarian Society Proceedings*, Vol. XXIX, (1922).

"The Siege of Fort Mifflin," *The United States Magazine*, (May, 1779). Brackenridge, Hugh Montgomery, ed.

Stewart, Frank H. Series of Articles on the Revolution in Southern New Jersey, *Year Book, 1928, of The New Jersey Society of Pennsylvania*.

Whitehead, John, ed. "The Battle of Red Bank and The Battle of Princeton," *Proceedings of the New Jersey Society of the Sons of the American Revolution*, (Morristown, N. J., 1893).

Printed Sources: Letters, Diaries, Journals

Adams, Charles Francis, ed. *Familiar Letters of John Adams and His Wife Abigail Adams, During the Revolution, with a Memoir of Mrs. Adams.* New York, 1876.

Allen, James. *Diary of James Allen, Esq., Philadelphia Counsellor-at-Law, 1770–1778. Pennsylvania Magazine of History and Biography,* Vol. IX (1885–1886).

André, John. *Major Andrés Journal: Operations of the British Army Under General Sir William Howe and Sir Henry Clinton, June, 1777, to November, 1778.* Edited by William Abbatt. New York, 1930.

Barney, Mary, ed. *A Biographical Memoir of the Late Commodore Joshua Barney.* Boston, 1832.

Baurmeister, Carl Leopold, "Letters of Major Baurmeister During the Philadelphia Campaign, 1777–1778." Edited by Bernhard A. Uhlendorf and Edner Vosper. *Pennsylvania Magazine of History and Biography,* Vols. LIX and LX (1935–1936).

Biddle, Charles. *Autobiography of Charles Biddle.* Philadelphia, 1883.

Buettner, Johann Carl. *Narrative of Johann Carl Buettner in the American Revolution.* New York, n.d.

Bushnell, Charles J. "Memoir of Samuel Smith, 1776–1786." *Crumbs of Antiquarians.* 2 vols. New York, 1864–1866.

Chastellux, Marquis François Jean de. *Travels in North America in the Years 1780, 1781 and 1782* (revised translation). Edited by Howard C. Rice, Jr. 2 vols. Chapel Hill, 1963.

Clark, John, Jr. "Letters from Major John Clark, Jr., to General Washington during the Occupation of Philadelphia by the British Army." *Bulletin of the Historical Society of Pennsylvania,* Vol. I (1845–1847).

Clausen, Baron Ludwig von. *The Revolutionary Journal of Baron Ludwig von Clausen, 1780–1783.* Evelyn M. Acomb, ed. Chapel Hill, 1958.

Collin, Nicholas. *The Journal and Biography of Nicholas Collin. 1746–1831.* Amandus Johnson, ed. Philadelphia, 1936.

David, Ebenezer. *A Rhode Island Chaplain in the Revolution: Letters of Ebenezer David to Nicholas Brown, 1775–1778.* Jeanette D. Black and William Green Roelker, eds. Providence, 1949.

Drinker, Elizabeth. *Extracts from the Journal of Elizabeth Drinker, from 1759 to 1807, A.D.* Henry D. Biddle, ed. Philadelphia, 1889.

———. "Extracts from the Journal of Mrs. Henry Drinker, from Sept. 25, 1777, to July 8, 1778." *Pennsylvania Magazine of History and Biography,* Vol. XIII (1889).

Du Coudray, Philippe Trouson. "Observations on the Forts Intended for the Defense of the Two Passages of the River Delaware, July, 1777." *Pennsylvania Magazine of History and Biography*, Vol. XXIV (1900).

Howe, Admiral Lord Richard. "Excerpts from the Master's Log of His Majesty's Ship *Eagle*, Lord Howe's Flagship, 1776–1777." Edited by William F. Mervine. *Pennsylvania Magazine of History and Biography*, Vol. XXXVIII (1914).

Ford, Worthington C., ed. "Defenses of Philadelphia in 1777." *Pennsylvania Magazine of History and Biography*, Vols. XVIII, XIX, XX and XXI (1894–1897).

Franklin, Benjamin. *The Writings of Benjamin Franklin*. 10 vols. Albert Henry Smyth, ed., New York, 1905–1907.

Galloway, Joseph. *The Examination of Joseph Galloway, Speaker of the House of Assembly of Pennsylvania Before the House of Commons*. Second Edition. London, 1780.

———. *Historical and Political Reflections on the Rise and Progress of the American Revolution*. London, 1780.

[Galloway, Joseph]. *Letters to a Nobleman on the Conduct of the War in the Middle Colonies*. Second Edition. London, 1779.

Greene, Colonel Christopher. "Orderly Book October 11, 1777, to November 20, 1777." *Year Book, 1928, of the New Jersey Society of Pennsylvania*.

Howe, William. *The Narrative of Lieut. Gen. Sir William Howe in a Committee of the House of Commons, on the 29th of April, 1779, relative to His Conduct during His Late Command of the King's Troops in North America*. Second edition. London, 1780.

Huth, Hans, ed. (C. V. Easum trans.) "Letters from a Hessian Mercenary." *Pennsylvania Magazine of History and Biography*, Vol. LXII (1938).

Kemble Papers. Collections of the New-York Historical Society for the years 1883–1884. 2 vols. New York, 1884–1885.

Kirkland, Frederic R., ed., *Letters on the American Revolution*. 2 vols. Philadelphia, 1941–1952.

Lamb, R. *An Original and Authentic Journal of Occurrences during the Late American War, from Its Commencement to the Year, 1783*. Dublin, 1809.

Laurens, John. "Letters of John Laurens, November, 1777." Frederic R. Kirkland, ed. *Pennsylvania Magazine of History and Biography*, Vol. LXV (1941).

————. *The Army Correspondence of Colonel John Laurens in the Years 1777–8: Now First Printed from the Original Letters Addressed to his Father Henry Laurens, President of Congress.* William Gilmore Simms, ed. New York, 1867 and 1969.

Lee, Henry. *Memoir of the War in the Southern Department of the United States.* New York, 1870.

"Letters to Earl Harcourt and Lord Nuneham." *Pennsylvania Magazine of History and Biography*, Vol. VIII (1884).

Logan, Sarah. "A Diary of Trifling Occurrences, Philadelphia, 1776–1778." Nicholas B. Wainwright, ed. *Pennsylvania Magazine of History and Biography*, Vol. LXXXII (1958).

Maitland, John, and John Henry. "Reports of Major John Maitland and Captain John Henry on the Bordentown Affair, May 8 and 9, 1778." The *Universal Magazine of Knowledge and Pleasure*, Vol. LXII (London, 1778).

Marshall, Christopher. *Extracts from the Diary of Christopher Marshall kept in Philadelphia and Lancaster during the Revolution, 1774–1781.* William Duane, ed. Albany, 1877.

Martin, Joseph Plumb. *A Narrative of Some of the Adventures, Dangers and Sufferings of a Revolutionary Soldier.* George F. Scheer, ed. New York, 1962.

Montresor, John. "Journal of Captain John Montresor, July 1, 1777, to July 1, 1778. G. D. Scull, ed. *Pennsylvania Magazine of History and Biography*, Vols. V and VI (1881–1882).

Moore, Frank, ed. *The Diary of the Revolution.* 2 vols. New York, 1969.

————, ed., *Materials for History* (letters to and from Henry Laurens). New York, 1861.

Morris, Margaret. *Margaret Morris: Her Journal with Biographical Sketch.* John W. Jackson, ed. Philadelphia, 1949.

Morton, Robert. "The Diary of Robert Morton, Kept in Philadelphia while that city was occupied by the British army in 1777." *Pennsylvania Magazine of History and Biography*, Vol. I (1877).

Muhlenberg, Henry Melchior. *The Journals of Henry Melchior Muhlenberg.* Theodore G. Tappert and John W. Doberstein, trans. 2 vols. Philadelphia, 1942–1945.

Paine, Thomas. "Letter of Thomas Paine to Dr. Franklin: Military Operations near Philadelphia in the Campaign of 1777–78." *Pennsylvania Magazine of History and Biography*, Vol. II (1878).

Peale, Charles Willson, "Journal of Charles Willson Peale." *Pennsylvania Magazine of History and Biography*, Vol. XXXVIII (1914).

"Popp's Journal 1777–1783." *Pennsylvania Magazine of History and Biography*, Vol. XXVI (1902).

Proud, Robert. "Letters of Robert Proud." *Pennsylvania Magazine of History and Biography*, Vol. XXXIV (1910).

Reed, Joseph. "General Joseph Reed's Narrative of the Movements of the American Army in the Neighborhood of Trenton in the Winter of 1776–77." *Pennsylvania Magazine of History and Biography*, Vol. VIII (1884).

Reed, William B. *Life and Correspondence of Joseph Reed.* 2 vols. Philadelphia, 1847.

Robertson, Archibald. *Archibald Robertson, Lt. General Royal Engineers: His Diaries and Sketches in America, 1762–1780.* New York, 1930.

Ryden, George Herbert, ed. *Letters to and from Caesar Rodney, 1756–1784.* Philadelphia, 1933.

Schultz, Charles R., comp. *Inventory of the Silas Talbot Papers.* Mystic, Conn., 1965.

Scull, G. D., ed., *The Evelyns in America.* Oxford, 1881.

Serl, Ambrose. *The American Journal of Ambrose Serl, Secretary to Lord Howe.* Edward H. Tatum, ed. San Marino, Cal. 1940.

Seybolt, Robert Francis. "A Contemporary British Account of General Sir William Howe's Military Operations in 1777." *Proceedings of the American Antiquarian Society.* New Series, Vol. XL (1931).

Smith, Samuel. "Papers of General Samuel Smith." Henry B. Dawson, ed. *The Historical Magazine and Notes and Queries Concerning Antiquities, History and Biography of America,* Second Series, Vol. VII (1870).

Sparks, Jared, ed., *Correspondence of the American Revolution.* 4 vols. Boston, 1853.

Stone, Edwin M. *The Life and Recollections of John Howland.* Providence, 1857.

Washington, George. *The Writings of George Washington with a Life of the Author.* Jared Sparks, ed. 12 vols. Boston, 1834–1838.

―――. *The Writings of George Washington from the Original Manuscript Sources, 1745–1799.* John C. Fitzpatrick, ed. 39 vols. Washington, 1931–1944.

[Whitall, Job]. "Two Generations of Quakers: An Old Diary." Logan Pearsall Smith, ed. *Atlantic Monthly,* July, 1903.

Young, William. "Journal of Sergeant William Young, written during the Jersey campaign in the winter of 1776–77." *Pennsylvania Magazine of History and Biography,* Vol. VIII (1884).

Secondary Sources: Books and Pamphlets

Allen, Gardner W. *A Naval History of the American Revolution.* 2 vols. Boston, 1913.

Almon, J., *The Remembrancer or Impartial Repository of Public Events.* 12 vols. London, 1775–1783.

Ashmead, Henry Graham. *History of Delaware County, Pennsylvania.* Philadelphia, 1884.

Bill, Alfred Hoyt. *The Campaign of Princeton, 1776–1777.* Princeton, 1948.

Barber, John W. (assisted by Henry Howe). *Historical Collections of New Jersey: Past and Present.* New Haven, 1868.

Boyd, Thomas. *Mad Anthony Wayne.* New York, 1929.

Callahan, North. *Henry Knox-General Washington's General.* New York, 1958.

―――. *Royal Raiders—The Tories of the American Revolution,* Indianapolis, 1963.

Carrington, Henry B. *Battles of the American Revolution, 1775–1781.* New York, 1876.

―――. *Washington the Soldier.* New York, 1899.

Chapelle, Howard I. *The History of the American Sailing Navy.* New York, 1949.

―――. *The History of American Sailing Ships,* New York, 1935.

―――. *The Search for Speed Under Sail, 1700–1855.* New York, 1967.

Clark, Thomas. *Naval History of the United States.* 2 vols. Second edition, Philadelphia, 1814.

Clark, William Bell. *Captain Dauntless: The Story of Nicholas Biddle*, Baton Rouge, 1949.

———. *Gallant John Barry, 1745–1803*. New York, 1938.

———. *Lambert Wickes, Sea Raider and Diplomat*. New Haven, 1932.

Coffin, Charles C. *The Boys of '76*. New York, 1876.

Cowell, Benjamin. *Spirit of '76: in Rhode Island*. Boston, 1850.

Davis, Charles L. *A Brief History of the North Carolina Troops on the Continental Establishment in the War of the Revolution*. Philadelphia, 1896.

Dawson, Henry B. *Battles of the United States by Sea and Land*. 2 vols. New York, 1858.

Dunbar, Seymour. *History of Travel in America*. 4 vols. Indianapolis, 1915.

Eelking, Max von (translated by J. G. Rosengarten). *The German Allied Troops in the North American War of Independence 1776–1783*. Baltimore, 1969.

Emmons, Lieut. George F. (comp.). *The Navy of the U. S. from the Commencement 1775–1853*. Washington, 1853.

Fisher, Sydney George. *The Struggle for American Independence*. 2 vols. Philadelphia, 1908.

Fortescue, Sir John W. *A History of the British Army*. 13 vols. London, 1911–35.

Freemen, Douglas Southall. *George Washington*. 7 vols. New York, 1948–1957.

Gardner, Asa Bird. *The Rhode Island in the Continental Army and Its Society of Cincinnati*. Providence, 1878.

Gordon, William. *The History of the Rise, Progress and Establishment, of the Independence of the United States of America*. 4 vols. London, 1788.

Greene, Francis Vinton. *The Revolutionary War and the Military Policy of the United States*. New York, 1911.

Greene, George Washington. *The Life of Nathanael Greene*. 3 vols. New York, 1867–1871.

Griffin, Martin I. J. *Stephen Moylan*. Philadelphia, 1909.

Gruber, Ira D., *The Howe Brothers and the American Revolution*. New York, 1972.

[Hall, Captain]. *The History of the Civil War in America* (by an Officer of the Army). Second edition, Vol. I all published, London, (1780).

Hastings, Everett. *The Life and Works of Francis Hopkinson*. Chicago, 1926.

Haven, C. C. *Thirty Days in New Jersey, Ninety Years Ago—Washington and His Army in 1776 and 1777.* Trenton, 1867.

Society of Gentlemen. *The History of the British Empire.* Second edition, 2 vols. Philadelphia, (1803).

An Impartial History of the War in America between Great Britain and the United States, 3 vols., Boston, (1781–1785).

Jameson, J. Franklin, ed. *Essays in the Constitutional History of the United States in the Formative Period 1775–1789,* "The Predecessor of the Supreme Court, by J. Franklin Jameson." Boston, 1889.

Kain, C. Henry. *The Military and Naval Operations on the Delaware in 1777.* Philadelphia, 1910.

Kapp, Friedrich. *The Life of John Kalb.* New York, 1884.

Leake, Isaac Q. *Memoir of the Life and Times of General John Lamb.* Albany, 1850.

Lee, Francis B. *New Jersey as a Colony and as a State.* 5 vols. New York, 1902.

Lincoln, Charles H., *Naval Records of the American Revolution.* Washington, 1906.

———. *The Revolutionary Movement in Pennsylvania 1760–1776.* Cos Cob, Connecticut, 1968.

Lossing, Benson J. *Pictorial Field Book of the American Revolution.* 2 vols. New York, 1860.

Lowell, Edward J. *The Hessians and the Other German Auxiliaries of Great Britain in the Revolutionary War.* New York, 1884.

Lundin, Leonard. *Cockpit of the Revolution—The War for Independence in New Jersey.* Princeton, 1940.

Malone, Dumas, ed. *Dictionary of American Biography.* 22 vols. New York, 1928–1958.

Marshall, John. *The Life of George Washington.* 5 vols. Citizens Guild edition, Fredericksburg, Va. 1926.

Merlant, Captain Joachim. *Soldiers and Sailors of France in the American War for Independence (1776–1783).* New York, 1920.

Mickle, Isaac. *Reminiscences of Old Gloucester: or Incidents in the History of the Counties of Gloucester, Atlantic and Camden.* Philadelphia, 1845.

Nolan, J. Bennett. *The Schuylkill.* New Brunswick, N. J., 1951.

[O'Beirne, Thomas L.], *A Candid and Impartial Narrative of the Fleet, Under the Command of Lord Howe, from the Arrival of the Toulon Squadron, on the Coast of America, to the Times of His Lordships Departure for England. . . ,* taken from second edition, revised. New York, 1969.

Parry, Edwin S. *Betsy Ross, Quaker Rebel.* Philadelphia, 1930.

Paullin, Charles O. *The Navy of the American Revolution.* Cleveland, 1906.

Quarles, Benjamin. *The Negro in the American Revolution.* Chapel Hill, 1961.

Ramsey, David. *The History of the American Revolution.* 2 vols. Trenton, 1811.

Rankin, Hugh F. *The North Carolina Continentals.* Chapel Hill, 1971.

Reed, John F. *Campaign to Valley Forge July 1, 1777–December 19, 1777.* Philadelphia, 1965.

Sabine, Lorenzo. *Biographical Sketches of Loyalists of the American Revolution.* 2 vols. Boston, 1864.

Sargent, Winthrop. (New edition with notes by William Abbatt.) *The Life and Career of Major John Andre, Adjutant-General of the British Army in America.* New York, 1902.

Scharf, J. Thomas and Westcott, Thompson. *History of Philadelphia, 1609–1884.* 3 vols. Philadelphia, 1884.

Schermerhorn, Frank Earle. *American and French Flags of the Revolution 1775–1783.* Philadelphia, 1948.

Siebert, Wilbur H. *The Loyalists of Pennsylvania.* Columbus, Ohio, 1905.

Smith, George. *History of Delaware County, Pennsylvania.* Philadelphia, 1862.

Smith, Samuel Stelle. *Fight for the Delaware, 1777.* Monmouth Beach, N. J., 1970.

Stedman, C. *The History of the Origin, Progress, and Termination of the American War.* 2 vols. London, 1794.

Stewart, Frank H., ed. *Foraging For Valley Forge by General Anthony Wayne in Salem and Gloucester Counties, New Jersey.* Woodbury, N. J. 1929.

Stewart, Frank H. *History of the Battle of Red Bank.* Woodbury, N. J., 1927.

———, comp. & ed. *Notes on Old Gloucester County.* 3 vols. Camden, N. J., 1917–1937.

Stille, Charles J. *Major-General Anthony Wayne and the Pennsylvania Line in the Continental Army.* Philadelphia, 1893.

Stone, Edward Martin. "The Invasion of Canada in 1775." *Collections of the Rhode Island Historical Society,* Vol. VI. Providence, 1867.

Strittmatter, I. P. *The Importance of the Campaign on the Delaware During the Revolutionary War—1777,* Philadelphia, 1932.

Stryker, William S. *The Battles of Trenton and Princeton.* Boston, 1898.

————. *The Forts on the Delaware in the Revolutionary War.* Trenton, N.J. 1901.

Trevelyan, Sir George Otto. *The American Revolution.* 6 vols. London, 1909–14.

Tuckerman, Henry T. *Life of Silas Talbot.* New York, 1850.

Wagner, Frederick. *Submarine Fighter of the American Revolution, The Story of David Bushnell, New York,* 1963.

Wallace, John William. *Colonel William Bradford, the Patriot Printer of 1776.* Philadelphia, 1884.

Ward, Christopher. *The Delaware Continentals.* Wilmington, 1941.

————. John Richard Alden, ed. *The War of the Revolution.* 2 vols. New York, 1952.

Watson, John F. (Enlarged, with revisions and additions by Willis F. Hazard.) *Annals of Philadelphia, and Pennsylvania in the Olden Time.* 3 vols. Philadelphia, 1884.

Weiss, Harry B., and Grace M. *The Revolutionary Saltworks of the New Jersey Coast.* Trenton, 1959.

Wertenbaker, Thomas Jefferson. "The Battle of Princeton," *The Princeton Battle Monument.* Princeton, 1922.

Williams, Mrs. *Biography of Revolutionary Heroes.* Providence, 1839.

Winsor, Justin, ed. *Narrative and Critical History of America.* 8 vols. Boston and New York, 1887.

Index

Bird, Jacob, 350
Black Duck (vessel), 102, 304, 351–52, 428n12
Blair, James, 337, 421n12
Blakely house, Carpenter's Island, 159, 222, 223, 230
blankets, 54; scarcity, 32, 33, 34, 75, 79
Blast (vessel), 116, 348, 349
Blewer, Joseph, 267, 286, 424n3; quoted, 102, 201; *Augusta* salvage list, 202–203, 320–21; chevaux-de-frise and, 365; on Pennsylvania Navy Board, 85, 86, 87, 128, 138, 145, 268, 282, 300, 341, 435n27
Bombay Hook, 30, 115, 414n22
Borden, Joseph, 288–89, 297
Bordentown, New Jersey, 76, 77, 78, 122, 127, 128, 207, 208; "battle of the kegs" and, 288–89; British raid (1778), 294, 295–98, 434n26; fleet quarters (1778), 283, 286, 290, 291, 292; Hessian camp, 80, 172; privateer recruitment in, 285; State navy disbandment and, 294
Bordentown Creek, 147
Boston, Massachusetts, 23, 31
Boston (vessel), 312, 314
Botham, John, 446n70
Bow Creek, 221–22
Bowman, Thomas, 97
Boyd, Thomas, cited, 412n3
Boys, Nathan, 115, 133, 203, 285, 328, 338; chevaux-de-frise and, 367; Davidson affair and, 421n12; fort garrisons (1779) and, 327–28; patrol squadron command, 303, 304, 321, 322, 323, 325, 334, 336; resignation offer (1781), 329, 339
Bradford, Joseph, 344
Bradford, Thomas, 286, 326
Bradford, William, 143, 210, 331, 340, 455n33; the *Augusta* and, 197, 201, 202, 204, 348; at Billingsport, 131, 133, 134; on chevaux-de-frise removal, 140–41, 366; on *Delaware* burning, 347; on fire ship sinking, 347, 348; fleet disbandment and, 290, 291–92, 293, 294; on Fort Mercer defeat, 277; Fort Mifflin defense (1777) and, 159, 164, 456n42; on Hazelwood, 139, 268; Moncrieff and, 144; Navy Board activities of, 86,

128, 282–83, 300, 435n27, 450n16, 460n2
Bradford, William C., 210, 299, 328, 335, 450n18
Bradley, Colonel, 138
Brandywine, battle of, *vii*, 118, 119, 121, 128, 339; Mitchell at 433n23
Brewington, Marion V., cited, 309
Brice, John, 102, 349, 462n24
Bridges, Cornelia, 17, 408n39
Brimstone (vessel), 115, 341, 342, 417n13, 421n9; sale, 340
Bristol, Pennsylvania, 77, 79, 128, 294; ammunition stores in, 273; hospital, 282; Maitland in, 297; ship repairs at, 266–67, 282, 283; troop ferry in, 129, 155, 274
British Admiralty, 35, 202
British Army, 3–4, 5, 20, 77; Bordentown raid (1778), 295–98, 434n26; Fort Mercer defeat by, 269–79, 282; Fort Mifflin defeat by, 227, 230–69; lists of river fort ordnance (1777), 402–404, 442n14; New York occupation by, 18, 59, 72, 95, 97, 104, 329, 330, 397, 398–99; Philadelphia attack strategy, 104, 117, 119, 120–24, 128, 400, 401; Philadelphia evacuation, 282, 294, 299, 325, 394, 397; redoubt construction, 138 (*See also* British Army. Engineers); Whyte in, 394, 398; winter pause (1776), 76, 84–85, 95; winter pause (1777), 281
British Army. Artillery, 272, 280, 402–404
British Army. Dragoons, 122, 223, 272, 280
British Army. Engineers, 60, 455n33; redoubt construction, 138, 141–45, 149, 157, 158–59, 161, 164, 166, 168, 170, 212, 213, 222–23, 230, 245, 259, 271
British Army. Hessian Grenadiers, 172, 272. *See also* Hessians
British Army. Jägers, 172, 176, 180, 184, 187, 272, 280. *See also* Hessians
British House of Commons, 5
British Navy, 11, 295–98; Billingsport chevaux-de-frise and, 134, 136, 138, 139, 140–41, 171; on Chesapeake Bay, 105, 111–12, 128, 400, 401; colonial smuggling and, 68–69; Delaware Bay

Morris, Robert, 8, 9, 24, 63, 396; Whyte and, 394, 395

Morris, Samuel, Jr., 9; chevaux-de-frise and, 356, 363, 364; on Pennsylvania Navy Board, 86, 435*n*27; Whyte and, 394, 395, 396

Morris, Samuel C., 308

Morrison, James, 82

Morristown, New Jersey, 97, 193

Morton, Robert, 124, 257; quoted, 122

Mosquito (vessel), 434*n*26

Moulder, John, 339

Mount Holly, New Jersey, 79, 273, 276, 277

Moylan, Stephen, 358

Mud Island: fortification of, 10, 15, 60, 103, 105, 156, 161, 367; timber of, 369. *See also* Fort Island; Fort Mifflin

Muhlenberg, John Peter, 209, 275

Murderkill River, 30, 41, 414*n*22

Murdock, John, 190

Murphy, Daniel, 93–94, 114

muskets, 26, 39, 276; arrows *versus*, 354; at Fort Mercer, 180, 182–83, 185, 190, 192; at Fort Mifflin, 227, 254, 265

muster masters, 29, 335, 339, 413*n*14; warrant, 389

muster rolls, 24, 37, 65, 333–36; of Boys' patrol squadron, 321; on Continental frigates, 207; on crew numbers in *Roebuck* alarm, 42; on crew numbers in Trenton campaign, 82; of floating batteries, 344–45; of the *General Greene*, 311, 313; naval ranks and, 66–67; on Negro enlistment, 416*n*50; on skilled recruits, 92

Myers, Jacob, 336

Nash, Francis, 100

Nassau Hall, Princeton, 356

National Park, New Jersey, 151, 176

Nautilus (vessel), 35

"Nauticus," 15

Naval Records of the American Revolution (Lincoln), 463*n*8

Negro in the American Revolution, The (Quarles), 416*n*50

Negroes, 37, 173, 314, 439*n*74

Nesbit, John Maxwell, 335, 413*n*14

Nesbitt & Company, 307

neutrals, 4, 8, 78

Newark, New Jersey, 374

New Brunswick, New Jersey, 95

New Castle, Delaware, 52, 54, 136, 428*n*9; British anchorage, 223; the *General Greene* and, 312, 313, 316

Newcomb, Silas, 133, 149, 154, 216, 220; Hessian retreat from Fort Mercer and, 188, 189

New England, 3–4, 44–45, 180

New Jersey, 11, 18, 71, 106, 354; British invasions of, 72, 74–75, 81, 95, 104, 108, 125, 129, 295–97, 322; chevaux-de-frise removal (1783), 367; Fort Mercer defense (1777) and, 173–74, 187–88; Fort Mifflin defeat and, 234, 244, 252, 258, 397; the *General Greene* and, 311, 314; naval defense costs and, 59; the *Roebuck* and, 47, 52, 401; Varnum in, 216, 271, 273, 276, 277. *See also specific placenames*

New Jersey Gazette (newspaper), 456*n*42

New Jersey Militia, 128, 215, 220, 331; at Billingsport, 96, 100, 102, 131, 133; Bordentown raid and, 296, 297; Cornwallis and, 278, 279; at Fort Mercer, 154, 155, 188–89, 206, 269; Fort Mifflin defeat and, 243, 269; Lafayette and, 280; at Trenton, 79; Whyte capture by, 394, 398

Newport, Rhode Island, battle (1778) of, 439*n*74

New York City, New York, 312, 316, 409*n*41; Bay chevaux-de-frise, 353, 358, 374, 376; British occupation of, 18, 59, 72, 95, 97, 104, 329, 330, 397, 398–99

New York State, 18, 27, 59, 75, 209

New York State Legislature, 376

Nice, John, 90, 428*n*9

Nicholson, Samuel, 314

Nicola, Lewis, 10, 14–15, 113, 323

Nixon, John, 54, 364, 371, 411*n*73

Nolan, J. Bennett, quoted, 92

Norris, J. P., quoted, 200

North Carolina, 100, 434*n*26

Notes on Old Gloucester County (Stewart), 192–93

oars, 16, 18, 21, 22, 23, 24; Durham boats and, 433*n*19; impressment for, 82, 83; practice on, 386

088578